DECOLONIZING KNOWLEDGE

UNU/WIDER

Studies in Development Economics embody the output of the
research programmes of the World Institute for Development
Economics Research, which was established by the United Nations
University as its first research and training centre in 1984 and started
work in Helsinki in 1985. The principal purpose of the Institute is to
help identify and meet the need for policy-oriented socio-economic
research on pressing global and development problems, as well as
common domestic problems and their interrelationships.

Decolonizing Knowledge

From Development to Dialogue

Edited by

FRÉDÉRIQUE APFFEL-MARGLIN
and
STEPHEN A. MARGLIN

A study prepared for the World Institute for Development
Economics Research of the United Nations University (UNU/WIDER)

CLARENDON PRESS · OXFORD
1996

Oxford University Press, Walton Street, Oxford OX2 6DP

Oxford New York

Athens Auckland Bangkok Bombay
Calcutta Cape Town Dar es Salaam Delhi
Florence Hong Kong Istanbul Karachi
Kuala Lumpur Madras Madrid Melbourne
Mexico City Nairobi Paris Singapore
Taipei Tokyo Toronto

and associated companies in
Berlin Ibadan

Oxford is a trade mark of Oxford University Press

Published in the United States by
Oxford University Press Inc., New York

UNU/WIDER: World Institute for Development Economics
Research of the United Nations University, Katajanokanlaituri 6B
FIN-00160 Helsinki, Finland

British Library Cataloguing in Publication Data
Data available

Library of Congress Cataloging in Publication Data
Decolonizing knowledge: from development to dialogue / edited by
Frédérique Apffel-Marglin and Stephen A. Marglin.
p. cm.—(Studies in development economics)
"A study prepared for the World Institute for Development
Economics Research of the United Nations University (UNU WIDER)."
Includes bibliographical references.
1. Economic development. 2. Economic development—Social aspects. 3. Technological
innovations—Social aspects. 4. Knowledge, Sociology of. I. Marglin,
Frédérique Apffel. II. Marglin, Stephen A. III. Series.
HD75.D435   1996   95–46913
338.9—dc20
ISBN 0–19–828884–0

1 3 5 7 9 10 8 6 4 2

Typeset by Best-set Typesetter Ltd., Hong Kong
Printed in Great Britain
on acid-free paper by
Bookcraft (Bath) Ltd., Midsomer Norton, Avon

CONTENTS

LIST OF CONTRIBUTORS

FRÉDÉRIQUE APFFEL-MARGLIN, Smith College, Northampton, Mass.

GUSTAVO ESTEVA, Opción Sociedad Civil, Oaxaca, Mexico

RAMACHANDRA GUHA, Nehru Memorial Museum and Library, Delhi

NANCY E. GUTMAN, University of Massachusetts, Amherst

STEPHEN A. MARGLIN, Harvard University, Cambridge, Mass.

ASHIS NANDY, Center for the Study of Developing Societies, Delhi

MARJA-LIISA SWANTZ, WIDER, Helsinki

AILI MARI TRIPP, University of Wisconsin, Madison, Wis.

SHIV VISVANATHAN, Center for the Study of Developing Societies, Delhi

FRANCIS ZIMMERMANN, Écoles des Hautes Études en Sciences Sociales, Paris

1

Introduction: Rationality and the World

FRÉDÉRIQUE APFFEL-MARGLIN

The fall of communism can be regarded as a sign that modern thought—based on the premise that the world is objectively knowable, and that the knowledge so obtained can be absolutely generalized—has come to a final crisis . . . It is a signal that the era of arrogant absolutist reason is drawing to a close and that it is high time to draw conclusions from that fact.

Vaclav Havel[1]

Vaclav Havel's 'arrogant absolutist reason' has a lead role in the drama of development, as it had in the communist experiment. The expertise informing development projects earns its label precisely by being 'based on the premise that the world is objectively knowable, and that the knowledge so obtained can be absolutely generalized'. The knowledge of the experts—engineers, technicians, economists, anthropologists, and many others—can be exported world-wide and applied in varying contexts because of this premiss. Local knowledge, in contrast, is just that, local. Universality is the privilege of this modern mode of thought. It is this privilege which has enabled this mode of knowing to confidently override local ways of knowing and doing, secure in its ability to deliver superior results. The First World is 'developed' and the Third World is 'developing' or 'underdeveloped'. In these phrases the *telos* of development stands revealed and the superior results are there already, luring everyone 'forward'. Simultaneously, this logic transmutes all alternative visions rooted in local knowledge as going 'backwards', a charge that acquires its clout wholly from a progress-oriented notion of development.

At the end of the twentieth century the ideology of progress is badly frayed. The downside of progress, from the latest revelations about US radiation experiments on its citizens to the many grassroots movements resisting development world-wide, along with the environmental disasters this century has witnessed, has become visible to all. It is no longer just the collapse of the former communist block that can predispose us to see reason as arrogant and absolutist, but the daily reports in the press.

The romance with development gripping the governments of the so-called Third World is undoubtedly rooted in the power that the modern form of thought is able to deliver. Cartesian rationality has been the motor that has fuelled the Industrial Revolution as well as its spread world-wide. The desirability of this form of thought seemed self-evident given the power and the goods that it delivers. What seems to be emerging at the end of the century is a realization that the price one pays for the goods industrialization and development bring is not only environmental destruction and social fragmentation but the colonization of the mind. In other words the undisputed validity, regardless of context, of this form of knowledge is beginning to be questioned. What is at stake is the privilege that this form of thought enjoys due to its claims to universality, not whether it is itself a valuable addition to the repertoire of ways of knowing and doing.

It is not only animal and plant species that are becoming extinct at an ever faster pace but human forms of life and thought. The latter can only be justified by a belief in progress, in the replacement of 'outmoded' ways of knowing and doing by more advanced ways of knowing and doing. The downside of progress and of development is creating a mood congenial to revisiting local forms of knowledge as well as to questioning the claims to universality of modern thought.[2] What is happening in the world, whether the First or the Third, looks more and more like loss: loss of environmental integrity, loss of a diversity not only of plant and animal species but of human ways of doing and knowing. What only yesterday looked outmoded, today looks sustainable.

The claim to universality of this modern form of knowledge is challenged in the essays gathered in this volume. Once the universality of Cartesian rationality or more generally of the dominant modern form of knowledge is questioned, progress begins to look less like improvement or advance and more like colonization. Given the entrenchment of the developmental enterprise in the ideology of progress, its kinship with colonization is brought into focus by such an exercise.

A century and a half ago, Christianity was spoken of in Europe as a rational religion and on that ground was confidently exported outside the West for the people's own improvement and/or salvation (see Detienne, 1981). We are perhaps approaching a time when more and more people are perceiving the developmental enterprise as we now perceive the nineteenth-century missionizing enterprise.

Like Vaclav Havel, I see a certain form of rationality to be at the heart of the universalizing impetus of modern forms of thought. A brief perusal of the emergence of this form of rationality in the West seems a fitting manner of introducing the volume as a whole before turning to the individual essays. My intent is not to offer an in-depth history of the emergence of Cartesian rationality, a task historians are much better equipped to undertake, but rather to highlight very briefly the cultural rootedness of this particular form of cognition. This form of cognition will be contrasted with other modes of cognition rooted in other cultural contexts. It is hoped that by so doing one may begin to perceive this form of thought as only one among many other forms of local knowledge, rather than as a prefiguring of everyone's future.

Since the emergence of Cartesian rationality took place among a rather small Western European élite, a brief look at the manner in which it first deployed itself throughout Western society and later throughout the world will enable us to clarify the link between the present dominance of this form of knowledge and the processes of development.

THE EMERGENCE OF CARTESIAN RATIONALITY

The modern form of knowledge which is dominant in the world today is one of the offshoots of the scientific revolution and of the Enlightenment, both of which were Western European phenomena.[3] It is characterized by a form of rationality that disengages the mind from the body and from the world. Charles Taylor has identified the genesis of this disengaged stance towards the body and the world in Descartes's work (Taylor, 1989: ch. 8). Disengaging rationality from the body and from the world has been seen by many as having roots in Classical Greece, although Classical Greek thought differs in other important respects from the modern system of knowledge inaugurated by Descartes. Taylor's manner of articulating the difference simultaneously clarifies the meaning of the disengagement of rationality from the world and from the body:

This very different view of knowledge and the cosmos means that Descartes' dualism of soul and body will be strikingly different from Plato's. For Plato, I realize my true nature as a supersensible soul when I turn towards supersensible, eternal, immutable things . . .

For Descartes, in contrast, there is no such order of Ideas to turn to, and understanding physical reality in terms of such is precisely a paradigm example of the confusion between the soul and the material we must free ourselves from. Coming to a full realization of one's being as immaterial involves perceiving distinctly the *ontological cleft* between the two, and this involves grasping the material world as mere extension. The material world here includes the body, and coming to see the real distinction requires that we disengage from our usual embodied perspective . . . We have to objectify the world, including our own bodies, and that means to come to see them mechanistically and functionally, in the same way that an uninvolved external observer would (Taylor, 1989: 145; emphasis added).

The ontological cleft between reason and the world means that the world is no longer a meaningful order, that it is expressively dead. Understanding the world was no longer a matter of attunement with the cosmos, as it was for the Classical Greek thinkers. The world, as Weber put it, became 'disenchanted', silent as to the good or the beautiful. The cosmos became what it is for citizens of the modern world, a despiritualized mechanism to be grasped by concepts and representations constructed by reason.

Descartes saw this grasping in terms of instrumental control and mastery of nature:

For they [some general notions concerning Physics] caused me to see that it is possible to attain knowledge which is very useful in life, and that, instead of that speculative philosophy which is taught in the Schools, we may find a practical philosophy by means of which, knowing the force and the action of fire, water, air, the stars, heavens and all other bodies that environ us, as distinctly as we know the different crafts of our artisans, we can in the same way employ them in all those uses to which they are adapted, and thus render ourselves the masters and possessors of nature (*Discours de la méthode*, VI: 61–2; quoted in Taylor, 1989: 149).

The utter separation between mind and matter left the world and the body empty of meaning and thoroughly subjectivized mind. This subjectivization of mind, this radical separation between mind and world, placed human beings in a position external to the body and the world, with an instrumental stance towards them. Our minds could no longer attune themselves to the order in the cosmos, the material embodiment of mind, nor could they hope to reach that order through faith in God as St. Augustine had urged.

Truth, goodness, and beauty no longer reside in the world. Truth is attained by following the right method. Humans by their own autonomous powers of reasoning can attain certain truth provided they follow specific canons of thought. With Descartes a major shift takes place that has the effect of making thinking an internal, subjective activity rather than a turning towards or an attuning to the world. Although modern science has criticized Descartes's method, and much disagreement has been voiced as to the precise nature of this method, modern reason is still conceived of as a procedure rather than in terms of substantive beliefs (Taylor, 1989: 156).

For the Greeks, understanding the world was an ethical pursuit. Modern rationality by contrast is disengaged not only from the body and the world but from ethics as well, or rather the world for us is no longer a sacred cosmos and the laws of nature are silent as to the good and the beautiful. I can do no better here than to reproduce Einstein's words on this issue: 'The concepts which [the scientific way of thinking] uses to build up its coherent systems do not express emotions. For the scientist, there is only 'being', but no wishing, no valuing, no good, no evil—in short, no goal' (1953: 779; quoted in Maxwell, 1984: 131). The separation demanded between the pursuit of truth and ethical concerns about the good is explicitly claimed to be necessary in the various methodologies devised to arrive at verifiable and therefore certain knowledge.[4]

The Good that inhered in the cosmos for the Classical Greek was eventually replaced by the Good that faith in God enables one to attain. St. Augustine 'retains the Platonic notion of an order of things in the cosmos which is good' (Taylor, 1989: 143) but because of sin this Good can only be attained by an inward turn towards God.[5] With Descartes, the term 'idea' began being used for the workings of the human mind rather than for God's. This profound shift is an important part of the making of the human mind into a 'mirror of nature' in Richard Rorty's phrase (Varela *et al.*, 1991: 141).

The Church's monopoly on articulating this Good was fractured by the Reformation. Descartes's disengaged rationality arose in an immediate historical context of bloody religious conflicts. Stephen Toulmin (1990) makes a persuasive argument that the new knowledge was a way to a new certainty outside the conflicting religious certainties. Out of the chaos of clashing certainties, disengaged rationality, freeing the knower from religious, cultural, and historical context, offered a neutral road to certainty and order.

What made the new mode of knowing ultimately triumphant beyond the immediate contingencies of history highlighted by Toulmin is the fact that the new neutral ground created by it did not fundamentally challenge Christian doctrine, either Catholic or Protestant. The new mechanistic view of the world in which nature and natural bodies become despiritualized objects of knowledge contrasted in that respect with Renaissance magic: alchemy, astrology, sorcery, and witchcraft.[6] In particular Calvin's notion of an omnipotent God as designer of the universe was very close to the notion of a God who had designed and who acted through regular laws of nature. Such a cosmology eventually found expression in the mechanistic philosophy of Descartes, in which all physical events were governed by mechanical motion. According to Tambiah (1990: 17–18) this 'alliance between Protestant theology and modern science lasted for a century and a half' until it broke down with Darwinism. This new understanding of the lack of conflict between Christian theology and the new mechanistic science's cosmology contrasted to Hermetic cosmology made, to use von Wright's phrase: 'The new science . . . a welcome ally in fighting heresies and exorcising the inferior ghosts, leaving the one superghost, the Christian Trinitarian God, sovereign ruler of the universe.' (von Wright, 1991: 17). Furthermore, the new mode of knowing not only did not challenge the Christian godhead but, by making nature into a great machine, its cosmology positively implied a Great Maker.[7]

Tambiah's review of Keith Thomas's work shows that Thomas's distinction between religion and magic, prayer and spell, was a Protestant legacy taken over uncritically by Thomas as well as by anthropology. This view of magic—the mechanical manipulation of the divinity—as strongly opposed to religion—the supplication of the divinity through prayer—was not challenged in anthropology until quite recently. The now established view that magic and religious ritual should not be two separate categories owes a great deal to Tambiah's own work. Tambiah's use of Wittgenstein's critique of Frazer, as well as Austin's work on the performative use of language, is central to the movement in anthropology away from magic or ritual as 'bad science' and towards magic or ritual as 'rhetoric art' and performative utterances with illocutionary force.[8]

Tambiah's critique of Thomas's work bears on the distinction Thomas makes between magic and religion or ritual. Magic as actions designed to affect the external world was initially classified in anthropology as a primitive or false science. This is due to the fact that its explicit aim was to transform the external world. Tambiah's critique of magic or ritual as bad science and his redefinition of magic or ritual as rhetoric art and performative utterances shows how these practices are aimed at influencing humans and not at transforming the external world. In other words Tambiah does not scrutinize critically the very separation between humans and the 'external' world.

The 'ontological cleft' between mind and the world and body that Taylor attributes to Descartes was prefigured in the works of certain reformers, particularly of Huldricht Zwingli (Uberoi, 1978: 40; Burke, 1990). Zwingli postulated two radically separate aspects of reality: namely, what is intrinsically so or the literal, and what is symbolically true, which refers to the invisible deity which in Descartes's thought became ideas in men's minds (Varela et al., 1991: 141). In this new world-view, God and humans could only be united in the mind through belief and faith, whereas God and the external world—including the body—became radically estranged. Later developments, such as the Cartesian cogito, could not have taken place without the Reformation and Zwingli's work in particular. Jit Singh Uberoi (1978: 40 and passim) argues that with the latter's separation between the literal and the symbolic, the separation between the material and the spiritual had enormous implications:

Ever afterwards in modern European thought and life the symbol was thus a mere allegory or metaphor, ritual was just an outward form, and myth of itself a fairy tale . . .
   Under the new dispensation, God, man and the world could be still united in theoretical belief and faith, the internal vision, but they definitely seemed to have parted in the external world to the outward eye and for all practical purposes.

In other words modern persons cannot act towards the external world in any other way but on the premiss that it is devoid of spirit or of any inherent meaning. The separation between the human mind or spirit and the world is absolute. That separation now has the status of an 'ontological cleft' to use Taylor's phrase. Only science and effective rational technical action can affect the world; ritual affects only humans.

The earlier view of magic or ritual as bad science precluded an understanding of the performative and rhetorical dimensions of magic and ritual. We must, however, beware of remaining caught in a dualism of efficacious, instrumental action versus rhetorical and/or performative action. Efficacious instrumental action—that is properly technical action devised by the use of rationality—presupposes a radical separation between a rational agent and the world which is acted upon. What from the standpoint of Cartesian rationality is called rhetorical and performative, affecting only humans, may in fact be efficacious action upon a world from which mind has not been siphoned off and exclusively lodged in a human subject.

Other cultures do not necessarily make a separation between efficacious, technical or rational action and magical or ritual action. This is basically because the particularly modern, Western, radical separation between a mind subjectivized in humans and the world does not exist.

CONTRASTING CULTURAL STYLES OF COGNITION

In Chapter 8 Francis Zimmermann asserts that in Indic civilizations (Hindu, Buddhist, and Jain) the Cartesian separation between mind and world does not exist. In Indic civilizations the works of humans come under the same rule as the rest of nature. In the following passage the contemporary Indian philosopher-saint Gopinath Kaviraj explains to his interlocutor, the Swiss psychologist Medard Boss, this contrast between the two civilizational views:

Nevertheless, not only man but everything that is, all animals, plants and inert things, are, by their very nature, of the same origin. If, in fact, the openness that makes up my nature, if—in other words—my understanding/perceiving of things as what they are, were separated from them by a radical gulf between me and them, between my and their ground-nature, there could never be any real contact with them, any real knowledge of them. However, if no difference by nature is possible, then the nature of the other entity that can be understood by me must be of the same luminating kind as myself. If anything at all, even I, were only 'consciousness' matter by nature—which is the only alternative possibility—there would again be no experiencing and knowledge of anything. And this would be so, because pure matter bare of an illuminating, opening-up ground-nature can have no knowledge. If that is the case, the true nature of everything that is, is based on the nature of 'brahman' or, as the Buddhists say, is in accord with, and corresponds to, the enlightening nature of 'Buddha'.

. . . However, the true reality recognized by Vedanta as ultimate and undisguised far surpasses the One, and the Many, and the Void. We have to leave it at the negative designation of Vedanta as the 'Advaita' doctrine, the doctrine of the non-dual, the non-excluding truth (in Boss, 1966: 130, 138).[9]

I have quoted Kaviraj extensively in order to attempt to communicate the radical contrast between this form of epistemology and ontology and the modern Western one. What is of particular interest in this case is that Indic civilizations did originate a materialist epistemology and ontology quite similar to the modern one. I am referring to the *carvaka* school of materialism. Kaviraj elsewhere explains how this school of thought was defeated and marginalized in Indic civilizations.

It is interesting to note that an endeavour similar to what Kaviraj attributes to Buddhist and Advaita thought has been undertaken by a group
of cognitive scientists in the West. Francisco Varela, Evan Thompson, and
Eleanor Rosch have recently argued for a way out of what they perceive as
the impasse reached by Western philosophy and cognitive science. They
turn to the Madhyamika school of Buddhism. It is impossible to do justice
to their arguments here, but the following passage makes clear that their
critical endeavour focuses on the ontological cleft between a subjective
mind and an objective outer world:

By treating mind and world as opposed subjective and objective poles, the Cartesian
anxiety oscillates endlessly between the two [nihilism and absolutism] in search of
a ground . . .
    We have already seen in our exploration of human experience through the
practice of mindfulness/awareness [a Buddhist meditative practice] that our grasping after an inner ground is the essence of ego-self and is the source of continuous
frustration. We can now begin to appreciate that this grasping after an inner ground
is itself a moment in a larger pattern of grasping that includes our clinging to an
outer ground in the form of the idea of a pregiven and independent world. In other
words, our grasping after a ground, whether inner or outer, is the deep source of
frustration and anxiety. This realization lies at the heart of the theory and practice
of the *Madhyamika* or 'middle way' school of the Buddhist tradition (1991: 141,
143).

The alternative to the 'inner and outer ground', or to put it differently to the
subject–object dichotomy, is sought in a perception of reality as a constantly changing web of relationships in which neither the mind nor the
world nor the body are points of departure, tangible things, or grounds.
    Lest one gain the impression that the Indic world may be exceptional in
this regard, I will adduce one more example from a very different part of the
world. I will let the voice of an indigenous Mochica writer from the Andes
speak of a world that is alive and in dialogue with humans. It is striking how
Eduardo Grillo Fernandez's (1993) words echo those of Gopinath Kaviraj:

The Andean world is a world that is alive and life-giving, although what is relevant
is not life in itself, since that is an abstraction, but rather the concrete living beings
which inhabit it in symbiosis with its great diversity and complexity, the great
multitude of forms of life, the innumerable organic processes which it harbours.
    We are dealing with an animal-world in whose bosom everything that exists is
itself alive: the people, the animals and the plants, but also the soils, the waters, the
streams, the valleys, the mountains, the stones, the winds, the clouds, the mists, the
rains, the forests, and everything that exists (my translation).

As Grillo goes on to point out, in this cosmology the name of a thing or
person is not a representation invented by humans, rather it is that thing
or person's mode of presenting itself to others as it is simultaneously the
mode by which others recognize it. By naming a being—a person, tree, or

rock—one brings the presence of that being to the place where it has been called or named. This is so because there is no division between the material and the ideational, the subject and the object, the literal and the symbolic.

Grillo describes how Andean peasants have reclaimed lands rendered waste by either plantation or government-created co-operative agricultural schemes. The peasants recreate the ancient terracing and care for the land. They have successfully rendered fertile these wasted lands. When asked how they have done it, they respond by saying that they converse with the soil, the rocks, and the plants and receive answers from these.

Eduardo Grillo Fernandez and some collaborators are engaged in a task akin to that of Varela and his collaborators, namely that of turning to another cultural context (the indigenous Andean mode of knowing and doing for Grillo and Buddhist thought for Varela *et al.*) as an alternative to modern Western forms of knowledge. These authors' abandonment of the modern form of knowledge is not undertaken as a purely philosophical endeavour, but rather as a practice, a cultural politics. It is motivated by what they perceive as the utter failure and destructiveness of the developmental enterprise in Peru and other Andean countries. Many of them come from ideological backgrounds inspired by the socialist or communist experiment, the heritage of which seems to have led them to the same conclusion as that voiced by Vaclav Havel in the opening epigraph to this chapter.

I will conclude this section by mentioning the work of some anthropologists who have investigated the relevance of the nature–culture dichotomy to other cultural contexts. The nature–culture dichotomy is closely related to the subject–object and mind–body dichotomies (see Chapter 4): like them it is an exclusive dichotomy in which one of the terms is defined by the absence of the other. Culture is that which is transformed or created by the action of the human mind and will, whereas nature is that which is not so transformed or created. In this opposition, nature is what is devoid of mind, that which exists apart from and before any human intervention. In a book of essays edited by McCormack and Strathern (1980) with examples from many parts of the world, the authors concur that the nature–culture dichotomy is not a given of reality but a particular Western construction not found in other parts of the world. The absence of a nature–culture dichotomy means that the human mind is not subjectivized and that the world is not emptied out of mind. In other words it means that there is no ontological cleft between the world and the mind.

This foray into contrasting cultural styles of cognition, though extremely brief and sketchy, should suffice to alert us to the cultural specificity of the Western ontological cleft between the human mind and the rest of the world that Taylor has highlighted as the defining characteristic of Cartesian rationality.

THE DEPLOYMENT OF CARTESIAN RATIONALITY

The modern Western form of knowledge not only outlived the circumstances of its birth, but also spread far beyond an élite circle of scientists and philosophers. This is, of course, the process which was characterized by Max Weber as the rationalization of society.

The new science claimed disengagement from historical contingency; it is this very characteristic which gave it global aspirations and universal pretentions. As Weber has argued (1950), it is the decisive role the new scientific rationality played in the Industrial Revolution that has made it dominant in the West. The instrumental stance of reason towards nature and the body was a crucial element in the instrumental use of labour and of natural resources for increased production. The instrumental use of various resources transformed the human body as the source of labour into a commodity, along with those parts of nature that industrialization exploited. Through the process of commoditization the body and the world became factors of production. This process implies a radical separation between thought and the world or body; in fact it could hardly occur without such a separation.

The process of commoditization affects not only the particular resource which is being commoditized, but also transforms the whole environment, human and non-human. The process of commoditization necessitates the extraction of the commodity-in-the-making from the context in which it was embedded, as well as its transformation into a quantifiable entity, so that it can become available to be bought and sold in the market economy. Vandana Shiva (1993) shows how the transformation of certain tree species into commodities simultaneously transforms other tree species into weeds. The non-commoditized trees' role in protecting the earth from the top-soil-eroding impact of torrential rains, in retaining ground moisture through their root system, or in providing green fodder for the local agro-pastoralists, becomes invisible, unquantified, unmeasured, in sum non-existent. Commoditizing one species of tree does not leave the rest of the natural environment intact. Other non-commoditized species, having become weeds, not only lose all importance but become noxious, inviting extermination through monoculture. The local communities for whom these weeds are life-sustaining, particularly the women, are delegitimized, since their purpose is that of sustaining life, a non-commoditized form of work. This work has suffered a fate similar to that of non-commoditized plant species: stigmatized by the label 'subsistence', sustaining life becomes unimportant and backward. The relationship between the commoditized and the non-commoditized species becomes hierarchical, one being valued and visible, the other devalued and invisible. This hierarchization leads to a radical transformation of the natural environment and affects the social environment as well.

Processes that have transformed forestry as well as agriculture have their parallel in the historical processes which created labour as a commodity. Labour is an abstract quantifiable entity owned by a person. The context in which labour as a commodity-in-the-making is embedded is the communities to which the labourer belongs. In non-commoditized societies, various members of the community such as kin groups and neighbours can claim the labour of a person. Many community endeavours such as festivals and life-cycle ceremonies mobilize the labour of many members of the community. With the extraction of labour from its context, these events become relegated to a private domain which must take a secondary and dependent position in relation to the public domain of wage labour. In fact, the development literature is replete with references to such community celebrations as a waste and a drain of productive resources. Such community events are transmuted by the development perspective into the equivalent of weeds in the case of trees. The result is that the resources in labour and in kind expended on community events come to be perceived as drains on the economy as well as obstacles to it. The result is that the sociality created and maintained by such activities becomes eroded, eventually leading to social alienation and fragmentation.

The reason for this process must be sought in the utilitarian rationality integral to commoditized relations. The imperative to maximize utility and self-interest logically leads to a reckoning in which the environment—both human and non-human—becomes either an input or an obstacle to increased production. The consequences on the social and natural environment of the exercise of utilitarian rationality are labelled 'externalities'. Those features of the environment which do not contribute to this maximizing logic become defined as obstacles. When the removal of these obstacles brings about unforeseen deleterious consequences, these are labelled 'externalities'. They are therefore lost as potential sources of self-criticism.

This type of rationality travelled outside the West with trade, colonialism, and the spread of industrialization and the market economy. Political decolonization has changed the ethnic composition of the teams but not the game itself. Ranajit Guha (1989: 222–9) has shown the correlation between colonialism and a universalizing knowledge by arguing that the transformation of the colonies into capitalist market economies required the extension of practices and modes of thought declared to be universal, and hence applicable everywhere.[10]

In the context of development what is remarkable is that the modern form of knowledge is not only the knowledge system of the Western expert but of experts in general, as well as of governments. The Indic (Buddhist, Hindu, Jain) style of cognition hinted at above has not become the knowledge used by the state or taught in state educational institutions in India.[11] This is not only true of India but also of Peru and many other nations. The formerly colonized nation-states have continued the knowledge system imported by their erstwhile colonial masters. The nexus between scientific and technological knowledge and the military and organizational might of Western nations made a deep impression on the subjugated peoples. The dominant system of knowledge maximizes instrumental control and renders its wielders not only 'the masters and possessors of nature', as Descartes put it, but also the engineers of social reality (Bauman, 1989). Such mastery and control emerges from the use of the right method by a rational mind. This method is not restricted to the natural sciences, as we know, but extends to the social sciences, rendering the wielders of this kind of knowledge the masters and possessors of the social world as well. The ability to represent the world conceptually and symbolically enables the disengaged observer to manipulate that world—using quantification and measurements such as statistics, censuses, maps, etc.,[12]—without himself or herself being directly affected by such manipulation.

Many a thoughtful observer of the contemporary scene has pointed out that this spread of rationalization is or has become 'unreasonableness' (von Wright, 1991), 'irrational' (Maxwell, 1984), 'political domination' (Habermas, 1971), 'discipline and surveillance' (Foucault, 1965; 1970; 1975; 1977), 'a powerful ideological fiction' (Haraway, 1989), or 'morally bankrupt' (Bauman, 1989). Such scepticism is no doubt inspired by the mounting evidence of the enormous cost in terms of social and ecological health of the modern form of knowledge. These costs, these losses, are leading more and more people to question the universal validity of the modern mode of thought and to the recognition that it is just as culturally rooted, just as local, as other modes of thought. After political decolonization must now follow a decolonization of the mind.

INTRODUCING THE ESSAYS

Political decolonization has not meant the decolonization of minds. This is nowhere more evident than in the case of Tanzania. Swantz and Tripp's case-study of a fisheries project in Tanzania perfectly illustrates what we mean when we advocate the decolonizing of development knowledge and therefore fittingly introduces the first part of the volume.

Julius Nyerere, president of Tanzania at the time, articulated a commitment to building upon rather than jettisoning the 'traditional knowledge accumulated in [the] tribal past' and warned that if Tanzanians were to save this traditional knowledge: 'we cannot afford the arrogance which our technical superiority tempts us to assume' (Nyerere, 1973 quoted in Chapter 2 , below). Nyerere's party unambiguously articulated warnings against expert knowledge, against top-down development, and against dismissing the wisdom and knowledge accumulated from the tribal past.

In the actual practice of the project jointly carried out by the Tanzanian government and the Norwegian Ministry of Development Co-operation (NORAD), these pronouncements and commitments from Nyerere were radically contravened. If we take the example of the Mbegani Fisheries Development Centre (MFDC) that resulted from this co-operation between the Tanzanian and Norwegian states as emblematic of what has happened and continues to happen in Tanzania, it is clear that disregard for indigenous knowledge was less pronounced among Norwegian experts than among Tanzanian government officials. It is clear from the detailed historical account in Swantz and Tripp's chapter that the Norwegian development agency cannot be primarily, nor even solely, responsible for the near total disregard of indigenous practices and knowledge, as well as needs and aspirations, which in fact took place. There is no avoiding the fact that this disregard came from Tanzanian state officials themselves. In fact, before signing the agreement between Tanzanian government officials and NORAD concerning the fisheries project, the Norwegians expressed their desire to strengthen the artisanal sector, but in the agreement itself their desire was disregarded. Norwegian fishery experts may have made no secret of their confidence in the superiority of their form of knowledge, with the corollary of disregard and indifference towards indigenous fishing craft (in both senses of the term), but the creation of two sub-projects in which the MFDC did co-operate with local people, (namely, a boatbuilders' project and a women's project), are concrete instances of the Norwegians paying more than lip-service to local artisanal knowledge.

This case-study makes abundantly clear that development, even in the case of Tanzania with its explicit commitment to people's knowledge and people's involvement, is not meant to benefit local populations but rather is meant to transform the nation-state into a modern, industrialized power. Nyerere's rhetoric notwithstanding, its government embarked on an extensive resettlement of its rural population. The villagization programme was a coercive move, in which villagers were forced to destroy their own houses or have them destroyed by soldiers or police. As the authors point out, this resettlement was reminiscent of German and British colonial schemes for similar purposes of ease of administration, tax collection, and transport of commodities. In Operation Villagization, as Swantz and Tripp relate, little attention was paid to 'local ecological and social conditions and local methods of cultivation, often with disastrous results.' The government replaced local social and cultural practices with co-operatives with the justification that this type of organization replicated the people's own way, historically, of sharing. The reason given by the authors for the dismal failure of co-operatives is that their 'impersonal form of organization which were isolated from the social and cultural base people are familiar with, leading to distrust and abuses of power.' The government language of replicating people's own form of sharing shows itself to be empty rhetoric since, as the authors show unambiguously, this, along with villagization and development by experts, is also a method for controlling people.

Although the newly independent Tanzanian state made one of the sharpest ideological breaks with colonialism among Third World nations, its commitment to industrialization and modernization—that is to development—necessarily made empty rhetoric of its pronouncements. By replacing people's own community-based social and cultural organizations with governmental ones, through such schemes as resettlement and government co-operatives, the state achieved the destruction of the context in which people's knowledge emerged and could be practised. In the resulting vacuum and atomization, the form of knowledge associated with industrialization and modernization—namely the dominant Western form—encounters little resistance and can even be perceived as the only alternative. It is instructive to note that in the United States a similar destruction of community institutions was the prerequisite for the modernization and industrialization of agriculture (see Chapter 6).

There is no reason to doubt the sincerity of Julius Nyerere regarding people's knowledge and participation. This commitment, no doubt shared by Tanzanians in general, was the antithesis of colonial governance. The requirements of development, however, necessitate the mobilization of people for increased production. In such an endeavour, a natural alliance emerges between a system of knowledge which gives mastery over nature and the world and the state. The decolonizing of development knowledge may require of the Tanzanian state a relinquishing of power which it may be unwilling to allow.

The only well-articulated alternative to industrialization, namely Mohandas Gandhi's vision (as presented *inter alia* in *Hind Swaraj*, 1938), was discarded by independent India's first prime minister Jawaharlal Nehru. In opting for industrialization and the form of knowledge which is necessary to it, Nehru reflected an overwhelming consensus in favour of Western-style industrialization among the Indian élite.[13] It is possible that with the growing ecological crisis and increasing global economic inequality, such a consensus may be beginning to weaken in India and elsewhere.

In the arena of development the discipline of economics—central as it is to development knowledge and practice—contributes powerfully to the delegitimization of local knowledge and the continuing colonization of the mind. Economics models itself methodologically on physics and claims that its methodology enables it to attain verifiable and certain truth (see Chapter 3). Although the object of its study is part of the social world, which is constantly changing and contingent on historical and cultural context, its methodological stance of disengaged rationality transmutes its object of study into what Adam Smith has characterized as 'a great, an immense machine, whose regular and harmonious movements produce a thousand agreeable effects' (quoted in Chapter 3, below).[14] This epistemological stance grants economics a privileged status as a knowledge system, separating it from historical and cultural contingency. From such a perspective, local knowledge, mired as it is in historical and cultural contingency, is no serious competitor in claims to truth.

Nancy Gutman's reading of Keynes as a crypto-pragmatist (in Chapter 3, below), reveals the epistemological and ontological assumptions implicit in the rationality postulate at the heart of the discipline. The pragmatist school of philosophy rejects the ontological cleft between rationality and the world and the view of mind as a 'mirror of nature'.[15] In the words of a pragmatist philosopher 'worlds are as much made as found . . . knowing is as much remaking as reporting' (quoted in Chapter 3). This view, one that rejects the possibility of an Archimedean point from which disengaged rationality can objectively represent the world, is fundamentally at odds with the rationality postulate of economics and its corollary, methodological individualism.

Although I use the term crypto-pragmatist to refer to Gutman's reading of Keynes—because Keynes himself never fully articulated the philosophical basis for his views—Gutman makes a persuasive argument for Keynes as a pragmatist. She shows how Keynes's critique of probability as a method to deal with uncertainty (in his first work *The Treatise on Probability*, originally an essay submitted in competition for a college fellowship at the University of Cambridge in 1908, and not published until 1921), led him in *The General Theory* to emphasize that the sole authority underlying economic agents' decisions in the presence of uncertainty was common practice: the conventions and precedents of everyday life.

According to Gutman, Keynes's neo-classical successors devoted their energies to interpreting him in a rationalist-positivist epistemological framework, thereby accomplishing 'precisely what Keynes had been opposed to, namely the construction of another mechanical model of the economy, which would lead to correct outcomes in the hands of technocratic policy-makers'. Even though most economists, both before and after Keynes, have treated issues of 'uncertainty' in probabilistic terms, Keynes himself was unambiguous about the matter:

By 'uncertain' knowledge let me explain, I do not mean merely to distinguish what is certain from what is only probable. The game of roulette is not subject, in this sense, to uncertainty; nor is the prospect of a Victory bond being drawn . . . The sense in which I am using the term is that in which the prospect of a European war is uncertain, or the price of copper and the rate of interest twenty years hence . . . About these matters there is no scientific basis on which to form any calculable probability whatever. We simply do not know (quoted in Chapter 3).

Keynes emphasized that most events relating to economic decision-making did not possess the uniformity and replicability of such events as cointossing, to which probabilistic calculations can confidently be applied. In the face of irreducible ignorance, Keynes is not led to a position of radical subjectivity or analytic nihilism. In the *General Theory*, Keynes argues that in situations of ignorance coupled with the necessity to act, typical in the realm of the economy, agents rely on conventions. Conventions are sets of ideas, perceptions, values, and beliefs shared by a particular group of people. What characterizes conventions is their variability both in time and in space. In other words, rather than grounding economic agents' decision-making in rational calculus, Keynes recognizes it to be contingent and historical. This, as Gutman shows, amounts to a profound epistemological break from the dominant paradigm in economics, which grounds agents' economic decision-making in disengaged rationality—a universal capacity unsituated in time and place. If incorporated into economic theory, Keynes's view of the agent's decision-making process would dethrone economics from its status of privileged knowledge. In Keynes's own words: 'I also want to emphasize strongly the point about economics being a moral science . . . not a natural science.'

Gutman argues that Keynes's epistemology destroys the hierarchy of knowledge between these two. By grounding the economic decision-making of individual agents in conventions and world-views rather than in a universal utility-maximizing rationality, Keynesian economics abandons a progress-based paradigm of knowledge. The political implications of Keynes's views are in direct conflict with the project of development. For him economic agents are not acting on the basis of a universal rational calculus since such a calculus cannot be used for economic phenomena. These phenomena are not stable and repeatable: they vary through time and across place. Neither can economic agents base their decisions on universal, pre-linguistic instincts or intuitions. Gutman shows that Keynes had a pragmatic view of agents as actively constructing their cultural terrains in the context of the conventions of their particular group. In other words, Keynes thoroughly grounded his understanding of the economy and of economic agents in particular social contexts. By thus removing from the domain of the economy any transcendental, universal, or context-free factor, Keynes emphasized the contextual, historically contingent nature of both economic decision-making and economic theorizing.[16]

This last factor, above all others, accounts for the vigour with which neoclassical economists have fitted Keynes into their own epistemology, and the equal vigour with which they have marginalized other readings of his work. Keynes's view on the economy and on economics has the radical consequence of nullifying the privileged status of economics and hence its ability to travel essentially unchanged to markedly different social and historical contexts. Keynes's epistemology contradicts the universalizing movement inherent in the process of commoditization, and upholds a view of economics and economic processes as grounded in culturally and historically variable contexts. Such a reading of Keynes directly threatens the power held by the dominant neo-classical version and therefore continues to be marginalized. The dominant system of knowledge marginalizes those systems of knowledge—both in the West and outside of the West—that challenge and threaten its privileged status with regard to truth. Such a privileged status is fiercely protected, since it ensures the power of that system to dominate all other systems of knowledge and impose its practices world-wide.

With the contemporary focus on 'sustainable development', environmental issues have become central in development knowledge and practice. A critical look at the basic epistemological and ontological assumptions underlying mainstream environmental knowledge is essential in a project of decolonizing development knowledge. In Chapter 4, Ramachandra Guha focuses on two of the most influential of American environmentalist movements: Progressive Conservation and Wilderness Thinking. These two movements see themselves as adversarial, whereas in Guha's perspective their complementarity is highlighted. Guha reads these movements from the standpoint of a student of the Indian popular resistance to relationships with nature representative of these two movements. This standpoint allows him to identify what the two share epistemologically, in spite of the fact that the Wilderness Movement contradicts one of the fundamental premises of Progressive Conservationism.

Guha's discussion of the two movements in the United States is particularly sensitive to their power dimension both at home and abroad. Progressive Conservationism in fact modelled itself on colonial Britain's Scientific Forestry Programme as well as on colonial Britain's vast water conservation programme. The Wilderness movement grew in importance during the post World War II period and originated in the United States. America has exported its vision of Wilderness Thinking to the Third World with catastrophic results as Guha informs us.

Progressive Conservation arose in the United States at the turn of the century in reaction to the excesses and environmental ravages of *laissez-faire* capitalism. From the start it was located in governmental agencies such as the Forest Service and the Bureau of Reclamation, centralized and in the hands of experts: forestry scientists, engineers, and other water-management experts.

Like their model, the colonial Forestry Programme and Water Management Programme in India, Progressive Conservationists saw themselves as the bearers of a superior form of knowledge which superseded democratic processes; in the blunt words of one of its spokespersons, Harold Loeb, 'it is stupid deciding an issue by vote or opinion when a yardstick can be used.' In other words the use of expert knowledge and of science in general rendered local opinions and desires irrelevant.[17] Scientific forestry as well as water-management expertise were both used in the service of the rational utilization of natural resources, which meant bringing ever greater portions of nature under human dominion for increased production as well as a sustained yield of valuable resources.

With the shift in emphasis in America from production to consumption, as well as with the first warnings of the extent of the environmental damage which industrial civilization had wreaked on nature, a new movement arose. As Progressive Conservation was 'a chapter in the history of production, the Wilderness Movement is a chapter in the history of consumption'. The Wilderness Movement is a direct revolt against sentiments such as those of John Widshoe, special advisor to the Bureau of Reclamation: 'The destiny of man is to possess the whole earth and the destiny of the earth is to be subject to man.' Unspoiled, wild nature needed protection from such rampant colonizing for various lofty purposes. Guha masterfully disentangles the multiple strands motivating this movement, most of which fall under what Shiv Visvanathan has called the 'museumization of life' (see Chapter 9). Guha in particular highlights the disastrous results which the export of Wilderness Thinking and the creation of National Parks in Third World countries like India has had. Wilderness thinking is fundamentally hostile to subsistence agriculture and to pastoralism, since it sees human intervention in nature as inherently destructive.[18] Guha points out that Wilderness Thinking disembeds the spiritual from the material and livelihood from nature. In this fundamental characteristic, Wilderness Thinking contrasts sharply with peasant and tribal practices in which spirituality, livelihood, and nature are intertwined. In this very characteristic, Wilderness Thinking reveals its epistemological kinship with Progressive Conservation.

Both movements speak a language of universalism and both are allied with Western science: Progressive Conservation 'insists it is the most "scientific" and "rational" system of resource utilization', while Wilderness Thinking has the support of the sciences of ecology and conservation biology, which require wilderness preserves as databanks (on this point, see also Chapter 9, below). It is clear that the alliance between Western science and both these American movements is more than a legitimating ploy. Guha shows that these two movements have contradictory views about the proper relationship between humans and nature, but that they share the more basic characteristic of separating the man-made world from the natural world. This is how he pithily formulates this point: 'Progressive Conservation places society above ecology (Nature must follow the dictates of Man), in Wilderness Thinking ecology is placed over society (Man must follow the dictates of Nature). Peasant culture, by embedding ecology in society, transcends both these perspectives.' The alliance between Western science and both these movements, however, has deeper roots than mere opportunism. The ontological separation between the man-made world and the natural world is the same cultural matrix in which the practitioners of Western science disengage rationality from the body and the world. The alliance of Progressive Conservation and Wilderness Thinking with Western science is based on an intimate epistemological and ontological kinship. Even though the two movements are in a sense contradictory, they share an epistemology and ontology with Western science.

Guha concludes his chapter by calling for the subordination of 'science to morality and politics [so that] we can pave the way for a more open and symmetrical dialogue between different environmental traditions'. To heed such a call science would have to abandon the objectivist claim of an Archimedean point with its Cartesian rationality disengaged from nature and from the world of morality and politics.

In Chapter 5 I continue the historical summary of the emergence of Cartesian rationality with a brief look at the deployment of this form of rationality throughout society. This exercise is a prolegomenon to looking at the practices of certain villagers in coastal Orissa (India). The necessity for this historical prolegomenon is that certain categories of description or analysis such as biology or ritual present themselves as neutral and universal. I argue that in fact they are not so but carry within themselves a particular modern Western epistemology and ontology. The categories of 'biology' and 'ritual' are focused upon because the practices that will be the entry-point for understanding certain aspects of Oriya villagers' lives concern the festival of the menses.

This discussion is necessary to make visible the non-universal and non-neutral character of these categories. This exercise is necessary to prevent the invisible violence the uncritical use of these categories perpetrates on others' reality. This exercise is also necessary in order to reveal that another style of cognition, radically different from Cartesian rationality, is at play in that context. Making this visible allows us to perceive these villagers not as pre-modern, but as contemporary actors. It therefore militates against such people being perceived as in need of modernization, advancement, or development.

Control of the passions and the body is a constitutive feature of the form of rationality inaugurated by Descartes and still dominant today. It is this instrumental relationship to the body and the passions which made Cartesian rationality a tool and an ally in the creation of the commoditization of labour required by the new mode of production and the full development of a capitalist economy.

Although Cartesian rationality is genderless—a corollary of its disengagement from the body—its instrumental relationship with the body resulted in a sharp differentiation in the manner in which it deployed itself among men and women. This differentiation between the deployment of rationality among men and women arose from the role that rationality played in the formation of the commoditized form of labour. Reproduction, regeneration, and nurture are human activities that do not evince an instrumental relationship between rationality and the body. In the nineteenth century these processes came to be seen as specifically feminine and as belonging to a sphere where instrumental control—as well as the maximization of self-interest—had no place. The domestic sphere became increasingly separated from the world of productive activity, while generation and regeneration became naturalized. The instrumental relationship between rationality, the body, passions, and nature had the effect of depriving those activities in which the relationship between the mind and the body or passion is not instrumental, namely the activities of generation and regeneration, of rationality. In other words, it had the effect of at once naturalizing and mechanizing them. Generation has become biology, emptied out of mind and managed by what Nancy Gutman calls the upper division of knowledge, or what Stephen Marglin calls epistemic knowledge.

Given that the modern construction of selfhood is built around this Cartesian disengaged rationality and its instrumental—as well as unitary—relationship to the body and the emotions, women have found it difficult to achieve a sense of self within the domestic sphere. Women are increasingly entering the public sphere and have long since rejected the antinomy between rationality and generation and regeneration posited in the nineteenth century. Such a rejection, however, has not on the whole changed the view of generation and regeneration as biological phenomena; in other words it has not reconsidered the emptying out of mind from generation and regeneration.

The epistemological and ontological assumptions underlying the biologization of generation and regeneration are the same as those underlying the ontological cleft between the human-made world and nature discussed in Guha's chapter. There is thus a link in advanced industrial countries between the emergence of a deteriorating social ecology and a deteriorating natural ecology.

By looking at farming communities in coastal Orissa which have been only marginally affected by the commoditization of labour, one can see what things look like when generation and regeneration are not emptied out of mind, when generation and regeneration are the central concern of the society as a whole, of both men and women; when generation and regeneration are not subordinated to production and not relegated to a private domain. What emerges from listening closely to these villagers' voices is that they do not apprehend nature as wholly outside them. This is made clear in the phrases used to speak of the relationship between the earth, the goddess, and women—all three of whom menstruate. The relationship is not conceptualized as a symbolic or representational one but as a substantive one. I characterize this form of thought as 'embodied or enactive cognition' following Varela and colleagues; it is a non-Cartesian form of rationality. This form of cognition leads us to reconsider the category of 'ritual' and particularly its opposition to 'effective instrumental action'.

This form of non-Cartesian rationality forces us to rethink the boundaries created by classifying religion, ritual, and belief as separate from science or philosophy. These classificatory acts begin to emerge as entailments of Cartesian rationality and they begin to blur when a different form of rationality is envisaged. Social engineering—of which development is an instance—presumes the ontological divide between subject and object. The violence such engineering inevitably brings in its wake often remains invisible to those who bring it about, since they are not the object of the engineering. Where that divide does not exist, as in these Oriya villagers' world, when violence erupts, all parties to the conflict belong to the same world; violence can only remain invisible with difficulty. This leads to practices aimed at healing and regenerating social relationships. Regeneration is not left to the private domain and thereby sentimentalized, but becomes a core concern of the collectivity, thus preventing a steady deterioration of social ecology.

The case of the Oriya villagers gives evidence for Ramachandra Guha's claim that peasant (and tribal) societies embed society in nature. Therefore the environmental options that have emerged in the United States do not constitute universal solutions. They are rooted in a particular historical and cultural context and presume a certain epistemology and ontology. Environmental development is as much in need of decolonizing as other branches of the dominant system of knowledge.

The essays in the second part of the volume explore in specific contexts a variety of encounters between the dominant modern form of knowledge and a variety of other forms of knowledge. Although the encounters vary from a simple transfer-of-technology approach to the quest by a Western scientist for transforming his knowledge by settling in India, all the authors are exploring alternatives to the dominant transfer-of-technology approach. This expression is used here more metaphorically than literally, following Ashis Nandy's usage in Chapter 10. It refers to the import via state officials or international agencies of modern Western forms of knowledge with an accompanying marginalization or out-and-out destruction of local knowledge. A recurring question raised by the authors is the possibility of transforming a colonizing dynamic between these various forms of knowledge into a relationship based on dialogue.

Before introducing Stephen Marglin's essay in detail, some paragraphs will be devoted to a discussion of Marglin's theoretical framework first elaborated in our 1990 publication and further refined in his Chapter in this book. This discussion aims at clarifying certain differences in our views concerning the universality of the *episteme/techne* distinction made by Stephen Marglin.

Stephen Marglin (1990 and Chapter 6 in this volume) uses the term *episteme* to refer to a Cartesian method of arriving at true knowledge, but he also considers *episteme* to be a universal category referring to a type of knowledge found in all cultures. To the extent that the Cartesian method entails a culturally specific ontology—as was argued in the first part of this introduction—the universality of *episteme* seems to me problematic. It remains to be seen whether the concept can be usefully generalized to non-Western cultures, as Marglin believes. Marglin contrasts the specifically Western form of *episteme* as Cartesian method with what he terms *techne*. *Techne* reveals itself only through practice, its theory being implicit and usually unavailable to practitioners. *Techne* is embodied as well as embedded in a local social, cultural, and historical context. In other words, *techne* is at once practice and knowledge. Marglin's distinction between *episteme* and *techne* is very close to Bourdieu's distinction between theory and practice. The theoretical and logical fuzziness of practice, as Bourdieu has shown (1990: 80 ff.), is necessary to its success, since it has to be incorporated, embodied as a habit (Bourdieu uses the term *habitus*) to generate appropriate responses in diverse circumstances. Such embodiment of what Bourdieu calls a generative scheme requires that it remain at a general and simple level so that it can generate appropriate actions in many different circumstances, thereby defying strict logic.

When *techne* is translated into epistemic terms it is reduced, appropriated, and distorted.[19] The domination and appropriation that such a translation into epistemic terms effects on the *techne* of people has been investigated by Stephen Marglin among industrial workers (1974; 1990) and among peasant farmers (this volume). A clear example of it is Taylorism or scientific management, where the *techne* of the worker—the knowledge lodged in the worker's hands and body—is epistemized, that is translated into the knowledge of the expert. That expert knowledge then becomes the tool for extracting from workers what the entrepreneur requires, namely greater productivity. It takes away from the worker her ability to control her work. Work ceases to be part of the way of life of the worker or the farmer and becomes simply the means to an economic end.[20]

This illustrates how what Stephen Marglin calls the 'ideology of knowledge' affects knowledge as practice. Western ideology recognizes only epistemic knowledge as knowledge. The knowledge of the disengaged, objectivist observer and the tools constructed by this knowledge are privileged: they give the experts their authority and power.

The question has been raised as to whether the distinction between *episteme* and *techne* is a universal one. The definition of *episteme* 'could have been cribbed from Descartes . . . for it practically paraphrases the method of arriving at true knowledge expounded in the *Discourse on Method* and the *Meditations on First Philosophy* (Marglin, this volume). In this sense *episteme* is a Western historical product with a particular epistemology and ontology. In particular the ontological cleft between mind and world characteristic of the Cartesian method is one not found in other non-Western systems of knowledge.

However, in Marglin's thought, *episteme* also refers to what he might call a human—hence universal—ability to reason. Such an ability is contrasted with another modality of knowing, namely *techne*. For Marglin the implicit, practical, and embodied character of *techne* is central:

> Possessors of *techne* often find it impossible to articulate their knowledge. They are generally aware that they possess special knowledge, but their knowledge is *implicit* rather than explicit. It is revealed in production of cloth or creation of a painting or performance of a ritual, not in manuals for weavers, artists, or priests . . .
>
> *techne* is intensely *practical*, to the point that, as has been suggested, it reveals itself only through practice. This is not to deny the existence of an underlying theory, but the theory is implicit rather than explicit, not necessarily available, perhaps not even usually available, to practitioners (Marglin 1990: 234–5).

To the extent that some non-Western systems of knowledge are self-conscious, theoretical, and non-implicit, they are not *technai* in Marglin's sense of the term. To the extent that they do not share in a Cartesian ontology they do not belong to the category of Western *episteme*.

Until an *episteme* which is not rooted in Cartesian rationality can be demonstrated to exist, it is difficult to accept *episteme* as an aspect of our universal humanity rather than a culturally rooted mode of cognition carrying with it an implicit cosmology, an aspect of a Western-style humanity. *Episteme* does not present itself as such; it takes the gulf between mind and world as a given, a universal fact, part of reality itself, and relegates the thought of those who question this givenness to the realm of religion, belief, or ritual. In my view the distinction between *episteme* and *techne* is a powerful and useful tool for looking at modern Western forms of thought. It highlights an ideology of knowledge which privileges one kind of knowing. What I question is the validity of this distinction for other cultural contexts, since for me *episteme* is thoroughly implicated in a particularly modern Western epistemology and ontology.

In the first part of Chapter 6, Stephen Marglin details the history and the pre-history of one of the first transfers of technology under the rubric of development: the bringing of what later came to be known as the Green Revolution from the US to Mexico during World War II. The man who first discussed the idea of exporting the seed revolution to Mexico with President Avila Camacho in 1940 was Henry A. Wallace, scion of an Iowa family long prominent in the movement to make agriculture more 'progressive', founder of a seed company that commercialized hybrid corn (maize), Secretary of Agriculture, and the Vice President-elect of the United States.

High-tech agriculture increased output dramatically, at least commoditized output. But at the same time it seriously eroded farming as a way

of life in the US as well as abroad. In the US farmers either became technocratic agribusinessmen or left the farm. In the Third World farmers are
increasingly becoming mere cogs in an agri-industrial complex. Was the
game worth the candle? Were there alternatives that might have increased
output without replacing agriculture as a way of life with agribusiness as a
way of making a living? Marglin's history of the development of hybrid corn
in the US in the 1920s, 1930s, and 1940s shows that its eventual success in
that country came after decades of research and work on a huge scale.
Research results from the 1950s show that alternative methods of increasing plant yield through open pollination and schemes of recurrent selection,
all methods used by traditional farmers, could produce yield increases
comparable with those obtained through genetic manipulation in the lab.
These alternative methods were not pursued.

What is also remarkable is that the prophetic voice of an early critic of
high-tech agriculture, Carl Sauer, was totally dismissed. Carl Sauer, a well-
established academic geographer, was touring Mexico studying its native
plants and farming practices in 1940–1 when his advice was sought by the
Rockefeller Foundation. The Foundation, following up on Wallace's ideas,
was investigating the possibility of exporting an agricultural revolution
based on hybridization. In a letter to the head of the social sciences division
of the Rockefeller Foundation dated February 1941 Sauer foresaw the
disaster which in fact has since taken place (on this see also Chapter 7).

The possibilities of disastrous destruction of local genes are great unless the right
people take hold of such work. And Mexican agriculture cannot be pointed toward
standardization on a few commercial types without upsetting native economy and
culture hopelessly. The example of Iowa is about the most dangerous of all for
Mexico. Unless the Americans understand that, they'd better keep out of this
country entirely. This thing must be approached from an appreciation of the native
economies as being basically sound (quoted in Chapter 5, below).

Sauer pointed out that the use of such cultivars as maize and bean were of
a much greater variety than in the US, being part not only of the staple diet
but of religious and other complexes. He also recognized the need to work
on the selection of ecologically adjusted native seeds. In other words Sauer
advocated embedding research in local ecologies and local cultural practices. But as Marglin wryly points out 'science was the one true god
worshipped universally at the altar of modernity . . . from capitalist to communist' and Sauer was dismissed on the grounds of wanting to preserve 'the
picturesque folk ways' of the Mexican peasants. By cloaking themselves in
the mantle of science, the modernizers could monopolize claims to
progress. The contextualized knowledge of Mexican farmers was damned
for being 'traditional', a word made synonymous with backwardness and
stagnation. Science and progress replaced the discredited colonial legitimi-
zation of the 'civilizing mission' which had the marked disadvantage of

racism and ethnocentrism. The invocation of science by any state has the distinct advantage of presenting a supposedly socially, religiously, and culturally unsituated legitimation irresistible to élites the world over. In their eagerness to inherit the ability to 'master nature and the world' bequeathed to them by their former colonial masters they ignored the colonizing implicit in importing science and technology.

Developments since the early days of the creation and export of high-tech agriculture (hta)—in particular the difficulties encountered by hta in various Third World settings—have led experts and researchers to a new-found respect for the knowledge of indigenous farmers. From early contempt for such indigenous practices as intercropping, experts moved by the late 1970s to a new-found respect for what was labelled 'indigenous technical knowledge' (itk). The second part of Chapter 6 is an attempt to assess this latest trend. Are we witnessing the mutual enrichment of traditional and modern forms of knowledge and therefore the beginnings of a genuine decolonizing movement? In order to answer these questions Marglin analyses the knowledge of expert and farmer in terms of *episteme* and *techne*.

Marglin insists that all knowledge and action is a combination of *episteme* and *techne*, but that the ideology of knowledge in the West denies this, elevating *episteme* to a position of either superior knowledge or knowledge *tout court*, and that it is this ideological factor which accounts for the colonizing behaviour of *episteme*.

Having first defined the categories of *episteme* and *techne* in an ideal-typical manner Marglin gives us a historical account of the emergence of *episteme* in the West. *Episteme* has deep roots reaching as far back as Classical Greece. But, as discussed above, there are both continuities and discontinuities between *episteme* and Classical Greek thought. Its modern incarnation dates from the scientific revolution and is particularly associated with Descartes and the historical situation in Europe in the first half of the seventeenth century. Descartes participated in the religious wars as a volunteer in the army of Prince Maurice of Nassau. As noted above, the Reformation had given voice to what Marglin calls a 'cacophony of claims to ultimate truth'. Pluralistic scepticism and tolerance *à la* Montaigne having failed politically, Descartes's method offered a path to certain knowledge that by-passed rival religious claims while at the same time rejecting Hermetic cosmology and challenging neither Catholic nor Protestant beliefs concerning the relationship between Creator and Creation. In a world torn apart by religious controversy, the search for certainty in a non-religious form had obvious appeal.

This search for certainty led later in the century, with the Port-Royal logic, to the birth of the modern idea of probability. Here Marglin's discussion of the relationship between probability and uncertainty reinforces Gutman's discussion of Keynes on the same concepts. Marglin argues that the probability calculus 'assimilates the uncertain into the realm of the true, certain, knowledge.' The taming of uncertainty is directly related to the discrediting of *techne* as a form of knowledge adapted to uncertainty.[21]

Ultimately Marglin makes a plea for the preservation of a plurality of types of knowledge as our safeguard for the future. Since *episteme*, as a consequence of the dominant Western ideology of knowledge, destroys *technai*, an exclusive reliance on epistemic knowledge would be suicidal. Because agriculture is inherently fraught with uncertainty, because the only thing that is certain about the future is that it will bring surprises, we must rely on the resources of many *technai* since '*techne* is the knowledge system of uncertainty'. In order for *episteme* to cease behaving in a colonizing manner we in the West must abandon our ideological claims that *episteme* is all knowledge and instead recognize that it is inextricably bound up with *techne* and therefore that actions and thinking embody both kinds of knowledge. In Marglin's view pure epistemic knowledge does not exist except as an ideology.

Marglin is sceptical as to whether a dialogue between expert knowledge and indigenous knowledge is possible. Given our ideology, adepts at epistemic knowledge will only understand what they can translate, necessarily leaving a residue of 'superstitions and beliefs', non-knowledge; our ideology permits us to recognize as true knowledge only what we can epistemize. In fact in traditional farmers' practices it is impossible to disentangle the technical, social, religious, aesthetic, and other characteristics.[22] To do so does violence to indigenous modes of knowing and living and by so doing endangers these. In other words, the so-called dialogue between expert and indigenous knowledge, by virtue of the ideology of knowledge, continues to be a colonizing activity. One is left with the question of how *episteme* can be decanonized, how we can be led to abandon this ideology. As Marglin rightly insists, recognition of the *de facto* intertwining of *episteme* and *techne* is an essential first step, but it is not clear where to go after this.

The title of Chapter 7 'Hosting the Otherness of the Other' refers to what Gustavo Esteva, following Raimundo Panikkar (1990), calls a 'dialogical dialogue': such a dialogue between holders of different knowledge systems takes place in a context of radical pluralism, where the otherness of the other is taken for granted or hosted. The intention of such dialogue is not to reduce one system to another or transcend difference in a new synthesis (thus differentiating itself from a dialectic between knowledge systems) but to accept the tension, even the conflict, of radical pluralism. Esteva concludes that Western science is incapable of such a dialogue because of its inherent power dimension. Science by disengaging itself from what Esteva calls the social context, claims a privileged form of knowledge transcending the particularities of human historical communities. His plea, therefore, is for the recontextualizing of knowledge in the socio-cultural context of human societies. This would recreate a situation of radical plurality among knowledge systems and thus of life-forms that were eroded during the scientific revolution in seventeenth-century Europe.

Esteva's argument is made on the terrain of the Green Revolution through the biographies of three remarkable Mexican personalities whose lives he interweaves as the essay unfolds. He first introduces us to Don Fidel Palafox, born in 1895 into a family of indentured *peons* (landless labourers) on a *hacienda*. Don Fidel spent a lifetime practising agriculture, half of it as a supervisor in *haciendas*. At the age of 40 he began writing down the sum of his knowledge acquired in the practice of agriculture in one region of Mexico. The manuscript was ready by 1940 but Don Fidel refused to have it published.

The reason for Don Fidel's refusal is used by Esteva as a comment on the fate of peasant knowledge in Mexico during those years. Don Fidel's refusal lasted over the period of the most intense marginalization of peasant knowledge and his recent agreement to publish is the outcome of a current surge of interest in local knowledge and disillusionment with developmentalist approaches to Mexican agriculture. Fortunately for us, and possibly as a portent of a more pluralistic future, Don Fidel's reticence was overcome in 1988 and his book was published.

This narrative is interwoven with that of the lives of Marte Gomez and Don Efraim Hernandez Xolocotzi. As Don Fidel exemplifies peasant knowledge, Marte Gomez is the spokesman of a transfer of technology approach to agriculture in Mexico. Highly placed and influential—he was minister of agriculture under two governments—he secured the enthusiastic collaboration of Henry Wallace, the hybrid seed entrepreneur turned US Vice-President mentioned in Chapter 6. At this point, Esteva's account intersects with that of Marglin concerning Wallace's influence on agriculture. Esteva focuses on Marte Gomez's approach to knowledge rather than on a socio-economic critique of the Green Revolution. Marte Gomez's career illustrates a sustained belief that scientific research is the only legitimate and acceptable source of knowledge. His substantial influence on the creation of schools of agronomy, extension programmes, and institutionalized collaboration with US experts contributed mightily to the marginalization of peasant knowledge. It is this marginalization that made Don Fidel Palafox recoil from publishing his work to protect himself from merciless criticism as well as from inevitable misunderstanding. It created a climate in which peasants could not contribute to agronomic science.

Don Efraim Hernandez Xolocotzi represents the recontextualizing of scientific knowledge in tradition. Although educated in the US since his high-school years (with a post-graduate degree in agronomy from Cornell), Don Efraim had wide-ranging experience with Mexican peasants which made him realize very early on that agronomic science would never be appropriate in the context of rural Mexico. Agronomy excludes the peasant's socio-cultural context as part of its own knowledge production.

Esteva contrasts Don Efraim's mode of relating to the peasant with that of Nobel Peace prize-winner Norman Borlaug, emblem of the Green Revolution. Borlaug also advocates listening to and learning from the peasant, but such listening and learning is done with the aim not of creating a new form of knowledge but of finding the information necessary to better facilitate the peasant's participation in agronomic knowledge packages.[23] In sum it is not a dialogue with the peasant but rather the obtaining of 'field information' to smooth the process of the transfer of technology. This view parallels closely Marglin's discussion in the second part of his chapter on the power aspect of the relationship between the knowledge of experts and the knowledge of farmers.

Don Efraim consistently refused to reduce traditional agriculture to the categories of agronomy, to separate agriculture from ethical and social concerns. In Esteva's view it is just such a separation between the science of agronomy and the humanities that has catastrophically reduced the biological, technical, and cultural diversity of Mexico, exactly as Carl Sauer had predicted in 1941 that it would. Don Efraim's work represents the direction which Esteva would like to see knowledge relating to agriculture to take, a direction opposite to that taken by the Green Revolution. Unthinkable a decade or two ago, the spectacular failures of developmentalism in Mexico and the recent peasant revolution in Chiapas as a result of NAFTA's destructive effect on indigenous agriculture may have created a mood favourable to just such a dialogical knowledge now. It is this very mood that made Don Fidel Palafox finally agree, in his 90s, to have his manuscript published.

In the first part of Chapter 8, Francis Zimmermann invites us to read the great British geneticist J. B. S. Haldane's move to India in 1957 in the broader context of the politics of knowledge. In the second part of the essay he takes up where Haldane left off in an emerging pursuit of contextualizing biology and genetics in tradition. Even though Haldane was one of the pioneers in applying statistics to population genetics, and therefore part of the classical, tough-minded tradition in population genetics, the central piece of the Darwinian legacy for him was not fitness and the idea of 'the survival of the fittest'. In particular, he was critical of Social Darwinism and its implications. For Haldane the concept of diversity in Darwin was of far greater importance than that of evolution. Haldane ascribed the greater influence of Darwin's ideas of evolution to its challenge to Christian theology, which drew a sharp distinction between humans and other living beings. He recognized that such a division had not been made in Hindu, Buddhist, and Jain cosmology.

Haldane's attraction to India was not only to pursue a lifelong interest in field observation where polymorphism—the exuberant multiplicity of species—was so abundant, but also the possibility of exploring biology in a cultural milieu where the common rule of Nature includes the products of the human mind and imagination.

Zimmermann argues that ultimately Haldane's narrow scientific training—i.e. his lack of cultural, historical, or linguistic training—prevented him from breaking new epistemological ground. Zimmermann himself sketches the outlines of a science in which natural and cultural diversity both come under the same rule of Nature. Relying on Caillois's critique of the concept of fitness, he points out its deep anthropomorphism, born as it was in the context of nineteenth-century evolutionism. Zimmermann shows that Caillois's position, far from being a retrograde movement toward mysticism, is a natural history without a transcendental subject. From Hegel's transcendental subject who saw all that is contingent and contextual, all that is of the body and of the world as fetters to the freedom of the spirit,[24] to Sanskrit medicine and astrology, Zimmermann sketches an anthropology in which humankind is radically decentred. This, he claims, would amount to a second Copernican revolution; to an anthropology of biological facts for which well-being, a quiet life rooted in a healthy soil, happy connections and conjunctures, celebrates local knowledge as well as locality.

In Chapter 9, 'Footnotes to Vavilov', Shiv Visvanathan explores the relationship between cultural diversity and genetic diversity. The great Soviet geneticist Nikolai Vavilov—who died in prison in 1943, a victim of Lysenkoism and Stalinism—was an enthusiastic and indefatigable field botanist. He mapped what are now called the 'Vavilov Zones', where the first cultigens were domesticated and also the greatest diversity of cultivars is found. He identified eight such zones in the world and pointed out a correlation between genetic diversity and cultural diversity.

Shiv Visvanathan does not take up where Vavilov left off; rather, he explores the correlation of diversities through readings of various contemporary biologists' works. Visvanathan makes his point initially through an examination of the contrasting works of two field biologists: E. O. Wilson's *Biophilia* (1984) on the forest and Edgar Anderson's *Plants, Man, and Life* (1967) on agriculture. Humans are excluded from Wilson's forest, whereas for Anderson, the greatest genetic diversity in plants came about through the first agricultural revolutions. Wilson's biology is a form of knowledge which did not grow from living in the forest; in spite of his love of the forest, it remains an Other to him. Visvanathan calls this kind of knowledge and love a case of the museumization of life. The danger in such forms of knowledge is that the securing of information, in this case the preservation of gene-plasm, overrides the concern for the continued life of the forest.

This danger is amply confirmed in the experience of anthropology, where the fate of communities studied can almost be said to be inversely proportional to the size of their ethnographic archives.[25] Visvanathan calls this the narcissism of science, a narcissism that undermines concern over the fate of the forest.

In Visvanathan's reading of Anderson, it is the embeddedness of human communities in nature which has given rise to the greatest explosion of new cultigens. The synthesis of new plants and new varieties carried out by traditional agricultural communities throughout the world is, according to Anderson, a legacy that agronomy and genetic engineering are still scavenging off. According to Anderson, nature's multidimensionality is mimicked in traditional agriculture. Multiple cropping, crop rotation, the multiple use and meaning of plants, from food to medicine, to magic, music, work, play, and more mirror nature and contrast with the unidimensionality of agronomy and genetic engineering. In the latter two, the logic of commoditization and the rationality of the market renders this multidimensionality mere noise. The language of economism is unidimensional and it is not the language of nature. By disengaging rationality from nature Western science is similarly unidimensional and therefore ultimately hostile to nature.[26]

In the last two parts of the paper Visvanathan basically argues that by separating nature and our knowledge of it from the human world we are destroying diversity, both genetic and cultural. He pleads for the urgent necessity of a dialogue between Western science and traditional knowledge. It is clear, however, that given the destructiveness of the dominant form of knowledge, he does not envisage a dialogue that would leave that hegemonic knowledge intact.

In Chapter 10 Ashis Nandy details for us what happened when Freud's psychoanalytical method arrived in India. Nandy's reading of the works of the first Indian psychoanalyst constitutes both a critique of Freud and a description of the contextualizing of psychoanalysis. Girindrasekhar Bose (1886–1953) founded the Indian Psychoanalytic Society (IPS) in 1922, only three years after the British Psychoanalytic Society was formed. Nandy focuses on the works of Bose and of the only two non-Indian members of the IPS, Berkeley-Hill and Daly. All three wrote and practised in India; Bose never went to Europe, while the two British members of the IPS were trained and analysed in England by Ernest Jones.

Berkeley-Hill and Daly were to pioneer psychoanalytical studies of national character in India. As Nandy observes, their hope was to introduce this branch of knowledge in India as 'a partial cure for the worst affliction the Indians suffered from—Indianness'. Berkeley-Hill and Daly's work embodies what Nandy calls the 'transfer-of-technology' model of knowledge inherent in the positivist aspect of Freud's work. Bose's work, in contrast, is presented as a continuation and adaptation of India's age-old philosophical interest in theories of consciousness. Bose made extensive use of India's manifold epic narratives, creatively indigenizing Freud's method. Bose never seems to have explicitly criticized Berkeley-Hill and Daly's use of psychoanalysis to further the colonialist project. Nandy, however, invites us to recognize in Bose's work a check against the Social Darwinist and evolutionist potential of psychoanalysis, actualized in the two British members of the IPS. Ultimately, though, what Nandy sees as Bose's hope to anchor the new discipline outside the colonial progressivist discourse failed.

Berkeley-Hill and Daly's colonial extension of the early and mature positivist Freud, and Bose's creative indigenizing of what later became the metaphorical Freud, coexisted peacefully in the bosom of the Indian Psychoanalytical Society. One could argue that such non-conflictual coexistence replicated their non-conflictual existence in Freud's own thought. To dislodge psychoanalysis from progressivism and its offspring, colonialism, Bose would have had to confront the colonizing nature of Freud's model of the self, something he seems never to have done. However, by insisting on seeing psychoanalysis as continuous with an ancient Indian philosophical tradition in which introspection played a central role, Bose *de facto* decolonized this Western import. In the face of an explicit rejection of introspection by Freud and by psychoanalysis ever since, Bose's embrace of introspection as a primary method of accessing the unconscious and of attaining self-awareness in effect transforms psychoanalysis into a genuinely Indian knowledge.

Nandy disentangles two contradictory sides of Freud. When Freud was a young medical student he came under the influence of four experimentalists who transformed physiology into a hard science. It was in the lab of one of these, Ernst Brucke, that Freud fashioned his own self-concept as a hard scientist. In this milieu, clinical observation was demoted in favour of experiments in the lab. Reductionism was at a premium and life was to be understood ultimately in terms of energy and matter. This side of Freud competed with another Freud in which metaphorical thought and interest in religious philosophy predominated. In Nandy's view Freud kept this metaphorical side strictly in check until his late 50s. He had to do this in order to be academically accepted. Girindrasekhar Bose all but ignored Freud's positivist and progressivist side, and anticipated by several decades a focus on what became Freud's later metaphorical period. Berkeley-Hill and Daly, on the other hand, actualized the racist content and oppressive potential which positivism had for the South in deriving their version of psychoanalysis from Freud's earlier phase. Bose, however, by not directly confronting the oppressive potential in psychoanalysis's Eurocentricity, as well as by paying lip-service to Freud's progressivist language, ultimately failed to bring out fully the subversive potential of psychoanalysis and to emancipate it from its links with imperial structures of thought.

Nandy argues that the controversial status of Freud's ideas in Victorian Europe essentially derived from the fact that Freud brought the 'disowned underside of the self' out of its Victorian closet. This disowned underside of the self had been both created and denied by the process of the Industrial Revolution. Disengaged rationality transmuted great parts of the self into dark and unspeakable recesses. This very form of rationality, Ashis Nandy's 'scientific rationality', played a central role in stabilizing everyday culture in the wake of the disruptions created by the Industrial Revolution. Freud shocked the Victorians by naming what was denied and unspeakable. But, more fundamentally, he took over the notion of a disengaged rationality and set about charting ways in which it could successfully conquer those parts of the self which commoditization had exiled to disowned and nether regions. The critical edge of Freud's work can be likened to the critical force in that part of the gay movement which fights to end invisibility and unspeakability—destroy the closet—but not the categories which conflate sexual behaviour and a unitary identity and thereby create the gay, the lesbian, and the bisexual.[27]

Ultimately Bose's work remained of interest only to a small section of Indian society and did not challenge the dominant progressivist discourse. Nandy's reading of Bose in the context of a critique of psychoanalysis's Eurocentric aspect reclaims the subversive potential in the work of the first Indian psychoanalyst.

CONCLUSION

A frequently voiced theme in these essays is that scientific or epistemic knowledge endangers diversity. As Marglin points out, high-tech agriculture promotes monoculture with its attendant impoverishment of native cultigens. Visvanathan, relying on Vavilov's and Anderson's work, shows that traditional agriculture has produced the highest variety of cultigens. Haldane pursuing an interest in diversity, goes to India sensing that its traditions of knowledge, where the products of the mind are not separated out from the natural world, have much to teach him.

Diversity, of cultigens as much as of cultures, succumbs to an *episteme* geared towards instrumental control of nature and the world. Research and development funds are poured into epistemic types of research while alternative ways of increasing productivity based on local knowledge are not investigated. The transfer-of-technology model dominates development thinking. Even where this model is adapted in order to draw upon local knowledge, the latter is distorted and impoverished when translated into epistemic terms.

Several authors advocate the contextualizing of epistemic knowledge into the local socio-cultural context. This contextualizing for Marglin means the abandonment of the ideology of knowledge which only recognizes *episteme* as knowledge. Therefore it means the explicit recognition that all knowledge is always a combination of *episteme* and *techne*. In the case of the first Indian psychoanalyst, Nandy's study of Bose shows that he did recontextualize psychoanalysis in Indian philosophical traditions but that his failure to deal head-on with the positivist Freud ultimately destroyed his project of indigenizing psychoanalysis.

If we understand the intertwining of *episteme* with *techne* as the contextualizing of *episteme* in locality, it may be that this by itself may not be sufficient to transform the relationship between *episteme* and other forms of knowledge into a dialogical relationship. We must ask ourselves whether the hierarchical relationship between *episteme*, various *technai*, as well as other types of non-Western knowledge systems may not be the corollary of the ontology gathered within it. An *episteme* based on Cartesian rationality posits the existence of a mind outside the world; a mind not situated, contextualized, or otherwise rooted in any particular context. The transcendental nature of this mind places it outside and above all other manifestations rooted in particular contexts. In other words forms of knowing that do not share in this ontology are by definition 'below' *episteme*; by being of the body, of the world, and of nature they are, from the point of view of a transcendental mind, fettered, and therefore limited. *Episteme* can recognize *techne* and other knowledges, make them part of itself even, but cannot remain *episteme* and forgo its transcendental nature, hence its superiority. The case of the pragmatists discussed by Nancy Gutman makes this clear. Pragmatist thinkers have abandoned certainty and absolute truth. The immense resistance within the profession of economics to recognizing Keynes as a pragmatist stems from this—most often implicit—recognition that such a reading would rob economics of its privileged status and thus of its political clout.

Zimmermann phrases the question clearly: what would biology look like without a separation between mind and world? What would natural history be like without Hegel's transcendental subject? Haldane came to India sensing that there, in a context where the common rule of Nature includes the products of the human mind and imagination, he would learn to understand diversity. It may be that for a genuine dialogue to take place *episteme* might have to alter itself profoundly to the point of self-negation. This, however, does not mean that science would stop. Haldane was willing to do science differently and there have been others since him (and probably some before him) similarly inclined.[28] It may mean that development will cease to be a one-way export from the North to the South. The traffic will go both ways and Haldane's journey would no longer seem such an unusual one.

NOTES TO CHAPTER 1

1. Vaclav Havel 'The End of the Modern Era', *New York Sunday Times* editorial, 1 Mar. 1992.
2. In our previous publication (Apffel-Marglin and Marglin, 1990) we have called this modern form of thought the dominant system of knowledge.

3. It is by no means the only system of knowledge in what can be called 'the West' and one can speak of Western knowledge systems in the plural. With conquests, world trade, colonialism, and development, however, what the West exported, and continues to export world-wide, is a particular form of rationality which is dominant today. The terms 'dominant' and 'Western' are used in a basically relational or situational manner rather than in an essentialist manner. A system of knowledge becomes dominant from the perspective of other systems of knowledge and the term 'Western' clearly does not refer to a unified place or civilization; the West emerges as a monolith only in opposition to another culture, only when one situates oneself in worlds such as that of the Tanzanian craft fisherpeople discussed in Ch. 2, or the Oriya subsistence agriculturalists discussed in Ch. 5, or the Mexican peasants discussed in Chs. 6 and 7. The relationality of these two terms means that the characteristic of 'dominance' or of something that can be labelled 'Western' becomes visible through contrast. It does not mean that the characterization is illusory or empty.

4. Robert Proctor (1991) gives us a detailed history of the emergence of the separation between scientific pursuits and ethical questions.

5. Taylor traces the continuity—as well as the discontinuity—between Descartes's turn inward and Augustine's inwardness. Descartes's subjectivization of rationality owed much to Augustinian piety, but unlike St Augustine, who located the moral sources outside humans, Descartes relies on rationality as a subjective activity for discerning the right conduct (1989: 143).

6. As Carolyn Merchant points out in her book *The Death of Nature*, this contrast between the new mechanistic cosmology and Renaissance magic created another powerful alliance against various heresies between the new science and Christianity.

7. On the new alliance between Christian doctrine and the new mode of knowing see also Abram, 1991; in the case of primatology Haraway calls it Judeo-Christian science (1989: 9).

8. Tambiah's path-breaking series of essays on magic and ritual are now gathered in a volume of his essays (1985).

9. Medard Boss in his interviews does not refer to his interlocutor by name but only as 'the sage'. The identity of this sage as the scholar-saint Gopinath Kaviraj of Uttar Pradesh is well known in India (personal communication, Giri Deshingkar).

10. Partha Chatterjee has also developed this idea in *Nationalist Thought and the Colonial World* (1986).

11. On the alliance between the Indian state and Cartesian rationality see the work of Shiv Visvanathan (1985; 1988).

12. On the role of statistics, censuses, maps, historical monuments, museums, etc. for the colonizing of South-East Asia and their adoption by nationalist movements see Anderson, 1989. On the foundational role that the idea of social engineering played in the holocaust see Bauman, 1989.

13. For a commentary on and development of Gandhi's ideas and vision of an alternative to industrial civilization see the works by the Kumarappa brothers (1946; 1949). Michael Adas (author of *Machines as the Measure of Men*, 1989) is currently engaged in writing a book on Gandhi's own and Gandhian alternatives to industrialization. Adas is motivated by the conviction that industrial

civilization must profoundly alter its course if it is to avoid both natural and social-ecological disaster.

14. This is the kind of effect which Bourdieu (1990) claims is the result of an objectivist, theoretical perspective.

15. In rejecting this separation between mind and world, the pragmatist's stance is the same as that of the Indic systems referred to above. However, it differs in other respects from the Vedantic or Madhyamic stance. The pragmatists share with those schools the conviction that there is no absolutely certain starting-point. The pragmatist view that the value of intellectual tools is measured by their practical success refers only to success in the world and not to something affecting the knower herself. In the Indic schools referred to, the life and character of the knower is transformed in the activity of knowing.

16. For a similar understanding of economics as being embedded in culture see Gudeman (1986). See also Dumont (1977) for a focus on the embeddedness of Marx's economics in the modern individualist construction of the person.

17. For a similar anti-democratic utilization of 'superior' Western science see my cultural and historical study of smallpox eradication in India (1990).

18. Colin Turnbull's book on the Ik, *The Mountain People* (1972), illustrates not only the disastrous effects of the creation of a wildlife preserve on a hunting and gathering people, but also the ethically bankrupt nature of a system of knowledge which adheres to an objectivist stance. Turnbull's book is an 'objective' description of what happens to a community when it is dying of hunger. He shows no ethical discomfort in pursuing anthropological scientific observation in a situation where he was not only well fed and protected but also knew the cause of the desperate predicament of his subjects and chose to carry on prolonged fieldwork rather than immediately addressing their plight. The Kidepo valley in North-east Uganda was the major source of game for the Ik until it was transformed into a wildlife park and they were excluded from it. Their hunting and foraging took them from Uganda to Sudan and Kenya. Turnbull does not give a date for the creation of the Kidepo Park nor any precise details as to the manner in which the Ik became settled agriculturists. The year he met them (in the mid-1960s) he found them in the grip of a drought and an acute famine. Turnbull's anthropological voyeurism is compounded by the fact that this book is a popular introductory ethnography in many American colleges and universities, intended to edify generations of American students by informing them of the depths to which humans can sink in extreme conditions.

19. This view is again very similar to Bourdieu's. The latter states that instruments of objectification, or what Marglin would call epistemization—such as maps, diagrams, and statistics—destroy the logic of practice (1990: 11).

20. For a clear example of the violence that epistemization wreaks on the *techne* of individuals see James Clifford's (1988) account of the Mashpee Indian court case and the manner in which the oral testimony of members of that community was disregarded in favour of the written and epistemic testimony of experts.

21. Ernst and Christine von Weizsacker (1987) make a similar argument in the context of theories of evolution and argue that along with 'fitness' an equally

crucial concept is that of 'error-friendliness'; they argue that in the face of uncertainty, the unpredictability of the future, room must be made for what from a particular present orientation are errors. These errors can become tomorrow's successes.

22. For examples on this issue see Schlesinger's (1982) article on Indian peasant practices; see also Appadurai (1990); and Savyasaachi (1993); on this issue see also the work of Stephen Gudeman and Alberto Rivera (1990).

23. This position is the one that has opened up a role for anthropologists in the development project. For a critique of development anthropology similar to Esteva's critique of Borlaug see Escobar (1991).

24. On the misogyny of Hegel's devaluation of all that is of the body and the world see Lloyd, 1984: chs. 4, 5, and 6.

25. For a humorous as well as deadly critique of the inverse relationship between ethnological records and the well-being of living peoples see Ch. 4 of Deloria, 1988.

26. Christine von Weizsacker (1988) makes an argument similar to Visvanathan's concerning the insufficiency and ultimate danger of preserving genetic diversity solely through gene-banks, and advocates the preservation of traditional agricultural practices as the only reliable safeguard of diversity.

27. For a critique along these lines of the category of 'homosexuality' I refer the reader to Foucault's *History of Sexuality*, (1980), and to Marilyn Strathern's discussion of so-called homosexuality in some Melanesian boys' initiation rites in *Gender of the Gift* (1988).

28. One such is C. V. Seshadri, who has created a grassroots scientific research centre in Madras, India; see his *Equity is Good Science* (1993). Another is Herb Bernstein, co-author with Marcus Raskin of *New Ways of Knowing*, who has created the Institute for Science and Interdisciplinary Studies in Amherst, Mass.

REFERENCES

ABRAM, D. (1991), 'The Mechanical and the Organic: Epistemological Consequences of the Gaia Hypothesis', in S. Schneider and P. Boston (eds.), *Scientists on Gaia*, Cambridge, Mass: MIT Press.

ADAS, M. (1989), *Machines as the Measure of Men: Science, Technology, and Ideologies of Western Dominance*, Ithaca, NY: Cornell University Press.

ANDERSON, B. (1989), 'Census, Map, Museum: Notes on the Origins of Official Nationalism in Southeast Asia', paper presented at the WIDER conference on Systems of Knowledge as Systems of Domination, Karachi, Pakistan.

APFFEL-MARGLIN, F. (1990), 'Smallpox in Two Systems of Knowledge', in F. Apffel-Marglin and S. A. Marglin (eds.), *Dominating Knowledge: Development, Culture, and Resistance*, Oxford: Clarendon Press: 102–44.

——and S. A. MARGLIN (1990) (eds.), *Dominating Knowledge: Development, Culture, and Resistance*, Oxford: Clarendon Press.

APPADURAI, A. (1990), 'Technology and the Reproduction of Values in Western India', in Apffel-Marglin and Marglin (1990).

BANURI, T. and APFFEL MARGLIN, F. (1993) (eds.), *Who Will Save the Forests? Resistance, Knowledge, and the Environmental Crisis*, London: Zed Books.

BAUMAN, Z. (1989), *Modernity and the Holocaust*, Ithaca, NY: Cornell University Press.

BERNSTEIN, H. (1987), 'Idols of Modern Science and the Reconstruction of Science', in M. G. Raskin and H. J. Bernstein (eds.), *New Ways of Knowing: The Sciences, Society, and Reconstructive Knowledge*, Totowa, NJ: Rowman & Littlefield: 37–68.

BOSS, M. (1966), *A Psychiatrist Discovers India*, trans. H. A. Frey, Calcutta Allahabad Bombay: Rupa.

BOURDIEU, P. (1990), *The Logic of Practice*, Stanford, Calif.: Stanford University Press.

BURKE, P. (1990), 'Historians, Anthropologists and Symbols', in E. Ohnuki-Tierney (ed.), *Culture Through Time*, Stanford Calif.: Stanford University Press: 269–83.

CHATTERJEE, P. (1986), *Nationalist Thought and the Colonial World: A Derivative Discourse*, London: Zed Books.

CLIFFORD, J. (1988), *The Predicament of Culture*, Cambridge, Mass.: Harvard University Press.

DELORIA, V. (1988 edn.), *Custer Died for Your Sins*, Norman London: University of Oklahoma Press.

DETIENNE, M. (1981), *The Creation of Mythology*, Chicago: University of Chicago Press.

DUMONT, L. (1977), *From Mandeville to Marx: The Genesis and Triumph of Economic Ideology*, Chicago: Chicago University Press.

ESCOBAR, A. (1991), 'Anthropology and the Developmental Encounter: The Making and Marketing of Development Anthropology', *American Ethnologist*, 18/4: 658–82.

FOUCAULT, M. (1965), *Madness and Civilization: A History of Insanity in the Age of Reason*, New York: Random.

——(1973), *The Birth of the Clinic*, New York: Pantheon.

——(1970), *The Order of Things*, New York: Pantheon.

——(1977), *Discipline and Punish*, New York: Pantheon.

——(1980), *History of Sexuality: An Introduction*, New York: Vintage Books.

GANDHI, M. K. (1938), *Hind Swaraj or Home Rule*, Ahmedabad: Navajivan Publishing House.

GRILLO, E. F. (1993), 'La Cosmovision Andina de Siempre y la Cosmologia Occidental Moderna', in *Desarrollo o Descolonizacion en los Andes?* Proyecto Andino de Tecnologias Campesinas (PRATEC), Lima, Peru.

GUDEMAN, S. (1986), *Economics as Culture: Models and Metaphors of Livelihood*, New York: Routledge & Kegan Paul.

——and RIVERA, A. (1990), *Conversations in Colombia: The Domestic Economy in Life and Text*, Cambridge: Cambridge University Press.

GUHA, R. (1989), 'Dominance without Hegemony and its Historiography', in R. Guha (ed.), *Subaltern Studies*, vi, Delhi: Oxford University Press.

38   INTRODUCTION: RATIONALITY AND THE WORLD

HABERMAS, J. (1971), 'Technology and Science as Ideology', *Towards a Rational Society*, ch. 6, London: Heineman.

HARAWAY, D. (1989), *Primate Visions: Gender, Race, and Nature in the World of Modern Science*, New York London: Routledge.

KUMARAPPA, B. (1965), *Capitalism, Socialism, or Villagism?* (1946 report) Benares: Varanasi.

KUMARAPPA, J. C. (1949), *Why the Village Movement?* 5th edn., Madhya Pradesh: Wardha.

LLOYD, G. (1984), *The Man of Reason: 'Male' and 'Female' in Western Philosophy*, Minneapolis: University of Minnesota Press.

MACCORMACK, C. and STRATHERN, M. (1980), *Nature, Culture and Gender*, Cambridge: Cambridge University Press.

MARGLIN, S. (1974), 'What do Bosses Do?', *Review of Radical Political Economy*, 6: 60–112.

——(1990b), 'Losing Touch: The Cultural Conditions of Worker Accomodation and Resistance', in Apffel-Marglin and Marglin (1990), 217–82.

MAXWELL, N. (1984), *From Knowledge to Wisdom: A Revolution in the Aims & Methods of Science*, Oxford: Basil Blackwell.

MERCHANT, C. (1980), *The Death of Nature: Women, Ecology and the Scientific Revolution*, San Francisco, Calif.: Harper and Row.

PANIKKAR, R. (1990), 'Religious Pluralism: The Metaphysical Challenge', *Interculture*, 23/3: 25–44 (Montreal).

PROCTOR, R. N. (1991), *Value-Free Science? Purity and Power in Modern Knowledge*, Cambridge, Mass.: Harvard University Press.

SAVYASAACHI (1993), 'An Alternative System of Knowledge: Fields and Forests in Abhujhmarh' in Banuri and Apffel-Marglin (1993).

SCHLESINGER, L. (1982), 'Agriculture and Community', in G. Dalton (ed.), *Research in Economic Anthropology*, iv: 233–74.

SESHADRI, C. V. (1993), *Equity is Good Science: The Equity Papers*, Madras: MCRC, Tharamani.

SHIVA, V. (1993), *Monocultures of the Mind: Biodiversity, Biotechnology and 'Scientific' Agriculture*, London: Zed Books and Third World Network.

STRATHERN, M. (1988), *The Gender of the Gift*, Berkeley, Calif.: University of California Press.

TAMBIAH, S. J. (1985), *Culture, Thought and Social Action*, Cambridge, Mass.: Harvard University Press.

——(1990), *Magic, Science, Religions, and the Scope of Rationality*, Cambridge: Cambridge University Press.

——(1989), *Sources of the Self: The Making of Modern Identity*, Cambridge, Mass.: Harvard University Press.

TOULMIN, S. (1990), *Cosmopolis: The Hidden Agenda of Modernity*, New York: Free Press.

TURNBULL, C. (1972), *The Mountain People*, New York: Simon & Schuster.

UBEROI, J. S. (1978), *Science and Culture*, Delhi: Oxford University Press.

VARELA, F. J., THOMPSON, E., and ROSCH, E. (1991), *The Embodied Mind: Cognitive Science and Human Experience*, Cambridge, Mass.: MIT Press.

VISVANATHAN, S. (1985), *Organizing for Science*, Delhi: Oxford University Press.

——(1988), 'From the Annals of the Laboratory State', in A. Nandy (ed.), *Science,*

Hegemony, and Violence, Delhi: Oxford University Press.

WEBER, M. (1950), *General Economic History*, Glencoe, Ill.: Free Press.

WEIZSACKER, C. VON (1988), 'Seed Options: Four Approaches to the *in situ* conservation of local crops', MS, Bonn, March.

WEIZSACKER, E. VON and WEIZSACKER, C. VON (1987), 'How to Live with Errors? On the Evolutionary Power of Errors', *World Futures*, 23/3: 225–35.

WRIGHT, G. H. VON (1991), 'Images of Science and Forms of Rationality' in S. J. Doorman (ed.), *Images of Science: Scientific Practice and the Public*, Aldershot Brookfield Hong Kong Singapore Sydney: Gower: 11–29.

PART I

Decolonizing Development Knowledge

2

Development for 'Big Fish' or for 'Small Fish'?: A Study of Contrasts in Tanzania's Fishing Sector

MARJA-LIISA SWANTZ AND AILI MARI TRIPP

Probably no other African nation has adopted so explicitly a people-first orientation as Tanzania. The ideological impetus for this thrust came from Julius Nyerere, who stepped down in 1985 from his 24-year tenure in the office of the presidency. The approach was evident in the country's ambitious public service programmes, especially in the areas of adult education and health care. In the 27 years after Independence, Tanzania raised life expectancy from age 42 to 51 and adult literacy from 10 to 79 per cent. In addition, about half the population had access to potable water (Helleiner, 1985: 21).

Tanzania's commitment to basic needs was coupled with a populist emphasis on mass participation in the development process. In the ruling Party's 1971 Mwongozo Guidelines the policy orientation was unambiguous: if development is to benefit the people, the people must participate in considering, planning, and implementing their development plans. The duty of our Party is not to urge the people to implement plans which have been decided upon by a few experts and leaders. The duty of our Party is to ensure that the leaders and experts implement the plans that have been agreed upon by the people themselves (Clause 28).

Nyerere expressed this even more forcefully in a 1968 speech:

We have to be a part of the society which we are changing; we have to work from within it, and not try to descend like ancient gods, do something and disappear again. A country, or a village, or a community, cannot be developed; it can only develop itself. For real development means the development, the growth, of people. Every country in Africa can show examples of modern facilities which have been provided for the people and which are rotting unused. We have schools, irrigation works, expensive markets, and so on. Things by which someone came and tried to 'bring development to the people'. If real development is to take place, the people have to be involved (1973: 25).

Local ten-house cells were to serve as mechanisms in mobilizing democratic grassroots participation in the political and development processes. These cells were the building-blocks of a hierarchical political structure that included branches, wards, districts, and regions.

The stated policies were not only geared towards popular participation in the development process, but also towards incorporating people's own knowledge. In a 1968 speech Nyerere explained:

Knowledge does not only come out of books . . . We have wisdom in our own past, and in those who still carry the traditional knowledge accumulated in that tribal past . . . We would be stupid indeed if we allowed the development of our economies to destroy the human and social values which African societies had built up over centuries. Yet if we are to save these, we cannot afford the arrogance which our technical superiority tempts us to assume (1973: 27).

Given the unusual sensitivity the nation's political leadership exhibited towards starting from the people themselves in charting development plans, one has to ask, why in practice was a 'top-down' approach the rule rather than the exception. Rarely were people's own priorities, values, working arrangements, and technologies taken into account or taken as a starting-point for development programmes initiated by the government and/or external donor agencies. 'Progress' came to mean something that existed externally to the 'objects' of development schemes, i.e. to people themselves. Their so-called traditional practices would have to be eradicated before 'development' could occur. Development was generally something 'done to' people or imposed on them in the form of directives, projects and campaigns rather than being a collective interactive endeavour.

At its worst, this thinking led to coercion, as seen at times in the forced removal of people from their homes during the massive Operesheni Vijijini campaign to resettle the rural population into villages from 1972 to 1975. The more benign manifestations of this kind of thinking involved the paternalism leaders expressed in their interactions with local people. This paternalism was reflected, for example, in the comments of a senior official involved in the Shinyanga villagization scheme, who stated that 'Tanzania could not sit back and watch the majority of its people leading 'a life of death'. The state had, therefore, to take the role of the 'father' in ensuring that its people chose a better and more prosperous life for themselves' (quoted in Bernstein 1981: 45).

Perhaps the greatest fallacy of the development ideology is that it relegated people who adhered to traditional beliefs and practices to being passive receptacles of progress, denying them agency in their own lives, and refusing to recognize their own choices and rationales for asserting these preferences. One Party cell leader put it poignantly: 'You can't force people to go along on the narrow road. People have their own minds (*akili*). They aren't going to go along with force' (Tripp, 1989).

One of the key factors militating against a bottom-up approach was the emphasis on the role of the state, i.e. the Party, the government, and its administrative, legal, extractive, and coercive institutions. In Tanzania, as in other parts of the Third World, much of the expansion of the state's role in society had to do initially with the post-War thinking emerging in the West. This thinking was influenced by the market failures of the 1930s and the reconstruction policies of the 1940s and 1950s, and looked to the state to maintain trade and maintain a macroeconomic balance. The views of development economists, who saw an even greater need for state intervention in the economies of developing countries, were fused with those of radical Third World nationalist leaders. In Africa these nationalists looked to the state as an instrument for exerting domestic interests over those of foreign interests. The state also gave politicians a base from which to enhance their personal power by manipulating markets via the state. Furthermore, at Independence, there was only a small African entrepreneur class, which meant that the state had to fulfil functions that might otherwise have been undertaken by the private sector (Wilson, 1988: 25; Brett, 1987: 31).

The newly independent Tanzanian state made a sharp break with the colonial state in its ideological emphasis on egalitarianism, communalism, and self-reliance. However, various structures and administrative practices inherited from the colonial state proved more difficult to transcend. One clear example of this was the 1970s villagization programme that was seen as a way of bringing about rural socialism. Most of the rural population was resettled in this programme.

Villagization was designed both to ease the distribution of social services and to facilitate administration of the rural population. The operation was reminiscent of the German and British colonial schemes to resettle people along the roads to make it easier to administer them and transport export crops. In the 1930s, for example, the British colonialists created 'minor settlements' as adjuncts to larger towns. Their purpose was to make it easier to carry out tax collection, judicial administration, and trade. Sisal and other plantations were similarly used to create reservoirs of labour. The majority of people at that time, however, chose to stay away from areas of tight administrative control and the plantations, preferring their own areas where they grew food and cash crops (Mascarenhas, 1981: 147–8).

As in the colonial days, those implementing 'Operation Villagization' paid little attention to local ecological and social conditions and local methods of cultivation, often with disastrous results. In the villagization process, Boesen writes, 'the existing agricultural and land use systems were often disregarded although they were the basic elements in the adaptation to the ecology of different areas of the peasants' vital demand for security and for the main tenance of their family development cycles' (1979: 136). Some of the consequences of the disruptions of villagization were food shortages and hunger. People were forced to huddle in temporary shacks in the cold and rain when their houses were demolished. They tended to shun working in communal fields and now had to walk farther to their own fields. Fields close to the village often suffered from over-cultivation resulting in soil infertility. People also had to walk further to collect firewood and water (Raikes, 1986: 120).

The example of villagization shows that even one of the cornerstone programmes of the nation was not an entirely new creation of the socialist state but had its precedent in the colonial regime. In spite of its socialist rhetoric and nationalism, the new state faced many of the same dilemmas of governance as the colonial state, frequently resorting to similar measures to deal with these problems. Moreover, the post-colonial state, aided and abetted by foreign donors, frequently encroached on and distorted local initiatives and practices.

This chapter explores the case of the fishing sector in Tanzania, examining the presuppositions often made by donors, development planners, and experts in their dealings with local people they have targeted for development.[1] It looks at a foreign-sponsored training project in the fishing sector situated in the midst of a local fishing community 50 miles north of Dar es Salaam. The project's emphasis on sophisticated trawling technology in effect reduced the needs, interests, and technological development of artisan fishermen to virtual irrelevance. Like many other capital-intensive operations, this project tied up precious foreign exchange and increased dependence on donors for spare parts and other equipment. It became so costly to operate that the prospects of turning a profit were not in sight even fourteen years after it began to receive major financial assistance from abroad. In contrast, the artisan fishermen, who caught 98 per cent of the total fish catch in Tanzania, mainly used local inputs in making their boats and equipment. They primarily served local markets, providing people with cheaper fish than industrial fishing was able to offer.

This case-study examines why this development project gave so little consideration to the people it was initially designed to reach, undermining the very goals Tanzania and the donor countries set out to accomplish. It reveals the depth of the rift between 'expert knowledge' and 'local knowledge' and the lack of concern by experts for local conditions, wisdom, and values. In Tanzania, as in other developing countries, the dominant economic and political interests support proponents of 'scientific knowledge', which they consider superior knowledge. This chapter critically evaluates the utility of the Western notion of universal scientific and technical knowledge in the context of this empirical study.

BACKGROUND: COASTAL ARTISAN FISHING

Approximately 13,000 artisan fishermen operate 3,500 small boats along Tanzania's 800 km. Indian Ocean coastline, with yields of close to 40,000 tons of fish a year and a shrimp catch of 1,000 tons a year (NORAD, 1986: 5). The best fishing is between December and March during the north-east monsoon, but it is also good from August to December, especially after the rough south-east monsoon. Some say, 'Fish are like mangoes, they have the same seasons.' During the fishing seasons, larger teams of fishermen come from Zanzibar, Pemba, the southern coast, or from inland lakes like Lake Nyasa (Lake Malawi) to fish at different locations up and down the coast.

Fishermen along the Indian Ocean operate primarily five types of boats: dug-outs (*ngalawa, mtumbwi,* and *hori*) and plank-built boats (*mashua* and *kidau*). The *ngalawa* have outriggers. Of these boats the *ngalawa* is the most common in the Dar es Salaam–Bagamoyo area (Sassoon, 1970: 200).[2] Most fishermen fish in groups of two or three using handlines and hooks. They use squid, octopus, or small fish to catch rock cod, horse mackerel, kingfish, wrasse, and a variety of small fish in addition to large sharks, swordfish, and skate. They also catch lobster, crayfish, and shrimp.

Various nets of different sizes and mesh are used, depending on the fisherman's financial means and the general availability of gear. One man can fish alone in shallow waters using a cast-net, which he throws in front of him. Weights rapidly sink the net, while he pulls the ropes, catching the fish in the bag that forms. More commonly two fishermen carry a small gill-net of $\frac{1}{2}$–3" mesh into knee-deep water forming a circle while beating the water with their hands. One checks the net for fish while the other holds it (Wenban-Smith, 1963: 173).

Those working in teams fish with a beach seine (*juya*) at low tide. They attach one end to the beach, dragging the other end out in a boat, while a dozen others form a semicircle to pull it in. Larger drag-nets employing a similar principle are used in deeper waters, where they are pulled by about eight men in each boat. Some swim (with the aid of goggles) and loosen the net if it gets caught in coral or seaweed.

Gill-nets of 6" mesh (*jarife*) are dropped in deeper waters on reefs overnight to catch larger fish, while smaller gill-nets are placed in reefs in shallow waters. As the tide recedes it leaves fish caught in the net, which are collected at low tide (Hassett, 1985: 103).

Only men's fishing activities are referred to as 'fishing', regardless of whether or not they use boats and nets. Women's manner of catching fish is not considered 'fishing'. Women wade through shallow waters to entrap schools of small fish (*dagaa*) in calico sheets, hence their fishing is referred to by the word meaning the spreading of the cloth or net, *kutanda*. In the past women used their black *kaniki* cloth or men's white *shukas* to catch fish. Later mesh nylon became popular (Landberg, 1969; Hassett, 1984: 97). Women fish these small *dagaa* both for consumption and for sale. *Dagaa* have become especially popular in recent years as people have found it harder to afford meat and larger fish. In describing their hardships, people often refer to their diet of *dagaa* and spinach as a poor person's diet of 'nails and small brooms' (*misumari na ufagio*).

Children, youths, and women are most often found collecting shellfish, octopus, squid, sea-slugs, and eels in shallow waters on reefs when the tide has receded. For these seafoods the investment is minimal: a sharp stick with which to poke around in the reefs, and a spear or club which is used to catch octopus and squid, and possibly goggles. Aluminium pots are used to collect the shells and sea-slugs are thrown into gunny sacks. These seafoods are collected both for consumption and for sale in small income-generating projects. The sea-slugs are sold to people who cook and dry them for resale to South-East Asia and China. In some villages, like Mlingotini near Bagamoyo, the youths and women themselves prepare the slugs for sale.[3]

The most common trap is a hexagonal basket (*dema*), which is 1m. in diameter and made of bamboo strips and float-markers. Baiting the traps with turtleweed, crushed shellfish, or offal, fishermen lay them on reefs where fish feed. They collect the entrapped small fish or crayfish the following day during the low tide. The traps can also be laid by boat in deeper waters.

Until recently, several long fence-traps (*wando*) could be seen on the low beaches, but they decreased in popularity in the 1980s. It consists of a fence of chicken-wire attached to a row of mangrove poles going out in a straight line. When the tide is high, the fish swim up the mesh and are caught in a trap at the end of the fence, where they are collected when the tide has receded.[4]

PANDE FISHERMEN AND THE MBEGANI FISHERIES DEVELOPMENT CENTRE

Since the mid-1960s the Tanzanian government's goal in the fishing sector has been to increase fish production, to increase internal consumption in order to improve nutrition, to raise the incomes of fishing communities, and to generate foreign exchange from fish exports. Although policy-makers were divided over how best to achieve these aims and how to prioritize them, the goals, nevertheless, remained the same over the years.

In 1964 Tanzania formed a separate Fisheries Division within the Ministry of Agriculture, Food and Cooperatives.[5] Ten years later a state-owned Tanzania Fisheries Corporation (TAFICO) was established to supervise the use of new 'modern' boats obtained through development aid (Hallensvedt and Hersoug, 1985: 20). The Fisheries Division also established three training centres, including the Megalith Fisheries Development Centre (MFDC), which was built close to the quiet fishing village of Pande in 1966. In 1972 the Tanzanian government asked Norway, which had already indicated a general interest in providing assistance to Tanzania's fishing sector, to send a fisheries expert to advise on how to organize its fishing sector.[6] The Norwegian expert recommended that Norway assist Tanzania in developing the Mbegani Fisheries Development Centre. After further studies and consultations, in 1976 Norway agreed to provide NOK 17.5 m. ($4 m.) in financial assistance to develop Tanzania's fishing sector. That same year the official Norwegian aid agency, the Royal Norwegian Ministry of Development Cooperation (NORAD), hired FIDECO, a Norwegian firm of fisheries consultants made up of twenty Norwegian fishing companies, to develop the MFDC. Two years later a NORAD evaluation commission found that the Centre was not progressing as planned because of FIDECO's inability to organize the training and Tanzania's inability to meeting its planning and construction obligations.

As a result of the evaluation NORAD decided to take direct responsibility for Norway's commitments to the MFDC. A new agreement was worked out between Tanzania and NORAD in 1979, and in 1980 NORAD granted another NOK 85 m. ($20 m.) to operate and expand the MFDE. It hired two Norwegian firms to supervise the planning and construction of the MFDC. Two years later the Centre received its first students and in 1983 the majority of the construction at the MFDC had been completed. By the end of 1984 the Centre was operating close to full capacity with 117 students (NORAD, 1986: 26–9). By 1984 the MFDC had cost a total of NOK 212.4 m. (approximately $50 m. in 1984 prices) with additional operational costs for 1984–7 of up to NOK 36 m. (approximately $1.8 m. a year) with comparable sums allotted for expatriate costs (NOK 32.2 m.). Norway was to contribute 75 per cent and Tanzania 25 per cent of the yearly operating costs. This meant that Tanzania's share in the project added up to one half of the total expenditure on the country's fisheries sector (NORAD, 1986).

The history of the MFDC provides a useful case-study of the way in which foreign donors and Tanzanian officials collaborated in a project that elevated expert knowledge from the outside over the knowledge of local people. It shows the wasted efforts and potential that resulted from ignoring existing know-how, technologies, and forms of organization.

The MFDC was built in a location near Pande, a village 7.5 miles south of Bagamoyo, with a population of around 1,120 and 279 households (1986 statistics). It had grown considerably since 1974, when it was only a small hamlet (neighbouring Mbegani had a population of approximately 500). Its inhabitants were primarily of Zaramo ethnic origin, but a number of Ngindo and Ndengereko had also settled in the area. Of the 491 working adults, the majority were engaged in agricultural production, growing mostly cassava and rice, and to a lesser extent coconuts and cashew-nuts as cash crops. Many of the men who fished also farmed, along with their wives and other household members, although some considered themselves full-time fishermen.

Over half of the Pande women were involved in small income-generating activities like extracting coconut oil and making and selling buns (*maandazi*), rice cakes (*vitumbua*), and cooked beans (*maharage*). Most women were also skilled in mat-making, while a number made pottery for local sale (Masaiganah, 1986: 92). They obtained considerable amounts of cash from the sale of fried fish. We calculated that from fish bought both locally and at the Centre, about 110–20 women in the surrounding seven villages fried and sold fish two or three times a week, and that one quarter of their families ate small amounts of fish one or two days a week, while the other three-quarters did so irregularly.

In 1974–5, during the period of Villagization, the inhabitants of Pande and the nearby hamlets were directed to move to the adjacent village of Mlingotini. Many demolished their own houses under orders or watched as field-force units tore them down. Villagers sent a delegation to the National Party Headquarters to complain and the Party halted the action, thus preventing the further destruction of their homes. Pande was then established as a separate village. However, in the course of the Villagization operation many had been forced to move their houses to another site. There were those who more than ten years later still considered their new houses to be temporary structures.

It was in this setting that the MFDC was established. Since the population surrounding Mbegani derived a considerable portion of its subsistence from activities related to the ocean, including fishing, transporting or selling fish, and building boats, they could potentially have benefited considerably from the Centre being located in their midst.

However, from the outset the MFDC's interest in developing the artisan sector was limited and problematic, as this chapter will show. The limitations came from both the Tanzanian fishing officials and from the Norwegians involved with the MFDC project. The general aim of the MFDC was to train professional personnel for operative positions within Tanzania's coastal and inland fisheries, including training aimed at developing the country's traditional fisheries. A secondary aim was the provision of training for Tanzania's coastal fleet (NORAD, 1986: 22).

In the process of hammering out an agreement between NORAD and Tanzania over the MFDC in 1979, it became apparent that the Tanzanian bureaucrats disapproved of the goal of strengthening the artisan sector. Their emphasis was on training technically skilled experts and not extension workers. To them it did not make sense to invite external experts to teach what the country already knew. However, the officials' interest in high technology did not involve considerations of how useful and appropriate it was in the Tanzanian context. NORAD had disagreed with the Tanzanian officials' emphasis on theoretical expertise, pressing for more training in practical skills and training of local fishermen in order to improve coastal artisan fishing. However, when the 1979 agreement between NORAD and

Tanzania was signed, no mention was made of how the MFDC was to assist the artisan fishermen.

Thus, the Centre's initial aim to help artisan fishermen was virtually lost among other goals which gained predominance: namely, the promotion of industrial fishing aimed at earning foreign exchange through the export of fish and prawns. The project emphasized the training of skippers, engineers, and fishing officers in nautical science, marine engineering, fish-processing and refrigeration engineering, marketing, and boat-building. Trainees practised on a larger Norwegian trawling vessel, M/V Mafunzo, equipped with large-scale cold storage and freezing capacity, i.e. facilities for large industrial capital-intensive fishing.

To satisfy its original commitments to the small-scale fishing sector, the Centre started three-month courses in Pangani in 1983 and later in Mbegani itself, in addition to the courses being held in Musoma on Lake Victoria. These courses mainly served groups of young men, and later also a few women, chosen from various fishing villages in the respective areas. Teaching consisted of net-making, trawling, and learning to operate an engine and a motor-boat. The short courses suffered from being unrelated to the villagers' own fishing methods and technology. A 1986 NORAD evaluation team visited five of the villages from which the students had come and met some of the students. In one village north of Tanga the village itself had made an effort to provide the young people with some equipment and make use of the skills they had learned. But many of the villagers complained that they did not have enough gear to make use of the learning. The young trainees were restricted in their use of fishing technology because of their inability to purchase more sophisticated equipment, motor boats, and fuel at affordable prices. This made the training frustrating to young people who would have wanted to start experimenting with motorboats. At one point those who completed the course received some (non-motorized) equipment. But overall, the courses suffered from not responding to the real needs of fishing villages.

The gap between the aims of the MFDC and the needs of artisan fishermen became most obvious in relation to Pande fishermen, who continued to keep their boats only 20 m. from the main MFDC office yet remained virtually superfluous to the project. Physically coexisting, the MFDC created and perpetuated a distance between the project and the local fishermen. Similarly, one local fish-trader was refused space in the Mbegani freezers for transporting prawns from the northern coastal town of Sadani to Dar es Salaam, while several big fishing companies were permitted to store their catch there.

The separateness of the practitioners of the two technologies was further underscored by the erection of a fence around the MFDC compound, ostensibly to prevent theft. Nevertheless, it curtailed social interaction between those inside and outside the fence. Although local fishermen, traders, and buyers were permitted to use the beach within the MFDC grounds, many complained of restrictions on their movement in and out of the compound (NORAD, 1986: 56–7, 62).

The development of the fishing project paralleled the underdevelopment of local fishing. Fishermen experienced a decrease in their catches as a result of competition from large trawlers. Breeding and nursing grounds for various fish were disturbed, while trawling for prawns near Bagamoyo allegedly interfered with the stationary nets of artisan fishermen in waters deeper than 20 m. The MFDC vigorously denied that its trawlers competed with small-scale fishing (NORAD, 1986: 35). Mlingotini fishermen complained that the building of the Centre put an end to their beach seining. By 1989 Mlingotini boats were moving to fish from the Kaole beach near Bagamoyo town. Records from 1977–84 show a steady decline of boats bringing in fish at the Pande landing station. From a one-time high of 55 boats, in 1977 41 boats landed fish at the station; by 1983 the number of boats had decreased to 29; and by 1985 they had dwindled to a mere nine (Swantz, 1986: 32). The declining number of operating fishing boats is reflected in the numbers of fishermen in Pande: 90 of Pande's residents were recorded as fishermen in 1985, while only 70 were recorded a year later, and of these not even 30 fished on a regular basis (Swantz, 1988).

The main reason for this decline was the lack of fishing gear. Moreover, the scarcity of spare parts and fuel meant a shift away from engine-propelled boats to the use of boats with sails in the larger villages of Mlingotini and Mbweni, where a few motor-boats had been operating earlier. Artisan fishermen were especially hard-hit by shortages of equipment in the late 1970s and early 1980s, when Tanzania fell into a serious foreign exchange crisis. It became nearly impossible to obtain basic fishing gear like handlines, hooks, casting nets, gill-nets, scoop-nets, and seines. Even locally made goods dependent on inputs requiring foreign exchange were scarce, and the little fishing equipment available was prohibitively expensive. Consequently, small-scale fishing along the coast decreased drastically during this period. Even when supplies became available after the 1984 trade liberalization it took some time before fishermen were once again in a position to purchase equipment. Moreover, the price of fishing gear remained high, regardless of the grade, mesh-size, or whether it was imported from Japan, China, Kenya, or made locally. In 1986/7 a small fishing net cost anywhere from Tsh. 500 ($ 5 according to the 1987 exchange rate) to Tsh. 3,000 ($ 30) and the largest gill-nets of 400 yds. ran as high as Tsh. 15,000 ($ 150) to Tsh. 18,000 ($ 180) (Swantz, 1988: 45; Tripp notes).

As a result of the equipment shortages, fishermen became more dependent on patrons or 'big men' who had the capital to buy imported supplies or pay high prices for smuggled gear. They had the wherewithal to invest in upgrading boats and equipment and the means to offer loans and credit to poorer fishermen. In Bagamoyo district, the ratio of fishermen to a boat was roughly 3:1 in 1983. Generally the owner of the boat was one of the fishermen. Fishermen who used only hooks and handlines generally shared the equipment and use of the boat. Those without boats could compensate with their labour. If the owner of the boat was not one of the fishermen, he would claim about 20 per cent of the catch and the rest was divided equally between the fishermen. But if the equipment also belonged to the boat-owner, then he could claim one-half to two-thirds of the revenue. In larger boats, the owner often claimed even larger portions, but then the catches generally brought in greater returns. With the increasing reliance on patrons, the financiers were less likely to be fellow-fishermen. More often they entered into fishing on a commercial basis and were also involved in the transport business and in trading fish. Consequently they were more inclined to demand larger portions of the proceeds, making it increasingly difficult for fishermen to extricate themselves from debt and dependence.

It was during the period when fishing gear was in short supply that the contrast between the artisan fishermen and 'development fishing' became especially acute. The well-stocked MFDC store stood literally yards from where the artisan fishermen launched their boats, yet these supplies were inaccessible to the local fishermen. The Centre claimed that the Ministry of Natural Resources and Tourism had not granted it permission to loan or to sell gear, engines, or boats to the fishermen. Similarly, fishermen requested that the Centre keep a motor-boat available in the event that a fisherman's boat were to capsize, but the Centre failed to pursue the matter.

There were two aspects of the work of the MFDC which suggest how the work of the Centre could have developed without creating such a large gap between the goals of the fishing communities and the goals of developing the new technology sector. These breakthroughs were made in the areas of boat-building and the training of women. Their success, although limited, could be attributed to individuals who pursued a different vision of what developing the fishing sector could mean. These two exceptions also illustrate how difficult it was to deviate from the dominant view of priorities. They show what lengths people had to go to in order to make small gains, even when the benefits were clearly visible.

LEARNING FROM LOCAL BOAT-BUILDERS

Boat-building was one of the earliest projects started by the Centre when it was under FIDECO supervision. The Centre's aim was to improve the standard of local boats and to offer training in improved boat-building technology. Without any investigation of local boat-building skills and knowledge, the MFDC experts started the training project, simply taking for granted the superiority of their imported technological skills. This ill-fated project ended with the beaches of Mbegani and Bagamoyo strewn with rusting unused boats that local fishermen could not repair because they lacked the necessary equipment and supplies.

Later, after NORAD had taken over the MFDC, training in boat-building was given primarily by three young Norwegian boat-builders who took turns working at the Centre. The second Norwegian boat-builder, whom the fishermen called Heriki, continued where the first had left off. He learned Swahili and began to explore what had been written about the coastal boat-building traditions. He started by acquainting himself with the work of the coastal boatmen. He did not have to look far in order to discover the superb skills and aesthetic quality of local boat-building. For example, around the time he was at MFDC in the mid-1980s, a team of Tanzanian and Kenyan men were building a large 40-ft. vessel called a dhow on the main Bagamoyo beach. With a set of chisels, a hand-drill, hammers, and saws the men created the graceful boat, sawing thick tree trunks into planks and placing them together. They formed large nails by hammering smelted scrap iron on a small anvil, patiently working on the boat for months. Similar smaller plank-boats were crafted in the coastal towns of Mafia, Pangani, and Kaole.

The MFDC boatyard decided to employ a local boat-builder and his assistant. They were introduced to techniques using electric handsaws and drills, circular saws, water-levels, planers, clamps, and galvanized nails. The local boat-builder later appropriated these new skills when he set up his own boat-building business next to the boatyard in order to be able to make use of the Centre's equipment when needed (Engebrigsten, 1985b). The man ended up working in the government-run boatyard in Dar es Salaam as a master-builder.

The incorporation of the local boat-builder meant that the MFDC students could, at least potentially, learn some old skills in addition to the new ones, and could experiment with a variety of boat models. As a result of this training, one of the students decided to become a boat-builder. He took on an order to build a *mashua* boat and started a small-scale fishing enterprise for himself.

Heriki also continued the efforts to modify the popular *ngalawa* outrigger boat. He tried to alter the outriggers and the sail but faced difficulties. Looking at his failed efforts, a workman at the MFDC boatyard suggested that he talk to a local *ngalawa*-maker (Engebrigsten 1985a). After consultations with a local expert and a fisherman, the *ngalawa* boat was modified and improved. The best qualities of the old boat were kept while the boat was made safer, more stable and larger than the original model. The *ngalawa* hull is generally carved from the trunk of a mango or a teak tree. The hull of the new version of the *ngalawa* was made lighter with planks, yet the same basic shape with the outriggers and the single sail was kept intact (Engebrigsten, 1985a).

The fisherman, who was doing the experimenting with the modified *ngalawa* for the boatyard, gave the builders continual and valuable feedback on his experience with the boats and the boat-builders made alterations based on his suggestions. After eight different outrigger boats had been built a prototype was finally chosen. Through this kind of interaction with local fishermen, an outrigger boat was developed which proved to be in high demand, not only from local fishermen, but also from the owners of fishing boats in Dar es Salaam and even as far away as Tanga. In addition, the MFDC introduced an outrigger boat for fishing in Lake Victoria and a couple of the Pande fishermen were sent to demonstrate how to use the boat. This represented a big change from the attitudes initially expressed by MFDC administrators.

One problem with the MFDC boat-building project was that it made contact primarily with only one fisherman and not with a group of them. This meant that the testing of the boat did not become a common concern and ultimately the boat-yard programme failed to create sustained co-operation between the Centre and the fishermen. Moreover, communication with local boat-builders was neither extensive nor intensive. Like the local fishermen, they had not been invited to visit the boatyard.

As time went on, the boatyard gave preference to the production of larger boats for financial reasons. By the late 1980s the demand for these boats grew to exceed the capacity of the boatyard to produce them. Subsequently, the price of the boats almost doubled from one year to the next, making them unaffordable to local fishermen.

In general, this boat-building programme worked out well, but did not receive much support from either the Norwegian or Tanzanian authorities. The Norwegian in the Boat-building Department worked out a plan to extend the training and to introduce the making of the improved local boat to the local boat-builders along the coast. He submitted it to NORAD but it was rejected (Engebrigsten, 1985*b*). Similarly, the boat-building team's suggestion to extend the Mbegani boatyard to nearby boat-building sites also met with disapproval. As a result, the boat-building section failed to expand co-operation between the MFDC boatyard and local boat-builders on a larger scale.

Although the boat-building project indicated the necessity of mutual learning in the development of new technologies and skills from a combination of local and new technologies, the MFDC administrators were loath to admit this. To them, the improvement of the outriggers was a one-way process, or as one administrator put it: 'We have upgraded the local boatbuilders skills.' It was evident from such remarks that the experts did not feel they needed to acknowledge in any way that they were indebted to local skills and knowledge of the environment.

The differences between the two technologies went deeper than simply different techniques or types of equipment. The differences reflected two profoundly divergent concepts of training. To the local boat-builders, training involved the task of teaching skills through apprenticeship and experience. It included paying attention to the impact of small details on the total outcome of the product, like the relationship between the quality of wood, boat-building techniques, and the seaworthiness of the boats. For the experts, the key was to teach a technique in order to carry out a particular task on the boat in an atomized fashion, with little emphasis on the relation of the individual tasks to the end product. Even though both forms of training produced skilled boat-builders, the piecemeal approach used by the Centre meant that the average student of boat-building would leave the Centre without the ability to build an entire boat.

THE WOMEN'S PROJECT AT THE MFDC

If artisan fishermen had been ignored in the MFDC project, women in the fishing communities were completely overlooked. The MFDC did not provide courses for local women in fishing or marketing. The primary interaction of local women with the Centre was in purchasing fish from MFDC trawlers. Women, who came twice a week to the Centre, were permitted to purchase up to 3 kg. of left-over fish. The students took the more valuable fish to the Dar es Salaam and Kibaha markets to practise marketing. Some fish were also sold locally to traders and to large institutions like the prisons.

There were days on which women walked to the Centre and waited hours for their fish, sitting along the walls of the cold store, only to return empty-handed because fish were not available or they were of poor quality. Frequently, the defrosted fish sold to the women became soft and spoiled after being carried home on their heads in the midday heat. After spending their cash on daily household needs, women were not able to save in order to buy larger fish. In fact, the Centre made a clear distinction between the larger male traders and the women, selling the poor quality fish to the women from a different door than the fish sold to boys who were purchasing fish for the larger traders. The illiteracy of the coastal women, coupled with male attitudes against women selling in public places, had until recently kept them from entering into public marketing.

However, pressure on NORAD from women's groups in Norway helped to change the Centre's direction in working with women. In 1985 NORAD responded by organizing a small research project in co-operation with the Women's Study Group of the Institute of Development Studies (IDS), at the University of Dar es Salaam to look into the potential for women's participation in the fisheries sector.

As a result of the study, some women's courses were organized to which women responded enthusiastically. A group of women living in the vicinity organized themselves into a co-operative with the help of two women teachers at the MFDC who had been asked to stay on the staff after they finished the diploma course. Women in the co-operative sewed clothes and sold them, saving the money to help buy a rice-mill, which received substantial support from the MFDC and NORAD. NORAD provided the premises for the mill and built a house for the women's co-operative activities. The women had a sense that the mill came as a result of their efforts, but their role was not publicly recognized at the celebration to mark the opening of the mill. Instead, the Centre representatives congratulated themselves on having made this donation to the local women.

The researchers made substantial contacts with women from the three nearby villages of Pande, Mlingotini, and Mbweni. Women had the opportunity to express themselves in discussions and to determine how to implement goals that they had set as priorities. NORAD responded to these initiatives by offering various grants and loans. The villages selected fifty women of all age-groups to attend a four-day training seminar, which the women attended without missing a day, tirelessly walking each morning to the Centre with their small children on their backs. Regardless of their age, the women were not afraid to tackle new skills, such as mending and weaving nets or smoking fish. During the seminar the women made plans for future income-generating activities. The women, who were grouped according to village and age, obtained a loan from NORAD to help them start these planned activities with which they would pay back the loan.

The younger Mlingotini women's group decided they would earn income initially by selling fish. Ultimately, they planned to buy a pick-up car to transport people and goods. They bought one of the improved outrigger boats to transport fish from the MFDC back to Mlingotini, where they packed the fish and took them by truck to Dar es Salaam early in the morning. They hired a fisherman to do the fishing for them. The project went well until the fisherman claimed that the boat had been stolen and the nets torn at sea. MFDC responded to the recommendations of the seminar by sending its students to conduct one part of their practical training in Mlingotini village in order to have first-hand contact with fishermen and women. The students were to provide special support to women's initiatives, such as building a kiln for smoking and marketing fish.

After the seminar, women from Pande continued to learn net-making at the MFDC, each making a net for herself. Pande women also started marketing fish in small quantities. Mbweni women decided to open a co-operative shop in order to sell fish locally. There was considerable demand for fish since the fishermen supplied fish only for their own families' daily consumption, while the fish-traders transported the fish to Dar es Salaam to obtain better prices, selling none to local retailers. The Mbweni women had difficulties in registering their co-operative shop and ended up paying several bribes to a man at the regional Party office who had offered to help them obtain the necessary documentation. Mbweni women also planned to start fishing, even though it was commonly believed that it was dangerous for women, especially pregnant women, to go out in the ocean. It was believed that a woman who fished would bring bad luck, but the women were ready to show that they no longer feared these taboos.

In spite of various setbacks, the seminar showed the remarkable openness in women's attitudes and their willingness to go ahead with their plans. Women faced numerous obstacles, having to fight against both the prejudices of the officials and those of family members. In development projects women are frequently relegated to the 'second phase', as it is called in Tanzania. This also happened in the MFDC, where women's training needs were addressed only because of the special efforts of women advisers in NORAD. As long as development agencies only assist women in isolated projects, the sustainability of support for women is not guaranteed. The MFDC leadership continued to consider the work with local women to be outside the responsibility of the Centre. Consequently it did not allow the women teachers to use their working hours to follow up on the women's projects. They had to do it in their leisure time and without transport help. Having their own families to care for and many other duties, this did not allow sufficient opportunity to be involved in new initiatives. It was yet another example of how little significance the technically weighted programme of the MFDC gave to village contacts. Pressure from the women, however, eventually forced a change, so that the women teachers were given more time to work with the village women and also to conduct courses in Musoma District. One teacher lived with the women for a month, planning and conducting courses which built on women's know-how and needs.

The research project brought to light a number of particular problems the women faced. The way in which powerful aid money is distributed can exacerbate existing conflicts or create new tensions depending on how it is disbursed. In the case of the village women it sometimes engendered envy between those who had participated in the women's project and those who had not, thus destroying mutual trust. The women's project also revealed the particular problems women confronted because of the customary deference they are expected to show to men. Men found it easy to cheat women, who were new to business and unaccustomed to defending their rights against the various machinations of unscrupulous men. Also women's small trade was taxed more heavily than the larger trade of men. Consequently, their profits remained small. A man selling a whole array of vegetables, fruit, and fish on a stall in one of the villages surrounding Bagamoyo paid a levy of two shillings a day, while a woman sitting next to the stall had to pay one shilling simply to sell one plate of fish. Similarly, someone selling only a couple of hundred shillings worth of fish might have to pay the same levy as the trader selling thousands of shillings worth of fish. Thus, the larger the scale of trade, the lower the proportionate levy.

The women's project at the MFDC showed the necessity of integrating women into all development initiatives, while giving them the freedom to organize themselves. The difficulty that all such projects face is how to render support through, for example, consulting services and courses in management procedures, without interfering excessively in people's own plans. These cases illustrate the precarious situation that all development efforts face where external personnel and money are involved. People's use of their own know-how and resources ultimately conditions all efforts to improve their lives. The two cases, problematic as they are, show both the possibilities and limitations of such development initiatives.

PEOPLE'S KNOWLEDGE VERSUS THE EXPERTS' KNOWLEDGE

What one saw in the case of the MFDC and the artisan fishermen in nearby villages was two technologies coexisting, yet the perceptual distance had set them worlds apart. This distance can be conceptualized both in terms of space and time. 'Local space' was set apart from the 'expert space', as manifested so often in external technical assistance projects that adopt a top-down approach (Swantz, 1989; Sitari, 1988).

Johannes Fabian's concept of allochronism is applicable here (1983). He refers to the denial of coevalness, or the refusal to allow the 'Other' to be in one's own time, which is present time. Fabian is primarily critiquing the anthropologists' distancing of their subjects through such a denial of coevalness, but the critique could easily be extended to the activities of donor agencies, states, and other institutions involved in development programmes. Underlying the idea of development is the notion that those in need of development are to be brought from where they are in their traditional practices and beliefs, from their past into the present of the developer. Many involved in so-called 'modern' training institutions like the MFDC perceive the local technology as situated back in time. Thus they create a temporal distance between, for example, those who fish in *ngalawa* outrigger boats and those who operate the trawlers. As Fabian writes:

coevalness aims at recognizing contemporality as the condition for truly dialectical confrontation between persons as well as societies. It militates against false conceptions of dialectics all those watered-down binary abstractions which are passed off as oppositions: left vs. right, past vs. present, primitive vs. modern. Tradition and modernity are not 'opposed' (except semiotically), nor are they in 'conflict'. What are opposed, in conflict, in fact, locked in antagonistic struggle, are not different societies at different stages of development, but different societies facing each other at the same Time. (1983: 154–5)

The language of the MFDC students and staff reflected how they disparaged the technology, practices, knowledge, and organization of the artisan

fishermen. One graduating MFDC student explained the difference between what he had learned and the technology of the artisan fishermen this
way: 'What we learn here is such high technology and it goes higher and
higher [demonstrating with his hands how high] so that it has nothing to do
with ordinary fishermen.' He had been trained to do extension work in the
districts and would undoubtedly end up working with artisan fishermen.
Another extension officer who had been placed in the Lake Victoria–
Nyanza area echoed these same sentiments. He had been complaining
because he did not have a means of transport necessary to do his work.
When it was suggested that he use the same vessels as the fishermen did, he
responded: 'How can I teach them progress if I use the same equipment
that they use.'

The remark that the MFDC technology was so 'high' it had nothing to do
with the local fishermen and the comment on how the fishermen were
in need of 'progress' are reflections of the consciousness of the 'experts'. It
is indicative of the way in which they produce and reproduce knowledge in
a fashion that makes them distance themselves from the 'Other' fishermen.
This distancing allows the 'experts' to ignore the people's own technologies
and practices, dismissing them as 'traditional'. It explains how a fishing
development project could coexist physically side by side with artisan
fishermen yet virtually ignore interacting with them, denying them access to
equipment on the grounds of a technicality at a time of shortages when
fishermen could have really benefited from having a place to purchase
equipment. The artisan technology was seen as so inferior to the high
technology of trawling that it was pointless to work with fishermen.

While government development officers may harbour the perception that
they can dispense with local technologies, their jobs often bring them into
contact with the proprietors of these technologies. In these instances,
distancing can be accomplished by taking refuge in regulations. One extension worker explained how fishermen benefited from his work as a government representative: 'They benefit much. We register them.' When further
pressed on what benefit registering bestowed on the fishermen, he said: 'We
can control the fishing.'

The attempt to control is a key element in all these distancing ploys. It is
doubtful whether such control was even a reality, but the assertion of
authority was implicit in this distancing. One of the main ways the government asserted control of the fishing and other artisan sectors was by
determining the ways in which artisans and fishermen ought to form themselves into economic co-operatives. They were thought by government and
Party authorities to be an equalizing form of organization and close to
people's way of sharing historically. In fact, co-operative forms of organization were made a pre-condition for obtaining the few government loans
and credit arrangements available to small-scale entrepreneurs. Nevertheless, artisan and manufacturing co-operatives have for various reasons had

a dismal record of success in Tanzania. One of the main reasons co-operatives failed was their impersonal form of organization which was isolated from the social and cultural base people are familiar with, leading to distrust and abuses of power. Many co-operatives resisted registration as co-operatives in order to avoid being subjected to high sales taxes and price controls. Others found the registration process itself too cumbersome because of the bribes demanded by petty officials who issued the permits (Bagachwa, 1982: 345; Tripp, 1989). Moreover, as the fishermen in the Pande co-operative found, they were subject to numerous petty intrusions on their freedom to operate as they saw fit.

Like many other such institutions, the fishermen's co-operative in Pande has had a rocky existence since its formation in 1978. The co-operative was revived in 1986 because its 25 members wanted to determine their own prices for the fish they sold, and operate free of price controls set by large patrons. They did not deem it necessary to re-register their co-operative since it was a continuation of the earlier one. One day they were selling their fish on the floor of the co-operative when a fishing officer who had not been there for months dropped by. Instead of being happy to see the rare spectacle of a co-operative in operation, he angrily demanded to know why the floor had not been swept and then why were they operating as a co-operative without proper registration.

The consequences of not taking people on their own terms are disastrous as the examples from the fishing sector show. The artisan fishermen around the MFDC suffered from the presence of the Centre in their midst because trawling interfered with their fishing. In addition, they experienced set-backs because of a lack of inputs which could have been prevented had the MFDC store permitted sales of gear to the fishermen. But most regrettable was the lack of interaction between the MFDC and local fishermen. Had such interaction been carried out on the basis of equality and mutual respect for the different technologies, the Centre would have been able to begin to have an important impact on the sector that represents the majority of Tanzania's fishermen.

CONCLUSIONS

The experience at the MFDC offers numerous general lessons for multilateral co-operation in development assistance programmes. First, being capital-intensive and import-dependent, the MFDC suffered the fate of many other high-technology projects dependent on foreign exchange. The MFDC trawler operating costs exceeded revenues accrued by the vessel. The MFDC project was not alone in this regard: the Tanzania Fishing Corporation (TAFICO) was also unable to bring in sufficient foreign exchange to maintain its trawling vessels. In nine years its catches had amounted to a mere 7 per cent of its initial investment (Bryceson, 1985: 12). Japan was the prime beneficiary of a joint fishing development endeavour between the Tanzania Fisheries Corporation and Japan, which ended up buying fish from Japanese-run trawlers. Similarly, the BAFICO fishing project in Bagamoyo town eventually went out of business because the operation of trawlers became too costly.

Had the Mbegani Fisheries Development Centre actively supported the local fishermen and women, even their goal of bringing in foreign exchange would have seen better results. An increasing number of artisan fishermen in this coastal area had seized opportunities presented by the 1984 liberalization of trade. They took the initiative of selling prawns and other seafood for export, in spite of their limited means and connections.

The second point relates to the perceptions of the beneficiaries of so-called aid, who are considered the 'targets'. Two contradictory practices are in force. On the one hand, the artisans are ignored because they are not seen as developed, their practices are not those of progress, so they are irrelevant to development projects like the MFDC. They would have to 'develop', or more to the point, they would have to 'be developed' before they could be taken on their own terms. On the other hand, when artisan fishermen were engaged, it was in highly temporally distancing terms: they were seen as 'backward' and undeveloped, which presupposes being 'controlled'. The 'developers' have generally avoided taking people's own technologies, values, ways of life, and priorities on their own terms, as a basis for development endeavours.

Furthermore, those in charge of the development did not take seriously the need to define the artisan fisherman's needs and develop a programme based on those needs. This gap between expert knowledge and people's knowledge creates mutual contempt between those with new technological skills and those with local skills and know-how.

Because of this gap, people may become suspicious of the experts and keep them at a distance in order to create space in which they can preserve their own decision-making power and autonomy. This suspicion of expert knowledge thus becomes a hindrance to even communicating useful ideas.

The third issue is that of the definition of expertise. Norway was asked to assist in developing Tanzania's fishing sector because of its international reputation of being a leader in the fishing industry. However, its expertise with fishing in the northern seas was not necessarily compatible with the kind of expertise needed in developing the fishing sector in tropical oceans and lakes, as became evident in other NORAD projects in Kerala, India, and in Turkana, Kenya. Like the MFDC project, Norwegian-sponsored fishing projects in both countries did not start principally from the interests and needs of the primary population, in setting its goals or planning the project. As a consequence, boats of unsuitable fibres were brought to the Turkana lakes, and trawling in Kerala led to the destruction of the fishing grounds of small-scale fishermen. These examples of Norwegian assistance did not affirm the often repeated truism that a country ought to give expertise in the areas it knows best. Being an expert in one environment does not guarantee good results in another environment. Ironically, it might even be argued that a country that is itself gaining new knowledge in a field might do better giving technical and practical assistance. The experts would be more compelled and willing to work with people at the local level and to gain from their experience and knowledge. The familiar proclamation of an expert that: 'We have nothing to learn. We know this business' promises the least in terms of success. A person trained in his/her home country with a long history of technical expertise in a particular field often has a narrow view of his/her field of expertise and frequently is not open to alternative ways of doing things. The expert's uncertainty in new conditions tends to limit freedom to experiment. The expert feels that he/she has to demonstrate expertise in order to be trusted. Unfortunately the local expertise quickly discovers the shallowness of the foreigner's knowledge.

Finally there is the question of criticism. Norway, like any other donor country, has borne its share of criticism for its assistance programmes. Norway has responded even to sharp criticisms of its work with grace. Sometimes the failures are simply brushed off by counter-criticism against the local management and policies of the recipient country. Those criticisms that are taken seriously frequently centre around the poor quality of experts or the high cost of various projects. But such criticisms fall short of getting to the heart of the main problems with donor assistance. As the two examples of boat-building and the women's project show, it does not take large sums of money or state-of-the-art equipment and know-how to make real and important changes in people's livelihood. More importantly, it does not require all the hardware and expertise that the donor country and its companies want to sell. But it does take attention paid to specific local resources, needs, and forms of organization and an appreciation of existing knowledge and skills.

A much more thorough understanding of what people's strategies are would be needed to train workers in any sector of rural development. When extension staff in fisheries, in agriculture, or in community work are not trained even to be in day-to-day contact with those for whom their services are intended, whether they are ordinary fishermen and women, boat-builders, small-scale farmers, or traders, they simply cannot learn their wisdom, know-how and ways of acting and thinking.

As we have seen in this chapter, the fact that the experts viewed the local fishermen and women as backward did not change the reality that the latter were anxious to improve the quality of their gear and craft (using motors when they had the capital to do so), to adopt less exploitative forms of organization (as those in the Pande fishing co-operative demonstrated), and to expand their markets, even outside Tanzania. In fact, the fishing communities never stopped trying to make the most of their situation, using what materials and resources they had even during difficult times. There is little doubt that Tanzania's fishermen and women, as well as other artisans and craftspeople, would respond creatively to a socio-economic and administrative environment more responsive to their needs. Their openness to new ideas and change needs to be matched by equally creative and innovative approaches from 'above' that start from their existing knowledge, technologies, and organizational forms.

NOTES TO CHAPTER 2

1. Information in this paper draws heavily on the fieldnotes of both authors. Swantz was one of the six consultants in a joint Tanzanian and Norwegian evaluation team that reported on the Mbegani Fisheries Development Centre in May 1986 (NORAD, 1986).

2. The *mashua* (8 m. long) has a single mast, a triangular (lateen) sail, and a stern with a deck. It requires at the minimum a crew of three people, but usually has a crew of six to eight. The *ngalawa* (4 to 6 m. long) is a narrow boat with spoon stem, a pointed stern, and a lateen sail, usually hewn by local craftsmen from a mango trunk. The *mtumbwi* (3 to 5 m. long) has a semi-circular section. It may or may not have a sail and rudder. The *hori* is about the same length as the *mtumbwi*, is made of planks, and has a narrow flat bottom. The *kidau* is a small, open, flat-bottomed boat with a lateen sail and sloping bow and stern (Sassoon, 1970; Swantz notes). All can be propelled with a paddle or punting stick (*pondo*), especially in shallow waters.

3. In the past the Chinese, who started this trade, prepared the slugs. These days local young men and some women are able to generate an income by processing the slugs themselves. Those who prepare the slugs pour 200–300 of them into a barrel filled with 5–10 buckets of sea-water, bringing them to a boil and stirring well until they become round. The slugs are then poured into a hole in the sand and left until next day. When they have become swollen they are pounded and trodden on until the skins peel off. They are boiled a second time and laid in the sun to dry thoroughly so that they can be easily transported. Altogether it takes about three days to prepare them for sale. In 1985 one kilo of sea-slugs was worth Tsh. 21 near Bagamoyo. In Zanzibar in 1987, people who cooked slugs bought them from women and children for one shilling a piece. Having processed them they would sell to wholesalers gunny sacks filled with 1,200 slugs at 1,600 Tsh. per sack. In one month one person could make as much as Tsh. 10,000 in this line of work (Swantz, 14 June 1989; Tripp, 23 Dec. 1987).

4. This method of fishing became less popular in the 1970s as poles and chicken-wire became scarce and costly and the erosion of the sand beaches also adversely affected the environment for the traps. This information is from the year 1986. The data in general was gathered during 1985–9. Fishermen always take a share of the catch for family food, however small their catch. On the other hand, they prefer to sell the fish to city traders, since they get a better price than if they were

to sell the fish at the village market (Hallensvedt and Hersoug, 1985: 20; Swantz, 1986: 27; NORAD, 1986).
5. In 1970 the Fisheries Division was brought under the Ministry of Natural Resources and Tourism.
6. Norway had become involved in fisheries development in India in 1952, and later in other major recipient countries such as Kenya and Sri Lanka.

REFERENCES

BAGACHWA, M. S. D. (1982), 'The Dar es Salaam Urban Informal Sector Survey', Technical Paper no. 7, in *Basic Needs in Danger*, Addis Ababa: International Labour Office, Jobs and Skills Programme for Africa.

BERNSTEIN, H. (1981), 'Notes on State and Peasantry: The Tanzanian Case', *Review of African Political Economy*, 21: 44–62.

BOESEN, J. (1981), 'Tanzania: From Ujamaa to Villagization', in B. U. Mwansasu and C. Pratt (eds.), *Towards Socialism in Tanzania*, Toronto: University of Toronto Press: 125–44.

BRETT, E. A. (1987), 'States, Markets and Private Power in the Developing World: Problems and Possibilities', *IDS Bulletin*, 18/3: 31–8.

BRYCESON, I. (1985), *Tanzanian Marine Fisheries and the Mbegani Centre*, International Seminar on Fisheries Development, Solvaer, Lofoton, Norway: Royal Ministry of Development Co-operation.

ENGEBRIGSTEN, E. (1985a), *Preliminary Report on Ngalawa Program*, Mbegani Fisheries Development Centre.

—— (1985b), *A Report on Traditional Boatbuilding in Tanzania and a Proposed Project to Assist Local Boatbuilding*, Mbegani Fisheries Development Centre.

FABIAN, J. (1983), *Time and the Other: How Anthropology Makes its Object*, New York: Columbia University Press.

HALLENSTVEDT, B. and HERSOUG, B. (1985), *The History of Mbegani FDC*, Oslo: NORAD.

HASSETT, D. (1984), 'Economic Organization and Political Change in a Village of South East Tanzania', Ph.D. thesis (Cambridge).

—— (1985), 'The Development of Village Co-operative Enterprise in Mchinga II Village, Lindi Region', in R. G. Abrahams (ed.), *Villagers, Villages, and the State in Modern Tanzania*, Cambridge African Monograph, no. 4, Cambridge: Cambridge University Press.

HELLEINER, G. K. (1985), 'Stabilization Policies and the Poor', paper presented at conference on Government Policy and the Poor in Developing Countries, Institute for Policy Analysis and Development Studies, University of Toronto.

LANDBERG, P. (1969), *The Economic Roles of Women in a Tanzanian Coastal Community*, Department of Sociology, University of Dar es Salaam (mimeo).

MASAIGANAH, M. S. (1986), *Pande Village: A Summary Report*, Oslo: Royal Norwegian Ministry of Development Co-operation.

MASCARENHAS, A. (1981), 'After Villagization What?' , in B. U. Mwansasu and C. Pratt (eds.), *Towards Socialism in Tanzania*, Toronto: Toronto University Press, 145–65.

NORAD, Royal Ministry of Development Co-operation (1986), *The Evaluation Report of the Mbegani Fisheries Development Centre*, Report from the joint Tanzanian/Norwegian evaluation team, Evaluation report 4.86.

NYERERE, J. K. (1973), *Freedom and Development: A Selection from Writings and Speeches, 1968–1973*, Dar es Salaam: Oxford University Press.

RAIKES, P. (1986), 'Eating the Carrot and Wielding the Stick: The Agricultural Sector in Tanzania', in J. Boesen, K. J. Havnevik, J. Koponen, and R. Odgaard (eds.), *Tanzania: Crisis and Struggle for Survival*, Uppsala: Scandinavian Institute of African Studies.

SASSOON, C. (1970), 'Notes on Smaller Craft in the Region of Dar es Salaam', *Tanzania Notes and Records*, 71: 200.

SITARI, T. (1986), 'The Spatial Consequences of Transfer of Technology from a Developed Area to an Underdeveloped Area', MS.

—— (1988), *Technology Transfer to Developing Countries: From Place to Place or Space to Space*, University of Helsinki, Institute of Development Studies, Report 15, B. Teco Publication No. 17.

SWANTZ, M.-L. (1986), *The Role of Women in Tanzanian Fishing Societies: A Study of the Socioeconomic Context and the Situation of Women in Three Coastal Fishing Villages in Tanzania*, University of Dar es Salaam, Institute of Development Studies Women's Study Group.

—— (1988), 'Strategies for the Fishing Communities', paper presented at the Annual Meeting of the African Studies Association, Chicago.

—— (1989), *Transfer of Technology as an Intercultural Process*, 24, Helsinki, Finland: Finnish Anthropological Society.

TRIPP, A. M. (1989), 'Defending the Right to Subsist: The State vs. the Urban Informal Economy in Tanzania', Helsinki, Finland: UNU/WIDER Working Paper no. 59.

WENBAN-SMITH, H. B. (1963), 'The Coastal Fisheries near Dar es Salaam', *Tanganyika Notes and Records*, 61: 165–74.

WILSON, E. J. (1988), 'Privatization in Africa: Domestic Origins, Current Status and Future Scenarios', *Journal of Opinion*, 16/2: 24–9.

3

The Economic Consequences of Pragmatism: A Re-interpretation of Keynesian Doctrine

NANCY E. GUTMAN

> Peace and comfort of mind require that we should hide from ourselves
> how little we forsee. Yet we must be guided by some hypothesis. We
> tend, therefore, to substitute for the knowledge which is unattainable
> certain conventions, the chief of which is to assume, contrary to all
> likelihood, that the future will resemble the past. That is how we act in
> practice.
>
> J. M. Keynes, Collected Writings, xiv. 24.

INTRODUCTION

The task of this chapter is to show how John Maynard Keynes attempted to reclaim the authority of economic agents' lived experiences as a basis for economic theorizing. The need for such an effort was as great in Keynes's day as it is in our own, given the continuing bias of mainstream theory against experiential knowledge. Keynes, in an effort to rectify this defect, took as his starting-point the events and formidable changes that marked the period in which he wrote. In so doing, he extended his innovations beyond economic theory to the very methodology of economic thought.

Keynes's work is far too subtle to admit of any single 'hidden meaning', and this chapter does not attempt to find one. Instead, it takes up and develops certain salient themes in Keynes's work; themes that are the unintended consequences of his life-long effort to establish an ineluctable link between human beliefs and human conduct. It pursues connections, insights, and consequences of Keynes's thought that Keynes himself did not pursue, and of which he remained largely unaware.

Specifically, this chapter attempts to show, first, that the methodology Keynes employed in his seminal work, *The General Theory of Money, Interest, and Employment* (1937), marked an epistemological shift in his own approach to economic theorizing, and second, that this methodology created a foundation for an entirely new field of economic enquiry, one free of the unrealistic and misleading micro-foundations of mainstream economics.

Keynes's approach discarded 'utility maximization' and narrow definitions of instrumental 'rationality' as a basis for macroeconomic theories of economic decision-making and co-ordination. Having abandoned such a quest for micro-foundations, Keynes was thereby prompted to redefine the basis for economic decision-making in a manner that clearly repudiated the algorithmic, certainty-equivalence approach of neo-classical theory. Instead, he identified the common practices, conventions, and precedents of everyday life as the sole authority underlying agents' decisions and actions: in particular, their savings and investment decisions. And by substituting conventional knowledge for agent's rational self-interest, Keynes was essentially subverting the epistemic underpinnings of neo-classical theory, as well as the axiomatic methodology in which it is embedded. In its place, he inserted his theory of conventional decision-making (see Dow, 1993: 60; 1993: 119–20): an alternative, non-neoclassical theory of economic co-ordination, in general, and investment behaviour, in particular.

Thus, while mainstream theorists generally start with some variant of Jeremy Bentham's maxim that the best way to maximize everyone's utility is to have free markets in which everyone is able to act in his or her own interest—subject to exogenously imposed constraints—Keynes's *General Theory* presents a radically different epistemic point of departure, one which affords economists the opportunity to shift the focus of economic theorizing from the realm of empirical uniformity to that of thinking agents whose reasons and grounds for their beliefs are culturally and historically contingent, and therefore subject to tremendous variation and incompleteness.

Keynes's theory of decision-making implies, specifically, that agents' economic decisions are neither fundamentally 'voluntary', as Lockean-inspired theories argue, nor essentially and explicitly 'coerced', as Hobbesian-derived explanations insist. In other words, Keynes's innovative methodology enables us to dispute the validity of the liberal neo-classical or contractarian representation of economic decision-making and co-ordination in a modern capitalist system. Accordingly, a non-liberal, non-neoclassical approach, based on Keynes's methodology, implies that political and economic co-ordination can emerge without the Hobbesian's invocation of an explicit and coercive exercise of the 'visible hand' of authority, or the Lockean's invocation of a 'hidden hand' guided by agents' rational self-interest. Economic decision-making is instead guided, in the words of the philosopher Philip Petit, by an 'intangible hand'. Hence, Keynes's non-neoclassical alternative avoids the contractarian tradition's dichotomous approach to economic decision- and policy-making in its insistence (to paraphrase Jon Elster), that collaboration arises out of tacit co-ordination (1990: 104). As a result, it affords economists significantly different criteria for determining how society should assign tasks to the market mechanism and the state, thereby enabling them to avoid the false choice between rigid regulation of the market and non-intervention in the economy.

Keynes accomplishes this theoretical and political feat by discarding the methodological individualism (see Elster, 1990: 87), and hence the 'rationality postulate', upon which his neo-classical contemporaries' work was founded: namely, the idea that a rational act is the best way an agent can satisfy her desires, given her beliefs (Keynes, 1931: 312). The problem with this postulate arises not so much from its unrealistic assumption that the beliefs, desires, and actions of the individual must be consistent with themselves and with each other; or from the further assumption that an action must not only be rationalized by one's desires and beliefs, but, rather from the belief that these beliefs, desires, and actions must also be caused by deliberative strength, not mere weakness of will (Elster, 1986; 1989*a*: 36–7, 45–9).

Even rational-choice theorists who presume that there exists what Elster characterizes as 'consistent, future-oriented and instrumentally efficient behavior', readily acknowledge in light of historical experiences, casual observation, introspection, and literary representations, that non-rational behaviour is nevertheless widespread (Elster, 1989*b*: 27–8). As Isaiah Berlin has written, '[t]he rational egoists of Hobbes, Locke or Spinoza are arbitrary and unhistorical; if men had been as they are depicted by these thinkers, their history becomes unintelligible' (Berlin, 1982: 103).

Keynes carefully demonstrated the limitations of the rationality postulate in his *Treatise on Probability* (1921) a work concerned with the task of rigorously modelling the logic of inductive reasoning. The rejection of the rationality postulate (and its philosophical corollary, methodological individualism), was to have a profound effect upon the methodology employed by Keynes in his *General Theory*. It is precisely this methodology—which emphasizes the importance of convention, precedent, and common social values to the economic agent's decision-making ability—that was discarded by Keynes's followers, even as they retained some of Keynes's central doctrines. Adherence to the rationality postulate prevented the so-called 'Keynesians' from recognizing the indissoluble bond between the questions Keynes chose to investigate and the methods he used to analyse them. Having provided a broader perspective and a different theoretical framework than that offered by mainstream discussions, Keynes enables theorists and policy-makers alike to go beyond the sterile controversy over the relative merits of the state and market as co-ordinating mechanisms in a decentralized economy.

RATIONALISM, POSITIVISM, AND THE KEYNESIAN TRADITION

In the almost half-century since his death, Keynes's writings have been subject to many, often divergent, interpretations. Thanks in large part to Joan Robinson's untiring efforts (1961; 1964; 1973; 1978), it has become possible to detect fundamental differences between the standard 'bastard

Keynesianism' of the dominant neo-classical synthesis (Hicks, 1936; 1937; 1967; 1981; Hansen, 1949; 1953; 1970; Patinkin, 1958; 1982; Samuelson, 1939; 1947; 1958; Tobin, 1955; 1958; 1965; 1969; 1972a; 1972b; 1980) and the marginalized interpretations of the post-Keynesians. Thus it has been left to a vocal minority of non-neoclassical Keynesians—including the Cambridge, England neo-Keynesian school[1] and the American post-Keynesians[2]—to sustain and extend Keynes's critical perspective *vis-à-vis* the neo-classicals.

Above all, post-Keynesian economists credit Keynes with a fundamental critique of Say's Law and hence of the many theories of output and employment that it spawned. In addition, they emphasize the inherent instability of the capitalist macroeconomy (as did Keynes throughout his later economic writings). The post-Keynesians take issue with the neo-classical synthesis because it ignores:

1. Capital–labour conflict. This strand of post-Keynesianism originates with Kalecki (1954; 1971), who, taking his cue from Marx, argues that the level of effective demand is determinate only with respect to a given class distribution of income. This is manifested in the relationship between prices and money wages which consequently gives rise to the notion of cost-determined prices at the micro-level of the enterprise (Robinson, 1933; 1954; 1962; 1973; 1977; Kaldor, 1956; 1960; Eichner, 1973; 1978; Kregel, 1971; Eichner and Kregel, 1975; Sawyer, 1982; Eatwell and Millgate, 1983; Marglin, 1984; Rousseas, 1986; Bhaduri and Marglin, 1990).

2. The problems of uncertainty and information (Shackle, 1967; 1972; 1974; Davidson, 1972; Robinson, 1973; Weintraub, 1973; 1975; Vickers, 1984; 1985a; 1985b; Dow, 1985).

3. The role of investment, money, the behaviour of financial markets and asset prices; and of industry and finance conflict in generating economic instability and industrial decline (Harrod, 1972; Clower, 1967; Davidson, 1972; Rousseas, 1972; 1978; 1986; Kregel, 1973; 1980; Minsky, 1975; 1986; Kindleberger, 1978; 1985; Vickers, 1978; Kaldor, 1983; Chick, 1983; Crotty, 1983; 1985; 1989; Dow, 1985; Rapping, 1978; 1988; Bhaduri, 1986; 1988; Bhaduri and Marglin, 1990; Amadeo, 1989; Boyer, 1990).

4. Keynes's methodological and epistemological innovations (Clower, 1965; 1967; Leijonhufvud, 1968; Kregel, 1976; Hutchison, 1977; 1984; Coddington, 1972; 1982; 1983; Crotty, 1980; Dow, 1985; Brown-Collier and Bausor, 1985; Lawson, 1985; Bateman, 1987; Bateman and Davis, 1991; Carabelli, 1988; Fitzgibbons, 1988; Rotheim, 1988; O'Donnell, 1989, 1991; Skidelsky, 1994).

This paper is in line with some of these critiques, especially those which have taken Keynes's methodological innovations as their point of entry into the debate concerning the relationship between 'Keynesian economics and the economics of Keynes' (Leijonhufvud, 1968).

One of the central concerns of the post-Keynesians has to do with the relationship between Keynes's *Treatise On Probability* and his treatment of expectations in *The General Theory*. Specifically, they attempt to trace the roots of Keynes's concern with economic uncertainty in the *General Theory* back to his theory of probability in the *Treatise*. In particular, they are divided over the question of whether Keynes's model of economic decision-making follows, in the words of Anna Carabelli, the 'logic of certainty' or the 'logic of opinion' (see Carabelli, 1988: 99–100, 145–8)—a question whose answer, it turns out, has rather important political implications. Thus, while the neo-classical Keynesians—who have adopted the former interpretation—tend to regard Keynes as the father of a mechanistic and technocratic approach to policy-making, the post-Keynesians, by contrast, have embraced the latter interpretation of Keynes's theory of rationality, and consequently been led to question why the very term 'Keynesian' has come to serve as an abbreviation for a set of assumptions regarding the privileged nature of economics as a discipline and the privileged place of economic policy-makers in society.

The debate within the discipline over the nature of rationality, in general, and its relationship to economic theory and/or behaviour, in particular, can be divided roughly into two opposing philosophical camps: the rationalist branch of the discipline, which gives special epistemological status to initial premisses by virtue of their 'realism'[3] (von Mises, 1949; 1960; 1978; Robbins, 1949; Knight, 1940; 1964; Buchanan, 1962; 1972; 1979*a*; 1979*b*; Lucas and Sargeant, 1978), and the positivist strand, which asserts that the validity of a theory depends solely upon the accuracy of its predictions and not on the realism of its assumptions[4] (Hutchison, 1938; 1964; Friedman, 1953*a*; Samuelson, 1963; 1964; 1965).

Despite the heated debates over method that have raged in the profession in general (Caldwell, 1982), and between Keynesians and Monetarists (Kindleberger, 1985), in particular, it can be argued that the rationalist and positivist traditions are simply two sides of the same epistemological coin, in that they both represent attempts to uncover the intrinsic, i.e. unchanging, qualities of reality, albeit by different routes (Berlin, 1982; Quine, 1953).

Keynes may be read, however, as ultimately rejecting both the rationalist and positivist traditions' (see Carabelli, 1988) partition of knowledge into 'an upper and lower division', to use Richard Rorty's phrase (1982: p. xvi), the former consisting of invariant universal truths, and the latter of histori-cally contingent human judgements and opinions. Instead, Keynes threads his way through this rationalist–positivist distinction by questioning their common presupposition that there is, in Rorty's words, 'an invidious dis-tinction between [the two] kinds of truths' (1982: p. xvi).

Instead, Keynes asks us to regard economic knowledge as the product of a culture in which, according to Rorty, 'neither the priests nor the physicists nor the poets' (nor the policy-makers) are regarded as ' "more rational", or "more scientific", or "deeper" than one another' (Rorty, 1989: p. xxxviii). Their aims and purposes might be quite different from one another, but their various efforts to 'make things hang together' (Sellars, 1967: 160) would nevertheless be treated as being on the same footing.

Thus Keynes may be seen as a philosophical Pragmatist[5] or 'post-Wittgensteinian', (Carabelli, 1988: 134), in the company of the Pragmatists John Dewey (1916; 1922; 1925; 1927; 1929; 1930; 1935; 1936; 1938; 1939*a*; 1939*b*; 1946; 1969; and Bentley, 1932–51); William James (1950; 1907; 1912); Isaiah Berlin (1980; 1982; 1991); Hilary Putnam (1975; 1978; 1981); Richard Rorty (1979; 1982; 1989); Wilfrid Sellars (1967; 1968); Nelson Goodman (1951; 1972; 1978), as well as the company of followers of the later Wittgenstein (e.g. Ryle, 1949). And since it is not my claim that he held these views self-consciously, I shall proceed to build my case using the following steps. In the first part of the essay I shall try to set the stage for Keynes's theoretical innovations by summarizing some of the methodological issues which concerned him. Next I will try to illustrate the argument by examining the contextual, i.e. pragmatic, nature of economic agents' investment and savings decisions, in contrast to the disembedded or epistemic nature of finance. Finally, I will contrast this interpretation with the approach taken by the neo-classical-Keynesian synthesis.

A 'PRAGMATIC' APPROACH TO ECONOMICS

> Economics is a science of thinking in terms of models joined to the art of choosing models which are relevant to the contemporary world. It is compelled to be this, because, unlike the typical natural science, the material to which it is applied is, in too many respects, not homogeneous through time.
>
> J. M. Keynes, *Collected Writings*, xiv. 96.

Since the turn of the century there has been a constant temptation to take natural science theory as a model for social theory (Berlin, 1982; 1990; Mirowski, 1990); that is, to see theory as offering an account of underlying processes and mechanisms of society, and as providing the basis of a more effective planning of social life. Keynes, however, recognized that despite all the superficial analogies, economics as a social theory can never really occupy this role (*CW* x. 262).[6] This is because it is part of a significantly different activity. And economics, which Keynes referred to as a 'moral science' (*CW* xiv. 300) is a significantly different activity because its formulations can serve more than descriptive purposes.

In addition, economics can affect our social practices because it can alter our self-understandings and social identities. And it is precisely for this reason that we recognize the deficiencies of both the rationalist and positivist traditions in representing agents as either passive instruments of pre-linguistic intuitions or of universally valid scientific laws. Keynes's pragmatism, by contrast, rejects the enervating fatalism of both rationalist and positivist traditions and offers, in its place, the notion that economic agents, in forgoing the myth of decision-making as an act of objective calculation, must, according to Rorty (1982), actively make, rather than passively discover, the maps of their cultural terrain.

ECONOMICS AS MECHANICAL IDEAL OR 'MORAL SCIENCE'

In his *Theory of Moral Sentiments* Adam Smith wrote: '[h]uman society when we contemplate it in a certain abstract and philosophical light, appears like a great, an immense machine, whose regular and harmonious movements produce a thousand agreeable effects' (1759: 316). The explanatory ideal to which these words give expression is deeply rooted in Western intellectual history and is adhered to by social scientists to this day. The Western intellectual tradition sees the natural order of society as a system of stable relationships between interdependent but autonomous structures. The descriptions of these relationships are called theories, which satisfy the dual requirements of empirical proof and conditional predictability.

According to this well-entrenched doctrine, questions of value are considered to be resolvable by reference to a set of independent facts. Faced with incontrovertible facts, we are led, i.e. have no choice but to adopt a limited number of value positions. It is this philosophical belief which, because of its immense influence amongst both natural and social scientists, has contributed to the privileged status of economics as a genuine science, since its proclaimed search for economic facts, by definition, gives its (theoretical and policy) conclusions the same intellectual weight as all scientific facts, which also give no moral guidance, no way to distinguish between right and wrong.

Keynes argued that economics does not evolve in the same manner as physics. 'Economics is essentially a moral science and not a natural science', he wrote to Roy Harrod. It employs introspection and judgements of value (*CW* xiv. 297). It deals with motives, expectations, and psychological uncertainties (*CW* xiv. 300). Yet Keynes never addressed some essential questions concerning the relationship between the so-called moral and natural sciences. For example, he never fully explained why moral science, contrary to Adam Smith's vision, could not usefully employ the method of natural science. According to Klant, Keynes 'virtually confined himself to remarking that economists should do it differently. He wrote that "to convert a model into a quantitative formula is to destroy its usefulness as an instrument of thought" (*CW* xiv. 299), but he did not explain this' (Klant, 1985: 81).

Thus Keynes never explicitly stated whether he viewed political economy as an art or a science. But in refraining from mathematical formalization of his theories, Keynes seems to have been following Marshall,[7] who believed that economics as a moral Science (1925: 171) was meant to better the world and thus remain comprehensible to anyone (Klant, 1985: 82). The rejection of mathematical formalization, more importantly, illustrated Keynes's belief that economic decisions, especially those regarding savings and investment, necessarily reflect the influence of convention, precedent, intuition, and common social values, rather than the authority of some abstract criteria of economic calculus.

KEYNES AND THE CAMBRIDGE TRADITION: ECONOMICS AS 'A BOX OF TOOLS'[8]

In describing economics as 'a method rather than a doctrine, an apparatus of the mind, a technique of thinking, which helps its possessors to draw correct conclusions' (*CW* xiv. 296), Keynes was theorizing in the manner and spirit of Marshall, who described economic theory 'not as a body of concrete truth, but an engine for the discovery of concrete truth' (1925: 159). The discovery of such truths, however, could not be guaranteed by virtue of the economists' reliance upon either a strictly deductive or inductive methodology. Economists deal with a world which is incessantly changing. They study facts which 'by themselves are silent' (1925: 166), and 'are so complex that they generally teach nothing directly; they must be interpreted by careful reasoning and analysis' (1890: i. 769 n.). Marshall believed that the more plain and simple an economic doctrine appears to be due to 'it[s] skillful exposition[,] the more mischievous it is.' He continued, '[a] man is likely to be a better economist if he trusts to his common senses, and practical instincts, than if he professes to study the theory of value and is resolved to find it easy' (1890: i. 368).

Accordingly, economic analysis is not undertaken in an effort to produce a model which lends itself to making predictions, but instead because it can serve as a device for agents with practical instincts who must interpret and sort through a multiplicity of facts in the pursuit of good policy choices. Marshall's particular kind of instrumentalism is thus a far cry from either the rationalism of von Mises, Knight, Weber, Robbins (1935), and certain early economists like Cairnes and J. S. Mill (Blaug, 1980), which stressed the subjectivism, methodological individualism, and self-evident nature of basic postulates of economic theory (Blaug, 1980; Caldwell, 1982), or the positivism of Hutchison, which fostered the belief amongst economists, beginning in the 1930s, that economics is an objective, scientific, and value-free discipline (Hutchison, 1938).

Despite their obvious methodological differences, both the positivist and rationalist traditions none the less share a conviction that the structure of economic theory itself is isomorphic to the reasoning processes of economic agents. The only real point of difference between the two traditions, then, concerns the logical status of the rationality postulate,[9] or the real source of rationality: is it analytic, i.e. does it reside beyond time and place, in pre-linguistic intuitions, as the Austrians, Robbins, and the rational expectationists believe; or is it synthetic, that is, subject to direct verification as Friedman, Machlup, and Samuelson have asserted? The assumptions of rational conduct and perfect expectations, however, have never been called into doubt. The disputes have thus centred solely on the competing notions that economics is a science (1) due to its methods of investigation (the rationalists' claim); or (2) due to the certainty of its results (the positivists' position). By contrast, Keynes eschews the search for (rational) foundations as well as the quest for certainty, given their irrelevance to his goal of creating a moral science.

THE PRAGMATIST CRITIQUE

As Horkheimer and Adorno noted long ago, the Enlightenment's 'dissolvant rationality' led to a rupture or decoupling of Enlightenment liberalism from Enlightenment rationality (Horkheimer and Adorno, 1944). In other words, the identification of progress with critical rationality, which is the epistemological underpinning of the scientific method, dialectically destroys faith in rationality as a means of achieving such progress. As Horkheimer and Adorno put it, 'every specific theoretic view succumbs to the destructive criticism that it is only a belief—until even the very notions of spirit, of truth and, indeed enlightenment itself have become animistic magic' (p. 11).

Following Rorty (1982; 1989), the pragmatist position can be seen as a reaction to and critique of the rationalist as well as positivist tendencies to equate rationality or rationalization with progress. The Pragmatists argue that the attempt to locate a *deus ex machina* in either the rational recesses of our minds or in the impersonal operations of physical laws cum market forces is antithetical to the ambitions and ideals of a genuinely liberal culture. Because we have incorrectly attributed an ontological status to physics on the basis of its instrumental and functional successes, we have also mistakenly inferred that the reductionist, mathematical vocabulary of physics can provide us with a vocabulary that will unlock all aspects of the universe by means of the scientific method. This belief has led 'a host of philosophers [to spend] years trying to use notions like "objectivity", "rigor", and "method" to isolate science from non-science.' (Rorty, 1982: 192). This project in turn has led to the construction of a knowledge hierarchy, with first-rate, discovered (scientific) truths located in the upper division, leaving second-rate created (artistic) truths to languish in the lower division.

The Pragmatist alternative views economics (and any other discipline for that matter) as a vocabulary which describes situations and actions as entirely accidental and contingent. Rather than being a 'mirror of nature' (Rorty, 1979), economics can instead be seen as consisting of various languages which constantly offer competing explanations and understanding of our sentences, situations, and actions. The economist's choice of vocabulary (whether Ricardian, Marxian, Keynesian, etc.,) will ultimately depend upon the degree to which she finds that particular vocabulary useful in her efforts to both predict and understand economic events. Successful prediction, by this account, however, cannot be guaranteed a priori by virtue of some mechanistic and axiomatic methodology which presumes to 'speak nature's own language' (Rorty, 1982). Thus economics, as a theory, has two functions: the first is prediction or description of how things work; while the second is to provide descriptions which help us to understand and choose between our justifications or reasons for believing the things we do. It has been mistakenly assumed by neo-classical economists that the second goal can be satisfied by achieving the first: that in resolving questions of fact we can also resolve questions of value, i.e. the question of how one should live.

KEYNES'S PRAGMATISM

It is because Keynes consistently[10] expressed concern about the relationship between the distinct requirements of prediction and evaluation within economics that he should be categorized as a Pragmatist writer, even if he never articulated the philosophical basis of his argument. His 'view that the bare bones of economic theory are not worth much in themselves and do not carry one far in the direction of useful practical conclusions' (*CW* x. 196) is very much in keeping with the Pragmatist project of eliminating the search for 'nature's own language' (Rorty, 1982).

As we know, Keynes ultimately abandons the quest for certainty and the search for foundations (Davidson, 1972). The path that led him to this position began with *The Treatise On Probability*, in which he expressed dissatisfaction with the explanatory value of the neo-classical mechanistic perspective. His dissatisfaction led him, in turn, to develop an alternative, specifically pragmatic, approach to economic theory. The purpose of this alternative approach is not to 'furnish a body of settled conclusions immediately applicable to policy. It is a method rather than a doctrine, which helps its possessor to draw correct conclusions' (*CW* xii. 856). The logic of the pragmatic ('organic') method, in contrast to the mechanistic (axiomatic) method, (according to Carabelli), is the logic of opinion, rather than truth (1985: 167; 1988: 99–100, 145–8).

This epistemological shift reflects a change in focus from the realm of empirical uniformity, to that of thinking agents whose reasons and grounds for their beliefs are culturally and historically contingent, and therefore subject to tremendous variation and incompleteness. As Keynes wrote in his essay on Edgeworth (1926):

[t]he atomic hypothesis which had worked so splendidly in physics breaks down in psychics. We are faced at every turn with the problems of organic unity, of discreteness, of discontinuity—the whole is not equal to the sum of its parts, comparison of quantity fails us, small changes produce large effects, the assumptions of a uniform and homogeneous continuum are not satisfied. (*CW* x. 262)

Keynes is stating here that precise mathematical methods are appropriate for unravelling the atomic constitution of the universe, because they proceed on the assumption that there are calculable and limited effects between defined bodies. However, if knowledge is organic, i.e. pragmatic, then mechanistic methods will be defeated by subtle and complex feedback effects. If theory tries to abstract from these effects by means of partial analysis, then the more significant part of the story will always be left out of account. Organic or pragmatic knowledge thus requires a logic of metaphorical understanding, which is fundamentally unquantifiable, and consequently not susceptible to mechanistic attempts to create privileged or first-rate forms of knowledge.

There are, of course, significant political consequences which follow from the adoption of either one of these epistemological positions. In the mechanistic approach, just as there is assumed to be a uniformity of laws governing natural events, so too is there assumed to be a uniformity of purpose associated with all social, political, and productive activity within society. Furthermore, just as the possibility of discovering these uniformities in nature presupposes and requires the application of a highly specialized and mechanistically developed intellect, so too does the requirement of rational social organization, based upon an assumed uniformity of purpose, necessitate the creation of a body of mechanistically oriented specialists to ensure the realization of this uniformity of purpose.

The political implications of the logic of opinion or judgement are equally clear: no epistemologically credible grounds exist for the construction of privileged knowledge systems, which implies that no legitimate reasons exist for the special social and political status accorded to those persons who claim to possess such privileged, i.e. first-rate, mechanistic knowledge, at least in the realm of social affairs.

THE INDUCTION PROBLEM: POSSIBILITIES FOR A SCIENCE OF ECONOMICS

I also want to emphasize strongly the point about economics being a moral science . . . not a natural science . . . [i]t seems to me that economics is a branch of logic, a way of thinking; and that you do not repel sufficiently firmly attempts . . . to turn it into a pseudo-science.

J. M. Keynes, letter to Harrod, *Collected Writings*, xiv. 296.

Keynes's belief that modelling cannot be mechanized but is instead highly judgemental stems from the theories and arguments he developed in his *Treatise on Probability*. In his attempt to solve Hume's induction problem,[11] Keynes is led to reject the notion that economics can be modelled upon the natural sciences, since economic theories, which describe a complex world subject to unpredictable structural changes, cannot be falsified. The 'principle of the uniformity of nature' which provides the epistemological underpinning of the scientific method, thus cannot be applied to economic events since, as Keynes believed, the condition of a constant environment is not met (*CW* xiv. 316).

This does not imply, however, that Keynes's methodology was 'subjectivist' (e.g. Dow and Dow, 1985; Fitzgibbons, 1988) or 'analytically nihilistic' (e.g. Shackle, 1967, 1974). Nor is it susceptible to a rational-expectationist interpretation (e.g. Meltzer, 1981; Coddington, 1983). Keynes gave two reasons to support his belief in the inappropriateness of an aleatory (frequency) theory in economics. The first is that no economist to date, including Tinbergen, had made enough observations under different types of circumstances to be able to legitimately make the assumption of stability that would be necessary to employ an aleatory conception of probability (Klant, 1985; Bateman, 1987). Keynes's second reason for objecting to the use of an aleatory theory of probability was that its use, while legitimate in certain of the natural sciences (given the efficaciousness of the principle of the uniformity of nature), was inappropriate within economics, given the nature of the material under study, which makes long-run stability unlikely. This position, however, does not entail a repudiation of empirical analysis or a nihilistic rejection of the practical uses of economic theory. There is nothing in the *Treatise* or in any of Keynes's subsequent writings that suggests that economic theorizing should be discontinued. To the contrary, Keynes optimistically points to the possibility of creating more useful economic theories and models once the chimera of scientific method is abandoned in favour of a pragmatic or contextual analysis.

THE TREATISE ON PROBABILITY: SIMPLIFIED RATIONALISM

Economics, according to Keynes, is first and foremost a moral science. What he meant by this is that economics as a discipline is concerned chiefly with human judgement and its social impact. Unlike his Utilitarian predecessors,[12] Bentham (1879) and J. S. Mill (1848), and contrary to the thorough-going scepticism of David Hume (1748), Keynes believed that a relationship could be established between the principled beliefs (values) of individuals and their actions, and that the discipline of economics constituted the chief link between the abstract and concrete spheres of human behaviour.

Keynes's characterization changed dramatically over time, however, as first expressed in his Cambridge fellowship thesis entitled the *Treatise on Probability*, and later redefined in his seminal work *The General Theory of Employment, Interest and Money*. In his autobiographical essay (*CW* x) Keynes described the evolution of his own thought in terms of a progression from the Platonic Dialogues to Plato's *Republic* and then to Plato's *Laws*. Keynes understood the Dialogues to enquire into the meaning of ideals and virtues, the *Republic* as establishing the nature of the ideal state which would express and balance the virtues, and the *Laws* as considering how best in practice to approximate the ideal state by means of laws and customs. Overall, there is a connection drawn within the Platonic framework, from ideals to political action. Consistent with this classic progression, in the two decades between the publication of the *Treatise* and the *General Theory*, Keynes attempted to achieve what his mentor, Moore, and his own disciples, the Keynesians, assumed to be impossible: a bridging of the chasm between values and public policy.

In the *Treatise*, for example, Keynes believed that he had bridged the chasm with a new ethics which would bear on practical issues (Fitzgibbons, 1988; Carabelli, 1988; O'Donnell, 1990). The overriding goal of the *Treatise*, then, was to reconnect ethics and politics under conditions of subjective epistemic probability (Bateman, 1987).

In the *Treatise*, Keynes was concerned chiefly with the task of rigorously modelling the logic of inductive reasoning, i.e. the process of decision-making when justification of rational belief is based upon argument by analogy. He argued that induction by itself, the mere counting of instances, does not tell us anything. Since any theory must depend on analogy if it is to say anything about the real world, knowledge itself—including scientific knowledge—is more limited than previously understood. 'There is no direct relation between the truth of a proposition and its probability', he wrote. 'Probability begins and ends with probability' (CW viii. 356).

The Treatise's epistemic or logical theory of probability implies that we cannot rely on observation by itself. Instead we must rely upon and utilize the logic of metaphorical understanding. For example, when we recognize that knowledge is the degree of belief that one has in a hypothesis given some evidence, we must also acknowledge that we do not ever know when all the relevant circumstances of two scientific tests are genuinely identical, which means that we never know when a general law has been refuted. Keynes emphasized this point, noting:

We cannot always weigh the analogy against the induction, or the scope of the generalization against the bulk of the evidence in support of it. If we have more grounds than before, comparison is possible; but, if the grounds in the two cases is quite different, even a comparison of more or less, let alone numerical measurement, may be impossible. (CW viii. 32)

Consequently, Keynes did not agree with Hume or J. S. Mill that knowledge is more advanced by the refutation of general laws than by the accumulation of evidence in their favour. He argued that Mill and Hume failed to recognize that the habits of nature are general tendencies rather than invariable laws, and that nature's possible contingencies are too numerous to be covered by a finite number of experiments (CW viii. 259; 295–8).

In short, inductive method can only work if the potential variation of instances is not arbitrarily large. Keynes believed that in the natural sciences the presumption of the uniformity of nature warranted the assumption of limited potential variability.[13] This uniformity, however, was peculiar to what Keynes referred to as 'atomic uniformity'. Accordingly:

The system of the material universe must consist, if this kind of assumption is warranted, of bodies which we may term . . . legal atoms, such that each of them exercises its own separate, independent and invariable effect, a change of the total size being compounded of a number of separate changes each of which is solely due to a separate portion of the preceding state. Each atom can, according to this theory, be treated as a separate cause and does not enter into different organic combinations in each of which it is regulated by different laws. (CW viii. 259)

He concluded, however, that there is no reason to assume that all systems exhibit such uniformity:

Now an assumption that all systems of fact are finite . . . cannot, it seems perfectly plain, be regarded as having an absolute, universal validity in the sense that such an assumption is self-evidently applicable to every kind of object and to all possible experiences . . . The most which can be maintained is that this assumption is true of some systems of fact, and further, there are some objects about which, as soon as we understand their nature, the mind is able to apprehend directly that the assumption in question is true. (CW viii. 262; emphasis in original)

Keynes labelled as 'organic' systems which do not exhibit such atomic uniformity. The behaviour of such systems as a whole, accordingly, cannot be construed as a simple aggregation of their parts. Specifically, variation in the whole is not proportional to variation in other components.

> Yet there might well be different laws for wholes of different degrees of complexity, and laws of connections between complexes which could not be stated in terms of laws connecting individual parts. In this case natural laws would be organic and not, as is generally supposed, atomic. If every configuration of the universe were subject to a separate and independent law, or if very small differences between bodies . . . led to their obeying quite different laws, prediction would be impossible and the inductive method useless. (*CW* viii. 277)

Therefore, with regard to organic systems it is impossible to gain either knowledge of a part from knowledge of another part or to predict a change in the whole given a change in one of the parts. 'In them, inductive method working up from atomic constituents is unjustifiable' (Brown-Collier and Bausor, 1982: 9).

In order to determine whether the conditions under which a theory is tested are identical, we are again forced to depend upon a judgement of similarity. Thus judgement inevitably underlies all knowledge. The moral here is that scientific knowledge is as limited as any other form of knowledge, since judgement must determine which strands of the causal web come to the attention of science.

In rejecting the premise of modern science, namely that laws of regular causation are discoverable, Keynes was rejecting in turn the mechanical theory of the external world, which supposes a unique correspondence between 'facts' and 'mind'. His message (as paraphrased by Fitzgibbons) is that: '[e]xperience tells us nothing . . . unless it elaborates an initial insight, and this insight, though it may be mistaken, is not arbitrary and relates to something definite' (Fitzgibbons, 1988: 27).[14] To the contrary, Keynes did not hold that all concepts have an independent reality. Instead, he drew a sharp distinction between 'direct' and 'indirect' knowledge, 'between the part of our rational belief which we know directly and that part which we know by argument' (*CW* viii. 12). The distinction apparently refers to the source of our belief that acceptance of a proposition is justified. Thus Keynes writes:

> our knowledge of propositions seems to be obtained in two ways: directly, as the result of contemplating the objects of acquaintance; and indirectly, *by argument*, through perceiving the probability-relation of the proposition about which we seek knowledge, to other propositions. In the second case, at any rate at first, what we know is not the proposition itself but a secondary proposition involving it. (*CW* viii. 12; emphasis in original)

Direct knowledge, then, is the result of 'things . . . we may be said to *experience*', such as 'our own sensations . . . ideas or meanings, about which we have thoughts and which we may be said to *understand*' (*CW* viii. 12; emphasis in original). Indirect knowledge, on the other hand, refers to those things which we may have good reason to believe are true, but which are neither perceived directly, nor logically entailed by directly appre-hended propositions. Keynes used this distinction to argue that 'our logic is concerned with drawing conclusions by a series of steps . . . from a limited body of premises', and 'in the actual exercise of reason we do not wait on certainty, or deem it irrational to depend on a doubtful argument' (*CW* viii. 3).

The distinction between direct and indirect propositions runs throughout the *Treatise on Probability*, and, as will be argued below, formed a guiding criterion for Keynes's distinctive macroeconomic constructions in the *General Theory*. While the *Treatise* emphasizes that 'indirect' (or a priori) knowledge can serve as a reasonable basis for belief and action, in the *General Theory*, 'direct' knowledge is held to engender greater confidence, thereby providing a more reliable source of political judgement.

THE GENERAL THEORY: THE 'REPUBLIC' REJECTED

Although not published until the 1920s, most of *The Treatise* was written before the intellectual watershed of the Great War had brought home to Keynes and his contemporaries the full force of human irrationality (see Skidelsky, 1994). Hence it is marked by the unabashed idealism and simpli-fied rationalism of the pre-war period. By contrast, *The General Theory of Employment, Interest and Money* expresses Keynes's later belief in the preva-lence of non-rational behaviour. In particular, Keynes said there that inves-tors are typically unable to resolve uncertain situations and thus must fall back upon conventional rules and intuition (Marglin, 1987). 'Tis not, therefore, reason which is the guide of life, but custom. That alone deter-mines the mind, in all instances, to suppose the future conformable to the past. However easy this step may seem, reason would never, to all eternity, be able to make it' (*CW* xxviii. 52). Judgement about the proper course of behaviour and action thus comes to be founded not upon 'rational intui-tion' but instead upon:

public opinion in the broadest sense . . . based on our view of the temper of the country, its motives and ideals . . . and the sort of people likely to be in power from time to time in the near future. It is on such judgement alone, that we can arrive at a reasonable conclusion whether we wish this country to be strong or weak. (*CW* xxviii. 52)

Here Keynes seems to be saying that while judgement is complex, relying upon custom or social convention is as likely, if not more likely, to produce a reasonable, i.e. desirable, outcome as relying upon intuitively rational judgement.

The transition from rationalism, with its attendant faith in the ability of transcendent intuitions to govern the nature of our actions, to pragmatism, with its emphasis on the unavoidable contingency of all decision-making, marks a significant transformation of Keynes's epistemological orientation, as well as his political-economic programme. The practical consequence was to shift the focus of economic thought away from a priori theorizing and towards an openly sociological study of modern capitalist economies.

In one powerful stroke, then, Keynes undermined the conceptual bases of both *laissez-faire* and mercantilism. Specifically, the construction of an economy devoted to the twin aims of full employment and an equitable distribution of income could neither be left to the vagaries of the free-market system nor to the whims of a financially self-serving state. Instead, optimal social and economic arrangements would reflect conventional values created through a process of social consensus, rather than the outcomes of either impersonal market forces or indifferent autocratic decision-making.

Thus we have the following progression in Keynes's ideas: by focusing on and emphasizing the importance of uncertainty and probability, he brought out the salience of conventional and non-rational elements in human decision-making. This led him to contrast the logic of truth with the logic of opinion, (and, in the realm of policy-making, the logic of axiomatic micro-models), to that of pragmatic macro-models.

This account of Keynes's behavioural theory is necessary to reach the substantive conclusions of Keynesian theory: the absence of any automatic tendency to full utilization of resources (including employment) in the short run, or to a natural rate of growth in the long run. But there is a more important point to be made as well, one that concerns the connection between Keynes's behavioural theory and its consequences for mainstream theory's social construction of reality.

Keynes's successors accepted his policy prescriptions as well as his particular macro model, but none the less devoted their energies to interpreting them from an axiomatic perspective. Thus, they accomplished precisely what Keynes had been opposed to: namely, the construction of another mechanical model of the economy, which would lead to correct outcomes in the hands of technocratic policy-makers.

Neither the neo-classical synthesis nor the technocratic application of Keynes's macro-theory would have been possible, however, if the so-called Keynesians had understood Keynes's conclusions regarding the impossibility of using an axiomatic probability calculus as a basis for decision-making in general, and investment, savings, and finance decisions in particular. The development of these ideas is taken up in the next section.

THE FOUNDATIONS OF KEYNES'S METHODOLOGY:
THE GENERAL THEORY

I should therefore conclude your theme rather differently. I should say
that what we want is not no planning, or even less planning; indeed, I
should say that we almost certainly want more. But the planning should
take place in a community in which as many people as possible, both
leaders and followers, wholly share your own moral position. Moderate
planning will be safe if those carrying it out are rightly oriented in their
own minds and hearts to the moral issue.

J. M. Keynes, letter to Hayek, *Collected Writings*, xxvii. 387.

Keynes said that the readers of the *General Theory* would have to undergo
'a struggle of escape from habitual modes of thought and expression' (1936:
viii) if his efforts to undermine the prevailing orthodoxy were to be successful. The orthodoxy to which he referred was the axiomatic or mechanistic
approach that was embedded in the writings of his classical contemporaries.
In terms of their macroeconomic models, the classicals relied upon the
axiomatic approach to demonstrate or derive the result that the economy,
as a whole, is simply the sum of its parts. During his own escape from
economic orthodoxy, Keynes developed an alternative vision of an organic
or interdependent economy whose macroeconomic variables cannot be
straightforwardly derived from disaggregated phenomena. His rejection of
the micro-founded economics of Marshall and his followers was based
upon certain insights, first developed in *A Treatise on Probability*, concerning
the severely limited and circumscribed character of knowledge garnered
through 'atomistic' induction. And whereas his repudiation of piecemeal
economics had led him to adopt an over-simplified rationalism or intuition-
ism in the *Treatise*, it instead led him, with the publication of the *General
Theory*, to emphasize the contextual, historically contingent nature of economic decision-making and, hence, theorizing.

*Microeconomic Innovations: Uncertainty and the Endogeneity of
Behavioural Relations*

In Keynes's day, as in our own, the analysis of economic decision-making
was dominated by neo-classical postulates and methods. This approach
asserts the unproblematic nature, in principle, both of agents' knowledge
and of their application of this knowledge to economic decisions such as
consumption, investment, savings, wage-bargaining, etc. These claims pre-
suppose a number of assumptions which need to be made explicit, mostly
having to do with the future and its relation to agents' knowledge and
decision-making.

First, neo-classical theorists generally presume that agents can know the future. Less baldly, they assume that agents learn from mistaken choices in the past and that the basic structure of economic relationships (behavioural, institutional, etc.), in the future will not differ significantly from those that obtained in the past. Hence, agents' knowledge of the past is assumed to provide an ample and reliable basis on which to form correct, or at least rational, expectations. Typically, of course, agents will not have the information they need to evaluate their present choices *vis-à-vis* the future. They must make decisions in the present under uncertainty regarding the future.

Keynes adopts a very different approach to the analysis of economic decision-making. He offers a much less sanguine view of agents' knowledge, particularly their knowledge of the future, than do the neo-classicals. His behavioural assumptions and relationships in the *General Theory* emphasize 'the extreme precariousness of the [agents'] basis of knowledge'. Agents' knowledge is never sufficient to know (i.e. predict) the future. Keynes's analysis is thus fundamentally different from Walrasian general equilibrium approaches which posit a knowable future (Chick, 1983; Crotty, 1985; Minsky, 1975; 1986). One could even argue that Keynes is conceptualizing economic agents who are genuinely different from those of neo-classical theory. That is, he is not using the same agents with less information, but rather agents affected at their core by their uncertain environment.

Keynes's approach can be characterized in terms of four concepts: uncertainty, convention, expectation, and confidence (Davidson, 1972; Minsky, 1975; Kregel, 1976; Marglin, 1984; Dow and Dow, 1985; Crotty, 1985). Uncertainty, for Keynes, is a general feature of all economic decisions that implicate the future. It refers to the troublesome fact that, despite their profound ignorance of the future, agents must take action in the present. They must therefore form opinions, however vague or incomplete, about future circumstances in order to act in the present with some semblance of quasi-rationality. Superficially, this seems little different from the neo-classical problem of 'imperfect information'. Yet the two approaches are quite distinct:

> By 'uncertain' knowledge let me explain, I do not mean merely to distinguish what is certain from what is only probable. The game of roulette is not subject, in this sense, to uncertainty; nor is the prospect of a Victory bond being drawn . . . The sense in which I am using the term is that in which the prospect of a European war is uncertain, or the price of copper and the rate of interest twenty years hence . . . About these matters there is no scientific basis on which to form any calculable probability whatever. We simply do not know. (Keynes, 1937: 213–14)

Most economists, both before and after Keynes, have treated issues of uncertainty in probabilistic terms. For them uncertainty refers to a situation in which all the potential outcomes are neither 100 per cent likely nor 100 per cent unlikely. Given a knowable future, however, rational agents can

discern the probability distributions associated with these various possibilities. Put differently, it is possible for agents to know, with certainty, both
the expected outcome (the probabilistic mean) and the relative likelihood of
this outcome *vis-à-vis* all other possible outcomes (the variance about the
mean). Keynes criticized this conception of uncertainty in his *Treatise on
Probability*. His main line of argument there is that probability theory is an
inappropriate tool for the study of agents' expectations (Shackle, 1974: 40–
2; Lawson, 1988: 48–9). Whereas the former requires a series of repeated,
identical events (like coin-flipping), the latter undergo change continuously
as part of history and therefore must be understood not as a uniform series
of trials but as conjuncturally determined and hence unique phenomena. In
sum, Keynes was highly critical of these 'certainty equivalence' approaches
which, in his view, failed to address the key problems of forecasting and
decision-making under uncertainty by reducing them to a mere probability
calculus.

Pursuing these arguments one step further, Keynes's concepts of expectation and confidence must be distinguished from the roughly analogous
concepts of the probabilistic mean and its variance. Expectation refers to an
agent's best guess at any given moment about some future circumstance
(e.g. the nature of competition in a particular industry five years hence). In
tandem with this idea, Keynes defines confidence as the extent to which an
agent believes her best guess to be correct. Neither of these concepts can be
defined or theorized in terms of a probability calculus. Insufficient and
unevenly disseminated information poses one set of problems along these
lines.

More fundamentally, however, the very concept of agents' rationality is
also at issue (Robinson, 1962: 17, 73). Whereas neo-classical theories
presume that all individuals share a common form of reasoning (a common
form of rationality), Keynes assumed that agents' decision-making criteria,
along with their perceptions of the world around them, generally differ
across individuals. It is this fundamentally radical insight, then, which
constitutes Keynes's most significant epistemological break with the neo-
classical tradition, which assumes the prevalence of agents' rational, i.e.
utility-maximizing, behaviour.

At this point, the concept of convention enters Keynes's micro-theory, as
an attempt to explicate and revise those ideas presented in the *Treatise on
Probability* concerning the formation of expectations and confidence in their
development through time. A convention, for Keynes, is akin to a Kuhnian
paradigm. That is, it refers to a set of beliefs and ideas about the world—
past, present, and future—which are held in common, more or less, by a
particular (usually local) group of people (Robinson, 1962: 9, 13, 18).
Conventions thus provide a theoretical framework, of sorts, by means of
which agents who must try to make sense out of an otherwise chaotic
present and an otherwise unknowable future, attempt to construct this

sense collectively. These conventions are merely social constructions and, as such, are subject to change and revision whenever society so chooses: 'We shall use the new found bounty of nature quite differently from the way the rich use it today, and will map out for ourselves a plan of life quite different from theirs' (CW ix. 328–9). They provide the basis for agents' knowledge and hence for their expectations and confidence as well.

Several important implications may be drawn from this discussion, all of which serve to differentiate Keynes's method of microeconomic analysis from those of the neo-classical theorists. First, Keynes's theory enables one to understand the development of agents' expectations and confidence as a fundamentally social, rather than individual, process (Robinson, 1962; Davidson, 1972; Kregel, 1980; Brown-Collier and Bausor, 1985). Agents' knowledge, their decision-making criteria, and their actual economic decisions (to save, invest, consume, etc.) are not produced atomistically, in isolation from other individuals. They develop and change very much in response to the surrounding economic and social environment, which includes other agents' attitudes and behaviour. They are endogenous, in other words, in relation to the social structure at large, and are therefore always subject to change (Shackle, 1974: 38–9, 73, 76–7).

Second, in extending these micro-level problems of agents' knowledge to the macro-level, Keynes points out a number of important repercussions. These have mainly to do with co-ordination failures (i.e. market failures), such as when supplies and demands in financial markets keep interest rates higher than would be consistent with a full-employment equilibrium. The issues of uncertainty, convention, expectation, and confidence raised by Keynes suggest massive potential for this kind of market failure along with the instabilities and potential downturns they might entail (Crotty, 1985). Here he departs sharply from neo-classical micro and macro analysis, in so far as the latter do not recognize the existence of uncertainty or convention (in Keynes's senses of the terms), and therefore rule out, a priori, the co-ordination problems that are central to Keynes's vision of a modern capitalist economy.

As a specific instance, consider the decision to save. Given their current income, individuals must make a two-fold savings decision: how much, if any, of their current income they wish to save; and simultaneously, the particular form(s) in which these savings will be held, given the available range of financial instruments. In Keynes's analysis, the first of these is determined by individuals' propensity to consume, while the latter is determined by his or her degree of liquidity preference. Liquidity preference refers to individuals' desire to hold savings in money form (i.e. short-term, relatively liquid assets) as opposed to holding them in bond form (i.e. longer-term, relatively risky assets). Assuming a constant propensity to consume, the volume and composition of aggregate savings depends, therefore, on the aggregate impact of individuals' liquidity preferences. In other words, a shift in liquidity preference will alter equilibrium income and therefore, given the marginal propensity to consume, will alter aggregate savings as well.

Unlike the neo-classical theories of savings behaviour, in which savings (i.e. 'the supply of loanable funds') is treated as a function of interest rates alone, Keynes introduces additional determinants, via the concept of liquidity preference, which yield conclusions quite different from those produced by the neo-classical approach. Specifically, Keynes assumes that liquidity preference depends upon the differential degrees of risk (or safety) associated with the alternative assets, as well as upon assets' differential rates of return (Chick, 1983: 194–218). This is not to suggest that Keynes's critique and reformulation of the neo-classical theory can be reduced to an introduction of risk as a determinant of portfolio choices. In that case, his criticism would be largely misplaced, since most neo-classical theories of financial markets incorporate a notion of risk as part of their conception of the market interest rate (i.e. arguing that risk differentials are assessed and transmitted within the financial markets via interest-rate differentials). Where Keynes departs from the neo-classical approach is in his treatment of the future in terms of the behavioural concepts discussed above (Marglin, 1984: 69, 430–1).

From a neo-classical perspective, savings decisions are straightforward. Given individuals' rates of time preference and the existing pattern of market interest rates, savers simply maximize the expected rate of return on their investments. Implicit here is the idea that savings will tend to flow into the higher-yielding, long-term securities through which these funds are made available for private investment, thereby facilitating an expansion of capital investment at the aggregate level which is consistent with the establishment or maintenance of full employment.

Keynes, on the other hand, argues that savings decisions are both complex and potentially unstable at both the micro- and the macro-levels. Existing patterns or risk and return are always perceived differently by different individuals, say Keynes, each of whom will interpret these figures through his or her own convention-based lens. By means of these interpretative frameworks, savers form expectations about future interest rates (and hence the potential for capital gains and losses) which they hold with differing and ever-fluctuating degrees of confidence. Clearly, then, from this perspective, there is no reason to assume—as the neo-classical theory does—that variations in the interest rate can effect an obedient, well-orchestrated flow of loanable funds into long-term securities. There is no reason to assume, in other words, that the decisions of savers and investors will be co-ordinated and made to coincide with full employment through the workings of supply and demand in financial markets (Chick, 1983: 174–93). The importance of uncertainty, and hence convention, at the level of individual decision-making thus creates potential (if not inherent) instability for the macroeconomy in so far as interest rates and financial markets cannot co-ordinate savings and investment decisions as they are claimed to do by neo-classical theory (CW ix. 318).

Thus, only if we assumed an economy that was perpetually at its full-employment equilibrium, could we reasonably theorize agents whose liquidity preference was so low that the neo-classical savings theory would follow. Similarly, only if the macroeconomy was assumed to have been at equilibrium forever could we produce rational agents who could reproduce it. Ironically, then, neo-classical theorists (including the 'rational expectation' school) implicitly need a special macro (historical) foundation for their micro-theories.

MACRO-LEVEL INNOVATIONS: THE CRITIQUE OF SAY'S LAW AND AUTOMATIC SELF-ADJUSTMENT

Though logically inseparable from his innovative microeconomic principles, Keynes's macroeconomic analysis in the *General Theory* is widely regarded as his most valuable contribution to economic thought. His analysis included not only a critique of Say's Law and its associated theories of output and employment, but also an exposition of his own alternative approach. On both counts, his chief innovation was to develop an analysis of the capitalist macroeconomy in which supply and demand relations, as traditionally conceived, are not the fundamental determinants. The *General Theory* showed that an adequate explanation of how output and employment are determined, within the institutional context of twentieth-century capitalism, cannot be derived from the neo-classical method of supply and demand analysis. For this method simply assumes, despite all evidence to the contrary, that capitalism is a self-correcting system in which competitive market pressures act to propel the economy ever nearer to full employment.

Briefly, let us consider the logical structure of the neo-classical vision. Neo-classical theories are based on the concept of general equilibrium. All economic transactions (whether an exchange of labour-power for wages, credit for interest plus principal, or goods and services for cash or credit) are treated identically, as market transactions between buyers and sellers. In the absence of institutional barriers or imperfections, the aggregate levels of output and employment (i.e. 'quantities') will gravitate naturally towards equilibrium, full-employment levels in all markets, simultaneously. Thus, all markets will clear, leaving no products unsold and no factors involuntarily unemployed.

The interest rate and the market for loanable funds both play key roles in these general equilibrium theories. At a macroeconomic level, general equilibrium implies an equality between total planned saving and total planned investment at full employment. Intertemporally, this aggregate equality is established and maintained through the market for loanable funds, with the interest rate acting as the equilibrating mechanism. Thus, the interest rate is understood to be a scarcity price, reflecting the relative scarcity of loanable funds. Like any other competitively determined price, it serves to co-ordinate the choices of buyers and sellers in the market—in this case, co-ordinating demands for deferred consumption (the supply of loanable funds) with demands for borrowed money. Given these supply and demand relations, the volume of savings in the economy is thereby determined directly by the rate of interest. Moreover, these savings are assumed to flow directly and entirely into private investment.

Wages (both nominal and real) are similarly understood within a Walrasian, general equilibrium schema as a scarcity price and hence as an equilibrating mechanism acting to maintain equality between demands and supplies for labour. As a basis for macroeconomic analysis, this schema therefore posits a decentralized, self-regulating economy which—barring 'structural' imperfections—will never deviate systematically from a full-employment equilibrium.

From Keynes's perspective, this approach is seriously flawed, inasmuch as it can only explain the determination of the best of all possible worlds (full-employment equilibrium), and then only by assuming institutional conditions which cannot exist in reality, such as highly flexible wages and interest rates. Keynes, by contrast, rejects the proposition that factor-market competition tends to produce market-clearing rates of interest and wages. Labour and capital markets, he argues, tend not to clear, that is, tend not to eliminate involuntary unemployment and under- or over-investment. Significantly, however, his argument for non-clearing does not appeal to market imperfections *per se* ('sticky' wages or interest rates). Keynes points instead to insufficient effective demand, which, he argues, is characteristic of modern capitalist macroeconomies in which the processes of savings and investment tend to clash with one another—not to harmonize or mutually adjust—both cyclically and secularly.

The concept of effective demand, rather than relative prices, forms the centrepiece of Keynes's macroeconomic theory. Effective demand refers to the total volume of expenditures, measured in money terms, during a given period of time; or, in short, national income. Keynes employs this concept to argue not only that the aggregate level of economic activity is determined by the level of effective demand, but also that aggregate saving and investment are equalized, not by the interest rate, but by movements in the aggregate levels of output and income.

The concept of 'macroeconomic equilibrium' which emerges from this analysis is altogether different from the natural, full-employment, centre of gravity notions employed by neo-classical theory. In the closed, private-sector economy Keynes considers, equilibrium implies a temporary balance, in money terms, between planned saving and planned investment.

This balance can occur at any level of employment and output, however; it neither requires nor necessitates full employment. For Keynes, it is changes in effective demand which effect changes in the volumes of saving and investment, while, in turn, changes in the path of the economy over time also affect the savings and investment functions. The volume of current savings is determined by the current level of national income, assuming a stable propensity to consume. The determination of investment expenditure, while more complex in character, is similar in kind. Current effective demand enters here into the formation of investors' and savers' expectations and confidence, both of which affect their respective MEC (marginal efficiency of capital) estimates and degrees of liquidity preference, with the latter then placing pressure (upward or downward) on long-term rates of interest. At any point during this process, the volume of new investment is determined jointly by investors' estimated MEC schedules and the rate of interest on long-term securities.

Keynes's concept of macroeconomic equilibrium may be distinguished even further from its neo-classical counterpart by considering how these concepts are used within their respective theories to explain inter-equilibrium adjustments. Most Walrasian-based theories, (including 'bastard Keynesianism'), use the method of comparative statics for this purpose. For instance, an autonomous decline in investment demand would be analysed as follows: assuming an initial state of general equilibrium, falling investment reduces the demand for loanable funds and hence creates an excess supply in the money market; this excess supply will push down the interest rate, inducing both marginal increases in consumption and marginal decreases in savings, eventually re-establishing an equilibrium between demand and supply, at which point the interest rate becomes stationary at its new, higher level. The new economy shows more consumption and less investment than before, as well as a lower rate of interest. Methodologically, the analysis is time-less. The economy is conceptualized solely as a stationary, market-clearing state. Nothing is explained about the step-by-step process whereby the economy moves from disequilibrium to equilibrium, except by an appeal to supply and demand adjustments in the market for loanable funds. But this is inadequate, since changes in this market can be analysed *ceteris paribus* with respect to all other markets in the economy if the analysis in question is indeed general equilibrium in scope. Thus, the method of comparative statics, as applied in the analysis of macroeconomic systems, merely presumes that the economy will move towards full employment and only then indicates the direction and magnitude of price changes that must occur in order to effect this tautological result.

Keynes's method of dynamic analysis, as exhibited in the *General Theory*, proceeds quite differently. Above all, his reasoning excludes the notion of a 'stationary state', i.e. a macroeconomic situation, sustainable indefinitely, in which there exist no endogenously generated pressures for change. So,

for example, to analyse the effects of falling investment demand, the point
of departure is not full employment equilibrium, but instead, a specific set
of short-period circumstances in which the level of employment is generally
below full employment. But in any case, regardless of the starting-point, a
Keynesian analysis of falling investment demand would proceed as follows:
with current investment demand falling, the level of effective demand must
be falling as well, thus creating, or simply reinforcing, the expectation of a
downturn among private investors. Informed by these revised expectations,
these agents may well become more cautious and risk-averse, tending to
produce lower MEC estimates and higher degrees of liquidity preference,
with the latter placing upward pressure on long-term interest rates. The
initial contraction of investment will thus be worsened, contributing to a
further weakening of effective demand and thus a further decline—not an
expansion, despite the higher rate of interest—in aggregate saving. The
duration and outcome of a cumulative, self-reinforcing slump such as this
are not determinate a priori within the logic of Keynes's theory. The only
general proposition advanced is that changes in the volumes of planned
saving and planned investment will each depend, in different ways, on the
level of aggregate economic activity, as represented by the level of effective
demand. To the extent that they are brought into equality with one another,
the level of effective demand will modulate their respective movements.
There is no presumption, however, that the level of effective demand at
which planned savings equals planned investment will correspond to, or
tend towards, a full employment level of activity.

Keynes thus projects a strikingly non-teleological image of macroeconomic adjustments in which no natural or necessary centres of gravity
are presupposed, and in which both micro-level and macro-level relationships are understood to develop and change endogenously.

THE NEO-CLASSICAL–KEYNESIAN SYNTHESIS:
A COUNTER-REVOLUTION?

The preceding discussion has employed a post- or neo-Keynesian interpretation of *The General Theory*, arguing against the neo-classical–Keynesian
synthesis view of Keynes as an 'imperfectionist' Walrasian. If one believes
it possible to construct a coherent and insightful economics which is not
based on the principles of Walrasian general equilibrium, then it becomes
possible to see in Keynes a distinctly non-Walrasian analysis of the capitalist
macroeconomy (Davidson, 1972; Minsky, 1975).

The majority of economists in the United States today do not give much
credence to this possibility, however. To the extent that Keynes is granted
any stature at all within contemporary mainstream macroeconomics, his
relevance is generally limited to the analysis of short-term market imperfec-

tions—e.g. 'sticky' prices, especially wages or interest rates, monetary inter-
ferences with the workings of the real economy, monopoly pricing, etc.—all
of which prevent markets from operating perfectly and which therefore
impede the otherwise spontaneous movement of the economy toward full
employment. The post- and neo-Keynesians are quite strongly opposed, of
course, to this imperfectionist interpretation, since it masks Keynes's political and ideological rebellion against *laissez-faire* capitalism, which is for
them the central message of the *General Theory*. So, having discussed the
analytical differences between these two approaches, it may be instructive
at this point to consider a specific imperfectionist argument and a post- or
neo-Keynesian response to it.

The proposition that money wages are downwardly rigid is widely understood to be Keynesian. While all might agree that the idea is, in general,
consistent with Keynes's vision of the capitalist macroeconomy, its theoretical role within this broad vision remains an issue of deep disagreement.

The neo-classical–Keynesian tradition represents rigid money wages as
a postulate of Keynes's theory, upon which, from their perspective, is
predicated his heretical conclusion regarding non-clearing labour markets
and involuntary unemployment. By contrast, many non-neoclassical
Keynesians have argued that rigid money wages are a result—not a presupposition—of Keynes's analysis in *The General Theory*. For instance, in
chapter 19 of *The General Theory*, Keynes argues that flexible wages could
lead to full employment if and only if the reduction in wages caused interest
rates to fall and capital investment correspondingly to rise by amounts large
enough to equate planned saving and planned investment at a level consistent with full employment. This is generally an impossibility, according to
Keynes, since firms' expected profitability, and hence their demand for
borrowed funds, are likely to remain weak during a macroeconomic slump
despite the reduced rates of interest. If Keynes's argument on this point
is well founded, then downwardly rigid money wages follow as an
implication: specifically, as an implication of his critique of neo-classical
macroeconomics. If, as Keynes theorized, the interest rate cannot serve the
macro-equilibrating function ascribed to it by Walrasian-grounded macro-
theories, then it is entirely unnecessary for Keynes to postulate labour-
market imperfections in order to explain persistently high unemployment.
Unemployment may be understood, following Keynes, as a problem of
insufficient effective demand. Rigid money wages are thereby seen not as an
impediment to growth, but as an important prop for aggregate demand,
particularly so under the depressed conditions of the 1930s. Under those
circumstances, as Keynes often argued, falling money wages would have
weakened aggregate demand and thereby added further instability and
deflationary pressures to an already severe macroeconomic depression.

Thus, contrary to the neo-classical–Keynesian view of Keynesian economics as a specialized imperfectionist branch of Walrasian general-equilib-

rium economics, these arguments support the post- or neo-Keynesian view of Keynesianism as a full-fledged alternative theory of output and employment in a capitalist economy. The distinctiveness of Keynes's economics, from this perspective, has nothing to do with imperfections in the market for labour or any other market; it has much more to do with his critique of the neo-classical theory of interest rates and investment and his reformulation of these in terms of uncertainty, convention, and liquidity preference.

UNCERTAINTY AND INVESTMENT

The themes of uncertainty, convention, expectation, and confidence continually resurface in *The General Theory*, especially in discussions of investment, which Keynes believed to be a crucial economic problem in capitalist economies. Once again, experience, habit, judgement, and other modes of decision irreducible to any systematic algorithm, form the basis of Keynes's analysis of investment behaviour.

Expectations 'upon which business decisions depend', make their first full-fledged appearance in chapter 5 of *The General Theory*. They fall into two groups. The first, referred to as 'short-term expectation', is the price an entrepreneur expects to receive from sales of currently produced output. The second, termed 'long-term expectation', reflects the expected future yield on investment in additional capital equipment (*CW* vii. 46–7).

Keynes gives considerable attention to the effects of the general state of expectations on the level of production and employment. Past expectations influenced previous levels of output and investment. Consequently, they remain 'embodied in to-day's capital equipment with reference to which the entrepreneur has to make to-day's decisions'. For this reason, 'it will often be safe to omit express reference to short-term expectation, in light of the fact that in practice the process of revision of short-term expectation is a gradual and continuous one, carried on largely in the light of realized results' (*CW* vii. 50). This argument permits Keynes to concentrate his attention on 'The State of Long-Term Expectation' (ch. 12). Many post-Keynesians see this shift in focus as significant (Davidson, 1972; Minsky, 1975; Robinson, 1973; Shackle, 1972; 1974).

Long-term expectations

Post-Keynesians have long argued that long-term expectations are formed not merely in the context of risk, to which a definite probability can be assigned, but also with regard to the basic uncertainty surrounding the outcome of future events for which 'there is no scientific basis on which to form any calculable probability whatever' (*CW* xiv. 114). Long-term expectations are guesses formulated with minimal information regarding future economic, as well as other related, events. In addition, there is the question of the confidence with which we make such forecasts (*CW* vii. 148). Typically, entrepreneurs lack information which is essential to their attempts to make sound estimates of future investment yields. The degree of confidence attached to these estimates will depend on the quantity and the quality of available information. Since these estimates are little more than guesses, they are tentative and precarious by nature. Lacking solid and incontrovertible evidence, such calculations can be revised with startling rapidity, given any significant changes in the economic or political climate.

Despite the precariousness of investment decisions in the face of uncertainty, the 'necessity for action and decision' compels the entrepreneur to act as if she had a 'good Benthamite calculation of a series of prospective advantages and disadvantages, each multiplied by its appropriate probability, waiting to be summed.' What criteria are to be used given such pervasive uncertainty?

We assume that the present is a much more serviceable guide to the future than a candid examination of past experience would show it to have been hitherto [and] that the existing state of opinion as expressed in prices and the character of existing output is based on a correct summing up of future prospects . . . Knowing that our individual judgement is worthless, we endeavour to fall back on the judgement of the rest of the world which is perhaps better informed. That is, we endeavour to conform with the behaviour of the majority on average. (*CW* xiv. 114)

Decisions are taken, then, on the basis of past conventions.

There can be little doubt, then, that Keynes saw the concepts of uncertainty, convention, and expectation as central to his theory of investment behaviour. In writing of 'enterprise', a term he used interchangeably with 'investment', Keynes distinguished investment in real assets from the alternative meaning of purchasing financial or other liquid assets:

There is much of great importance which can be said, quite independently of the rate of interest, concerning the state of long-run expectation and the methods by which the prospective yield of investment is estimated by the market, as distinct from the methods by which this prospective yield is capitalized or converted into present value. It is a subject to which practical men always pay the closest and most anxious attention under the name of the *state of confidence*. But economists have not analysed it carefully and have been content, as a rule, to treat it in general terms. (*CW* xiv. 464–5; emphasis in original)

Clearly Keynes regarded the state of long-term expectations, and the state of confidence upon which they are based, as important to both speculative and non-speculative transactions. Furthermore, he argued that:

This does not mean, of course, that the rate of interest is the only fluctuating influence on [the] prices [of capital assets]. Opinions as to their prospective yield are themselves subject to sharp fluctuations, precisely for the reason already given, namely, the flimsiness of the basis of knowledge on which they depend. It is these opinions taken in conjunction with the rate of interest which fix the price. (1937: 217)

However, in addition to the importance which Keynes attaches to confidence, he also states that his analysis has an inductive basis of 'actual observation of markets and business psychology' which reveals a degree of institutional detail unusual for the General Theory (CW xii. 149).

Ultimately, the overriding effect of Keynes's approach to uncertainty is to render suspect all mathematical calculations of any precision with respect to real asset values. Keynes argued that a precise value for real assets is impossible to ascertain given the uncertainties involved. No probability statistic can be derived as to the likely returns, since information about future events is necessarily inadequate. Consequently, the valuation of capital assets is affected in the following ways. First, liquidity preference is altered, as confidence in the future rises and falls. An optimistic outlook leads portfolio holders to value liquidity less, leading to a fall in the interest rate, as bonds and other long-term securities are substituted for money balances. The falling interest rate directly increases the present value of investment goods. Second, future costs and revenues are anticipated values. Thus not only is there a risk, quantifiable in probability terms, that estimates will be off, but there is also uncertainty of the non-quantifiable variety. Consequently, present value is undefined over a very wide range in many realistic investment situations.

Since uncertainties cannot be reduced to probability statements (not even to a mean expected value, let alone other moments), Keynes saw the rational investor or entrepreneur as having to resort to other forms of guidance. Optimism, awareness of conventional opinion, and work as an end in itself can replace, or supplement, algorithmic assessments of present values. Thus, according to Keynes, confidence, along with the rate of interest, technological advance, and other variables, plays its part in determining investment. Changes in confidence, by altering investment levels, expand or contract investment, and with it aggregate demand and the level of income and employment. Indeed, knowledge of the present, or the past, may be scant, and thus a poor guide to the future, but the decisions of enterprise will necessarily rest on convention, habit, and daring, rather than on abstract economic calculus.

As we have seen, the themes of uncertainty, convention, expectation, and confidence did not turn up for the first time in The General Theory, but were already present from the Treatise onwards. The configuration of an economic system at a given moment was for Keynes the result of decisions and behaviour put into action in the past on the basis of forward-looking expectations. In the draft of *The General Theory* he wrote: 'When ... I say that the level of employment is determined by the expectations of entrepreneurs, I must be taken to mean, not merely the existing expectations, but all the expectations which have been held in the course of the relevant past period' (*CW* xiv. 394; *CW* vii. 50).

Under such conditions, where the present is squeezed between the unrepeatable past and the unknowable future, in which time is irreversible and decisions irrevocable, the economic behaviour of investors will be constrained by uncertainty. Such uncertainty unavoidably challenges the neoclassical rationality postulate:

Generally speaking, in making a decision we have before us a large number of alternatives, none of which is demonstrably more 'rational' than the others, in the sense that we can arrange in order of merit the sum aggregate of the benefits obtainable from the complete consequences of each. To avoid being in the position of Buridan's ass, we fall back, therefore, and necessarily do so, on motives of another kind, which are not 'rational' in the sense of being concerned with the evaluation of consequences, but are decided by habit, instinct, preference, desire, will, etc. All this is just as true of the non-economic as of the economic man. But it may well be, as you suggest, that when we remember all this, we have to abate somewhat from the traditional picture of the latter. (letter to Townshend, 1938; *CW* xxix. 294)

The starting-point of Keynes's approach to the problem of expectations, therefore, was his criticism of the neo-classicals' ideal economic agent, who is presumed capable of quantitatively rendering deterministic judgements. To the contrary, according to Keynes, '[w]hen all is said and done, there is an arbitrary element in the situation' (*CW* xxix. 289). So he stressed again, as he had done in *A Treatise on Probability*, that the field of probability as a whole could not be brought 'within the dominion of reason' (*CW* viii. 90).

CONCLUSION

Inevitably, economic theorizing cannot be properly conceived as detached from economic practice or behaviour. The concepts of macroeconomic theory, if they are to earn their theoretical living, must be infused with meaning by the daily efforts of economic agents and theorists trying to understand and react to their economic fortunes and misfortunes. Economic concepts must be grounded in the activities of economic agents for them to have any life.

This relationship between the theories employed by professional economists and the habits or practices pursued by economic agents is an especially important issue for Keynes, who only dimly perceived its far-reaching implications for economic theorizing itself. It means that successful economic analysis will require that the economic theorist develop analyses based upon his or her own economic practices. It means that the professional theorist, like the non-professional theorist is capable of creating and making use of good enough—rather than perfect or infallible—hypotheses and interpretations. The achievement of a good enough interpretation is signalled by the agent's step from passivity to activity: from a position in which her life is lived by meanings over which she has little understanding or control to a position in which she actively lives according to meanings she has helped to shape.

Keynes recognized that economic agents—workers and managers alike—actively attempt to fashion what they can regard as good enough interpretations of their economic environments. Whether he believed that such a pursuit constituted a worthy aspiration of the professional economist is open to dispute. But what is not open to dispute are the far-reaching implications of Keynes's behavioural theory for the discipline of economics in general, and its pursuit of scientific rigour, in particular.

The primary significance of Keynes's methodological innovations lies in an unintentional elimination of the accepted hierarchical relationship between economic theorists and economic agents. In underscoring both the implausibility and incoherence of the central behavioural assumptions of mainstream economic theory, Keynes undermines the professional economist's claim to possess a potentially perfect, and therefore privileged, form of economic knowledge. Due to the pervasive uncertainty which confronts all economic decision-makers, economic theorists (and agents alike) will have to adjust their epistemological aspirations to reflect the more realistic goal of providing merely good enough interpretations of economic events. Accordingly, theorists are no longer entitled to assume that they possess the right to perform an active role, while economic agents are relegated to a merely passive role, in the relationship between professional and non-professional economists.

Keynes's methodological legacy, in other words, is to show that the professional economist's search for the sole, true, objective explanation of economic events is not merely Utopian in practice, but incoherent in concept. In contrast, a good enough interpretation must acknowledge the values and actions it is trying to explain. A good enough interpretation would reflect the role of the theorist who may care for and depend upon his environment, but who is essentially differentiated from it.

To discard the ideal of theoretical neutrality and infallibility for the sake of an alternative criterion, such as a good enough interpretation, may seem theoretically suspect. It is justifiable, however, on the grounds that different individuals have had different values at different times, and under different circumstances. Conflict among these values is a permanent feature of life, one which no single system or theory is likely to remove (Berlin, 1991: 79–80).

The notion, then, that science constitutes such a definitive system is either wrong or irrelevant. From this follows another important consequence of Keynes's methodological innovations: namely that our current view of economic science must be re-evaluated and broadened to reflect the value, purpose, and meaning underlying all economic activity. In other words, if we reject the idea that economic activity is devoid of value, purpose, and meaning, we must also reject the idea that the science we use to investigate economic activity is itself neutral or without purpose. Consequently, if science is to capture economic reality, then its boundaries and methods must be redrawn.

By demonstrating that economic science requires a capacity for imagination, memory, and intuition, Keynes broadens the concept of economic science to one which is never reducible to inductive or deductive rules of scientific research. A truly Keynesian economic science would attempt to understand the diversity and incompatibility of human values out of a recognition that there is no single way to harmonize or systematically order our deepest values. It would reject the neo-classical assumption that our various values can somehow be harmoniously realized—or at least ranked in importance—by the efforts of some especially wise thinker, clever politician, religious saviour, or sympathetic sociologist, or by the use of some scientific or philosophical method, or some technological invention.

As Keynes clearly understood, there is no permanently stable background of standards against which we can appraise the alternatives, no universally valid criterion whereby a rational decision between them can be made. There are just competing alternatives; we must somehow choose one of them. Such choices cannot be made with reference to facts which have yet to be discovered. Instead, they require a decision, an impulse which makes one moral attitude towards the problem our own. To reduce such conflict, and the uncertainty which it inevitably entails, superficially and artificially by logical, theoretical, or technological means is a form of (individual and cultural) self-deception which yields particularly pernicious results.

The practical consequences of Keynes's ideas have yet to be fully explored. This chapter has merely attempted to identify the central ideas implied by Keynes's methodological innovations. These include both the reconceptualization of the relationship between the economic theorist and the economic agent, and the recognition of the diversity of human values and moral outlooks, with the attendant responsibility of having to make radical, that is non-rational, choices. Keynes's ideas thus lead to the unavoidable conclusion that our conception of economic science must be broadened to reflect the special kind of understanding or knack required to gain a direct grasp of events initiated by thinking, planning, human beings and their cultures.

NOTES TO CHAPTER 3

1. This category most notably includes Victoria Chick, Sheila Dow, John Eatwell, Roy Harrod, Nicholas Kaldor, David Moggridge, Joan Robinson, Malcolm Sawyer, and G. L. S. Shackle.
2. This group includes Amit Bhaduri, James Crotty, Paul Davidson, Alfred Eichner, Jan Kregel, Stephen Marglin, Hyman Minsky, Leonard Rapping, Stephen Rousseas, Douglas Vickers, and Sidney Weintraub.
3. Economists in the rationalist tradition believe that economic theory is not amenable to verification or refutation on purely empirical grounds. Instead, they believe that economics is a system of a priori truths, a product of disembodied reason, a system of pure deduction from a series of postulates.
4. For example, the validity of the theory of perfect competition, according to Friedman, does not depend at all on the nature of the markets which the theory uses for predictive purposes (Friedman, 1953a: 8–9, 14, 16–18). Of course, neither Samuelson nor Friedman would appreciate being grouped together in this way! None the less, both Samuelson's revealed preference theory and Friedman's demand-for-money function can be seen as attempts to restructure economic theory along positivist lines (Samuelson, 1947: chs. 5–6; Friedman, 1959: 327–51).
5. Pragmatism is widely regarded as a distinctively American philosophy. It originated with the American Charles Sanders Peirce (1839–1914). Early adherents included William James (1842–1910) and John Dewey (1859–1952). Recent philosophers who have made important contributions to pragmatic philosophy include W. V. O. Quine, Nelson Goodman, Hilary Putnam, Richard Rorty, Wilfrid Sellars, and Isaiah Berlin. Despite the diversity and heterogeneity of thinkers within this tradition, all of these Pragmatists share a common goal: the formulation of a clear and persuasive alternative to the rival positions of rationalism and empiricism. Unlike the Cartesian tradition, for example, which holds that all genuine knowledge is achieved through reflection, Pragmatism argues, instead, that knowledge must be attained by a process of trial and error. An absolutely certain starting-point is neither available nor possible; we must ultimately create our own principles in the empirical sciences, as well as logic and mathematics, and then try them out in the course of inquiry. The value of our intellectual tools, accordingly, must always be measured by their practical success. This holds in logic just as it holds in physics; the usual distinction between a priori and a posteriori forms of knowledge, from the pragmatist's point of view, then, is simply a mistake.
6. The abbreviation CW refers to the Collected Writings of John Maynard Keynes, 14 vols. (1973).
7. This is not to say that the substance of Keynes's economic theories did not differ significantly from Marshall's economics, which held that the economy was automatically self-regulating and tended towards full employment in accordance with Say's Law. As stated above, one of the most distinctive tenets of Keynes's economics, from a post-Keynesian perspective, is precisely his theoretical repudiation of Say's Law.
8. Joan Robinson labelled her approach to price theory, 'a box of tools' (1948: 3). This was in keeping with the anti-Ricardian sentiments of Marshall, who held

that economic theories are neither true nor false, but only more or less useful, given any specific task. Accordingly, a theory's value should be evaluated for its adequacy, not its realism. In this sense Marshall is an instrumentalist.

9. In its simplest formulation, the rationality postulate asserts that atomistic economic agents pursue their own self-interest: that consumers or households seek to maximize utility and that firms maximize profits. The model of maximizing behaviour has also been applied to political agents (McKenzie and Tullock, 1978).

10. In addition to the *Treatise On Probability*, which was published in 1921, Keynes also wrote about his theory of induction in response to Frank Ramsey's review of the *Treatise*, entitled 'Truth and Probability', and again in the September 1939 *Economic Journal* in the form of a review of Tinbergen's work on multiple regression analysis.

11. Inductive reasoning entails the formulation of assertions about events or propositions that go beyond the evidence available. Even though inductive reasoning may support certain laws or regularities, we have no means of knowing whether they will persist. In order to render existing laws or regularities feasible for future needs, an appeal is often made to the 'principle of the uniformity of nature'. This states that laws or regularities that have held in the past will continue to hold in the future. The difficulty with this argument is that it is circular. One is employing an inductive argument to justify induction. This is known as the 'problem of induction' and is posed by our inability to provide rational or logical grounds for justifying induction.

12. See Keynes's Essays on Jevons and Edgeworth (*CW* x. 109–60; 251–66), which critique these neo-classical writers' reliance upon the Benthamite calculus which combined and compounded the errors of utilitarianism and mathematical probabilism.

13. In an effort to provide rational grounds for employing inductive reasoning, Keynes argued that it was necessary to start from an a priori finite probability concerning the truth of any generalization, otherwise the accumulation of inductive evidence would not raise the probability above zero (*CW* viii, ch. 22). Keynes realized that one of the difficulties in obtaining such a finite a priori probability is that there are innumerable characteristics associated with all the phenomena of the world. Consequently, he needed to 'bind up' all of these characteristics into a finite or limited number or groups. This was achieved by his 'principle of limited independent variability.'

14. In this, Fitzgibbons further notes, Keynes 'seems to have followed G. E. Moore; "It is indifferent to their nature", Moore had said, in reference to concepts, "whether anybody think them or not. They are incapable of change."' (Moore, 1899, cited in Fitzgibbons, 1988: 27).

REFERENCES

AMADEO, E. J. (1989), *Keynes's Principle of Effective Demand*, Bookfield, Vt.: Edward Elgar.

APFFEL-MARGLIN, F. and MARGLIN, S. A. (1990) (eds.), *Dominating Knowledge: Development, Culture and Resistance*, Oxford: Clarendon Press.

BATEMAN, B. W. (1987), 'Keynes' Changing Conception of Probability', *Economics and Philosophy*, 3: 97–120.

—— and DAVIS, J. B. (1991) (eds.), *Keynes and Philosophy: Essays On The Origin of Keynes' Thought*, Brookfield, Vt.: Edward Elgar.

BENTHAM, J. (1879), *Introduction to the Principles of Morals and Legislation*, Oxford: Clarendon Press.

BERLIN, I. (1980), 'Alleged Relativism in Eighteenth-Century European Thought', *British Journal for Eighteenth Century Studies*, 3, repr. in *The Crooked Timber of Humanity: Chapters in the History of Ideas*, (ed.) Henry Hardy, (1991), New York: Knopf: 70–90.

—— (1982), *Selected Writings*, iii. *Against the Current: Essays in the History of Ideas*, ed. Henry Hardy, New York: Penguin, 1st pub. 1955–79.

—— (1991), *Selected Writings*, v. *The Crooked Timber of Humanity: Chapters in the History of Ideas*, ed. Henry Hardy, New York: Knopf, 1st pub. 1959–90.

BHADURI, A. (1986), *Macroeconomics: The Dynamics of Commodity Production*, Armonk, NY: M. E. Sharpe.

—— (1988), 'Industry, Finance and the Reserve Currency Status', Helsinki, Finland: World Institute of Economic Research (UNU: WIDER), mimeo.

—— and MARGLIN, S. A. (1990), 'Profit Squeeze and Keynesian Theory', in S. A. Marglin and J. B. Schor (eds.), *The Golden Age of Capitalism: Reinterpreting the Postwar Experience*, Oxford: Clarendon, WIDER Studies in Development Economics: 153–86.

BLAUG, M. (1980), *The Methodology of Economics: Or How Economists Explain*, New York: Cambridge University Press.

BOYER, R. (1990), 'The Forms of Organization Implicit in the General Theory: An Interpretation of the Success and Crisis of Keynesian Economic Policies', in A. Barrere (ed.), *Keynesian Economic Policies: Proceedings of a Conference held at the University of Paris I–Pantheon-Sorbonne*, London: Macmillan, 117–39.

BROWN-COLLIER, E. and BAUSOR, R. (1982), 'The Epistemological Foundations of *The General Theory*', University of Massachusetts, Amherst, mimeo.

BUCHANAN, J. (1962), *The Calculus of Consent: Logical Foundations of Constitutional Democracy*, Ann Arbor: University of Michigan Press.

—— (1972), *Theory of Public Choice: Political Applications of Economics*, Ann Arbor: University of Michigan Press.

—— (1979a), *What Should Economists do?*, Indianapolis: Liberty Press.

—— (1979b), 'Is Economics the Science of Choice?' in Buchanan (1979a): 39–63.

CALDWELL, B. (1982), *Beyond Positivism: Economic Methodology in the Twentieth Century*, London: George Allen & Unwin.

CARABELLI, A. (1985), 'Keynes on Cause, Chance and Possibility', in Lawson and Pesaren (eds.): 151–80.

—— (1988), *On Keynes's Method*, London: Macmillan.

CHICK, V. (1983), *Macroeconomics After Keynes: A Reconsideration of The General Theory*, Cambridge, Mass: MIT Press.

CLOWER, R. W. (1965), 'The Keynesian Counterrevolution: A Theoretical Appraisal', in F. H. Hahn and F. P. R. Brechling (eds.), *The Theory of Interest Rates*, London: Macmillan: 103–25.

—— (1967), 'A Reconsideration of the MicroFoundations of Monetary Theory', *Western Economic Journal*, 6: 1–9.

CODDINGTON, A. (1972), 'Positive Economics', *Canadian Journal of Economics*, 5: 1–15.

—— (1982), 'Deficient Foresight: A Troublesome Theme in Keynesian Economics', *American Economic Review*, 72: 480–7.

—— (1983), *Keynesian Economics: The Search for First Principles*, London: George Allen & Unwin.

CROTTY, J. (1980), 'Keynes and Classical Economic Theory', University of Massachusetts, Amherst, mimeo.

—— (1983), 'On Keynes and Capital Flight', *Journal of Economic Literature*, March, 59–65.

—— (1985), 'Macroeconomics II: Economics 706', University of Massachusetts, Amherst (personal lecture notes).

—— (1989), 'The Limits of Keynesian Macroeconomic Policy in the Age of the Global Market Place', in A. MacEwan and W. Tabb (eds.), *Instability and Change in the World Economy*, New York: Monthly Review Press: 82–100.

DAVIDSON, P. (1972), *Money and the Real World*, London: Macmillan.

—— (1982), 'Rational Expectations: A Fallacious Foundation for Studying Crucial Decision-Making Processes', *Journal of Post Keynesian Economics*, 5/2: 182–98.

DEWEY, J. (1916), *Democracy and Education*, 1961 edn., New York: Macmillan.

—— (1922), *Human Nature and Conduct: An Introduction to Social Psychology*, 1930 edn., New York: Modern Library.

—— (1925), *Experience and Nature*, 1958 edn., New York: Dover.

—— (1927), *The Public and its Problems*, 1954 edn., Denver: Swallow Books: 96–7.

—— (1929), *The Quest for Certainty: A Study of the Relation of Knowledge and Action*, 1960 edn., New York: Minton, Balch.

—— (1930), 'From Absolutism to Experimentalism', in R. J. Bernstein (1960) (ed.), *John Dewey on Experience, Nature and Freedom*, New York: The Library of Liberal Arts.

—— (1935), *Liberalism and Social Action*, New York: G. P. Putnam's Sons.

—— (1936), 'Authority and Social Change', repr. as 'Science and the Future of Society' in J. Ratner (ed.), *Intelligence in the Modern World: John Dewey's Philosophy* (1939), New York: 343–63.

—— (1938), *Experience and Education*, New York: Macmillan.

—— (1939a), Freedom and Culture, New York: Putnam.

—— (1939b), *Theory of Valuation*, Chicago: University of Chicago Press.

—— (1946), 'Philosophy of Education', in *Problems of Men*, New York: Philosophic Library.

—— (1969), *The Early Works of John Dewey*, Carbondale, Ill.: Southern Illinois University Press.

DOW, A. and DOW, S. (1985), 'Animal Spirits and Rationality', in T. Lawson and H. Pesaren (eds.), *Keynes' Economics: Methodological Issues*, Armonk, NY: M. E. Sharpe: 46–65.

DOW, S. (1985), *Macroeconomic Thought: A Methodological Approach*, Oxford: Basil Blackwell.

—— (1993), *Money and the Economic Process*, Brookfield, Vt.: Edward Elgar.

EATWELL, J. L., and MILGATE, M. (1983), *Keynes's Economics and the Theory of Value and Distribution*, Oxford: Oxford University Press.

EICHNER, A. (1973), 'A Theory of the Determination of the Mark-up Under Oligopoly', *Economic Journal*, 83: 1184–1200.

—— (1978) (ed.), *A Guide to Post-Keynesian Economics*, Armonk, NY: M. E. Sharpe.

—— and KREGEL, J. A. (1975), 'An Essay on Post-Keynesian Theory: A New Paradigm in Economics', *Journal of Economic Literature*, Dec., 1293–1314.

ELSTER, J. (1986) (ed.), *Rational Choice*, Oxford: Blackwell Publisher.

—— (1989*a*), *Nuts and Bolts for the Social Sciences*, New York: Cambridge University Press.

—— (1989*b*), *Solomonic Judgments: Studies in the Limitations of Rationality*, New York: Cambridge University Press.

—— (1990), 'Marxism, Functionalism and Game Theory', in S. Zukin and P. DiMaggio (eds.), *Structures of Capital: The Social Organization of the Economy*, New York: Cambridge University Press: 88–118.

FITZGIBBONS, A. (1988), *Keynes's Vision: A New Political Economy*, Oxford: Clarendon Press.

FRIEDMAN, M. (1953*a*), *Essays in Positive Economics*, Chicago: University of Chicago Press.

—— (1953*b*), 'The Methodology of Positive Economics', in Friedman (1953*a*): 3–43.

—— (1977), 'Nobel Lecture: Inflation and Unemployment', *Journal of Political Economy*, 85: 451–72.

GOODMAN, N. (1951), *The Structure of Appearance*, 2nd edn. (1966), Indianapolis: Bobbs-Merrill.

—— (1972), 'The Way the World Is', in *Problems and Projects*, New York: Bobbs Merrill, 24–32.

—— (1978), *Ways of Worldmaking*, Indianapolis: Hackett.

HALL, P. A. (1989) (ed.), *The Political Power of Economic Ideas: Keynesianism Across Nations*, Princeton: Princeton University Press.

HANSEN, A. H. (1949), *Monetary Theory and Fiscal Policy*, New York: McGraw-Hill.

—— (1953), *A Guide to Keynes*, New York: McGraw-Hill.

—— (1970), *A Survey of General Equilibrium Theory*, New York: McGraw-Hill.

HARROD, R. F. (1939), 'An Essay on Dynamic Theory', *Economic Journal*, 49: 14–33; repr. in R. F. Harrod, *Economic Essays*, 2nd edn. (1972), New York: Macmillan.

HICKS, J. R. (1936), 'The General Theory: A First Impression', *Economic Journal*, 46, repr. in Hicks (1967).

—— (1937), 'Mr. Keynes and the "Classics"', *Econometrica*, 5; repr. in Hicks (1967), 147–59.

—— (1967), *Critical Essays in Monetary Theory*, Oxford: Oxford University Press.

—— (1981), 'IS-LM: An Explanation', *Journal of Post-Keynesian Economics*, 2: 291–307.

HORKHEIMER, F. and ADORNO, T. (1944), *Dialectic of Enlightenment*, 1972 edn., New York: Seabury Press.

HUME, D. (1748), *An Inquiry Concerning Human Understanding*, ed. Charles W. Hendel, 1955, New York: The Liberal Arts Press.

HUTCHISON, T. W. (1938), *The Significance and Basic Postulates of Economic Theory*, London: Macmillan, 1938; repr. New York: A. M. Kelley, 1960.

—— (1964), *Positive Economics and Policy Judgments*, London: Allen and Unwin.

—— (1977), *Knowledge and Ignorance in Economics*, Chicago: University of Chicago Press.

—— (1984), *The Politics and Philosophy of Economics: Marxians, Keynesians and Austrians*, New York: New York University Press.

JAMES, W. (1890), *The Principles of Psychology*, 2 vols., 1950 edn., New York: Dover.

—— (1907), *Pragmatism*, New York: Longmans, Green; repr. 1981, ed. Bruce Kulick, Indianapolis: Hackett.

—— (1912), *A Pluralistic Universe*, New York: Longmans, Green.

JOHNSON, E. S. and JOHNSON, H. G. (1978), *The Shadow of Keynes*, Oxford: Basil Blackwell.

KALDOR, N. (1956), 'Alternative Theories of Distribution', *Review of Economic Studies*, 23: 83–100.

—— (1960), *Essays on Value and Distribution*, London: Duckworth.

—— (1983), 'Keynesian Economics after Fifty Years', in D. Worswick and J. Trevithick (eds.), *Keynes and the Modern World*, Cambridge: Cambridge University Press, 1–48.

KALECKI, M. (1954), *Theory of Economic Dynamics*, New York: Cambridge University Press.

—— (1971), *Selected Essays on the Dynamics of the Capitalist Economy*, New York: Cambridge University Press, 1st pub. 1933–1970.

KEYNES, J. M. (1923), *A Tract on Monetary Reform*, repr. in *The Collected Writings of John Maynard Keynes*, iv (1973), New York: St Martin's Press.

—— (1931), *Essays in Persuasion*, 1936 edn., New York: W. W. Norton.

—— (1936), *The General Theory of Employment, Interest and Money*, 1964 edn., New York: Harcourt, Brace, Jovanovich.

—— (1937), 'The General Theory of Employment', *Quarterly Journal of Economics*, 51: 209–23.

—— (1973), *The Collected Writings of John Maynard Keynes*, New York: St Martin's Press (vols. iv. *A Tract on Monetary Reform*; v. *A Treatise on Money, i. The Pure Theory of Money*; vi. *A Treatise on Money, ii. The Applied Theory of Money*; vii. *A General Theory of Employment, Interest and Money*; viii. *A Treatise on Probability*; ix. *Essays in Persuasion*; x. *Essays in Biography*; xi, xii. *Economic Articles and Correspondence*; xiii. *The General Theory and After, Part I, Preparation*; xiv. *The General Theory and After, Part II, Defence and Development*.

—— (1973–9), *The Collected Writings of John Maynard Keynes*, ed. D. E. Moggridge, 29 vols., London: Macmillan.

KINDLEBERGER, C. P. (1978), *Manias, Panics and Crashes*, New York: Basic Books.

—— (1985), *Keynesianism and Monetarism and Other Essays in Financial History*, London: George Allen & Unwin.

KLANT, J. (1985), 'The Slippery Transition', in Lawson and Pesaren (eds.): 80–98.

KNIGHT, F. H. (1940), '"What is Truth" in Economics?', *Journal of Political Economy*, 48: 1–32.

—— (1964), *Risk, Uncertainty and Profit*, New York: Augustus M. Kelley.

KREGEL, J. A. (1971), *Rate of Profit, Distribution and Growth: Two Views*, London: Macmillan.

—— (1973), *The Reconstruction of Political Economy: An Introduction to Post-Keynesian Economics*, London: Macmillan.

—— (1976), 'Economic Methodology in the Face of Uncertainty: The Modelling Methods of Keynes and the Post-Keynesians', *Economic Journal*, 86: 209–25.

—— (1980), 'Markets and Institutions as Features of a Capitalistic Production System', *Journal of Post-Keynesian Economics*, 3/1: 32–48.

LAWSON, T. (1985), 'Keynes, Prediction and Econometrics', in Lawson and Pesaran (1985).

—— (1988), 'Probability and Uncertainty in Economic Analysis', *Journal of Post-Keynesian Economics*, 9/1: 38–65.

—— and PESARAN, H. (1985) (eds.), *Keynes' Economics: Methodological Issues*, Armonk, NY: M. E. Sharpe.

LEIJONHUFVUD, A. (1968), *Keynesian Economics and the Economics of Keynes*, Oxford: Oxford University Press.

LUCAS, Jr., R. E. and SARGEANT, T. J. (1978), 'After Keynesian Macroeconomics', in eid. (eds.), *Rational Expectations and Econometric Practice*, 2 vols., Minneapolis: University of Minnesota Press, 259–319.

McCLOSKEY, D. (1983), *The Rhetoric of Economics*, Madison: University of Wisconsin Press.

McKENZIE, R. B. and TULLOCK, G. (1975), *The New World of Economics*, New York: Richard D. Irwin.

—— and TULLOCK, G. (1978), *Modern Political Economy: An Introduction to Modern Economics*, New York: McGraw-Hill.

MARGLIN, S. A. (1984), *Growth, Distribution and Prices*, Cambridge, Mass.: Harvard University Press.

—— (1987), 'Investment and Accumulation', in the *New Palgrave*, ii, London: Macmillan: 986–91.

—— (1988), 'Losing Touch: The Cultural Conditions of Worker Accommodation and Resistance', repr. in F. Apffel-Marglin and S. A. Marglin (eds.), *Dominating Knowledge* (1990), Oxford: Clarendon Press.

—— (1990), 'Economics as a System of Knowledge', unpublished paper, World Institute of Development Economic Research (WIDER), Helsinki, Finland.

—— and SCHOR, J. B. (1990) (eds.), *The Golden Age of Capitalism*, Oxford: Clarendon Press.

MARSHALL, A. (1890), *Principles of Economics*, 8th edn. (1961), London: Macmillan.

—— (1925), 'The Present Position of Economics', repr. in A. C. Pigou (ed.), *Memorials of Alfred Marshall* (1966), London.

MELTZER, A. H. (1981), 'Keynes' General Theory: A Different Perspective', *Journal of Economic Literature*, 19: 34–64.

MILL, J. S. (1848), *Principles of Political Economy*, ed. W. Ashley, 1961, New York: Kelley.

MINSKY, H. P. (1975), *John Maynard Keynes*, New York: Columbia University Press.

—— (1986), *Stabilizing an Unstable Economy*, New Haven, Conn.: Yale University Press.

MIROWSKI, P. (1990), *More Heat Than Light: Economics as Social Physics, Physics as Nature's Economics*, Port Chester, NY: Cambridge University Press.

MISES, L. VON (1949), *Human Action: A Treatise on Economics*, 3rd rev. edn. (1963), Chicago: Henry Regnery.

—— (1960), *Epistemological Problems of Economics*, trans. George Reisman, Princeton: Princeton University Press.

—— (1978), *The Ultimate Foundation of Economic Science*, 2nd edn., Kansas City, Mo.: Sheed, Andrews and McMeel.

MOORE, G. E. (1899), 'The Nature of Judgment', *Mind*, 8 (April 1903), 176.

—— (1903), *Principia Ethica*, Cambridge: Cambridge University Press.

O'DONNELL, R. M. (1989), *Keynes: Philosophy, Economics and Politics*, London: Macmillan.

—— (1991) (ed.), *Keynes as Philosopher–Economist*, New York: Macmillan.

PATINKIN, D. (1958), *Money, Interest and Prices*, New York: Harper and Row.

—— (1982), *Anticipations of the General Theory and Other Essays on Keynes*, Oxford: Basil Blackwell.

PUTNAM, H. (1975), *Mind, Language and Reality*, Cambridge: Cambridge University Press.

—— (1978), *Meaning and the Moral Sciences*, London: Routledge & Kegan Paul.

—— (1981), *Reason, Truth and History*, Cambridge: Cambridge University Press.

QUINE, W. V. O. (1953), *From a Logical Point of View*, 2nd edn. (1963), New York: Harper Torchbooks.

RAPPING, L. A. (1978), 'The Domestic and International Aspects of Structural Inflation', in J. H. Gapinski and C. E. Rockwood (eds.), *Essays in Post-Keynesian Inflation*, Cambridge, Mass.: Ballinger.

—— (1988), *International Reorganization and American Economic Policy*, New York: New York University Press.

ROBBINS, L. (1935), *An Essay on the Nature and Significance of Economic Science*, 2nd edn. (1949), London: Macmillan.

ROBINSON, J. (1933), *The Economics of Imperfect Competition*, 2nd edn. (1948), London: Macmillan.

—— (1937), *Introduction to the Theory of Employment*, 2nd edn. (1969), London: Macmillan.

—— (1954), 'The Production Function and the Theory of Capital', *Review of Economic Studies*, 21: 81–106.

—— (1961), 'Prelude to a Critique of Economic Theory', *Oxford Economic Papers*, 13: 53–8.

—— (1962), *Essays in the Theory of Economic Growth*, London: Macmillan.

—— (1964), *Economic Philosophy*, Suffolk: Penguin Books.

—— (1956), *The Accumulation of Capital*, 3rd edn. (1969), London: Macmillan.

—— (1973), *Economic Heresies: Some Old-fashioned Questions in Economic Theory*, New York: Basic Books.

—— (1977), 'Michal Kalecki on the Economics of Capitalism', *Oxford Bulletin of Economics and Statistics*, 39: 7–17.

—— (1978), *Contributions to Modern Economics*, Oxford: Basil Blackwell.

RORTY, R. (1979), *Philosophy and the Mirror of Nature*, 1980 edn., Princeton: Princeton University Press.

—— (1982), *Consequences of Pragmatism: Essays: 1972–1980*, 1989 edn.,

Minneapolis: University of Minnesota Press.

RORTY, R. (1989), *Contingency, Irony and Solidarity*, New York: Cambridge University Press.

ROTHEIM, R. J. (1988), 'Keynes and the Language of Probability and Uncertainty', *Journal of Post-Keynesian Economics*, 11/1: 82–99.

ROUSSEAS, S. (1972), *Monetary Theory*, New York: Random House.

—— (1978), *Capitalism and Catastrophe*, New York: Cambridge University Press.

—— (1986), *Post-Keynesian Monetary Economics*, Armonk, NY: M. E. Sharpe.

RYLE, G. (1949), *The Concept of Mind*, London: Hutchison: 42–3.

SAMUELSON, P. A. (1939), 'Interactions between the Multiplier Analysis and the Principle of Acceleration', *Review of Economics and Statistics*, 21: 75–8; repr. in J. Lindauer (ed.), *Macroeconomic Readings*, New York: Free Press.

—— (1947), *Foundations of Economic Analysis*, Cambridge, Mass.: Harvard University Press.

—— (1958), 'An Exact Consumption-Loan Model of Interest, With and Without the Social Contrivance of Money', *Journal of Political Economy*, 66: 467–89.

—— (1963), 'Problems of Methodology: Discussion', *American Economic Review*, papers and proceedings, 53: 231–6.

—— (1964), 'Theory and Realism: A Reply', *American Economic Review*, 54: 736–9.

—— (1965), 'Economic Forecasting and Science', *Michigan Quarterly Review*, 4: 274–80.

SAWYER, M. C. (1982), *Macroeconomics in Question: The Keynesian-Monetarist Orthodoxies and the Kaleckian Alternative*, Armonk, NY: M. E. Sharpe.

SELLARS, W. (1967), *Science, Perception and Reality*, London: Routledge & Kegan Paul.

—— (1968), *Science and Metaphysics*, London: Routledge & Kegan Paul.

SHACKLE, G. L. S. (1967), *The Years of High Theory: Invention and Tradition in Economic Thought 1926–1939*, 1983 edn., Cambridge: Cambridge University Press.

—— (1972), *Epistemics and Economics: A Critique of Economic Doctrines*, Cambridge: Cambridge University Press.

—— (1974), *Keynesian Kaleidics*, Edinburgh: Edinburgh University Press.

SKILDELSKY, R. (1994), *John Maynard Keynes*, ii, New York: Allen Lane.

SMITH, ADAM (1759), *The Theory of Moral Sentiments*, ed. D. D. Raphael and A. L. Macphie, 1976, Oxford: Clarendon Press.

TAYLOR, C. (1985), *Philosophy and the Human Sciences: Philosophical Papers*, ii, 1985 edn., New York: Cambridge University Press.

TOBIN, J. (1955), 'A Dynamic Aggregative Model', *Journal of Political Economy*, 63: 103–115.

—— (1958), 'Liquidity Preference as a Behavior Towards Risk', *Review of Economic Studies*, 25: 65–86.

—— (1965), 'Money and Economic Growth', *Econometrica*, 33: 671–84.

—— (1969), 'A General Equilibrium Approach to Monetary Theory', *Journal of Money, Credit and Banking*, 1: 15–29.

—— (1972a), 'Inflation and Unemployment', *American Economic Review*, 62/1: 1–18.

—— (1972*b*), 'Friedman's Theoretical Framework', *Journal of Political Economy*, 78/2: 852–63.

—— (1980), *Asset Accumulation and Economic Activity: Reflections on Contemporary Macroeconomic Theory*, Chicago: Basil Blackwell.

VICKERS, D. (1978), *Financial Markets in the Capitalist Process*, Philadelphia: University of Pennsylvania Press.

—— (1984), 'The Uncertainty about Uncertainty', *Eastern Economic Journal*, 10/1: 71–7.

—— (1985*a*), 'On Relational Structures and Non-equilibrium in Economic Theory', *Eastern Economic Journal*, 11/4: 384–403.

—— (1985*b*), *Money, Banking and the Macroeconomy*, Englewood Cliffs, NJ: Prentice-Hall.

WEINTRAUB, S. (1973), *Keynes and the Monetarists*, New Brunswick: Rutgers University Press.

—— (1975), ' "Uncertainty" and the Keynesian Revolution', *History of Political Economy*, 7/4: 530–48.

4

Two Phases of American Environmentalism: A Critical History

RAMACHANDRA GUHA

[Commissioner of Reclamation] Dominy began to talk dams. To him, the world is a tessellation of watersheds. When he looks at a globe, he does not see nations so much as he sees rivers, and his imagination runs down the rivers building dams. Of all the rivers in the world, the one that makes him salivate most is the Mekong. There are chances in the Mekong for freshwater Mediterraneans—huge bowls of topography that are pinched off by gunsight passages just crying to be plugged. 'Fantastic. Fantastic river', he says, and he contrasts it with the Murrumbidgee River, in New South Wales, where the Australians have spent twenty-two years developing something called the Snowy Mountains Hydroelectric Scheme—'a whole lot of effort for a cup of water.'

(McPhee, 1971: 222)

If biologists want a tropics in which to biologize, they are going to have to buy it with care, energy, effort, strategy, tactics, time, and cash.

(Janzen, 1986: 306)

THE PARADOX OF AMERICAN ENVIRONMENTALISM

There have been millions of words written on the American environmental movement, mostly by Americans themselves, and virtually all celebratory in tone. If chroniclers of the triumphant march of American environmentalism have tended to be long on praise and short on criticism, they have good reason. For since John Muir made his impassioned plea for the protection of the Western wilderness at the turn of the century, the United States has created what is unarguably the most extensive and best managed system of national parks in the world. And having effectively protected large chunks of wilderness from the threat of 'development', the environmental movement has in recent decades turned its attention to controlling the hazardous by-products of modern industrialization. Despite the stone-walling of both industry and government (especially under Republican administrations), here too it has been remarkably successful, forcing Congress to enact over seventy environmental measures into law. Among these is the comprehensive National Environmental Protection Act of 1969, a model of its kind and the envy of environmentalists in other countries struggling to enforce minimum standards on their own governments.[1]

Indeed, 'since the beginning of the seventies, the environmental movement has probably shown more staying power and vitality than any other public movement' in America (Gendlin, 1982: 39). Its influence is 'demonstrable at all levels of government in extraordinary quantities of legislation, regulations, and budgetary allocations, as well as in continuing media attention' (Andrews, 1980: 221). In the early 1970s conservative critics had confidently predicted the movement's early demise (see Downs, 1972). To their dismay, the movement has gone from strength to strength.[2] While public opinion polls consistently show over two-thirds of the public in support of even stricter measures for environmental protection, the environmental agenda is increasingly influencing the outcome of local, state, and federal elections.[3] Despite attempts (by, for example, Douglas and Wildavsky in the work cited earlier) to push it to the margins, the environmental movement's centrality to contemporary American culture and politics is beyond dispute.

From a larger, more global perspective, of course, this success has not been without its costs. For 'no other nation [has] equalled the American people in their paradoxical ability to devastate the natural world and at the same time mourn its passing' (Ekirch, 1963: 189). And not just its own environment. For if within its borders America has been remarkably successful in the cause of environmental protection, it has simultaneously had by far the most negative impact on other ecosystems. With 6 per cent of the world's population, it consumes close to 40 per cent of the world's resources. To maintain current standards of living, American society draws upon the physical resources of many, if not most, of the countries in the world, fostering in the process imprudent and ecologically unsustainable practices elsewhere.[4] Moreover, for Americans the global environment is not only a source of raw material, it is also a sink for the disposal of waste. Illustrative here is the case of the garbage barge from New York, whose cargo was rejected by eight states and three countries (the Mexican navy having to stop it at gunpoint from dumping its load in the Gulf of Mexico), before it turned reluctantly for home after more than three months at sea (Branigin, 1987: A-20).

Although its neglect of over-consumption is a serious weakness of the American environmental movement, it need not detain us here. For it is a narrow view that judges a movement solely in instrumental terms, balancing its successes against its failures. American environmentalism is far more than a sum of legislative enactments and failures to stem the excesses of consumerism. For many of its participants the movement's appeal lies not so much in the policy changes it has wrought as in the compelling moral vision (more accurately, visions) it offers of human attitudes to the natural world. One can identify two distinct phases in the history of American environmentalism, each characterized by distinct values and perceptions of nature. Of course, their adherents do not themselves see these systems as being bounded either by culture or history. On the contrary, Americans have typically insisted that the language of environmentalism is universal, although its presence may be more or less marked in different societies and at different times. Support for this view comes from two sources. One is science. Since the scientific understanding of natural processes (and human intervention in these processes) has provided a powerful justification for environmental intervention, and as science is by definition universal, so are (in so far as they are based on science) environmental values. Indeed, ecologists even claim a privileged status for their discipline in redefining those areas of human activity normally regarded as 'outside' science. Echoing their judgement that ecology is a 'subversive science', the historian Donald Worster believes it has 'mounted a powerful threat to established assumptions in society and in economics, religion, and the humanities, as well as the other sciences and their ways of doing business' (Worster, 1977: 22–3; cf. also Shepard and McKinley, 1969).

The scientific claim for the universality of environmental ideas is buttressed by a moral argument. The development of ethics, it is argued, makes the protection of rocks, plants, animals, and other elements of (non-human) nature a moral imperative for human beings.[5] In this perspective, since it is indicative of a society's philosophical and cultural maturity, there is, or should be, a universal striving for the protection of nature. 'The Third World', claims the Executive Director of the Sierra Club, 'looks upon having a system of national parks and protected areas as an indication of a country's level of development' (McCloskey, 1984: 36).

Challenging these claims to universality will be a major task of this essay. The sections that follow analyse sequentially the two dominant phases in American environmentalism, which I call (following American usage) Progressive Conservation and Wilderness Thinking respectively. Embedded within Progressive Conservation and Wilderness Thinking are distinct perceptions of nature, particular evaluations of the existing and ideal relationships between society and nature, and, finally, concrete manifestos aimed at bringing the existing relationship into line with the preferred model of human–nature interactions.[6] In defining the central features of these two phases, we shall uncover their cultural and ideological moorings.

PROGRESSIVE CONSERVATION AS A WORLD-VIEW

In this section, I reconstruct the world-view of the Progressive Conservation movement that arose around the turn of the century. For its votaries, who stood for greater state intervention in the management of natural resources, conservation was above all the 'gospel of efficiency'.[7] Conservation was part of the larger movement away from *laissez-faire* capitalism towards a greater role for the state in regulating economic processes. Blaming 'chaotic individualism' for the concentration of wealth 'in the hands of a few irresponsible men', the influential founder of the New Republic had declared in 1911: 'In becoming responsible for the subordination of the individual to the demand of a dominant and constructive national purpose, the American state will in effect be making itself responsible for a morally and socially desirable distribution of wealth' (Croly, 1912: 23).

In the sphere of natural resource policy, perhaps the decisive factor in this transition was the official closing of the frontier in 1890. No longer could the American state rely exclusively on a settlement policy which treated land (and other resources) as inexhaustible (Turner, 1893). A more 'rational', intensive use of resources was the order of the day. By far the two most important resources were forests and water. As Theodore Roosevelt, the President who put his weight behind the Progressive Conservation Movement, emphasized in his first address to Congress, 'the forest and water problems are perhaps the most vital internal questions for the United States' (Pinchot, 1947: 191).

In the years ahead, foresters and irrigation engineers were to dominate the conservation movement. The institutions their efforts gave rise to, the United States Forest Service and the Bureau of Reclamation, are to this day closely identified with the utilitarian aims of their founders. Forestry was the first of the resource-management professions; indeed 'conservation as a national policy began with nineteenth century fears of a timber famine' (Gray, 1983; see also Steen, 1976). However, scientific forestry arose primarily as a defensive measure, seeking to reverse the deforestation of the past decades with a policy of 'sustained yield' timber management. By contrast, irrigation represented the assertive and more forward-looking strand in conservation. The pioneer irrigators saw themselves as the vanguard of a momentous social movement, the transformation through technology of the arid Western desert into a cultivated garden. For the most part, however, the two strands worked in harness, and their histories are closely interwoven. They subscribed unitedly to the basic tenets of conservation ideology. These tenets are the following.

First, there is the hostility to private control of natural resources. Not only are private individuals and enterprises notoriously short-sighted, there is always the chance of monopolies emerging to the detriment of the public good. 'When storage works are built and controlled as private enterprises', a leading irrigator observed, 'there is danger that the owner of such works will trade upon the necessities of farmers, and when their fields are suffering from drought, will charge such high rates of water that the prosperity of irrigated agriculture will be threatened' (Mead, 1902: 25). At least as far as forests and water were concerned, market forces were to be held firmly in check, and 'Big Money' (one of the conservationists' favourite targets) would not be allowed to exercise its pernicious influence (Pinchot, 1947: 29). This opposition to private control was not however an argument for locking up resources—on the contrary, it was a pre-condition for wise use. To quote the founder of the Forest Service, Gifford Pinchot, 'the job was not to stop the axe, but to regulate its use.' Indeed, irrigators frequently justified dams on the ground that they efficiently utilized 'water resources which would otherwise go to waste' (Newell, 1909: 10–11).

This abhorrence of waste, and the emphasis on use, were embodied in the very definition of conservation as 'the greatest good of the greatest number of the longest time', the last phrase giving a distinctive twist to the well known utilitarian maxim. In theory, the long view was available only to the state. As the profit motive was incompatible with conservation, 'the community, or rather the government, State or Federal, can alone afford to establish such an experiment [in forest preservation]' (Fernow, 1892: 334). Most conservationists in fact explicitly favoured federal, as opposed to state, control, on the grounds that conservation was in essence a 'national, interstate problem' (Pinchot, 1921: 11–12). Others, notwithstanding their hostility to private control of natural resources, even talked admiringly of the 'captains of industry' who had 'demonstrated in their combinations . . . that success is attained not so much by process or invention as by the economies which are possible in operations on a large scale' (Newell, 1909: 10–11). In this Hegelian equation of the communal will with the state, and the stress on centralization, lay the roots of domination by experts. A statement by Pinchot is revealing here: 'These public forests held this attraction for a forester, they were under one and only one ownership and control [and] Congress by a single act could open the way for the practice of Forestry upon these enormous stretches of public forest lands' (Pinchot, 1947: 79).

Rational planning would ensure the 'great error' of waste (Collingwood, 1885) was done away with, but more importantly would leave the experts firmly in charge. Once in control, Progressive Conservationists promised their fellow citizens a bounteous future. Wise and efficient use, they were convinced, 'would provide a resource base for unlimited growth' (Hays, 1958b: 42). In sharp contrast to Malthusian forebodings, Gifford Pinchot claimed the United States could easily support a population of eight hundred or even a thousand million people (Pinchot, 1910: 3). 'The sum to be added to the world's wealth and comfort by the conquest of the waste places', claimed an early proponent of large irrigation, 'is literally beyond the dreams of avarice, even in a day when avarice has large conceptions' (Smythe, 1905: 121).

In holding out a vista of unending progress and prosperity, the conservation movement invoked one of the deepest and most enduring veins in

American culture—the agrarian ideal. Scientific forestry was best suited to industrial timber production, yet even Pinchot could insist that the aim of conservation was to make America a 'nation of homes'. This clearly involved serving the agrarian sector, since the 'farmer who owns his land is still the backbone of the Nation [and] the first of home makers' (Pinchot, 1910: 22–3). The connection between irrigation and the realization of the Jeffersonian ideal was more clear-cut. For irrigation was the very epitome of 'scientific' agriculture; with pesticides, chemical fertilizers and co-operative marketing to follow, the traditional peasant would undergo an entirely willing transformation and become a modern, forward-looking farmer (Mead, 1925; Worster, 1985: 112–15).[8]

A distaste for private control, the worship of centralization, and the placement of science in the service of the Jeffersonian ideal—these are the defining features of Progressive Conservation. While perfectly in tune with the larger movement towards collectivism and the coming of age of the 'expert' (cf. Haskell, 1984), it also drew inspiration from what is at first glance a most unlikely source—British India. If Gifford Pinchot is to be believed, even the word 'conservation' was derived from 'Conservator', the title of senior forest officials in colonial India (Pinchot, 1947: 326).

The influence of Indian forestry was effected largely on a personal level. Pinchot, and following him other early American foresters, learnt their science at the feet of Sir Dietrich Brandis, the German expert who had set up the Indian Forest Department for the British. Brandis, by now in retirement in Bonn, took charge of the education of Pinchot and his colleagues, and continued to advise them after they had returned to the United States. Although American forest historians seem to have overlooked this connection, in his own writings, Pinchot repeatedly acknowledges his debt to Brandis. 'Measured by any standard of achievement, [Brandis] was the first of living foresters', he says in his autobiography, 'but what came first with me, he had done great work as a forest pioneer, [and] had made Forestry to be where there was none before. In a word, he had accomplished on the other side of the world what I might hope to have a hand in doing in America' (Pinchot, 1947: 9). Here, the element of personal projection is marked. However, other American foresters also admired the achievements of the British in India, who 'under the lead of German influence' had established there 'one of the largest, if not the most efficient, forest departments in the world' (Fernow, 1907: 320).

Unlike their forester counterparts, American irrigators actually visited British India to study the extensive systems of canal irrigation in operation there. In fact, George Perkins Marsh, the author of 'Man and Nature' and arguably the first of the scientific conservationists, had himself marvelled at 'the truly stupendous network of canals lately constructed in India by the British Government' (Marsh, 1874: 17). Marsh visited his praise from afar; other American engineers travelled extensively in the Indian subcontinent, bringing back a wealth of detail on the design, construction, and mainten-ance of the Indian canal system. Nor did they restrict themselves to the gathering of technical information, being interested equally in the legal and administrative framework within which the Indian Irrigation and Public Works Departments operated. Outlining the differences and similarities with respect to geography and culture, these early scientific pilgrims were interested above all in the lessons the history of irrigation in British India had for the United States. Here, what impressed Americans was not merely the scale and technical sophistication of Indian constructions, but the fact that they were carried out exclusively by the state, and were from start to finish under the control of engineers. The Indian example was repeatedly invoked by Americans as proof that dam building could not be left to the whims of private enterprise but must be carried out by the government itself (see, *inter alia*, Davidson, 1875; Wilson, 1890; Worster, 1985).

At one level, this interest was reflective merely of the aspirations of science to be a universally applicable system of knowledge. Modern science has very rarely conceded that technological developments can be specific to particular ecological contexts; never that they are specific to particular cultural contexts. From this perspective, the Progressive Conservationists only hoped to do in America what the British (in their reading) had already done, with great success, on the other side of the globe. Significantly, on the eve of Indian independence, the 'transfer of technology' began to flow in the reverse direction. Thus the Tennessee Valley Authority, in many ways the culmination of the conservationist project, became the model for a far-reaching programme of multi-purpose river valley projects in post-colonial India.

But there is more to it than meets the eye. It was not merely the search for the most up-to-date technology which interested American experts in the systems in operation in British India. A closer look at the specific features of colonial forestry and irrigation which attracted Progressive Con-servationists may in fact tell us a great deal about the latter.

Progressive Conservationists were impressed, above all, by the scale of the colonial enterprise. If British India had by far the most extensive system of state forestry,[9] the 'finest examples of canal construction' were also to be found there, for 'in length, cross-sectional dimensions, discharging ca-pacity, number and aggregate mileage, the Indian canals are the greatest in the world' (Flynn, 1892: 4). Compared to the British, the Americans were mere novices—indeed, in India the former had already 'met and answered many questions which still confront the American forester' (Pinchot, 1905: 75) (and, we may add, irrigators as well).

However, these victories had been achieved only after a long struggle. This was the second lesson—if conservationists were to succeed in America, they would have to become more politically astute, combining the roles of expert and lobbyist. Brandis, remarks Pinchot, overcame the multiple obstacles of 'an insufficient or a wrong conception of the interests involved, the personal bias of lumbermen, [and] the alternating support and opposition of the men in power.' If Brandis's victory was 'brilliant, conclusive and lasting', it was only because he was able to place conservation in a much wider perspective. For 'Sir Dietrich was not only a forester', he was 'preeminently a statesman', whose 'conception of the Indian forest policy as a means for nation-wide statesmanlike ends was greatly imagined and greatly carried out' (Pinchot, 1891; 1908: 62–3).

To intervene effectively at the macro level, Progressive Conservationists had therefore to be 'interested in everything that had to do in a large way with the progress of the Nation' (Pinchot, 1908: 62); in other words, convince the political élite of the links between effective conservation and the 'national interest'. An awareness of larger political forces did not blind conservationists to the need for close control and supervision over micro operations. In the United States, irrigators complained, the completion of an irrigation system was an excuse for dispensing with the services of the engineer: whereas in India they continued to be in charge of monitoring and distribution. 'On the skill of the patrolmen and superintendent largely depends the successful operation of a canal system [in India]', remarked one expert, yet it was 'this branch of the service which is most neglected and least thought of in the administration of American canals' (Wilson, 1891: 166–7).

Finally, Progressive Conservationists managed to convince themselves of the wider social acceptability of colonial forestry and irrigation. Pinchot, for example, had no doubt of the peasants' acquiescence in the system of forest management devised by Brandis (see e.g. Pinchot, 1908: 60–1). And 'the modern development of irrigation', held an American admirer, had 'not only freed India from the dread of the fearful famines which used to decimate her population, but is enabling her to export in addition such large quantities of grain that she is becoming one of America's chief competitors in the wheat markets of the world' (Wilson, 1890: 220–1). Apparently peace and stability followed close on the heels of prosperity. Indian irrigation, a British engineer told an admiring audience at the International Engineering Congress in St Louis in 1904, was

not only a profitable property, a sound financial investment, but, far better, an active force over potent to tie the population to their rulers, to render them happy in their homesteads and contented with their surroundings; a condition which cannot but tend to political advantage and security. The Swat River canal on the borders of the Punjab has probably done more in ten years to still the turbulence of a quarrelsome frontier tribe than all the police of the Province could have done in half a century (Brown, 1905: 16).[10]

These words must have been sweet music to American ears. For they provided confirmation of their own deepest yearnings: for the construction of an equivalent system on American soil. There is little doubt that irrigation engineers in British India and the United States did not see themselves only as technologists; rather, they imagined themselves (and their works) to be the ultimate guarantor of prosperous, growing, but ultimately subservient agricultural communities. Governance, as much as science, was their mission, and here the British example was of paramount importance. George Davidson, of the Coast Survey, the first of the irrigation pilgrims, had already drawn attention to one significant similarity. The 'qualities of the English governing race in India', he wrote, 'are almost identical with those of our own people' (Davidson, 1875: 9). It took Henry Luce another half a century to proclaim Pax Americana as the rightful successor to Pax Britanica, but the Progressive Conservationists had seen it coming all along.

As its admiration of British imperialism makes evident, despite its democratic rhetoric the Progressive Conservation movement was anti-democratic in its operations. Conservationists were comfortable with, and indeed welcomed, the enormous powers large forestry and irrigation systems vested in them—believing with Pinchot that 'the use of power to good ends is one of the greatest of all pleasures' (Pinchot, 1947: 381). These powers were justified in the name of 'science' and 'expertise', the system of knowledge they believed legitimized decision-making by experts regardless of the will of the public or its elected representatives. They would very likely have echoed the belief of technological utopians that 'administration in a technocracy has to do with material factors which are subject to measurement. Therefore, proper voting can be largely dispensed with. It is stupid deciding an issue by vote or opinion when a yardstick can be used' (Loeb, 1985: 30).

Centralization and the affirmation of expert control had as its obverse the contempt for the knowledge systems of the ordinary cultivators who were at the receiving end of their projects. Indeed, one of the major hurdles Progressive Conservationists had to overcome was the reluctance of settlers to adopt their technology. Reflecting on the problems scientists faced in manipulating human beings, one irrigator noted that in India 'the prejudices [sic] and the difficulties encountered in inducing the people to make use of the water furnished, were probably quite as great as we will have to contend with in encouraging immigration to our now desolate wastes' (Wilson, 1890: 218). The recalcitrance did not deter American engineers—on the contrary, the lesson they drew from the first two decades of reclamation work was that 'people and their agricultural institutions had to be reshaped to make the technology work efficiently' (Worster, 1985: 186–7).

Domination of human beings was only one element—domination of nature was equally important to the Conservationist project. The latter sentiment found its fullest expression in the writings of John Widstoe, President successively of the Utah Agricultural College and the University of Utah and a special adviser to the Board of Reclamation. 'The destiny of man', he was convinced, 'is to possess the whole earth, and the destiny of the earth is to be subject to man'.[11] Clearly irrigation was the cutting edge of this process of conquest and subjugation. For it was 'one of the great world movements for subduing the waste-places of the earth'—in the American West, irrigation represented a 'continuous conquest of the untoward forces of the desert', finally bringing the 'empire west of the 100th parallel under the subjection of mankind'. The agents of this 'continuous conquest' were themselves a chosen people, for 'the history of irrigation . . . is virtually the story of the most progressive peoples of historical times' (Widstoe, 1913: 53; 1912: 23; 1920: p. ix).

The mission of Progressive Conservation, therefore, was nothing less than the total reordering of nature and society in the image of their technology. Yet neither nature nor society were entirely willing accomplices in this project of domination. There is by now a substantial literature on the ecological costs of scientific forestry and scientific irrigation respectively—the former in terms of its simplification of complex ecosystems into single species stands and the failure of 'sustained yield' methods to ensure adequate regeneration, the latter with respect to the serious problems of soil salinity, waterlogging, and high rates of siltation which have beset large irrigation projects all over the world. For American scientists whose self-image rests heavily on their contribution to the Jeffersonian ideal, the problem of a recalcitrant yeomanry has proved to be as intractable. A telling commentary on the failure of scientific conservationists to carry the farmer with them is provided by Donald Worster in his summary of the life and work of Elwood Mead, Commissioner of the Bureau of Reclamation from 1924 to 1936:

All his life he showed a 'passion for orderliness': he loved efficiency, hated waste, insisted on rules. Directing the flow of water in the desert satisfied him immensely. The farmers, however, would never behave quite so well as the water did, would never run in the ditches he had dug for them. Not seeing that he had their best interests at heart, they repeatedly broke the rules, refused to become organized, were unthrifty, and made foolish demands. Irrigation, Mead had hoped, would be a training ground for a new breed of farmers, but the debacle of the federal program in its first two decades demonstrated how much work with rural folk remained to be done (Worster, 1985: 183).

But perhaps the problem lay with Mead and his philosophy, and not with the farmers who refused to follow the narrow and straight path he had mapped out for them. For, while professing to serve the farmers, Progressive Conservation recognizes neither the local user's knowledge about local conditions nor his/her definitions of natural resources and priorities in their use. A totalizing and exclusivist system of knowledge, it can only treat cultivators as objects of manipulation, not as creative agents with their own systems of knowledge and action. Indefensible even in the American context, this separation of resource management from resource use has, in many parts of the Third World, seriously affected the social and ecological viability of agricultural production systems (Fortmann and Fairfax, 1987).

In fact, the most devastating indictment of Progressive Conservation is the history of the reception of scientific forestry and irrigation in India itself. For the British experts the American conservationists so admired were not operating in a scientific vacuum; rather, they sought to impose their own project of large-scale, centralized resource management on a vast network of pre-existing, traditional systems of forest and water management. In their relationships with nature, Indian peasants drew upon a reservoir of shared community values and ecological knowledge whose sophistication and depth is only now beginning to be appreciated. While undermining these indigenous knowledge systems, state forestry and irrigation projects in British India sought to substitute an inflexible system of external controls for the decentralized and flexible set of internal constraints which characterized village systems of forest and water management. Not only were the new systems socially inappropriate, they were also based on an imperfect understanding of the natural environment in which they intervened. Far from creating a prosperous, contented, and stable agricultural community (as the Americans fondly imagined) conservation management in British India was bitterly resisted by the peasants adversely affected by its workings. More recently, the continuing mismanagement of soil, water, and plant resources by the successors of the colonial forest and irrigation departments has created substantial (in many cases irreversible) ecological damage and led to widespread discontent.[12] In contemporary India, the two issues around which a vigorous environmental movement has crystallized are precisely the excesses of commercial forestry and large irrigation respectively. If the work of colonial foresters and irrigators greatly inspired the first wave of the American environmental movement, in their original home the reception has been quite different.[13]

WILDERNESS MANAGEMENT AS A WORLD-VIEW

In the fashion of innumerable social movements, Progressive Conservation, which arose as a movement of protest against the excesses of unregulated capitalism, was transformed over time into an instrument of state power. Institutionalized in the Bureau of Reclamation and the United States Forest Service, and bolstered by the emphasis on state intervention during the New Deal, by the Second World War Conservationists were very much in charge. The war and its aftermath, in giving tremendous boost to the American economy, apparently confirmed their prognosis of unending economic growth. Science was the 'endless frontier', technology the 'inexhaustible resource'; working in harness, they would dispel any thoughts of temporary or permanent resource shortages. As for Mother Earth itself, it had 'enough and to spare' (see, *inter alia*, Bush, 1945; Mather, 1944).

This optimism proved to be short-lived. The first salvo was fired by a gentle, retiring, woman scientist to whose exposé of ecological damage by pesticides is conventionally assigned the credit for stimulating the modern environmental movement. The American public had been prepared for Rachel Carsons's *Silent Spring* by the growing concern with radioactive fallout from nuclear testing (Lutts, 1985; Boyer, 1985). While Carsons limited herself to the impact of chemicals on the living world, the ecologists who came in her wake were pessimistic about the survival of civilization itself. Among these 'prophets of doom' we may single out two schools: one emphasized population as the main cause of environmental degradation, the other blamed modern technology.

Among those who pointed their finger at population growth, we may further distinguish between Soft and Hard Malthusians (Guha, 1985*a*). The former, whose main spokesman was the Stanford biologist Paul Ehrlich, viewed strict population control (in the United States, but especially in the Third World) and a coercive state as inevitable if ecological disaster was to be forestalled. The Hard Malthusians (or Social Darwinists), pre-eminent among whom was Garret Hardin, preferred to abandon the Third World altogether. In the 'lifeboat ethic' it professed, the West, with a far more favourable land–man ratio, could, if it did not waste its time and money on basket-cases like India and Bangladesh, safely come through the current crisis, albeit with reduced living standards.

The Malthusians (of both varieties) were given a fitting reply by Barry Commoner, the St Louis biologist who had cut his political teeth in the campaign against nuclear testing. While pointing to the self-evident fact that the population-resources balance was threatened far more by over-consumption in the West than high birth-rates in the Third World, Commoner held modern technology (more precisely, technology under capitalism) primarily responsible for the ecological crisis. At a theoretical plane, he attacked the reductionist framework of modern science; practically, he deplored the developments in nuclear physics and synthetic chemistry which introduced hazardous substances into the environment. A professed socialist, Commoner, like the Progressive Conservationists of an earlier era, placed his faith in technical change and state intervention. Admittedly, the alternative technologies he advocated were far more sensitive to ecological considerations. However, Commoner squarely rejects the notion of 'limits to growth'. And as an orthodox socialist, he apparently believes that the state is the only reliable agency for environmental regulation and policing.[14]

These trends were not confined to the universities. Malthusian ideas resonated strongly with enduring American concerns, for as the cultural critic Howard Mumford Jones pointed out many years ago, 'in contradiction to the professed theory that the United States is a haven for the oppressed, the fear of overpopulation weighs heavily on the American spirit' (Mumford Jones, 1946).[15] The organizational forum of the Neo-Malthusians has been Zero Population Growth, a group founded by Paul Ehrlich. Likewise, Commoner's concerns with the dangerous by-products of industrial production (though not always his socialist values) have been widely shared by large sections of the urban population. Noteworthy here are the many local initiatives against the dumping of hazardous wastes by chemical companies (cf. Geiser, 1983).

In terms of popular support, both these trends have been eclipsed by what is unarguably the dominant strand in modern American environmentalism—the wilderness movement. Neither ZPG nor anti-pollution initiatives are able to match the popular support and organizational strength of groups such as the Sierra Club or the Wilderness Society, whose main concern has been with the preservation of wild areas. John Muir may have died a bitter man, but his spirit and mission have been triumphantly vindicated by the march of the wilderness crusade across the United States. Cutting across the political spectrum, the power of the wilderness movement is visible in its influence over policy-making, and even more so in its capacity to evoke such strong sentiments among the members of its far-flung constituency.

Our concern here is with the ideology of the wilderness movement, its overarching world-view. We must first understand the reasons for the movement's success. According to the historian Samuel Hays, this can be explained by the tremendous expansion of the industrial economy and consumer society in the decades following World War II. The satisfaction of basic material needs, the advent of the private automobile, and the growth in leisure time all allowed Americans the opportunity and instruments to avail themselves more fully of the system of National Parks that was already in place. Thus an 'increasing number of Americans came to value natural environments as an integral part of their rising standard of living.' This interest, Hays is at pains to point out, 'was not a throwback to the primitive, but an integral part of the modern standard of living as people sought to add new 'amenity' and 'aesthetic' goals and desires to their earlier preoccupation with necessities and conveniences.' If Progressive Conservation, as an attempt to utilize natural resources more efficiently, was one chapter in the history of production, the contemporary environmental movement is more appropriately viewed as a chapter in the history of consumption (Hays, 1982).

Buttressing the 'objective' factors which made wild areas accessible and attractive to the American public were powerful scientific and moral arguments. The Sierra Club had early on made the claim that preservation of natural areas was of 'inestimable worth' for scientific study—in fact, wilderness was the 'ecological baseline', the perfect standard of 'ecological health' (Brower, 1947; McCloskey, 1972). Of late, the revolution in genetic engineering and the strong economic arguments in favour of biological diversity have strengthened the 'scientific' rationale for retaining representative areas in their undisturbed state (cf. Soule, 1986). The wilderness movement also draws upon moral arguments—viz. the intrinsic right to existence of non-human species, and the responsibility of human beings to allow other species to realize their 'evolutionary potential'. This critique of anthropocentrism is in part a reaction to the strictures passed on the Judeo-Christian ethic by Lynn White in his germinal essay 'The Historical Roots of our Ecologic Crisis'; its acceptance is also related to the greater familiarity with animals enabled by the popularity of household pets in modern Western society (see Passmore, 1980; Thomas, 1983).

Economics, science, and morality collectively provide only part of the answer: it is only in the domain of culture that we can find a satisfactory explanation for the tremendous popular support enjoyed by wilderness preservation in the United States. For if the wilderness ethic 'has had an important impact on the form and content of American environmental goals', it is because it represents 'the most vital and broadly accepted contemporary expression for human meaning in the landscape' (Graber, 1976: 2). The concern for wilderness, in cutting across conventional party lines, resonates deeply with the historical experiences and cultural aspirations of the American people. The national parks are a vivid reminder of the formative experience of the American nation—its engagement with the untamed frontier. The parts are a 'richly endowed showcase' of American history, which reflect 'the aspirations of a free and independent people': here, wilderness lovers can symbolically re-enact the experiences of the pioneer settlers and explorers (Sax, 1980: 15, 50, 111–13, etc.).

While providing a continuing link with the frontier, the wilderness movement is also a powerful antidote to the chronic insecurity which is one of the most striking features of America as a nation. In the eyes of the rest of the world (and especially Europe) Americans have always felt discomfited by their nation's comparative youth and the identification of material pursuits as its defining characteristics. Advocates of wilderness preservation have played on both these fears. In fact the creation of the national park system had little to do with ecological values—on the contrary, it was the expression of cultural nationalism, the 'search for a distinct national identity' that lay behind the movement for scenic preservation. When compared with the stunning achievements of European civilization, the new nation had little to show by way of art, architecture, or epic literature—but it did have natural landscape unparalleled in its majesty and diversity. Thus monumentalism, rather than environmentalism, was the driving-force behind the national park idea. The 'agelessness of monumental scenery instead of the past accomplishments of Western civilization was to become the visible symbol of continuity and stability in the new nation.' Cultural nationalists favourably compared the Rockies to the Alps and the Mississippi to the Nile in terms of size; others took solace in the fact that the great Sierra redwoods had begun to grow even before the dawn of the Christian era (Runte, 1979: pp. xi–xii, 11–22, etc.).[16]

The protection of wild areas from commercial exploitation also helped allay fears that the pursuit of wealth would become the nation's overriding concern. John Muir's life-work, a famous editor reflected, was an important step towards throwing off the 'two shackles which retard our progress as a nation—philistinism and commercialism—and advance with freedom towards the love of beauty as a principle' (Johnson 1922: 21–2). This sharp separation of material and spiritual values (with wilderness preservation equated with the latter) also found expression in the later definition of a conservationist as 'the man (or part of him) concerned with what natural resources do for his spirit, not his bank balance' (Brower, 1956: 3). Conceived as a movement of spiritual uplift, the wilderness crusade could also help elevate America's standing in the international community. Even as one historian complained that those critics 'who say that Americans think only of the present', had not looked at the national park system, another was hopeful the rest of the world would heed the voices of wilderness thinkers, which were articulated from a deep stratum of the national experience and are 'surely as American as those of Joseph Coors and Union Carbide' (Winks, 1984; Turner, 1984).

Driven by these sentiments, wilderness nationalism inevitably spilled over into wilderness internationalism. By the end of the Second World War, America had created a 'national park system which [was] the unrivalled adornment of the hemisphere' (Huth, 1947: 76). It was time to take the movement overseas, and no organization was more enthusiastic about its proselytizing mission than the Sierra Club. For the United States, wrote one Club executive in 1957, wilderness was a 'powerful diplomatic weapon': its advocacy would not only overcome the 'less than friendly attitude towards the United States in many countries', it would be 'one of the most effective answers' to the belief that America was merely an 'industrial nation with a dollar sign for a heart' (Talbot, 1957). A quarter of a century later, its Executive Director likewise reflected that having nurtured the national park idea in America since its inception, it was time for the Club to be 'in the forefront of efforts to protect parks everywhere in the world' (Gendlin, 1982; cf. also Coan, 1971).

We may now conveniently summarize the basic tenets of wilderness thinking. These are the practical emphasis on the preservation of wilderness areas (as opposed to the 'wise use' of natural resources advocated by Progressive Conservationists); the claim that both science and ethics provide a powerful justification for such protection; the fusion of the wilderness crusade with cultural nationalism; and finally, the 'export' of the national park idea to the rest of the world. At this point, Wilderness Thinking bifurcates into two distinct streams. One, the so called Deep Ecology, elevates 'anti-anthropocentricism' into an overriding moral imperative, the touchstone of ecological conscience. It calls for a substantial (for some, up to 90 per cent) reduction in human populations and the reversion to a hunter-gatherer society, so as to allow the recovery of wilderness and of species threatened by human activity. Although it has been receiving some publicity of late, Deep Ecology is actually a marginal trend with little popular support.[17] Far from advocating a reversal to earlier modes of production, major spokesmen of the wilderness movement are unequivocally modernist in their outlook. For them, wilderness is the latest stage in the progress of human civilization—it is, in a sense, the culmination of industrialism itself. Here the appreciation of natural beauty and variety becomes an unerring indication of a society's successful transition to 'post-industrialism' (or 'post-materialism') (cf. Inglehart and Rabier, 1986). And if we were 'to measure the maturity of a civilization by the regard it pays to non-material values' (Griffith, 1958: 20) then wilderness lovers are akin to a chosen people, the 'advance guard for a higher level of civilization' (Graber, 1976: 30).

This interpretation is not entirely novel—it provides the analytical basis both for Ronald Inglehart's study of modern European politics and Samuel Hays's work on American environmentalism (Inglehart, 1977; Hays, 1987). But wilderness thinkers have given it a distinctive twist, elevating a time- and culture-bound explanation into a universal theory of history. In his enormously influential history of the wilderness crusade, Roderick Nash divides the countries of the world into two categories—those which are rich and sophisticated enough to appreciate wilderness (whom he calls 'nature-importing') and those who are too poor and primitive to do so ('nature-exporting'). This deceptively simple and attractive, but ultimately false and pernicious theory of history is graphically depicted by Nash in Fig. 1.

In this framework, wilderness and civilization are not contradictory (as the Deep Ecologists like to portray them) but two equally important parts of an internally consistent whole. Nash's ideas accurately reflect the goals of the American wilderness movement. From its inception, the movement has been not so much a rebellion against as a fulfilment of modernization. Many preservationists (including Nash) yield to no one in their admiration, and even worship, of modern science and technology; and it must not be forgotten that until some years ago the Sierra Club, while opposing hydro-electric projects which submerged wild areas, enthusiastically embraced nuclear power as the embodiment of a clean and efficient modern technology (cf. Schrefper, 1983: 16, 18; Nash, 1965).

As a linear theory of history, Nash's formulation has some striking similarities to the modernization theory of economic development. It draws upon the same Judeo-Christian roots in representing human (but especially

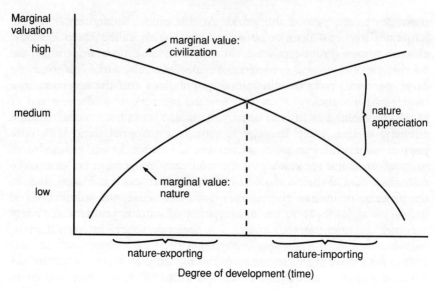

FIG. 1   Changing attitudes towards nature and civilization with development

Western) civilization as marching steadily upwards, and in assigning the role of history's chosen agents to a select few who have crossed a frontier in their own lives and are now preparing to lead the rest of humanity out of darkness into light. Not only is this theory of environmentalism (like its counterpart in economic development) self-serving, it is also at variance with the facts. For it is only Americans who have possession of a vast, beautiful, and sparsely populated continent and the political and economic clout to draw upon resources elsewhere to sustain their ever-rising standard of living. The juxtaposition of the world's most consumerist society and the best system of national parks within the borders of one nation, is a historic accident, made possible only by a unique combination of ecological and political factors. In representing a country's development as autonomous, wilderness thinking is guilty of a most elementary analytical error. For just as the underdevelopment of Asia and Africa was central to the development of Europe, the ecological wisdom displayed at home by the United States is only made possible by its ecological imperialism abroad.

Significantly, this linear and isolationist theory is reinforced by the hostility to the mode of existence of hundreds of millions of people around the world—subsistence agriculture and pastoralism. From Muir onwards, wilderness lovers have consistently represented these life-sustaining activities in pejorative terms. For Muir 'marauding shepherds' and their sheep (whom he called 'hoofed locusts') were the greatest threat to his beloved Sierra (see e.g. Muir, 1895). Modern nature-lovers, mostly from the cities, invariably condescend to the farmer and 'take for granted the dependence of both city and country on the agricultural base' (Graber, 1976: 21–2). With the transnationalization of the movement, this hostility is carried over to Asian, African, and Latin American farmers and pastoralists. Apropos the wildlife of the Ngongoro crater in East Africa, one writer complained: 'Here one can also see the Masai and their herds of economically worthless [sic] cattle . . . They have already overgrazed and laid waste too much of the 23,000 square miles of Tanganyika they control [and] are illustrative of the threats to what is left of the world's wilderness' (Talbot, 1957: 28). The sentiments of wilderness tourists are strongly echoed by American biologists working in the tropics. Moaned one: 'Where will be taxonomists and evolutionists when cows and corn dominate the earth?' (Iltis, 1967: 37). Another, more well-known ecologist asked his colleagues' help to protect the 'tropical agroscape' from being 'populated only by humans and their mutualists, commensals and parasites' so as to leave untouched areas available for scientific study (Janzen, 1986: 305).

There are two fundamental flaws in this way of thinking. First, it confuses the American frontier ethic—of what one might call 'cut and run' agriculture and grazing—with agriculture as a culture, a traditional mode of livelihood. Second, it is symptomatic of the sharp separation of the material and spiritual domains in wilderness thinking. Most wilderness lovers only 'season their lives with wildness' (see Schmitt, 1969: 6–7)—having taken their holiday in a national park, they return to the city (or suburb) and their resource-wasteful lifestyles. There is thus a sharp separation of nature from work and livelihood in the daily life of the average American. This is in sharp contrast to the peasant cultures they so deplore, many of which have endured for centuries precisely because of a successful integration of nature with livelihood. In fact, Asian (and sometimes European) environmentalists uphold the peasant as an exemplar of ecological responsibility. And with good reason—for sustainability, perhaps the ecological ideal, and one that will be forever beyond the reach of industrial man, was well within the grasp of many (if not most) non-modern cultures. Perhaps the most devastating indictment of wilderness thinking's undiscriminating contempt for agriculture is provided by the life and work of a man otherwise acclaimed as one of its founders—Aldo Leopold. Leopold, who spent his last years on a small farm in Wisconsin and actually died while working on it, was clear that sustainable agriculture, and not a combination of wilderness and civilization, was the ecological ideal worth striving for. As Donald Fleming (in a germinal but sadly neglected history of American environmental thought) observes, for Leopold

the virtue of small farms and rural living was the homely private transactions with nature to which they lent themselves, the untremendous and unpremeditated encounters knit into the fabric of daily life. National parks and national forests were seen as the goal of a pilgrimage, holy places set apart under the care of a jealous priesthood of conservationists, against the day when a lay believer, once in a lifetime, would conform to the faith in some cathedral-of-pines. This was the core of Leopold's objections to the Transcendentalist posture towards nature. It was irrevocably coupled to the idea of retreats from practical life, and worse still, to a corresponding devaluation of the workaday world as an appropriate arena for cherishing the natural environment. Leopold's own purpose was exactly the opposite. He wanted to strip the conservation ideal of its remote and sacred aspects and make cultivation of a loving and wondering attitude toward other organisms and toward the land itself a matter of voluntary daily practice in modest contexts, particularly when men were unobserved and unintoxicated by the gigantic and patently sublime (Fleming, 1972: 20).

Among the perspectives Wilderness Thinking barely acknowledges, and at times suppresses, are three that are *raisons d'être* of environmental movements elsewhere: equity, whether across nations, classes, or generations; sustainability, a mode of livelihood that is not exploitative of nature but can be sustained across time; and peace, an ethic for regulating social behaviour which acquires added significance in view of the threats to human survival today (see e.g. Bahro, 1984; Agarwal, 1986).

The lack of concern with equity is of course related to the absence of a socialist tradition in the United States. It is reinforced by the emphasis on individual experience in wilderness thinking. As one devotee laments, in the wilderness there can be only one worshipper at a time, 'since two people create a society' (Cohen, 1984: 150). We have also shown that its philosophy of history sidesteps the question of sustainability, an ecological ideal undermined by Americans daily but within the grasp of many of the cultures so despised by wilderness thinking. As for peace, there has actually been a close link between wilderness, masculinity, and militarism. If, for the founder of the Wilderness Society, one of the prime benefits of wild areas was that it nurtured 'physical independence' (see Marshall, 1947), for the Forest Service chief wilderness had 'given bodily vigour, self-taught resourcefulness, and moral stamina to . . . generations of Americans' (Greeley, quoted in Schmitt, 1969: 175). By helping Americans 'build up their bodies', wilderness also helped prepare them for war, a fact well recognized by that arch imperialist and lover of the wild, Teddy Roosevelt. 'A fine, generous national park system is absolutely essential', wrote a wilderness nationalist in 1911, 'to the proper handling of an American War Fleet in case of a great war, or to the establishment and maintenance of an army which, in the event of such a catastrophe shall be invincible against the armed hosts of the world' (Marshall, quoted in Runte, 1979: 95–6). This emphasis on physical strength and experience has been picked up by the modern wilderness movement and linked to the pioneer ethic (cf. Sax, 1980). It also explains why wilderness thinking is largely a male preserve and looked upon with suspicion by many feminists (see King, 1987).

While suppressing other ways of seeing, Wilderness Thinking also assigns a privileged place to science and scientists. In its privileging of expertise it is at one with Progressive Conservation—no matter that it 'lays off' rather than dominates nature. The backing of science has proved especially useful in the movement's international expansion. A scientist acclaimed by his peers as 'the dean of tropical ecologists' is open in his territorial ambitions, claiming that:

A seeming goal of humanity is to convert the world to a pasture designed to produce and sustain humans as draught animals. The challenge, in which the tropical ecologist is a general, knight, foot soldier, and technical specialist, is to prevent humanity from reaching this goal. The true battle, is, however, to reprogram humanity to a different goal. The battle is being fought by many more kinds of professionals than just ecologists; however, it is a battle over the control of interactions, and by definition, the person competent at recognizing, understanding, and manipulating interactions is an ecologist (Janzen, 1986: 307).

While its appearance in a prestigious scientific journal was noteworthy, Janzen's article was only reiterating a well-worn theme. Over twenty years ago, an identical claim had been made by a botanist from the University of Wisconsin:

If there is anybody who should provide leadership in the preservation movement it is the systematic or environmental biologist . . . We are not only citizens and humans, each with individual desires. We are not only trained taxonomists and ecologists, each perhaps wishing to preserve the particular organisms with which we work. But we, the taxonomists and ecologists, are the only ones in any position to know the kinds, the abundance, and the geography of life. This is a knowledge with vast implications for mankind, and therefore vast responsibilities. When nobody else knows, we do know where the wild and significant areas are, we know what needs to be saved and why, and only we know what is threatened with extinction (Iltis, 1967: 36–7).

The support of scientists has been crucial in the overseas expansion of the wilderness crusade. It is well known that tropical ecosystems have a far greater variety of plant, animal, and insect life. The search for new pastures for scientific research, coupled with the aesthetic preferences of Western wilderness lovers, has fuelled a massive growth in the global network of national parks. Spearheading this drive are the International Union for Conservation of Nature and Natural Resources and the World Wildlife Fund, multinational organizations which exercise an enormous influence on the governments of many Third World countries.

A study of conservation imperialism is long overdue. It has a peculiar yet symmetrical relationship with the more conventional form of economic imperialism. Economically, politically (and above all, intellectually) subordinated to Western societies, the Third World is subjected on the one hand to the modernizing rhetoric of the World Bank and on the other to the gentler but equally insidious persuasions of Wilderness Thinking. If the message of the former is that massive hydroelectric projects and nuclear power are the indices of progress, the latter insists that an extensive system of national parks is an infallible index of a culture's maturity. Anxious to please both sets of masters, Third World élites obligingly put these ideas into practice, with catastrophic effect. For trapped in between the show-pieces of development and the showpieces of conservation are the bulk of the rural population, with no stake in either and who often have to make way for both.

In my own country, national parks already cover 3 per cent of the land surface, and there are proposals to double this area by the end of the century. In displacing peasants without proper rehabilitation, prohibiting traditional hunting and gathering within the reserve, and exposing villages on the periphery to the threat of crop damage, cattle-lifting, and man-slaughter, the parks are (as they stand) inimical to the interests of the poorer sections of agrarian society (see Agarwal et al., 1982: ch. 10). This is not to say that preservation of biological diversity is not important, only that it should proceed on different principles. For in India, as in other parts of the Third World, national park management is heavily imprinted by the American experience. In particular, it takes over two axioms of wilderness thinking: the monumentalist belief that wilderness has to be 'big, continu-ous wilderness' (cf. Devall, 1985; Brower, 1956) and the claim that all human intervention is bad for the retention of diversity. These axioms have led to the constitution of massive sanctuaries, each covering thousands of square miles, and a total ban on human ingress in the 'core' areas of national parks.

These axioms of 'giganticism' and 'hands off nature', though cloaked in the jargon of science, are simply prejudices. When it is realized that the preservation of plant diversity is far more important than the preservation of large mammals, a decentralized network of many small parks makes far greater sense. The widespread network of sacred groves in India tradition-ally fulfilled precisely these functions.[18] Yet modern wilderness lovers are in general averse to reviving that system: apart from rationalist objections, they are in principle opposed to local control, 'seeking instead scientific [i.e. centralized] land management' (Schrefper, 1983: 32). The belief in a total ban on human intervention is equally misguided. Studies show that in fact the highest levels of biological diversity are found in areas with some (though not excessive) intervention. In opening up new niches to be occu-pied by insects, plants, and birds, partially disturbed ecosystems often have a greater diversity than untouched areas. The dogma of total protection can have tragic consequences. In the famous Keoldeo Ghana bird sanctuary in Bharatpur in 1982, scientists forbade villagers from exercising traditional grazing rights—when villagers protested, police opened fire, killing several. When the ban was enforced in following years, the population of key bird species (e.g. waterfowl and the Siberian crane) actually declined. Grazing, by keeping down the tall grass, had helped these species forage for insects. Grazing was thus beneficial to the park, but the pill was too bitter to swallow and in subsequent years park managers have refused to lift the ban.[19]

In sum, wilderness thinking, in common with Progressive Conservation, shuts out other ways of apprehending and transforming nature, while it centralizes power in the hands of a few certified 'experts'. The ultimate irony perhaps is that it is based on bad science. The wholesale transfer of a movement culturally rooted in American conservation history can only result in the social uprooting of human populations in other parts of the globe.

LESSONS FROM WITHIN AND WITHOUT

It has been aptly remarked that Americans often forget that America is a place not an idea. While viewing other cultures 'through its own unique, self-interested prism', the United States seeks to impose its vision of the good life on the rest of the world. It sees itself as the norm, the ideal to which other cultures must aspire. When they find these cultures are not always willing to conform, Americans are alternately bewildered and hurt. Believing themselves to be the injured party, they either retreat into their shell (the isolationists) or (the internationalists) redouble their efforts to spread the American Dream overseas.[20]

Isolationists and internationalists operate in economic, political, and cultural spheres. Economic isolationists, forgetting the dependence of the consumer society on foreign produce, put up trade barriers; internationalists try and convert other nations to their energy-intensive, capital-intensive, and market-oriented brand of development. Political isolationists want to pull out of NATO and UN agencies; internationalists distinguish between authoritarian and totalitarian regimes (our dictators versus theirs), supporting the former and instigating guerrilla movements against the latter. Cultural isolationists resist the penetration of American society by foreign music, theatre, and cuisine; internationalists eagerly export the ethic of disposable containers (of all sizes, from plastic cups up to the automobile) and *Dallas*.[21]

This essay has dealt with the representatives of these generic tendencies within the American environmental movement. Ecological isolationists are easily identified as the Neo-Malthusian proponents of the lifeboat ethic (who, incidentally, advocate a ban on further immigration into the United States), and just as easily dismissed as irrelevant. Far more important are the internationalists, among whom we have identified two schools: the Progressive Conservationists, who held sway from the turn of the century until after World War II, and Wilderness Thinkers, who have been in the ascendant ever since.

My analysis of these two strands has located them in their historical and cultural contexts and reconstructed their world-view. I further argued that the impact of these movements on Third World ecologies and societies has been, on the whole, adverse. While conceding their claim to be the cutting edge of American environmentalism, I have challenged the further claim that they are, or should be, the cutting edge of the global environmental movement.

Among the two strands, Progressive Conservation has been for years an instrument of state power; it is identified by environmentalists in America itself as a major adversary. On the other side, Wilderness Thinking continues to see itself as a movement of revolt; like many such movements (*vide* Marxism) it takes solace in a theory of history which guarantees it an ultimate victory.

In challenging the universalistic pretensions of Wilderness Thinking, we are left with a number of unanswered questions. Is this another argument for cultural relativism? Can there only be 'national' environmental movements? Is there any common ground on which different national traditions can converge? Can we at least work towards a multinational environmental ethic, if not a multinational environmental movement?

Space does not permit a comprehensive treatment of these issues, and what follows are only some pointers. Both Wilderness Thinking and Progressive Conservation, we have argued, strongly reinforce the links between knowledge and domination. The severing of these links then becomes a matter of central concern. How can the experience of environmentalism in other cultures help us here?

But we are not done with America yet. While Progressive Conservation and Wilderness Thinking have at different times been the dominant environmental tradition, there have been other trends as well. Take for example the cultural traditions of self-reliance and working on the land that have surfaced from time to time in American history, acting as a valuable corrective to 'the excesses of materialist individualism' (Shi, 1985: 277 and *passim*). Since the late 1960s, these traditions have been given an ecological twist by the concern with 'sustainable' agriculture, ways of working on, and living off, the land which are more in tune with nature as compared with agribusiness. By integrating nature with work and livelihood, the organic farming movement provides a sharp if largely unnoticed contrast with the antinomies of wilderness thinking.[22]

Searching for individuals (rather than tendencies), we can do worse than settle for Lewis Mumford. Mumford is better known as a historian of technology and the city, yet his 'organicist' philosophy was deeply ecological. His varied concerns all converge on the problem of defining an ethic which could fuse the classical socialist concerns with justice and what we would today call environmental values. When Mumford 'caught the eco-logical tide with *The Pentagon of Power* in 1970', he was in fact 'merely reconstructing and amplifying the themes of a lifetime' (Fleming, 1972: 74). A formidable critic of modern technology, Mumford displayed an early concern with the health hazards of industrialization and the decline of the urban environment. While appreciative of biological diversity, he did not fetishize wilderness; on the contrary, he was a lifelong admirer of traditional agricultural systems which he believed were gentler with nature and sus-tainable in the long run. A relentless opponent of isolationism, Mumford's internationalism was of a qualitatively different kind too—based on a deep respect for, and willingness to learn from, other cultures. A fierce opponent of nuclear energy, he accurately predicted that the fruits of atomic secrecy would be atomic proliferation. Finally, while an implacable foe of Stalinism and the bureaucratic state, Mumford never wavered from his socialist values, upholding in opposition to Marxism-Leninism the decentralized and community-based socialism of Kropotkin and Morris.[23]

Mumford provides a refreshing contrast to Wilderness Thinking. Far from worshipping modern science, he is one of its ablest critics. He also provides the perspectives of peace, sustainability, and equity missing from the wilderness movement. He can be an authentic spokesman for American environmentalism, whose voice would resonate world-wide.

So much for lessons from within. What are the lessons which environ-mentalism in other countries (in this case, India) has for Wilderness Thinking?

A comparison of American and Indian traditions reveals the charac-teristic interpretation of scientific and moral–political arguments in environmentalism. Here the cultural distinctiveness of moral–political claims is quite apparent. For example, in the United States the defence of wilderness as 'sacred space' is linked both to the frontier ethic (of independence and individual engagement with nature) and the nationalist search for cultural icons unique to America. While some American writers (notably Roderick Nash) equate environmentalism with wilderness preser-vation, the dominant environmental tradition in India is quite different. In the absence of a frontier, industrialization in India has had to contend with a shrinking resource-base and rapid environmental degradation. Urban and industrial development, while not even successful on its own terms, has wreaked tremendous havoc on the countryside, pauperizing millions of people in the agrarian sector and depleting the stock of soil, water, and plant resources at an alarming rate. Degradation of the land and vegetative base, with all it implies for the subsistence and survival of rural communi-ties, is thus the focus of the Indian environmental movement, which has paid comparatively little attention to industrial pollution or the loss of biological diversity. At the same time, the movement has put forward an alternative strategy of economic development which could be more sensitive to the needs of the rural population and have a greater awareness of ecological limits.

In this sense, the thrust of the Indian environmental movement is quite different from the two American traditions discussed in this chapter. At the same time, in their search for an authentic lineage Indian environmentalists also draw upon powerful cultural symbols—in this case, the memory of Mahatma Gandhi and the peasant movements orchestrated by him against British colonialism. The defence of agrarianism then becomes a defence of tradition. Gandhi's successors, by adopting a pattern of development which is unmindful of ecological considerations and biased against the peasants who fought so heroically against the British, are charged with betraying the Mahatma's sacred trust.[24]

The cultural rootedness of environmental traditions means that the transfer of even individual traits across cultures is an exercise fraught with danger. For example, many wilderness thinkers draw selectively on Eastern traditions. They frequently invoke Hindu and Buddhist sayings which apparently suggest that humans should subordinate themselves to nature. At the same time, American 'Orientalists' show little interest in the ways in which these religious injunctions are embedded in concrete social practice. This selective borrowing is influenced by the radical individualism that is so much a feature of American culture, coupled with a spirituality whose ultimate basis is rootlessness. In agrarian society, however, relations with nature are invariably communal rather than individual. Moreover, they are firmly rooted in the continuity of cultural experience. Thus if Progressive Conservation places society above ecology (nature must follow the dictates of man), in Wilderness Thinking ecology is placed over society (man must follow the dictates of nature). Peasant culture, by embedding ecology in society, transcends both these perspectives.

What then of the scientific component in environmentalism? Modern science has always claimed to be of universal applicability. Many writers (including the contributors to the last WIDER project)[25] have challenged this claim to universality, and our analysis in this paper reinforces that challenge. The question is, why then do environmental movements claim the backing of science? Quite simply, because 'in American culture science is the ultimate source of epistemological authority. Scientists are the high priests of nature, for claims that are valid according to the methodological principles of science are most likely to attain the unchallengeable status of 'facts' about nature' (Downey, 1986: 398). If Progressive Conservation insists it is the most 'scientific' and 'rational' system of resource utilization, Wilderness Thinking for its part claims the support of the 'frontier' sciences of Ecology and Conservation Biology. Significantly, both movements also feel the need to claim the backing of 'scientific' theories of history (collectivism and post-materialism respectively).

Here too India is something of a contrast. Unlike in the United States, where science is a hegemonic ideology, in India the culture of science is not, at least as yet, pervasive (though its instruments and institutions are). This could actually work to the benefit of environmentalists. They are not obliged to talk the language of science and can more forcefully present the moral and political aspects of their case. 'Equity', 'justice', and especially 'community' and 'culture' are concepts which do not admit of scientific treatment; they are beyond the realm of science. Thus the Chipko movement succeeded not because it had the backing of science, but because its location in an area rich with religious and cultural significance and its veneer of Gandhism struck a sympathetic chord in the hearts of the Indian public, forcing the hand of the state (Guha, 1989*b*: ch. 8). Undoubtedly, the ultimate justification of development projects is that they are scientific; while retaining a healthy scepticism about such claims, it is more pertinent to point out that the displacement of populations as well as the transformation, mostly for the worse, of nature are not matters on which scientists can legislate. Rather than accept the terms of discourse laid down by their adversaries, environmentalists would do well to follow Mahatma Gandhi by placing culture and history outside science.

By subordinating science to morality and politics, we can pave the way for a more open and symmetrical dialogue between different environmental traditions. The recognition of a multiplicity of such traditions would first of all reject the pernicious theories of history which refuse to recognize any environmental tradition other than those prevailing in the more 'advanced' nations. For example, the influential journal *World Development*, in outlining its research foci, includes a concern for the 'implications for the development efforts of the Third World of Western concerns for the environment'.[26] If the arguments of this paper have any validity, it is now time to ask: 'What are the implications for the development efforts of the West of Third World concerns for the environment?' But that is another story, to be taken up another time.[27]

NOTES TO CHAPTER 4

1. For a comprehensive historical treatment of the American environmental movement, see Hays, 1987.
2. A recent conservative attack on the movement is Douglas and Wildavsky, 1982. In its low level of scholarship (very little evidence is presented in support of its sweeping pronouncements) and hysterical tone, this work is most unbecoming of the two senior scholars.
3. For a review of these polls, see Hays, 1987. Cf. also Oakes, 1986.
4. The classic case is the infamous 'hamburger connection', wherein millions of acres of Amazonian rainforest were destroyed to raise beef for the American market.
5. A philosophical journal of some influence devoted almost exclusively to this

theme is *Environmental Ethics*, edited by Eugene Hargrove at the University of North Texas.

6. Like any other socio-cultural phenomena, Progressive Conservation and Wilderness Thinking can be analysed across three dimensions: cognitive, normative, and conative (corresponding to thinking, evaluating, and acting): see Worsley, 1984: 42–3.

7. A phrase popularized by the standard work on the movement—Hays 1958*b*.

8. For the Jeffersonian ideal's ambivalence toward modern technology, see Marx, 1964.

9. By 1947 over one-fifth of India's land area was controlled by the Forest Department, making it by far the biggest landlord in the subcontinent.

10. In 1875 the American George Davidson had written that 'together with the other grand and humanizing British works and projects, [irrigation] will in time induce kinder feelings and sympathies from the native population': 1875: 11.

11. Widstoe, quoted in Worster, 1985: 188.

12. The state systems of forests and water management in independent India are modelled closely on their colonial predecessors.

13. For an analysis of traditional forestry and irrigation systems, their suppression by the 'scientific' systems introduced under colonialism, and the ensuing social conflicts, see Guha, 1983, 1985*b*; Sengupta, 1980; 1985.

14. See Commoner's interesting retrospective on the first two decades of the environmental movement (Commoner, 1987).

15. Jones lists Malthus's 'An Essay on the Principle of Population' second in a list of fifty books he feels are basic to the understanding of American culture. Cf. also Hofstadter, 1944, *passim*.

16. For an early critique of monumentalism, see Adams, 1945.

17. For a more detailed treatment of Deep Ecology, see Guha 1989*a*.

18. On sacred groves as the traditional form of forest preservation, see, *inter alia*, Gadgil and Vartak, 1976; Brandis, 1897; Edwardes, 1922.

19. This paragraph is based on discussions with Madhav Gadgil.

20. See the interesting collection edited by Ungar, 1985.

21. To the extent that the internationalists succeed, they are helped along by elements in the host society only too eager to embrace American values.

22. See, for example, the writings of Berry, especially his *The Unsettling of America*, 1977.

23. Mumford's thoughts on politics and ecology are scattered throughout his books, but are expressed more forcefully in his many articles in journals such as *The New Republic, The New Leader, Atlantic Monthly*, etc.: see Guha, 1991.

24. See the 'Statement of Shared Concern', in Agarwal and Narain, 1985.

25. See Apffel-Marglin and Marglin (eds.), 1990, and Banuri and Apffel-Marglin, 1993.

26. See *World Development*'s advertisement in Economic and Political Weekly, 21 May 1988.

27. This essay was written in 1989, and does not take account of subsequent developments. But I believe its main arguments stand; indeed, in hindsight the essay might be seen as providing the historical context for understanding the controversies that erupted at the Earth Summit of 1992, and which continue to dog environmental relations between North and South.

REFERENCES

ADAMS, A. (1945), 'Problems of Interpretation of the Natural Scene', *Sierra Club Bulletin*, 30/6.

AGARWAL, A. (1986), 'Human–Nature Interactions in a Third World Country', *The Environmentalist*, 6/3.

—— and NARAIN, S. (1985) (eds.), *India: State of the Environment 1984–1985: A Citizens Report*, New Delhi: Centre for Science and Environment.

—— CHOPRA, R., and SHARMA, K. (1982) (eds.), *India: The State of the Environment 1982: A Citizens Report*, New Delhi: Centre for Science and Environment.

ANDREWS, R. N. L. (1980), 'Class Politics or Democratic Reform: Environmentalism and American Political Institutions', *Natural Resources Journal*, 20/2.

APFFEL-MARGLIN, F. and MARGLIN, S. A. (1990) (eds.), *Dominating Knowledge: Development, Culture, and Resistance*, Oxford: Clarendon Press.

BAHRO, R. (1984), *From Red to Green*, London: Verso.

BANURI, T. and APFFEL-MARGLIN, F. (1993) (eds.), *Who Will Save the Forests? Resistance, Knowledge, and the Environmental Crisis*, London: Zed Books.

BERRY, W. (1977), *The Unsettling of America*, San Francisco: Sierra Club Books.

BOYER, P. (1985), *By the Bomb's Early Light: American Thought and Culture at the Dawn of the Atomic Age*, New York: Pantheon.

BRANDIS, D. (1897), *Indian Forestry*, Woking: Oriental Institute.

BRANIGIN, W. (1987), 'Garbage Barge Returns towards U.S. Waters', *Washington Post*, 26 Apr.

BROWER, D. R. (1947) (ed.), 'The Sierra Club and Science', *The Sierra Club: A Handbook*, Sierra Club Bulletin, 32/10.

—— (1956), 'Scenic Resources for the Future', *Sierra Club Bulletin*, 41/10.

BROWN, H. (1905), 'Irrigation under British Engineers' (paper presented to the International Irrigation Congress, St Louis, Missouri, October 1904), in *Transactions of the American Society of Civil Engineers*, 54, pt. C, no. 31.

BUSH, V. (1945), *Science: The Endless Frontier*, Washington: National Science Foundation (repr. 1960).

CARSON, R. (1962), *Silent Spring*, Boston: Houghton Mifflin.

COAN, E. (1971), 'The International Role of the Sierra Club: A Proposal', *Sierra Club Bulletin*, 57/1.

COHEN, M. (1984), *The Pathless Way: John Muir and American Wilderness*, Madison: University of Wisconsin Press.

COLLINGWOOD, F. (1885), 'The Preservation of Forests', *Transactions of the American Society of Civil Engineers*, 19/311.

COMMONER, B. (1987), 'A Reporter at Large: The Environment', *New Yorker*, 15 June.

CROLY, H. (1912), *The Promise of American Life*, New York: Macmillan.

DAVIDSON, G. (1875), *Irrigation and Reclamation of Land for Agricultural Purposes, As Now Practised in India, Egypt, Italy, etc.*, 44th Congress, 1st Session, Senate Exec. Doc. 94, Washington, DC.

DEVALL, B. (1985), 'David Ross Brower', *Environmental Review*, 9/3.

DOUGLAS, M. and WILDAVSKY, A. (1982), *Risk and Culture: An Essay on the Selection of Technical and Environmental Dangers*, Berkeley, Calif.: University of California Press.

DOWNEY, G. (1986), 'Risk in Culture: The American Conflict over Nuclear Power', *Cultural Anthropology*, 1/4.

DOWNS, A. (1972), 'Up and Down with Ecology: The "Issue Attention Cycle"', *The Public Interest*, 38.

EDWARDES, S. M. (1922), 'Tree Worship in India', *Empire Forestry*, 1/1.

EKIRCH, A., Jr. (1963), *Man and Nature in America*, New York: Columbia University Press.

FERNOW, B. E. (1892), 'Economic Conditions Antagonistic to a Conservative Forest Policy', in *Proceedings of the American Association of the Advancement of Science*, 46, sect. I.

—— (1907), *A Brief History of Forestry in Europe, The United States, and Other Countries*, Toronto: Toronto University Press.

FLEMING, D. (1972), 'Roots of the New Conservation Movement', in D. Fleming and B. Bailyn (eds.), *Perspectives in American History*, Cambridge, Mass.: Charles Warren Center for Studies in American History.

FLYNN, P. J. (1892), *Irrigation Canals and Other Irrigation Works*, San Francisco: George Spaulding and Co.

FORTMANN, L. and FAIRFAX, S. (1987), *American Forestry Professionalism in the Third World: Some Preliminary Observations*, Berkeley: University of California (mimeo).

GADGIL, M. and VARTAK, V. (1976), 'Sacred Groves of Maharashtra', *Economic Botany*, 30/2.

GEISER, K. (1983), 'Toxic Times and Class Politics', *Radical America*, 12/2–3.

GENDLIN, F. (1982), 'A Talk with Michael McCloskey', *Sierra*, 67/2.

GRABER, L. (1976), *Wilderness as Sacred Space*, Washington, DC: Association of American Geographers.

GRAY, G. C. (1983), 'Conservation Movement', in R. C. Davis (ed.), *Encyclopaedia of American Forest and Conservation History*, i, New York: Macmillan.

GRIFFITH, E. (1958), 'Main Lines of Thought', in Jarrett (1958).

GUHA, R. (1983), 'Forestry in British and Post British India: A Historical Analysis', *Economic and Political Weekly*, 10 Oct., 5–12 Nov.

—— (1985a) 'Eco-Development Debate: A Critical Review', *South Asian Anthropologist*, 8/1.

—— (1985b), 'Forestry and Social Protest in British Kumaun, c. 1893–1921', in R. Guha (ed.), *Subaltern Studies, iv. Writings on South Asian History and Society*, New Delhi: Oxford University Press.

—— (1989a), 'Radical American Environmentalism and Wilderness Preservation: A Third World Critique', *Environmental Ethics*, 11/1.

—— (1989b), *The Unquiet Woods: Ecological Change and Peasant Resistance in the Himalaya*, New Delhi: Oxford University Press.

—— (1991), 'The Forgotten American Environmentalist: Lewis Mumford: An Essay in Rehabilitation', *Capitalism, Nature Socialism*, 8.

HASKELL, T. (1984) (ed.), *The Authority of Experts: Studies in History and Theory*, Bloomington: Indiana University Press.

HAYS, S. (1958a), 'The Mythology of Conservation', in Jarrett (1958).

—— (1958b), *Conservation and the Gospel of Efficiency: The Progressive Conservation Movement, 1880–1920*, Cambridge, Mass.: Harvard University Press.

—— (1982), 'From Conservation to Environment: Environmental Politics in the United States since World War Two', *Environmental Review*, 6/2.

—— (1987), *Beauty, Health and Permanence: Environmental Politics in the United States*, New York: Cambridge University Press.

HOFSTADTER, R. (1944), *Social Darwinism in American Thought*, Boston, Mass.: Beacon Press (repr. 1960).

HUTH, H. (1947), 'Yosemite: The Story of an Idea', *Sierra Club Bulletin* 33/3.

ILTIS, H. (1967), 'Whose Fight is the Fight for Nature?', *Sierra Club Bulletin*, 52/9.

INGLEHART, R. (1977), *The Silent Revolution*, Princeton, NJ: Princeton University Press.

—— and RABIER, J. R. (1986), 'Political Realignment in Advanced Industrial Society: From Class-Based Politics to Quality-of-Life Politics', *Government and Opposition*, 21/4.

JANZEN, D. (1986), 'The Future of Tropical Ecology', *Annual Review of Ecology and Systematics*, 17.

JARRETT, H. (1958) (ed.), *Perspectives on Conservation: Essays on America's Natural Resources*, Baltimore: Johns Hopkins Press.

JOHNSON, R. U. (1922), 'John Muir', a commemorative tribute, in *Academy Notes and Monographs 1916*, New York: American Academy of Arts and Letters.

KING, Y. (1987), 'What is Ecofeminism?', *Nation*, 12 Dec.

LOEB, H. (1985), *Life in a Technocracy: What it Might Be Like*, quoted in H. P. Segal, *Technological Utopianism in American Culture*, Chicago: University of Chicago Press.

LUTTS, R. (1985), 'Chemical Fallout: Rachel Carsons' *Silent Spring*, Radioactive Fallout, and the Environmental Movement', *Environmental Review*, 9/3.

McCLOSKEY, M. (1972), 'Wilderness Movement at the Crossroads', *Pacific Historical Review*, 41/3.

—— (1984), 'World Parks', *Sierra*, 69/6.

McPHEE, J. (1971), *Encounters with the Archdruid*, New York: Farrar, Strauss and Giroux.

MARSH, G. P. (1874), *Irrigation: Its Evils, the Remedies and the Consequences*, 43rd Congress, 1st Session, Senate Misc. Doc. 55, Washington.

MARSHALL, R. (1947), 'The Problems of the Wilderness', *Scientific Monthly*, Dec. 1930, repr. in *Sierra Club Bulletin*, 32/5.

MARX, L. (1964), *The Machine in the Garden; Technology and the Pastoral Ideal in America*, New York: Oxford University Press.

MATHER, K. (1944), *Enough and to Spare*, New York: Harper and Brothers.

MEAD, E. (1902), 'Irrigation Works: An Informal Discussion at the Annual Convention', *Transactions of the American Society of Civil Engineers*, 49/233.

—— (1925), 'Community Farming', 18 Feb.

MUIR, J. (1895), 'Address on the Sierra Forest Reservation', in *Sierra Club Bulletin*, 1/7.

MUMFORD JONES, H. (1946), 'Fifty Guides to American Civilization', *Saturday Review of Literature*, 12 Oct.

NASH, H. (1965), 'Grand Canyon Dams: A Necessary Evil?', *Sierra Club Bulletin*, 50/10.

NEWELL, F. H. (1909), 'Irrigation: An Informal Discussion at the Annual Convention, June 25th 1908', *Transactions of the American Society of Civil Engineers*, 62/1092.

OAKES, J. B. (1986), 'Back to Environmentalism', *New York Times*, 10 Nov.

PASSMORE, J. (1980), *Man's Responsibility for Nature*, London: Duckworth.

PINCHOT, G. (1891), 'Government Forestry Abroad', *Publications of the American Economic Association*, 6/3.

—— (1905), *A Primer of Forestry: Part II: Practical Forestry*, Washington, DC: Department of Agriculture.

—— (1908), 'Sir Dietrich Brandis', *Proceedings of the Society of American Foresters*, 3/1.

—— (1910), *The Fight for Conservation*, New York: Doubleday, Page and Co.

—— (1921), *The Economic Significance of Forestry*, Washington, DC: National Conservation Association.

—— (1947), *Breaking New Ground*, Seattle: University of Washington Press (repr. 1972).

RUNTE, A. (1979), *National Parks: The American Experience*, Lincoln: University of Nebraska Press (repr. 1984).

SAX, J. (1980), *Mountains Without Handrails: Reflections on our National Parks*, Ann Arbor: University of Michigan Press.

SCHMITT, P. (1969), *Back to Nature: The Arcadian Myth in Urban America*, New York: Oxford University Press.

SCHREFFER, S. (1983), *The Fight to Save the Redwoods: A History of Environmental Reform*, Madison: University of Wisconsin Press.

SENGUPTA, N. (1980), 'The Indigenous Irrigation Organization of South Bihar', *Indian Economic and Social History Review*, 17/2.

—— (1985), 'Irrigation: Traditional versus Modern' (special number, Aug.), *Economic and Political Weekly*.

SHEPARD, P. and McKINLEY, D. (1969) (eds.), *The Subversive Science: Essays toward an Ecology of Man*, Boston, Mass.: Houghton Mifflin.

SHI, D. (1985), *The Simple Life: Plain Living and High Thinking in American Culture*, New York: Oxford University Press.

SMYTHE, W. E. (1905), *The Conquest of Arid America*, New York: Macmillan.

SOULE, M. (1986) (ed.), *Conservation Biology: The Science of Scarcity and Diversity*, Sunderland, Mass.: Sinnauer Associates.

STEEN, H. K. (1976), *The United States Forest Service: A History*, Seattle: University of Washington Press.

TALBOT, L. M. (1957), 'Wilderness Overseas', *Sierra Club Bulletin* 42/6.

THOMAS, K. (1983), *Man and the Natural World*, Harmondsworth: Penguin.

TURNER, F. (1984), 'So Necessarily Elite', *Parks in the West and American Culture*, Sun Valley, Idaho: Institute of the American West.

TURNER, F. J. (1893), 'The Significance of the Frontier in American History', in his *The Frontier in American History*, 1986 edn., Tucson: University of Arizona Press.

UNGAR, S. (1985) (ed.), *Estrangement: America and the World*, New York: Oxford University Press.

WIDSTOE, J. (1912), 'The Irrigation Problem of Today', in *Official Bulletin of the National Irrigation Congress*, 1/3.

—— (1913), 'The Rational Use of Water in Irrigation', in *Official Bulletin of the International Irrigation Congress*, 1/7.

—— (1920), *The Principles of Irrigation Practice*, London: Macmillan.

WILSON, H. M. (1890), 'Irrigation in India', *Transactions of the American Society of Civil Engineers*, 23/454.

—— (1891), 'American Irrigation Engineering', *Transactions of the American Society of Civil Engineers*, 25/492.

WINKS, R. (1984), 'Concern and Values', *Parks in the West and American Culture*, Sun Valley, Idaho: Institute of the American West.

WORSLEY, P. (1984), *The Three Worlds: Culture and World Development*, London: Weidenfeld and Nicholson.

WORSTER, D. (1977), *Nature's Economy: The Roots of Ecology*, San Francisco: Sierra Club Books.

—— (1985), *Rivers of Empire: Water, Aridity and the Growth of the American West*, New York: Pantheon Books.

5

Rationality, the Body, and the World: From Production to Regeneration

FRÉDÉRIQUE APFFEL-MARGLIN

> Western civilization has articulated its struggle for domination in terms of the holy battle of humanity against barbarism, reason against ignorance . . . science against magic, rationality against passion . . . Western, modern society is defined as *civilized* society . . .
>
> What in fact has happened in the course of the civilizing process, is the redeployment of violence . . . violence has been taken out of sight, rather than forced out of existence.
>
> Bauman, 1989: 96–7

INTRODUCTION

In the introduction to this collection I presented a brief summary of the historical emergence in Western Europe of Cartesian rationality. In this chapter I find it necessary to continue the historical summary in the first part of the chapter and examine the deployment of this new rationality, that is the way it spread throughout society and affected not only the pursuit of knowledge but everyday practice and the very construction of experience. This historical work seems to me a necessary exercise before I introduce the reader to the contemporary lived experience of a segment of the population in a region of coastal Orissa in India. The necessity of this historical work bearing on implications of Western *episteme* as a prolegomenon to approaching the contemporary reality of some non-Western people derives from the fact that Western epistemic knowledge presents itself as having universal validity and application. This is nowhere truer than in the field of development, both as knowledge and as practice. Development relies heavily on expert knowledge, particularly on economics, but on all the other social sciences as well, anthropology being the newest comer (Escobar, 1991). This expert social scientific knowledge is largely epistemic in character. This means that its practitioners do not perceive themselves as the carriers of a particular cosmology or ontology rooted in particular historical and cultural contexts but rather as the wielders of a neutral method that enables them to accomplish certain goals. These goals—be they individual preferences or the choices of governments—are seen as being the legitimate loci for values, but the tools, methods, and means to attain them are themselves seen as neutral. This is particularly true of economics but applies as well, in various degrees, to the other social sciences.

The following brief historical argument is intended to make visible the culturally and historically specific nature of certain categories such as 'biology' or 'ritual'. It is not offered as a piece of original historical scholarship—a task I am not equipped to undertake—but, drawing on the work of historians and others, is undertaken for the limited aim of making visible the non-universal, non-neutral nature of key categories of thought and analysis and revealing their historico-cultural specificity. These categories in their modern sense co-emerge with Cartesian rationality. The 'biological' (like the 'natural') is a category that is opposed to the 'cultural' or 'symbolic', i.e. a category bereft of cognitive ability or of mind whereas 'ritual' is a category that is opposed to effective rational or technological action (Leach, 1972). I will argue that these categorizations are dependent on the emergence and subsequent deployment of modern Western Cartesian rationality and therefore carry within themselves the same cosmological and ontological implications. Without some such preliminary work, the use of categories that are thought of as neutral, descriptive, or universal will end up doing invisible violence to different realities and in the process rob them of their power to be perceived as possible resources for alternatives to modernity. This is in part because cognitive activity becomes monopolized by Cartesian rationality and other types of activities are perceived as devoid of cognition. This becomes consequential in a development context since it facilitates intervention or perhaps even simply makes it possible.[1]

The categories of 'biology' and 'ritual' are the focus of the critical historical efforts in the first part of this chapter in preparation for the second part, which will focus on the practices of some people in coastal Orissa on the occasion of the festival of the menses of women and of the earth. Besides making visible the violence that the use of the categories of rationality, biology, and ritual perpetrate on these practices, the second part of the essay attempts to make visible an alternative form of cognition. This is not undertaken for archival or theoretical purposes but rather to reveal this form of cognition as a potential resource for alternatives to modern rationality. It is also undertaken to demystify any possible perception of these practices and the world these villagers live in as pre-modern, that is as somehow pre-dating modernity and therefore perceived as potentially in need of modernization, advancement, or development. The oft-expressed criticism that presenting non-Western practices as resources for alternatives to modernity amounts to 'going backwards' is a corollary of the invisibility of the ontological assumptions carried within rationality and the many other categories it has given rise to.

The first part of this chapter focuses on the manner in which Cartesian rationality deployed itself throughout society and some of the effects such a deployment brought about. Cartesian rationality did not remain within the circle of a small intellectual élite. With the Industrial Revolution, production found in Cartesian rationality an indispensable tool and ally. The industrial mode of production required the commoditization of labour, the transformation of labouring activity into a homogeneous, hence quantifiable, as well as disciplined activity. The first part of the chapter tries to show how Cartesian rationality fitted into the project of taming labour to the needs of industrialization.

Descartes, rather than advocating the repression of the passions, advocated instead their harnessing in order to fuel thought. This instrumental relationship between rationality and passions came to serve the purposes of the industrial mode of production very well. Rationality was used to control the body and the passions in the service of the commoditized form of labour. This instrumental character of rationality in relationship to the body and the passions of a singular, atomized agent, came to be felt as an intrinsic quality of rationality itself. This became so much a part of lived reality that those activities in which the relationship between rationality and the body or the passions is not an instrumental one came to be seen as devoid of rationality.

Generation, regeneration, and nurture, are human activities where there is no instrumental relationship between rationality and the body or passions, and where the agent-in-relationship is emphasized more than the singular, atomistic agent, maximizing his self-interest. Generation, regeneration, and nurture became increasingly seen as belonging to a separate, feminine realm; a realm of nature or at least closer to nature than the public sphere, where men used their minds to control their bodies and their passions. Given the prominence of women's bodies in those processes, women's generative activities came to be seen as antithetical to reason.

Given the centrality of the autonomous, rational agent in the formation of the modern sense of self, women have found it difficult to achieve a sense of self from activities within the domestic sphere. Autonomous instrumental control of one's body and emotions is a central part of the modern sense of self. This has led to the naturalization—the biologization—of generation and regeneration. Generation and regeneration have become reproduction and the servicing of the labour force. Generation and regeneration have become akin to 'natural resources' controlled and exploited for the benefit of increased production in the public sphere.

Women's increasing access to the ranks of the labour force has had the effect of rejecting the antinomy the nineteenth century saw between women and rationality. It has not had the effect of rejecting the biologization of generation and regeneration as well as its status of 'natural resource' for the productive sphere.

The second part of the chapter listens closely to the voices of certain Oriya villagers: we hear of a world where generation and regeneration are at the centre of collective life. In this world where the commoditization of labour has only marginally penetrated, Cartesian rationality does not exist. What one finds is a different form of rationality, a different style of cognition. Relying on the work of Varela, Thompson, and Rosch (1991), I call this style of cognition 'embodied (or enactive) cognition'.[2] It is a style of cognition which actualizes the Indic lack of separation between the human, animal, and inert natural realms, and one in which mind has not been siphoned off into a transcendental subject, but rather is shared among both the human and the non-human world. From the perspective of embodied cognition the boundaries between categories such as 'ritual'—along with 'religion', 'beliefs', and others—and the category of 'efficacious rational action' become blurred.

The second part of the chapter also gives a specific instance of what Ramachandra Guha means in Chapter 4 when he asserts that peasant (and tribal) societies do not separate the social–cultural and the natural world; that they embed the spiritual in the material.

Development knowledge will remain a colonizing type of knowledge as long as it continues to take such categories as 'technology', 'ritual', 'science', 'religion' as givens rather than constructed on the basis of a certain Western epistemology and ontology. The people to whom development is brought will continue to be perceived as engaging in irrational or wasteful behaviour. Decolonizing development knowledge requires the questioning of a world constructed by the categories of the dominant system of knowledge.

The ramifications of the deployment of a Cartesian rationality with an instrumental relationship to the body, the passions, and to nature are far-reaching. Just as the instrumental control of nature has seen the emergence of a severely deteriorating natural ecology, the signs of a severely deteriorating social ecology are everywhere. As long as mind has departed from the realms of nature, of the body, and lodged itself in a transcendental subject, generation and regeneration will be seen as inferior to production, to achievement. Men have already abandoned the realm of generation and regeneration and women have been unable to find meaning and fulfilment in it. Putting generation and regeneration at the centre may entail a different style of rationality. The social and ecological crises pose a challenge that may require such a profound transformation.

PART I

The Deployment of Instrumental, Cartesian Rationality

An earlier era would have looked upon atomistic agents pursuing their self-interest as unbridled selfishness. As Dumont's work (1977) on the emergence of individualism in Europe has pointed out, before the commoditization of capital could take place a revolution in mores had to happen; usury had to transform itself from a sin to a positively valued necessity. More generally, the association between rationality and the atomistic agent—that is the individual—was powerfully enhanced by the print revolution. Reading and thinking gradually became solitary, asocial activities. As Walter Ong's work (1982) on orality and literacy has shown, it is only with the advent and wide availability of printed texts that thinking can become totally detached from an immediate social context. Descartes's widely influential *cogito* could not have emerged without the ready availability of the printed word.[3]

Descartes's *cogito* articulates a new style of thought, one disengaged not only from particular social contexts—from the world—but disengaged also from the passions. The world is now disenchanted matter, no longer the source of humans' moral guidance. In this, the Cartesian *cogito* differs profoundly from classical Greek rationality where the 'ultimate criterion of rationality [was] conformity with this order itself' (Taylor, 1989: 156). Disengaged reason, to use Charles Taylor's phrase, achieves a self-sufficient certainty by following the right method. The vagaries of passions and of a dynamic, changing social and natural world are deliberately kept at bay so as to attain certainty. The passions are not to be repressed or denied but controlled so as to tap embodied energies that can fuel thought. Descartes admires 'great souls . . . whose reasoning powers are so strong and powerful, that although they also have passions, and often even more violent than is common, nonetheless their reason remains sovereign' (quoted in Taylor, 1989: 150). The emergence of a form of rationality where instrumental control of the passions was a constitutive feature was a necessary requirement in the commoditization of labour. The latter development, alongside the commoditization of the other two factors of production, namely land and capital (Polanyi, 1944), was essential to the full-fledged development of a market economy. With the establishment of a market economy, a Cartesian *cogito* harnessed to the pursuit of self-interest deployed itself throughout the public sphere.

Cartesian rationality played a key role in the formation of labour as a commodity creating a new, typically modern, self with a particular relationship to the body, to others, and to nature. Given the differential relationship between specifically feminine bodily functions and commoditization, Cartesian rationality deployed itself differentially among men and women.

With industrial capitalism, productive labour became a commodity separated out from work performed in personalized social contexts such as kinship or other community relationships. Work became progressively detached from an unmediated relationship between work activity and the task accomplished as well as from social relationships. The characteristic features of capitalist production as contrasted with craft production are the removal of the worker from a familial or community setting as well as the fragmentation of tasks (see Marglin, 1974). Let me examine both these features, starting briefly with the former.

With the birth of the factory, the household ceased to be the main locus of productive activity. The rhythms of work were profoundly altered by this shift, which strictly separated out labouring activity from all other activities, since the entrepreneur paid for time actually worked. This transformation created time as money to be saved, spent, or wasted. E. P. Thompson, in his classic article on time and work discipline in industrial capitalism (1967), documents the lengthy and difficult transformation from pre-industrial work rhythms to industrial discipline, a process he pithily summarizes as resulting in the separation of work and life.

It is the creation of the concept and reality of work as an abstract, quantifiable, and homogeneous commodity separated from what Thompson calls 'life' that gave to the two separate spheres of the public and the private their particular configuration. Much of what E. P. Thompson calls 'life'— particularly the body and generation—and eventually most women, became confined to the latter (Tilly and Scott, 1987; Ehrenreich and English, 1979; Oakley, 1984). The process of industrialization and commoditization did not, however, leave the private sphere untouched; it profoundly transformed it. These transformations were slow and complex and unevenly distributed geographically and in terms of class. One can, however, summarize them by stating that the nuclear family became the dominant form. Industrialization and commoditization destroyed the extended household with kinsfolk and servants besides the nuclear couple (Flandrin, 1979).[3] This made it much more difficult for women to work outside the household and when they did because of dire necessity the toll on infant mortality was very high (Flandrin, 1979). This explains why working-class women supported the unions' demand for a family wage (Mullings, 1986).

In conjunction with enclosure of the commons and the mobility of the labour force necessary to the functioning of the labour market, the shrinking of households to nuclear dimensions contributed powerfully to the eroding of community life. Such an erosion weakened the sources where customs and conventions held in common by a local group flourished and elicited people's allegiance. In the resulting vacuum individualism and rationality flourished in the public sphere, while the private sphere became feminized and naturalized. Before proceeding with a consideration of the naturalization and the feminization of the private sphere—to which we shall return below—we must first understand the effects that the industrial mode of production had on workers' bodies and minds and the differential impact of these effects on men and women.

Let me now turn to the second characteristic of the industrial mode of production, namely the fragmentation of the task at the product level. As Stephen Marglin has shown, this development did not take place due to any sort of technological imperative but due to a political imperative in the form of the entrepreneur's need to control the workers. This controlling requirement of the bosses in factory production is supported and enhanced by the development of a whole state apparatus to map, control, measure, and socialize people. In hospitals, schools, workshops, and the army, discipline was impressed on bodies and on psyches in order to make people useful and compliant (Foucault, 1975; 1980).

In order to appropriate productive labour, labour itself had to become an abstract force, that is divorced from the concrete activity involved in making a completed object or a completed task. As E. P. Thompson has shown it took a long time in England to create the disciplined worker capable of sustained and concentrated labour in a setting where work activity has no immediate relationship to a finished product ('immediate work'), nor is carried out as part of personalized social relationships ('personalized work') (Thompson, 1967). In immediate and personalized work the relationship between bodily activity and task is unmediated: the constraints emerge from the task itself as well as from the social relationships involved in the carrying out of a task. These constraints impinge directly on the body of the worker. This unmediated impinging determines the pace and rhythm, as well as the bodily movements of the worker. Stephen Marglin has characterized the knowledge necessary for this type of work by the word *techne* and he illustrates it by the example of craft work (Marglin, 1990; Ch. 6, below). Craft skills are normally acquired by direct bodily mimesis during a period of apprenticeship. The acquiring of a particular craft skill is not mediated by abstract generalization of the work process, or by a purely intellectual analysis of the way the body must perform in order to achieve the desired end result. The verbal accompaniments to apprenticeship are not in the nature of analyses (decomposing and elucidating the relationship between components) but in the nature of directives to imitate, judgements as to the quality of the results, encouragements, or reprimands. In a word they are social in nature, grounded in the master–apprentice relationship, a relationship made visible by bodily mimesis. The craft of the carpenter, wheelwright, or weaver is embodied in him or her in full. This contrasts with the knowledge of the production process under capitalism. The embodiment of this knowledge, i.e. its physical execution, is fragmented among several types of workers producing different parts of the product. In turn, the embodied knowledge, namely the physical movements required to produce something, is separated out from the purely intellectual knowledge of the production process, typically in the possession of the entrepreneur or of experts hired by the entrepreneur. The distinction is not primarily one between physical and mental work but between two kinds of knowing: one in which the knowledge is unmediated by analytic reason—in other words a knowledge lodged as it were in the body—and a knowledge mediated by analytic reason, lodged as it were in the mind. I intentionally use the expression 'as it were', since the kind of knowledge embodied in a craftsperson must clearly engage mental faculties as well as bodily co-ordination, and the knowledge of the engineer has to materialize itself if not in the actual making of a product at least in the mapping of such activity in the form of diagrams, computer programs, or some other such concrete form.

The form and rhythm of industrial work is monotonous, regular, sustained; it requires discipline and punctuality. These requirements emerge from the standpoint of the entrepreneur, who pays not for a finished product but for time actually worked. It does not emerge from the standpoint of the worker, whose activity derives neither from an interaction with a given task nor from personalized social interactions. The actualization of this form of work in a sustained and reliable manner, requires more than the necessity of survival. The phenomenon of 'Saint Monday' as reported by Marglin (1974), in which the workers spent their Monday (not to mention the previous week's) pay at the tavern, shows clearly the limitations of economic incentives for the reliable actualization of the commoditized form of labour.

What needed to happen to bring about the spontaneous and reliable actualization of the type of labour required by its commoditization was that it should become internalized, that is, become a habit. Only then would the worker reliably exhibit this type of labouring activity by developing the appropriate working habits. In order to achieve this, the commoditized form of labour could not appear in the eyes of the workers as a necessity born from the requirements of the buyers of labour, the bosses. Such a necessity would have no legitimacy for workers. Discipline, punctuality, sustained attention, and the precise execution of tasks needed to acquire their own legitimation, outside any specific social, political, or religious context. In other words, in order to be internalized, this kind of labouring activity would have to be associated not with the bosses' or the state's need to control the worker but with the worker's own desire to control himself. What was required was a legitimating factor that would be decontextualized, socially unsituated, politically and morally neutral, yet one with the very form of commoditized labour.

Cartesian rationality had established itself since the seventeenth century as the privileged mode of thought for attaining certain knowledge. What made it relevant for the creation of appropriate factory work habits was its instrumental relationship to passions. Strong passions were not in themselves decried, a radical departure from the traditions of the Stoics (Taylor, 1989: 150). Controlled, the passions could actually fuel the thinking process. This internal dynamic between the mind and the passions, enlarged to encompass the relationship between the mind and the body, is precisely what was required by entrepreneurs. A strong, able body disciplined and made compliant by the mind.

By the mid-nineteenth century education became compulsory and free state schools trained the young in the use of rationality, with its disengaged stance towards the social and natural world and its instrumental stance to the passions and the body. The necessity of education for the development of what today are called human resources imposed itself. The commoditized form of labour was produced through reason pertaining to an agent, controlling the actions and passions of a body.

The nineteenth century also saw the fruition of a development in the professionalization of medicine which created the 'medicalized body'. The body became a 'natural' object, owned by an agent. As a natural object the body had no will of its own (only in a metaphorical sense), no reasoning capacity. Like nature, it had to be controlled so as to extract its resource, namely labour, and its workings were to be investigated by medical and biological science.[4] The secrets of the body had to be unveiled in a manner parallel to that of the secrets of nature (see Jordanova, 1980; 1989). The body became an object to be disciplined and controlled through the proper training of the mind, as well as an object to be known through the exercise of scientific knowledge. Bodily mimesis grounded in personalized relationships such as parent and child, craftsperson and apprentice, took second stage to formal (and rational) institutions of learning. In a world where the commoditized form of labour has to be learned by all, that is all those able, willing, as well as unable not to enter into the market (due to the steadily eroding basis for subsistence living) and sell their labour power, these institutions needed to be accessible to all.

Experiences and relationships came to be mediated by a proprietary agent, owning the capacity to reason. Of course such a configuration—a unitary agent as possessor of an instrumental rationality—became internalized, became a learned habit of being, or a *habitus* as Bourdieu would prefer us to say (1990). This is different from embodied cognition, which as we will see in the second part of the essay, entails a very different epistemology and ontology.

State schools with curricula devised and controlled by a central government also functioned to loosen the allegiance of the new generation to particularistic world-views, customs, and conventions. In France, for example, regional languages and cultures were suppressed and even banned in the state-school system. Disengaged rationality taught one not only to control the body and the emotions but detachment from local allegiances, the customs, beliefs, and values passed on by the older generation. By the first half of the twentieth century Sigmund Freud could develop a theory in which mental health is understood as a strengthening of that part of the self which makes one independent from received wisdom—i.e. the teachings of the elders, custom, and convention—and which tames or colonizes bodily passions and drives: 'To strengthen the ego, to make it independent of the superego, to widen the field of perception and enlarge its organization so that it can appropriate fresh portions of the id, where id was there ego shall be. It is a work of culture.' The id, like the non-productive lunatics and vagrants of all kinds in seventeenth- and eighteenth-century Western Europe, and the lazy, incorrigible natives of the colonies in the nineteenth and twentieth centuries, has to be subjected to a repressive, controlling apparatus. As in the colonized areas, the intra-psychic colonizing was necessary in order to mobilize productive labour. The relationship of independence to superego, representing the accumulated wisdom of a local, particular group, facilitated the allegiance to both a centralized state—by distancing people from traditions—and to rationality with its reliance not on received wisdom but on the right method. All of this worked together towards the creation of atomistic agents making decisions in terms of their own self-interest instead of in terms of the values, duties, and expectations of a local group. In the context of a thoroughly commoditized market economy this meant that people were sufficiently pried loose from local allegiances to respond to economic incentives. The enclosure movement which destroyed the commons and intensified the commoditization of land in England was an indispensable background to these other transformations, eroding the viability of local communities.

Although industrial work as compared with pre-industrial work is non-gendered (indeed, women and children outnumbered men in the first manufactories), the process summarized by Thompson as the separation of work and life along with the progressive nuclearization of the family eventually established as the norm that waged employment became the province of men and home the province of women. This transformation of the private sphere culminated and found its ideological articulation in the nineteenth century with what feminist scholars have termed the 'domestication of women'. In the articulation of this ideology the relationship between women's reproductive activities and rationality became central. As the domestic sphere became feminized and naturalized it transformed an originally gender-neutral concept of rationality[6] into the maleness of rationality.

Women's Bodies and the Domestication of Women

Women presented a particular problem to the onward march of reason. Reason came to be seen in the eighteenth and nineteenth centuries as antithetical to the experiences of menstruation, gestation, birth, and lactation. The rigorous training of the mind of post-menarchal girls was seen as a direct danger to their ability to bear normal and healthy children.[7] An inverse relationship between the development of the mind and that of the uterus was posited: as the former grew, the latter shrivelled. Feminist historians have rightly pointed out the sexist nature of such beliefs. But there are other lessons to draw from this inverse relationship between the female body and rationality. Whereas the male body's ability to act productively was enhanced by the development of reasoning capacities, in the case of specifically female bodily functions, the development of the same capacities was seen as a threat.

Female generative processes were progressively thought about in terms of production processes as the very word reproduction indicates.[8] The woman herself came to be seen as the one who (re)produced the baby. This individualization of 'reproduction' undoubtedly owed a great deal to the shrinking of community life as well as to the nuclearization of the family. The whole process of generation separated itself out from wider kin and community involvement as well as from rationality. For us, situated in a culture which takes individualized reproduction as the norm, the idea of non-individualized generation may be difficult to understand. Its meaning will become clearer when our discussion shifts to the communities of Oriya villagers.

The reproductive force of female bodies, however, did not enter the market in the same way that the productive forces of male bodies did. Labour as a commodity can be sold in the first place because it is owned by an agent. This agent, in turn, owns both a body and a mind, the latter controlling the former. It is precisely by the unitary proprietary relationship between an agent and a mind and body which excludes others that labour can become a commodity on the market. (This is what makes commoditized labour 'free' as opposed to slave or serf labour; it also distinguishes it from labour subject to the claims of kinspeople in kin-organized societies.) Another basic requirement for constituting labour as a commodity is its transformation into a quantifiable, measurable entity. The body had to respond no longer to the requirements of performing a completed task done to rhythms set by the household and the wider community, but rather to the abstract and epistemized requirements of the industrial mode of production. The control of the body became internalized; this control took the form of a socially unsituated agency, namely the reasoning capacity of the mind to tame and control the 'natural' body. This capacity of the reasoning mind was the same capacity that enabled humans to tame and control external nature so as to transform it into marketable products. We can therefore discern at least two reasons why the relationship between the reproductive force in women's bodies and their reasoning capacities were seen as antithetical. First, the instrumental relationship between the mind and the body was intimately connected to the constitution of a marketable commodity, namely labour. A similar connection with regard to the relationship between female minds and bodies would conjure up the spectre of either the sale of one's body or the product of one's body's labour, namely a child. This was inadmissible since it would justify prostitution or slavery or both. Second, the unitary proprietary status of an agent with regard to its mind and body, essential in the constitution of labour as a free commodity would, in the case of women's generative powers, exclude men as co-owners of those capacities or rather of those capacities' products.

Ironically, the use of the production metaphor to think about the re-lationship between labour and its products contributed powerfully to seeing women as the sole authors of 'reproductive labour'. Reproductive labour became individualized in contrast to non-commodity societies where new people are 'grown' by the work not only of the father and the mother but by a whole array of other persons socially relevant to that task.[9] Here the word 'grown' is not to be confused with commoditized societies' notion of 'socialization'. It involves the growth of the child in the mother's body as well as the physical growth of the child outside its mother's body; 'growth' refers at once to a physical process as well as to a social process. Physical growth is not something that happens 'naturally', independently of the contributions to that process by socially relevant others.

Because of the reproduction metaphor, 'making babies' came to be seen as an exclusively female activity. This in turn created the necessity on the part of men to establish their claims on children thus produced. This could not be done in the way the buyers of labour asserted their claims on the product of labour, namely by paying wages and thereby alienating the product of labour. The way the contradictions generated by the production metaphor were resolved was to assimilate women's reproductive powers to the natural fertility of external nature. This resolution had several advan-tages: it located the control of such powers with an agency external to women in the same way that the control of nature allowed its domestication and the appropriation of its products by human culture seen as external to it. This in turn resolved the risk involved in allowing women's minds to control their specifically female bodies. The external agency controlling these natural powers was men as husbands, as medical professionals, as biologists, psychiatrists, and others.[10] Until the middle of the eighteenth century women's knowledge about their own generative activities was fully embodied in them, just as the knowledge of the craftsperson was fully embodied in that person. Women were the only source of knowledge as to whether they were pregnant or not, whether what they bore was a child or just some kind of growth (such as a *mola*), and that knowledge was legit-imate (on this point see Duden, 1991). With the biologization of the body and the 'naturalization' of the generative functions of women, the epistemic knowledge of different kinds of professionals has completely replaced the knowledge of the woman about her body.[11] The woman gives her body up to the investigation of its interior by medicine and to the management of her pregnancy by various medical experts and their technologies.[12]

The commoditization of labour separated out work from all other human activities, such as socializing, gossiping, and resting, bringing about what E. P. Thompson has called the separation of work and life. Bodily life came to be restricted to the private domain and that is where new life was produced, where bodily activities such as sexuality, elimination, cleaning, and resting took place. Due to the contradiction generated by the production metaphor of making babies, the private domain became the natural sphere of women. The private sphere was strongly feminized—the realm of the care of the body and of the emotions—in opposition to the realm of reason, efficiency, achievement, and market relations.

The nineteenth century saw a positive explosion in the ideology of domesticity as the natural calling of women. Woman's very physiology and anatomy at once destined her to the domestic realm and disqualified her from full participation in the public sphere. Menstruation, as a regularly recurring phenomenon seen as plunging women into dysfunctionality and irrationality, epitomized women's unreliability. Menstruation proved that women had a weaker grip on will and reason than men. The following excerpt from an address by the President of the American Gynecology Society delivered in 1900 captures this with rhetorical flair:

Many a young life is battered and forever crippled on the breakers of puberty; if it crosses these unharmed and is not dashed to pieces on the rock of childbirth, it may still ground on the ever-recurring shallows of menstruation, and lastly upon the final bar of the menopause ere protection is found in the unruffled waters of the harbor beyond reach of sexual storms.[13]

Woman's nature, her very physiology destined her to the domestic realm, to maternity, to emotionality. The maleness of rationality and of will was stated quite explicitly in the nineteenth century. The French nineteenth-century historian Michelet, for example, writes of 'manly rationality' and of the powers of deduction and calculation as a 'virile art' (Michelet, 1842: 174, 176).

The production metaphor used in discussions of generation, along with the erosion of community life and the nuclearization of the family, all contributed to the individualization of reproductive labour, captured in the phrase 'women make babies'. This individualization of generation, however, did not extend to the woman as a person. This was accomplished by naturalizing generative functions and biologizing the body. Although the woman's body by itself makes the baby, the removal of rationality, of will and consciousness from the process effectively removes the woman from the sphere of instrumental Cartesian rationality (Martin, 1987: 61). The ideology of domesticity used women's biology to argue that women's destiny was motherhood. Although the young unmarried woman became able to exercise her free choice in choosing a husband, once married she had to obey and follow her husband. This preserved a sphere of life where human relatedness would not be eroded by the atomizing forces of individualism. The price was the patriarchal family and the sacrifice of women's access to individualism. Eighteenth- and nineteenth-century thought 'extolled women as custodians of morality and religion, now reduced to the virtues of the home' (Fox-Genovese, 1991: 136), creating the home as the refuge for men from a tough and unfeeling world of competition and self-seeking. This view of the private and public sphere implicitly acknowledges that human relatedness, sociality, and more generally social cohesion could not be left to the workings of the market (Fox-Genovese, 1991: 130).

At the tail-end of the twentieth century, the ideology of domesticity is frayed beyond repair, in spite of the strenuous efforts of the extreme Right to revive it. The balance which ideally should have been struck between the morality of the home and that of the market has been steadily destabilized by the fateful association of the private sphere with the body and with reproduction seen as a biological, natural phenomenon. What this means in a culture where nature is radically separated from human rationality and consciousness and where rationality—along with its corollary, individualism—are the core values of the polity, the economy, and the culture at large, is best captured in these words of Simone de Beauvoir (1961: 59):

On the biological level a species is maintained only by creating itself anew; but this creation results only in repeating the same Life in more individuals. But man assures the repetition of Life while transcending Life through Existence [i.e. goal-oriented, meaningful action]; by this transcendence he creates values that deprive pure repetition of all value. In the animal, the freedom and variety of male activities are vain because no project is involved. Except for his services to the species, what he does is immaterial. Whereas in serving the species, the human male also remodels the face of the earth, he creates new instruments, he invents, he shapes the future.

The clarification in brackets is from Sherry Ortner (1974: 75), whose comments on this passage from *The Second Sex* makes explicit its implications for women and men:

In other words, woman's body seems to doom her to mere reproduction of life; the male, in contrast, lacking natural creative functions, must (or has the opportunity to) assert his creativity externally, 'artificially', through the medium of technology and symbols. In so doing, he creates relatively lasting, eternal, transcendent objects, while the woman creates only perishables—human beings.

Both de Beauvoir and Ortner write in the universalistic mode, presenting these views not as specific to industrial capitalism but to humankind. The brief historical perusal of the deployment of Cartesian rationality through the commoditization of labour and the individualism which it entailed (given the necessity to buy and sell one's own labour) should already alert us to the historical specificity of such views.

The second part of this chapter discusses village communities in coastal Orissa that belong largely to a subsistence way of life and that are only marginally integrated into a market economy. It presents us with a way of life in which generation and regeneration is a creative, meaningful human activity. This concrete instance of generation and regeneration as meaningful and not emptied out of mind belies the universality de Beauvoir and Ortner claim for their views.

These two texts by de Beauvoir and Ortner, which have been immensely influential in the wave of feminism in the U.S. which started in the late 1960s, make it clear why the ideology of domesticity could not withstand the dual blow of associating women with nature, and all creativity, all human worth, with the products of a rational mind lodged exclusively in humans and particularly in human males.

It is only from an individualist or rationalist perspective that one can speak of human beings as 'perishables'. The individual ends with death but the person-in-relationships regenerates relationships and the web of relationships endures. As long as generating new human beings and regenerating the web of social relationships is seen as the 'mere repetition of Life', a sphere of activity that does not distinguish us from brute animals and from nature, and as long as creativity is confined to the non-natural—i.e. the specifically human domain of culture—social and natural ecology will be casualties. De Beauvoir's choice of words to characterize male transcendence of Life, namely '[he] remodels the face of the earth, he creates new instruments, he invents, he shapes the future' emphasizes that human creativity lies in making new things not in repeating the same. The word 'regenerating' means renewing, recreating something that already exists. This characterizes the workings of nature and is therefore considered by de Beauvoir as mere repetition devoid of creativity.

De Beauvoir's contrast between regenerating and creating is drawn much too starkly as well as short-sightedly. From an evolutionary perspective nature is a most prolific creator of new forms. At any one point in time, however, nature may seem to simply be generating and regenerating, that is continuing the same Life. A parallel can be drawn with non-modern, non-commoditized societies, especially kin-organized societies. At any given time people claim simply to follow the path of their ancestors, of custom and convention, but the work of ethno-historians has shown us that this seeming sameness over the longer run reveals itself to be constant change.[14]

I would argue that de Beauvoir's choice of the third person masculine to speak of human/male creativity is not merely a stylistic strategy: he remodels the face of the earth, he creates new instruments, he invents . . . It is the individual 'he' using his rationality—not the wisdom of his forebears—to transform the earth and make new things. A member of a non-modern society would be much more likely to credit either the gods or the ancestors for the tools and implements he uses, and would be unlikely to speak proudly of 'remodelling the shape of the earth' with its tones of mastery and control over nature. I would argue that the understanding of generation and regeneration as the mere repetition of life, as mere biology, is a direct corollary of a style of cognition which requires the autonomous agent, disengaged from both nature and others, relying cognitively not on an apprenticeship with nature or on the wisdom of elders and forebears but on a right method, called rationality. Today the phrase 'remodelling the shape of the earth' is as likely to invoke polluted waters, deforested wastes, or salinized lands as it is to invoke the ingenuity and creativity of man.

The challenge posed to us by the social and natural ecological crises in a country like the United States requires us to rethink generation and regeneration and its opposition to rationality and individualism. The view of nature and of human generation and regeneration as mere repetition of life is in fact a necessary corollary to the creation of atomistic agents rationally pursuing their self-interest, and more generally to an understanding of rationality as the use by disengaged individuals of a right method. To begin to construct generation and regeneration as a creative human endeavour requires us as a first step to deconstruct rationality and individualism. A second step would be to ask new questions about non-commoditized societies. Such an exercise should also thoroughly transform our notions of the private and public spheres as well as of the economy.

De Beauvoir's formulation is a contemporary variant of the Cartesian *cogito* in that it sets up a clear boundary between a level called 'biology', a level of the body, and a level of the mind, consciousness, will, and reason. Biology is a category that fits within the broader category of nature. This domain of the biological and natural is stated to be a universal domain, shared by all living beings, including humans. Variation enters with the diverse cultural constructions put upon the biological or natural realm. The cultural constructions put upon the bed-rock of the 'facts of life' belong to a symbolic domain (Schneider, 1968: 116).[15]

When anthropologists encounter cultures which do not separate a natural and a cultural domain, this is generally seen as a local cultural construction made possible by the lack of scientific knowledge of biology. But where what we call biology is infused with mind, it is difficult to draw a boundary between what is of the body and what is of the mind. The category of biology as that which is different from the human-made, from products of the mind, has, from the perspective of our Cartesian mode of thought, a givenness to it. It is not seen as itself a cultural construction, rather it is the bed-rock upon which all cultural constructions rest; in other words it is a universal category. I hope that the foregoing has succeeded in showing that the category of biology is dependent on that of rationality or mind and thus carries within itself the same ontological entailments as the latter categories.

The distinction between a symbolic order and a biological and natural order is key to the manner in which we (moderns) construct the category of 'ritual'. We consider ritual action to be opposed to instrumental action, the latter consisting of actions upon domains that are wholly outside the rational mind and whose purpose is to transform that domain (or aspects of it). The category of 'ritual' is dependent on the legacy of the Reformation and particularly of Zwingli's work, in which a categorical distinction between the literal and the symbolic was drawn (see the Introduction). It is also dependent on the subsequent emergence of Cartesian rationality.

In Chapter 4 Ramachandra Guha characterized Progressive Conservation and Wilderness Thinking as corresponding to the production and consumption phases of industrial capitalism. What both these movements share, in spite of their radically opposed views, is the separation between a human and a natural domain, a separation which at bottom is a corollary of the Cartesian *cogito*. The *cogito* disengages the mind from the world as well as from the body. It also sets up an instrumental relationship between the mind and the world or body. The former characteristic entails the categories of nature and culture as mutually exclusive and mutually defining realms. Nature is what culture is not and vice versa. The latter characteristic, namely the instrumental relationship between the mind and the world or body, means that by transforming nature the mind will domesticate it and transform it into culture. The word 'culture' with its roots in agriculture and cultivate implies domesticating and taming (Wagner, 1981). This is how Freud uses the word culture when he characterizes the work of the ego as that of appropriating portions of the id 'to widen the field of perception and enlarge [the ego's] organization so that it can appropriate fresh portions of the id . . . It is a work of culture.' (see n. 5).

The work of culture is to constantly appropriate new portions of the id, this internal wilderness. The Wilderness movement responded to the ever-widening encroachment of culture into untamed, unspoiled nature. Its response was inevitably that of setting apart portions of wilderness and protecting these from the work of culture. The Wilderness movement has materialized in the form of wilderness preserves, an essentialist or universalist understanding of nature. Nature in the raw is not something out there; rather it comes into being by thinking that there are parts of the world untouched, untransformed by the human mind. Where mind pervades the living as well as the non-living world, as it does for Indic and many other peoples, there cannot be such a thing as nature in the raw. Wilderness preserves from which humans are excluded make no sense to the people living in them.

Of course, the Wilderness movement has not stopped the trend of appropriating new portions of nature. Now, with genetic engineering, *in vitro* fertilization, and other reproductive technologies, the reach of the *cogito* has made a quantum leap. With the Onco-mouse, genetically engineered by DuPont by adding an onco-gene so that the mouse will develop cancer (these mice are sold to cancer research laboratories), we are not seeing the 'implosion of nature and culture' as Haraway would have it, but the reach of instrumental Cartesian rationality into ever fresh portions of the world.[16] Less and less of the world will remain undomesticated—or undeveloped—by this dominant rationality whose transcendental and instrumental nature propels it to control ever fresh portions of the world. This, however, will not lead us to the 'implosion of the categories of nature and culture'; for that to happen the form of rationality itself must be changed.

Guha contrasts both Progressive Conservation and Wilderness Thinking to peasant cultures which 'by embedding ecology in society, transcend[s] both these perspectives'. The following look at the practices of certain Oriya villagers will allow us to understand how ecology can be embedded in society and how such an embedding is related to a style of cognition I will call, following Varela and colleagues, 'embodied or enactive cognition'.

PART II

Generation and Regeneration among Oriya Villagers

My own observations have focused on a particular site, some 20 km. south of the coastal city of Puri. There the festival of the menses (Raja Parba) is marked by a fair at the temple of Goddess Haracaṇḍī. The temple sits atop a small hill and is surrounded by a small sacred grove of mostly tamarind, neem, and banyan trees. The temple on the hill is set apart from fields and settlements. During the four days of the festival men from some sixty villages in a 20 km. radius around the hill set up tents and camp there. The women celebrate in the villages and many of them come for a day-trip to the temple of Haracaṇḍī. This festival on the hill is the occasion of a fair attracting many merchants selling wares to villagers. Since the construction of a tarred road leading to the foot of the hill some 15 to 20 years back, the fair has attracted a much wider group of people. Only male villagers pitch village tents, where male representatives from each household in the villages sleep, regardless of caste. Many other people come to visit for the day, including residents from the city of Puri.

The festival is observed by men and women of all castes, including untouchable castes, except brahmins. The temple priests, however, celebrate the festival with special observances in the temple, but the wives of the brahmin temple priests (there are non-brahmin priests as well) do not observe the festival. Many tents include the village brahmin. These brahmins come in their capacity as village temple priests and household priests. They respond when queried that this is not their custom and observance, since their women folk do not observe the festival at home. Similarly, Muslims from neighbouring villages participate in various capacities, as cleaners of the sacrificed sheep, as vendors, and in other ways.

The brahmins and the muslims belong to the same villages as the men and women who consider this their festival but they do not participate in all the practices that make up this festival.

On the occasion of Purna Chandra Mishra[17] and my second visit to the sacred grove of Haracaṇḍī in June 1990, P. C. Mishra did a complete survey of all the tents and interviewed at least one man per tent.[18] He discovered that several 'youth clubs' from a few villages had organized tents for the purposes of keeping law and order at the fair. One of these youth clubs was a Muslim one from the village nearest to the site of the fair. These were relatively recent developments (having occurred in the last 4 to 5 years), a response to events which occurred on two other sites where the festival of the menses is also observed. There, a contingent of young men and women from college came to visit and some of the women were raped. Since the sacred grove of Haracaṇḍī is a popular spot for picnics with middle-class urbanites in the region, one can well imagine that these young male urban college students came to these isolated spots to act up and 'have a good time'.

The rape of women at these other two temple sites motivated the creation of the youth club tents at Haracaṇḍī, since rape would constitute a major affront and insult to the Goddess, who, during the four days of the festival, is called Draupadī, the heroine of the great Indian epic Mahābhārata. The theme of rape is in fact central to the events of these four days and I will return to it below. The fact that the villagers responded to the news of rape in these other two sites by organizing youth clubs for the purpose of keeping order at the fair also betrays their lack of confidence in the police's ability or willingness to prevent rape. Rape would constitute such a major catastrophe and so fundamentally jeopardize the welfare of all villagers that they are not willing to let the police do this work. Some policemen are regularly sent to the fair to keep the crowds in order. From the villagers' point of view, however, the police, along with any other representatives of the state, hail from the same urban milieu as the college students, which is perceived as alien to their own.

The Muslims, the brahmins, the young college students, and some of the vendors, as well as policemen and other government officials participate in the festival in some capacity, but do not consider it their festival. The observances and commentaries we elicited at the fair and in the villages are from those men and women whose festival this is. Their views and practices are not shared by all segments of the regional population. Their voices represent only one viewpoint among many. In fact, the young male students who either committed rape or condoned it, can be said to hold views diametrically opposed to those we will shortly present. Opposite views are not only held by more modernized segments of the population, but also by certain groups from what is considered a very traditional segment of the population, namely temple brahmin priests of certain temples.[19] The villagers whose festival this is are not only well aware of differing views and observances, but when these views and actions directly threaten their own, they take active precautions to prevent them from trespassing into their space.[20]

I have chosen to focus on the practices of the villagers whose festival this is because this will allow me to make visible another form of cognition. The voices of the villagers themselves,[21] as they responded to my questions and those of P. C. Mishra, introduce their practices and their views. Here is what Sisulatá, a woman in her 40s, said to me:

FAM: What is Raja?

S.: Haracandī is at her menses for three days. On the fourth day is the bath of the goddess. The girls and young women will also take a bath on that day. Red colour will be thrown on the goddess so it will appear as if she is bleeding. The cloth on which red is thrown will be put in a bucket of water so the water will be red. The priest will show the pilgrims, and say: 'This is the blood of Thākurāṇī [the goddess]'. People out of joy will take and drink that water.

FAM: Why do only the men come and camp in the sacred grove of Haracandī?

S: Thākurāṇī is menstruous so all the men have to come there, to cook and be merry. It is a rule [niyama] that they cannot stay at home. If we don't do this, the goddess will not preserve the world. For these four days of the festival husband and wife will not sleep together. Those men who stay in the village leave the women alone. That is because Thākurāṇī is at her periods. We have this condition [of menstruating] from her and because of that the men leave. The women stay in the village . . . This festival is almost like our menstruation; we do not bleed but we follow the same rules as during our menses since we are of the same kind as her. She is a woman and we are all women. We are parts [anśa] of her.

This is how Bhikari Paridā, a man from another village, answered a similar query from P. C. Mishra:

Women are prakriti, the creative energy [ṣrusti śakti] and we are puruṣa [male] and we come here to worship the greater energy [adiśakti], the Mother [mā]. We come here now because She is at Her periods which is good for each and everyone. This means that She is ready, that She will give forth. She will give us good crops and cause many things to grow. Women are reflections of the Mother and of the earth [pruthibī]. The Mother, the earth, and women are the same thing in different forms. During the four days of Raja the earth, the Mother, is bleeding . . . We think that women are bleeding too, not really but symbolically [sanketika] and that the Mother bleeds through them. During the menses of the earth women do no work; they play and sing with their friends. The sole reason is for them to rest, just like during their monthly periods when they do no work and must not be disturbed, they should not be touched, they are then untouchable. When the Goddess is bleeding we also stop all work in the fields, and not only we farmers but all other men, blacksmiths, carpenters, potters, washermen, barbers, etc. It is incumbent upon us that we should please the Goddess and women at this time. Young women [i.e. pre-menopausal] celebrate Raja because they are the centre of creation and we want to make them happy and please them.

What both Sisulatā and Bhikari—and all other men and women we spoke to—state clearly is an identity between women, the earth, and the Goddess. The nature of this identity is of a different type from that between a thing and something else that stands for that thing. The relationship between the water reddened by red powder and menstrual blood is spoken of by Sisulatā as an 'as if' relationship. The reddened water is not really menstrual blood. Similarly Bhikari says that 'we think women are bleeding too [during Raja], not really but symbolically'. These phrases express a difference between the literal and the symbolic, metaphorical, or representational. The manner of speaking of the relationship between the earth, the Goddess, and women is different. Sisulatā says that women are parts or portions (anśa) of the Goddess. Bhikari says that women are reflected images (pratibimba) of the Mother and of the earth; also that the Mother, the earth, and women are the same thing in different forms. Other persons spoke of women as the substitute (pratinidhi) of the Goddess and the earth.

The identity between women, the earth, and the Goddess is a substantive one; it is not representational or symbolic. Women do not stand for the earth nor for the Goddess, as red-powdered water stands for menstrual blood: they are the earth and the Goddess, portions or reflections of these. More precisely, they are the earth and the Goddess in a different form. By the same token the relationship between the earth and the goddess is like that too. It would be a distortion to speak of the Goddess as a symbol or a representation of the earth or of women.[22]

How are we to understand these statements of identity? Clearly it is not a question of the Oriya villagers' inability to distinguish between the literal and the symbolic, since they make those distinctions in the passages I have just quoted. The form varies, so that identity is not based on similarity of form;[23] it is based on the perception that women, the earth, and the Goddess do similar things. It is in what women, the earth, and the Goddess do that they are the same. The following excerpts from villagers' speech makes this clear:

Mā is at Her periods, which is the right time for Her to manifest and to produce through nature. We feel that our women and our lands are the representatives, the duplicates of our Mā. SHE produces through these two: women and the land. (Satyabādi Pahalā)

Women are connected with production [or giving forth; utpanna]. We consider them the source of production. They are like the land and in that way they are considered as Bāsudhā Mā [mother earth]. They experience pain to produce from their wombs. [Sahadeb Palāi]

Mā maintains creation, so also our wives maintain our lineage; so they are the same and we keep ourselves away from them [during Raja] even if they are not at their periods, but . . . we understand women are reflected images or shadows of Mā and Pruthibī.

(Sadasiba Jena)

The villagers in these passages give voice to a very ancient identification between women and the earth. This identity is enacted in lived experience in various contexts.

I think it is important to take a close look at the manner in which this identity is enacted in order to understand that this identity is not simply a belief, i.e. a purely mental phenomenon. This identity is rather what could be called an 'enactive cognition'. The distinction is crucial for recognizing a different style of cognition, as well as for understanding what embedding ecology in society means, and I will return to it below.

Let us start by looking at the oft-reiterated statements that during Raja Parba, as during women's monthly menses, husbands and wives should not have intercourse. Women at their menses are untouchable and so is the Earth during Raja Parba; all agricultural work ceases and the earth is not penetrated. This is spoken of in terms of women and the earth needing to rest. During their menses women do no work and the earth does no work during her period of fallow. This no-work period is a period of rest necessary for women and the earth to regenerate their strength in preparation for their generative activity.

The Goddess menstruates once yearly in mid-June. This is the articulation between the hot and dry season and the rainy season. The hot and dry season is a period of fallow, when nothing grows.[23] The rainy season is the season when the newly planted seeds germinate. During the hot and fallow season, there is a separation between the earth and the clouds, whereas during the fertile rainy season there is a union between earth and clouds. Women are the earth and the rain clouds are the virile Indra, King of the gods.[24]

The articulation of the seasons is called *ritu*, a word which also means 'menses'. The etymology of *ritu* that Emile Benveniste gives us suggests a way of looking at the practices surrounding menstruation among these villagers:

With the aid of an abstract suffix -*tu* Indo-Iranian formed the Vedic *ritu*, Avestan *ratu*, which designated order, particularly in the seasons and periods of time, and also rule and norm in a general sense. All these forms are referrable to a root -*ar*, which is well known because of numerous formations outside Indo-Iranian and belong to several of the formal categories just mentioned. The root is the Greek *ararisko* 'fit, adapt, harmonize' (Arm. *arnel* 'make'), which is connected with a number of nominal derivatives. Some with the suffix—*ti* . . . others with -*tu*, e.g. Lat. *artus* 'joint' and also with a different form of the root *ritus* 'rite'. (Benveniste 1973: 380)[25]

Today in Oriya the word *ritu* means both the articulation of the seasons and women's menses. The notion of order may be implicit in the notion of articulation and particularly in the connection between the articulation of the seasons and the 'articulation' of women's periods (of time). In the case of women's menses, *ritu* as well as the other words designating it (such as *raja*), refer not only to the periodic flow of blood but also to the actions taken by men and women during that time. Even the flow of blood is spoken of as an action by women and the earth. The earth and women bleed rather than something happening to women or the earth.[26]

In the Greek version of this Indo-Iranian root *-ar*, the nature of the activity is specified: *ararisko* means to fit, adapt, harmonize. This suggests a way of seeing these practices. The activity of bleeding and of observing the rules of menstruation—the two being of a piece—articulate humans to the order in the articulation of the seasons. This articulation between humans and the seasons is constituted by human activities and practices such as bleeding periodically, resting, keeping men and women separate, doing certain things and not doing other things. The actions of humans must articulate with the movements of the clouds, with their separation from and convergence with the earth. Women and men recapitulate in a monthly rhythm the cosmos' yearly rhythm. The separation of rain clouds and earth during the fallow hot season is enacted by men and women keeping each other separate during women's periods.[27] After the purificatory bath on the fourth day of the menses, husband and wife are supposed to unite. Among the learned classes, the husband is supposed to recite a Sanskrit verse at the time of this union, called *ritu-samgamana*. The verse ends with the following: 'I am the sky, thou art the earth' (Kane, 1974: 202). The women like the earth are fixed; they stay in a room during their menses, they stay in the village during the festival. The men come and go like monsoon clouds. These actions enact in the daily life of humans the identity between women and the earth, men and the clouds, as well as bringing about the articulation between humans and the cosmos.

All these human activities will ensure order as well as the continuity of life. The ordered movement of the sun, and of the seasons, guarantee the continuity of life. In lived experience this order is enacted through the separation of men and women during Raja Parba and during women's monthly menses. Such an enactment creates a cosmic rhythm in which humans are participating actors along with the earth, the clouds, the sun, and so forth.

When the cosmic order is violated, chaos and dissolution are the results. Violation of the human order also brings threats to the continuity of life. When I asked women and men what would happen if women's menses were violated, the responses invariably involved a story from India's great epic, the Mahābhārata.[28] The Mahābhārata is ever present during the Raja festival, because during that time Goddess Haracaṇḍī is considered to be Draupadī, the heroine of the epic. Furthermore, the area is considered to be Virāta's kingdom, an important locus in the epic. The fateful scene in the epic, which motivates the whole subsequent action, is that of the gambling match where Draupadī's five husbands—the Pandava brothers—play dice with their rival cousins, the Kaurava brothers. The Pandavas stake their wealth, their kingdom, their selves, and finally their common wife, and lose all. The winner, the eldest Kaurava, has Draupadī seized and dragged by the hair into the men's hall. At that time Draupadī was menstruating: her garment was stained with blood and her long black hair was unbound (Hiltebeitel, 1980a; 1980b; 1981).

This is what Sisulatā told me about this scene:

Duḥśāsana [brother of elder Kaurava] came to the room where Draupadi was and dragged her away. Then Draupadī said: 'When I will see your blood then I will bind my hair.' Duḥśāsana died in the great battle that followed, and so did all the Kauravas. Then the binding of the hair was done.

The following is a conversation concerning these epic events I had with a young washerman called Ramacandra Nayak at the festival:

FAM: What happened at the dice match?
RN: Draupadī cursed Duḥśāsana and he died. The whole lineage of the Kauravas was destroyed because of this sin.
FAM: What sin?
RN: She was disturbed during her *ritu*; she was taken by the hair and she was angry and the result was very bad. Everything was destroyed, blood was shed.
FAM: What would happen if you did the same thing the Kauravas did and disturbed the earth during Raja?
RN: We would get afflictions [*doṣa*]. Everything would be spoiled. If you plow, it will not give results. That is why we give sufficient rest to women during their menses. If they rest it will be good for them. They do no work; they are untouchable; we do not disturb them. So the mother goddess should take rest at this time.

The curse of Draupadī mentioned by Ramacandra Nayak is enunciated by Sisulatā: namely, Draupadī tells her tormentor that she will not bind her hair until she sees his blood, that is until he dies.[29] Draupadī was not only humiliated in the men's hall, but, as Hiltebeitel argues, by forcing her to sit on his thigh, the elder Kaurava makes it clear by word and deed that rape is intended and symbolically enacted. Draupadī vows to remain in a symbolic menstrual state—signalled by her unbound hair—as long as her tormentor lives. It is her vow and curse which propel the men towards the great battle (Hiltebeitel, 1980a). The point being made here by both Sisulatā and Ramacandra Nayak is that disturbing a woman at her menses is itself an abhorrent act, which also has connotations of rape. Such an act brings about frightful consequences which threaten the continuity of life. It is not only the death of individuals such as Duḥśāsana that is the result of this 'sin', but the end of the Kaurava's lineage, since they and all their male offspring were killed. The death of a lineage is true cessation of life; the death of an individual does not have the status of a threat to the continuity of life.

Ramacandra Nayak responds to my question about disturbing the earth during Raja by saying that everything would be spoiled and nothing would grow. He follows this statement by saying that this is why women must rest during their menses. For him, letting the earth rest and letting women rest is the same, since both are the source of the continuity of life in the form of crops and in the form of the lineage.

The enactment of the identity between women and the earth is more fine-grained than I have intimated so far. The earth comes in two varieties: cultivated and uncultivated lands. The temple of Goddess Haracaṇḍī is situated in the midst of a sacred grove which is a piece of uncultivated land. The trees are never cut and cultivation is never undertaken in the sacred grove. This is where the fair of the festival of the menses takes place. During their menses women must not only refrain from work but must sit separately, apart from where the life of the home takes place. Women do not bathe, bind or comb their hair, or cut their nails during the three days of menses.[30] Furthermore, as I was told by several women that they are not supposed to cut, grind, or paste any vegetables or plants. These practices identify women with the sacred grove of the Goddess. The sacred grove is situated apart from fields and settlements, apart from people's daily activities; no cultivation must take place in the grove. Women's loose, unbound, and uncombed hair is as the uncut, untrimmed trees and plants in the grove.[31] In order to be the sacred grove, women should refrain from cutting, grinding, or pasting any plant food, for these actions are the continuation of cultivation. Women process the food cultivated by men and that processing is understood as the continuation of the work of creating food to sustain life. During their menses women are the virgin forest garment of the earth; in between their menses women are the cultivated fields.[32] The virgin forests dotting the subcontinent in the form of sacred groves are the source of the herbs and plants used in Ayurvedic medicines, which regenerate the lives of people. It is not only biologists who see the virgin forest as indispensable to regeneration but also the common people. Haracaṇḍī's sacred grove also harbours a spring said to have healing properties; the link between forest cover and water sources is well understood by the people. Continuity of life necessitates the alternation between cultivated field and virgin forest and the enactment of such alternation by humans. This enactment is seen in the alternation between everyday work[33] and the wild, fallow state of menstruation observed by women and men each in their own ways.

Another crucial requirement for the continuity of life is the regeneration of a wider net of social relations beyond the household. This is enacted by the men in the sacred grove and by the women in the village during the four days of the festival. Sociality, harmony, and peace between co-villagers of different castes and between different villages are actively and carefully planned for and pursued.

Different aspects of sociality are regenerated by the women in the villages and by the men in the sacred grove. For the sake of brevity I will discuss only one of these here: namely, what the men do at the hill of Haracaṇḍī. Frayed social relations are healed and regenerated and new ties are forged in the form of marriage arrangements. This healing is accomplished not simply by holding the value of co-operation and harmony but by enacting specific actions that are carefully planned and orchestrated. In fact the very process of planning requires a modicum of co-operation. When there is so much conflict that the required co-operation cannot be reached the festival cannot be held, thereby exposing the villagers to the anger of the Goddess. The anger in the community becomes the anger of the Goddess. That anger, in its turn, spells disaster for the villagers. Incentives to achieve harmony are very pressing.

The time of the festival of the menses heals and regenerates not only the land and women but also a wide network of social relations. These village communities depend on each other for marriage exchanges as well as for other exchanges. The ritual of the menses creates a space apart from the daily activity and toil of the villagers to heal and regenerate sociality and social cohesion. Once again, I chose representative voices to convey what is done and how it is done.

Raghaba Sāhu, a 55-year-old man of the village of Caṇḍiput speaks of the organization of the festival:

I called a meeting (in the village) before the festival and we all agreed to contribute 80 rupees per household ... We are poor and we know that we have to spend money here for four days. Still then we like to come here and worship our Goddess. Only one man per household comes here. If the father comes the son won't, but it rotates every year so every man can come in time. Everybody in the family knows about the amount of the contribution; we make it the same for everyone in the village to create a good feeling among everyone. The women know about this money and they don't object. They are 'our treasuries. We deposit everything in their hand. They remind us to give the contribution in time; they like to keep up the prestige of our families ... The money goes into the village fund. We have a village project begun by the government of Orissa of cultivating shrimps in the village pond. The profit from the sale goes into the village fund and we are all happy to spend that money here in the festival. With that project's profit we bought four rams to offer to the Goddess; it costs us a little over 2,000 rupees. Because of the village fund it is possible for us to have a good feast every day up to the end of the festival.

Raghaba's account is typical of all the other accounts we recorded from men in the tents during the festival. The amount of the contribution from villagers varies somewhat between villages (between 50 and 120 Rs.) and the nature of the village commons also varies. But the majority of villages have either fields, ponds, or groves in common and those that do not have any common land or pond collect a portion of each household's harvest for the common fund. All men reported that women are the treasuries and are in charge of household finances. The cash contributions are supplemented by contribution of food grains and vegetables. The bulk of the expenses go towards the feast the men cook four times a day during the four days of the festival. Preparing and distributing the food is a focal activity in the process of regenerating social relations. This is what Rajana Palāi, in charge of distributing the food at the feast, says:

The distribution of the food at our feasts is very important and I take great care with it. I know who will eat what and how much—that is my sixth sense. I balance everything between the rich and the poor, the younger boys, the grown men, and the old ones. I am very careful about that. I eat only after everyone has been fed and is fully satisfied. Especially when the meat curry is served then I forget about the face of anyone and only look at their leaf plates, serve them, and go to the next in line. In this way I go from first to last. Every day, four times I have to do this to keep my villagers happy, this is why they trust me [to be the tent leader].

Rajana Palāi articulates clearly the care with which he carries out the actions that foster fellow feeling and deflect envy, competition, and resentment. In order to have a sense of the social composition at such feasts let us listen to the voice of Kishore Routray:

We are all castes here except brahmins (there is no brahmin in our village[34]) and this is very good for us. We have six *doms* (untouchable caste). We have no feeling of high and low; we are cultivators, sweet-makers, scribes, barbers, *doms*. We eat together and sleep together; we are friends.

The caste composition of the various villages varies somewhat but what is striking is that all castes including untouchables will sleep and eat together. This contrasts sharply with everyday life in villages where different castes do not eat or sleep together. Several men remarked that this is easier when no brahmin is present and that feelings 'of high and low' are brahmin concerns which they do not share.[35] In any case what was consistently reported was the careful planning and deliberate fostering of fellow feeling and harmony between co-villagers through specific actions of feasting. This is accomplished through deliberations in village meetings, use of common funds, setting of equal amounts for the contributions and the manner in which the food is cooked and distributed at the festival. These concrete actions enact the healing and regeneration of intra-village sociality.

The manner in which intra-village sociality interdigitates with inter-village sociality is made clear in the words of Siddheśwara Nāyaka:

We feel that this tent is our home during the four days and we are members of the same household. So there is no feeling about 'this is mine and this is another's'. Our tent leader (*murabi*) . . . treats everyone equally and shares the tasks among us like cutting vegetables, fetching fuel and water, etc. . . . Everyone takes the responsibility for his task very seriously. No one goes away from the tent before having completed his duties. If one were not to do this, it would anger the tent leader and he might report this to the village headman. Villagers feel very bad about any sort of allegation brought by the tent leader. They feel that by this the reputation of the village will be damaged. Preserving the reputation and prestige of the village is extremely important because if it is ruined nobody will want to give their daughters in marriage to our village and no villagers will want to take our daughters. Our image will be spoiled, then our life deserts us. So we co-operate and we do not quarrel. After finishing our duties in the tent we go visiting in other tents. Our relatives and in-laws all come from this area of Brahmagiri [the market town in this area of sixty villages]. We talk about many things: about cultivation, fertilizing and land, water problems. Sometimes we meet persons who are very knowledgeable in agriculture or about ayurvedic medicinal plants and leaves to cure many kinds of diseases. We also often discuss possibilities of marriages between grown sons and daughters and about the money involved. Meeting so many friends and relatives from other villages is a very big pleasure for us.

The sixty villages that participate in the festival at Haracaṇḍī belong to one marriage exchange circle. Marriages are always arranged between mates of different villages (they practise village exogamy). The bride leaves her natal village to go and live in her groom's parents' house in another village. The festival is a time when marriage prospects are initially explored and the reputation of a village is crucially important in that process. Arranged marriages join two lineages rather than two individuals and the quality of a village's sociality is paramount in the choice of a groom or a bride. Therefore the regeneration of intra-village relationships is directly relevant to the eventual generation of new social ties between villages as well as the generation of new people and thus the continuity of life. This is why Siddheśwara says that if his village's reputation is spoiled—and the reputation bears on sociality, not on material factors—'then our life deserts us.'

Inter-village sociality is enacted at the festival by the men from all the sixty villages in the marriage circle living in tents closely spaced in the small sacred grove. The language used by several of the men refers to the tents in the sacred grove as one big village and all the men as the children of Goddess Haracaṇḍī. This is how Banambar Saralā expresses this:

Coming to the place of the Mother at this fair we forget everything, all our problems, our individual responsibilities. We feel that we are all the children of Mother Haracaṇḍī and that we are all the same. Except for the fact that we eat with our fellow villagers, we do not feel as if we belong to one particular village. Here all the men feel as brothers since She is the Mother and we have come here to receive Her blessings. There is no feeling of inferior or superior. There is competition—we play cards, we have song fests—but there is no quarrel among us; we do not lose our tempers. Even if there is some quarrel between some people or between some villages, we carefully manage it so as to resolve it and forget our quarrels. We do not allow such disturbances to develop and destroy the peace and beauty of the festival. If there is peace [śanti] then She becomes peaceful and gives us peace. When She is *śanti* then She does everything good for us. Whether we get food or not is not the most important thing, but we need peace. We try to do constructive things; we don't want to bring any harm or destruction. We do not show our individual greatness or express our power and dignity. We try to keep peace and order in this sacred place. Nobody has bought this land to become master over another; the sacred grove belongs to everybody. With all the tents in it it looks like one big village, the tents are the houses and we all are the children of the Mother. The Mother's temple is our village temple.

The sacred grove is not only the place where the earth regenerates itself but this regeneration is enacted by the men as well. Their long tents pitched under the trees relate them to each other as the leaves of a tree and the different tents as the trees that form one grove. The village communities and the larger group of villages in the marriage exchange circle regenerate their sociality. This regeneration is enacted deliberately, with forethought and great care. The Goddess is the focal point, enabling the villagers to relate to each other as her children, thereby muting inequality, dissension, and conflict.[36] The sacred grove as a commons is the material embodiment of the Goddess as mother of all the villagers.

The pattern we described above of an alternation between a productive period and a period of fallow or rest as being necessary to the continuity of life is here enacted in a different register. This register encompasses the widest social circle and enacts an alternation between hierarchical and egalitarian inter-caste relationships. Order and continuity consist of this very alternation or articulation; order and continuity are a rhythmic pattern rather than a fixed structure. It is the centrality of our own architectural metaphor of structure when speaking of social order that propels us to look for 'the' structure and predisposes us to consider the enactments during festival times as a special bracketed time and space. The egalitarianism enacted during the festival is discounted as 'ritual activity' opposed to the real activity that takes place in everyday life.

Activity during this festival cannot be contrasted to instrumental activity; what the villagers do during Raja can be thought of as instrumental to the regeneration of the land, the body, and the community. It is also helpful to keep in mind that villagers perform certain actions which, from a rationalist point of view, seem to be non-instrumental—such as patterned behaviour learned from the elders, usually categorized as 'ritual activity' by anthropologists—when they carry out what to us are thoroughly instrumental activities such as ploughing, sowing, weaving, making pots, cooking, etc.

Our root architectural metaphor of structure combined with our categorization of ritual as opposed to rational instrumental action conspire to prevent us from seeing continuity and order as a dynamic pattern of alternations between different moments.[37]

Human beings enact the cosmic rhythm by articulating their activities with the articulation of the seasons and of women, both called *ṛitu*. In that enactment they create a dynamic order as well as the continuity of life. This enactment represents an alternative style of cognition. Following the school of 'enactive cognition' of Varela, Thompson, and Rosch, I would argue that the environment is not objectively given but emerges out of sensorimotor interactions with it in a particular context. This enactment is a creative activity, since both the perception of alternation in the world and the enactment of alternation by humans are not givens. They emerge out of particular interactions between humans and the world. These interactions are particular rather than universal because they are not determined in any sense but depend on how the humans in question perceive, think about, and act in the world. It is therefore not an imitation of nature but a creative, intelligent activity motivated by our embodied condition. Nature is not a given independent from our sensorimotor interaction with it. In other words we are not separate from the world, but enfolded within it.

Enactive cognition is a type of action and cognition in which sensorimotor activity creates the world that humans inhabit. The terms 'enfolded' and 'participation' are not quite right since they presume a pre-given world that humans are enfolded by or that they participate in. Enactive cognition is a mode of being, acting, or thinking where there is no ontological gulf between the mind and the world or body.

We must be careful not to fall into a dualism of rhetorical or performative action versus effective rational action. The categories of enactive cognition transcend the dichotomy between ritual and effective rational action however 'ritual' may be defined or understood. In Stanley Tambiah's distinction between participation and causality, his view of ritual as rhetorical or performative action is subsumed under the rubric of participation and contrasted to cognition and science:

It is possible to suggest that a meaningful way to contrast participation and causality is through a comparison of religion and science as contrasting and complementary orientations to the world. What our discussion so far has led to is the plausibility of at least two modes of ordering the world that are simultaneously available to human beings as complementary cognitive and affective interests, and which in the self-conscious language of reflexivity and analysis might be labelled as 'participation' and 'causality' . . . (1990: 108).

For Tambiah, therefore, ritual belongs to religion, to affectivity, to rhetorical and performative action. Cognitive activity belongs to causality, to science. As the term 'enactive cognition' indicates, we are dealing with a cognitive and not only with an affective phenomenon. The category of 'enactive cognition' dissolves the boundary between science and religion, between performative action or speech (i.e. ritual) and effective rational action.

Enactive cognition also transcends the boundary between a realm of the world wholly outside humans and the human realm of culture. Such a style of cognition precludes the hands-off attitude towards nature propounded by Wilderness Thinking. As Shiv Visvanathan makes clear in his discussion of E. O. Wilson's *Biophilia* (Chapter 9, below), the naturalist's love of the untouched forest excludes humans from it. It is a love which did not arise from living in and with the forest; the forest remains an Other for Wilson, akin to a museum where precious biodiversity is carefully preserved from human depredation. Visvanathan worries that when all the information and all the samples of genetic material from the forest are stored in databanks, these will have more importance than the continued life of the forest.

The concern of the Oriya villagers, both men and women, is the continuity of life, the generation and regeneration of people and of relationships. Productive activity is not understood as being only that activity which produces food or wealth, but also as the activity of men and women in generation, or the activities of women in processing food. In the work of generating new people (i.e. sexual intercourse between husbands and wives) as in the work of producing food, the work of both men and women is required. Both generating new people and producing food are called work because the former is not a mindless natural or biological activity but a fully creative activity involving cognition. There is no category of biology or of nature devoid of creativity, cognition, or will.

Regenerating social relations or sociality in general is also called work, even though it may take place in a heightened fashion during festivals. It is work which is cognitive (as well as affective) and instrumental. In other words the categories of biology, ritual, and effective rational action are blurred. This, I have tried to argue, is so because our category of rational effective action that assumes the transcendental subject whose rational faculties are radically separate from the world and from the body is absent. Rational effective action presumes an agent radically separated from a world (or body) that is devoid of mind and upon which the agent acts. Society, with the deployment of Cartesian rationality, of rational bureaucratic modes of organization, and of the market economy, likewise became an object upon which rational effective action could be targeted. Society could be socially engineered, which is one way of looking at what development is. Such a process of social engineering always involves invisible violence. As Zygmunt Bauman has argued in the context of the Holocaust, this violence is made possible by the phenomenon of distanciation (Bauman, 1989: 98 and *passim*). The perpetrators of the violence do not see the results of their actions and are not held responsible for them. They are not members of the groups their actions are targeted towards. This is also true in the context of development (Sachs, 1992).[38]

The regeneration of social relations carried out by Oriya villagers during the festival of the menses is carried out in a language of kinship relating not only most of the inhabitants of a single village but most inhabitants of several villages. This language of kinship highlights the fact that the actors are emphatically not separate from what they are acting out. Such actions become ritual only when Cartesian rationality monopolizes all cognition. The action undertaken to heal social relations also means that violence in this type of society is visible. The visibility of violence is precisely what leads people to devise ways to heal the effects of violence and of conflict. What I have called the regeneration of sociality is precisely the actions that bring about this healing. The example I have focused upon is the phase of healing and of regenerating sociality, and so people spoke of that and not of violence. This is emphatically not meant to be construed as meaning that there is no violence in this society. Conflict and violence exist everywhere, but when they are visible and the perpetrators of the violence are not separated from those on whom the violence is perpetrated, healing and regeneration can take place.

CONCLUSION

The embeddedness of these villagers' world in nature is made possible by a style of cognition which I have called, following Varela and colleagues, 'enactive cognition'. Unlike Cartesian rationality, which is both transcendental and instrumental, this style of cognition is an embodied one, emerging from our embodied condition and enacted in actions that relate us to the world around us and to each other. This mode of cognition is not only embodied but also embedded in the knowledge, conventions, and beliefs of a historical collectivity. Unlike the Freudian ego it is not independent of the superego, the knowledge and wisdom of the elders, nor does it control our embodied passions and instincts. It is fundamentally a mode of cognition which arises from human activity interacting with others and with the world.

Such a mode of cognition places a premium on relationships and is in marked contrast to the disengaged stance of rationality towards the body, the world, and others. The latter stance has proved dramatically successful at creating material abundance and technological advance but disastrous at maintaining both social and natural ecology. The latter stance brings about an invisible violence.

To naturalize the body and generation is to separate us from nature and at the same time to deprive that nature of cognitive creativity. That in itself sets up a hierarchical relationship of dominance between humans' rationality and an unthinking, unknowing, disenchanted nature. This, as is obvious now at the close of the twentieth century, has spelled disaster for natural ecology. The monopolizing of cognition in the mind of a rational transcendental subject also results in the objectification of society. Society—or the economy—becomes the target of various social engineering projects. The violence that these may, and often do, perpetrate is rendered invisible by the distanciation between the actors and those who are the targets of these actions. With enactive cognition that separation evaporates—this is emphatically not the same as saying that violence evaporates. Violence and conflicts of course erupt frequently, but they are visible. Enactive cognition makes possible actions designed to breach the rifts and heal the conflicts and pain. It could be said that the anthropological category of 'ritual' has functioned as a way of keeping invisible or unquestioned the separation between the thinking agent and what is thought about.

The concept of 'enactive cognition' which I have tried to illustrate in one concrete case could become a resource for thinking about possible alternatives to modernity and development. The concrete example given is not offered as a model to emulate—even if this was possible for us modern Westerners—but to show how enactive cognition manifests itself in the lived experience of a contemporary people. Looking at this contemporary example through the lens of enactive cognition has allowed us to see these people not as pre-modern and therefore in need 'of being brought into the 21st century' by development or any other social engineering scheme but as contemporary people. The impossibility of emulating these people arises not from the fact that this would mean going backwards but from the fact that the experiences of the past so many centuries in the modern West cannot be wished away, they can only be transformed and perhaps transcended.

NOTES TO CHAPTER 5

1. I thank the participants in the Harvard South Asia Seminar, where I gave portions of this paper on 8 October 1993, for prodding me to clarify the issues I raise in this chapter. I am particularly grateful to William Fisher, Kunal Parker, Benjamin Schwartz, Joseph Prabhu, John Mansfield, and John Carman.

     I am well aware that similar critiques or deconstruction of Cartesian rationality abound in these post-modern times. My aim is to bring to bear such critical deconstructive work on a development context where what some have called 'high modernity' still reigns.

2. Ong argues that manuscript culture is not that far removed from a style of thought grounded in specific social contexts.

3. Flandrin's study focuses on France and paints a different picture than MacFarlane does for England in *The Origins of English Individualism* (1989); besides regional differences in these processes and the prevalence of the nuclear family in England, the nuclear family as it is known in industrialized societies exists in a very different social context than the nuclear peasant households that MacFarlane discusses in pre-industrialized England. The latter existed in a social context in which kin and fictive kin networks played a crucial role in communities. The mobility of labour required by the industrial mode of production has made serious inroads into those networks and the cohesiveness of communities.

4. The work of the historian Barbara Duden (1991) shows with meticulous attention to a multi-volume text recording the practice of a German doctor of the early 18th cent. how the biologization of the body happened in the latter part of the 18th cent. and how previous to this, experience was fully embodied. She has focused exclusively on case histories of females in the text.

5. Freud (1968), 106, quoted in Ahmed (1989). Ahmed makes a most insightful analysis of the relationship between the internal colonizing ego using will and reason to repress the dark and dangerous forces of the id characteristic of the modern self and the actions of the contemporary state apparatus in a country like Pakistan towards minorities of various kinds.

6. Descartes, when describing this faculty, makes no gender distinctions: 'I have noticed, on examining the nature of many different minds, that there are almost none of them so dull of understanding that they are incapable of high feeling, and even of attaining to all the profoundest sciences, were they trained in the right way': quoted in Schiebinger, 1989: 171.

7. See Lefkowitz Horowitz, 1984: ch. 5, where the author conducts a historical study of the 'Seven Sisters', the seven élite women's colleges of the North-East of the U.S. Of particular interest for the point being made here is her discussion of the debate that raged at the time of the creation of Smith College, the first women's college to offer women the same intellectual regimen and training as the élite Ivy League schools for men such as Harvard, Yale, and Princeton. The debate centered around the conviction on the part of men that subjecting women to such rigorous mental exercises would inevitably lead to reproductive disorders, such as shrivelling of their uteri or the birth of defective children. This was a direct threat to the survival of the upper classes and caused great alarm. The college survived with its curriculum modelled after the Ivy League's curriculum, but the price it had to pay was that its graduates would marry élite men and use their education only to train their sons. If women graduates wanted a career of their own they had to forgo marriage. It was not until the late 1960s that marriage was no longer seen as disqualifying a woman from pursuing a career. The first woman president of Smith came there in the late 1970s. For a history of the arguments made by biologists for excluding women from the Academy see also Hubbard, 1990: 36–41.

8. On the production metaphor for the generative processes of women see Martin, 1987, in which the author analyses the language of gynaecological textbooks used in the second half of the 20th cent. in medical schools in the U.S.

9. The term 'grown' is used in a Melanesian context; see Weiner, 1976; Strathern, 1988.

10. The scholarship on men's control of female sexuality in the West includes Foucault, 1980; Ehrenreich and English, 1979; Oakley, 1984; Delamont and Duffin, 1978; Wertz and Wertz, 1977; Martin, 1987; and Strathern, 1988 have shown that the understanding of alliance in general and affinal exchanges in particular in terms of men's need to control female sexuality is a result of our own Western commoditized concepts and logic.

11. This change is obviously fraught with enormous political implications for women. It gave a way for the state—and other agencies as well—to enter into the domain of the control of women's fertility.

12. This 20th cent. development has given rise to various forms of protest and resistance on the part of women. Women have vigorously and fairly successfully revolted against what we came to feel was an inhuman approach to childbirth and demanded to be present as people during the birth of our children rather than removed through sedation. Another result of this invasion of medicine has been an alarming rate of unnecessary ceasarean sections and hysterectomies, as well as a marked increase in iatrogenic diseases, giving rise to many self-help women's movements. The most well-known resulted in the series of publications on women's health by the Boston Women's Health Collective, 1971; 1981; 1983; 1984; 1987. Along with a rise in inhuman birthing techniques and iatrogeny, this kind of knowledge has also brought women many health benefits and has dramatically lowered the rate of infant mortality. For a balanced assessment of the ambiguous effect of this development on women see Riessman, 1983.

13. S. Hall, *Adolescence*, ii (1905), 588, quoted in Ehrenreich and English, 1979: 110. For the medical view of women's physiology in France see Moreau, 1982. In her 1987 book, Emily Martin reviews 20th-cent. opinions on the role of menstruation in discouraging or encouraging women in the workforce; she shows how medical research, in times of labour shortages such as World War II, tended to show that menstruation did not lower women's productivity, whereas research findings showed the opposite in times of labour surplus: ch. 6.

14. For a critique of the ahistoricality of 'traditional' societies see in particular Wolf, 1982; Sahlins, 1985; and Parmentier, 1987.

15. In his work on American kinship the anthropologist David Schneider argues that there is no natural fact *per se*, only cultural interpretations of them; however, he stops short of saying that the category of 'biology' is constructed. He states that there *are* natural facts which are determined by science, the so-called 'facts of life'. Cultural constructions are symbolic phenomena placed over and above the bed-rock of these natural facts. He therefore continues to privilege biological scientific knowledge. I have relied on Sarah Franklin's 1988 MS for my critique of Schneider.

16. Donna Haraway, lecture delivered at Smith College, 22 Jan. 1993.

17. I have been carrying out fieldwork in Orissa since 1975 and have done field research with the help of my collaborator there, Purna Chandra Mishra, who is a brahmin from Puri. This turned out to be an advantage, since, when interviewing the men, he was able to ask for basic information, since he did not know anything about these practices.

18. I was meanwhile speaking to women in one of the villages and participating in their observances there.

19. For a very different, and negative, view of menstruation on the part of temple brahmin priests of a temple in Bhubaneswar, see Richard Schweder's 1985 study. Schweder, however, presents these views on menstruation as representative of Oriyans in general and even of 'Hindus'. They are in fact very contrary to the views held by the villagers P. C. Mishra and I spoke with. For a discussion of the implications on how women are viewed in different traditions within Hinduism see my article 'Female Sexuality in the Hindu World', 1985*b*.

20. The villagers also took measures that allowed them to keep the police at a safer distance. When we first came there in June 1987 the place was thronged with

policemen, due to violent conflicts that had erupted in a nearby village where a faction of the villagers had bribed the Police Commissioner. By 1992 stone retaining walls and steps around the temple effectively prevented police trucks from discharging their contingents at the centre of the festival.

21. From now on, the expression 'the villagers' will refer only to those villagers whose festival this is. It excludes the brahmin and the Muslim villagers.

22. In Peircian terminology women are indices of the earth and of the Goddess rather than icons or symbols. I am relying on Richard Parmentier's (1985) work on Peirce.

23. In Peircian terms, the relationship is not an iconic one.

23. I am speaking here of rain-fed agriculture; irrigation permits a third crop to be grown during the hot season.

24. In Puri, the temple town in coastal Orissa, people speak of rain as Indra, since Indra is the master of rain; cf. Apffel-Marglin, 1985a: 97.

25. The word *rita*, cognate of *ritu*, is a central one in the earliest Sanskrit literature, the Vedic hymns. There, *rita* is the ordered cosmos, opposed to chaos and dissolution. *Ritu* is the activity which creates *rita*; *ritu* is an articulating activity. The sun by its dynamic activity (*ritu*) articulates a well-ordered continuity according to Lillian Silburn (1955). Human beings, by their dynamic articulating activities (*ritu*), create, by participating in cosmic activity, order and continuity. Of course I am not suggesting any continuity across 3,000 years of history. Rather, these indigenous ideas serve to lead me in certain interpretative directions rather than in others.

26. This contrasts with the manner in which women of all classes and ethnic backgrounds speak of menstruation in the U.S. today. As Emily Martin (1987: 78) has shown in her extensive interviews, menses is something one has. The woman's body is passively subjected to this phenomenon.

27. During their menses women are considered extremely hot.

28. In fact the villagers were referring to the vernacular Oriya Mahābhārata by the 16th-cent. Oriya poet Sarala Das, and not to the Sanskrit epic ascribed to Vyāsa and dated by scholars between the 2nd century BC and the 2nd century AD. Their knowledge of Sarala Das's epic was an oral one, based on listening and watching plays.

29. The symbolism of Draupadī's hair, which she keeps loose for the 13 years of the Pandavas' exile, is complex and rich. It is explored by Alf Hiltebeitel in 'Draupadī's Hair', 1981. In 'Draupadī's Garment' (1980a), he explores the symbolism of menstrual blood and of garments. For the purposes of my argument here, it is not necessary to enter into this fascinating and rich terrain, and I refer the reader to Hiltebeitel's work on the Sanskrit Mahābhārata.

30. These actions also signal the women's state of impurity which renders them untouchable. But menstruation is also auspicious. On the distinction between the categories of purity and auspiciousness see Carman and Apffel-Marglin, 1985.

31. Hiltebeitel (1980a; 1981) has shown that in the Sanskrit Mahābhārata, women's hair and garments represent the vegetation on the earth.

32. The biologist Madhav Gadgil has shown that the sacred groves found all over India are the last places where the primal, original forest cover remains today. He points out that with the drastic genetic impoverishment brought about by

monoculture and the green revolution, regeneration of indigenous gene plasm can take place thanks to the sacred groves (Gadgil 1987; Gadgil and Berkes, 1991).

33. The Oriya word I translate by the English 'work' is *kāma*, from the root *kar-* meaning 'hand'. That word is used not only to refer to what we would consider productive work, such as agricultural or craft activities, but also to what anthropologists would classify as 'ritual' activity, to women's work of food processing and cooking, of cleaning, of feeding people and animals, as well as the intercourse between husband and wife. All these activities are necessary to the generation and regeneration of life and are therefore all referred to as 'work'.

34. Generally the village brahmin will come to the festival but this is not a brahmin festival. The wives of those brahmins who do come because they serve the villagers do not celebrate Raja. Raja is a non-brahmin festival.

35. It is relevant to note that these interviews with men from the tents were conducted by P. C. Mishra, who is a brahmin from Puri. So these remarks are certainly not motivated to please a Western woman probably suspected of valuing equality. These remarks emphasize that during the festival hierarchical considerations are seriously muted; they do not mean that at other times these hierarchical considerations are equally muted. The works by Gloria Raheja (1988) and Nicholas Dirks (1987) have in their own ways dislodged hierarchy from the central place it has had in the understanding of caste relations.

36. For a related argument based on fieldwork among Maharashtrian agriculturalists, see Schlesinger, 1982. He reports that farmers refuse to calculate the cost and benefit of their sharing activities during the ploughing season in order to preserve and foster sociality. This is done on a daily basis and not at special festival times.

37. The festival of Raja could be seen as a rite of passage in a Turnerian manner, marking the passage from the hot/dry season to the fertile rainy season. Turner (1966) would read the egalitarianism at the festival as typical of the liminal phase of such rites, characterized by inversion and by the erasing of social differences. Turner takes over van Gennep's (1908) tripartite schema for rites of passage, as well as van Gennep's architectural metaphor for social structure. In fact, Turner understands liminality as the absence of social structure; liminality 'reveals . . . some recognition of a generalized social bond that has ceased to be and has simultaneously, yet to be fragmented into a multiplicity of structural ties' (1966: 96). Such an understanding of rites of passage conceives the actors as dynamic, moving through a fixed structure. In thresholds they are neither here nor there and this is expressed variously, often by egalitarianism and inversions. I think such an understanding is constrained by the static idea of structure. Rather, order is itself moving and dynamic. The actors do not move through a fixed house, rather both actors and the world move.

38. Grassroots resistance to development projects, such as, for example, the resistance in India to the Narmada dams project, involve the local population that will be affected by the dams. Those who support the building of the dams will not have their homes, temples, and villages wiped out.

REFERENCES

AHMED, D. S. (1989), 'Monotheism and Violence: A Psychological Analysis of Ethnic Conflict in Karachi', paper presented at the WIDER conference on Systems of Knowledge as Systems of Domination, Karachi, Pakistan.

APFFEL-MARGLIN, F. (1985a), *Wives of the God-King: The Rituals of the Devadasis of Puri*, Delhi Oxford New York: Oxford University Press.

——(1985b), 'Female Sexuality in the Hindu World', in C. Atkinson and C. Buchanan (eds.), *Immaculate and Powerful*, Cambridge, Mass.: Harvard University Press.

BAUMAN, Z. (1989), *Modernity and the Holocaust*, Ithaca, NY: Cornell University Press.

BENVENISTE, E. (1973), *Indo-European Language and Society*, Coral Gables, Fla.: University of Miami Press.

Boston Women's Health Collective (1971), *Our Bodies, Ourselves*, Boston, Mass.: Free Press.

——(1981), *Changing Bodies, Changing Lives*, New York: Random House.

——(1983), *Our Jobs, Our Health*, Boston: The Massachusetts Coalition for Occupational Safety and Health.

——(1984), *The New Our Bodies, Ourselves*, New York: Simon & Schuster.

——(1987), *Ourselves Growing Older*, New York: Simon & Schuster.

BOURDIEU, P. (1990), *The Logic of Practice*, Stanford, Calif.: Stanford University Press.

CARMAN, J. and APFFEL-MARGLIN, F. (1985) (eds.), *Purity and Auspiciousness in Indian Society*, Leiden: Brill.

DE BEAUVOIR, S. (1961), *The Second Sex*, New York: Bantam Books.

DELAMONT, S. and DUFFIN, L. (1978) (eds.), *The 19th Century Woman: Her Cultural and Physical World*, New York: Barnes & Noble Books.

DIRKS, N. (1987), *The Hollow Crown: Ethnohistory of an Indian Kingdom*, Cambridge: Cambridge University Press.

——(1991), *The Woman beneath the Skin* (trans. from German, 1987), Cambridge, Mass.: Harvard University Press.

DUMONT, L. (1977), *From Mandeville to Marx: The Genesis and Triumph of Economic Ideology*, Chicago: University of Chicago Press.

EHRENREICH, B. and ENGLISH, D. (1979), *150 Years of the Experts' Advice to Women*, New York: Anchor Books.

ESCOBAR, A. (1991), 'Anthropology and the Developmental Encounter: The Making and Marketing of Development Anthropology', *American Ethnologist* 18/4: 658–82.

FLANDRIN, J.-L. (1979), *Families in Former Times: Kinship, Household and Sexuality*, Cambridge: Cambridge University Press.

FOUCAULT, M. (1975), *Surveiller et punir: Naissance de la prison*, Paris: Gallimard.

——(1980), *The History of Sexuality: An Introduction*, New York: Vintage Books.

FOX-GENOVESE, E. (1991), *Feminism Without Illusions: A Critique of Individualism*, Chapel Hill/London: University of North Carolina Press.

FRANKLIN, S. (1988), 'The Virgin Birth Debates: Biology and Culture Revisited', MA thesis (New York).

FREUD, S. (1968), *New Introductory Lectures on Psychoanalysis*, trans. W. J. H. Sprott, London: Hogarth.

GADGIL, M. (1987), 'Culture, Perception and Attitudes to the Environment', in P. Jacobs and D. Munro (eds.), *Conservation with Equity: Strategies for Sustainable Development*. Gland, Switzerland: IUCN.

—— and BERKES, F. (1991), 'Traditional Resource Management Systems', *Resource Management and Optimization*, 18/3-4: 127-41.

HILTEBEITEL, A. (1980a), 'Draupadī's Garment', *Indo-Iranian Journal*, 22: 98-112.

——(1980b), 'Śiva, the Goddess, and the Disguises of the Pandavas and Draupadī', *History of Religions*, 20: 147-74.

——(1981), 'Draupadī's Hair', *Puruṣārtha*, 5: 179-214.

HUBBARD, R. (1990), *The Politics of Women's Biology*, New Brunswick/London: Rutgers University Press.

JORDANOVA, L. (1980), 'Natural Facts: A Historical Perspective on Science and Sexuality', in C. P. MacCormack and M. Strathern (eds.), *Nature, Culture, and Gender*, Cambridge: Cambridge University Press.

——(1989), *Sexual Visions*, Madison: University of Wisconsin Press.

KANE, P. V. (1974), *History of Dharmaśāstra*, ii, pt. 1, Poona: Bhandarkar Oriental Research Institute.

LEFKOWITZ HOROWITZ, H. (1984), *Alma Mater: Design and Experience in the Women's Colleges from their 19th Century Beginnings to the 1930's*, New York: Knopf.

MACFARLANE, A. (1989), *The Origins of English Individualism*, Oxford: Basil Blackwell.

MARGLIN, S. A. (1974), 'What do Bosses do?', *Review of Radical Political Economy*, 6: 60-112.

MARTIN, E. (1987), *The Woman in the Body*, Boston, Mass.: Beacon Press.

MICHELET, J. (1842), *La Femme*, Paris, Grevin.

MOREAU, T. (1982), *Le Sang de l'histoire: Michelet, l'histoire, et l'idée de la femme au XIXième siècle*, Paris: Flammarion.

MULLINGS, L. (1986), 'Uneven Development: Class, Race, and Gender in the U.S. before 1900,' in E. Leacock and H. I. Safa (eds.), *Women's Work*, Hadley, Mass.: Bergin and Garvey.

LEACH, E. (1976), *Culture and Communication*, New York: Cambridge University Press.

OAKLEY, A. (1984), *The Captured Womb: A History of the Medical Care of Pregnant Women*, Oxford: Basil Blackwell.

ONG, W. (1982), *Orality and Literacy: The Technologizing of the Word*, New York: Routledge.

ORTNER, S. (1974), 'Is Female to Male as Nature is to Culture?' in M. Zimbalist Rosaldo and L. Lamphere (eds.), *Woman, Culture, and Society*, Stanford, Calif.: Stanford University Press.

PARMENTIER, R. (1985), 'Semiotic Mediation: Ancestral Genealogy and Final Interpretant', in E. Mertz and R. Parmentier (eds.), *Semiotic Mediation: Sociocultural and Psychological Perspectives*, San Diego, Calif.: Academic Press.

——(1987), *The Sacred Remains: Myth, History, and Polity in Belau*, Chicago: University of Chicago Press.

POLANYI, K. (1944), *The Great Transformation*, Boston, Mass.: Beacon Press.

RAHEJA, G. (1988), *The Poison in the Gift: Ritual, Prestation, and the Dominant Caste in a North Indian Village*, Chicago: University of Chicago Press.

RIESSMAN, C. K. (1983), 'Women and Medicalization: A New Perspective', *Social Policy*, 14: 13–18.

SAHLINS, M. (1985), *Islands of History*, Chicago: Chicago University Press.

SCHIEBINGER, L. (1989), *The Mind has no Sex? Women in the Origins of Modern Science*, Cambridge, Mass.: Harvard University Press.

SCHLESINGER, L. (1982), 'Agriculture and Community', in G. Dalton (ed.), *Research in Economic Anthropology*, 4: 233–74.

SCHNEIDER, D. (1968), *American Kinship: A Cultural Account*, Englewood Cliffs, NJ: Prentice-Hall.

SCHWEDER, R. (1985), 'Menstrual Pollution, Soul Loss, and the Comparative Study of Emotions', in A. Kleinman and B. Good (eds.), *Culture and Depression: Studies in the Anthropology and Cross-Cultural Psychiatry of Affect and Disorder*, Berkeley, Calif.: University of California Press.

SILBURN, L. (1955), *Instant et cause: Le Discontinu dans la pensée philosophique de l'Inde*, Paris: Librairie Philosophique, J. Vrin.

STRATHERN, M. (1988), *The Gender of the Gift: Problems with Women and Problems with Society in Melanesia*, Berkeley, Calif.: University of California Press.

TAMBIAH, S. J. (1990), *Magic, Science, Religion and the Scope of Rationality*, Cambridge: Cambridge University Press.

TAYLOR, C. (1989), *Sources of the Self: The Making of the Modern Identity*, Cambridge, Mass.: Harvard University Press.

THOMPSON, E. P. (1967), 'Time, Work Discipline, and Industrial Capitalism,' *Past and Present*, 38: 56–97.

TILLY, L. and SCOTT, J. (1987), *Women, Work and Family*, New York: Methuen.

TURNER, V. (1966), *The Ritual Process: Structure and Anti-Structure*, Glenside, Pa.: Aldine.

VAN GENNEP, A. (1908), *The Rites of Passage*, 1960 trans., Chicago: University of Chicago Press.

VARELA, F., THOMPSON, E., and ROSCH, E. (1991), *The Embodied Mind: Cognitive Sciences and Human Experience*, Cambridge, Mass./London: MIT Press.

WAGNER, R. (1981), *The Invention of Culture*, Chicago/London: Chicago University Press.

WEINER, A. (1976), *Women of Value, Men of Reknown*, Austin: University of Texas Press.

WERTZ, R. and WERTZ, D. (1977), *Lying In: A History of Childbirth in America*, New York: Schoken.

WOLF, E. (1982), *Europe and the People without History*, Berkeley, Calif.: University of California Press.

PART II

Decolonizing the 'Transfer-of-Technology' Model

6

Farmers, Seedsmen, and Scientists: Systems of Agriculture and Systems of Knowledge

STEPHEN A. MARGLIN

HI-TECH AGRICULTURE

1. The Triumph of Science or Disaster in the Making?

This chapter examines agriculture through the lens of knowledge. Is hi-tech agriculture (hta) a triumph of science or a disaster in the making? Or both? Is the answer to the limitations of hi-tech agriculture more science? Or does the answer lie in incorporating the virtues of traditional agriculture into the agronomic *episteme*? Is this feasible?

We shall approach these questions by retelling the story of hta and its global diffusion, a story whose outlines are familiar enough. It begins with the development of hybrid corn (maize) in the United States in the first three decades of this century, its commercialization in the 1930s, and the near 100-per-cent replacement of traditional open-pollinated varieties by hybrids in the 1940s and 1950s. Next is the export of the philosophy of seed manipulation from the Corn Belt to Mexico in the early 1940s. Wheat varieties developed in Mexico in the 1950s became the basis for the Green Revolution's greatest production successes, not only in Mexico itself, but also in the Punjab region of India and Pakistan. Meanwhile, the International Rice Research Institute in the Philippines, inaugurated in 1960 as a joint venture of the Ford and Rockefeller Foundations, began to do for rice what Nobel Prize winner Norman Borlaug and his colleagues had done for wheat in Mexico. The common thread is the synthesis of new varieties which under favourable conditions respond to high doses of fertilizers and significantly out-yield the 'land races' that cultivators have evolved over millennia of experimentation.

Writing this paper has created many debts. First, to Shankar Ramaswami for excellent research assistance, particularly on the first section of this chapter. Secondly, for a number of important criticisms of earlier versions which are reflected in this version: Donald Duvick, Thomas Glick, Arthur MacEwan, Siddiq Osmani, Mohan Rao, Vernon Ruttan, and Jonathan Sauer. These criticisms helped me to tighten and clarify the presentation, and in some cases made me change the argument. Finally, I should like to thank the Rockefeller Archive Center, and its director, Darwin Stapleton, for permission to quote from the documents in its possession.

By the time of America's entry into World War II, hybrid corn was clearly a success, but this success was only the beginning. Once the principles had been mastered, corn could be manipulated to various ends. As early as 1925, Henry A. Wallace noted in the pages of *Wallace's Farmer* that the uniformity of hybrids developed from in-breds made them suitable for machine harvesting (Crabb, 1947: 172), a characteristic that would guide plant breeders for years to come. But the most dramatic demonstration of the possibilities of hybridization appeared when the nitrogenous fertilizer industry came of age as a by-product of the expansion of munitions production during World War II. Open-pollinated varieties responded to nitrogen only up to a certain point; after this point, the plants would become, as it were, too big for their britches and fall over ('lodge' in the jargon), making harvest more difficult and exposing the plants to possible damage by rain and hail. By selective breeding, the roots could be strengthened and the stalks shortened, considerably extending the limit of responsiveness to nitrogen and increasing the optimal density of planting. Successive generations of hybrids were planted more closely together and given more fertilizer, and yields continued to climb (Duvick, 1984).

As American hta was transformed into the Green Revolution, the same principle of selection was followed. Crucial to the strategy of both the wheat programme and the rice programme was the synthesis of strains that could accept massive doses of nitrogenous fertilizer without lodging. The expansion of Third World consumption of fertilizer at an annual rate of 12.4 per cent between 1960 and 1975 and 7.1 per cent over the next decade is testimony to the size of this endeavour (Alexandratos, 1988: table 4.6). The expansion of wheat production, first in Mexico then in Pakistan and northwestern India, and of rice production in Indonesia are testimony to the success of the strategy under favourable conditions.

Food production has increased enormously, but at a price: first, considerable narrowing of the genetic base, as a relatively small number of new cultivars displaced the great variety of genetically diverse land races; second, dependence of the new varieties on abundant water, fertilizer, and pesticides; third, transformation of economic relationships occasioned by the expansion of the role of inputs purchased off the farm. The narrowing of the genetic base raises questions of vulnerability, the dependence on water, fertilizer, and pesticides questions of environmental degradation and resource exhaustion, and the economic transformation questions of political stability. The three sets of questions can be brought together under the rubric of sustainability.

The term 'sustainability' is relatively new, but not the questions. Rachel Carson's *Silent Spring* (1962) was a turning-point in creating public awareness of the environmental degradation caused by pesticides. The Club of Rome's *Limits to Growth* (Meadows *et al.*, 1973) raised the spectre of resource exhaustion and, coinciding as it did with the first oil shock, had an important impact on thinking about the problems of basing agriculture on fossil fuels both to power equipment and to manufacture chemical fertilizers and pesticides. After an encounter with corn blight that became a near disaster because of the genetic uniformity of hybrid corn (see below), the narrowness of the genetic base of hta became an important concern (National Research Council, 1972). Finally Wendell Berry's *The Unsettling of America* (1977) questioned the ethical and political consequences of the transformation of agri*culture* into agri*business*. For Berry disconnectedness from the land endangered the very fabric of the society; no gain in efficiency could make good this loss.

Keith Griffin (1974), Cynthia Hewitt de Alcantara (1976), Andrew Pearse (1980), among others, criticized the Third World version of hta, the so-called Green Revolution, largely on the grounds that the skewed distribution of land ownership and access to credit concentrated the benefits of development disproportionately amongst the rich. Indeed the poor, especially the landless who survived off the sale of their labour, could be made absolutely worse off if mechanization figured prominently in Green Revolution innovation.

In the 1980s critics took a different tack. The issue became not the neutrality or lack of neutrality of Green Revolution innovations with respect to different classes of cultivators, but the neutrality of agricultural science itself. Among others Edward Oasa and Bruce Jennings (1982), Jennings (1988), Jack Kloppenburg Jr. (1988), and Robert Anderson, Edwin Levy, and Barrie Morrison (1991) have developed this theme, arguing that politics and economics shape the application of science whether or not individual scientists are aware of it, that the institutional biases of the private foundations at the cutting edge of the Green Revolution were themselves shaped by the political and economic interests of the societies in which they are embedded.

This two-part chapter draws freely on all these earlier critiques. The first part in particular, which attempts to balance up the pluses and minuses of hta, is a variation on themes introduced by Anderson *et al.*, Jennings, Kloppenburg, and Oasa and Jennings. The novelty is the emphasis on the knowledge that undergirds agriculture, specifically the interplay between the *episteme* of the experts and the *techne* of the farmer in different agricultural systems.

2. We Have Bought You Time

A balance-sheet of hta is difficult to draw. Enthusiasts claim that hta has prevented the Malthusian nightmare from becoming a reality. The population of India, Bangladesh, and Pakistan, for example, has more than doubled in the past 40 years. Yet, despite the persistence of malnutrition and even hunger, twice the number of people are eating at least as well, and probably better, than their grandfathers and grandmothers ate at the time of Independence and Partition.

A similar story applies to large parts of China, South-East Asia, and Latin America. Indeed the significant exception to this story is Africa, and it is a matter of continuing controversy whether the African problem is more plausibly attributed to the lack of a Green Revolution, that is, in the inability thus far to develop a suitable hta for the semi-arid and arid tropics, or to the inappropriateness of the Green Revolution model (for the second view, see Dommen, 1988).

The most persuasive argument is that hta is a stopgap, an emergency measure necessitated by the rapid increase in population practically everywhere in the Third World. Norman Borlaug, awarded the Nobel Peace Prize as representative and emblem of the Rockefeller effort in Mexico, explicitly took this line in a letter to a critic quoted in a laudatory piece that appeared in the *Atlantic Monthly* after environmental criticism of the Green Revolution began to mount (Bourjaily, 1973: 75):

You are barking up the wrong tree. The correct tree is population growth but why then attack the Green Revolution? . . . I know the population explosion cannot be stopped immediately . . . education must lead the way . . . So what is to be done? Are we to sit idly by and watch the world starve? This I cannot watch! . . . Do you think for a moment they will die peacefully? A biologist knowing anything about animal behavior can't be that naive.

I have spent my professional lifetime trying to increase world food production . . . and through this process buy time—perhaps two or three decades— in which to permit population control programs to become more effective and dynamic.

Is the so-called Green Revolution expected to correct all the social ills that have accumulated since the days of Adam and Eve, and then on the Sabbath (while resting) solve the population problem as well? How stupid can educated people be? What has happened to the indispensable, rare character called common sense in the over-populated, over-sophisticated, over-computerized so-called educated American society?

Food production need not be the number one problem for the next twenty or thirty years. We have bought you time. Use it wisely . . . sell the need for population control.

I am sure my colleagues feel as I do that the most unfair of all criticism are those that . . . say we have created more problems than we have solved. Perhaps we have, but we have also generated hope where there was despair.

Observe that this line of argument does not require us to attribute all the increase in agricultural production to hta. Even without hta greater numbers would have increased production: each mouth came with a pair of hands, so production would have risen quite apart from new seeds, additional fertilizer, and so on.

This much Malthus himself would concede. The Malthusian case hinges not on stagnant production, but on the inability of production to keep pace with population. The extra hands accompanying each mouth are quite consistent with Malthusian misery, since each pair of hands came without a proportionate share of tools, land, and water.

A more serious difficulty with the 'buying time' argument is that it takes population growth as wholly exogenous. I do not mean here to invoke the endogeneity associated with the population growth stimulated by hta itself—among other things greater availability of food would almost certainly have decreased infant mortality. This secondary endogeneity is consistent with the primary exogeneity—clean drinking water, vaccination, and the like—to which the Norman Borlaugs of the world see themselves as responding.

But there is another, more primary, sense in which population growth may be endogenous; it is possible that the development process itself has precipitated the population explosion. Development everywhere has meant the wholesale destruction of local institutions, but we know little about the impact of this onslaught on population growth. These dislocations may have had as much impact on population as have improved material standards of living. It would be surprising indeed if traditional modes of population control were the sole survivors of the juggernaut of modernity. If population growth is the consequence of a breakdown of indigenous institutions of control, and the breakdown is caused by modernization on the Western model, then the stopgap argument evidently loses much of its force.

The last two decades have been kind to Borlaug's 'buying time' argument. In parts the Third World population growth rates have fallen markedly, and moreover these are regions in which agricultural growth, thanks to the Green Revolution, has been strong. Asia and Latin America have both experienced significant reductions in total fertility (the number of children born to each woman on average) over the quarter-century between 1965 and 1990, and both regions also experienced relatively high rates of agricultural growth between 1965 and 1980.

By contrast, Sub-Saharan Africa has had a much lower rate of agricultural growth and a much lower fall in overall fertility over the same periods. The only exception to this pattern is the Middle East and North Africa, where agricultural output has grown rapidly but the fall in fertility has been modest (World Bank, 1992, World Development Indicators: 221 and 271, tables 2 and 27).

We might none the less try to go beyond the conventional wisdom on the population explosion, to go beyond the improvements in public health, medicine, and so forth that are usually given credit for the acceleration in population growth in the first two-thirds of this century. Indeed, it is worth considering to what extent the population explosion is the result of modernization itself.

The destruction of traditional communities, for which the Green Revolution may be held accountable at least as an accessory, may bear more of the responsibility than is generally acknowledged. Indeed many demographers contend that non-modern societies have been able to stabilize birth and death rates at levels well below their maximum biological potential. (This claim has been contested however: see Caldwell *et al.*, 1987.) In pre-modern Europe, for instance, delayed marriage and permanent celibacy have been identified as means of social control—Dr Malthus's preventative checks—over population growth. If pre-modern Europe did indeed control population by these or other social norms, then it becomes relevant to ask how the norms fared under the pressure of modernization. Suppose, as Dr Malthus himself argued (1976: 34–5), that a principal means of regulating the age of marriage was a customary wealth qualification: a couple could not make a respectable marriage unless resources could be mobilized to sustain the couple and their presumptive off-spring in a manner appropriate to class and station. Then we can ask whether the upsurge in population resulted from the continued operation of the same norm—under conditions of growing prosperity the resources necessary for respectability were more easily mobilized—or from the breakdown of this norm under the dissolving forces of modernity.

If the answer is that the norms broke down, then we should be less surprised to find analogous transformations in the Third World today. But whatever the case in the transition to modernity in the West, it would be at best suggestive evidence with respect to present-day population dynamics. And we know surprisingly little about the social control of population in contemporary non-Western societies. For example, it remains controversial whether the traditional practice of post-partum sexual abstinence in Sub-Saharan Africa is (was) a means of limiting population growth or—by enhancing child survival—a means of increasing the rate of growth (Caldwell, *et al.*,: 31)!

Whatever might be concluded about the role of social control and its breakdown, it can be argued that the population explosion is a real and present danger, one that ought to make us thankful for the Green Revolution. Two arguments make Borlaug's vindication premature. First, it is to say the least controversial whether population growth is the ecological culprit, as Borlaug alleges. The claims on sources and sinks—on non-reproducible resources like petroleum and on places to dispose of wastes—of the First World of wealthy, industrialized countries and the erstwhile Second World of the disastrously inefficient Soviet empire are many times greater than the claims of the Third World, and in the First and Second Worlds populations are stable or growing slowly and are much smaller than the population of the Third World.

Second, the last two decades will have been borrowed rather than bought time unless the Green Revolution is sustainable over the long haul, exactly what is at issue between Borlaug and his critics. If the increases in agricultural output cannot be sustained, then according to Borlaug's own logic Malthusian misery will have been postponed, not conquered. If the gains of the Green Revolution prove to be transitory, Malthus will have the last laugh.

3. What Has Been Lost?

A second benefit widely claimed for hta is that it has freed enormous numbers of people to work in industry: 'Each American farmer feeds 56 others'.

This claim invites many questions. First, it presupposes an answer to the question Wendell Berry immediately asks of Secretary Butz: freed for what? For industrial jobs that offer the worker nothing but a pay-check at the end of the week in return for work that is boring, stultifying, and—worst of all— meaningless (Marglin, 1990)?

Paradoxically, the 4 per cent left on the farm in the 1970s (the percentage is now less than 2) have survived the industrialization of agriculture better than those that industrialization has made redundant. Evidently the spread of hta involved not only a new kind of farming, it also required a new kind of farmer. Indeed a condition of the industrialization and modernization of agritechnology was the industrialization and modernization of the psyche of the farmer.

What is perhaps less obvious is that industrialization and modernization were themselves predicated on a political as well as a psychological transformation; industrialization and modernization could not have taken place without the destruction of the political institutions which shaped and expressed the existence of the rural community. Indeed, from the late nineteenth century, modernization and industrialization were seen as an antidote to the populist political movements that periodically swept rural America like prairie fire (Kimmelman, 1987: 23).

The struggle centred chiefly around the local school and church, seen by (largely urban) improvers as inefficient and backward, and inconsistent with the full participation of rural folk in the twentieth century (Bowers, 1974; Danbom, 1979). In the end, the modernizers won, and the regional school and the town church replaced the one-room school and church which had identified, sustained, and expressed the local community. The breaking of community ties contributed significantly to the change in the farmer's identity that made him receptive to new agricultural technologies. Without the institutions that gave meaning to community, farming gradually became less a way of life than a way to make a living; the farmer became the agribusinessman.

This oversimplifies. It would be more accurate to distinguish between two classes of farmers: the educated, skilled, relatively well-heeled, aggressive go-getters, and the more ordinary folk, the garden variety dirt farmer. The political, technological, and economic revolution that produced hta had very different effects on these two groups: it enriched and empowered the first while it disenfranchised the second. The first group—having access to credit and capital; possessing either the skills and knowledge to implement modern technologies or the resources to command these skills in the market; standing on an equal footing with the bureaucrats and technocrats of government, industry, and finance—the agribusinessmen thrived under the new conditions. As one member of a family which owns and operates a multi-million 'family farm' put it to me, the new division of labour and specialization freed his brothers to do what they do best: manage.

Meanwhile the second group largely disappeared from the American scene. It was these folks who traded the plough for the assembly-line, the country for the city. Once farming ceased to be a way of life, their departure was all but inevitable. Or they stayed but transformed themselves into agribusinessmen. Either way, the dirt farmers were on their way out, and few mourned their passing.

History repeats itself, goes the cliché. Certainly, the twentieth-century transformation of American agriculture bears more than a passing resemblance to the early modern transformation of English agriculture known as the 'enclosure movement'? The name mistakes the form for the substance, for enclosing the land (by hedge-rows or other physical markers) was only the last act of a drama, the point of which was the invention, construction, and imposition of modern ownership claims by the powerful, as a means to eliminate the complex of coexisting and overlapping claims, duties, and rights over the land in which all segments of the community had a share, and with this elimination the destruction of the political and economic base of the erstwhile 'copyholders' (those whose claims were based on copies of manorial court rolls). In the usage of the times 'enclosing' was paired with 'engrossing', roughly the equivalent of monopolizing: indeed engrossing was the greater evil in the eyes of contemporary critics, for this was the act of power and aggression, on which enclosing the land merely put a physical seal. At the end of the drama, the smallholders of medieval and early modern England became the yeomen and landless labourers of the modern era. The first group, a privileged few, remained on the land as proprietors; the second, the meaning of their existence eroded as their economic, political, and social ties to the land were eroded, became the first 'agriproletarians', remaining on the land at the sufferance of their masters. From there it was a short social step—however long a geographical one—into the 'reserve army' that constituted the labour-force for England's industrialization (Lazonick, 1974).

A. Richard Crabb, the hagiographer of hybrid corn and its inventors, innovators, and promoters, thought it was to the credit of hybrid corn that it advanced the transformation of the American farmer into a passive dependent of the agro-industrial complex (1947: 286):

Hybrid corn has helped develop in farmers a receptive frame of mind. When his county agent, the state experiment station, a seed company, or any other organization in which he has confidence brings out a new product such as a new strain of hybrid oats, a new selection of wheat, or even a new hybrid chicken or hybrid hog, this farmer is immediately receptive, ready and willing to give such new products a thorough testing.

Liberty Hyde Bailey, plant breeder, apostle of agricultural science, Dean of the agricultural college at Cornell University in the early years of this century, and chairman of the Country Life Commission appointed by Theodore Roosevelt in the waning months of his presidency, not only anticipated the intrusion of the expert into every phase of rural life but also lived long enough to see the transformation of which Crabb wrote. Sensitive though he was to the importance of independence in the many-faceted web of the farmer's connections to the land, Bailey did not see the expert as a threat to this independence. For shortly after the Country Life Commission submitted its report, Bailey described the coming kingdom of the expert with enthusiasm (1911: 203; quoted in Kimmelman, 1987: 360): 'There will be established in the open country plant doctors, plant breeders, soil experts, health experts, pruning and spraying experts, forest experts, recreation experts, market experts . . . housekeeping experts . . . needed for the purpose of giving special advice and direction.'

Bailey, while emphasizing the spiritual and religious dimensions of farming (Bailey, 1919; especially 24, 32–3), apparently thought the land could accommodate both the servants of God and Mammon. Here is Bailey on the lack of a sustainable agriculture and the need for moral vision to fulfil the lack (pp. 26–7):

Probably we have not yet evolved a satisfying husbandry that will maintain itself century by century, without loss and without the ransacking of the ends of the earth for fertilizer materials to make good our deficiencies. All the more is it important that the problem be elevated into the realm of statesmanship and of morals.

But Bailey's solution is not a republic of yeoman farmers; he is careful to provide a place for agribusiness in his scheme for regulating 'Holy Earth' (the title of his 1919 tract, pp. 53–4):

Yet we are not to think of society as founded wholly on small separate tracts, or 'family farms,' occupied by persons who live merely in contentment; this would mean that all landsmen would be essentially laborers. We need to hold on the land many persons who possess large powers of organization, who are managers, who can handle affairs in a bold way: it would be fatal to the best social and spiritual results if such persons could find no adequate opportunities on the land and were forced into other occupations.

Bailey evidently hoped that a managerial élite would provide the leadership that would permit farming communities to survive as communities. Ironically, Bailey's leaders are the sole survivors of the transformation wrought by hta. The followers are all gone, or at best surviving on the land thanks to non-agricultural employment.

Of course the managers are dependent in a way that no apostle of Jeffersonian self-sufficiency would find acceptable. But the dependence is not of the kind that kills the spirit. The managers of a multi-million-dollar family farm may depend on bankers for credit, on industrial suppliers for fertilizers, pesticides, tractors and other equipment, and on government extension agents for advice not only on farming but on complying with myriad regulations. But theirs is a dependence that can coexist with at least the aspiration to equality. It is, first of all, a mutual dependence: the agribusinessman depends on bankers, suppliers, and government as a producer in a complex social division of labour. It is not far-fetched to liken this dependence to the interdependence of the butcher, the baker, and the candlestick-maker.

Second, this dependence leaves a measure of control of product and a larger measure of control of process in the hands of the agribusinessman. He remains in a very real sense his own boss, in charge of his day-to-day activities. He may not be the exact equal of the banker or bureaucrat, but neither is he the subordinate of the one or the other.

This is a far cry from the situation of the assembly-line worker, the filing clerk, or the hired hand, whose dependence is marked by subordination and inferiority. Indeed, the very structure of industrial work, I have argued (Marglin, 1974; 1979; 1984; 1990), reflects the boss's goal—and for these purposes it matters little whether the boss is a capitalist or a commissar—of substituting his control over process and product for the worker's, the better to maintain the dependence and subordination of the worker to a system which provides neither meaning for work (other than the instrumental meaning of the pay-check) nor any opportunity for using one's work to create one's own meaning.

Transplanted abroad as the Green Revolution, hta has had very different consequences for the cultivator. The first, although clearly inspired by the hybrid-corn revolution in the United States, the Rockefeller programme never had the success it anticipated with corn. Under Mexican conditions hybridization was in practice unable to improve markedly on what farmers, particularly the large number whose corn was rain-fed, were able to achieve on the basis of their own experimentation with land races and materials introduced from outside (Wellhausen, 1978: 80-1). Early on the Mexican Agricultural Program, as the Rockefeller project was called, turned the bulk of its attention to wheat, which in Mexico is largely irrigated.

But it would be a mistake to over-emphasize the technical side of the story, if for no other reason than, as we shall see, hybrid corn took off in the United States precisely because of its ability to withstand drought better than open-pollinated varieties in the disastrous year of 1934. In Mexico wheat was more amenable to manipulation not only for technological reasons but because it was grown by modern agribusinessmen whose orientation to agriculture was essentially instrumental; the resilience of local peasant communities stood in the way of innovation in corn production, particularly innovation that increased dependence on outsiders.

Not that much sleep has been lost over the destruction of peasant communities where this has proved feasible. These communities are generally despised as remnants of a past of backwardness, superstition, ignorance, and laziness. When Henry A. Wallace, Secretary of Agriculture and Vice-President Elect of the United States, attended the inauguration of the successor to the populist Lázaro Cárdenas in December 1940, he found that not only the Right of the political spectrum (represented by the new president, Avila Camacho), but also the Left (as the murals of Diego Rivera from this epoch strikingly reveal), considered industrialization to be the future of Mexico. However much they disagreed on tactics, Left and Right were agreed on the goal, and implicitly on the instrumental role for agriculture in the process. In this respect not much has changed since 1940.

An important difference between hta at home and abroad is the pace of change. In the United States the rationalization of agriculture has eliminated some 80 per cent of the farmers over the past two generations. From over 30 million, the farm population has declined to fewer than 5 million souls. The Green Revolution, by contrast, has been accompanied by a shrinking agricultural population in percentage terms but a rising absolute number of people trying to win a living from the land. In India, for example, there are approximately 50 per cent more people on the land today than at the time of Independence.

In the American situation the competitive pressure to survive has left a remnant of the fit; the survivors are people who are still in charge of their lives in important dimensions, in control of resources both natural and human that allow them to interact more or less as equals with the rationalizers. The American farmer retains the possibility of entering into meaningful relationships with work, land, and others. He retains a position of dignity, and remains a person of dignity.

In the Third World, where the selection process has been less severe, rationalization has degraded the peasant as a person as part and parcel of making him more prosperous. He becomes an ancillary of the machinery of credit, supplies of hi-tech inputs, official advice, in short, a cog in the agro-industrial machine. Dependent and subordinate to bankers and bureaucrats, his knowledge of the land, the micro-climate, and other specifics of his world are rendered obsolete or irrelevant by the requirements of stand-ardization built into hta, and the peasant comes increasingly to resemble the industrial worker Adam Smith described in *The Wealth of Nations* and Karl Marx described in *Capital*. Here is Smith (1776: 734):

In the progress of the division of labour, the employment of the far greater part of those who live by labour, that is, of the great body of the people, comes to be confined to a few very simple operations, frequently to one or two. But the understandings of the greater part of men are necessarily formed by their ordinary employments. The man whose whole life is spent in performing a few simple operations, of which the effects too are, perhaps, always the same, or very nearly the same, has no occasion to exert his invention in finding out expedients for removing difficulties which never occur. He naturally loses, therefore, the habit of such exertion, and generally becomes as stupid and ignorant as it is possible for a human creature to become.

And here is Marx (1867: i. 645):

[W]ithin the capitalist system all methods for raising the social productiveness of labour are brought about at the cost of the individual labourer; all means for the development of production transform themselves into means of domination over, and exploitation of, the producers; they mutilate the labourer into a fragment of a man, degrade him to the level of an appendage of a machine, destroy every remnant of charm in his work and turn it into a hated toil; they estrange from him the intellectual potentialities of the labour-process in the same proportion as science is incorporated in it as an independent power; they distort the conditions under which he works, subject him during the labour-process to a despotism the more hateful for its meanness; they transform his life-time into working-time, and drag his wife and child beneath the wheels of the Juggernaut of capital . . . in proportion as capital accumulates, the lot of the labourer, be his payment high or low, must grow worse.

Similarly, the Third World farmer is immiserized no matter how much hta might increase his economic returns. But if control is the measure, it may not be far off the mark to say that the industrialization of agriculture, which has transformed American agriculture into agribusiness and the surviving American farmers into agribusinessmen, has in the Third World transformed peasants into agri-proletarians, just as surely as the first mod-ernization, the modernization of England in the sixteenth century, transformed copyholders into landless labourers.

4. Is the Unsustainability Critique Sustainable?

In the previous section I have taken a different approach from that of more conventional critiques based on unsustainability—be it the unsustainability of dependence on non-renewable resources, particularly energy, the unsustainability of the environmental degradation associated with hta, the unsustainability of a narrow genetic base, or the unsustainability of a process which—according to the critics—destabilizes rural society by enriching the haves and impoverishing the have-nots. This change of emphasis is deliberate: I am less than persuaded that environmental degradation, no matter how deplorable on other (ethical or aesthetic) grounds, is unsustainable, and I find the resource-exhaustion argument to be, at the very least, overdone. Genetic sustainability or unsustainability seems to me a matter about which we have very little knowledge at all, and the evidence on the distributional bias of hta is no more compelling.

Energy, I would argue, is a molehill rather than a mountain. Consider the numbers. In the late 1980s fertilizer use world-wide peaked at almost 150 m. Tonnes in terms of plant nutrients N, P_2O_5, and K_2O (Worldwatch Institute, 1994: Fertiliz. WK 1), about half of which is consumed in the Third World. This required about 6,000 PJ of energy, the equivalent of 1 bn. barrels of oil. This seems like a lot, but like all numbers even a billion is relative. Relative to the energy consumption of the United States, for example, it is a modest number, indeed no more than 8 per cent of the total. That is, the total energy used to produce fertilizer all over the world amounts to about one month's energy utilization in the United States.

Another way to gain perspective on the use of energy in agriculture is to compare the total energy used to grow food with the energy used to process it. The numbers are sobering: in the mid-1970s (the only data I have been able to find), more energy was used to prepare food in the American home than was used to grow food on the American farm, 3,000 PJ as against 2,200 PJ. In total, on-farm energy consumption, both direct (as in fuel consumption of tractors) and indirect (as in fertilizers and pesticides), amounted to less than 20 per cent of the total energy used to grow, process, and prepare food and only about 3 per cent of total US energy use (Lovins et al., 1984: table 2). I count myself among those who believe the wolf of fossil fuel exhaustion is real, but how long we can keep the wolf at bay depends little on how we grow our crops. Rather it is one of how we live our lives—the space we occupy (and heat), the cars we drive, and so on. No change in agricultural practices is going to make a significant change in the energy picture.

A second line of criticism of hta focuses on water, and this line I find much more persuasive than the energy argument. The strategy of hta, particularly in its export form, was to focus on cultivars which performed well under favourable conditions—adequate water, fertilizer, and protection of plants against disease and insects. These conditions involved considerable complementarity, but water has been the *sine qua non* of the Green Revolution. As of the early 1980s more than half the world's wheat and rice was already produced on irrigated land, and the percentages for these staples and other crops are expected to rise in the near future (Alexandratos, 1988: fig. 4.5).

The problems are myriad. Possibilities for river diversion without storage have long since been exhausted, as have the more favourable locations for storage of surface water. Consequently, incremental costs of surface water have risen sharply all over the world (Postel, 1989: 9–10), as has the opposition to large dams and reservoirs from the local people who would be uprooted by them. Ground-water aquifers have been exploited at rates far in excess of recharge, and some, so-called 'fossil' aquifers, receive practically no recharge at all (National Research Council, 1989: tables 2–9; Postel, 1989: table 3). We are not running out of water, but its cost is increasing dramatically. And without assured supplies of water, hta, certainly as it has evolved over the last half-century, is not an economic proposition, at least not outside the temperate zone.

Quite apart from whether or not the resource base is adequate, hta has come in for severe criticism because of its effects on the environment. Water quality is a significant problem: contamination of both ground and surface waters from the residuals of fertilizers and pesticides is perhaps the most worrying aspect (National Research Council, 1989: 98–108), but the discharge of sediment and salts into rivers and other waterways from soil erosion and even just from normal irrigation practice (National Research Council, 1989; Postel, 1989: 15 ff.) is also a cause for alarm.

Irrigation on alkaline desert soils is another source of trouble. Postel (1989: table 2) has estimated that salinization has damaged almost one-quarter of the irrigated land in the five countries of the world with the most irrigated land—India (36 per cent), China (15 per cent), US (27 per cent), Pakistan (20 per cent), and the Soviet Union (12 per cent). In India, along with the damage to 20 m. ha., salinization has led to the abandonment of another 7 m. ha (Postel, 1989: 16).

Hta also stands accused of aiding and abetting soil erosion, masking the deleterious effects on productivity by ever-greater applications of chemical fertilizers. Animal manures, crop rotations, and other soil-building practices are conspicuous by their absence in hta. Even its partisans have on occasion expressed concern. Lester Pfister, a prominent developer of hybrid corn, said this (quoted in Crabb, 1947: 243):

The thing that concerns me most is whether or not we are taking proper care of our soil. In this new hybrid corn, we have one of the most efficient mining machines ever devised by man. This capacity of hybrid corn to mine our soil fertility quickly and convert it into increased amounts of food was a godsend during the great war [World War II], but I wonder now that the war is over whether we will map adequate programs to maintain and improve the condition of our soil.

You know my Grandfather Haas came out here and broke eighty acres of virgin prairie with four oxen and a walking plow. If he had had tractors and power farm equipment and modern hybrid corn, he would have raised a hundred and twenty bushels of corn on every one of those acres. Today [in the mid-1940s] we average about sixty bushels to the acre. How much will we be getting sixty years from now? Our biggest single problem is to maintain our soil fertility. Not only the future of the

Corn Belt, but the very future of America depends on how we meet this problem. One thing we must never forget; there never was land so good that it couldn't be ruined.

This leaves the most serious environmental charge of all: that hta is an accessory to global warming and the greenhouse effect. This is probably a bum rap: it is simply the other side of the coin of the energy-intensiveness of hta and as little persuasive. This is not to take a position one way or the other on global warming, but only to remind ourselves that, since hta does not account for a large part of energy consumption, it is unlikely to be a big part of any energy-related problem.

Genetic vulnerability is more problematic. There was a close call in 1970 in the United States. In that year a devastating attack of leaf blight was traced to the presence in 80 to 90 per cent of the corn seed of a genetic trait bred into the corn along with a particular form of cytoplasmic male sterility ('cmsT'), which had been introduced to facilitate hybridization (Steele, 1978: 37–8). There appears, more recently, to have been a less well-publicized near miss in Indonesia. In 1986 irrigation and pesticides combined with the narrowness of the genetic base of the new rice cultivars to produce a near disastrous epidemic of brown plant-hopper. Year-round irrigation eliminated the fallow season which used to break the plant-hopper's life cycle, and pesticides did more damage to plant-hopper predators and parasites than to the pest itself (Sterba, 1990: A10).

Finally, no summary of the negatives of hta would be complete without at least reference to the voluminous literature on the distributional effects of the Green Revolution. Whereas enthusiasts have always maintained the scale neutrality of Green Revolution agricultural practices, critics have argued that preferential access to credit, technical knowledge, and physical inputs have biased actual results in favour of the larger and richer culti-vators (Pearse, 1980). The enthusiasts have countered with the argument that the Green Revolution increases the demand for labour for all phases of the production cycle from planting to harvest, which works to the advan-tage of the poorest of the agricultural poor, the landless labourers. Each side can and has buttressed its arguments with statistical data, and the results are something of a stand-off.

My own hunch—too impressionistic to justify the label view, except that it agrees with the analysis by Yurijo Hayami and Vernon Ruttan (1985: 341–5)—is that the critics are right about the early stages of particular Green Revolutions, but that the technologies do, for better or worse, trickle down with the passage of time. This means that, where cultivators of different classes cultivate the same crops, as do, say, rice farmers in the Ganges–Brahmaputra delta in Bangladesh, the long-run effects on income distribution are likely to be more favourable than the short-run effects. However, trickle-down logic is limited by crops and geography: little if anything can have trickled down from the wheat farmers of Sonora and Sinaloa to subsistence farmers of other areas of Mexico.

In any case, significantly improving the well-being of farmers may not have been the highest priority. It has already been remarked that in the cradle of the Green Revolution, Mexico, Right and Left may have agreed on little else but an instrumental role for agriculture in accelerating industrialization. Indeed, there is a sense in which increasing agricultural productivity could hardly play any but an instrumental role: this is certainly the logic of a competitive economy. A large number of small producers means that the market holds sway in agriculture to a degree unknown in more centralized, oligopolistic industries. Consequently agricultural innovation can never by itself bring anything but transitory prosperity to the cultivator—unless it is limited by natural considerations or artificial ones. Without these limits, competition will work against the farmer; additional production will only find a market at lower prices. If the innovations are specific to a place, the owners of land will enjoy enhanced rents, imputed or actual. But if the innovations are generalizable and replicable, rents need not rise at all. In either case, returns to labour will settle at their pre-existing level.

This is not to say that nobody benefits. In countries like Mexico, lower food prices will accelerate the process of industrialization, and low food prices translate into low wages. The first beneficiaries will be industrialists, although eventually workers and farmers might benefit too—as consumers, if and when generalized industrialization has raised productivity across the board.

So farmers, like other groups, attempt to bend and limit the market whenever they have the political power to do so, using price supports, subsidies, allotments—the repertoire differs from country to country but the purpose is similar. In Third World terms the problem becomes one of reconciling the need to increase the marketed surplus at low cost (either for export or to feed the cities) with the interest of the producer in high prices, the interest of the landless labourer in steady employment, the interest of the smallholder in social and economic, if not physical, survival—and, last but surely not least—the interest of the agro-industrial complex in expanding markets for seeds, fertilizers, pesticides, and equipment. Since this is something like squaring the circle, it is not surprising that the economist's version of the golden rule holds: he who owns the gold makes the rules.

The best that conventional critics can hope for, I think, is a Scots verdict of 'not proven'—somewhere between guilty and innocent. It may be the case that hta is poisoning the water and (and this is not the same thing), that our land and water resources base is inadequate to sustain further expansion of hta over an extended period. And even though genetic disaster has been avoided so far, this does not mean that the narrowness of the genetic base is no longer an issue. And I may be altogether too sanguine on the energy front; the contribution of hta to fossil-fuel exhaustion may be a greater problem than my calculations indicate. Finally, the effect of the Green Revolution on income distribution and politics may be more pernicious than my trickle-down notions suggest.

For the critics a not proven verdict is a kind of Pascal's wager, more than sufficient grounds for refusing to go further down a path fraught with dangerous uncertainties. But the enthusiasts demand proof: what may be the case may otherwise not be the case. And from their point of view, there are good reasons for leaving well enough alone: 'if it ain't broke, don't fix it'.

In the first place, it will be argued, the critics misunderstand the nature of the process. Hta was not offered as a once-and-for-all technological fix. Scientists knew all along that although problems require solutions, solutions also generate problems. Eternal vigilance is the price not only of liberty, but also of sustainability. Paul Mangelsdorf, corn breeder, Harvard professor, and adviser to the Rockefeller Foundation in the formative years of its agricultural programmes, put it this way in a survey on the evolution of wheat written for the *Scientific American* (Mangelsdorf, 1953: 59): 'the growing of new varieties over large acreages increases the hazards from those diseases to which they are susceptible. The result is a never-ending battle between the wheat breeders and the fungi.' Unstated is Mangelsdorf's confidence, nay certainty, that the wheat breeders will win. When Mangelsdorf's article appeared in 1953, the scientists were clearly in the intellectual saddle. After Three Mile Island, Bhopal, and Chernobyl, not to mention acid rain, ozone depletion, and other problems that scientific engineering has thrown up, the balance is perhaps more even. Perhaps the most frightening analogy is the career of antibiotics. The medical profession proclaimed victory over infectious disease only to find the effectiveness of antibiotics seriously compromised by mutant microbes. Here too, the scientists put their faith in a process rather than a quick fix. 'Man and microbe have been in a footrace', according to one researcher, Richard Wenzel of the University of Iowa, quoted in a recent *Newsweek* cover story (Begley, 1994: 46–51). But confidence in the scientists' ability to keep their lead is waning, even among the scientists themselves. Listen to Dr Wenzel: 'Right now the microorganisms are winning. They're so much older than we are . . . and wiser.'

The scientists' confidence in their ability to stay one step ahead of the problems that their solutions generate must be recognized as no less an assertion of faith than is the critics' conviction that sooner or later the solutions will run out. Both positions rest upon a number of propositions that can be justified by faith alone.

5. *Triumph of Science, Triumph of Capital*

Whence comes the faith of the agricultural scientists? To answer this question, we must go back to the beginning, to the story of hybrid corn. The struggles of a George Shull, an Edward East, and a Donald Jones to apply Mendelian genetics to the practical needs of humankind, while not quite the stuff of Arthurian romance, are legend enough, and like all myths contain at least a grain of truth.

But Triumph of Science is not the whole truth. There is also the truth of Jean-Pierre Berlan and Richard Lewontin (Lewontin and Berlan, 1986; Berlan and Lewontin, 1988), who see the history of hybrid corn as a deliberate attempt by seed companies to insinuate themselves into the production process. An examination of the Berlan–Lewontin thesis puts the triumph of science in perspective. The basis of the Berlan–Lewontin theory is that the offspring of hybrids of open pollinated crops (corn is the most important) are genetically unstable and, unlike their parents, generally fall far short of traditional varieties in yield. Consequently, hybrid seeds must be produced anew in each generation under controlled conditions, which implies an unprecedented role for the seed companies.

As a matter of fact, seed companies like Henry A. Wallace's Pioneer Hi-Bred made a fortune on hybrid corn, and it was the same Henry Wallace who first broached the idea of exporting the seed revolution to Mexico at the inauguration of President Manuel Avila Camacho in 1940. By then Wallace was Secretary of Agriculture and Vice-President Elect. The plot thickens.

Henry A. Wallace was the scion of an Iowa family that had long been prominent in the agricultural community. His grandfather, 'Uncle Henry' Wallace, had founded *Wallace's Farmer* as the voice of agricultural progressivism and served on the prestigious Country Life Commission chaired by Liberty Hyde Bailey. Henry A.'s father, Henry C. Wallace, carried on *Wallace's Farmer* and became Warren Harding's Secretary of Agriculture, serving in that capacity until his death, shortly before Harding's own, in 1924.

And therein hangs a tale. At the request of father Henry C., whose appointment to Agriculture had not yet been announced, Henry A. visited the Department in Washington to evaluate (surreptitiously) the work of C. P. Hartley and his staff. Hartley was Principal Agronomist in charge of Corn Investigations for the Office of Cereal Investigations. Having tried hybridization early on, and concluded 'that it offered no possibilities for corn improvement' (Crabb, 1947: 98) he had turned his attention elsewhere. Young Henry A., who had already become persuaded of the promise of hybridization, was to say the least underwhelmed. He much preferred F. D. Richey to Hartley, for Richey had been carrying out research into hybridization for several years. And in due course, on 16 February 1922 to be exact, Secretary Wallace (père) appointed Richey to succeed Hartley. (Soon after, Hartley's career in the USDA ended badly and sadly: a broken man, Hartley was fired for insubordination in the mid-1920s.)

For the conspiratorially inclined, the sequel is irresistible. Richey and Wallace fils developed a close association. In Crabb's words (1947: 190–1)

That the hub of Richey's program would be in Iowa was a natural development for several reasons. The new Secretary of Agriculture, Henry C. Wallace, was an Iowa man. He had brought about Richey's promotion to the position held by Hartley because he felt that Richey would inject new life into the federal investigations. Furthermore, Professor H. D. Hughes, Iowa State College's respected agronomist [and author of the preface to Crabb's book], had been Richey's teacher at the University of Missouri, something that could be counted on to pave the way for effective co-operation at Ames. In addition, Henry A. Wallace, who had befriended Richey, could be counted to give strong support through his associations at Iowa State College and his connections with *Wallace's Farmer*.

Henry A. Wallace was in fact an innovator in the commercialization of hybrid corn, setting up the Pioneer Hi-Bred Seed Company. And one of the parents of the first Wallace commercial hybrid was supplied by, yes, F. D. Richey of the United States Department of Agriculture.

Nor were researchers unaware of the benefits to the breeder of hybridization over other strategies of improvement. Donald Jones, who is generally credited with realizing the commercial possibilities of successively crossing inbred varieties of corn (hence the name 'double cross'—to which Berlan and Lewontin might attach a more sinister significance), wrote the following in 1919 (East and Jones, 1919: 224; quoted in Becker, 1976: 2):

it is something that may easily be taken up by seedsmen; in fact, it is the first time in agricultural history that a seedsman is enabled to gain the full benefit from a desirable origination of his own or something that he has purchased. The man who originates devices to open our boxes of shoe polish or autograph our camera negatives, is able to patent his products and gain the full reward for his inventiveness. The man who originates a new plant which may be of incalculable benefit to the whole country gets nothing—not even fame—for his pains, and the plants can be propagated by anyone. There is correspondingly less incentive for the production of improved types. The utilization of first generation hybrids enables the originator to keep the parental types and give out only the crossed seeds, which are less valuable for continued propagation.

This is of course from an age before patent protection was even a gleam in the eye of seedsmen and their attorneys, a very different world from our own.

Since 1970 the Plant Variety Protection Act has given US plant-breeders two important privileges (Butler and Marion, 1983; quoted in Knudson and Ruttan, 1988: 55):

'(i) the exclusive right to sell or advertise and to license other persons to sell plants of the registered new variety and/or the reproductive material of those plants; (ii) the right to levy and collect royalties from persons selling or using new varieties registered under the Act'. More recently, these privileges have been extended by international treaty. A principal objective of the United States in the recently concluded Uruguay Round of negotiations to liberalize international trade was to protect so-called intellectual property rights, of which plant breeders' rights are one instance. With the approval of the new version of GATT, an important step has been taken to protect the scientific contributions of seedsmen—while doing nothing to protect the contributions of nameless and countless cultivators whose patient labours have improved indigenous varieties over centuries and even millennia.

There is more to the story. Even before hybrids took over in the corn-belt, the burgeoning seed industry and the Department of Agriculture developed a cosiness that would make the present-day military–industrial complex envious. Crabb innocently reports (1947: 119ff) that in 1918 a USDA experiment station was established on the farms of the Funk Bros. Seed Company.

While in the capital, he [one of the brothers temporarily on loan to the USDA during World War I] was largely responsible for securing a special appropriation from Congress which provided for establishing six more field stations in the corn belt at which corn disease problems were to be studied. The first of these was located on Funk Farms, partially in recognition of Funk's profound interest in the problem (p. 120).

This was the beginning of a symbiotic relationship between private seedsmen and the USDA which allowed seedsmen to capture an important share of the benefits of hybrid corn. James Ransom Holbert, to take one example, moved from Funk Bros. to the USDA experiment station—not physically exhausting since the experiment station was, as we have seen, located on Funk Bros. property. In 1937 the Federal Field Station on Funk Farms was closed, having in Crabb's words (1947: 138) 'accomplished the original purpose for which it was established and much more ... corn diseases ... with the development of high yielding hybrids resistant to disease, were no longer a major problem. Holbert 'returned' to Funk Bros. as Vice President in charge of research!

Lester Pfister is another example of the benefits of close co-operation with government research stations. Having endured his neighbours' ridicule to the point that he attempted to hide his experiments with hybrids, Pfister hit the jackpot when he 'double-crossed' one of his own single crosses with two single crosses supplied by government researcher Holbert. As Crabb tells the story (1947: 243), '[w]hat had in 1934 been the experimental hybrids 'Illinois 360' and 'Illinois 366' became in 1935 Pfister's 360 and 366. The net result was that [Pfister] became the sole possessor of the two greatest hybrids developed up to that time for the central and north central corn belt.' It need hardly be added that Pfister's bank-balance also developed considerably. Presumably his standing among his neighbours did too.

Finally, against the myth of science triumphant is the likely exaggeration of the claims made on behalf of hybrid corn. The distinguished econometrician Zvi Griliches estimated a benefit:cost ratio of 7:1 (Griliches, 1958) by comparing yields on hybrid varieties with unimproved traditional varieties. But, as N. W. Simmonds noted in a survey of plant breeding a decade ago (1983: 12):

The evidence from maize is that excellent progress in economic characters can be made by diverse population improvement methods [references omitted]. But no one has ever had the time and money to push big populations thus for decades. Hybrid maize is successful but it took decades of work on a huge scale to succeed. What would happen if we put a similar effort into population improvement?

Since, as Simmonds points out, the requisite research has never been carried out, the comparison must remain hypothetical, but population improvement seems a more plausible counterfactual than unimproved varieties. Research initiated by C. O. Gardner of the University of Nebraska in the 1950s, for example, suggests that yield improvement of the same order of magnitude as achieved by hybridization is possible with various schemes of recurrent selection. His experiments produced yield increases of 30 to 40 per cent after ten or so generations of selection (Gardner, 1978: 213–22). This is twice the yield increase Griliches imputes to hybridization, and so allows a reasonable margin for the difference between what can be achieved under experimental conditions and what is achievable in farmers' fields.

The comparison may be flawed: Donald Duvick has pointed out to me that '[Gardner's] populations lacked the all-around strong points needed on the farm. In particular they had weak roots and stalks, if my memory is correct.' None the less, Duvick supports the idea that population improvement can produce results comparable with those of hybridization, but firmly denies that the conditions necessary for this strategy were present in the 1920s (personal communication, 1993):

As a byproduct of hybrid corn breeding, George Sprague almost single-handedly invented population improvement for corn. With much assistance from the new science of quantitative genetics he and fellow geneticists devised practical methods of population improvement that allow for progress about as fast as that attained by the inbred–hybrid method. (I have published some experimental results that demonstrate this.) But his work was done under the stimulus of (and with research money brought in by) the success of hybrid corn. It simply could not have been done in the 1920s, and might not have been done at all if hybrid corn-breeding needs had not stimulated the research that led to development of the new population improvement methods.

But this fails to address Simmonds's basic question: 'What would [have] happen[ed] if we [had] put a similar effort into population improvement?' Berlan and Lewontin argue that the reason no such effort was made in the 1920s was not technical, but that hybrid corn was a way for seedsmen to claim a central role in the production process.

So a case can be made for a conspiracy theory, and this case has an obvious appeal to someone like myself, sympathetic to the general proposition that technological innovation responds to the exigencies of control as much as, if not more than, to the exigencies of efficiency, and even more sympathetic to the specific proposition that capitalist production is shaped by the concerns of capitalists to create, and then to maintain, a place for themselves in the production process (Marglin, 1974). But Berlan and Lewontin do not require a conspiracy to make their case; all that is required is that the individual seedsman enjoy sufficient advantage from the barriers to entry by potential competitors (including the farmers themselves) which he puts up by following a strategy of hybridization. No doubt the ilk of Funk and of Wallace understood the positional advantage afforded by a strategy of hybridization as against one of improving open-pollinated varieties.

It is, of course, going too far to argue that hybridization created a role for the commercial seed company where none had existed before—(notwithstanding the exception of Wallace's Pioneer Hi-Bred). Funk Bros., as we have seen, was around long before hybrid corn hit the market, and an improved open-pollinated corn, developed and marketed as Funk's 176A, was by 1920 'on its way to becoming the most outstanding and popular open-pollinated corn ever developed and distributed by the Funk Company' (Crabb, 1947: 119). In more recent times the preferred strategy for improving yields of the chief Green Revolution crops, rice and wheat (which are self-pollinating) has been to synthesize genetically stable varieties, not to rely on unstable hybrids. These varieties nevertheless have a very short life cycle in the field, susceptible as they are to insects and fungi to which land races have acquired immunity. They must therefore be replaced by newly synthesized varieties after a few years, which keeps the seed companies in business. Wheat varieties, for example, may last as little as five years in the field (Myers, 1983: 34).

Even before the introduction of hybrids, C. P. Hartley (the one who lost out to Richey) was urging farmers to specialize in crop production and to leave seeds to the seedsman (Hartley, 1920: 5):

Well-conducted corn breeding requires special methods that farmers generally do not have time to apply. If there is in your locality a corn breeder who demonstrates each year the superiority of his corn, you can afford to pay him well for his superior seed. Five dollars a bushel [hybrid corn hit the market a few years later at eight dollars] should prove a profitable price for both parties under ordinary conditions. Such corn breeders are improving various kinds of corn, just as cattle breeders are improving various breeds of live stock by breeding from the most profitable individuals.

The general farmer is a producer rather than a breeder of corn. He profits by the careful work of the corn breeder by adopting the higher yielding strains for his general crop. However, he must remember that all the corn grown from the bushel of purchased seed is not necessarily as good for seed as was the original bushel. Some of it may be better, but much of it is likely to be poorer. Corn is constantly producing variations and mutations, and can be improved thereby or allowed to 'run out.'

Moreover, hybridization facilitated, but did not necessitate, the division of labour between seedsman and farmer. Crabb exaggerated when he wrote (1947: 267) that 'the methods of producing and processing seed corn had been completely revolutionized, converted from a job that almost any careful farmer could do with little special machinery, into a high-precision business which required both knowledge and equipment beyond the means of the farmer who selected seed corn'. For he himself had just described the attempts in Wisconsin to adapt the technology of hybrid seed production to the small farmer (pp. 206 ff.). In Wisconsin, perhaps as an indirect legacy of the Progressive tradition, the hybridizers (Crabb, 1947: 107; see also Kloppenburg, 1988: 106 and references) 'worked out the administrative procedures and even devised and invented special machines which would make it possible for the individual farmer to produce seed for hybrid corn of high quality as a small-farm operation'.

As Kloppenburg emphasizes, technology was not determining. Seed production was, to borrow a phrase Richard Edwards (1979) has used in a different context, a 'contested terrain'. Much more important than the technology itself were the policies pursued by the USDA in diffusing the technology. These policies, in practice if not in theory, favoured the seed companies in terms of providing access to the fruits of publicly sponsored research.

But even so the practice was less sinister than attention to the balance-sheet of a Wallace or a Pfister makes it appear. Indeed, according to Donald Duvick, who, after a long career in plant breeding, retired in 1990 from Wallace's Pioneer Hi-Bred as Senior Vice President in charge of research, says 'the story that is still told in Pioneer had more than a little truth to it regarding all the early hybrid corn breeders. The story is that H. A. Wallace founded his company in order to make enough money to support his passion for corn breeding' (personal communication, December 31, 1993). Until the mid-1930s hybrid corn was far from being a practical success. In 1935 less than 0.5 per cent (1 out of 200 acres) of US corn acreage was planted to hybrid corn (Kloppenburg, 1988: table 5.1). And the enthusiasts of Henry A. Wallace's Department of Agriculture were able to claim no more than a 10 per cent yield advantage for hybrid over open-pollinated varieties on the basis of the margin of what it normally takes to convince farmers to innovate, especially where the incremental cost of hybrid seed was high relative to the potential yield improvement. A 10 per cent improvement would return the Iowa farmer something like 3 to 4 bushels per acre, which at $0.66 per bushel (the US season average for 1935) (Kloppenburg, 1988: table 5.1—I have not been able to obtain an Iowa-specific figure) would mean a return of $2.00 to $2.50. But at $9.25 per bushel (the 1937 Iowa price—1937 is the first year for which figures exist: United States Department of Agriculture, 1963: 100) and at a seeding rate of 6 to 7 lb. per acre (Berlan and Lewontin, 1988: 30), the cost of hybrid seed would have come to $1.00 per acre. (This expense would be offset somewhat by the saving of open-pollinated seed, but unless seed was purchased commercially, this saving would not be of much account.) So the gain would be of the order of $1.00 to $1.50—if the experiment succeeded. For a farmer whose returns (at $0.66 the bushel) would have fallen in the range of $20 to $25 per acre, this worked out at little more than a 5 per cent increase in income. In subsequent years the yield advantage of hybrids improved, and the economics changed. But this is to get ahead of the story.

In short, as late as the mid-1930s the commercialization of hybrid corn must have looked much more distant than it proved to be. In this context researchers and enthusiasts on the two sides of the public–private fence very probably did see themselves as engaged in a common endeavour, for which the free flow of information both ways was essential and for which no apology was necessary. Lester Pfister, for example, was not only a beneficiary of publicly funded research, he was also a benefactor (Crabb, 1947: 236–7). In 1932 Pfister provided F. D. Richey with one of the inbreds he had developed on his own, and this was quickly released to experiment stations and then to farmers.

Things changed as the practical potential of hybrid corn began to be realized. (Pfister, perhaps, was an unwitting and even unwilling benefactor. Donald Duvick recounts a story he heard during his many years as a plant breeder and senior officer of Pioneer, 'that Pfister did not intend that Richey would distribute his prize inbred, but Richey either did not understand that, or disregarded what he heard,' personal communication, 1993). The drought that made 'dustbowl' a word of common language served as a spur to the diffusion of hybrid corn: the yield differential in the Iowa Corn Test for the disastrous year of 1934 was more than 15 per cent. By 1940 15 per cent of US corn acreage was planted to hybrids and five years later over half. In anticipation the dollar value of hybridization eclipsed its intellectual value so that in 1936 Merle Jenkins, Principal Agronomist in the division of the USDA charged with responsibility for corn research, could complain (1936: 479)

information is available on so few of the lines developed by private breeders that they have not been included [in a listing of principal hybrid lines]. Among the private corn breeders and producers of hybrid corn, a tendency seems to be developing to regard the information they have on their lines and the pedigrees of their hybrids as trade secrets which they are reluctant to divulge. This has interfered with obtaining complete information at the present time. It would seem to be an extremely short-sighted policy, and one that probably will have to be modified in the future when the purchaser of hybrid seed corn demands full information on the nature of the seed he is buying.

Jenkins had the disease right but not the cure. As has been observed, patent protection for genetic engineering was not yet a gleam in the eye of the most imaginative entrepreneurs or lawyers.

In a way I wish I could tell a different story. It would simplify my problem as a critic both of hta and of the critics of hta if hybrid corn could be written off as the attempt of entrepreneurs like Henry Wallace to insinuate themselves into the production process. But, although history may be a construction, it is not a free construction. The facts do constrain, and the facts do not support the Berlan–Lewontin thesis. Without buying the triumph of science story lock, stock, and barrel, one cannot read the history of hybrid corn without allowing a considerable role for science. Indeed the prestige of science gave an incalculable boost to the strategy of hybridization. For it made the plant breeder, a tinkerer operating on largely hit-or-miss lines, into a geneticist. Prestige guided research along scientific lines—as against the more empirical approach of population improvement along the lines of recurrent selection.

Never mind that in practice hybridization was also largely a hit-or-miss affair: as scientists, Shull and his followers could claim the mantle of Mendel and this added considerably to the status of a field at or near the bottom of the pecking-order (Kimmelman, 1987: chs. 1, 7). In some cases the transformation was almost instantaneous. In the years before 1912 Ernest Brown Babcock of the agricultural college of the University of California had taught courses in agricultural education, plant pathology, and had just begun to offer a course in plant breeding in the division of horticulture—despite his lack of systematic training in this last field. By 1914, as chairman of the new division of genetics, Babcock was well launched on the path of academic entrepreneurship that would occupy the rest of his career at Berkeley (Kimmelman, 1987: 308–38). He could even complain that his managerial duties were preventing him from carrying out 'research in genetics, which is the work I am supposed to be doing' (quoted in Kimmelman, 1987: 353–4). It is in this light, I think, that one ought to read the remarks by Donald Jones about appropriability quoted earlier in this section—as a matter of appropriating recognition, status, and prestige, not as a matter of material gain.

Moreover, genetics was a science for the times: it fit the interventionist, manipulationist temper of the early twentieth century, fresh from the conquests of the steam engine, electricity, telegraph and telephone, and, most recently, the internal combustion engine. A science that offered such vast vistas of improvement could easily become a transcendent cause worthy of dedication and sacrifice (Kimmelman, 1987: 377).

How easily, therefore, the model of research, if not precisely the techniques of hybridization, could be exported to Mexico and thence to Asia. Though other factors are important, the cloak of science was crucial. Science was the one true god worshipped universally at the altar of modernity. People of all shades of economic opinion—from capitalist to communist—worshipped there. All kinds of politics—from populist to plutocrat—were represented too. And colour was no bar either—black, brown, and beige could be found at the altar of science.

6. *The Globalization of hta: Attractive Promises to Hungry People*

In this perspective it is easy to see how the Green Revolution could have been imagined to be a neutral, scientific, non-political endeavour. Nobody took offence when it was said: 'Agriculture is nothing more than the application of the principles of biology and other natural sciences to the art of growing food' (Rockefeller Foundation Archives, Advisory Committee to the Rockefeller Foundation, 21 June 1951; quoted in Anderson *et al.*, 1991: 32). Well, almost nobody: there were, as we shall see in the next section, a few ant-collectors who objected to disturbing the ant-hills. But on the whole science and progress were doubly useful banners, on the one hand for enlisting the co-operation of Third World governments and élites; on the other for justifying global intervention to an America reluctant to take on the obligations of empire.

As the Cold War fades into memory there is a temptation to minimize the Cold War imperative. It would be a mistake to yield to this temptation: it must be remembered that the Green Revolution was formulated in the context of an imperial conflict. Food was seen as an essential weapon in the struggle for the hearts and minds (not to mention markets and resources) of the Third World. This indeed was a recurrent theme in the justification for intervening. A typical statement of the Cold War imperative was a 1951 document circulated by E. C. Stakman, Richard Bradfield, and Mangelsdorf within the Rockefeller Foundation, just a decade after the same team had, following a summer's investigation in the field, written the guidelines of the Rockefeller programme in Mexico (quoted in Oasa and Jennings, 1982: 39): 'Hungry people are lured by promises; but they can be won by deeds. Communism makes attractive promises to underfed people; democracy must not only promise as much but must deliver more.'

Under such circumstances, criticism of hta bordered on the unpatriotic.

Despite the rhetoric of science, the Rockefeller leadership recognized a political quagmire when they saw one. As the Mexican Agricultural Program's research began to bear fruit, the Foundation was advised to disengage. Two years before the Advisory Committee was defining agriculture as the application of biology and other natural sciences, John Sloan Dickey, President of Dartmouth College and Trustee of the Foundation, concluded after a visit to Mexico that Rockefeller should withdraw before the political fallout of 'some fairly difficult political, social, and economic decisions' tainted the Foundation. 'I am', Dickey went on to say (Rockefeller Foundation Archives, Dickey to Weaver, 20 October 1949, 1.1/323/3/19 p. 3),

perfectly sure that within three to five years the program will raise some very acute problems with respect to the political control of these benefits. Moreover, if these benefits hold the promise which they seem to hold and if the present land-use policies of the Mexican Government are continued, these very benefits may introduce fresh economic disparities within the Mexican economy, particularly the agricultural economy, which will present political problems not now even dimly perceived by many Mexicans . . . If I am probably right on this, here is a very affirmative reason for positive plans to be made now for the orderly termination of this program within the foreseeable future.

Such a strategy, Dickey recognized, would pose administrative problems: the project had accumulated an important 'asset' in its 'personnel and wisdom', an asset that might desert a ship about to be deliberately scuttled. Dickey's preferred solution was another such programme, preferably in Latin America (in order to capitalize on acquired skill in navigating the Spanish language and Latin culture), or failing that, to use 'many of these people in other areas of the world assuming a generally similar agricultural programme would be a desirable undertaking in these other areas'. Global hta was an idea whose time had surely come, even though a decade would elapse before the gleam in Dickey's eye was born as the International Rice Research Institute, a joint undertaking of the Rockefeller and Ford Foundations.

7. Sauer Grapeshot: A Prescient Critique of the Green Revolution

All this leaves two questions unanswered. First, is this critique anachronistic? Are we operating on the basis of 20–20 hindsight? Second, is there in fact an alternative to hta? This section will address the first question, and subsequent sections the second one.

Few indeed were the voices that questioned hta as a strategy for Mexico or later for Asia. But there were individuals who warned against the export of hta, even in the councils of the Rockefeller Foundation. One such voice was Carl Sauer's. Sauer—chair of the Geography Department at UC-Berkeley, past president of the Association of American Geographers, winner of the Charles P. Daly Medal of the American Geographical Society, and member of the selection committee for Guggenheim Fellowships—was consulted by the Rockefeller Foundation almost immediately after Henry A. Wallace, by this time Vice President, proposed that the Foundation become involved in Mexican agriculture. Writing from Mexico where he was on sabbatical leave, Sauer cautioned Joseph Willits, the head of the Social Sciences Division (Rockefeller Foundation Archives, Sauer to Willits, before 4 February 1941, 1.2/323/10/63, p. 2):

A grand job to be done or to be messed up beyond making good. The first step would be in economic geography: . . . Identify the occurrence and usage of every domesticated plant form together with its utility in the kitchen and in agricultural practice (soil, climate, seasonal labor in planting and harvest, tolerance of extreme weather, of pests). Secondly, make sure that every genetically fixed form is preserved and grown in adequate quantity for experimental purposes. Thirdly, set up breeding centers for the development of better strains. Remember that the gene range of maize, beans, etc., is enormously beyond that available to the American plant breeder, that an individual 'plant' like 'maize' has much more varied uses than in our commercial agriculture, that a large stock of native species is present which do not exist in the U.S., that a large number of old world Mediterranean plants are established. The possibilities of improvement by selection are enormous, but such selection should proceed from the local materials. A good aggressive bunch of American agronomists and plant breeders could ruin the native resources for good and all by pushing their American commercial stocks. The little agricultural work that has been done by experiment station people here has been making that very mistake, by introducing U.S. forms instead of working on the selection of ecologically adjusted native items. The possibilities of disastrous destruction of local genes are great unless the right people take hold of such work. And Mexican agriculture cannot be pointed toward standardization on a few commercial types without upsetting native economy and culture hopelessly. The example of Iowa is about the most dangerous of all for Mexico. Unless the Americans understand that, they'd better keep out of this country entirely. This thing must be approached from an appreciation of the native economies as being basically sound.

Returning from Mexico in January, Wallace had broached the idea of a Rockefeller Foundation programme in health, nutrition, and agriculture with Willits. Willits, who had known Sauer since at least 1934, when the two of them worked together on a committee of the Social Sciences Research Council (West, 1979: 97n.), turned to him for an appraisal of the Wallace proposal. Presumably Willits knew what to expect from Sauer and was not surprised by the letter which has been quoted at length just above. Whether for Sauer's reasons or for other reasons of his own to which we are not privy, Willits was sceptical, perhaps the only sceptic in a hive of enthusiasts. At a staff meeting called on 18 February to consider Wallace's ideas for a Mexican programme, Willits—following an intervention in favour of a technological fix involving both plant breeding and 'demonstration of existing knowledge'—sounded a cautious note. According to the minutes of the meeting, 'JHW. Makes one suggestion: hopes that before RF goes overboard too far it obtain formally invited criticism of Carl Sauer. Is in entire sympathy with importance of focussing on agriculture' (Rockefeller Foundation Archives, Staff Meeting Minutes, 18 February 1941, 1.2/323/10/63, p. 3).

It is not recorded whether the Foundation officially acted on Willits's advice, but a Rockefeller delegation visiting Mexico the next month did seek out Sauer's views on the agricultural programme, and Sauer again wrote at length to Willits (Rockefeller Foundation Archives, Sauer to Willits, 12 March 1941, 1.2/323/10/63, pp. 1–2). Sauer began by characterizing the Wallace proposal as political:

I do have something approximating the conviction that Mr. Wallace and the USDA (and his successor is still his lieutenant) should swing their own plans. Under Mr. Wallace's administration the USDA has developed an aggressive political philosophy with regard to agriculture. It now looks like an extension of that philosophy of the good life to our Latin neighbors. An agrarian philosophy in the USDA did not have its origin with Henry Wallace, but in the last years the bright young men of the Department have been mobilized and trained into an elite corps, as never before. I think they now admit that they know the kind of society they want and how to go about it. I like a fair share of their program, but I think it is necessary to be quite clear that the USDA is primarily a political organization today.

It seems that the USDA is taking steps for a penetration of L. A. There are already the agricultural attaches and now there are individuals and commissions to study the agricultural problems of individual countries. These persons seem to be selected as missionaries, not because of experience or detached interest in such lands. Politically, such moves may be sound. What I do not see is that this aegis is likely to provide the means of inquiry into other modes of life except insofar as we can influence them to our national advantage. This may be a worthy, or even necessary objective, but it lies in the field of politics, not in that of research.

If the Department [of Agriculture] now wishes to survey the whole of New World agriculture it can, especially in terms of world emergency, easily throw funds . . . into a Pan-American program. Let it do so if it wishes, rather than a foundation.

This said, Sauer once again states his own views clearly and forcefully:

Nor am I anxious to see the process of Americanization of the New World accelerated. It is going too fast to suit me as it is. Here in Mexico, I am appalled by the progress of the automobile, radio, and movie. Those whose credit is sufficient are in hock to the automobile dealers. Whoever can dig up ten pesos delivers himself into the hands of a radio merchant. Purchasing power needed for food is going into movie going. The United States are the mode now, as France was before the Revolution . . . We are looked up to as doing everything so much better that even our agriculture may be imitated excessively, if a sharp official drive gets under way. I've said before that I fear the irreparable loss of native crop forms by a rapid Americanization. American tools and methods may do a great deal of harm to soils by a too hasty introduction. (Witness what we have done to Porto Rico!? Perhaps the native stubbornness is a sufficient safe-guard, but our agriculture is geared to a level of production that either involves a great using up of soil fertility or the inversion of sums in amelioration (fertilizer bills, engineering works) beyond—far beyond the capacity of most of these lands. The simplest of our conservative solutions—that of an animal husbandry—encounters an entirely new set of problems in most of these countries. They must build on the preservation and rationalization of their own experience with slow and careful additions from the outside. Only the exceptional American agricultural scientist will see that there are these hazards of cultural destruction. He will be under the pressure of quick results. He will hardly have the life-time of learning that native practices represent real solutions of local problems, partly because he comes as an alien to a strange situation.

Willits must have been sympathetic: under his patronage the Rockefeller Foundation continued to support Sauer's expeditions to Latin America, beginning with a lengthy tour of the western rim of South America (Chile, Bolivia, Peru, Ecuador and Colombia) just as America entered World War II. Sauer's views of modernization were not softened by this trip. A sample will convey the flavour (Rockefeller Foundation Archives, Sauer to Willits, 22 February 1942, 1.1/200S/391/4631). On agriculture:

Our major stop [in the south of Chile] was in Chiloe, a sort of New World Hebrides. We managed to catch the two sunny days of the year and for the rest experienced the drenching rains of this part of the world. The Chilote is quite a different animal from the Chileno, a mestizo of different Indian background and different colonial history. It takes a steamer all day to get out to the island. Once there you can travel across the island on a 60 cm railroad, or else by little sail boats along the coast. We got down as far as Castro, or pretty close to the absolute southern limit of agriculture. Chiloe and the Chilote would be a swell subject of study—a microcosm of insular isolation. This is the supposed home of our Irish potatoes of the whole northern hemisphere and (in part) of the modern strawberry. Bewildering variety of potatoes here now, as also on adjacent mainland, and the big strawberries grow on the inner edge of the beaches. Horses and cattle are dwarfed, unless fresh blood introduced from mainland. The sea feeds all domestic life. Pigs and chickens work over the tide flats; seaweed the most important fertilizer, and some of it important food, green and cooked. Nothing being done about the native elements of culture. Quite well run agricultural school and experiment station (federal) at Anoud, which as Jonathan [Sauer's son, assistant, and travelling companion, then a graduate student in geography at the University of Wisconsin; now emeritus professor of geography at UCLA] said, might just as well have been in northern Wisconsin. With a large range of domestic potatoes (and they are good and thrive well) they have been laboring with Canadian seed potatoes. I wish to report with satisfaction that the Canadian potatoes are a flop. That, I fear, is the normal agricultural mind. Here you are in the ancestral home of all non-Andean potatoes, with an unknown wealth of genes, and the first thing they do is to try to introduce plants from the big commercial regions and to destroy what they have of their own. And that not because of any inadequacy of their own plant materials. The littler agricultural group imitates the bigger one. I fear that if you get enough Cornell and California trained agriculturists down here in South America, you will wipe out the thousands of years of plant breeding. The Chilote fortunately in contrast to the Chileno is culturally resistant (syn. unprogressive). (My Methodist church maintains a 'good' agricultural school and introduction center in the southern part of the Valley of Chile, and is a bodily transfer of the U.S. They even issue an elaborate catalogue with everything in it from Golden Delicious apples to Reid's Yellow Dent Corn.) Nor will I accept the answer that it is a question of survival of the fittest: the virtues of the poor little Chilean corns don't even get a hearing (I hope the agriculturist who sold us Americans on the Elberta peach rests uneasily.) But enough of diatribe.

On academia, this from Bolivia (Rockefeller Foundation Archives, Sauer to Willits, 15 March 1942, 1.1/200S/391/4633):

Were we doing this trip over, I should certainly provide for a stay at Sucre. I had hoped to get there from here [La Paz], but was misled by Bolivian official statements as to roads . . . At Sucre the old University of Chuquisaca, with strong clerical influence, but strong in historical and sociological studies. A center of sociologic studies being developed there is worth looking into. Here are the national archives, the national library, and the religious capital (seat of archbishop). I regret it very much, but we shall not see what I suspect is intellectually the most interesting place in this country.

Of the University of La Paz I have little to report. Its Rector, Ormachea Zalles is apparently a high-powered administrator and somewhat of a financial genius; he has increased the revenue of the university in six years from 240,000 bolivianos to sixteen million. They are now building a main sixteen-story building (in a city quite uncrowded for space) which will be for many years the tallest building in Bolivia. Still a young man, he drew the design for the present university when he was Minister of Finance. He also has drawn up an educational program for Bolivia from the first grade to the doctorate. He is also the principal social scientist, and calls himself a mathematical economist. Speaks English fairly well, and could soon pass in the U.S. as a successful dean or college president; affable go-getter with un-doubted business competence . . . Ormachea says, with a broad smile, that it is not now and will not be for a while, proper for the university to concern itself with research; that it has a curriculum to establish for training the young generation, and that this curriculum must be professional . . . [T]he conversation then tends to shift to a talk about what text books cover a certain course best. The atmosphere would be quite familiar in many an American school of commerce or even college of letters and science. And I think I've got the atmosphere straight; the skyscraper is a proper symbol of what is in the making. It was after seeing this southern version of the U. of——gh that I felt most regretful about not seeing Chuquisaca–Sucre. Another reporter might have had the opposite reaction.

Two questions beg for answers. First, why was Sauer so different from the others? That he was a geographer, and a historical geographer at that, may have contributed to the difference in perspectives. How many plant breeders (excuse me, geneticists) read the work of the Soviet botanist Nikolai Vavilov on centres of crop origins, a topic to which Sauer returned many times from the 1930s onward? (On Vavilov, see Ch. 9, below). Not many, I would guess. And even fewer would appreciate the significance for the hta strategy. But I doubt that this is the whole story. I should be surprised indeed if there were not geographers by the score willing and able to sing the hta tune.

More important, why was Sauer, so perceptive in observation and so cogent in argument, nevertheless so ineffective in shaping policy? In part, I think, because his arguments were wrongly construed as favouring an unchanging tradition over modernization. Read this way, Sauer's arguments are contradictory and even self-destructive. In Sauer's first evaluation of Wallace's proposal (Rockefeller Foundation Archives, Sauer to Willits, 5 February 1941, 1.2/323/10/63), he stressed that the problems of Mexico were economic and political rather than cultural. Mexicans are poor and oppressed, not lazy and ignorant. Poor public health and nutrition as well as poor agriculture are the consequence of this poverty and oppression, not the result of stupidity or misinformation. Here is Sauer on public health and nutrition.

1. *Public health*. Of course things are bad here by American standards but . . . [t]he chief obstacle is economic and political . . . What they need is socialized medicine, but the finances of the government will not permit it. The first people paid are the military, who constitute the gendarmerie that keeps the country in order and the government in power. Pay the generals and their staffs first.

Emphasize poverty rather than ignorance.

The major problem is economic. Find the funds for public hygiene and the Mexicans will make good use of them. Beware the attitude that if we instruct them, they will learn from us.

2. *Nutrition*. Same line of argument . . . They get an amazing lot for what they spend and dietary deficiencies are economic, not cultural . . . [D]on't get the idea that they would eat better if they had nutrition experts to advise them. I've had a good deal of interest in the Mexican kitchen and if there is any other country in which sound nutrition is better practiced as far as the pocketbook permits, I don't know it.

But if the problems are essentially economic, if modernization equals economic development, and if tradition is opposed to modernization—then tradition itself becomes the problem. Development becomes the only way to alleviate the poverty that stands in the way of health and nutrition.

Moreover, the motives of people like Sauer could be questioned. In the late 1940s, Edgar Anderson, a botanist at the Missouri Botanical Gardens in St Louis, 'one of the nation's foremost authorities on maize' (West, 1979: 18), and a close friend and collaborator of Sauer, made negative comments about the Mexican Agricultural Program to Warren Weaver, head of the Natural Sciences Division of the Rockefeller Foundation. Weaver was alarmed enough to ask Paul Mangelsdorf what if anything there was to Anderson's remarks. Mangelsdorf responded (Rockefeller Foundation Archives, Mangelsdorf to Weaver, 26 July 1949, 1.1/323/3/18):

I think I can find out what Anderson means when he refers to our Mexican agricultural work as 'not clicking very well'. Anderson and I were graduate students together, and we were in fact roommates for one year. I am in frequent correspondence with him and when I next write him, I propose to ask him quite casually exactly what he meant when he made such a statement. I think he will probably give me an answer.

Without consulting him I can say that Anderson, taking his cue from Carl Sauer, has been opposed to the Mexican agricultural program from the beginning. His argument is somewhat as follows: If the program does not succeed, it will not only have represented a colossal waste of money, but will probably have done the Mexicans more harm than good. If it does 'succeed,' it will mean the disappearance of many Mexican varieties of corn and other crops and perhaps the destruction of many picturesque folk ways, which are of great interest to the anthropologist. In other words, to both Anderson and Sauer, Mexico is a kind of glorified ant hill which they are in the process of studying. They resent any effort to 'improve' the ants. They much prefer to study them as they now are.

This is a caricature rather than a characterization of Sauer's position. As if in anticipation of Mangelsdorf's misunderstanding, Sauer had some years earlier stated a very different point of view. Writing to Willits in early 1945 from Oaxaca, Sauer ranged from the superiority of the *milpa* (small plots intensively cultivated by hand, in which corn, squash, and beans are grown at the same time) over the ploughed field in terms of both yield and resistance to erosion ('The fact is almost unknown to science'), through the destructive social effects of sugar-cane cultivation ('Sugar is a malignant thing as I know cane growing . . . It disturbs or destroys community life . . . The labor demands are very uneven and bring in hordes of workers. These live under appalling conditions though their earnings may be high; and they do not feel themselves members of a permanent community.'), to the role of squash as food and markers of centres of cultural diffusion, and the plight of the Native Americans ('They need to be encouraged that their ways are good and they need protection against exploitation'). Near the end of this letter (Rockefeller Foundation Archives, Sauer to Willits, 12 February 1945, 1.1/200/391/4636), Sauer wrote:

I am not interested in the Indians as museum pieces and I am also interested in non-Indian populations that have cultural values of their own as apart from the standard-izing tendencies which are flowing out from the urban centers to strip the country of its goods and ablest men and pauperize it culturally as well as often economically.

The choice was not necessarily between stagnant tradition and unreflective modernization. There was a third way, as Sauer had already indicated in 1941: 'They must build on the preservation and rationalization of their own experience with slow and careful additions from the outside' (Rockefeller Foundation Archives, Sauer to Willits, 12 March 1941, 1.2/323/10/63). Tradition, as Sauer understood better than Mangelsdorf, need not be something fixed and unchanging. Tradition can be, invariably is, actively constructed and dynamic—except when people have their backs to the wall and become frozen in archaic patterns. The issue for Sauer was the preser-vation of a space for a relatively autonomous transformation of indigenous cultures, not the preservation of cultures as static systems. A half century later, we face the same issue.

II. ALTERNATIVE AGRICULTURE

1. The Economic Impetus behind the Search for Alternatives

Is there an alternative? Is there a technology which will provide adequate food for the planet without risk to the resource base, to the environment, to genetic diversity, and—hardly least—without risk to the diversity of ways of coping, knowing, and experiencing the world which are encoded in the multiplicity of cultures human beings have formed? In the context of this question, the appearance of the National Research Council's book *Alternative Agriculture* in 1989 was a noteworthy event. *Alternative Agriculture* made a strong case for substituting human labour and intelligence and mechanical energy for pesticides, chemical fertilizers, and other purchased inputs. The arguments themselves were not novel: the American farmer had been in trouble for some time, and the high costs of hta had made the search for alternatives economically respectable.

A few figures tell why. (The figures in this and the next paragraph are taken from the *Economic Report of the President*, 1991, Tables B-95 to B-97.) Although gross farm income in current dollars rose six-fold between 1947 and 1989, net income increased only three times—because production costs rose by a factor of nine during the same period. Agribusiness is less and less agri and more and more business: the value of food and fibre is made up increasingly of inputs produced off the farm rather than in the field. To add insult to injury, by the middle of the 1980s, from one-fifth to one-half of net farm income has consisted of government payments.

Agricultural chemicals are a large part of the story of rising costs. Cheap energy and abundant production capacity (a legacy of the munitions industry developed during World War II) led to hugely expanded output at low and stable prices during the immediate post-war period and into the 1950s; and fertilizer prices actually fell during the 1960s. The result was that while agricultural output increased by 50 per cent between 1947 and 1972, the utilization of chemicals increased by 400 per cent. In the 1970s, as prices rose in line with energy costs, the use of chemicals levelled off, and in the 1980s, for the first time since the war, utilization actually declined. Taking the period since the first oil shock as a whole, the application of chemicals has more or less kept pace with output, in sharp contrast with the rapid expansion in the quarter century between World War II and the end of the First American Empire.

The direction and pace of change in the Third World has been similar. Off-farm inputs (feed, seed, fertilizer, pesticides, fuel and other agricultural mechanization operating costs, and irrigation operating costs), a category that hardly existed in 1947, was equal to 25 per cent of the value of output in 1982-4 (as compared with 50 per cent in the First World: Alexandratos,

1988: 134 and table 4.5). By the end of the 1980s, nitrogenous fertilizer use in the Third World accounted for approximately half the world total (FAO, 1989: table 2). As in the metropolis, the growth rate has slowed down considerably in recent years: as against 12.4 per cent in the period 1961–75, the annual rate of growth of fertilizer use between 1975 and 1985 was 'only' 7.1 per cent, and the FAO projects a further fall to 4.6 per cent over the rest of the century (Alexandratos, 1988: table 4.6).

Nothing in the foregoing will astonish anybody who has followed agriculture even to the extent of the reporting in the New York Times. The surprising thing about *Alternative Agriculture* is not the message but the medium: it was published not by the Rodale Institute or the New Alchemy Institute, but by the National Research Council, whose Governing Board, we are informed by a notice at the beginning of the book, is 'drawn from the councils of the National Academy of Sciences, the National Academy of Engineering, and the Institute of Medicine' (National Research Council, 1989: ii). As if more evidence of the respectability of the book were needed, the notice intones that 'the project that is the subject of this report was approved by the Governing Board' and that 'The members of the committee responsible for the report were chosen for their special competences and with regard for appropriate balance.' Indeed: the Chairman of the Board on Agriculture which appointed the committee responsible for *Alternative Agriculture* was William L. Brown of Pioneer Hi-Bred International. Take that, Union Carbide!

Alternative agriculture has emerged from the interstices and margins of the cranks into the bright light of the establishment. But the establishment refuses to modify its profit-oriented optic; the justification of alternatives is not a new land ethic, not the substitution proposed by Wendell Berry (1977) of nurturance for exploitation. It is not feminine or ecological, certainly not eco-feminist. A recurrent theme in *Alternative Agriculture* is that the innovators are solid, bottom-line oriented folks, not kooks. For instance (National Research Council, 1989: 263):

The Spray brothers did not stop using chemical herbicides because they were worried about the health and environmental risks associated with pesticide use. They stopped because herbicides were altering weed populations in such a way that weeds that had never been seen before were becoming problems.

Very possibly this exaggerates the profit orientation of the Sprays and their ilk. The innovators may have initially been attracted to alternatives because of their need to stem the haemorrhage of outlays on pesticides and fertilizers. But once involved with alternatives, I dare say that farmers found satisfaction and meaning in connecting to the land in ways that chemical agriculture had made more difficult. The case-studies that *Alternative Agriculture* summarizes make it abundantly clear that the real change brought about by alternatives is the substitution of the farmer's immediate skill and knowledge for the skill and knowledge bound up in the fertilizers and pesticides that characterize hta. This could hardly leave the farmer's relation to the land unchanged, however reluctant he might be to admit that he had changed religions.

It will not have escaped notice that *Alternative Agriculture* is situated in the United States, where land is in relatively abundant supply and capital is relatively cheap. Rotations of corn, beans, and oats, for instance, make sense where land is relatively abundant, and the substitution of mechanical tillage for chemical control of weeds makes sense where capital is relatively cheap.

It is much less clear that alternative(s) exist which meet the requirements of the Third World, namely, suitability where land is scarce and capital expensive. North America may do just fine with lo-tech alternatives to hta, but this may have little relevance for India or Indonesia. It would do no service to pretend that for most of the planet we can now give a positive answer to the question posed at the beginning of this section: the truth is that even the rudiments of an alternative strategy for feeding the people of the Third World are lacking. On the other hand, prudent readers will respond to the questions raised in Part I of this chapter with their own doubts about the wisdom of putting all our eggs in the hta basket.

2. The Question of Alternative Agriculture: Whose Head Will the Farmer Use?

In any case, the lesson that I draw from *Alternative Agriculture* is not the details of this practice or that, but the substitution of the farmer's wisdom, rooted in the experience of working the land, for the knowledge of plant breeder, chemist, or engineer, rooted in the laboratory or the experimental plot. And this lesson knows no boundary—political, economic, or climatological. We can certainly put questions about the feasibility of integrating farmers' and experts' ways of approaching agriculture, without limiting ourselves to one part of the world.

Indeed, the importance of traditional knowledge has been increasingly recognized since the 1980s. Wendell Berry set out the theme (1984: 25, 28):

The industrial version of agriculture has it that farming brings the farmer annually, over and over again, to the same series of problems, to each one of which there is always the same generalized solution, and, therefore, that industry's solution can be simply and safely substituted for his solution. But that is false. On a good farm, because of weather and other so-called variables, neither the annual series of problems nor any of the problems individually is ever quite the same two years running. The good farmer (like the artist, the quarterback, the statesman) must be master of many possible solutions, one of which he must choose under pressure and apply with skill in the right place at the right time. This solving requires knowledge, skill, intelligence, experience, and imagination of an order eminently respectable. It seems probable (in farming as in art) that such a mind will work best which is informed by a live tradition.

The good farmer's mind, as I understand it, is in a certain critical sense beyond the reach of textbooks and expert advice. Textbooks and expert advice, that is, can be useful to this mind, but only by means of a translation—difficult but possible, which only this mind can make—from the abstract to the particular. This translation cannot be made by the expert without a condescension and oversimplification that demean and finally destroy both the two minds and the two kinds of work that are involved. To the textbook writer or researcher, the farm—the place where knowledge is applied—is necessarily provisional or theoretical; what he proposes must be found to be *generally* true. For the good farmer, on the other hand, the place where knowledge is applied is minutely particular, not *a* farm but *this* farm, *my* farm, the only place exactly like itself in all the world. To use it without intimate, minutely particular knowledge of it, as if it were *a* farm or *any* farm, is, as good farmers tend to know instinctively, to violate it, to do it damage, finally to destroy it.

And so one of the reasons it is impossible to give a full description of a good farmer's mind is that the mind of a good farmer is inseparable from his farm; or, to state it the opposite way, a farm as a human artifact is inseparable from the mind that makes and uses it. The two are one. To damage this union is to damage human culture at its root.

Berry's theme has resonated throughout the Third World, especially in Africa. Under the rubric of 'indigenous technical knowledge', itk for short, it has spawned a mini-literature, of which David Brokensha *et al.* (eds.), *Indigenous Knowledge Systems and Development*, published in 1980, was an early, if not the first, contribution. The claims are generally less bold than Berry's: itk is seen more as complementary to the knowledge of outside experts than as actually opposed to it. But to speak in the same breath of the two kinds of knowledge was daring enough; to insist on the value of the local and particular knowledge of uneducated and often illiterate peasants represented a radical departure from agricultural orthodoxy.

Outside the mainstream, however, the theme is much older. The basis of Carl Sauer's insistence that the problems of Mexico lay in poverty and oppression was his belief in the fitness of the peasant's adaptation to his life situation, an adaptation which presupposed intelligence and wisdom rather than stupidity and ignorance.

Economists find themselves in a difficult position with respect to itk. Committed to calculation and maximization as behavioural norms of rationality, it is not easy to cast aspersion on the knowledge underlying the peasant's actions without opening the door to massive irrationality. But this puts the economist squarely on the other horn of the dilemma: on what basis then is development to be justified? What does development mean if not the replacement of the traditions and superstitions of backwardness by scientific knowledge?

Theodore Schultz resolved the dilemma by an ingenious ploy which allowed him to argue simultaneously the adequacy of peasant knowledge and the need to supersede that knowledge, and won him a Nobel Prize in the bargain. The traditional peasant, according to *Transforming Traditional Agriculture* (1964), was after all a good economic man, calculating and maximizing with the best of us. The peasant's problem was poor opportunities for gain, a lack of resources, including above all that oxymoron beloved of economists, 'human capital'. (So far nothing Carl Sauer would take offence at.) Peasants' knowledge may be adequate for rational action and efficiency within the age-old context of traditional agriculture, but this says nothing about the changed context of modern agriculture. New opportunities require new knowledge.

So development is necessary after all, with one important proviso: we need spend no time worrying about motivating the peasantry. As *homines economici* peasants will respond as they have always done, intelligently making the best economic use of their resources and opportunities.

Implicitly, economists like Schultz look forward to a happy marriage of expert knowledge and farmer wisdom. The farmer will pick and choose among the recommendations of the professionals according to what works; that is according to what is profitable. I am not so sanguine.

3. An Exemplary Tale: The Death and Resurrection of Intercropping

The history of intercropping—the practice of sowing many crops in one field—provides a good vehicle for me to express my doubts. At first blush, this story is an example of the death and resurrection of itk and thus supports Schultz's position. But for me this story is exemplary in another way: it illustrates the limits of the project of incorporating itk into the agronomic *episteme*. We start with the observation of that well-known heretic, Sir Albert Howard, whose *Agricultural Testament*, published in 1940 after a career devoted to agricultural research in India, has become one of the holy books of alternative agriculture (p. 13):

Mixed crops are the rule. In this respect the cultivators of the Orient have followed Nature's method as seen in the primeval forest. Mixed cropping is perhaps most universal when the cereal crop is the main constituent. Crops like millets, wheat, barley, and maize are mixed with an appropriate subsidiary pulse, sometimes a species that ripens much later than the cereal. The pigeon pea (*Cajanus indicus* Spreng.), perhaps the most important leguminous crop the Gangetic alluvium, is grown either with millets or with maize. The mixing of cereals and pulses appears to help both crops. When the two grow together the character of the growth improves. Do the roots of these crops excrete materials useful to each other? Is the mycorrhizal association found in the roots of these tropical legumes and cereals the agent involved in this excretion? Science at the moment is unable to answer these questions: she is only now beginning to investigate them. Here we have another instance where the peasants of the East have anticipated and acted upon the solution of one of the problems which Western science is only just beginning to recognize. Whatever may be the reason why crops thrive best when associated in suitable combinations, the fact remains that mixtures generally give better results than monoculture.

Notwithstanding Sir Albert's observations, the invading army of experts who were preparing the way for the Green Revolution in the early 1960s regarded intercropping as a sign of backwardness. I remember asking both farmers and experts about intercropping of chick-pea and mustard, a ubiquitous practice, during my first encounter with rural north-western India almost 30 years ago. The farmers' responses ranged from the uninformative ('That's the way we do it') to an argument in terms of insurance ('If rainfall is scarce, at least one of the two crops will survive'). As the experts understood the insurance argument, it made no sense: one could as well insure against inadequate rainfall with two plots of monocultures as by one of polyculture. It was easy to conclude that there was no good reason for traditional practice. Science was no closer in the 1960s than in Sir Albert's day to answering his questions, presumably because the scientists of the 1960s were satisfied that they already had the answers. The sole reference to intercropping turned up in a search of the archives of the Ford Foundation's India office for the decade of the 1960s was a dismissive statement by a consultant in agronomy (who by chance was an acquaintance of mine): 'In mixed cropping two crops are sown at the same time and actively complete (*sic*) with each other during the growing season. Mixed cropping is not generally compatible with the concepts of intensive agriculture' (Ford Foundation Archives, Dwight Finfrock 1965, AG 65–24(b), p. 8).

Interestingly, Indian scientists held a more sympathetic view. (Perhaps they were more scientific than their British and American counterparts.) A. K. Narayan Aiyer began a 100+-page survey commissioned by the Indian Council of Agricultural Research and published in the *Indian Journal of Agricultural Science* in 1949 by observing (pp. 439, 446).

The practice of mixed cropping . . . is a peculiar and widely adopted method of cropping in India and one which may indeed be said to mark it off sharply from the agriculture of many other parts of the world. By reason of its widely prevalent character and the large variety of crops and conditions of farming that it covers its importance as a subject for scientific examination and research is as great if not greater than that of many other subjects which have been taken up for study so far.

Depending upon the temperament of the visitor it is put down to ignorance of the importance of rotation of crops or as a remarkably clever adaption to the needs of the country full of practical wisdom and worthy of deep study.

Only once does Aiyer tip his hand. Recounting an experiment which I surmise to have taken place during his tenure on the staff of the Department of Agriculture of the princely state of Mysore, he quotes (Leslie) Coleman, presumably a colleague, as remarking (p. 473):

The belief is fairly common in Mysore that mixtures are grown because the cultivator has found them to yield more than any of the pure types if grown separately. The few experiments we have carried out do not in any way support this view. In fact the pure types have, in cases experimented upon, given a higher yield than the original mixtures from which they were isolated, and in some cases the differences have been very marked.

Aiyer adds 'It is of course arguable that the experiments relate to only two years, whereas the *ryots*' [farmers'] belief is based upon the experience of many years.' Further along in the article Aiyer adverts once again to experiments with the same mixtures and pure crops, this time over a somewhat longer period. He quotes Coleman directly (p. 495): 'The results indicate pretty clearly that the growing of a mixed crop is more profitable than the growing of a pure crop. If we exclude straw the average value per acre of the pure crops was roughly Rs. 18 and that of the mixed crop roughly Rs. 25 per acre.' But Coleman is not ready to throw in the towel:

notwithstanding this considerable difference it is still quite possible that the advantages which accrue from early ploughing which can be done only when a pure crop of *ragi* is grown would outweigh the undoubted increase due to the mixture with a pulse crop. This must however remain a subject for future investigation.

Aiyer reviews the evidence on a number of questions, including the capture of nitrogen by legumes and its availability to non-legumes in mixtures; the effects on soil moisture and its utilization; and the control of insects and disease. A final section deals with the economics of intercropping. The evidence is far from univocal, and the expected Scottish verdict is returned.

Meanwhile cultivators continued to intercrop, and occasionally, very occasionally, researchers took note. P. N. Mathur was one such observer, who noted both the ubiquity of the practice and its economic superiority (1963: 40). But for every Mathur, there was a Brian Trenbath, who in 1974 again turned in a Scottish verdict, but one tilting against intercropping. I quote at some length (1974: 205):

Most binary mixtures have been recorded as yielding at a level between the yields of the components' monocultures ... This ... is what might be predicted on the assumption of competition between components for the same resources ... This implies that the relative yield totals ... of mixtures would have values close to unity ... This is found in practice.

A minority of binary mixtures has been recorded as yielding ... outside the range defined by the yields of the components grown in monoculture. This suggests that the above proportional model may not always apply, but the frequent lack of repetition of experiments and the small margins by which the mixture yields transgressed the range between the monoculture yields usually make it impossible to say whether a given case ... was due to experimental error or to a real effect. *Since a series of mechanisms can be suggested that could plausibly lead to mutually beneficial effects between mixture components, it seems likely, or at least possible, that some of the observed cases of overyielding are due to such mechanisms* (emphasis added).

I have underlined the last sentence because it seems to me to raise an important issue, to which I shall return, namely, the status of practice (and the validity of the associated knowledge) for which Western science cannot adduce plausible mechanisms. This seems especially relevant for Trenbath in view of his acknowledgement further down the page of the limitations of science, or at least of current scientific models (pp. 205–6): 'Owing to the complexity and unpredictability of many agricultural eco-systems, the control over them which man claims he has is often only nominal.'

Meanwhile the Indian story of expert neglect, indifference, and even hostility to the indigenous practice of intercropping was repeated in Africa. David Norman (1974) noted that 'because such a system is usually associated with "subsistence" farmers it is not worthy of being a topic of serious research endeavor' (p. 4). He set out to correct the record, by describing his own, very serious, research designed 'to demonstrate that there are valid reasons of a technological, sociological and economic nature for farmers' reluctance to change to a sole cropping system' (p. 17).

Although Norman's purpose is to legitimize traditional practice, he shares more than perhaps either side would acknowledge with Trenbath. For Norman 'valid reasons' are reasons acceptable to a Western, or Western-trained, observer. The tone is not only defensive, it is manipulative as well. Norman argues for the development of intercropping as a way for extension agents to get a foot in the door (p. 17):

once the farmer has adopted an innovation that does not conflict too much with his present traditional outlook, e.g., improvement of his returns from mixed cropping it will then be easier for the extension worker to suggest more radical changes, e.g., sole cropping if evidence obtained under improved technological conditions indicates that this is desirable as far as farmers are concerned.

Shades of Richard Crabb and his encomium to hybrid corn as a foot in the door for more radical change!

Norman was, though perhaps he did not know it, part of a movement. At a workshop held at the Institute of Development Studies of the University of Sussex (England) in the late 1970s, Deryke Belshaw (1979) presented a paper with the suggestive title 'Taking Indigenous Technology Seriously: The Case of Inter-cropping Techniques in East Africa'. Belshaw makes a similar case to the one made a generation earlier by Howard and Aiyer in India, along with his own chronicle of official indifference and even hostility to prior efforts to legitimize indigenous practice (see especially Belshaw 1979: 25 n. 1).

But at about the same time as the IDS conference, official attitudes were changing. Already in 1975 the American Society of Agronomy had sponsored a conference on multiple cropping which looked sympathetically at intercropping, the proceedings of which subsequently appeared as a special publication of the Society (Papendick et al., 1976). In January of 1979 the International Crops Research Institute for the Semi-Arid Tropics, located near Hyderabad in India and known generally by its acronym ICRISAT, held an international conference that reviewed intercropping from Brazil to Africa (West and East), to India, and under several lenses at that, from plant physiology to plant protection against insects and disease to the economics and management of mixed crops. ICRISAT was the establishment's answer to the charge that research had neglected the marginal, dryland cultivator in concentrating attention on irrigated crops which exploit the responsiveness of newly synthesized varieties of wheat and rice to fertilizers. Without assured supplies of water, the massive doses of fertilizer mandated by hta would easily become counterproductive and possibly even disastrous.

So this was hardly any old conference. It was rather the official seal of approval on itk, even if explicit recognition of traditional knowledge is for the most part relegated to the occasional footnote, such as the following one from N. S. Jodha's contribution (1981: 289):

The highest extent of intercropping . . . was partly due to the tradition that every farmer should plant nine crops in at least one of his plots. This ritual practice known as *Nava Dhanyam* (nine grains) is guided by a belief that it is the duty of every farmer to preserve the germplasm, which nature has provided. This practice—prevalent in several parts of the country—is now fast disappearing due to more and more specialized farming.

Perhaps belatedly—but better later than never—the scientific establishment recognized the virtues of traditional practice and began to engage them scientifically, to bring traditional virtues under the umbrella of modernity. In 1986 Charles Francis brought together articles on various aspects of multiple cropping that gave considerable prominence to intercropping, and 1989 saw the publication of a treatise on intercropping complete with mathematical models (Vandermeer, 1989).

Can we now look forward not only to peaceful coexistence but even to the mutual enrichment of traditional and modern forms of knowledge? I think not, and I will give a short argument and then try, in the rest of this paper, to explain that short answer.

4. Systems of Knowledge

The short answer is that the Western ideology of knowledge prevents such a peaceful coexistence. The system of knowledge which underlies Western science might in theory coexist with other systems of knowledge, but, in practice, ideology drives this system of knowledge to universal and exclusive claims which preclude peaceful coexistence. The politics of Western *episteme* preclude not only appreciating, but even tolerating what it cannot comprehend and appropriate. Indeed in this system, what cannot be owned is not even accorded the status of knowledge. This would be bad enough, but there is worse. Since all systems of knowledge are partial, something is always lost in translation. What cannot be reduced to the terms of Western science, not counting as knowledge, is forgotten altogether. In the encounter of modern knowledge with itk, the real danger is not that modern knowledge will appropriate itk, but that it will do so only partially and will return this partial knowledge to the cultivator as the solid core of truth extracted from a web of superstition and false belief. What lies outside the intersection of modern knowledge and itk risks being lost altogether.

Let me now spell out the basis of this fear. I have elsewhere (Marglin, 1990) contrasted *episteme* with *techne* as distinct ways of understanding, perceiving, apprehending, and experiencing reality. My contention is twofold: first, that knowledge and action are based on a combination, a synthesis of *episteme* and *techne*, indeed, sometimes a tension between the two; but, second, notwithstanding this symbiosis in practice, that ideologically Western culture has elevated *episteme* to a superior position, sometimes to the point that *techne* is not only regarded as inferior knowledge, but as no knowledge at all. Except to the extent that *techne* can be justified by *episteme*, it remains superstition, belief, or prejudice. This ideological hierarchy, in my view, has had a powerful influence on the way *episteme* and *techne* interact in practice, rendering technic knowledge illegitimate and even invisible.

I should emphasize at the outset that I have no criticism to make of *episteme* as a system of knowledge. On the contrary: one can argue that we would not be human without our command of *episteme*. The problem is rather the claim made on behalf of *episteme* that it is all of knowledge, from which stems its proclivity to crowd out other, equally important, systems of knowledge. While *episteme* is essential to our humanness, so is *techne*. Indeed, it is our ability to combine *techne* and *episteme* that sets us apart both from other animals and from computers: animals have *techne* and machines have *episteme*, but only we humans have both. (Oliver Sacks's clinical histories (1985) are at once moving as well as entertaining evidence for the grotesque, bizarre, and even tragic distortions of human beings that result from a loss of either *techne* or *episteme*.) Needless to say, this view of human knowledge makes me sceptical of the possibilities of artificial intelligence. Until we understand more about how human beings are able to integrate *techne* and *episteme*, we can hardly hope to do so in a machine.

But I get ahead of my story; I cannot very well explore the relationships between different systems of knowledge before I lay out what I mean by this terminology. First, let me say what a knowledge system is not: the term does not refer to a specific domain of knowledge. Economists and physicists, chemical engineers and personnel managers, deal with different domains of knowledge. But this in no way prevents us from sharing a common practice or a common ideology with respect to the systems of knowledge we employ.

By a knowledge system I mean a way of organizing knowledge in terms of four characteristics: epistemology, transmission, innovation, and power. A particular system has its own theory of knowledge, its own rules for acquiring and sharing knowledge, its own distinctive ways for changing the content of what counts as knowledge, and, finally, its own rules of governance, both among insiders and between insiders and outsiders.

The point of the term system is twofold. Its first purpose is to suggest that epistemology, transmission, innovation, and politics are not attributes of knowledge in general but characteristics of particular ways of knowing. There is no single epistemology, but specific epistemologies which belong to distinct ways of knowing. Equally there are distinctive ways of transmitting and modifying knowledge over time. A particular way of knowing may go along with different power relationships among the people who share knowledge and between insiders and outsiders.

The links among these several characteristics are a second systematic aspect of knowledge. How we know and how we learn and teach, how we innovate and how we relate to power—these characteristics of knowledge mutually interact, as well as interacting with the basic constructions that underlie each particular way of knowing.

These ideas will hopefully become clearer if I flesh them out in the context of the two knowledge systems I have labelled *episteme* and *techne*. In the process I shall also explain what I mean by these Greek terms. Indeed, *episteme* and *techne* will be defined by a series of binary oppositions on the axes of epistemology, transmission, innovation, and power, not by approximate English equivalents of an ancient language; the Greek terms are intended to evoke, not to define.

On the one hand, *episteme* is knowledge based on logical deduction from self-evident first principles. It thus combines induction and deduction. Induction plays an important role in determining first principles, deduction in reaching conclusions at some remove from these first principles. 'Logical deduction' implies proceeding by small steps with nothing left out, nothing left to chance or to the imagination. Indeed, the canonical Western model of epistemic knowledge is Euclidian geometry, though Euclid's axioms turned out with the passage of time to be less self-evident than had once been supposed—we now have a variety of geometries each with its own axiomatic basis. Besides the mathematical theorem, the computer programme comes to mind as a model of epistemic knowledge.

Epistemic knowledge is analytic. It decomposes, breaks down, a body of knowledge into its components. It is thus directly and immediately reproducible. It is fully articulate, and within *episteme* it may be said that what cannot be articulated does not even count as knowledge. It is a matter of some controversy whether *episteme* inherently lays claims to *universality*, to being applicable at all times and places to all questions. It is certainly the case that many people, particularly in the West, often do not see *episteme* as one system of knowledge among many, but as knowledge pure and simple. But I have come to view this claim not as an inherent characteristic of *episteme*, or in any case not a characteristic of its epistemology, but a characteristic of the politics of knowledge in the West. Epistemic knowledge is purely cerebral. Mind is separate from body, and *episteme* pertains to the mind alone. The statement 'I feel there is something wrong with what you are saying', which is to say 'I sense something is wrong, but I cannot articulate what or why' has no place within *episteme*.

Even when pressed into action, *episteme* is theoretical. Once the tentative and provisional nature of any axiomatic scheme is recognized, epistemic statements are necessarily hypotheses. Indeed, without entering into the nuances of the debate between Karl Popper (1968) and his critics (Kuhn, 1970; Lakatos, 1970; Putnam, 1974), it can be said that *episteme* is geared one way or another to falsification and verification. Its very procedure, the insistence on small steps that follow immediately and directly upon one another, preclude discovery and creativity. To discover or to create through *episteme* would be like the proverbial monkey typing Shakespeare: he might some day do it, but we would be hard-pressed to find the wheat among the chaff.

Finally, *episteme* is impersonal knowledge. Like the Christian God (Rom. 2: 11), *episteme* is impartial; it is in principle accessible to all on equal terms. Thus *episteme* is not only theoretical knowledge, it becomes theoretical knowledge of theoretical equals. So far so good: who would not applaud a bias towards equality? The problem is that as the elevation of the Jewish tribal deity to the status of universal God historically led Christians to deny the possibility of salvation to unbelievers, so the ideological elevation of *episteme* to superior status led to the disenfranchisement of those outside this system of knowledge. It is an easy political step to universalistic claims for *episteme* and only a tad more difficult to the view that those lacking in *episteme* are lacking in knowledge itself.

In contrast with the basis of *episteme* in logical deduction from self-evident axioms, the bases of *techne* are as varied as the authority of recognized masters (and mistresses) to one's own intuition. One way or another, however, experience is of the essence. Opposed to the small steps of *episteme* are both received doctrine and the imaginative leaps which all at once enable one to fit the jig-saw puzzle together. Received knowledge doctrine and imaginative leaps are both knowledge of the whole, difficult to break down into parts. In contrast to the analytic nature of *episteme*, *techne* is indecomposable.

Techne is often difficult if not impossible to articulate. Those who possess it are generally aware that they possess special knowledge, but their knowledge is implicit rather than explicit. It is revealed in the production of cloth or creation of a painting or performance of a ritual or a forecast of economic activity, not in textbooks for student weavers, artists, priests, or economists. Whatever the status of *episteme* with respect to the opposition between universal and local knowledge, the position of *techne* is clear: technic knowledge makes no claims to universality. It is specialized in nature and closely allied to time and place. It always exists for a particular purpose at hand; *techne* is contextual.

Techne belies the mind–body dualism which is basic to *episteme*. Under *techne* one knows with and through one's hands and eyes and heart as well as with one's head. *Techne* is knowledge which gives due weight to Keynes's (1936: 161) animal spirits, what Martha Nussbaum and Amartya Sen (1989: 316) have called the 'cognitive role of the emotions'. It is also the knowledge of touch. Feeling, in both senses of the term, is central to *techne*; *techne* is at once both tactile and emotional.

Techne is intensely practical, to the point that, as has been suggested, it reveals itself only through practice. This is not to deny the existence of an underlying theory, but the theory is implicit rather than explicit, not necessarily available, perhaps not even usually available, to practitioners. Technic knowledge is geared to creation and discovery rather than to verification. Even a mathematical theorem is largely the product of *techne*, although the proof must, by the very requirements of the knowledge system on which mathematics is based, be cast in terms of *episteme*. Finally, where *episteme* is impersonal, techne is not and cannot be. It normally exists in networks of relationships and cannot be transmitted or even maintained apart from these relationships. The normal avenues of transmission—parent–child, master–apprentice, *guru–shisha*—are intensely personal.

These are not normally relationships among equals. There is a hierarchy blending age, power, and knowledge. But it should be observed that the hierarchy is typically linear rather than pyramidal, as wide at the top as at the base. Thus those at the bottom have a reasonable expectation (though no guarantee) of moving up to the top with the passage of time. It is the hierarchy of the guild, where every apprentice can expect to be a master, not that of the factory, where few workers can become foremen, let alone executives. It can also be a hierarchy of gender. (Carol Gilligan's well-known work, *In a Different Voice* (1982), can be interpreted as a defence of (feminine) *techne* against (masculine) *episteme*.)

Recognizing limits of time, place, and purpose, *techne*, unlike *episteme*, does not readily lend itself to a politics of knowledge which divides the world according to haves and have-nots. *Techne* is certainly not inherently egalitarian in terms of its external relations, but it is at least pluralistic.

In terms of the four characteristics that have been proposed to distinguish knowledge systems, the differences between *episteme* and *techne* are striking. *Episteme* recognizes as knowledge only that which is derived by the rules of logic from axioms acceptable as self-evident first principles. *Techne* by contrast recognizes a variety of avenues to knowledge, from authority to immediate experience: the test of knowledge is practical efficacy.

The transmission mechanisms are as different as the epistemologies. Epistemic knowledge in principle is accessible through pure ratiocination, but in practice, *episteme* is generally acquired through formal schooling. Indeed knowledge in the West has more and more come to be equated with what is taught in the schools, and the schools in general are dedicated to *episteme*, so much so that a nephew of mine suggested opposing 'book knowledge' and 'street knowledge' in place of the opposition between *episteme* and *techne*. (There are exceptions: the law and business faculties of my own university have since their inception given pride of place to the 'case method' of instruction, which attempts to condense the *techne* of the law office and the executive suite into a form accessible to students, and to allow learning to take place in a simulated environment in which mistakes are not too costly. But even these exceptions are coming increasingly under fire from the epistemic academic establishment.)

The canonical way of transmitting *techne* is, as has been indicated, through a personal nexus epitomized by the master–apprentice relationship. The master's example, more than any precept, instructs the apprentice, who absorbs almost unconsciously what he is taught. Almost anybody can acquire the rudiments of a craft in this way, but quality is a matter of intuition, of a heightened sense of touch and feel developed through years of practice.

Epistemic innovation leads a double life. The formal model allows one only to replace an erroneous logical derivation with a correct one or to change the assumptions. One can supplement existing axioms, or, more rarely, replace existing axioms by new ones, as Newton did for his predecessors and Einstein did for Newton. With new axioms one can proceed to new theorems by old methods: the new theorems are simply logical entailments of the new assumptions. In practice, as has been noted, a considerable admixture of *techne* is involved even in epistemic innovation: the innovator has to know where she is going and the map is provided by her intuition rather than her logic. Technic innovation is largely a matter of trial and error. This is not to say it is haphazard, but the underlying structure of technic innovation, like the *techne* it modifies, is often hidden from the innovator himself.

If knowledge is a text, the canonical form of epistemic innovation is *criticism*. Innovation takes the form of a direct assault, a challenge to logic or to first principles themselves. The canonical form of technic innovation, by contrast, is commentary, emendation and explanation of the text. The authority of the fathers is not challenged but reinterpreted. For this reason, epistemic innovation can flourish only in a community of equals, where respect for personal authority is relatively attenuated. The extent to which the attacks of a Peter Abelard on the doctrinal authority of popes and saints were taken seriously is a measure of the degree to which the West had, by the year AD 1100, come to regard religious knowledge as epistemic in nature.

Episteme and *techne* reverse internal and external power relations. As has been noted, *episteme* assumes, or at least flourishes in, a community of equals, and in the West this community of equals claims also that the superiority of their knowledge makes them collectively and individually superior to those outside. *Techne*, by contrast, presupposes a hierarchy of knowledge and a corresponding hierarchy of power. But to the extent that knowledge rests on *techne*, a community of shoemakers, farmers, or economists can relate in different ways to other communities. According to context, it can be more knowledgeable, and hence wield greater power, or less knowledgeable and correspondingly weaker.

It will be recognized that *episteme* and *techne* are ideal types. *Episteme* comes close to what many mean by science, and 'science' is indeed one of the words used to translate the Greek. ('Knowledge' is another translation, which suggests that the claims for the universality of *episteme* are of long standing.) *Techne* is more difficult to pin down. As the root indicates, it contains elements of 'technique'; 'art,' one translation of *techne*, conveys some of its flavour. But contemporary scholarship glosses both *episteme* and *techne* as 'science', a translation perhaps more congenial to my purposes in its emphasis on the common field of these terms, at least so far as practice is concerned (see Nussbaum, 1986: 444). *Episteme* may be the form in which science is written down, but *techne* is essential to the way science is done.

As with many of my favourite 'original' ideas, having elaborated the notion that *episteme* and *techne* constitute separate and distinct systems of knowledge, I found similar ideas everywhere. Perhaps the best known is Robert Pirsig's (1976) distinction between 'classical' and 'romantic' knowledge in *Zen and the Art of Motorcycle Maintenance*. The details are different, but Pirsig's classical knowledge clearly resonates with *episteme* and romantic knowledge with *techne*. (Recently I came across the following in the autobiography of Alexander Luria, the Soviet psychologist: 'At the beginning of this century the German scholar Max Verworn suggested that scientists can be divided into two distinct groups according to their basic orientation toward science: classical and romantic' (1979: 174). Luria, presumably paraphrasing Verworn, then goes on to characterize classical and romantic in terms strikingly like Pirsig's and mine. So far I have been unable to track down any essay by Verworn that makes such a distinction, but I have not given up.) Michael Polanyi (1958) characterized 'tacit' knowledge as a distinct way of knowing in which touch and feel play an important role—as they do in *techne*. In another context, Jerome Bruner (1962) distinguished 'right-handed' from 'left-handed' knowledge, the first based on logic, the second on intuition—a distinction which also characterizes *episteme* and *techne*.

5. Towards the History of an Ideology

The glorification of *episteme* in Western culture has a long history. The term, along with *techne*, is of course Greek, but there is much dispute among students of classical Greek civilization over how these terms were used and understood by different Greeks at different times. A formal distinction between the two terms somewhat along present lines is made by Aristotle in the *Nicomachean Ethics* (1934 edn.: 1139b, 14–40a, 24), but the salient issue is less the precise nature of the distinction between the two than the subordination of the one to the other. Aristotle, it should be observed, is inconsistent in his usage of *techne* and *episteme* (see Nussbaum, 1986: 444), and earlier writers, including Plato, appear to have used the terms almost interchangeably, at least in those areas that are of concern to the present inquiry (Lyons, 1969; Nussbaum, 1986: 444). In particular, Nussbaum ascribes to *techne* (pp. 94–6) many of the characteristics that I have not only ascribed to *episteme*, but have made pivotal in distinguishing between the two.

There is first of course class politics: in so far as *techne* referred to the craftsman's knowledge of production, it is to be expected that it would be subordinated along with the craftsman himself. But if Plato is any guide, the upper-class Greek conception of the craftsman must have been ambivalent: the craftsman figures prominently in the Platonic origin myth, creation itself being the work of a *demiurgos*, a craftsman; and the craftsman's *techne* appears and reappears in the Platonic dialogues as the model of purposive knowledge (Klosko, 1986: 28, 41; Vidal-Naquet, 1981: 293). The ambivalence may stem from a very real tension between the essential role of the craftsman and his knowledge to the well-being of the *polis* on the one hand and the inferior position of the craftsman on the other (Vidal-Naquet, 1983: 289–316).

But more than power politics is at issue: Greek theories of knowledge, Jean-Pierre Vernant has suggested, led to the devaluation of technical knowledge, the artisan's *techne*, because production involved contamination of pure knowledge, which deals with the unchanging and the certain, by the unpredictable. Unlike *episteme*, technical knowledge deals with approximation, 'to which neither exact measure nor precise calculation applies' (Vernant, 1965: ii. 51). Thus

Artisanal *techne* is not real knowledge. The artisan's . . . *techne* rests upon fidelity to a tradition which is not of a scientific order but outside of which would hand him over, disarmed, to chance. Experience can teach him nothing because in the situation in which he finds himself placed—between rational knowledge on the one hand and *tuche*, chance, on the other—there is for him neither theory nor facts capable of verifying theory; there is no experience in the proper sense. By the strict rules which his art necessitates, he imitates blindly the rigour and sureness of rational procedure; but he has also to adapt himself, thanks to a sort of flair acquired in the practice of his profession, to the unpredictable and the chancy, which the material on which he acts always has in greater or lesser degree (Vernant, 1965: ii, 59).

Citing the poet Agathon, Aristotle summarizes the problem succinctly (*Nicomachean Ethics*, 1140^{a}20): 'Art [*techne*] loves chance, and chance art', and this, if we follow Vernant's interpretation, must lower the status of *techne*.

The association of *techne* with chance recalls Pierre Vidal-Naquet's eloquent evocation of the opposition between order and disorder in the evolution of Greek thought and social institutions. Lacking a theory of probability, the Greeks identified chance with disorder, and knowledge of random variability was not knowledge at all (Hacking, 1975). One might suggest that for the Greeks *episteme* was not only the knowledge system of science but the knowledge system as well of social order, and its attractions were the attractions of stability. The craftsman and his *techne* represent—to borrow a phrase Vidal-Naquet employs in a different context—'disorder and the individual exploit' (1981: 174).

Worse, *techne*, certainly the artisan's *techne*, was bound up with *empeiria*, experience, and therefore further contaminated by its contact with the concrete and the practical. '*Empeiria*, experience . . . is neither experimentation nor experimental thought but practical knowledge obtained with the physically concrete, theory [i.e. *episteme*] loses its rigour and ceases to be itself. It is not applied to, but degraded in, facts' (Vernant, 1982: 52). Indeed, Plato appears to use the term *empeiria* to describe characteristics of craft production that I have described in terms of *techne*. In *Gorgias* (465*a*) Plato has Socrates say with respect to the art of cooking: 'I say it is not an art, but a habitude [*empeiria*], since it has no account to give of the real nature of the things it applies, and so cannot tell the cause of any of them. I refuse to give the name of art [*techne*] to anything that is irrational.' In *Philebus* (55*d–e*) Socrates asks his interlocutor to 'consider whether in the manual arts [*cheirotechnikai*] one part is more allied to knowledge [*episteme*], and the other less, and the one should be regarded as purest, the other as less pure?' He goes on to assert, 'If arithmetic and the sciences of measurement and weighing were taken away from all arts [*techne*], what was left of any of them would be, so to speak, pretty worthless.'

But whatever the names, the distinction between types of knowledge is central to Plato's philosophy. The *Republic* is categorical about the inferiority of the craftsman's knowledge. Socrates expresses the Platonic view in terms of the relation between the knowledge of the horseman who uses the bit and bridle and the craftsman who makes them. 'Is it not true', Socrates asks, 'that not even the craftsmen who make them know [how they should be made] but only the horseman who understands their use?' (601*c*). At issue is a difference not between *episteme* and *techne* but one between *episteme* and *techne* on the one hand and *ortha doxa* (right opinion) on the other. Socrates continues:

It follows, then, that the user must know most about the performance of the thing he uses and must report on its good or bad points to the maker. The flute-player, for example, will tell the instrument-maker how well his flutes serve the player's purpose, and the other will submit to be instructed about how they should be made. So the man who uses any implement will speak of its merits and defects with knowledge, whereas the maker will take his work and possess no more than a correct belief, which he is obliged to obtain by listening to the man who knows (601*e*).

The terminology may be different, but there is no question that the knowledge of the craftsman is of a different, and inferior, sort.

For Aristotle too the craftsman left to his own devices could lay claim only to an inferior grade of knowledge. Indeed Aristotle even takes over the parable of the flute-maker and the flute-player and with Plato stigmatizes the craftsman's knowledge as simply 'right opinion' (*Politics*, 1277^b27–30). (But it is for 'experts in the science of mensuration to elect a land surveyor and for experts in navigation to choose a pilot' (*Politics*, 1282^a9–10). Foolish consistency is the hobgoblin of little minds. Aristotle believed that there could be an *episteme*—albeit an inferior one—of even the slave's work, an *episteme* for instance of cooking (*Politics*, 1255^b26–32). In this respect, Aristotle is the true precursor of Frederick Winslow Taylor, the father of scientific management.

It is evidently too much to assert that the conception of knowledge, and particularly of craft knowledge, held by certain Greek philosophers determined the Western conception for all time. In the first place, alternative readings of the Greeks are possible, as modern scholarship has amply demonstrated. For instance, in contrast to the dominant reading of 'the Greek' (that is, Plato's and Aristotle's) conception of knowledge as limited to that which is logically derivable from self-evident first principles, which is my notion of *episteme*, Nussbaum (1986: 290 ff.) has recently suggested that Aristotle in particular had a much more elastic view. In Nussbaum's interpretation, Aristotle's conception of practical wisdom, the knowledge of life, differs from the *episteme* of mathematics and natural science precisely in its reliance upon the emotions, experience, and other aspects of what I have assigned to the realm of *techne*. In Nussbaum's reading, Aristotle assigns practical wisdom to a distinct plane from *episteme*, but it is not an inferior one.

It is significant however that such an interpretation has a relatively recent pedigree, whereas the dominant reading goes back at least to Thomas

Aquinas. And the dominant reading, while a matter of interpretation, is not an invention out of whole cloth. The power of *episteme* in the modern West is hardly conceivable without deep roots in the past.

But one need not go all the way back to the Greeks to recover this past. The very definition of *episteme* could have been cribbed from Descartes (and very likely was, albeit unconsciously—I thought I was copying Euclid), for it practically paraphrases the method of arriving at true knowledge expounded in the *Discourse on Method* and the *Meditations of First Philosophy* (Descartes, 1637/1641). But in a sense Descartes is a Greek once removed: mathematics was for him the model, and the model of the model was Euclid's geometry. An *episteme* mimicking the form of the mathematical theorem was the answer to the 'disunity and uncertainty' of contemporary knowledge (Descartes, 1637/1641: editor's preface, p. vii), an answer resounding with 'certainty, necessity, and precision'.

The context in which Descartes elaborated his project is important, for it sheds light on the appeal of *episteme*. As for the Greeks, *episteme* was for Descartes and his times the answer to the disorder that threatened to undo society. The religious controversies that had from Martin Luther's time torn Christianity apart now threatened to destroy European civilization: the time of Descartes was the time of the Thirty Years War and Descartes himself, a volunteer in the army of Prince Maurice of Nassau, had seen the threat at close quarters. Indeed, Stephen Toulmin (1990) argues that the Cartesian attempt to secure a new basis for knowledge came directly out of the failure of religious toleration as embodied in the pluralistic politics of Henry of Navarre and the pluralistic scepticism of Michel de Montaigne.

Scepticism must itself be seen in context (Popkin, 1979). It is hard to see the rise of scepticism in the early modern period other than as a response to the assertion of interior authority, (literally) self-evident truth—or truths, there turned out to be more than one—that Protestants invoked to counter the claims of papal authority. Scepticism, by attacking all claims to ultimate truth, sought to restore the legitimacy of claims most hallowed by time and tradition, and in Montaigne's version at least, to temper even these claims with moderation and tolerance.

The sceptics' project misfired badly, perhaps because Montaigne's temperate pluralism did not exactly meet the requirements of the Counter-Reformation. Instead of pluralism and tolerance, there was a cacophony of claims to ultimate truth. It was these conflicting claims that Descartes proposed to cut through with his new system of knowledge.

Descartes and his contemporaries, like the Greeks before them, equated uncertainty and doubt with disorder. *Episteme* was the knowledge system of rational order, and in consequence—or so one might hope—of social order. The endemic social disorder was epitomized by the Thirty Years War. But one need not be directly touched by war to feel the dislocations of the age. The birth of modernity was a socially painful one in myriad dimensions: all institutions—not only the church, but the home, the workplace, the state, and of course the land—were in flux.

In this respect, too, the context in which the modern incarnation of *episteme* took hold was similar to the ancient one. The classicist E. R. Dodds characterized the transition from the Homeric to the archaic age which saw the birth of Greek philosophy as a period of a heightened sense of insecurity, 'not a different belief but a different emotional reaction to the old belief' (1951: 30). Undoubtedly, the rise in insecurity had many causes, but the political and economic upheavals that marked the seventh and sixth centuries BCE loom large in Dodds's account (pp. 44 ff.). However, periods of political and economic insecurity came and went with monotonous frequency without giving rise to new ideologies of knowledge. So what was different about this particular period of insecurity? Because it seems to offer a parallel with the early modern period I am tempted to attach considerable importance to Dodds's suggestion that the breakdown of the family, specifically, the authority of the father, played an important role in the perception of growing social disorder. Personal authority is central to *techne*, and one of *episteme*'s attractions is precisely the challenge to this authority that it poses.

In view of the central role that uncertainty plays in this chapter, it is very much to the point that shortly after the death of Descartes, the intellectual attack on uncertainty and doubt took a decisive turn. As Ian Hacking (1975) tells the story, the modern idea of probability was born from the union of a stochastic conception of events with the new understanding of doubtful knowledge as differing in degree rather than in kind from certain knowledge. The first text to reflect these notions was the so-called Port-Royal Logic, Antoine Arnauld's *The Art of Thinking*, originally published in 1662. Hacking's work is a *tour de force*, brilliant as it is entertaining. But it errs, I think, in seeing probability as an attack on the idea, inherited from the Greeks, of knowledge as certainty. Hacking sees the Greek correspondence

knowledge : certainty = opinion : uncertainty

as being ruptured by the modern notion of probability. In Hacking's view probability shifts the boundary between knowledge and opinion so that knowledge can be brought to bear on uncertainty. Instead, Descartes and the Port-Royal logicians after him seem to me to affirm the boundary between knowledge and opinion but to break down the boundary between certainty and uncertainty so as to bring chance within the framework of certainty.

Probability is thus the opposite of an attack on certainty; it is an attack on uncertainty. The probability calculus assimilates the uncertain into the realm of true, certain, knowledge. Uncertainty and approximation— hallmarks of *techne*—are banished by the certainty and exactness of *episteme*. Uncertainty becomes risk, the object of calculation and maximization, as *techne* yields to *episteme*.

Like the sceptics' project, the probabilists' project didn't quite come off. Much has been achieved, as the insurance industry attests. Thanks to our understanding of probabilities, we can buy life insurance, fire insurance, and even medical insurance at more or less their actuarial value. But no amount of calculation can move the incalculable from the realm of *techne* to the realm of *episteme*. As Aristotle said, *techne* loves chance and vice versa. In short, *techne* is the knowledge system of uncertainty, and uncertainty is the blessing—or curse, depending on one's point of view—of life.

Indeed, much of economic life would dry up if it depended on epistemic calculation. John Maynard Keynes and Joseph Schumpeter, arguably the most creative economists of this century, found themselves at opposite ends of the (mainstream) political spectrum but agreed emphatically on this point. For Keynes, the commitment of capital to specific physical forms, the act of investment, depends on 'animal spirits' that 'urge to action rather than inaction'. In a celebrated passage of *The General Theory* (pp. 161–2) Keynes expanded on this theme:

there is the instability due to the characteristic of human nature that a large proportion of our positive activities depend on spontaneous optimism rather than on a mathematical expectation, whether moral or hedonistic or economic. Most, probably, of our decisions to do something positive, the full consequences of which will be drawn out over many days to come, can only be taken as a result of animal spirits—of a spontaneous urge to action rather than inaction, and not as the outcome of a weighted average of quantitative benefits multiplied by quantitative probabilities. Enterprise only pretends to itself to be mainly actuated by the statements in its own prospectus, however candid and sincere. Only a little more than an expedition to the South Pole, is it based on an exact calculation of benefits to come. Thus if the animal spirits are dimmed and the spontaneous optimism falters, leaving us to depend on nothing but a mathematical expectation, enterprise will fade and die.

Schumpeter wrote in a similar vein in *The Theory of Economic Development* (p. 85):

As military action must be taken in a given strategic position even if all the data potentially procurable are not available, so also in economic life action must be taken without working out all the details of what is to be done. Here the success of everything depends upon intuition, the capacity of seeing things in a way which afterwards proves to be true, even though it cannot be established at the moment, and of grasping the essential fact, discarding the unessential, even though one can give no account of the principles by which this is done. Thorough preparatory work, and special knowledge, breadth of intellectual understanding, talent for logical analysis, may under certain circumstances be sources of failure.

6. *Every Farm Should be a Laboratory*

For both Keynes and Schumpeter epistemic calculation to justify one course of action instead of another is to 'save the appearances' of the self as a rational being. The course of action must, for better or for worse, be determined largely by *techne* whenever we act in the face of overwhelming uncertainty.

No activity is inherently more uncertain, and therefore less amenable to epistemic calculation, than is agriculture. Indeed, the problems of hta generally, and the Green Revolution in particular, may be seen, at least in part, as the consequence of the difference between the disorderly, uncertain field of the farmer and the ordered laboratory of the scientist. Agronomic *episteme* attempts to bridge this gap in the only way it knows how: by trying to make the mountain come to Muhammad. The goal is to make the farmer's field as much like the experimental field as possible, to reproduce the controlled conditions of the experiment station under which hta produces high yields.

But this project always falls short of its goal. Differences of soil, lack of water, variations in micro climate, vagaries of the weather—any number of problems may arise. Moreover conditions change, in part on their own, in part in response to the interventions of agricultural science. As Paul Mangelsdorf said, the battle between the fungi and the plant breeder never ends. Realizing these problems, the enlightened expert attempts to tap the knowledge of the farmer, to initiate a dialogue in place of the one-way flow of information from the expert to the farmer.

But the ideological claims on behalf of *episteme* pose serious limitations for this dialogue. Though the expert operates with both *techne* and *episteme*, the ideology of knowledge under which he operates constrains him to the language of *episteme*.

The expert recognizes the *techne* of the farmer, in which itk is largely couched, and is happy to learn from the farmer. In return, the expert is more than willing to teach the farmer, to give back in epistemic reworking that which he has elaborated on the basis of the farmer's *techne*. But this is exactly where the trouble begins. The expert can give back only what he can translate from the farmer's *techne* into his own *episteme*. However, no two languages are even isomorphic, so translation is always partial and something is invariably lost. This is not, I hasten to add, the shortcoming of individuals. It is not a matter of the good will or bad will of the expert. It is rather a systemic problem, a problem of the knowledge system. For an expert to move from farm to farm, not to mention from district to district, or country to country, he must disembed, categorize, reduce, universalize. He must, in short, epistemize. Learning—as distinct from translating—the *techne* of the farmer is, like learning and *techne*, the work of a lifetime.

But this is just the beginning: because of an ideology of knowledge which devalues *techne*, what cannot be translated ceases to exist, or exists only as a residue of superstition, ignorance, and belief. (We know; they believe (see Kopytoff, 1981). 'Dialogue' becomes appropriation, reduction, and loss—without even the recognition of loss.)

There is worse. The problem is compounded not only by ideology, but also by the power of the experts who operate primarily in terms of *episteme* relative to the power of the farmers who operate in terms of *techne*. Indeed it is the combination of power and ideology which makes the encounter between expert and farmer in the Third World so malign. The American farmer might ask himself, as Wendell Berry (1984) urges, 'Whose head is the farmer using?' But the American farmer is certainly in a better position to defend himself than is the Indian or the African or the Mexican—Carl Sauer's 'native stubbornness' (see Pt. I, sect. 7, above) to the contrary notwithstanding. (Just reflect for a moment on the different connotations of 'agribusinessman' and 'peasant'!) The remarkable success of the innovations described in *Alternative Agriculture* (see Pt. II, sect. 1, above) would not have been possible, I expect, if the farmers were as powerless as peasants typically are. But this does not mean that power is the only issue, or even the central one: without the compulsion of ideology there would be no incentive or reason to reduce *techne* to *episteme* in the first place.

Perhaps there is no solution. But perhaps the requisite dialogue—the dialogue between the *techne* acquired by osmosis and the *episteme* acquired by formal education—can exist as an internal one, a dialogue with oneself. 'Every farm should be a . . . laboratory and every farmer a practical chemist and philosopher' wrote an American popularizer of scientific agriculture in the middle of the nineteenth century (Rodgers, 1850: 17; quoted in Rosenberg, 1976: 147). It is hard to see how else the peasant can be anything but an agri-proletarian, dependent upon the salesman who provides seed and fertilizer and pesticides, the banker who provides the credit, and the expert who puts the package together.

7. Sustainability as Resilience, Resilience as Diversity

The social virtue of the farmer's *techne* is that *techne* is the knowledge system of uncertainty, and we simply cannot know today what crises we shall face in the next century—from soil exhaustion to water pollution to global warming, none can be ruled out. The ability to respond to these shocks takes on added importance now that the issue of sustainability, once marginal to the development debate, has claimed centre-stage, and in a very real sense has come to set the terms of the debate as we prepare to enter the twenty-first century. Indeed, one of the core definitions of sustainable development, a definition elaborated in the context of sustainable agriculture, is that it be resilient, capable of adjusting to shocks (Pearce *et al.*, 1989; 40–3). If the only certainty about the future is that the future is uncertain, if the only sure thing is that we are in for surprises, then no amount of planning, no amount of prescription, can deal with the contingencies that the future will reveal. That is why ultimately there can be no agriculture for the people that is not agriculture of the people, agriculture by the people. People's knowledge developed over centuries, even millennia, is the most important safeguard against disaster and the most sure basis of a resilient, adaptive agriculture.

For this reason, diversity is as necessary to our development as human beings as it is to ecological balance. Diversity may indeed be the key to the survival of the human species. Just as exotic species like the snail darter maintain the diversity of the gene-pool (see e.g. Myers, 1983), so does a variety of practices maintain the diversity of forms of understanding, creating, and coping that the human species has managed to generate. But within the human species culture rather than instinct bears the primary load of the intergenerational transmission of knowledge. So the necessary diversity must be cultural rather than biological.

Cultural diversity is in short a hedge against the bet that we are going to find all the savvy, all the wisdom, we need to deal with the surprises of the future in our *episteme*. Maybe we will, but up to now *episteme* has proven far better at improving the way we get from one place to another, at getting from here to there faster and more efficiently, than at understanding why we're making the journey. It takes a special combination of arrogance and naïvety to be sure that *episteme* contains all the resources required to cope with the various contingencies of change.

This is not a condemnation of *episteme* as a system of knowledge. The achievements of Western science and technology are unthinkable without it. Knowledge disembodied and disembedded, knowledge based on the separation of mind and body and taken out of the contexts of time, place, and persons; knowledge instrumental and rational, knowledge based on the separation of ends and means and speaking only to means by logical deduction from 'self-evident' first principles—there is a place for such an *episteme* in any culture as the world enters the third millennium of the Christian era.

The problem comes when *episteme* refuses subordination to a cosmology, but pretends itself to be a cosmology, a theory of reality. As a cosmology, *episteme* leaves no room, at least on the ideological level, for other systems of knowledge, no place for the local and particular *technai* equally necessary for thought and action. All knowledge may be socially embedded, but there is a world of difference between a knowledge system elevated to the status of a cosmology and the embeddedness of a knowledge system within a culture. The first may easily lay claim to a Truth, or Truths, which transcend their cultural origins; the second cannot. (There may or may not be such transcendent Truths; there are without question transcendent falsehoods.)

As a cosmology, *episteme* gives us not only scientific agriculture, which increases output in ways that degrade the farmer, threaten the environment, and undermine the ability to respond to whatever surprises the future may hold in store; it has also given us scientific medicine, which provides more effective means of treating illness and disease but transforms the person into a set of laboratory readings (Apffel-Marglin, 1990; Nandy and Visvanathan, 1990); it gives us scientific politics and administration, which transfers disembedded and disembodied forms of instrumental and rational politics to the Third World, aiding and abetting the creation and main-tenance of authoritarian and repressive regimes, and, if the American past is any guide, undermining those rural institutions that have been central to making traditional agriculture a way of life rather than a living and therefore resilient to outside pressures to change (Appadurai, 1990; Marglin *et al.*, 1990).

This is a cosmology that calculates the incalculable and substitutes management based on calculation for an ethic of prudence. At its most egregious, such calculation purports to give us the optimal rate of pollution or resource exhaustion in situations where the very attempt to manage the environment, to balance benefits and costs, may open the door to environ-mental destruction.

In this sense I understand ecology just as John Maynard Keynes and Joseph Schumpeter understood innovation and investment—to be beyond the scope of calculation and therefore lying squarely in the realm of *techne*. And for the same reason: the overwhelming uncertainty and ignorance in which we must act. Of course there is an important difference. Where Keynes and Schumpeter saw the needs of their time as requiring entrepre-neurs whose animal spirits would make them willing to take chances and damn the consequences, I see the present environmental situation as re-quiring caution and prudence, a disposition not to take chances where there are safer alternatives available. This, I hasten to emphasize, is not because we know with certainty that fertilizers, pesticides, or a narrowing of the genetic base, will be disastrous, or, more generally, that ozone depletion, the greenhouse effect, acid rain, and so forth will be calamitous. It is rather precisely because we do not know one way or the other. Progress towards sustainability may require the subordination of an *episteme* of calculation and optimization to a *techne* of prudence and judgement.

8. A Two-Fold Plea

The argument for alternative agriculture is thus a double one. There is first an individualistic argument: namely, that hta eliminates the farmer as the subject of his life-world, either by driving him off the land, as in the

American case, or by reducing him to an appendage of the agro-industrial complex, as in the Third World case. The second argument is a social one: that the impossibility of a true dialogue between expert and farmer makes the farmer's knowledge the best hope for a resilient agriculture capable of responding to whatever shocks and crises the future may bring.

In the end, the two arguments may come to the same thing. Can a society of subjects, a community which is collectively the author of its own future, exist without a basis in its own knowledge? Conversely, can a community which legitimizes and honours, as well as actively uses and constructs, its own knowledge do other than construct its own future?

REFERENCES

AIYER, A. K. and NARAYAN, Y. (1949), 'Mixed Cropping in India', *Indian Journal of Agricultural Science*, 19/4: 439–543.

ALEXANDRATOS, N. (1988) (ed.), *World Agriculture: Toward 2000*, New York: New York University Press.

ANDERSON, R., LEVY, E., and MORRISON, B. (1991), *Rice Science and Development Politics*, Oxford: Clarendon Press.

APFFEL-MARGLIN, F. (1990), 'Smallpox in Two Systems of Knowledge', in F. Apffel-Marglin and S. A. Marglin (eds.), *Dominating Knowledge: Development, Culture, and Resistance*, Oxford: Clarendon Press: 102–44.

APPADURAI, A. (1990), 'Technology and the Reproduction of Values in Rural Western India', in F. Apffel-Marglin and S. A. Marglin (eds.), *Dominating Knowledge: Development, Culture, and Resistance*, Oxford: Clarendon Press: 185–216.

ARISTOTLE (1934 edn.), *Nicomachean Ethics*, trans. H. Rackham, Cambridge, Mass.: Harvard University Press.

——(1944 edn.), *Politics*, trans. H. Rackham, Cambridge, Mass.: Harvard University Press.

ARNAULD, A. (1662), *The Art of Thinking*, 1964 trans. J. Dickoff and P. James, New York: Bobbs-Merrill.

BAILEY, L. H. (1911), *The Country-Life Movement in the United States*, New York: Macmillan.

——(1919), *The Holy Earth*, Ithaca, New York: Comstock Publishing Company.

BECKER, S. (1976), *Donald F. Jones and Hybrid Corn*, Bulletin 763, New Haven, Conn.: Connecticut Agricultural Experiment Station.

BELSHAW, D. (1979), 'Taking Indigenous Technology Seriously: The Case of Intercropping Techniques in East Africa', paper presented to a workshop at the Institute for Development Studies, University of Sussex, Sussex, England; repr. in D. Brokensha, D. M. Warren, and O. Werner (eds.) (1980), *Indigenous Knowledge Systems and Development*, Washington, DC: University Press of America: 195–201.

BERLAN, J. P. and LEWONTIN, R. (1988), *Hybrid Corn or the Unsettled Question of Technological Change*, MS.

244   DECOLONIZING THE TRANSFER OF TECHNOLOGY

BERRY, W. (1977), *The Unsettling of America: Culture and Agriculture*, San Francisco: Sierra Club Books.

BEGLEY, S. (1994), 'The End of Antibiotics', *Newsweek*, 123/13: 46–51.

—— (1984), 'Whose Head Is the Farmer Using? Whose Head Is Using the Farmer?' in W. Jackson, W. Berry, and B. Colman (eds.), *Meeting the Expectations of the Land: Essays in Sustainable Agriculture and Stewardship*, San Francisco: North Point Press.

BOURJAILY, V. (1973), 'One of the Green Revolution Boys', *Atlantic Monthly*, 231/2: 66–76.

BOWERS, W. (1974), *The Country Life Movement in America, 1900–1920*, Port Washington, NY: Kennikat Press.

BROKENSHA, D., WARREN, D. M., and WERNER, O. (1980), *Indigenous Knowledge Systems and Development*, Washington DC: University Press of America.

BRUNER, J. (1962), *On Knowing: Essays for the Left Hand*, 1979 edn., Cambridge, Mass.: Harvard University Press.

BUTLER, J. W. and MARION, B. W. (1983), 'The Impacts of Patent Protection on the U.S. Seed Industry and Public Plant Breeding', MS, University of Wisconsin, Madison.

CALDWELL, J. P. and CALDWELL, B. (1987), 'Anthropology and Demography: The Mutual Reinforcement of Speculation and Research', *Current Anthropology*, 28/1: 25–43.

CARSON, R. (1962), *Silent Spring*, Boston: Houghton Mifflin.

CRABB, A. R. (1947), *The Hybrid-Corn Makers: Prophets of Plenty*, New Brunswick: Rutgers University Press.

DANBOM, D. (1979), *The Resisted Revolution: Urban America and the Industrialization of Agriculture, 1900–1930*, Ames: Iowa State University Press.

DESCARTES, R. (1637/1641), *Discourse on Method and Meditations on First Philosophy*, 1980 trans. D. Cress, Indianapolis, Ind.: Hackett Publishing Co.

DODDS, E. R. (1951), *The Greeks and the Irrational*, Berkeley, Calif.: University of California Press.

DOMMEN, A. (1988), *Innovation in African Agriculture*, Boulder, Colo.: Westview Press.

DUVICK, D. (1984), 'Genetic Contributions to Yield Gains of U.S. Hybrid Maize, 1930 to 1980', in W. R. Fehr (ed.), *Genetic Contributions to Yield Gains of Five Major Crop Plants*, Crop Science Society of America Special Publication no. 7, Madison, Wis.: American Society of Agronomy.

—— (1993), personal communication, letter to the author dated 31 Dec.

EAST, E. and JONES, D. (1919), *Inbreeding and Outbreeding: Their Genetic and Sociological Significance*, Philadelphia: J. B. Lippincott.

Economic Report of the President, Washington DC: United States Government Printing Office, 1991.

EDWARDS, R. (1979), *Contested Terrain: The Transformation of the Workplace in the Twentieth Century*, New York: Basic Books.

FAO (Food and Agricultural Organization of the United Nations) (1989), 'Fertilizer', *FAO Yearbook 1988*, 38, FAO Statistics Series no. 89, Rome.

Ford Foundation Archives, Ford Foundation, New York.

FRANCIS, C. (1986) (ed.), *Multiple Cropping Systems*, New York: Macmillan.

GARDNER, C. O. (1978), 'Population Improvement in Maize', in D. B. Walden (ed.), *Maize Breeding and Genetics*, New York: John Wiley & Sons.

GILLIGAN, C. (1982), *In a Different Voice: Psychological Theory and Women's Development*, Cambridge, Mass.: Harvard University Press.

GRIFFIN, K. (1974), *The Political Economy of Agrarian Change? An Essay on the Green Revolution*, Cambridge, Mass.: Harvard University Press.

GRILICHES, Z. (1958), 'Research Costs and Social Returns: Hybrid Corn and Related Innovations', *Journal of Political Economy*, 66: 419–31.

HACKING, I. (1975), *The Emergence of Probability: A Philosophical Study of Early Ideas About Probability, Induction and Statistical Inference*, Cambridge: Cambridge University Press.

HARTLEY, C. P. (1920), 'Better Seed Corn', *Farmers' Bulletin 1175*, Washington, DC: United States Department of Agriculture.

HAYAMI, Y. and RUTTAN, V. W. (1985), *Agricultural Development: An International Perspective*, 2nd edn., Baltimore: Johns Hopkins University Press.

HEWITT DE ALCANTARA, C. (1976), *Modernizing Mexican Agriculture: Socioeconomic Implications of Technological Change, 1940–1970*, Geneva: United Nations Research Institute for Social Development.

HOWARD, A. (1940), *An Agricultural Testament*, New York: Oxford University Press.

JENKINS, M. (1936), 'Corn Improvement', in *Department of Agriculture Yearbook.*, Washington, DC: United States Department of Agriculture.

JENNINGS, B. (1988), *Foundations of International Agricultural Research: Science and Politics in Mexican Agriculture*, Boulder, Colo.: Westview Press.

JODHA, N. S. (1981), 'Intercropping in Traditional Farming Systems', in ICRISAT (International Crops Research Institute for the Semi-Arid Tropics), *Proceedings of the International Workshop on Intercropping, 10–13 January 1979*, Hyderabad, India.

KEYNES, J. M. (1936), *The General Theory of Employment, Interest, and Money*, London: Macmillan.

KIMMELMAN, B. (1987), *A Progressive Era Discipline: Genetics at American Agricultural Colleges and Experiment Stations, 1900–1920*, Ann Arbor, Mich.: United Microfilms International (Ph.D. diss., University of Pennsylvania).

KLOPPENBURG, J., Jr. (1988), *First the Seed: The Political Economy of Plant Biotechnology 1492–2000*, Cambridge: Cambridge University Press.

KLOSKO, G. (1986), *The Development of Plato's Political Theory*, New York: Methuen.

KOPYTOFF, I. (1981), 'Knowledge and Belief in Suku Thought', *Africa*, 51/3: 709–23.

KNUDSON, M. and RUTTAN, V. (1988), 'Research and Development of a Biological Innovation: Commercial Hybrid Wheat', *Food Research Institute Studies*, 21/1: 45–68.

KUHN, T. (1962), *The Structure of Scientific Revolutions*, 2nd edn. 1970, *International Encyclopedia of Unified Science*, ii, no. 2, Chicago: University of Chicago Press.

LAKATOS, I. (1970), 'Falsification and the Methodology of Scientific Research Programmes', in I. Lakatos and A. Musgrave (eds.), *Criticism and the Growth of Knowledge*, Cambridge: Cambridge University Press.

LAZONICK, W. (1974), 'Karl Marx and Enclosure in England', *Review of Radical Political Economy*, 6: 1–59.

LEWONTIN, R. and BERLAN, J.-P. (1986), 'Technology, Research, and the Penetration of Capital: The Case of U.S. Agriculture', *Monthly Review*, 38/3: 21–47.

LOVINS, A., LOVINS, L. H., and BENDER, M. (1984), 'Energy and Agriculture' in W. Berry, W. Jackson, and B. Colman, (eds.), *Meeting the Expectations of the Land*, San Francisco: North Point Press: 68–86.

LURIA, A. (1979), *Cognitive Development? Its Cultural and Social Foundations*, Cambridge, Mass: Harvard University Press.

LYONS, J. (1969), *Structural Semantics: An Analysis of Part of the Vocabulary of Plato*, Oxford: Basil Blackwell.

MALTHUS, T. (1976 edn.), *An Essay on the Principle of Population*, ed. P. Appleman, New York: Norton (1st pub. 1798).

MANGELSDORF, P. (1953), 'Wheat', repr. in *Scientific American* v. 189/1 (July), 50–9.

MARGLIN, S. (1974), 'What Do Bosses Do? The Origins and Functions of Hierarchy in Capitalist Production, Part I', *Review of Radical Political Economy*, 6: 60–112; repr. in A. Gorz (ed.), *The Division of Labour*, Sussex: Harvester, 1976.

——(1979), 'Catching Flies with Honey: An Inquiry into Management Initiatives to Humanize Work', *Economic Analysis and Workers' Management*, 12: 473–87.

——(1984), 'Knowledge and Power', in F. Stephen (ed.), *Firms, Organization and Labour*, London: Macmillan: 146–64.

——(1990), 'Losing Touch: The Cultural Conditions of Worker Accommodation and Resistance', in F. Apffel-Marglin and S. A. Marglin (eds.), *Dominating Knowledge: Development, Culture, and Resistance*, Oxford: Clarendon Press: 217–82.

——in collaboration with F. Apffel-Marglin, T. Banuri, A. Nandy, and M.-L. Swantz (1990), 'Sustainable Development: A Systems of Knowledge Approach', *TOES/NA Newsletter*, 6: 5–8; repr. in *The Black Scholar*, 21/1 (1990), 35–42.

MARX, K. (1867), *Capital*, i. 1959 edn., Moscow: Foreign Languages Publishing House.

MATHUR, P. N. (1963), 'Cropping Pattern and Employment in Vidarbha', *Indian Journal of Agricultural Economics*, 18/1: 38–43.

MEADOWS, D., MEADOWS, D. et al. (1972), *The Limits to Growth*, New York: Universe Books.

MYERS, N. (1983), *A Wealth of Wild Species: Storehouse for Human Welfare*, Boulder, Colo: Westview Press.

NANDY, A., and VISVANATHAN, S. (1990), 'Modern Medicine and its Non-Modern Critics: A Study in Discourse', in F. Apffel-Marglin and S. A. Marglin (eds.), *Dominating Knowledge: Development, Culture, and Resistance*, Oxford: Clarendon Press.

National Research Council (1972), *Genetic Vulnerability of Major Crops*, Washington, DC: National Academy Press.

—— (1989), *Alternative Agriculture*, Washington, DC: National Academy Press.

NORMAN, D. W. (1974), 'Rationalising Mixed Cropping Under Indigenous Conditions: The Example of Northern Nigeria', *Journal of Development Studies*, 11/1: 3–21.

NUSSBAUM, M. (1986), *The Fragility of Goodness: Luck and Ethics in Greek Tragedy and Philosophy*, Cambridge; Cambridge University Press.

——and SEN, A. (1989), 'Internal Criticism and Indian Rationalist Traditions', in M. Krausz (ed.), *Relativism: Interpretation and Confrontation*, Notre Dame, Ind: Notre Dame University Press.

OASA, E. and JENNINGS, B. (1982), 'Science and Authority in International Agricultural Research', *Bulletin of Concerned Asian Scholars*, 14: 30–44.

PAPENDICK, R. I., SANCHEZ, P. A., and TRIPLETT, G. B. (1976) (eds.), *Multiple Cropping*, American Society of Agronomy Special Publication no. 27, Madison, Wis.: American Society of Agronomy.

PEARCE, D., MARKANDYA, A., and BARBIER, E. R., *Blueprint for a Green Economy*, London: Earthscan.

PEARSE, A. (1980), *Seeds of Plenty, Seeds of Want: Social and Economic Implications of the Green Revolution*, Oxford: Oxford University Press.

PIRSIG, R. (1976), *Zen and the Art of Motorcycle Maintenance: An Inquiry into Values*, London: Transworld.

PLATO (1925a edn.), 'Gorgias' in *Lysis, Symposium, and Gorgias*, trans. W. R. M. Lamb, Cambridge, Mass.: Harvard University Press.

——(1925b edn.), 'Philebus' in *Statesman, Philebus, and Ion*, trans. Harold N. Fowler and W. R. M. Lamb, Cambridge, Mass.: Harvard University Press.

——(1941 edn.), *The Republic of Plato*, trans. F. Cornford, New York/London: Oxford University Press.

POLANYI, M. (1958), *Personal Knowledge: Towards a Post-Critical Philosophy*, Chicago: University of Chicago Press.

POPKIN, R. (1979), *The History of Skepticism from Erasmus to Spinoza*, Berkeley, Calif.: University of California Press.

POPPER, K. (1968), *The Logic of Scientific Discovery*, New York: Harper & Row.

POSTEL, S. (1989), *Water for Agriculture: Facing the Limits*, Worldwatch Paper 93, Washington, DC: Worldwatch Institute.

PUTNAM, H. (1974), 'The Corroboration of Scientific Theories', in K. Schilpp (ed.), *The Philosophy of Karl Popper*, La Salle, Ill.: Open Court.

Rockefeller Foundation Archives, Rockefeller Archive Center, North Tarrytown, New York: 221–40.

RODGERS, M. M. (1850), *Scientific Agriculture*, 2nd rev. edn., Rochester, New York: Erastus Darrow.

ROSENBERG, C. (1976), *No Other Gods: On Science and American Social Thought*, Baltimore and London: Johns Hopkins University Press.

SACKS, O. (1985), *The Man Who Mistook His Wife for a Hat, and Other Clinical Tales*, New York: Summit Books.

SCHULTZ, T. (1964), *Transforming Traditional Agriculture*, New Haven, Conn./ London: Yale University Press.

SCHUMPETER, J. (1911), *The Theory of Economic Development: An Inquiry into Profits, Capital, Credit, Interest, and the Business Cycle*, 1934 trans. R. Opie, Cambridge, Mass.: Harvard University Press.

SIMMONDS, N. W. (1983), 'Plant Breeding: The State of the Art', in T. Kosuge *et al.* (eds.), *Genetic Engineering of Plants: An Agricultural Perspective*, New York: Plenum Press: 5–25.

SMITH, A. (1776), *The Wealth of Nations*, 1937 edn., (ed.) E. Canaan, New York: Random House.

STEELE, L. (1978), 'The Hybrid Corn Industry in the United States', in D. B. Walden (ed.), *Maize Breeding and Genetics*, New York: John Wiley & Sons.

STERBA, J. (1990), 'Indonesia Gives Rice Farming a Facelift: Pesticides are Succeeded by Pest Management', *The Wall Street Journal*, 16 Apr.

TOULMIN, S. (1990), *Cosmopolis: The Hidden Agenda of Modernity*, New York: Free Press.

TRENBATH, B. (1974), 'Biomass Productivity of Mixtures', in N. C. Brady (ed.), *Agronomy*, 26, New York: Academic Press.

United States Department of Agriculture (1963), *Prices Paid by Farmers for Seed*, Statistical Bulletin no. 328, Statistical Reporting Service, Crop Reporting Board, Washington, DC.

VANDERMEER, J. H (1989), *The Ecology of Intercropping*, Cambridge: Cambridge University Press.

VERNANT, J.-P. (1965), *Mythe et Pensée chez les Grecs: Études de Psychologie Historique*, ii, 1982 edn., Paris: Francois Maspero.

VIDAL-NAQUET, P. (1981), *Le Chasseur Noir: Formes de Pensée et Formes de Société dans le Monde Grec*, 1983 edn., Paris: La Decouverte/Maspero. (rev. and corrected).

WELLHAUSEN, E. J. (1978), 'Recent Development in Maize Breeding in the Tropics', in D. B. Walden (ed.), *Maize Breeding and Genetics*, New York: John Wiley & Sons: 59–84.

WEST, R. (1979), *Carl Sauer's Fieldwork in Latin America*, Ann Arbor, Mich.: University Microfilms International.

Worldwatch Institute (1994), *Worldwatch Database Diskette*, Washington DC: Worldwatch Institute.

World Bank (1992), *World Development Report 1992: Development and the Environment*, New York: Oxford University Press.

7

Hosting the Otherness of the Other:
The Case of the Green Revolution

GUSTAVO ESTEVA

Some families send their sons to Jesuit schools in England and the United States, which presents the rare situation that the Mexican youth, in order to be brought up in entirely religious principles, go to learn to be Catholics in Protestant countries.

Lucas Alamán (1852)

In this chapter I will explore the marginalization of a rich variety of knowledge systems practised in the name of the Green Revolution. In alluding to the relationships between traditional techniques and modern technological packages, I will carefully avoid the reduction—to each other—of the knowledge systems generating them. I do not want to use a monistic or dualistic approach to deal with their pluriformity, difference, variety, or diversity. I want to examine them under the assumption of radical pluralism. I am looking for a dialogical dialogue[1] among knowledge systems, as a substitute for the power games embedded in some of them.

After 50 years of polemic, the discussion between the apologists and the critics of the Green Revolution has become pretty nonsensical. I suggest replacing it with a controversy,[2] assuming that the world is a pluriverse, not a universe. It is not my purpose to examine the content, the impact or the implications of the proposal and the experience labelled as the Green Revolution. I have not organized my arguments to persuade or refute, nor will I look for a neutral or impartial observation point from which to describe, classify, or evaluate the positions or versions involved. I will disown neither the position I adopted while participating in the polemic, nor its present incarnation as one of the versions in the controversy I am suggesting. What I am trying to show, while refusing to budge from my place, is that hospitality, in the relationship with the other, is not only possible but necessary.

You can host the other even when you are disagreeing with his arguments, his versions. To be hospitable is not to follow the other, to adopt his views, to affirm him, or to negate him. Hosting the other simply means to open your own doors for him and to accept his existence in his own place. Hospitality is the opposite of tolerance, which is just a more discreet form of intolerance.

The 'Green Revolution' is the territory of my analysis. The positions and versions involved are presented as I perceive them incarnated in Fidel Palafox, Marte R. Gómez, and Efraím Hernández Xolocotzi, whose life stories I am telling through some fragmented episodes, hoping not to betray the spirit and meaning of the actions and reactions I am describing.

DON FIDEL'S RESISTANCE

For more than eighty years, throughout this century, Don Fidel Palafox worked the land. He spent half his life administering *haciendas*. As a careful and patient observer of natural processes and peasant practices, he constantly experimented with ways of enriching their interaction. Once he felt his experience was mature enough to be useful for others, he started to write down what he had learned. He was then 40 years old. Once his work was concluded, however, he postponed its publication, in spite of the insistence of his friends. Finally, in 1988, before new pressures, he warmly but firmly accepted the edition.

I want to reflect on the historical sequence creating three different sets of conditions: those fostering in Don Fidel the impulse for writing, those creating his resistance to publishing his writings, and those finally forcing him to accept the publishing. In this way, I am building an impure model of the transformations marginalizing one knowledge system while imposing another and later opening a dialogue among them.

Don Fidel's book is a jewel of peasant wisdom, a brief encyclopedia of concrete knowledge. Told in simple language, through the pertinent use of local, vernacular expressions, Don Fidel organizes and systematizes in it his lifetime's observations and experiences. He describes carefully, with patience and rigour, sensible agricultural practices for the region he learned to know so well.

Don Fidel uses, more than any other, the word perfect. He relies on an attitude that searches for perfection in every aspect of agriculture or life. The way he approaches the subject of forests illustrates his contention. Don Fidel conceives of the exploitation of forests as a human way of helping to keep them young and magnificent. Without the perfect exploitation of the forest, he says, 'in time there will only be old and rotten trees'; without it, 'from the trunk will not generate the abundant and healthy sprouts which should come from the well-pruned tree' (p. 22). More than money, claims Don Fidel, the land needs 'responsible men, with extensive knowledge, to work it'. 'It is not a mistake', he insists, 'to contend that the land asks for a little money and a lot of knowledge' (p. 50).

Don Fidel exposes explicitly some of the reasons behind his resistance to publish. 'Those of us who know little', he says with dignified and typical peasant modesty, resist teaching what we know 'to protect ourselves from severe criticism'. In addition, he did not want to be misunderstood nor for his book to be taken for what it is not. It is not, says Don Fidel, 'an agricultural treatise'. According to him, it cannot be; it is only 'the result of the experience acquired during many years of working with the land'. And he adds:

I will not use technical words or concepts, since I received my agricultural knowledge not in a school but behind the yoke, preparing the land for starting the cultivation. Given the affection I have always had for this hard but sublime work, to which I have dedicated most of my life, by making some trials as well as observing carefully the works done by competent farmers, or by my elders, who were also farmers, I was able to succeed in the agricultural labor in the farms which I had under my control. I am profitting from this to give its form to this pamphlet, by using words known by the peasants.

Don Fidel thinks that it is worthwhile to expose oneself to anything to help 'those who, even if they live and work in the fields, don't know a thing about it'. The proof that they don't know, says Don Fidel, 'is the terrible condition of most of the land that was formerly excellent arable land' (p. 20).

I am exploring Don Fidel's resistance to publish his writings. The present confusion of personal and mercantile values, now invading every aspect of daily life, is part of the story. In the new arrangement of the world, use values disappear, they become old-fashioned and at the end lose their character. In the 'era of disabling professions' thus established, 'ten years managing a farm may be processed in a pedagogic mixer, making them equivalent to a university diploma' (Illich, 1981: 25). The profession underestimates use values and people like Don Fidel cannot publish an agricultural treatise. But this is not enough to explain Don Fidel's behaviour. Perhaps some other elements of the context will help to complete the picture.

ORGANIZING EVERYTHING WISELY

Don Fidel Palafox belongs to the generation of Lázaro Cárdenas, the father of modern Mexico. He was born just a few days before him, on 24 April 1895, in the *hacienda* La Noria, in the county of Huamantla, of the estate of Tlaxcala, a little province next to Mexico City, in the centre of the country. Almost the whole county is in a valley, in the southern portion of which appear the foothills of the volcano La Malinche. The valley is sandy and the vegetation scarce, but the area has good communications and is good for the cultivation of cereals. The son of an indentured peon, Don Fidel lived in this condition, in the *hacienda* where he was born, during the last years of the dictatorship of Porfirio Díaz. He heard how the Revolution started, very near his home, in the city of Puebla, when he was 15 years old.

Seven years later, by mysterious means that Don Fidel prefers to forget, he appears as an administrator of the *hacienda* La Laguna, belonging to Don Romárico González. He would be in that position for the next ten years.

Don Fidel started his work the same year as the proclamation of the new Political Constitution, defining the new legal order of modern Mexico. Thus reformulated the agrarian question, the challenge of redistributing the *haciendas* still dominating the rural landscape, was opened. During the next decade, around Don Fidel, in Tlaxcala as in many other places, there was much ado about nothing in agrarian matters. Few peasants got land. The agrarian policy of local governments was even more restrictive than the federal one. True, anti-agrarian winds were blowing and resistance from the *hacendados* appeared, but the factor determining that policy was the concern of the revolutionary governments. In 1920 this was synthetized by President Obregón with his usual frankness: 'We should not destroy the large properties before creating the small ones. Otherwise, we will create a productive imbalance which may cause a period of hunger. I think we must be very cautious and must study these problems calmly and thoroughly' (García Treviño, 1953: 48).

In accordance with this mood, the pace of the agrarian reform became slower as the decade proceeded, and activity was usually the result of local dynamism. In Morelos, for example, the land of Zapata, the most important peasant leader of the Revolution, agrarian reform proceeded fairly quickly; in fact, it consisted of giving legal deeds to the Zapatista peasants already occupying the land. In southern Tlaxcala, in the middle of an intense peasant mobilization, a large number of small plots were distributed. Where Don Fidel was, by contrast, almost nothing happened. We have only limited information on the peasant movements of the area, but the apparent paralysis of the peons of the *haciendas* in northern Tlaxcala seems to be the consequence of impotence and fear, rather than of passivity or lack of initiative.

In 1928 Don José María Cajica took Don Fidel to work on his *hacienda* San Miguel in Huamantla. In 1931 Don Fidel moved to Acatzingo, Puebla, to administer the *hacienda* San Juan Macuila. He was found there by Don Alfredo Bretón, who persuaded Don Fidel to come with him, back to Huamantla, to administer his *hacienda* Santa Clara. Don Fidel worked there from 1938 on.

Mexico changed considerably in those ten years, and the rural landscape took on a completely different face. Between 1935 and 1938, President Cárdenas distributed more land than all previous revolutionary governments: 20 million hectares. The *ejidos* were no longer the spaces allowing the peasants 'to cut some wood' or 'to get some water', as President Obregón used to say. Nor did they constitute a transitory institution for the peasants to substitute the gun for the yoke while small property was created, as Luis Cabrera had proposed since 1912 and as many revolutionaries wanted. The *ejido*, as a form of land tenure, was already established in half the arable land of the country and became a permanent institution. In most of the *ejidos* the plots were owned in common but allocated individually for the private use of the *ejidatarios*, but in some places the *ejidos* worked collectively by *ejidatarios* were also flourishing.

Hopes were also moving forward in a different direction. In 1935 Ramón Beteta exposed the economic aspects of the Six-Year Plan (1934–1940) as follows:

We believe that Mexico finds herself in a privileged position to determine her destiny . . . By observing the effects of the last crisis of the capitalistic world, we think that we should be able to use the advantages of the industrial era without having to suffer from its well-known shortcomings. We think that we should attempt to industrialize Mexico consciously, intelligently avoiding the avoidable evils of industrialism, such as urbanism, exploitation of man by man, production for sale instead of production for the satisfaction of human needs, economic insecurity, waste, shabby goods and the mechanization of the workmen . . . We have dreamt of a Mexico of *ejidos* and small industrial communities, electrified, with sanitation, in which goods will be produced for the purpose of satisfying the needs of the people; in which machinery will be employed to relieve man from heavy toil, and not for so-called over-production. (Mosk, 1950: 58)

This is probably the best existing definition of 'the road not taken'. Ten years later Ramón Beteta, the official of the Cárdenas government present-ing those ideas in 1935, became the Minister of Finance for President Alemán, where he brilliantly promoted urbanism, production for the mar-ket, and industrialization, ideas which have dominated official policies since then.

The educational system reflected the redefinition of hopes marking the 1930s. The goals changed drastically: the Constitution proclaimed that education should be socialist and the Six-Year Plan promised to bring elementary education to all the peasants. Realities also changed: Peasant Regional Schools started to appear everywhere, and cultural missions ar-rived in many towns. Both modalities of education worked around three axes: agricultural and industrial practices, the direct relationship with the communities, and the involvement of everyone—the teachers, the students, the technicians, and the institutions themselves—in the agrarian claims of the communities. In technical matters, the rural teachers or the agrono-mists of the cultural missions had no agronomic credo to disseminate.

In El Mexe, Hidalgo, and Chamuxco, Puebla, not very far from Don Fidel's area, two Peasant Regional Schools were established in 1935. For the next year, many community schools were incorporated into the 'experi-mental circuits' of the Regional Schools and were implementing the most diverse initiatives.

Don Fidel saw himself immersed in such a process. He perceived clearly that those receiving land were not only real peasants or indentured peons of the *haciendas*. Small merchants, artisans or craftsmen, 'who had never been in contact with the arable land and its problems', were also getting land. The former—Don Fidel thought—had worked the land 'physically', but 'they lacked administrative or directive knowledges' and did not know how to organize everything wisely. The last lacked both the 'physical' experience and the knowledge. But all of them were dedicated to exploiting their plots and

to cultivating the land mistakenly, neglecting edges and ditches, with the result that a few years later, in the rainy season, the water runs everywhere and, since there is no protection, carries away the organic layer of the land, leaving only some sand that the winds carry away to the flat fields, leaving small banks of fertile land on the slopes, in the middle of great extensions of sandy land and, in the flat fields, great sand banks. This represents the terrible plague of soil erosion that we all regret (p. 19).

Don Fidel started to write. He was back in his place, with his people. He thought he could be useful to them. He proceeded slowly, but with decision and perseverance. When he accepted a post at the famous *hacienda* Zotoluca, which he administered until 1951, the work was concluded. By then, however, the country had changed again, and Don Fidel did not now dare to publish his work.

THE AGRONOMISTS ARRIVE

It was not so unusual that Don Fidel, an indentured peon son of an indentured peon, became administrator of all those *haciendas*. The agronomists never represented a real alternative to the rural labourers when the question was how to handle the *haciendas*, largely because the agronomists did not exist until the end of the *hacienda* regime. This is no secret: the *hacendados* were not seriously interested in the technical changes promised by the agronomists, nor did these professionals seem to have the skills or knowledge to fulfil their promises of improvement.

For most of the last century, only the peasants and the *hacendados* were cultivating land in Mexico. Almost without exception, their activity was based on a traditional knowledge system, which was not learned in school. It was purely Indian *techne*, knowledge dating from past millennia transmitted through differentiated cultural patterns. Or it was *techné mestiza*, Indian *techné* exposed to the practices introduced by the Spaniards and mixed with them. Both of them constituted an agricultural tradition, bearing a specific knowledge system. Hierarchy born from the popular stock: the wise man of the town, consulted for difficult decisions or in the case of calamity or predicament, as well as foremen or administrators of the *haciendas*, who had emerged from among the peasants, the peons.

How and when did things change? Don Efraím Hernández Xolocotzi offered me an interesting clue:

The marginalization of traditional wisdom did not start with the Rockefeller Foundation, in 1943, but with the creation of the National School of Agriculture in 1854. It was based in the European educational system, to train supervisors for the *haciendas*, thus including only technical careers. From then on the peasant knowledge started to be marginalized.[3]

The first formal institution dedicated to the production of agronomists, the National School of Agriculture was founded in Mexico by a decree of President Antonio López de Santa Ana, on 19 August 1853. It started to function in February of the following year, in the ex-convent of San Jacinto. Twenty years later it was languishing at the point of extinction: it had only twenty-eight students, because the *hacendados* still preferred rural labourers. The programme and organization of the school militated against it: they suffered the dispersion and superficiality common to almost all Mexican study plans of the time, thus reflecting the weaknesses of the French plans they were trying to imitate. The Jesuits clearly identified those deficiencies when they refused to adopt the pedagogic fashions of the times, creating in the students the illusion of knowing a lot when they were not learning much. '*Ex omnibus aliquid; in toto nihil*: A little of everything and nothing in substance' (Alamán, 1852: 911).

The period known as República Restaurada (1867–76) started with a firm move to renovate the educational system, which had a major impact in technical fields. The results, however, did not correspond to the hopes. In the case of the National School of Agriculture, it confronted problems both of organization and of perspective: 'The rich don't want to come and the poor cannot find a future.' The very limited expectations for employment or prestige did not compensate for eight long years of study, with subjects like applied chemistry and physics, botany, zoology, topography, and geometry (Cosío, 1956: 732–4).

During the dictatorship (1877–1910), the *haciendas* persisted in their extensive exploitation of their immense endowments of natural resources. The School was in very bad shape. Early in this century, however, as a consequence of the observations he made during a long trip to Europe and the United States, Lauro Viadas, then Director of the School, started an intense campaign to publicize the agricultural backwardness of Mexico and to promote ways of remedying it. He proposed a complete reorganization of the School, to prepare technicians to be employed by the government for promoting the transformation of Mexican agriculture. Once his plan was approved, Viadas brought to the School European and American experts who helped in the establishment of the first experimental fields existing in

Mexico. The Revolution found Viadas among the promoters of the agrarian reform. One of his main proposals consisted of giving the land to 'the best farmers': those renting land or coming back after working in the States, where they mastered more advanced techniques. Viadas was not able to implement his plans fully, because of the turmoil of the Revolution, but his ideas had enduring effects. They were carried forward by one of his students, Marte R. Gómez.

MARTE APPEARS

Marte R. Gómez was 13 years old, in 1909, when he entered the National School of Agriculture. The School was closed in May 1914, after a rebellion involving both teachers and students, but in 1917 he graduated from the Ateneo Ceres, which had been created to give those whose studies had been interrupted an opportunity to conclude them.

Gómez soon acquired impeccable titles as a radical agrarianist: between 1914 and 1916 he was part of the agrarian commissions organized by Emiliano Zapata in Morelos and by Salvador Alvarado in Yucatán. After graduating, he became assistant director of the National Agrarian Commission, where he enacted Order 51, in which 'the incompatibility between petty agriculture and machinery' was assumed, thus postulating a kind of collectivization of the *ejidos* sponsored and controlled by the government. (For many, that instruction was the ideological embryo for the 'bureaucratic–cacique dictatorship' that has since characterized the situation in rural Mexico.)

Very early in his life Gómez acquired the twin convictions that the peasants should receive the land and that they did not know how to work it. In all the various high-level political and administrative positions he occupied he promoted a techno-productive revolution, parallel to the redistributing of *haciendas*, which was to be implemented through scientific research and technology transfer. A phrase he pronounced in 1946, when he was at the height of this political career, illustrates his position well: 'Mexico is a country of agriculturalists looking for both agricultural land and agriculture' (Secretaría de Gobernación, 1946: 189).

Don Marte left an enduring mark in the National School of Agriculture, which he directed for two years starting in 1923. In 1925 he founded a Regional School of Agriculture, in Tamaulipas, to support the agrarian policy of Governor Portes Gil. By that time elementary agriculture schools were being established in the whole country, to become centres of education, experimentation, propaganda, rural organization, and agricultural credit. Marte R. Gómez thought that his school should not be elementary: the rural population of Tamaulipas knew well and even practised the 'agricultural techniques of Texas'. He endowed his 'intermediate' school with fields for selecting corn seeds and experimenting with other crops and practices (Gómez, 1925: 78).

Gómez continued the promotion of his ideas when he became Minister of Agriculture, between 1928 and 1930. He was forced to concentrate on urgent agrarian affairs, but he was also able to deal with professional formation in agriculture. He promoted it in many ways, such as the creation of nurseries and pilot farms, which were the immediate antecedent of the experimental stations which defined one of the main roads for research and extension in the following years. He called to the Ministry, to work with him, the senior agronomists he knew well, but he also opened all the doors to the new generation and supported them extensively. At the end of his term almost all the agronomists in Mexico had a job in one of the official institutions—this had been one of Viadas' dreams.

Immediately afterwards, Marte R. Gómez departed for a trip to Europe which had an enduring impact on him: it reaffirmed his ideas about models for agrarian and agricultural organization, which were always closer to those followed in Denmark and Holland than to the United States, as well as his convictions about the role of research and education for the transformation of agriculture. These ideas matured over a long period and he tested some of them while participating in the government of Tamaulipas, first as a senator and later as a governor (1937–40). When he again became Minister of Agriculture, in 1940 under President Avila Camacho, his agrarianist convictions were as firm as ever, but he was convinced that the time has come for consolidation. The challenge was no longer on the agrarian front, but in the field of production and particularly in technology.

For him, as for most Mexican agronomists of the time, there were no doubts about the road to technical improvement: the priority was the transfer to the peasants of new modern techniques, based on scientific research, professional formation, and extension. Agronomic science should provide the models, the instruments, and the technical creations. Appropriate academic centres should train competent professional personnel to disseminate these techniques. The institutions should create the conditions for the technicians to be able to perform their task.

Marte R. Gómez was loyal to the tradition of Lauro Viadas from the very day he came back to the Ministry of Agriculture. He profited from the presence in Mexico of Henry Wallace, Vice-President of the United States, whom he knew as a private entrepreneur in hybrids. Gómez tried to convince him of the need and convenience for the United States to support Mexico in the field of agricultural techniques. Wallace's reaction was highly enthusiastic. Since there was no aid agency in the American government, he looked for philanthropic organizations. In Mexico the Rockefeller Foundation had already had a successful involvement in the health field since

1918, when it had helped the struggle against yellow fever. The Foundation showed clear interest in the challenge: it fitted very well with its own plans for Latin America in the 1940s.

From then on, all developments proceeded in the same direction, leading naturally to the creation of the Special Studies Bureau, in the Ministry of Agriculture, to perform the activities that in time were filed under the label Green Revolution. Neither in this operation, nor in the affair of the famous Brazilian zebu cows which brought foot-and-mouth disease to Mexico, was Marte R. Gómez guilty of treason—of which he was unjustly blamed in 1947. The imperialism of the operation, which I am exploring, was the imperialism of one knowledge system over the others, practised in the name of science by its personifications in Mexican and by foreign scientists to this day. It was not economic or national imperialism, as it has often been denounced in connection with the Green Revolution.[4]

At the start of his second term, Marte R. Gómez strengthened the Agronomy Department, by encouraging the dissemination of information and establishing the Experimental Fields Department to undertake research. These field stations were no longer the experimental stations of the 1930s, which, although they had used technically orthodox approaches, shared the social commitments of the times and were, in some measure, at the service of the peasants and the agrarian revolution. The fields now tended to be more and more at the service of science, that is, dedicated to the production of knowledge packages to improve the techniques of the producers.

Long before the scientific method for improving Mexican agriculture showed its first theoretical or practical results, its predominance was well established. Such was the force of the faith underlying it. It was, literally, pre-dominant, based in pre-judices. Well before pondering alternative and feasible technical methods for reaching the desired results, even before including in the analysis any ethical or social considerations, the final sentence was pronounced.

In fact, no possible evaluation of the specific contributions of the Mexican system of research, teaching, and extension up to 1940 could validly support the decisions taken in that decade, which reformed, widened, and instituted it as the main and only legitimate source of knowledge, and the fundamental purveyor of ideas for formulating policies and implementing public and private plans and programmes. The decisions taken were based on a series of ideological premises that were almost never exposed to analysis, being, as they were, established in the perception as a priori categories of consciousness. Those premises still support the dominant knowledge system: among them, particularly, the conviction that so-called scientific research is the only legitimate and acceptable source of knowledge and that only by starting with it, through teaching and extension, is it possible to improve agricultural practices.

LEARNING TO LEARN

In Mexico the critique of the predominant approach and the denouncing of its blinkers are incarnated magnificently in the life and works of a prominent native of Tlaxcala, born in 1913 in the village of San Bernabé, a few kilometers from the area in which Don Fidel worked his whole life. When Marte R. Gómez had just returned from Europe, this man was ending his training as an agricultural technician in the United States. He consolidated his studies in agricultural sciences at Cornell University (1934–8). In 1939 he inaugurated his brand new diplomas in the job of assistant to the Regional Director of the official rural bank in Villahermosa, Tabasco. He was then 27 years old.

In addition to his regular professional degrees from Long Island, Cornell, and Harvard, Don Efraím Hernández Xolocotzi has received honorary doctorate degrees from various academic institutions, as well as national and international prizes of many kinds. He has published several books and more than a hundred essays and monographs. A member of fourteen scientific societies, he has presided over two of them. From time to time, he receives ardent homages from Presidents of Mexico, Ministers of Agriculture, national or international academic or research centres, or professional organizations connected with his activities. All this dramatizes, to an extreme, the incredible marginalization of his ideas and works, which are not taken seriously by those who formulate or implement public policies or by those who orient and control academic activities. The niches of education and research that he had succeeded in constructing through tenacity, prestige, and affection tend to operate in the form of ghettos, as untouchable as they are isolated. He is always invited to debates, seminars, and congresses, as a necessary part of the analytical spectrum. His absence is thus emphasized: through indifference or omission—the perfect forms of intolerance—or even worse, through the offence of the fake incorporation, of a distorting synthesis, he is marginalized in the very places and circumstances where he seems to be appropriatedly recognized.

Since the 1920s, the model for the creation of Mexican agronomists included, almost without exception, a postgraduate degree from a foreign country, preferably from the United States. As shown above, Don Efraím is not lacking in diplomas: he has plenty to spare. But his path followed, in reality, the direction opposite to the conventional direction. Born in a rural school, where his mother was the teacher, he completed all his studies—from elementary school on—in the United States. The original attraction of the land should not have been so great: as a child and adolescent he dreamed of studying other subjects. He began to be interested in agriculture when he visited his native village of San Bernabé, at the age of 19. From then on, he never abandoned this field.

The first thing he learned, upon his return to Mexico in 1938, was the value of informal networks formed in the school in order to get a job in a country like Mexico. No contacts, no job. It took him one year to find a job. In the time of Cárdenas, a regional director of the rural bank fulfilled the function of organizing credit and marketing, as well as the *ejido* itself, and also of giving technical assistance to the *ejidatarios*. For the young new-comer, such a task posed quite a challenge:

Fortunately, remembers don Efraím, I had the idea of leaving the running of the cultivation efforts we promoted to the experienced farmers, as almost no-one in the bank seemed to know how to develop these efforts technically. Curiously enough, I came to the conclusion that the experienced farmers were the ones who could best direct the works (Hernández, 1984: 208).

In 1942 Don Efraím had to face the frustrating experience of having been hired to open a new experimental field—of the kind being created by Don Marte—for which finance never arrived. He was still floating in that bu-reaucratic limbo when he was named as part of a Mexican–American commission to study and promote the cultivation of castor vine. The programme failed completely, when pests invaded the promoted culti-vations, but this allowed Don Efraím to get to know first-hand a good portion of the country and to meet many farmers. That experience was extended when the Special Studies Bureau hired him to collect seeds. Don Marte R. Gómez approved his designation personally, and established a condition, illustrating very well his own involvement in the activities of research and education: the condition was that he must accept a job teaching botany in the School of Agriculture when the person in charge of the subject decided to retire. Even in the middle of the turmoil of the final year of his term, Don Marte found time to put agricultural teaching on the right track and to leave the research systems well established.

During his postgraduate studies, in 1947–8, Don Efraím took a glance at the latest advances in agricultural techniques and confirmed his old feeling that the American model was not applicable in México. This view, as well as his continual insistence on the need to give a socio-economic context to agricultural research, seriously affected his relationship with Taboada and Limón, the two pioneers who created the Department of Experimental Fields and headed the Mexican groups in charge of research. He was never able to reach an understanding with them. For him, they were too rigidly bound to a foreign model, both in conceiving and in implementing re-search. Those in the field had to follow strictly the instructions handed down from the centre, often based on blackboard schemes, such as the hybrids constructed mathematically by Taboada.

The Special Studies Bureau did not have the budget limitations or the bureaucratic ties of the Department of Experimental Fields, nor the blink-ers of Taboada and Limón, but it did have its own dogmatic biases. Don Efraím suffered them first-hand. He was hired by the Bureau to study alternative crops in the area of Tlahualilo, Durango, an arid zone with some irrigation, where the reduction of the price of cotton was affecting the main crop. Don Efraím studied all the options suggested by the Bureau, but he also explored the idea of breeding goats, suggested by local peasants. He found that in the area a particular grass called russian thistle grew easily and in abundance. It is resistant to salts, requires neither irrigation nor special care, and is a highly nutritive food for goats. At the end, Don Efraím suggested taking that option. As a result, he lost his job. Following previous decisions, supported by generous financial appropriations, the peasants were induced to breed cattle, feeding them with irrigated crops. The project finally failed. The incident is a good illustration of bureaucratic stubbornness. What worried Don Efraím most, and worries me in this work, is not bureaucracy but stubbornness, the fact that even after eliminating the bureaucratic ingredient the stubbornness may persist.

Having been designed for the *hacendados*, although they never paid much attention to it, after the Revolution the National School of Agriculture was left at the service of the agrarian reform. For Don Efraím, however, 'the *shape* of the support continued to be the same and peasant knowledge continued to be seen as something useless and worthless'. Things did not change much during Cárdenas's time, because the 'researchers fell in the same trap, convinced that the problem was technological and that a modernizing push would be enough'. According to Don Efraím, they were perhaps right in technical or economic terms, given the size of the population and the prevailing conditions in rural Mexico at that time: a technical change could bring about an increase in production capable of assuring the national food supply. But they were never right in social terms, given the condition of all peasants. This was definitely Don Efraím's main objection in the 1940s, when the winds of the Green Revolution began to blow. Before any ecological concern, due to seed destruction or environmental damage, which only emerged in the following decade, it was the social question that worried him, the fact that the technological proposal excluded the situation and prospects of the majority of peasants from the analysis.

Don Efraím acknowledges that the Special Studies Bureau carried out the socio-economic studies that Taboada and Limón refused to do. But those studies did not focus on finding out the peasants' situation or examining their opportunities for transformation within their own contexts; they just wanted to 'discover how the peasant could be induced to adopt the "modern" techniques in the shortest time possible' (1984: 208). Don Efraím, by contrast, was considering the peasant as a thoughtful being, who should be listened to:

It is not a question of just telling the peasant: 'Look, you can do something like this', but a process of collaboration in the solution of the problem, which in the first place should be defined and clarified by both, so that both of them can be clear. One thinks: 'I've got it'. But there is a need for understanding so that the peasant may also say: 'Well, you see it that way, but you have not seen this or that' and so on and so forth. Then, as we have said, we want to understand the mechanism for achieving a collaborative effort between professional technicians and peasants in a common solution for a specific area. That is, in my view, a work of divulgation. On the other hand, I do not believe that this is the problem. The problem is: why do we not get the results we expect? This is what generally happens. (Hernández, 1984: 217)

All these expressions may seem familiar to those involved with rural work. They seem to define an approach presently incorporated into conventional wisdom. When presenting the Nobel Prize to Norman Borlaug, the president of the Norwegian Parliament recalled that he was 'a great admirer of the peasant' and that he claimed, among other things, that 'Although the peasant farmer may be illiterate, he can figure' (sic) (1970: 8). In his address after receiving the Prize, Borlaug himself explained how all factors limiting production were studied by an interdisciplinary team; how a system was organized 'to train a new generation of Mexican scientists' in the research techniques; how the best were sent abroad for postgraduate studies, 'in preparation for positions of leadership in Mexican agriculture', and how the research results were put into practice:

Farm demonstrations of new varieties and technology were made by the research scientists, who had developed them. Indeed, the revolution of wheat production in Mexico was accomplished before the extension service came into being. This forced the research scientists themselves to consider the obstacles to production that confronted the farmers. The same philosophy and tactic were used effectively to bring researchers in contact with the farmers' problems in the early years of the wheat improvement programs in India and West Pakistan. Later, however, the extension services were brought into the production programs in both countries. (1970: 23–4)

The theoretical and practical principle of 'listening to the peasant' is today almost banal. His psychology and sociology are studied exhaustively the better to deal with him and in order to facilitate his participation. But I want to emphasize the differences of perception and approach involved here. Don Efraím and Borlaug appear to be doing the same thing when in reality they are doing the opposite.

Don Efraím's researcher knows he does not know, or at least that he does not know everything. Through a dialogue with the peasant he tries to produce new specific knowledge, which did not exist before the dialogue. When the peasant says: 'You haven't noticed this or that', he is not complaining about the lack of accuracy in the observations; he is rather revealing differences in perception, in knowledge systems. He sees what the research did not see, because he has a different field of observation. Don Efraím's researcher explores with the peasant, in order that they should find together specific solutions for specific problems, jointly defined. Borlaug's researcher expects complementary information from the peasant, 'field information', which he gets through the appropriate method. That information will allow him to identify the problem technically. Afterwards he will persuade the peasant, through another method, to apply the pre-fabricated solution that Borlaug will pull out from his bag or produce in his laboratory.

Don Efraím's researcher should have old-fashioned qualities which have now fallen into disuse: 'perhaps those identifying the naturalists of the past, who looked for their knowledge with curiosity, tenacity, and inexhaustible enthusiasm' (Hernández, 1970, n.p.). For Don Efraím, for example, 'ethnobotanic exploration is an art based in several scientific disciplines ... [that] should constitute the intellectual and material bridge between the Indian agriculturalist and the farmer, the agronomist, the ethnobotanist, the biochemist, the geneticist, and the plant geneticist' (Hernández, 1970: 21).

Borlaug's researcher is not an artist, but a militant soldier, rigidly in-structed to participate, as a leader, in the confrontation between two contending forces: 'the scientific power of food production and the biologi-cal power of human reproduction' (1970: 10). The 'vital scientific leader-ship' of production will not only increase the food supply and protect it against physical and biological catastrophes, but in addition it will 'dissemi-nate the benefits of science to all mankind in the shortest possible time and at a minimum cost' (1970: 25).

Don Efraím disliked the foregoing, when he read this paper. He felt that it was unfair to Borlaug. 'Borlaug was a great agronomist and a great scientist', he told me. 'Through his personal commitment and hard work, he became a model for many Mexican scientists, carefully formed by him.' Don Efraím is right. Borlaug's personal qualities should be explicitly recog-nized. But the very core of the problem lies here: I cannot suppress the paragraph. The power dimension of Borlaug's knowledge system trans-forms him into a warrior for the implementation of his scientific or techno-logical discoveries. And he is pretty dogmatic about imposing the changes scientifically diagnosed. Don Efraím comments that Borlaug was fully aware of the social question; but 'he assumed it was something separate from his own work'. In fact, 'he thought that his work gave ten years to the politicians, to fix the social question'. For Don Efraím, it was not his fault that they wasted that opportunity. This is precisely the point here: the social and technological questions cannot be separated. The life and works of Don Efraím may be seen as a permanent commitment to put ethics and culture at the centre of society, now occupied by economy and technology.

After several decades of respectfully studying traditional agricultural technology, Don Efraím has identified, together with a prodigious store of knowledge, an agricultural art that cannot be learned in a formal school. The manual of the 'venerable and learned Fidel Palafox' seemed to him a magnificent illustration of the process of creation of traditional technology in agriculture, clearly showing its value in rain-fed land. For him, Don

Fidel's work identifies critical problems of both traditional and modern agriculture and reveals some of the limitations of traditional technology, especially for the verification of the knowledge obtained (Palafox, 1938: 5–6).

In mid-1945 Don Efraím was part of a research group studying agricultural practices in an area of the state of Tabasco. In the course of his research he found an oral calendar and map used to identify the low areas that flooded in spring, in order to plan their planting. In these areas they planted in March and harvested in June, using varieties of early maize and rice. This method allowed the harvesting of two tons of maize and beans per ha. annually, in some 6,000 ha., without using fertilizers or pesticides and harvesting by hand—a difficult task, but suited to the soil conditions. Developmentalists ignored all this to implement their decision to avoid flooding in the area by constructing canals and a dam. As a result, the subterranean water level dropped, creating the need for irrigation; in addition, the lime level in the soil (previously brought with the floods) was reduced, thus making the use of fertilizers indispensable. It began to be impossible to plant rain-fed crops. According to the scientific–technical criteria of the time, development plans for the area later required its deforestation: in the first year, machines razed 84,000 ha. of forest to the ground.

In 1955 Don Efraím was invited to comment on what the developmentalists were doing. He criticized the inexperience of the technical experts who were participating in the project. He made them see that the traditional slash-and-burn technique could be much more effective for clearing land, if clearing was what was necessary. He showed them the negative consequences of the forced collectivization of *ejidos*. These and other observations did not serve for much. The moment arrived when there were more government employees than farmers working in the project, but even then the plans were not properly implemented. Their machines could not harvest the crops due to the soil conditions. The dependence on fertilizers and irrigation ended up being as expensive as it was useless. And the peasants were turned into passive observers of a mechanized agricultural process, in which their only participation could be to carry bags of fertilizers to the land. The project, which could be studied now with an archaeological perspective to explore the ecological, social, and productive ruins left behind, is a typical case of techno-bureaucratic clumsiness. It also illustrates, in classic form, the marginalization of one system of knowledge by another.

For several decades Don Efraím has worked from within a system of research and education profoundly alien to him. He has succeeded in maintaining a tension of dialogue that defines his very life. He has acted as an intellectual bridge between the peasants, with whom he learns constantly, and the scientists who claim to teach them. He masters the technique and formalities of what today is called science, but he has not fallen into the temptation of reducing the traditional technique—which he knows as few do—to its scientific terms. He has resisted this 'idol of the human mind' (Shanin, 1986), conscious that simplification, necessary for any analytic effort and for the pedagogic process in the transmission of knowledge, requires 'eternal vigilance' in order to avoid falling prisoner to the instruments of our work, to the techniques that we design. For Shanin, reductionism is the most serious blow inflicted upon itself by modern historical understanding. For Don Efraím, if I have understood him correctly, reductionism is the core problem of the Green Revolution, of the agronomic sciences in general, and of the systems of research, education, and extension in agriculture. He is convinced that Mexican research follows the pattern adopted by the Americans around the year 1880—the land-grant college system. He thinks that Mexican education, according with the 1946 Law of Agricultural Education—another creation of Don Marte—is adjusted to a European, basically French, scheme. Far from being universal patterns, as is assumed due to their packaging as science (under science's universalist pretension) they are dated and localized approaches and schemes. To work in a different context, a clear detachment from them is in order. It is there, precisely at this threshold, that Don Efraím detains himself. That is the theme of my exploration in this work; it is what he illustrates, for me, with his life. But I feel we need to cross that threshold, to look into what appears beyond it, on the other side.

'Science', Don Marte used to say,

is not imported to a country as Scottish cod or olives from Seville; science must be predigested; that is, it must be learned by nationals who have a national intellectual preparation and a complete knowledge of the environment, but also the adapting capacity to absorb the best from the most advanced environment to which they are sent in order to prepare themselves. (Jiménez, 1984: 240)

It is clearly paradoxical that a man without 'national intellectual preparation' or 'complete knowledge of the environment', such as Don Efraím, a man who, on the contrary, was trained almost completely in the United States, should have ended up being 'the man of destiny' in order to 'predigest' the science that he learned and to put it in its place. In contrast, the system promoted by Don Marte tends to operate like a shopping mall, controlled by managers, stock-keepers, and transit agents, who dutifully take care of the 'packages of knowledge' that are produced and stored in the factories of diplomas, papers, monographs, and frustrations into which all our centres of agricultural research and education have been transmogrified. Don Efraím has tried to keep open the dialogue between the two worlds that he knows so well. He has felt it to be the path for creative rupture, in order to create a less sterile and harmful option. But he has not yet had much success.

THE SILENCE OF DON FIDEL

How to dare, in the setting prevailing from 1940 on, to publish the *Manual*? The peasant was no longer a source of knowledge. The careful observation of natural phenomena and the trial-and-error method for generating knowledge, as well as the art of carefully, lovingly, and efficiently applying the agricultural practices learned, had been discarded. In the decades of 1940 and 1950, with his *Manual* in hand, Don Fidel was left exposed—along with all his friends—to the new wisdom arriving from the institutions and through the experts. His own wisdom was transmogrified into ignorance. His abilities were converted into deficiencies. He lacked the formal knowledge now required to practice agriculture. Around him, the peasants were less and less capable of directing their activities on their own, in their own plots. Public and private experts were now in charge, and the moment arrived when the peasants stopped being involved heart and soul in their activities: the soul had to go somewhere else.

None of the damages charged up to now to the bulky account of the Green Revolution is comparable to the disvalue it caused. If technologies must be appreciated for their meaning and not their content, as Ashis Nandy wants, the Green Revolution should be evaluated for its contribution to the rooting of economic values in rural reality. And to establish economic value requires the devaluing of all other forms of existence and social interaction (Illich, 1978). This devaluing transmogrifies aptitudes into deficiencies, commons into resources, men and women into marketable labour, tradition into a burden, wisdom into ignorance, autonomy into dependence. It transmogrifies autonomous activities (incarnating desires, skills, hopes, and interactions with others and with the environment) into needs whose satisfaction requires the intermediation of the market.

Don Fidel continued to trust his experience, but he no longer dared share it with others. Sometimes even his own confidence was weakened in the face of experts' opinions. The self-sufficient regimes that he knew so well started to fade away little by little. The peasants became completely dependent on the market and its institutions. Scarcity emerged, even in the formerly abundant valley of Huamantla, and began to dominate in all spheres of life. Don Fidel also saw the progressive destruction of the physical and cultural spaces of the communities. He was hurt by rural emigration, and quickly perceived what the academics discovered much later: after the first dazzling years, when the peasants went to the cities attracted by the prospects of a good job or by urban fascination, the migrants abandoned their community because they could no longer manage to continue living in it. The peasants were turned into the cast-offs of development, and Don Fidel himself was turned into a kind of relic of the past, an archaeological curiosity looked upon by the others with a feeling of nostalgia which also began to invade him. Why publish the book? Children were no longer interested in his stories, stuck as they were to the television screen. The youth were just hunting for an opportunity to abandon the rural world. The old had lost all hope. No, Don Fidel was not moved to publish his *Manual*. Who would dare blame him?

THE CONSEQUENCES OF SIMPLIFICATION

Rustum Roy has observed that for almost half a century the Americans have been convinced that their science allowed them to win the war and impose hegemony over the planet. This conviction filled the curricula of their educational system with 'science', thus sacrificing technological education. Only one out of every thousand Americans knows that Japan surrendered before the bomb was dropped on her territory, and that 'it had surrendered because of superior U.S. munitions production technology'. Less than one in a thousand know that all the modern physics needed for the bomb had all been done in Germany, and that 'if science conferred any advantage, Germany should have won hands down'. The very brilliant scientists— physicists and chemists—who had been practising amateur engineering at Los Alamos returned to the civil sector convinced that it was 'American science (especially nuclear physics) which had won the war'. In the eu- phoria of victory, says Roy, 'no one even bothered to challenge this utterly preposterous claim' and the conviction remained firmly entrenched among the Americans (Roy, 1990: 3).

The merchandise called Green Revolution embraces an interpretation just as foolish and harmful. All the science necessary for the Green Revo- lution has been known in Mexico since the beginning of the century: many of the experiments carried out in experimental stations in the 1930s were based on it. Like the physics necessary for the bomb, the agronomy of the Green Revolution was developed in Germany. But the transfer was incom- plete: Marte R. Gómez would have observed that it was not well digested. The American scientists, like the Mexicans, did not appreciate the very serious reservations expressed by Von Leibig in the last part of his life, regarding the sustainability of an agriculture based on his ideas. American agricultural science, on the other hand, had little to do with the impressive advances in US agriculture in the first half of this century. Those advances were, like the bomb, a techno-economic creation.

Lester Brown, one of the scientists who came with the mission sent to Mexico after the conversations between Marte R. Gómez and Henry Wallace, later affirmed that the mission was meant to export to Mexico the American agricultural revolution. The official report of the mission, for its part, identified certain specific technical problems for the solution of which American co-operation could be offered. It excluded, however, the idea of co-operating in the organization of an extension service—one of the subjects that most interested the Mexicans—because there were few things to disseminate. Their advice was to begin with a top-down approach, concentrating on research for tackling the technical problems previously identified.

The mission was an impossible mission: revolutions cannot be exported. In the field of agriculture, the Americans discovered this before anyone else: the technical revolution of Jethro Tull, in the eighteenth century, did not operate in America as it did in Europe. The force of rainfall, much higher in America, created an erosion problem there that is today almost uncontrollable—four billion tons of topsoil are washed away each year.

But the 'American agricultural revolution' was a real fact, awakening great interest in Mexico and other countries. To export it was impossible, but the experience could have been taken advantage of. The history of agriculture in all parts of the world is but the continual circulation of innovations and the emergence of new ones through the extrapolation of experiments. Man has been acting thus since the neolithic era. A programme of co-operation based on the sensible and careful use of the American experiences applicable in the Mexican context would clearly have made sense and undoubtedly been of use. But that opportunity was changed in the hands of those who tried to make good use of it. Far from exporting the American agricultural revolution to Mexico, as some proposed, or to apply modestly some lessons of the American experience to Mexican agriculture, as seemed pertinent and feasible, it was the monopolistic and pernicious dominance of one system of knowledge over another that was exported to Mexico. The operation clearly reduced the technical and social options of the country, introduced rigidity and harmful simplifications in its productive structure and in its system of agricultural research and education, dangerously constrained the techno-cultural horizon of Mexico in this field, and perniciously reduced the biological, technical, and cultural diversity of the country, with grave damage and risk to its ecology and society.

Norman Borlaug is the epitome of the transformation that took place. He is also its most passionate defender. 'I am impatient,' he affirms; 'I do not accept the need for slow change and evolution to improve the agriculture and food production of the emerging countries. I advocate instead a 'yield kick-off' or a 'yield blast-off'. There is no time to be lost, considering the magnitude of the world food and population problem' (1970: 3). Borlaug seeks an explosion. He wanted to share his prize with 'the army of hunger fighters'. His metaphors are warlike, because he considers himself to be the commander in a great confrontation between 'scientific and biological powers'. He believes that he is winning the war: 'Man has made amazing progress recently in his potential mastery of these two contending powers', thanks to 'science, invention and technology' (1970: 10). Despite all his critics, Borlaug knows 'of no alternative to the path that we have taken' (1987: 22).

When the expression Green Revolution was coined in 1968 by Dr William S. Gaud of the US Agency for International Development, it achieved immediate and universal acceptance. The magic of the miracle seeds was already in operation. By packaging it as science, it was possible to stress and consecrate the universal character of the miracle: its strength and its tangibility. And Borlaug became a publicist of such perverted perception. He never saw himself as a technician, as a plant geneticist: he is a man of ideals and action, but he sees himself, first and foremost, as a scientist. He has never stopped insisting that the main contribution of the Green Revolution is to have initiated a new era in which the principles of modern science are successfully applied 'to develop indigenous technologies appropriate to the conditions of local farmers' (1987: 18). He is no doubt a first-class scientific researcher, but the era he helped to initiate prevents to this day the emergence of what he thought he was propitiating.

Apparently, the promoters of the whole experience were not fully aware of the dangers of simplifying, in analytical exercises and research efforts, without a clear notion of the limits and scope of such an operation. What resulted was a dangerous form of reductionism: first, by abstracting certain aspects from their context (after considering them not pertinent or beyond the researchers' responsibility); and second, by attributing a causal role to one disarticulated fragment of a whole, in consequences that can only result from the overall dynamics. Human reality is more diverse, more complex, and more contradictory than is assumed in this case. It is necessary to recall, at each step, the ethical ends and social contexts of the theoretical and analytical efforts—especially when they are given a relation to science. 'We should be on our guard', wrote Einstein in 1951, 'not to overestimate science and scientific method when it is a question of human problems' (Shanin, 1986: 315). Don Efraím always noted the absence of an ethical element in the theory and practice of the Green Revolution; that was the basic source of his dissatisfaction with the experiment.

To attribute to science a triumph of a technological nature and to ignore its social contexts may be viewed, at this point, as 'egregious errors' (Roy, 1990: 1). They are, of course, but they are also something worse: they conceal a simplified vision of the world that lacks both realism and precision. The impact of this vision on reality, once translated into policies and behaviour, engenders a dangerous simplification of the world—with great harm to nature and society. In the case of realities such as that of rural Mexico, it is much more realistic to assume the existence of diverse versions of truth, diverse systems of knowledge, the human creativity of alternatives, multi-directionality of developments, and the multiplicity of the time and rhythm of diverse social groups. In a context like this, the rigid division into cause and effect is spurious: what is lacking is a conception of non-determinist, irreducible, and dialectic approaches to take on the specific context (Shanin, 1986).

What is at issue here is not a comparison of two agricultural regimes, two kinds of farmers, or two systems of knowledge, to evaluate their comparative efficiency for different ends. It is a matter of realities that cannot be inserted into the same measurement system. When Don Efraím, after prolonged research, classified the traditional agricultural practices he had observed, he included in his list the practices of soil preparation or the definition of the agricultural cycle, just as he included the practices of prayer and rituals of gratitude. The logic of this inclusion is not only clear, in this system of knowledge, but indispensable. The same inclusion, in a scientific list, would constitute an unbearable anomaly. The traditional agricultural mentality has no problem in including, in its cosmovision, outside anomalies: it is an inclusive universalism, a kind of inclusive, hospitable ethnocentrism. Could the exclusive universalism of the scientific mentality accept this dialogue? Could the scientist take on a less rigid attitude when confronted with the otherness of the other? Could he give up the idea of dominating and subjecting him, first in a theoretical transgression and then in the practical invasion of his territory and his life? His science cannot: that is its limit and its incapacity. Could the scientist, being its personification, acknowledge without arrogance his own limits, accepting that the other exists and that his otherness should be kept as both a mystery and a reality? Could he do that, particularly, when the time comes to change that mystery and that reality, something that should be left to the other?

A HAPPY ENDING FOR DON FIDEL

For Don Fidel, as for many other Mexicans of his class and condition, the so-called crisis of the 1980s—'the lost decade for development'—had ambiguous impacts. On the one hand, its troubling effects on the conditions of life and the perspectives of the majority of people created new predicaments and difficult burdens to carry. But at the same time, unexpected opportunities appeared. When the official bank could no longer finance the farmers, due to budget cuts, many of them stopped planting the sorghum previously forced on them by the bank and went back to the traditional intercropping of maize and beans. At the end of the season they found that their family ate better from their own harvest, that the sale of their modest surplus left them with more funds than the balance given to them by the bank for their sorghum harvest, and that the intercropping improved their soils. The examples of concrete improvements of this kind multiplied, and brought a new awareness. The perceptions and practices of the majority of the population, devalued and marginalized until that point even by the 'marginals' themselves, began to acquire a new meaning. The crisis allowed them to recover confidence in ways of perception that they had almost abandoned, ways that were second nature to them, so devalued were they by the predominant views. They began to trust their noses again; to believe again that their experiences and orientations made sense.

Don Fidel also discovered, in the 1980s, that even the experts and authorities began to be interested in the knowledge and practices that they had previously ridiculed or discarded. For the first time in forty years various government strategies, such as the Mexican Food System and the National Food Program, proposed the goal of self-sufficiency. They also recognized the key role of the peasants in the efforts ahead. Some technicians and government promoters, especially the younger ones, began to ask before giving orders.

The agrarian debates of the 1970s did not reach Don Fidel. They were too academic, if not technocratic: they seemed alien to him. In the new discussions, however, he had something to say. The time had come to publish his book. When the new governor of Tlaxcala, daughter of one of his friends, added her name to the list of names asking him to publish his book, he could no longer resist. He accepted.

One of the things Don Efraím learned early on in his life was not to argue uselessly. He has avoided the polemic against the Green Revolution: he prefers the calm and the silence characterizing the centre of the storm. (But not always. Many fear the brief ironic comments he uses against those exceeding in conversations or seminars, the limits of prudence when rattling off nonsense.) From time to time his works fall victim to the many temptations of his contradictory life: he who seems to have the best intuition about the world of traditional agricultural technology, a man who has developed a marvelous art for exploring plants and the relationship between man and the plants, is at the same time an eminent emeritus professor of the greatest academic centre in Mexico for the scientific formalization of research and education in agriculture. He has offered there, in addition, ample proof of his aptitude as a researcher, easily fulfilling the highest norms and requirements of conventional wisdom.

Don Efraím has always lived within that tension, enjoying or suffering it, alternatively. From time to time he seems to be concentrated in an integrative effort, like many of his colleagues, following opposed impulses. Sometimes he looks as if he is incorporating traditional agricultural technology into the world of science, to enrich scientific theories, the activities of the scientists, or the professional formation of agronomists; at other times, he seems to be advancing in the opposite direction, as if he would want to give to traditional agricultural technology some formal technical tools, derived from science, in order to enrich it and to overcome some of its classical limitations.

It is my feeling that Don Efraím's path does not follow such directions. I have the suspicion that he discovered a long time ago that the world is not monist and that dualism is just a form of monism. He does not believe in the discourse between two sectors, an analytical tool long since exhausted. In clear contradiction with everything he learned in school and with most of the beliefs of his colleagues, he suspects that the world's essence is of a plural nature. He is perhaps suspecting that the radical diversity or pluriformity of plants, which he found a long time ago, may be in the society of men in the form of radical pluralism. Through corn, his main obsession, he obtained a clear insight into a very wide and mysterious spectrum of radically different attitudes toward the prodigious plant. I think that he finds it both silly and dangerous to try to reduce all of them to only one vision, to one classification, to only one parameter.

I am asking myself, with him, how we can facilitate an open, tense dialogue, with the creative tension of the real world, of concrete cultures, among those now trapped in their sterile polemic. I am asking myself if we can together cross the threshold of radical pluralism. The question is clearly posed, because we are in a situation in which '*praxis* compels us to take a stance in the effective presence of the other, when the *praxis* makes it impossible to avoid mutual interference, and the conflict cannot be solved by the victory of one part or party. Pluralism emerges when the conflict looms unavoidable.' (Panikkar, 1979: 201)

In fact, we have the problem radically posed, if we seriously consider the concrete practices to which we are exposed.

The problem of pluralism arises only when we feel—we suffer—the incompatibility of differing worldviews and are at the same time forced by the praxis of our factual coexistence to seek survival. The problem becomes acute today because contemporary praxis throws us into the arms of one another. (Panikkar, 1979: 201)

It is not a question of situations in which different opinions, views and attitudes may operate in dialectical interaction, situations that may be solved, politically, through democratic dialogue. Democracy offers only consolation prizes to the minority, and the hope that one day it may become the majority. It is something, and there are many situations in the present world where that is perhaps the best or the only feasible solution. But it does not solve the principle of confrontation, the implicit monism (masked as dualism or political pluralism). We need solutions that are neither monist nor dualist. These are the kind of solutions we are lacking, if the world, as many of us presently suspect, happens to be of a plural nature.

IS DIALOGUE POSSIBLE?

Ni contigo, ni sin ti	Neither with you, nor without you,
tienen mis males remedio.	do my maladies have a cure.
Contigo porque me matas.	With you because you kill me.
Y sin ti porque me muero.	And without you because I die.
	Sor Juana

Para dialogar	To have a dialogue
escuchar primero.	first listen.
Después,	And then,
escuchar.	listen.

Machado

In the year of Our Lord 1524 twelve priests arrived in New Spain who belonged to the order of Saint Francis. They were sent by Pope Adrian VI and the Emperor Charles V to convert the Indians. The priests were convinced, in the vein later exposed by Father Las Casas, that conversion should only be attempted through dialogue, colloquy, and peaceful confrontation, inviting and attracting 'like the rain and the snow falling from heaven, without violence, not suddenly, with gentleness and softness'. As soon as they arrived, the renowned priests started conversations with the Indian principals. A written record of those conversations was kept.

Forty years later Friar Bernardino de Sahagún, who for many years had been trying to understand Indian thinking and culture, found that record. He decided to give some order to the old papers and to put the text 'in polished Mexican language', with the help of the best 'Mexican scholars' he could find. There is not much left of what Fray Bernardino did, but there is enough to imagine what the encounter may have been like. It is the first written testimony of an attempted dialogue between Europeans and Americans, and it is one of the first in the world between people of such different languages and cultures. It was a dialogue among prominent persons, of both sides, which proceeded peacefully and gently, with infinite courtesy.

We have only two pages, two magnificent, fascinating pages, of what was said by the Indians. They come from only one of the many conversations. This sole answer, however, is enough to illustrate a style of dialogue in clear contrast to the priests' style. In the gentlest way imaginable, in the most inspired and learned way, carefully conceived for their audience, the priests tell the principals, the Indian noblemen and priests, that they are not involved in the affair of converting them by their own initiative or out of any mundane purpose. They were sent by God himself, through his vicar, and with no other reason or motive but the salvation of the Indians' souls. They show how the doctrine they bring is divine word, deposited and kept in the sacred book they have with them, and they describe in wonderful colours all the virtues and powers of God, as well as the miseries of the devils. To the latter they attribute the perversion of having created in the Indians the illusion that they are gods. Because devils, and nothing but despicable devils, punished by God, are the gods that the Indians adore. They are not guilty for that, because of having had no previous access to the divine word. But now that they have the opportunity to listen to the word of God, the time has come for them to abandon their beliefs, for their own good and for the salvation of their souls.

The answer of the principals is brief, or brief, at least, is what has been saved of it. With extreme courtesy the Indians recognize the priests as divine messengers, even as the incarnation of God; they accept them as the voice and the word of He who gives the life. They are thus confronted by God himself. And God asks them to negate their own gods, their ancient rules of life. What can they tell them? How to react to such an atrocious demand? They assume themselves as learned in the divine mysteries: they are the ones in charge of interpreting them for 'the queue and the wing'— that is, the people. But they recognize themselves as human, little people, and limited, belonging to the earth. And these beings tell the priests, with exquisite courtesy, with the best words of their language, but in all firmness ('even if we offend you'; 'Make with us whatever you want') that they cannot take as truth everything they are saying—even if they are the divinity itself, as they are accepting they are!

The gods gave command, dominion, and prestige. To them is owed life, birth, and growth. They have established a rule of life, transmitted from one generation to the next.

> We will not destroy the ancient rule of life,
> we don't want the gods to become angry with us,
> we don't want to provoke their fury, their anger.

There is a call for good sense, for prudence, and for wisdom:

> You must not do something to your queue,
> to your wing [your people],
> bringing disgrace to them, making them die.

A warning:

> And let's avoid that, because of this, the queue,
> the wing [the people] may be aroused,
> let's not, because of that, we may become excited,
> we may be bewildered,
> if we tell them so:
> There is no longer any need to invoke, there is no longer any
> need to implore.

And a conclusion:

> It is enough that we have left,
> that we have lost, that we have been deprived,
> that we have been deposed from
> the mat, the seat of honour [the command].

If the command and the power have been lost, let's preserve at least the ancient rule of life, the road to go nearer to the gods!

> Don't be afraid, beloved—answered the priests.
> You should not take for a bad omen

> our word, what we have said,
> how, in which way,
> none of your gods is the true god,
> none of those you are revering,
> those to whom you are imploring.

And immediately afterwards they explained to them, copiously and with words full of love, the Christian doctrine (Sahagún, 1986).

NOTES TO CHAPTER 7

1. I am taking the expression from Raimón Panikkar (1979: 219): 'The way to handle a pluralistic conflict is not through each side trying to convince the other, nor by the dialectical procedure alone, but through a dialogical dialogue, which leads to a mutual opening to the concern of the other, to a sharing in a common charisma, difficulty, suspicion, guidance, inspiration, light, ideal, or whatever higher value both parties acknowledge and neither party controls. The dialogical dialogue is art as much as it is knowledge, involves *techne* and *praxis* as much as *gnosis* and *theoria* and the difficulty is to re-enact it, even when one of the partners refuses to enter into such a relation'.

2. In ordinary conversation, 'polemic' and 'controversy' have become synonyms. Dictionaries reflect the fact by defining each word with the other. I appeal to the etymological origin of these words: to the Greek *polemos*, war; to the Latin *controversia*, opposite versions, a dispute in which the conflict does not imply eliminating or suppressing the other. Beyond the origins or classical uses of the words, I find in the word *controversia* the allusions I am looking for: the tense opposition, when diversity is not doomed to extinction and may survive indefinitely; a situation in which the debate, the conflict, or the dispute, does not imply the domination of one part by the other, neither in the reality nor in the intention; the condition under which the opposed versions on a matter keep themselves together because of the interest in the matter. *Controversiam habeo cum eo do re familiari. Cic.*: 'I have a difference with him, I have a question with him, on family matters'. There is a dispute, conflict; but the family continues. These allusions I am discovering in the word *controversy* allow me to contrast it sharply with *polemic*, with its war-like meaning, implying by definition the suppression of the other, the will of dominating him, of having a victory over him, of prevailing over him.

3. Except when a reference is indicated, all the quotes from Efraím Hernández Xocolotzi come from conversations with the author.

4. The suspicion has been expressed that the scientists promoting the programme could have been in connivance with transnational corporations, with the *hacendados*, or with Mexican or American agribusinessmen. I find no foundation for such suspicion. I have no doubt about the pertinence of class analysis to explain the constitution and the dynamics of the policies and practices associated with the Green Revolution. In México, the concentration of the subsidies on some crops, some producers, and some regions may be soundly attributed to the economic interests involved and to the political dynamics of class confron-

tations—at a certain level of analysis and for specific purposes. In the same vein, I have no doubt about the usefulness of the analysis of the socio-economic implications of the process, whose insuperable model is the UNRISD research (see Hewitt de Alcántara, 1976; Pearse, 1980). It may be used, among other things, to modify the policies and practices still in use. Both approaches present aspects of the polemic that are not completely sterile, even if they are—as I suspect—exhausted by now. Anyway, they are entirely alien to the focus of this essay.

REFERENCES

ALAMÁN, L. (1852), *Historia de México desde los primeros movimientos que prepararon su Independencia en el año de 1808 hasta la época presente*, 1985 edn., México City: Fondo de Cultura Económica.

BORLAUG, N. E. (1970), *The Green Revolution, Peace and Humanity*, Oslo: Norwegian Parliament.

—— (1987), 'Accomplishments in Maize and Wheat Productivity', *The Future Development of Maize and Wheat in the Third World*, México City: CIMMYT.

COSÍO VILLEGAS, D. (1956), *Historia Moderna de México, La República Restaurada, Vida Social*, 1974 edn., México City: Hermes.

GARCÍA TREVIÑO, R. (1953), 'Agrarismo revolucionario y ejidalismo burocrático', *Problemas agrícolas e industriales de México*, 5/4: 27–66.

GÓMEZ, M. R. (1925), *Cartas de Marte R. Gómez*, 1978 edn., México: Fondo de Cultura Económica.

HERNÁNDEZ XOLOCOTZI, E. (1970), *Exploración etnobotánica y su metodología*, Chapingo: Colegio de Postgraduados.

—— (1984), 'Doctor Efraím Hernández Xolocotzi,' in L. Jimenez (ed.), *Las Ciencias agrícolas y sus protagonistas*, i, Chapingo: Colegio de Postgraduados.

HEWITT DE ALCÁNTARA, C. (1976), *Modernizing Mexican Agriculture: Socioeconomic Implications of Technological Change 1940–1970*, Geneva: UNRISD.

ILLICH, I., ZOLA, I. K., McKNIGHT, J., CAPLAN, J., and SHAIKEN, H. (1978), *Disabling Professions*, 1981 trans., Madrid: Blume.

JIMÉNEZ, L. (1984) (ed.), *Las Ciencias agrícolas y sus protagonistas*, i, Chapingo, Colegio de Postgraduados.

MOSK, S. A. (1950), *Industrial Revolution in Mexico*, Berkeley, Calif.: University of California Press.

PALAFOX, F. (1938), *Manual del campesino*, pub. 1988, Tlaxcala: Gobierno del Estado de Tlaxcala.

PANNIKAR, R. (1979), *Myth, Faith, and Hermeneutics: Cross-Cultural Studies*, New York: Paulist Press.

PEARSE, A. (1980), *Seeds of Plenty, Seeds of Want: Social and Economic Implications of the Green Revolution*, Oxford New York: Oxford University Press.

ROY, R. (1990), 'The Relationship of Technology to Science and the Teaching of Technology', *Journal of Technology Education*, 1/2: 5–18.

SAHAGÚN, B. DE (1524), 'Coloquios y doctrina cristiana con que los doce frailes de San Francisco, enviados por el papa Adriano VI y por el emperador Carlos V, convirtieron a los indios de la Nueva España', in M. L. Portilla (ed.), *Los diálogos de 1524 según el texto de Fray Bernardino de Sahagún y sus colaboradores indígenas,* 1986, México City: UNAM-Fundación de Investigaciones Sociales.

Secretaría de Gobernación, Producción rural (1946), *Seis años de actividad nacional,* México: Secretaría de Gobernación.

SHANIN, T. (1986), *The Roots of Otherness: Russia's Turn of Century,* ii, London: Macmillan.

FURTHER READING

Agroecosistemas (1977–), *Boletín Informativo,* ed. Hernández Xolocotzi, Chapingo, México: Centro Botanico del Colegio de Postgraduados.

BHALLA, A., JAMES, D., and STEVENS, Y. (1984) (eds.), *Blending of New and Traditional Technologies,* Dublin: Ticooly International Publishing.

BONFIL BATALLA, G. (1987), *México profundo: Una civilización negada,* México City: CIESAS/SEP.

BRAUER, O., ANDRADE, F. J., ZEDILLO, V., JIMENEZ, L., and MARTINEZ REDING, J. (1968), *Diagnóstico de las ciencias agrícolas en México, Cuatro Ensayos,* México: Ediciones Productividad.

BUVE, R. (1980), 'Los gobernadores de estado y la movilización de los campesinos en Tlaxcala', in D. A. Brading (ed.), *Caudillos and Peasants in the Mexican Revolution,* 1985 trans., México: Fondo de Cultura Económica.

ECHEVERRÍA, L. M. (1954), 'Progresos recientes de la agricultura mexicana', *Problemas Agrícolas e Industriales de México,* 614: 9–114.

ESTEVA, G. (1983), *The Struggle for Rural Mexico,* South Hadley, Mass: Bergin and Harvey.

GLIESSMAN, S. R. (1978) (ed.), *Agroecosistemas con énfasis en el estudio de tecnología agrícola tradicional,* Cárdenas: Colegio Superior de Agricultura Tropical.

HANSON, H. (1982), *Wheat in the Third World,* Boulder, Colo.: Westview Press.

HERNÁNDEZ XOLOCOTZI, E. (1960), 'Las ciencias sociales y el desarrollo social de México', *Revista de la Sociedad Mexicana de Historia Natural,* 21/1: 19.

—— (1977) (ed.), *Agroecosistemas de México,* Chapingo: Colegio de Postgraduados.

—— 'El papel de la tecnología agrícola tradicional en el desarrollo agropecuario', *Narshí-Nandhá,* 6/7: 14–27 (Mexico City).

HEWITT DE ALCÁNTARA, C. (1976), *Modernizing Mexican Agriculture: Socioeconomic Implications of Technological Change 1940–1970,* Geneva: UNRISD.

Instituto Nacional de la Investigación Agrícola (1981), *Resúmenes de las ponencias del simposio nacional de la investigación agrícola, Veinte años del INIA 1961–1981,* México City: SARH.

JIMÉNEZ VELÁZQUEZ, M. A. (1990), 'La Fundación Rockefeller y la investigación agrícola en América Latina', *Comercio Exterior,* 40/10: 968–75.

MÚJICA VÉLEZ, R. (1969), *La investigación científica y su importancia en el sector agrícola, El Instituto Nacional de Investigaciones agrícolas,* México City: UNAM.

NATHAN, P. (1955), 'México en la época de Cárdenas', *Problemas Agrícolas e Industriales de México,* 7/3: 17–176.

PANIKKAR, R. (1990), 'The Religion of the Future', *Interculture,* 23/2: 3–24.

SEPÚLVEDA, M. M. (1976), *La política educativa y las escuelas rurales en la década de los treintas, El caso de las Escuelas Regionales Campesinas en 1936*, México City: ENAH.

WARMAN, A. (1988), *La historia de un bastardo: maíz y capitalismo*, México City: Fondo de Cultura Econòmica.

WETTEN, N. L. (1947), *Rural Mexico*, Chicago: University of Chicago Press.

8

Why Haldane Went to India: Modern Genetics in Quest of Tradition

FRANCIS ZIMMERMANN

INTRODUCTION

John Burdon Sanderson Haldane (1892–1964), a celebrated scientist, one of the founders of the mathematical theory of population genetics in the 1920s, and a prolific ideologue of Marxism in science, had occupied the Weldon Chair of Biometry at University College London for twenty years when he resigned and emigrated to India in 1957. At first, he taught and carried out his own research in genetics and mathematical statistics at the ISI (the Indian Statistical Institute) in Calcutta (1957–61). Conflicts and the strains of bureaucracy led him to resign again. After working for a short time with the CSIR (the Council of Scientific and Industrial Research) of the Indian Government (1961–2), he moved to Bhubaneswar in the state of Orissa to found his own Genetics and Biometry Laboratory under the patronage of chief minister Patnaik, the local strong man who wanted to raise the status of science in his state (1962–4). The story of Haldane's voyage to India has already been told twice (Clark, 1968; Dronamraju, 1985). The purpose of the following pages is not to tell the biographical facts once again, but to reflect on them. The first two parts of this chapter will discuss Haldane's reasons for leaving England and his reasons for choosing India, his protest against the dominant scientific paradigm in biology and his quest for a 'soil' in the metaphorical sense of the word explicated below. The latter part of the chapter was written, as it were, in the wake of Haldane, to pursue the study of the diversity of life on new grounds.

This chapter and the collection of which it is part are two-pronged. On the one hand, we propose to document forms of traditional knowledge and show that they are now underdeveloped forms of modern knowledge but, rather, offer alternative ways of constructing reality. On the other hand, we want to analyse the dominant paradigms in science and show that their adaptation to local contexts has distorting effects on science itself, and oppressive or disintegrative effects on the local, social, and natural ecology. We are addressing ourselves to the political issue of an indigenization of modern science. Population biology is a case in point, since the universalistic spirit of population genetics, a tough science first developed as a branch of applied mathematics, has placed limits on the understanding of life diversity and the study of context-sensitive, area-dependant aspects of population biology. Haldane's emigration to India was both a protest against the dominance of a particular knowledge and a quest for new epistemic paradigms. His choice of India was not motivated only by the fact that it offers an ideal terrain for field observation of biological polymorphisms, but also by an ethical and philosophical interest in Hindu revivalism, Gandhism, and non-violence. Naive as it may have been, the biologist's encounter with India is none the less significant. It allows for a comparison of modern science and tradition.

Far from being context-free, Haldane's biology was a fieldwork type of scientific research grafted upon a combinatory mode of thought. I am thus trying to characterize Haldane's position in population genetics. This branch of genetics was founded by mathematicians and statisticians, but it soon evolved as a new statistical approach to the wealth of biological forms in nature. Haldane used to combine the two methods applicable to the study of a given population: calculating statistics at his desk, and conducting surveys in the field. This twofold approach to the realities of life is very congenial to the Hindu scientific tradition, as will be shown in the last section of this essay. The key concepts of evolutionary biology, especially in the balanced theory of population structure formulated in the mid-1950s, are those of diversity and polymorphisms. And South Asia is the land of polymorphisms in all senses of the word: in the wealth of variegated life-forms as well as in the pundit's taxonomies. Haldane himself recognized the value of the Sanskrit tradition of classification as a tool for the modern taxonomist.

Furthermore, when dealing with populations, the biologist tends to escape the domination of the Western ideology of individualism. The facts of population genetics tend to transcend the limits of individual bodies, they occur between individuals, and between the body and the environment. Although Haldane had no training in history or anthropology, my surmise is that the practice of population thinking in biology gave him some sense of locality, and of the value of local knowledge. Medical historians have traced the origins of populational and transpersonal thinking in biology back to the Hippocratic concept of medical constitutions (Smith, 1981: 2 (*catastases*); Grmek, 1983: 437). The present author, who is a student of *ayurveda*, the traditional Hindu science of long life, would also like to cite the Sanskrit word *prakrti* as an exact rendering of Hippocratic 'constitution' in the Hindu medical texts. Prior to their meaning the physical nature of an individual body in regard to health, strength, vitality, etc., the word 'constitution' and its equivalents in Greek (*katastasis*) and Sanskrit (*prakrti*) were used traditionally to designate a given network of relationships between the climate and landscape of a given locality, the inhabitants' temperaments, and the endemic diseases. Haldane was not aware of these historical connections between the classical discipline of natural history, the concept of population, and the ancient theory of medical constitutions, but he felt that biology would benefit from indigenization. The wealth of life-forms in India, he thought, was a great asset: it offered wonderful material for the study of genetic diversity in nature. In that respect, the population geneticists of our time have been sharing the same enthusiasm for field observations in the tropics as the travellers who founded botany (see Dagognet, 1970: 29) in the early eighteenth century.

Haldane's voyage to India presents two aspects, which correspond to the two sides of our own endeavour in these pages. There is a critical side, and a constructive side. The most interesting of the two is not Haldane's protest against what he was theatrically rejecting, through resigning his academic position, emigrating, and eventually changing his British passport for an Indian one, but his subsequent career in India. First in Calcutta and then in Bhubaneswar, he tried to create new research institutions and to define his scientific domain anew. In studying the protest side of Haldane's story, the first part of this essay will raise the issue of knowledge and power, and thus meet the initial goal of our project, that was to show how the dissemination of the dominant Western systems of knowledge and their industrial and political impact on Third World societies have come to shrink the space for alternatives: alternative modes of thought and alternative ways of constructing reality. However, the second and third parts of this contribution aim to be less critical than prospective. Following in Haldane's footsteps, we are going in search of a new paradigm. The first part is more concerned with genetics and Western science, while the second and third parts give space to ethnography, philology, and local knowledge. Although I started from the history of population genetics in the 1950s, this was not to me an object of study but a point of departure. Transported to India in Haldane's hands, population genetics has changed from within, shifting to new problems and new frontiers. The Haldane case will teach us that indigenization is not always a sheer degradation, that the hard science of evolutionary biology may benefit from the help of softer anthropological pursuits, and that tough Western science may rhyme with the Sanskrit tradition.

AN INDIAN PERSPECTIVE ON DARWIN

The Suez Crisis, which lasted from 31 October to 6 November 1956, was the main pretext invoked by J. B. S. Haldane to justify his emigration to India on 24 July 1957. In his biography Ronald Clark wrote brilliant pages on the episode. Following newspaper reports, he features his hero on the apron at London airport. In a last-minute statement, Haldane gave some substantiation to the myth that he was going as a result of the Anglo-French aggression against Suez. He did not wish to live in a criminal country. For full measure, and the benefit of any American reporters present, he added: 'I want to live in a free country where there are no foreign troops based all over the place' (Clark, 1968: 203). He was alluding to the lingering presence of American contingents of GIs in Europe. This typical amalgamation was likely to stir up enthusiastic reactions among left-wing people. For the whole winter he had encouraged the story, Clark says, 'fuming to his friends at the slightest opportunity and delighting newspapers' with his statements that he was leaving his native land 'because of the mass murders of civilians in Port Said' (Clark, 1968: 203). Yet, the truth was not so dramatic and the Suez Crisis was merely coincidental. In fact, by 1 November 1956, the day of the ultimatum to Nasser, Haldane was actually writing to Prasanta Chandra Mahalanobis, the Director of the ISI, accepting the appointment offered at this Institute in Calcutta. If politics was at stake in Haldane's move, it was not the day-to-day policies of military intervention but politics in the arena of knowledge. Beneath his broadcasting of radical views in politics proper, I think we can decipher a more fundamental protest against the dominance of a particular politics of knowledge in the West.

Through the following reading of Haldane's career in India, I shall be reflecting upon the status of genetics, a highly sensitive area of modern science, which offers many opportunities for an anthropological analysis of ideology in scientific research. The two main domains of application of population genetics—agriculture and medicine—have much bearing on development economics. The Haldane case is a strategic case, onto which we can project a discussion of the prospective expansion and ominous dangers of genetic engineering in developing countries. Furthermore, it offers an appropriate terrain for a critique of the dominant position of mathematical thinking, since population genetics was the very first branch of modern biology to have evolved right from the beginning, in the 1920s, as a mathematical theory. Empirical confirmations only came afterwards, and, out of the three founders (Haldane, Fisher, and Wright), Haldane was the most instrumental in linking the mathematical theory to the more concrete problems of natural history (evolution of faunas and floras), husbandry (inbreeding), medicine (see, especially, his 1949 paper 'Disease and evolution'), human kinship, etc. Therefore, when Haldane moved to India, the indigenization of the kind of biology he was practising also meant a coming back from mathematics to natural history, ecology, and society. Whenever Haldane stated he was pessimistic about the future of Europe and believed that the opportunities for research were better in India (Clark, 1968: 206), the most immediate interpretation was a political one.[1] On previous journeys to South Asia, however, he had been overwhelmed by the richness, variety, and beauty of India's animals and plants, and he thought of tropical lands as reservoirs of polymorphisms. The bio-geographical experience gained from these journeys to the tropics was consonant with Haldane's interpretation of Darwinian evolutionism. In Darwin's theory, evolution is a two-stroke process: variation provides the materials, and natural selection gives it a direction. At a time when current interpretations of Darwin's theory tended to reduce it to an economical and utilitarian view of nature, where fitness would entail selection, Haldane was among the first students of Darwinism to recognize the central place of variation and diversity in Darwin's theory. This reappraisal of Darwin, with its political reverberations, was among Haldane's motivations in 1957.

The Peacock's Tail Argument

Haldane's insistence that Darwin's ideas of diversity and variation were more important than his ideas of fitness and selection has a clear political tenor.[2] I would like to illustrate this by a quotation from *The Causes of Evolution*, a book published in 1932 which came as a philosophical conclusion to the celebrated series of ten papers published from 1924 to 1932 under the general title *A Mathematical Theory of Natural and Artificial Selection*. One of the most brilliant pages of this book discussed a fundamental fallacy underlying Social Darwinism. Haldane's critique is still perfectly topical. The same fallacy has recurred again and again: eugenics in Haldane's life-time, sociobiology in the 1970s, and the idea of the so-called selfishness of genes are as many ideologies of the selective value of fitness.

The fallacy resides in our egotistic understanding of fitness, when we say that natural selection favours the survival of the fittest. This may be true when we consider rare and scattered species engaged in competing with other species. But as soon as a species becomes fairly dense, its members begin to compete with one another. Then, misled again by our egotistic prejudices, we are inclined to infer from the current adaptedness of a given genetic trait in today's living individuals the reasons for its origination in the past history of the species. However, there are cases where the genetic traits thus selected through evolution may have been advantageous for the individual, but ultimately disastrous for the species: for example, the enormous horns developed in some species of deers, which led to the species' extinction. There are many oddities thus selected which represent the contrary of fitness: for example, the cumbrous tail of peacocks. For a both accurate and accessible discussion of such oddities that would help to place Haldane's text quoted below in its proper perspective, one is referred to Stephen Jay Gould's popular books (1980; 1983; 1986) on the panda's thumb, hen's teeth and horse's toes, and the flamingo's smile.[3] It should be pointed out that Haldane's critique of the fitness fallacy is not inconsistent with the theory of natural selection. He simply calls for a rigorous definition of the Darwinian concept of fitness. The fitness, or selective value, of a given genetic trait varies in time, and according to population density. Fitness, statistically defined, is not to be confounded with a situation, intuitively perceived, of adaptation to the current environmental conditions.[4] The target of the peacock's tail argument was not the theory of natural selection in itself, but an ideological interpretation of the evolutionary process which overvalued selection and marginalized the study of variation. The following text (written in 1932) speaks of a 'poisonous nonsense', that is, the ideology of the survival of the fittest, the advent of nationalism, the cult of strength, pride, and aggressivity, 'before the [1914–18] war':

I must [now] . . . discuss a fallacy which is, I think, latent in most Darwinian arguments, and which has been responsible for a good deal of the poisonous nonsense which has been written on ethics in Darwin's name, especially in Germany before the war and in America and England since. The fallacy is that natural selection will always make an organism fitter in its struggle with the environment. This is clearly true when we consider the members of a rare and scattered species. It is only engaged in competing with other species, and in defending itself against inorganic nature. But as soon as a species becomes fairly dense matters are entirely different. Its members inevitably begin to compete with one another. I am not thinking only of the active and often conscious competition between higher animals, but also of the struggle for mere space which goes on between plants of closely packed associations. And the results may be biologically advantageous for the individual, but ultimately disastrous for the species. The geological record is full of cases where the development of enormous horns and spines (sometimes in the male sex only) has been the prelude to extinction. It seems probable that in some of these cases the species literally sank under the weight of its own armaments. Again, while modern research tends to show that sexual selection in birds is rather less important in making bright colour and structures such as the peacock's tail advantageous in male birds than Darwin supposed, there is still a good deal of evidence that it has certain selective value in securing mates. And none will contend that (except insofar as it has induced Hindus to regard him as sacred and Europeans as a suitable pet) the peacock's rather cumbrous tail has been of any advantage to him in the struggle with the environment. I could multiply such cases indefinitely, but they are all somewhat uncertain. To prove our case we should want statistics as to the number of offspring left on the one hand, and expectation of life on the other, of long- and short-tailed peacocks under natural conditions. (Haldane, 1932: 119–20)

I quoted this page for its political implications; it helps us to focus on the politics of knowledge around Darwinism, and I propose to read it in the light of the essential tension, in Darwin's theory, between selection and variation. It announces Haldane's later advocacy of field studies and of a return to the study of variation, hitherto neglected in the early history of population genetics.

The Study of Diversity in the Mid-1950s

The study of variation in natural populations—the fact is well-known—represented the specific contribution of Russian (Dobzhansky) and British (Ford) scientists to the genetic theory of evolution. Evoking his early years in the Soviet Union in the 1920s, Theodosius Dobzhansky pointed up the characteristic tendency of Russian biologists to study organic diversity in different environments (Mayr and Provine, 1980: 231). This preoccupation with natural populations emerged only later in the West. When Dobzhansky's researches in America eventually won recognition, in the 1950s, it was by engaging himself and his school in a major conflict with the establishment. By the mid-1950s a dominant view had established itself, according to which evolution was a purely genetic phenomenon and, consequently, mathematical population genetics was the only source for any understanding of evolution. The classical theory of natural selection thus devised was the mathematical theory supplemented with laboratory experiments—the induction and manipulation of drastic mutations in Drosophila—that seemed to confirm the calculations. H. J. Muller, the main protagonist of the classical school, 'saw the biological world through the medium of the classical genetics and cytogenetics of well-behaved mutants of strong effect, localizable on the genetic or cytological maps' (Lewontin, 1974: 29). This chequerboard or beanbag approach to evolutionary change, essentially presented as an input or output of genes (Mayr, 1959: 309), was not devoid of political overtones. Muller was a pessimist—genetic change could only be a change for the worse. To prevent degeneration, he advocated eugenics by means of artificial insemination. In contrast with these gloomy predictions and this élitism, Dobzhansky in America and E. B. Ford in Britain developed a newer approach characterized by the study of natural populations *in situ* and an increasing emphasis on the interaction of genes. They were pluralists and optimists, seeing the world as Darwin had seen it, in all the richness of its diversity—an immense reservoir of genetic variation. Thus, the classical theory of natural selection and Dobzhansky's 'balance theory'—as he himself named it in 1955—were placed at two opposite ends on the spectrum of existing epistemic paradigms.

Haldane remained intimately associated with the classical theory throughout his life. The basic ideas of genetic load and the cost of natural selection were his own. The word 'load' was introduced by Muller (1950) in an attempt to assess the impact of mutation on human welfare. But James F. Crow, in a paper that constitutes a definitive review of Haldane's work on this particular question, has shown that Muller independently rediscovered the Haldane Principle already formulated in the 1930s, according to which the impact of mutation on fitness is approximately equal to the mutation rate and is independent of the selection coefficient, that is, independent of the effect of the individual mutant on fitness (Crow, 1970: 129, 173). The year 1957 itself, the year of Haldane's voyage to India, saw the publication of his seminal paper on 'The Cost of Natural Selection'. He attempted to calculate how expensive it is to replace one allele in a large population by a selectively superior one. Too rapid a rate of simultaneous selection against too many genes might eliminate the entire population.

Crow has shown that the 1957 paper was in continuity with Haldane's conclusion reached twenty-five years earlier, that in systems of slow selection, the number of generations required for a change was inversely proportional to the intensity of selection (Haldane, 1932: 180; Crow, 1970: 159). In spite of criticisms voiced by naturalists like Ernst Mayr, who questioned the relevance of these calculations to real evolutionary events (Mayr, 1959: 315), the 1957 paper proved to be very influential in recent theoretical developments, and Haldane continued to write and publish in that line until his death.

However, his final years in India (1957–64) must be put back in the context of the grand debate between the classical and balance theories. In retrospect, Haldane's response to the controversies raging in the 1950s appears to have been twofold. On the one hand, he remained a protagonist of the neo-classical school of population genetics. On the other hand, through his move to India, he brought about a theatrical *rapprochement* between mathematical population genetics and field research at the grass-roots, and he justified it in terms that came quite close to the naturalists' arguments, as I shall now try to show.

A Return to Botany

Krishna Dronamraju's testimony on Haldane's Indian years is precious, when he recalls how often his teacher emphasized that Darwin's most original work was not his theory of evolution. 'Personally', Haldane wrote in a book review of 1962, 'I think Darwin's books on plant physiology, and the attitude revealed by them, may be more original than his theory of evolution, much of which has been developed independently by Wallace' (Dronamraju, 1985: 35). He advocated a return to both Alfred Russel Wallace (1823–1913), the celebrated author of *The Malay Archipelago* (1869), and botany, the botanical writings of Darwin himself.

Plants made an impressive contribution to Darwin's thinking, and botany played a major role in his writings, including *On the Origin of Species, Animals and Plants under Domestication, Fertilization of Orchids*, and *Cross- and Self-fertilization in the Vegetable Kingdom*. Botany, however, has faded with the advent of genetics and molecular biology and does not seem to have played any role in the modern evolutionary synthesis. In the 1930s and 1940s no botanist published a book comparable in impact to the major books published by geneticists, zoologists, etc. (Mayr and Provine, 1980: 137). From a prospective point of view, however, Haldane would have agreed to say, with our contemporary environmentalists, that the preservation of plant diversity is far more important than the preservation of large mammals (see Ch. 4, above). Wallace was more explicit than Darwin on the great difference between a tropical flora and a temperate one.

[Wallace] saw that certain biological problems are forced on one by a study of tropical life, which are by no means so obvious in temperate climates. Many ecological questions are fairly simple in the arctic regions, where a biotic community may consist of only twenty or thiry species; more difficult in the temperate zone, where a hundred or more species must be considered; and extremely complicated in a tropical rain forest, where it might become necessary to consider thousands of species, many as yet undescribed. (Haldane, 1960: 710; cited in Dronamraju, 1985: 37)

Defending botany, promoting tropical biology in the field, and preserving genetic diversity constitute one and the same task.

What did Haldane mean when speaking of 'the attitude revealed by' Darwin's books on plant physiology? In the space of a short essay, I can only summarize my readings and outline this 'attitude'. Let me set aside the formidable question of Darwinism, its social aspects, its philosophical impact, its links to Western individualism and economics. This is definitely not my subject. When pointing to Darwin's botany, Haldane simply tried to address himself to the purely biological question of genetic diversity and species variation. One celebrated series of lectures he delivered in India in 1958 was entitled 'The Unity and Diversity of Life'. To him at that time, and in a tropical country, the most important of all Darwinian concepts was not evolution but diversity. This is a very telling attitude for us today. I remember a noted French population geneticist once addressing a philo- sophical meeting with rhetorical questions like: 'Don't you think, as philosophers, that evolution is a fascinating subject?' Some years later, having abandoned true research in mathematical population genetics to become a Parisian intellectual and anti-racism activist, he started writing books not on evolution but on human diversity. Now, the recognition of genetic diversity as one of the most precious values entails the recognition of a common rule in nature, for the acknowledgement of which Westerners are not so well prepared as Hindus, Buddhists, or Jainas:

To Europeans and Americans, it inevitably seems that Darwin's greatest achieve- ment has been to convince educated men and women that biological evolution is a fact, that living plant and animal species are all descended from ancestral species very unlike themselves and, in particular, that men are descended from animals. This was an important event in the intellectual life of Europe, because Christian theologians had drawn a sharp distinction between men and other living beings. In view of Jesus' remarks about sheep, sparrows, and lilies, this sharp distinction may well be a perversion of the essence of Christianity. St. Francis seems to have thought so.

But in India this distinction has not been made; and, according to Hindu, Buddhist, and Jaina ethics, animals have rights and duties. (Haldane, 1959: 357; cited in Dronamraju, 1985: 35)

This is a denunciation of dualism, the dualism of body and mind, animals and men, which has plagued Western thought for about two millennia.[5]

We are only touching here upon an important turning-point in the history of biology, which would require my adducing many readings to be accounted for. In brief, Darwin's approach to diversity in plants imposed a paradigm shift: he replaced typological thinking by population thinking. In the older Western philosophies of nature, based on fixism and creationism, the various biological species were conceived of in terms of types, whereas modern taxonomists after Darwin have come to work on populations that evolve in various degrees of isolation, or else, symbiosis. Ernst Mayr has emphasized Darwin's contribution on this particular point. He has shown that Darwin's intellectual achievements were at least threefold: first, Darwin presented an overwhelming mass of evidence proving that evolution was a fact; second, he proposed a mechanism that might convincingly account for evolutionary change, namely, natural selection; and, last but not least, he replaced typological thinking by population thinking. The first two contributions, Mayr goes on to say, have been easily recognized, but the third has been almost consistently overlooked (Mayr, 1959, repr. in 1976: 27). The change thus brought about in the biologist's approach to nature has philosophical as well as methodological bearing. It announces the modern developments of statistics and probability thinking. It also promotes a new set of values. First of all, we have diversity as a value, and with the more recent advent of environmentalism, the preservation of genetic diversity in faunas and floras. Then, another value revived from ancient times is the bond of nature common to humans, animals, and plants. I shall elaborate on these new values in the third part of the present essay. Let me first describe Haldane's career in India from 1957.

A BIOLOGIST IN QUEST OF A SOIL

Haldane's experimental activity dates back to his school days, when he started assisting his father J. S. Haldane in research on respiratory physiology relating to deep-sea diving and inhalation of gases in mines. 'JBS' used to serve as subject-investigator in these experiments, and he published noted contributions to this field of study in 1924 and 1927 (Dronamraju, 1968: 267). Thus, he had always been acquainted with fieldwork, although in many respects he remained an armchair scientist. During the Indian period, a kind of division of labour was established between the research professor and his younger researchers. Haldane's work was mostly theoretical; it involved no equipment except pen and paper, not even a simple calculator. The old man preferred to perform all his calculations in long hand, and have one of the young associates check them, especially S. D. Jayakar, whose background was in mathematics (Dronamraju, 1985: 14, 19).

Simultaneously, he attracted to Calcutta a few Indian biologists like S. K.

Roy, K. R. Dronamraju, and T. A. Davis, who applied the theories and methods of population genetics to local observations. In the following review of these researches, I shall emphasize only one aspect, namely, the indigenization of population genetics. I shall postpone until the third part of this essay the discussion of the overall unity of researches initiated by Haldane's disciples in India, although their various pursuits and scientific interests appear somewhat disjointed to me, when I read Davis' 'Biology in the Tropics' (1968) and K. R. Dronamraju's recollections. But I shall also say a few words on more recent papers by Davis, which retrospectively shed light on their early orientations.

S. K. Roy's research projects dealt with a study of the amount of soil brought to the surface by earthworms (a typically Darwinian topic), variation in organs on the same plant over time, and interaction between rice varieties. The work on rice varieties was devised to confirm Haldane's thought that, because of the denseness of the tropical flora, one would expect a large amount of interdependence involving both competition and co-operation among many species growing closely together:

Thus India has over 20,000 species of flowering plants, a number far surpassing states of much larger areas. One would expect symbiotic relations between flowering plants to be much commoner in regions with a diverse flora than in those where a natural plant community often consists of few members. Further, while harvesting is not mechanized, there is often no difficulty in growing mixed crops . . . While the most obvious symbiosis to look for and to exploit, if discovered, to increase agricultural production, is between different species, particularly cereals and legumes, nevertheless if such symbiotic relations are common, they should be looked for between different genotypes of the same species. (Haldane, 1958, in Dronamraju, 1985: 31)

There might be an economic benefit in the 'outbreeding' of one crop's many varieties. Roy's experiments were conducted mainly in Giridih in Bihar where the ISI had a field station for experimental trials; cocoons of *Antheraea mylitta*, the tussore silk moth, whose life cycle was studied by Mrs Haldane, also came from the market-place in Ciridih. As for Dronamraju and Davis, both of them worked on plant genetics and biometry, animal behaviour and human genetics. Dronamraju is well-known for his studies of consanguineous marriages in Andhra Pradesh, the inheritance of hairy ears, the gene frequencies of colour-vision defects in Andhra and Orissa, and deaf-mutism among Bengali Kayastha settlers in Orissa. Davis is best known for his studies on foliar asymmetry in the coconut and floral asymmetry in most species of *Malvaceae*. One observation he made seemed to be promising, from an economic point of view: he found that the coconut palms with left-handed spirals gave 20.9 per cent more nuts than those with right-handed spirals. However, this observation is misleading because it suggests that Davis had devised his researches in the perspective of horticultural economics and was looking for a way of increasing yields in plantations. Actually, his intellectual attitude was essentially that of fascination for asymmetry itself; we shall come back to it later.

Mr and Mrs Haldane were not working in the field properly speaking, but the following extract from a letter to an American colleague will give an idea of their daily life as naturalists:

We are just starting up here [in Bhubaneswar]. But I don't expect we shall have much to show, except human genetics, animal history, and theory, for a couple of years. By animal history I mean that for the first time Jayakar and my wife have got the complete history of an animal community (a nest of Polistes [wasps]) in our bath-room in Calcutta. Except for the foundress, we know when each of about 100 individuals was laid, pupated, emerged, and died or did not return. We also have records of all the journeys of each of them to and from the nest, and at least a good lot of data on what they did. There are about 4000 pages of notes to be analysed. Nobody has done anything at all comparable. The nest came to an end. It was a failure, perhaps because it was too far inside the house, so many workers lost their way. But to decide that, we should need studies of a lot of nests. Each means 13 hours' work a day for many months, so it won't be in a hurry. (Haldane's letter from Bhubaneswar, September 1962, to Professor J. T. Boner, Princeton University, cited in Dronamraju, 1985: 110)

The retrospective portrait of Haldane in India published by Krishna Dronamraju more than twenty years after the death of his teacher might have been disappointing to those readers who prefer critical analysis to emotional anecdotes. It is nevertheless a most interesting ethnographic document. It does not provide only facts, it also formulates a disciple's interpretation. Let me paraphrase Dronamraju (1985: 8–9) on Haldane's leanings towards Hindu culture and philosophy. Haldane said he fell in love with India in 1918 when he was sent to Simla to convalesce. (He had been accidentally hit in the leg on the Mesopotamian front in 1917.) Later he spent a year at Mhow in central India as a bombing instructor. Unlike most British officers, he used to travel, eat, and mix with the local people. He was intrigued by Hindu social customs, such as cow worship. In *Daedalus*, or *Science and the Future*, his first book published in 1924, he commented that Hindus appropriately appreciated the physiological relationship with the cow. He read extensively about Hindu philosophy and mythology.

He began to eat less meat and became a strict vegetarian shortly after his arrival in India. It was significant that Haldane found a common bond between such aspects of Indian culture as non-violence, vegetarianism and beautiful animal sculptures on the one hand and the Darwinian theory of evolution on the other. Furthermore, in spite of his socialist beliefs, Haldane had an instinctive liking for some aspects of the caste system. As an intellectual, he identified himself with the Brahmins and wrote in an article in *Envoy* that he had a sneaking sympathy for that group. This was not surprising since many of his colleagues in research institutions and universities were of the Brahmin caste and were a substitute, in a sense, for his former colleagues in England (Dronamraju, 1985: 8).

According to this account, Haldane found a common 'bond between the Hindu values of non-violence and vegetarianism, the mythological lore and aesthetics of beautiful animal sculptures, and the Darwinian theory of evolution. One may well ask if this alleged bond is more than simply an a posteriori rationalization of Haldane's emotions and leanings. However, Haldane's (1959) paper delineating 'An Indian Perspective of Darwin', which was quoted in the first part of this essay, and all the consonant documents I have tried to bring together will expose the underlying idea, namely, that we have to change our system of reference. The Hindu values of non-violence and vegetarianism entail a necessary decentration of mankind. Man is not the centre of the universe, mankind is not that unique species which Christian theology had separated from other living beings. Animals have rights and duties, and the beauty of animal forms conveys this idea of a common rule between man and other species.

Haldane was interested in the learned tradition of Indian logic so much that he wrote a curious piece on *syadvada*, 'the assertion of possibilities', or modal statements made by Jaina philosophers like Bhadrabahu (fourth century AD), which compare with what was known in Europe as the modes of scepticism.[6] Sceptical statements on sensory data—'wood is hard [compared with clay] and soft [compared with iron]', etc.—served to illustrate the canonical set of modal statements: 'maybe it is', 'maybe it is not', 'maybe it is and it is not', 'maybe it is indeterminate', etc. Naive as they might have been, these elucubrations put us on the right track towards a new relationship between science (i.e. biology) and the humanities (i.e. Sanskrit textual studies). Haldane rightfully sensed that the learned tradition of inference and taxonomy in Sanskrit still had something to teach to modern scientists, although what exactly Sanskrit studies have to offer is not where Haldane thought it to be. The Sanskrit medical texts, for example, do contain a sophisticated system of modal logic (the *tantrayukti* system) and combinatorics (the *laksana* system), as I have tried to show elsewhere (Zimmermann, 1987; 1989).

But before we engage in such a reconciliation of philology and biology and address ourselves to the prospective part of this essay, let me conclude its historical part with the evocation of a visit to T. Antony Davis in 1989. At the end of his career,[7] Davis retired to Nagercoil in Tamilnad where he founded an association in memory of J. B. S. Haldane.[8] I am aware of the somewhat marginal position of topics discussed in Nagercoil compared to the developments of mainstream genetics and biometry in Calcutta or Bangalore. The spirit of improvisation and curiosity which was so well received by Haldane is now looked on with scepticism by younger Indian scientists, who are facing stiff competition to gain academic recognition. The problems and methods described in the following paragraph clearly belong with natural history rather than tough science. With respect to the current shifts and *rapprochements* in the overall classification of sciences, and the recent advent of ethnosciences, I think that the researches on asymmetry pursued by T. A. Davis are bound to reach a new topicality. When I visited him in early February 1989, I was on my way to Tuticorin and Tiruchendur to collect data on Chank fisheries (see below); that is to say, we were sharing a common interest in asymmetry and polarities of the right and left in living organisms. In the course of our conversation, Davis was kind enough to recount the beginnings of this long-standing passion in Calcutta under Haldane's influence.

Researches on the hibiscus intermingled with that on the coconut palm. Davis was a recognized expert on coconut physiology when he was recruited by Haldane. He had already conducted (in 1950–2) the experiments in controlled pollination between known coconut seed parents and pollen parents, that were to be adduced a few years later to prove the non-inheritance of asymmetry in *Cocos nucifera* (Davis, 1962). However, his interest in asymmetry itself was kindled by his observations of the hibiscus in Calcutta. *Hibiscus rosasinensis* is one of the most popular flowering shrubs in and around Calcutta. Its attractive flowers form an important part of the offerings during worship, and the perennial flowering nature of the plant induces many Hindus to grow one or more specimens in their houses (Davis and Ghoshal, 1966: 30). Davis used to pluck them without even thinking of it until he noticed the floral asymmetry. When viewed apically, about half the number of flowers are left-handed (i.e. the inner margin of a petal curves clockwise towards the periphery), and the rest right-handed (it curves counter-clockwise). Was this a case of balanced polymorphism? Haldane's reaction to the question raised by Davis was typical. Data were needed to substantiate ideas, and Haldane (quoted to me by Davis from his most vivid memories) used to tell his collaborators: 'You cannot come to my house without data.' Our young researcher soon found himself engaged in extensive surveys with the help of Mrs Davis. There were days when thousands of flowers were piling up on the dining-table, awaiting inspection. Over 80,000 flowers from 34 species of *Malvaceae* were examined,[9] including 23,492 flowers of *Hibiscus rosasinensis* which showed a statistically significant excess (51.19 per cent) of left-handers (Davis and Ghoshal, 1966: 33). At the same time, Davis began to investigate foliar asymmetry in the coconut palm. The leaves are arranged along five distinct spirals which are either right-handed (counter-clockwise) or left-handed. Davis went over the data previously collected in Kerala and demonstrated that asymmetry was clearly not controlled by Mendelian genetics; this negative conclusion was subsequently confirmed in Indonesia. Then, Davis investigated the reasons for asymmetry and he suggested a possible geophysical influence, adducing data that showed a statistically significant excess of lefts over rights in the northern hemisphere, and of rights over lefts in the southern hemisphere. He has more recently published papers in the same vein—on foliar spirality, antler asymmetry in deer, and on dextral and sinistral coiling in gastropod molluscs—which testify to his long-lasting curiosity about asymmetry as a salient feature in natural history. I have been dwelling on Davis's particular orientations, because they illustrate an implicit drift from biology into natural history.

Current researches in biometry and population genetics derive their sharpness and accurateness from their being inserted in an overall scientific design, a theory or a concept, which dictates their agenda and procedures. Such designs are consubstantial with the dominant paradigm in that they determine the way we write our applications for research funds, the way we submit our papers to peer review, etc. Haldane came to India with such designs in mind—for example, to calculate the cost of natural selection. However, in the field researches I have just described, a dissociation is noticeable or, so to speak, a decoupling from the dominant concepts. When Davis started investigating foliar asymmetry in the coconut, the overall design within the frame of which he worked was that of natural selection. Thus his first project was to prove or disprove the inheritance of asymmetry. However, he soon gave in to a kind of intellectual drift away from the constraining canons of evolutionary biology, to indulge in the study of *mirabilia* (the wonders of nature in Latin), the subject-matter of natural history.

NATURAL HISTORY AND LOCAL KNOWLEDGE

Asymmetry, polarities of the right and left, clockwise and counter-clockwise spirallings, and other strange arrangements of forms in nature have played an important role in Hindu religion and mythology. I shall only mention conch-shells, which used to be collected by divers in the Gulf of Mannar: the right-handed ones are very rare—about one out of 100,000 left-handed shells. They are kept in temples as precious and sacred items. The overall Hindu approach to these rare arrangements of forms in Nature comes very near to the philosophical attitude which Roger Caillois labelled 'generalized aesthetics' (*esthétique généralisée*). As soon as we ascribe some value to these forms, be it an aesthetic or a religious value, we are challenging the tenets of Western scientific thinking. The scientist is accustomed to take an economistic view of nature. Accordingly, the Darwinian theory of natural selection is based on the concepts of utility and fitness, the survival of the fittest. The recognition of rare beautiful living forms militates against this utilitarianism, and suggests an alternative view of biology: suppose nature were to produce them gratuitously! Elements of such an alternative view were present in Haldane's text quoted above: 'None will contend', Haldane argued, 'that (*except insofar as* it has induced Hindus to regard him as sacred . . .) the peacock's rather cumbrous tail has been of any advantage to him.' The peacock's fanning tail is cumbrous indeed, but so exotic! Which of the two criteria, fitness or beauty, should we apply to give the peacock his right place in nature? Let us dissociate two views of nature, and decouple natural history from evolutionary biology.

Defining Natural History

In our quest for alternative views of biology, Roger Caillois might be a source of inspiration.[10] A protagonist of the two adventures of Surrealism and the Collège de Sociologie, he was a disciple of Georges Bataille, from whom he borrowed the idea of 'fastuous consumption' which appears below. Caillois spent his life collecting samples or examples of rare arrangements in nature. It would be only too easy to deride this as mysticism. However, the following text will reveal Caillois's perfect agreement with Haldane on the critique of fitness.

A doctrine of natural selection readily admits, or even implies, that plasticity exists, which gives the fin in hydrophilus, the toothed harpoon in mantis, the excavator in mole cricket, but the same doctrine according to the same postulates refuses to accept the idea of a similar mechanism to explain decoration on the wings in butterfly. There seems to be here a deciding contrast between the necessary and the luxurious. Most people are persuaded that something useless is something ineffective. The idea of something useless is unacceptable. In other words, all that is superfluous seems *a priori* inexplicable.

I confess, to me it is just here that what I would like to call deep anthropomorphism is raging. People will at all costs avoid introducing art, beauty, blazon, or painting, into the description of butterfly wings, because these words speak only to human sensibility and history, no matter what care is taken to stress differences and contrasts. In order to avoid using these forbidden words, people commonly choose to set up fitness as an absolute criterion, fitness meaning survival in Nature. This Nature, however, is one where an enormous amount of dilapidation is the rule. As soon as we stop projecting man's specific reactions onto the other domains of biology, it becomes evident. A kind of fastuous consumption devoid of any intelligible purpose prevails in Nature, and there is absolutely no reason to deny its being a more general and more powerful rule [in biology] than vital interest, that is, the imperative of species survival.

We humans keep thinking that Nature never operates in vain [*que la nature ne fait rien en vain*]. Nearly everything around us is suggestive to the reverse, but we keep thinking we enjoy, if not the best, at least the most economical of all possible worlds. I find such a postulate very risky. I even wonder which criterion might be invoked to explain away the phrase 'in vain'. Only humans can judge. I suspect, here is the ultimate mistake of true anthropomorphists. Of course, I know it's me they will charge with being a delirious anthropomorphist: what's more ridiculous than daring to compare butterfly wings with paintings?

Nevertheless, my system of reference might appear to be the most *decentered* of all systems, for it *also* entails conceiving of paintings, the painter's works, as human varieties of butterfly wings (Caillois, 1960: 50–2).

Caillois is trying to dissociate two ideas which were systematically combined in Leibniz's time: utilitarianism and optimism; nature is always
economical, and this is the best of all possible worlds. These two values
were still underlying Darwinism two centuries later, and we have not yet
been able to escape them. Natural history constituted itself as a taxonomy
on the basis of a continuous network of beings, which was called the tableau
of Nature, and governed by the laws of continuity and finality. Just as to the
mind of our modern evolutionists, oddities (like the peacock's cumbrous
tail) are proofs of the reality of evolution, similarly in Leibniz's time,
monstrosities were understood as proofs of the continuity of nature through
catastrophes and ephemeral variations. 'Monsters were proving on the time
dimension and in theoretical knowledge a continuity which deluges, vol-
canoes and engulfed continents were blurring on the space dimension and
in day-to-day experience' (Foucault, 1966: 169).[11] The oddities and monstrosities we observe, far from destroying our sense of order, constitute the
background noise out of which the regularities are deciphered by the
scientist.

Natural history as I shall understand it from now on is not exactly the
same as histories which flourished in the sixteenth and until the middle of
the seventeenth century. Our modern historians of science, who, in the
wake of Bachelard's epistemology, have been addressing themselves to the
epistemic breaks and boundaries between different paradigms of science,
have come to acknowledge the existence of such a break in the seventeenth
century, contemporary with the advent of Cartesianism (Foucault, 1966:
140–3). The field of *Historia* then underwent a sudden split between two
different systems of knowledge hitherto confounded: tradition and observation. Until then, histories were an inextricable web of fables and symbols,
virtues, beliefs, and local customs, compiled by scholars from the literate tradition and superimposed on the observation of things themselves.
From Jonston onwards, who published in 1657 a *Historia naturalis de
quadrupedibus*, the *litteraria*, that is, testimonies from Aristotle, Pliny, and
other literary sources, were put back to the end of each chapter, and thus
implicitly disqualified. The author ceased being a compiler, to become a
naturalist.[12] This involves a closer grasp of the perceived world, focusing on
the more structured layers of sensory knowledge, and almost restricting
observation to only one sense organ, sight. Hearsay is disqualified, as well
as taste and smell. The visible aspects of a thing, for example the stamens
and pistil in a plant, are screened, sketched, and transcribed into language.
The sense of sight is cleared of hearsay and scholastic jumble. 'The adum-
bration will accurately contain the whole history of the plant', Linné said in
his *Philosophia botanica* (1751) (Foucault, 1966: 147). However, in emphasizing the epistemic break, or mutation, between these two models of
natural history—pre-scientific in the Renaissance, and then, born as a new
observational science with the advent of Cartesianism—historians are

working on a questionable assumption which has been rightfully denounced by anthropologists.

It is the positivist's assumption that pre-scientific thought is essentially pre-logical, affective, and mystical. Foucault, for example, in his account of traditional *Historia*, laid great emphasis on the unrestrained use of analogy and sympathy, blazons and signatures, while he described the birth of modern natural history in terms of rationality and disenchantment of the world. The prerequisite to the advent of natural history as a science was a liberation of our observational skills from the colourful spells of imagination, it was 'visibility freed from any other sensory input', only the sense-data of sight, 'and, furthermore, turned grey' (*passé à la grisaille*) (1966: 145). Foucault was playing on the connotations of greyness: nature was to be depicted in black and white, since colours were too elusive to serve as criteria for natural classification, and the new world of natural sciences was discoloured or disenchanted. There was a frank dualism of night (mysticism) and day (enlightenment) in Foucault's presentation, inspired by Bachelard's disciples in French epistemology. In such a perspective, the text by Roger Caillois quoted above seems totally antiquated. It reads like an admonition against rationalism and may be mistaken for a retrograde invitation to mysticism. Is it not reintroducing colours, beauty, sensibility, and aesthetics into the realm of natural history?

To give Caillois full credit, however, one should read him in the light of current developments in anthropology. I shall outline these researches now in progress, especially on two fronts: first, the reappraisal of Lucien Lévy-Bruhl's seminal ideas on primitive classifications, and secondly, the *rapprochement* between ethnography and philology in the study of literacy and the learned traditions. Anthropologists of classical Greece, India, and China have exposed one particular aspect of ancient science which had been neglected by historians. A great divide is usually drawn between science and scholarship—the latter covering the humanities, the liberal arts, and more precisely in French, *les matières d'érudition*—according to which geometry is a science, and grammar is not, biology is a science, and geography is not. This division is a sheer anachronism, as regards our Greek, Sanskrit, or Chinese sources, not to speak of Latin, Persian, and Arabic. One should not play down the scientific character of scholasticism, the driving-force of rhetoric and philology in the birth of rationalism, and the everlasting fusion of the scientist and the scholar.[13] In classical taxonomies and the long tradition of *Historia* down to the seventeenth century in Europe, artefacts used to be inventoried along with natural beings. This is perfectly logical as soon as we acknowledge the philological character of natural history, conceived of as a compilation of testimonies on the lived world, inclusive of natures, artefacts, and usages. Reciprocally, one should not overplay the so-called mysticism of ancient naturalists. When Foucault pointed to the central position of analogy, sympathy, blazons, and the doctrine of signatures in Renaissance histories, he should have reminded us that these symbolical modes of thought were not used uncritically but had been elaborated into a full-fledged organon, first by the Stoics and then in medieval logic. An increasing amount of literature is currently devoted to the reappraisal of ancient logic, and a striking convergence is observed between textual studies on the learned traditions and the ethnographic study of folk taxonomies.[14] Ancient logic and folk taxonomies seem to share a common predilection for connective rather than inclusive relations, which makes them closer to phenetics than to cladistics; I shall elaborate on this below. Another common feature is that poetics, imagination, and affectivity are reckoned among the foundations of inference and classification. Strange as they may seem in our own prejudiced view of rationality, there have been systems of knowledge in which an inference was a valuation, and a classification responded to an implicit axiology.[15] Caillois's aesthetics makes sense especially in the light of these non-Western or non-modern logics, and the text quoted above can now be read as inviting from us a decentration of mankind's place in Nature, completing Kant's Copernician revolution down to natural history without any transcendental subject.[16]

Because he said he noted everywhere in the universe the presence of a sensibility and of a quasi-conscience similar to ours, he was charged with anthropomorphism. Caillois himself, however, passionately argued that he was on the contrary praising a reversed anthropomorphism, anthropomorphism the other way round, in which man, far from attributing , sometimes condescendingly, his own emotions to the rest of living beings, participated with humility, maybe also with pride, in all that is included or infused into the three kingdoms. This great mind had experienced, so to speak, an equivalent of the Copernician revolution: no longer was man at the centre of the universe, save that this centre is everywhere; man pertained with the rest of things to the gearing of cog-wheels (Yourcenar, 1981: 18).[17]

The dominant scientific paradigm in biology, since it retains the age-old Western dualism of the mind and the body, overshadows this bond of nature where mankind shares a common rule with all the three kingdoms. Indeed, the Darwinian legacy has placed our natural bodies in a continuum with animals, but in radically separating the humanities from scientific pursuits it has made modern biologists ill-equipped for understanding this embeddedness.

The Conch-Shell Syndrome

A definition emerges from the foregoing readings which challenges our usual prejudice in favour of economistic explanations: the definition of nature as embeddedness. I have been using the word 'soil' as a metaphor to connote this embeddedness of all things in one another, localized and pictured in a particular landscape. A philological study of the traditional values of rural life—in the Sanskrit texts of medicine and astrology for example—would yield a large collection of indigenous words and phrases connoting well-being, welfare and quiet life rooted in a healthy soil, happy connections, happy conjunctures. These all revolve around the central issue of biology re-embedded: I mean, the task of bringing biology closer to the study of local forms of life. Unfortunately, the dominant paradigm in biology hampers this kind of rapprochement. It marginalizes a study of nature based on philological grounds, that would integrate living beings, artefacts, and traditions into a single field. It disqualifies local knowledge, that is, knowledge embedded in a landscape, a community, or a tradition, as mysticism.

Haldane, as we have seen, did not share this arrogance and condemnation of local knowledge. He sensed the need to break with the dominant views, in his pursuit of the diversity of life, but he could not throw off the yoke of natural selection. Unfortunately, his training as a geneticist imposed limitations on his ability to imagine the necessary changes. Two rearrangements, which I have just outlined in the preceding paragraph, were necessary to place natural history in a new perspective: one was to dissociate taxonomy from evolutionary thought, and the other was to integrate natural with cultural diversity. The limitations imposed upon Haldane by mainstream biology in the 1950s are all the more visible since the first of these two ideas—decoupling taxonomy from evolutionary systematics—was very much in the wind at that time. But it was only as a challenging view. The established theory of systematics, held by most biologists over the world, embodied the evolutionary synthesis achieved during the 1930s and 1940s; it integrated population genetics with natural history. Evolutionary systematics seemed to be inscribed in nature itself. The pathways of evolution were objectified in images of ancestry and descent, cladograms, or the branching trees of phylogeny. However, the assumptions and techniques of natural classification were gradually called into question by the protagonists of numerical and phenetic taxonomy, first propounded by Sokal, Sneath, and associates in 1957.[18] They tried 'to distinguish between the process of classifying and the subsequent process of generating hypotheses about evolution' (Sneath and Sokal, 1973: 422). They progressively emancipated themselves from the constraining imagery of cladistics. They dissociated the measure of relationship from hypotheses about kinship. The polythetic arrangements of things in phenetics are based on an overall similarity which does not carry with it any necessary implication as to common ancestry. No need to recall the far-reaching applications of numerical taxonomy in archaeology, anthropology, and the humanities. But the systematists belonging to the Establishment, such as Ernst Mayr, who worked on the natural classification of animals, misjudged this alternative view and accused it of being nominalist. The debate in the 1960s is a very good example of how the dominant system of knowledge, which objectified relationships and affinities in nature by reducing them to cladograms, narrowed the space for the development of challenging views.

   In writing this account of Haldane's themes and attitudes at the end of his life, which I suggest may still be inspiring to us, I have been pursuing some new developments in natural history which Haldane himself had foreseen without being able to tackle them, because first, they were irrelevant to evolutionary biology, second, they belonged with local knowledge and indigenous categories of thought, and third they were ambiguous in their extolling of life-forms at the interface of nature and society. I persist in tying these developments to natural history, in order to stress the intellectual genealogy of the discipline, although it has long since been taken over by symbolic and cognitive anthropology. The preferred objects of the kind of natural history I have been defending in these pages, in which aesthetics, ethics, and biology are not separated, are those in which man's intervention has given the final touch to a natural arrangement.[19] One of its important chapters is the study of kinship, and a first example of the kind of ambiguous developments I have in mind is found in Haldane's paper on consanguinity in human cousin marriage (Haldane and Moshinsky, 1939), where he contrasted the coefficient of consanguinity for a sex-linked rare recessive gene between cross-cousins ($f' = 1/8$) to that between parallel cousins ($f' = 3/16$). The kind of relationship studied in this paper is ambiguous in that it is at the interface of nature (inbreeding) and society (marriage). As early as the 1930s anthropologists showed how cultural institutions, such as the preference for cross-cousin marriage and the prohibition of parallel-cousin marriage, had elaborated the natural facts of consanguinity into a mixture of nature and culture, the cousin marriage syndrome. By syndrome I mean a set of beliefs, practices, and institutions that are characteristic of a particular condition inscribed in Nature itself.

   Haldane, it is true, was not equipped for a full understanding of such syndromes which fall within the scope of philology and call for linguistic analyses. He played the unconventional scientist in India, researching unusual phenomena armed with a pen and paper, and this attitude can easily be taken for that of a dilettante. He had the stamina to distantiate himself from the Establishment and the profession of Western science, but in dissociating his new pursuits from the mainstream of population genetics, he ran the risk of simply falling into a disjointed compilation of exotic observations. When a scientist comes down to grassroots research in unconventional surroundings, as Haldane did, in a sense he renounces the systematicity and professionalism of science (only thriving in the forefront labs), and for this voyage outside the realm of tough science to represent a credible alternative, he must strive to meet the same standards of professionalism in the philological register. This is because language and written testimonies (the subject-matter of philology) are part of the nature of the objects now under investigation. In Peircean terms, one could say that the appropriate models of explanation, then, are iconic and not indexical. Let me conclude with the example of one such object in which human discourses give the final touch to nature's arrangements. It is the conch-shell named 'chank' in India, the *Turbinella rapa* of naturalists, a good match for the peacock's tail with which I began. The gist of my argument, although I can only make an allusion to current debates in semiotics, is that beliefs, practices, and artefacts related to such animals as the Indian conch bear an iconic connection to them; in other words, they share some quality, they represent synecdoches of one another. The life of the chank is not confined to its body: once caught on the Tamil coast, it extends as far as Bengal and Nepal, on women's ankles and in the plan of sacred towns.

Dextral and sinistral coiling in gastropods is a topos of population genetics; we saw that Davis was interested in it. However, the first methodological shift to our own paradigm here is to restrict observations to only one species. *Busycon pervusus*, for example, is another conch species, where a dextral shell is considered precious because of its rarity, since the normal *Busycon* (unlike the *Turbinella*) is sinistral. But the *Busycon* is only an exotic life-form, whereas the chank syndrome is a whole world of beliefs, practices, artefacts, and life-forms. *Turbinella rapa* (syn. *Xancus pyrum*) is still the object of intense seasonal activity in the Gulf of Mannar. The fishery is a government monopoly. Large quantities of living shells are obtained from the muddy bottom of the sea. Up to a hundred country boats carrying ten divers can be seen making for the fishing-grounds every morning in the season, from November to March. Nowadays twenty conch-shells represent quite a good daily haul for one man, and the target for the 1988–9 season was eight lakhs (800,000 shells). The outlet for the entire production is the Bengali bangle market. After a few years during which the animals are allowed to rot and the shells to dry in government storehouses, the Tamil Nadu fisheries make a bid for the current stock to Bengali authorities, and the chanks are delivered to bangle-makers, who will saw them into narrow rings or bracelets that are traditionally worn by married Hindu women in Bengal. Now we must enter into the spirit of the chank syndrome, and this is our second methodological shift, to espouse the indigenous perspective. The biologists and the local people, in describing the shell, agree to place it vertically, with the apex up and the mouth down. But biologists used to say that the ordinary shell is dextral, meaning that the mouth is to the right of the columella. This conventional orientation does not carry any value-judgement. The local people's view is radically different, when they say that the shell is 'coiling up to the left', that is, from outside to inside and right to left around the columella. A taxonomy, then, is an axiology. The chank's coiling up is reminiscent of the ritual gesture of circumambulation. The very rare specimens 'coiling up to the right' are sacred in that they reproduce the auspicious orientations of circumambulation done from outside to inside keeping the sacred centre to your right. Innumerable illustrations of the chank's iconic connection to circumambulation are found in South and South-East Asia, including towns designed after the blueprint of a chank. Paraphrasing Yourcenar's formula about all that is infused into the three kingdoms of Nature, I would like to conceive of chanks as living a life of their own in all the three kingdoms of biology, language, and Hindu culture. I mean first in the muddy waters where divers catch them, then in the Sanskrit texts and taxonomies, and again in the artefacts made from them. Tradition has superimposed a second nature upon the life-form of the *Turbinella*, which dictates its place in nature and generates its various avatars.

CONCLUSION

Haldane's voyage to India in 1957 was an exemplary move. One of the leading population geneticists of the time was attempting to escape from the dominant paradigm of evolutionism. He undertook to develop local modes of scientific research in India. The first part of this essay described Haldane's reappraisal of the Darwinian heritage. Haldane emphasized that Darwin's most original achievement was not the theory of evolution but his field studies on the different forms of flowers of the same botanical species. But after Darwin, the evolutionary synthesis had separated the biological processes out from their clinical and ecological context, thus alienating biology from its soil. Biological mechanisms had been disembodied, disembedded, dissociated from real life. My second section evoked Haldane's interest in the logic and ethics of India, his advocacy of fieldwork in the tropics, and his inchoate efforts to link tropical biology with the study of indigenous modes of thought. There was in Haldane a precious quality of anger at the arrogance of Western conventional wisdom. In an attempt to elaborate upon Haldane's insights, in the third part of this chapter I worked my way towards an integration of natural history with philology and local knowledge. On the practical level, agriculture and medicine are the two domains upon which population genetics may exert a technological influence, through genetic engineering, genetic counselling etc. At the same time, in the Sanskrit tradition, agriculture and medicine represent the two complementary domains of outside—the fields—and inside—the body. By tackling modern science and traditional scholarship, agriculture and medicine, the outside and inside as a unique set of values and facts, and developing an appropriate semiotics of syndromes and iconic relations, we may be able to shirk the domination of some of the oppressive so-called universals of modern science, and shift, for example, from the domination of fitness to the recognition of embeddedness.

NOTES TO CHAPTER 8

1. Actually politics, personal issues, and the politics of knowledge were conflated in Haldane's decision to go to India. I am skipping the description of practical reasons for a move which included, for instance, Haldane's desire to find a new teaching post for his wife, Helen Spurway, also a noted scientist, whose appointment as Lecturer in London ran only to 1957.
2. I am thankful to Frédérique Apffel-Marglin for illuminating this issue in her discussion of an earlier draft.
3. The oddities, which represent later misappropriations of formerly useful functions, Gould argues, are the best proof of the reality of evolution; see e.g. essays 3, 4 and 11 in *Hen's Teeth and Horse's Toes*. The case of the peacock's tail is adduced in passing in *The Flamingo's Smile*.
4. The word adaptation has intuitive connotations and carries utilitarian ideas. In the scientific literature of population genetics, the word fitness is used as a synonym for the selective or reproductive value of a genotype. It may be either an absolute value, measured by the number of progeny per parent, or relative to some reference genotype.
5. In tracing its origins back to theologians of late antiquity, Haldane was taking a much sounder historical perspective of dualism than today's anthropologists who blame it on Descartes; but that is not the point.
6. Unfortunately, the English renderings of Bhadrabahu's modal statements in this paper (Haldane, 1985b), are so harshly simplified and out of context that they seem to contradict the principle of the excluded middle. Furthermore, Haldane tends to give an uninformed reader the idea that modern logic is deprived of any means of conceptualizing modalities. Not only the discoveries of modern logic are ignored, but also the revival of ancient logic.
7. Trupapur Antony Davis was a coconut physiologist attached to the Central Coconut Research Institute of Dayangulam (Kerala) from 1953 to 1960. He resigned to join Haldane at the ISI in Calcutta (see Clark, 1968: 219), where he held positions as research professor from 1960 to 1977. He obtained his doctorate under C. R. Rao in 1972, and worked at the Coconut Research Institute of Manado in Indonesia from 1977 to 1983 (see Davis et al., 1985: 165). I am most grateful to Professor Davis for his warm welcome, and the generous gift of rare offprints. I apologize for any mistake in my interpretation of our conversation.
8. This association, founded in 1981, is named the J. B. S. Haldane Research Centre, and its headquarters are at 'Cocos', Carmal Nagar, Nagercoil, Tamilnad 629 004, India.
9. Davis 1964: 515 is updated in Davis 1968: 329. Hibiscus surveys started in 1961, and preceded the paper on the non-inheritance of asymmetry in the coconut (Davis, 1962, 1963), itself based upon observations made in 1958 (Davis, 1968: 327). There was a kind of cross-fertilization between the two researches.
10. Roger Caillois (1913–79) published various essays on the imaginative haloes surrounding biological forms. The most elaborate was a small book on *The Octopus* (1973). His approach has been compared to sociobiology (Starobinski, 1979: 186), but, in my opinion, Caillois might be better under-

stood as a forerunner of the return of natural history as I shall try to define it below.

11. The pages on 'Monsters and Fossils' in Foucault, (1966), with quotations from J.-B. Robinet (1768), are most illuminating. Monsters are seen as a 'background noise' of natural history: this is his own phrase at p. 169.

12. The foregoing division of *Historia* (in the Renaissance) vs. natural history (in the later 17th and 18th cents.) follows from a rich body of specialized literature by historians and philosophers of science from Duhem and Doyre to Cassirer and Foucault—which, unfortunately, is too often ignored by anthropologists. For example, in Francesca Bray's 'Essence and Utility' (1989: 4) as well as in Georges Métailié's 'Histoire naturelle et humanisme en Chine et en Europe au XVI siècle' (1989: see esp. 361), my feeling is that natural history is a misnomer or anachronistic concept to designate what was simply *Historia*, i.e. a compilation of traditions. In both papers, written by two of our most distinguished anthropologists of Chinese science, the confusion between the two paradigms tends unfortunately to weaken the comparison of China and Europe.

13. A new domain of anthropology, the anthropology of indigenous scholarship, is emerging, which combines philology with ethnoscience. A preliminary bibliography would include Détienne, 1988 on Greece; Jullien, 1989a, 1989b on China; and Zimmermann, 1989 on India. Pollock, 1985 is an extremely rich and lucid essay on the concept of scholarship in Sanskrit.

14. Madame Claude Imbert's brilliant essay on Stoic logic and Alexandrian poetics (1980) offers a point of departure, on the textual studies side of this new branch of anthropology, the anthropology of logic. Convergent developments on cognition and affectivity are presented in Jorion, 1989 with an up-to-date bibliography.

15. Commenting on Bulmer's phrase about Kalam taxonomy—'mystical values' are ascribed to things—Jorion (1989: 534) speaks of 'affect values' (*valeurs d'affect*), and of a 'spontaneous axiology'. I myself tried to show (Zimmermann, 1987: 100, 149, 148) that, in Ayurvedic medicine, classification was a valuation, and taxonomy an axiology.

16. This is an allusion to Paul Ricoeur's celebrated definition of structural anthropology: 'Kantism without a transcendental subject'.

17. Marguerite Yourcenar was replacing Roger Caillois at the Académie Française and duly praising the previous incumbent of the chair.

18. See a retrospective account of the controversy surrounding numerical taxonomy in Sneath and Sokal, 1973: 418.

19. For example, I have tried to show elsewhere (Zimmermann, 1987: 59) that the clearance of forests through slash-and-burn cultivation gave the final touch to the distribution of *Antilope cervicapra* over the plains of India; it was both a natural and a cultural process.

REFERENCES

BRAY, F. (1989), 'Essence and Utility: The Classification of Crop Plants in China', *Chinese Science*, 9: 1–13.

CAILLOIS, R. (1960), *Méduse et Cie*, Paris: Gallimard.

—— (1973), *La Pieuvre: Essai sur la logique de l'imaginaire*, Paris: Editions de la Table Ronde.

CLARK, R. (1968), *J. B. S.: The Life and Work of J. B. S. Haldane*, London: Hodder and Stoughton.

CROW, J. F. (1970), 'Genetic Loads and the Cost of Natural Selection', in K. Kojima (ed.), *Mathematical Topics in Population Genetics*, Berlin Heidelberg New York: Springer-Verlag: 128–77.

DAGOGNET, F. (1970), *Le Catalogue de la vie: Étude méthodologique sur la taxinomie*, Paris: Presses Universitaires de France.

DAVIS, T. A. (1962), 'The Non-Inheritance of Asymmetry in *Cocos nucifera*', *Journal of Genetics*, 58: 42–50.

—— (1963), 'The Dependence of Yield on Asymmetry in Coconut Palms', *Journal of Genetics*, 58: 186–215.

—— (1964), 'Aestivation in Malvaceae', *Nature*, 201/4918: 515–16.

—— (1968), 'Biology in the Tropics', In K. R. Dronamraju (ed.), *Haldane and Modern Biology*, Baltimore: Johns Hopkins Press: 327–33.

—— and GHOSHAL, K. K. (1966), 'Variation in the Floral Organs of *Hibiscus rosasinensis Linn*', *Journal of the Indian Botanical Society*, 45: 30–43.

—— SUDASRIP, H., and DARWIS, S. N. (1985), *Coconut Research Institute, Manado, Indonesia: An Overview of Research Activities*, Manado: Coconut Research Institute.

DETIENNE, M. (1988) (ed.), *Les Savoirs de l'écriture en Grèce ancienne*, Lille: Presses Universitaires de Lille.

DRONAMRAJU, K. R. (1968)(ed.), *Haldane and Modern Biology*, Baltimore: Johns Hopkins Press.

—— (1985), *The Life and Work of J. B. S. Haldane with Special Reference to India*, Aberdeen: Aberdeen University Press.

FOUCAULT, M. (1966), *Les Mots et les choses: Une archéologie des sciences humaines*, Paris: Gallimard.

GOULD, S. J. (1980), *The Panda's Thumb: More Reflections in Natural History*, New York: Norton.

—— (1983), *Hen's Teeth and Horse's Toes*, New York: Norton.

—— (1986), *The Flamingo's Smile*, New York: Norton.

GRMEK, M. D. (1983), *Les Maladies à l'aube de la civilisation occidentale*, Paris: Payot.

HALDANE, J. B. S. (1924), *Daedalus, or Science and the Future, a paper read to the heretics, Cambridge on February 4th 1923*, London: K. Paul, Trench, Trubner and Co.

—— (1932), *The Causes of Evolution*, London: Longmans; repr. 1966, Ithaca, NY,: Cornell University Press.

—— (1949), 'Disease and Evolution', *La Ricerca scientifica*, Suppl., 19: 68.

—— (1957), 'The Cost of Natural Selection', *Journal of Genetics*, 55: 511–24.

—— (1958a), *The Unity and Diversity of Life*, New Delhi: Publications Division, Government of India.

—— (1958b), 'Syadvada System of Predication', *Sankhya*, 18: 195.

—— (1959), 'An Indian Perspective of Darwin', *Centennial Review Arts Sci. Michigan State University*, 3: 357.

—— (1960), 'The Theory of Natural Selection Today', *Nature*, 183: 710.

—— and MOSHINSKY, P. (1939), 'Inbreeding in Mendelian Populations with Special Reference to Human Cousin Marriage', *Annals of Eugenics*, 9: 321–40.

IMBERT, C. (1980), 'Stoic Logic and Alexandrian Poetics', in M. Schofield, M. Burnyeat, and J. Barnes (eds.), *Doubt and Dogmatism: Studies in Hellenistic Epistemology*, Oxford: Clarendon Press: 182–216.

JORION, P. (1989), 'Intelligence artificielle et mentalité primitive: Actualité de quelques concepts lévy-bruhliens', *Revue philosophique*, 114: 515–41.

JULLIEN, F. (1989a), 'Une vision du monde fondée sur l'appariement: Enjeux philosophiques, effets textuels (à partir de Wang Fuzhi)', *Extrême Orient–Extrême Occident*, 11: 45–52.

—— (1989b), *Procès ou création: Une introduction à la pensée des lettrés chinois*, Paris: Seuil.

LEWONTIN, R. C. (1974), *The Genetic Basis of Evolutionary Change*, New York: Columbia University Press.

MAYR, E. (1959), 'Where are we?', *Cold Spring Harbor Symposium on Quantitative Biology*, 24: 409–40; repr. 1976: 307 ff.

—— (1976), *Evolution and the Diversity of Life: Selected Essays*, Cambridge, Mass.: Harvard University Press.

—— and PROVINE, W. B. (1980) (eds.), *The Evolution Synthesis: Perspectives on the Unification of Biology*, Cambridge, Mass.: Harvard University Press.

MÉTAILIÉ, G. (1989), 'Histoire naturelle en Chine et en Europe au XVIᵉ siècle: Li Shizhen et Jacques Dalechamp', *Revue d'histoire des sciences*, 42: 353–74.

MULLER, H.J. (1950), 'Our Load of Mutations', *American Journal of Human Genetics*, 2: 11–176.

POLLOCK, S. (1985), 'The Theory of Practice and the Practice of Theory in Indian Intellectual History', *Journal of the American Oriental Society*, 105: 499–519.

SMITH, W. D. (1981), 'Implicit Fever Theory in *Epidemics* 5 and 7', in W. F. Bynum and V. Nutton (eds.), *Theories of Fever from Antiquity to the Enlightenment*, London: Wellcome Institute: 1–18.

SNEATH, P. H. A. and SOKAL, R. R. (1973), *Numerical Taxonomy*, San Francisco: Freeman.

STAROBINSKI, J. (1979), 'Saturne au ciel des pierres', *Nouvelle revue française*, 320: 176–91.

WALLACE, A. R. (1869), *The Malay Archipelago*, London: Macmillan.

YOURCENAR, M. (1981), 'Discours de réception à l'Académie Française', *Le Monde*, 23 Jan. 1981 (p. 18, col. 3).

ZIMMERMANN, F. (1987), *The Jungle and the Aroma of Meats: An Ecological Theme in Hindu Medicine*, Berkeley, Calif.: University of California Press.

—— (1989), *Le Discours des remèdes au Pays des Epices: Enquête sur la médecine hindoue*, Paris: Payot.

9

Footnotes to Vavilov:
An Essay on Gene Diversity

SHIV VISVANATHAN

INTRODUCTION

In his *Gulag Archipelago*, Alexander Solzhenitsyn has a series of moving observations about the Russian scientist Nikolai Vavilov. Vavilov, the leading Soviet geneticist, was director of the Research Institute of Plant Breeding. He was arrested in 1940 at the height of Lysenkoism. The scientist was forced to endure over 400 interrogation sessions, but even then he refused to confess at his trial on 9 July 1941. Sentenced to death, he was made to wait several months, confined to a small basement cell without a window. The sentence was later commuted, but Vavilov, already ill from torture, died in 1943. In a footnote, the relentless Solzhenitsyn adds that Vavilov's interrogator, Khvat, lives in peaceful retirement, spending his pension at 41 Gorky Street (Solzhenitsyn, 1973).

History has been doubly unfair to Vavilov. A great scientist, he saw his school of genetics destroyed by Stalin. The attempts to rehabilitate him have failed to do full justice to the potential complexity of his ideas and the debates around him have a truncated quality about them. Vavilov was the centre of two far-reaching debates, one of which is read stereotypically as the Lysenko affair and the other centres around the debate on the death of diversity. Together, the two constitute probably the most significant morality play of modern science.

The history of the Lysenko affair is rendered as a typical persecution story and these operate in science as the equivalent of creation myths. Vavilov was one of the pioneers of genetics in Russia. A student of Bateson, he returned from Cambridge to succeed Eduard Regel as director of the Institute of Plant Breeding. The plot then reads as a tragedy of how Lysenko the impostor destroys Vavilov and his school. The conflict is portrayed as one between the state and scientific expertise, science and ideology.

Dominique Lecourt (1977: 445–6) in his more subaltern reading, points out that there were two stages in the controversy. In the first, Lysenko was an object of fun for the leading scientists, who saw him as a local technician with his recipes for vernalization and crop rotation. In this limited sense,

Lysenko might have had a restricted relevance, which even Vavilov admitted. Vernalization did alter the maturation time of seeds and this was crucial for agriculture in winter climates. At this stage the conflict was a simpler one between a group of scientists pioneering in a new field (genetics) and technicians who challenged them to prove their practical relevance convinced that such 'genetics was an amusement like chess or football' (Sullivan, 1967: 276–98). It was only at a later stage that a system of recipes regarding crop rotation and vernalization acquired ideological baggage. This included a defunct Lamarckianism claiming that characteristics acquired in an organism's lifetime could be passed on to future generations.

Mature Lysenkoism, as Lecourt (1977: 47) and Sullivan (1967: 281) point out, began as a collaboration between I. I. Prezent, pedagogue and ideologist, and Lysenko. It was only then that a system of techniques became transformed into an imaginary science. Lysenko played the peasant Stakhanov who wanted to be his own Frederick Winslow Taylor. His was an attempt to create a revolutionary science which would help collectivization. The combination of Lysenkoism and collectivization proved devastating in human terms. The danger began when peasant knowledge claimed to be as universal as modern Western science, that is when the local and concrete was no longer celebrated as such but sought to transform itself into a revolutionary ideology. Lysenko, as the Savonarola of an imaginary Soviet science, emasculated a whole school of genetics.

Eventually, Lysenko was discredited and the conflict between ideology and science ended in the victory of the latter. There is also a tendency to isolate the Lysenko affair and deny the similar themes underlying it and the debates on diversity. Vavilov is once again read 'passively' and becomes a humanistic backdrop to the Green Revolution. The debates on gene diversity, of which Vavilov was once again at the centre, show that Lysenkoism is only one side of the story. It reveals that the Green Revolution of the future could be more problematic for scientific expertise than Lysenkoism.

A conventional reading of the Lysenko affair might suggest Vavilov as the paradigmatic expert, proud of the modern science of genetics. But Vavilov was deeply sensitive to the achievements of traditional agriculture and peasant knowledge. He realized that long before the advent of modern science, agriculture had produced generations of successful plant breeders. He would have agreed with Alphonse Candolle's observation that men have not cultivated within the last two thousand years a single species which can rival maize, rice, the sweet potato, the bread-fruit, the date, cereals, millets, sorghums, the banana, and the soya bean. He realized that modern agriculture was parasitic on these traditional forms, and to sustain itself it had to collect these traditional varieties periodically. Based on his law of homologous variations, Vavilov presented a theory which systematized such efforts. He proposed that there were eight major centres of domestication and diversity, later called the Vavilov Zones, six in the old world and two in the new. Vavilov originally claimed that these Zones were not only the centres of origin for plants but areas with the greatest number of domesticated forms (Isaac, 1970: ch. 4).

His institute of plant breeding organized a series of expeditions to centres of diversity all over the world: to the Andes for potatoes, Mexico for corn, and Ethiopia for barley. India was the only Zone that Vavilov was not allowed to enter. By 1940 Vavilov's collection had 250,000 entries including 30,000 accessions of wheat, 10,022 of corn, 23,636 legumes, and 17,955 vegetables (Leppik, 1969). The collections were shifted to Estonia during the war, where they were confiscated by the Germans but returned after the war; they were, however, ignored during the Lysenko era and lost much of their authenticity and vitality. Walter Sullivan narrates that Vavilov was arrested by the Russian authorities while collecting plants in Polish Galicia. His colleagues never met him again, 'although it is said that they ultimately received his briefcase, crammed with plants. At the top—the last specimen that he plucked before his arrest—was a previously unknown variety, the most important find of the expedition'.

The technical complexities of the Vavilov Zones need not detain us, but the formulation itself raised a series of questions in relation to archaeology, sociology, and politics. A search for the origins of agriculture became simultaneously a reflection on the future of agriculture and raised some questions.

Vavilov not only showed that modern agriculture was dependent on traditional agriculture, but also suggested there was a rough correlation between agricultural diversity and diversity of ethnic styles. Vavilov Zones were generally isolated areas where farming communities, by maintaining traditional forms of agriculture, had preserved and sustained these vital gene-pools. This immediately raised the question as to what should be the relation between scientific and traditional forms of agriculture? How should the Borlaugs and Swaminathans relate to the expertise of the maize planters of Mexico, the sorghum growers of Sudan, or the rice cultivators of India? In this discussion, science was forced to confront a whole series of others it had suppressed—tribal, peasant, and other forms of knowledge.

Finally, the Vavilov Zones raised issues about nature. What was modern man's attitude to nature? Was nature to be conceived as a form of heritage or a piece of property? What could be the life-saving attitude in science to nature as the great experimenter?

One must admit there was a certain innocence to Vavilov. The literature does not group him in the capacious list of colonial plant-hunters, though his was the biggest scientific collection in history. Today, this kind of collection is no longer possible. 'When Jack Harlan visited the Cilician Plain in Turkey in the 1940's the area bore virtually thousands of flax land races. When he returned in the 1950's, only one variety remained—and that was imported from Argentina' (Mooney, 1983: 13). This raises another set of questions. Has the Vavilov map inadvertently created a new generation of plant-hunters? Is Vavilov's theory of the zones of diversity a new map for the panopticonization of the globe, where the reserves sustain gene-pools while the world around them succumbs to monoculture?

The question of gene diversity has shown science at its self-reflective yet tragic best. It raises an array of problems about time, knowledge, property, efficiency, justice, and nature not as extraneous issues but from within the structure of the paradigm itself. An anthology of essays on gene diversity would have to select from the works of outstanding scientists like Edward Wilson, David Ehrenberg, Peter Raven, Richard Levins, Cary Fowler, and Daniel Janzen. In examining this vast literature the question I want to ask is a more limited one: how far can science at its self-reflective best go to create an ecological science? Note, I did not say a science of ecology, for that would only be a sub-discipline within the overall disciplinary and disciplining categories of science like biophysics or radioastronomy. Can we have an ecological science that can challenge and rework the categories and organizations of modern science as it exists?

The remaining sections of the paper are organized in the following way. The debate on gene diversity splits into two overlapping frames of forestry and agriculture. For an understanding of the forest I consider Edward Wilson's *Biophilia* (1984); as a frame to explore the relation between diversity and traditional agriculture I consider Edgar Anderson's *Plants, Man and Life* (1967). This is followed by a discussion of the nature of the Green Revolution. The problem of gene diversity adds to the usual questions of political economy the wider questions about knowledge and nature. In the last section I explore what reflections on genetic loss reveal about the character of science as a mode of thought.

DIVERSITY IN THE FOREST: E. O. WILSON'S *BIOPHILIA*

Edward Wilson is a controversial scientist and arouses an ire second only to Garret Hardin. He cannot be wished away as a Reaganite trend in biology, not merely because he is more literate but also because there is a deep passion and resilience to his scholarship. Wilson's *Biophilia*, while an intensely personal testament, cannot be dismissed as the extra-curricular anguish of a professional scientist.

At a time when the mysteries of science have become confined to the cosmological vastness of the universe or the problem of infinitely small particles, Wilson's field biology operates in the middle range. It captures the magic of everydayness. We have beautiful descriptions of trees, of the leaf-cutter ant and the bird of paradise, and of the intelligence of the peccary. Yet there is a sense of the totality of the forest that is somehow lost.

The forest is not a 'dwelling' in the Heideggerean or even tribal sense. Wilson inhabits the forest as a field biologist but does not dwell in it, nurturing it, preserving it or merely watching it unfold. The forest as a whole does not exist. One senses that before he has even entered it, it has already been resolved into a cluster of research programmes.

In *Biophilia*, there is a split-level sense about the loss of the forest. There is, first, the danger to man's biological need for the forest, and there is also the threat to the constant advance of science. To scientists like Wilson, the forest is literally a magic well from which science can draw endlessly. The forest is information. Wilson states that 'one lump of earth contains information that would just about fill all fifteen editions of the Encyclopaedia Britannica' (Wilson, 1984: 16). Yet there is a narcissism here for a few pages later he claims: 'In a tropical forest, with thousands of mostly unknown species all around, the number of discoveries per investigator, per day, is probably greater than anywhere else in the world' (Wilson, 1984: 28). The starkness of the scientific hubris is always present; what Wilson adds to it is the loss a field biologist feels for the forest, which adds to his hubris a sense of heroism.

One intuitively feels—I admit I might be a bit unfair—that Wilson suffers from what the philosopher Richard Bernstein has called 'Cartesian anxiety' (Bernstein, 1983: 16), the immediate need for opening the forest or any other object to the scientific eye. The way a scientist reads the forest immediately cuts it into the certainty of a series of visual fields through map, survey, census, hand-lens, and the microscope. Secondly, what appears as a series of discrete bits of information is then organized into a giant information system called science. The loss of the forest creates a series of gigantic holes in this cybernetic system. Between the cybernetic frame and the Cartesian eye the sense of the forest (despite the eloquence of the language), gets lost. Wilson claims: 'I open an ant hill like a Swiss watch, I am enchanted by the intricacy of its parts and the clean thrumming precision' (Wilson, 1984: 36).

Wilson loves the forest. But the forest he loves is the 'wilderness', hopefully untouched by man and history. Its only biography is the long story of evolution. Nature as wilderness is then juxtaposed to the city in which he finds 'lawn grass, potted plants, caged parakeets, puppies and rubber snakes inadequate' (Wilson, 1984: 118). Man needs nature and this need for nature when programmed epigenetically, Wilson calls 'biophilia'. The greatest threat to biophilia is the remorseless destruction of genetic and ecological diversity.

In fact, the baldest and most dramatic statement of the problem of gene diversity is Wilson's. He states:

Everyone agrees, defense ministers and environmentalists alike, that the worst crisis possible is a global nuclear disaster. If it occurs the entire human species is endangered, life as normal human beings wish to live it would come to an end. With that terrible truism acknowledged, it must be added that if no country pulls the trigger the worst thing that can happen—in fact is already under way—is not energy depletion, economic collapse, conventional war, or even the expansion of totalitarian governments. As tragic as these catastrophes would be for us, they can be repaired in a few generations. The one process that will take millions of years to correct is the loss of genetic and species diversity by the destruction of natural habitats. This is the folly our descendants are least likely to forgive us. (1984: 121)

In cataloguing this destruction, scientists have produced an obituary that sounds like a census. Wilson notes that the current rate of extinction is 1,000 species a year. By the 1990s the figure has risen to ten thousand species a year (one species per hour). During the next thirty years fully one million species could be erased.

The question we must ask concerns how scientists perceive this fact of death, this everydayness of extinction. Reading the literature one notices that science has no mourning rituals. Caught in the credo of objectivity, impersonality, and number, it hides grief in arithromorphism. Somehow the scientist seems to feel that the litany of number can be a substitute for mourning rituals. Maybe this has to do with the current preoccupation with the death of civilization. Time and collective death in Western industrial society intersect in the vision of the apocalypse. Such a view is captured in one of the most famous magazine covers, that of the *Bulletin of the Atomic Scientists*. It portrays a clock with the hour-hand at 12. The minute-hand stands a few minutes from 12, conveying the imminence of extinction. Depending on the event—the Cuban missile crisis, SALT, *perestroika*—the minute hand is moved back and forth.

The ability to calibrate time gives one a sense of control. In fact, this juxtaposition of clock-time, apocalypse, and number embodies a notion that number can divide time and measure risk and that even an atomic experiment or one in genetic control can be a calculated risk. A parade of numbers hides both the irresponsibility and the ignorance of this approach. Scientific time has swung too often between mechanical time and apocalyptic time, between the ahistorical and history's end. The problem of gene diversity moves beyond the time of mechanistic physics and introduces a variety of other times, emphasizing in particular the intersection of evolutionary and historical time. Peter Raven remarks that 'not since the end of the cretaceous period, 765 million years ago, has such a rate of extinction occurred, it has been calculated that the process of extinction is about 1,000 times higher than during the past million years' (Raven, 1988: 549–60).

It is the problem of time that becomes fundamental to ecology. Ecology demands an unravelling of the various kinds of time in science and the various kinds of time concealed in concepts like extinction, death, obsolescence, memory, particularly in terms of how science conceives nature and other cultures. The debate about gene diversity is a typical futurological exercise ambivalent, even contemptuous, about the past, yet scavenging off it. Probably the simplest way of understanding it is by contrasting the polysemic richness of the word 'seed' with the semantic impoverishment of the word 'gene'. The seed is one of the richest and most pregnant metaphors of modern man. The seed is memory, the seed is the past, it is tradition and also the future as a responsibility. If the seed is memory, then the gene is information. The logic of language is noticeable here. You can talk of the death of the seed, but merely of the obsolescence of information. The basis of modern science is not memory, embedded in life-forms, but information subject to constant erasure. If ecology is to survive, it must fight a life-and-death struggle against concepts such as obsolescence, a notion of time encoded in the market and in science. The word 'obsolescence' is anti-traditional, linear, splitting life and death into separate systems rather than seeing them as integrated processes. If the seed is embedded, then information is abstract, and science as a knowledge system thrives on obsolescence, a modern kind of forgetting, privileging one kind of knowledge above all other forms.

Once the tropical forest is seen as an information system, then its process of extinction becomes easier. Once information is abstracted, classified, and filed, the forest as a life-form may even disappear. This contrast of the forest as information and the forest as a dwelling, a presence, a memory may provide a key to how scientists have looked at the destruction of the tropical forest. Someday one should compare a tribal view of the forest with Wilson's perception of it. There is poetry in the latter, even guilt and loss; but eventually the poetry, guilt, and loss are overshadowed by its intrinsic scientific verve. In fact, the sense of tragedy at the death of the forest is always vitiated by the narcissism of science seeking to collect the last plant, like the anthropologist pursuing the last savage. Peter Raven of the Missouri Botanical Garden observes with the delicate care of a curator, that

in collecting plants in the tropics, we should be aware that in many cases they may be obtaining the last samples of a given species that may be gathered. Unlike curators of art or historical material, biologists rarely regard the preservation-conservation of their specimens as a matter of much importance. Implicitly they operate as if there is always an abundant supply of material in the field ready to be obtained when it is needed, when regrettably that is not the case. (1988: 556–7)

It is this museumization of life-forms that is ingrained in science, where the other as nature or as culture is presented as disembodied and abstracted from context. The museum is the recognition of the other but always through the smell of formaldehyde. One must admit that this framework is slowly weakening. Robert Leo Smith has observed that 'The bare accumulation of data does not advance the cause of conservation and there is danger in believing it will. For a few species we have accumulated considerable quantities of data, which now rests in books and journals, while the species themselves have ceased to exist' (Smith, 1976: 33–5).

In his *Biophilia* Wilson shows that man needs nature and recreates primordial memories of nature repeatedly even in the backyards of the city (Wilson, 1984: 94–5). Since nature is an evolutionarily determined need, Wilson speculates on the possibility of a conservation ethic. Following Aldo Leopold, Wilson defines an ethic as 'a set of rules invented to meet circumstances now new and intricate, or else encompassing responses so far in the future, that the average person cannot foresee the final outcome' (1984: 120). Such an ethic must be biologically rooted and must seek a kinship with nature. He cites Darwin's notebooks in another context as saying, 'He who understands the baboon would do more for metaphysics than Locke' (1984: 47). Yet the kinship he posits towards nature is of a contractual kind, despite the moving section on his encounter with the almost human chimpanzee, Kanzi. He suggests that the work of Christopher Stone (1975) and Peter Singer (1975) about plant and animal rights be given a wider hearing. Yet as a biological realist he retreats into a oneness with Garret Hardin in contending that the facts of biology do not allow the circle of altruism to easily include plants, animals, or even future generations. 'The only way to make a conservation ethic work is to ground it in ultimately selfish reasoning—but the premise must be of a new and more potent kind' (Wilson, 1984: 131). He warns that 'ecological and evolutionary time are intellectualist constructs without immediate impact' (Wilson, 1984: 120) because 'natural selection has programmed people to think mostly in physiological time' (Wilson, 1984: 120). Acute as Wilson or Hardin are at the level of biology, they get trite beyond it. Their celebration of nature contrasts with the bleakness of their cultural categories restricted to utility and contract. To survive, biophilia has to move beyond the facts of biology. One is doubtful whether ecopiety or an ecological ethic can be constructed out of the poverty of sociobiology alone.

Yet, Wilson has wise and interesting ideas to offer. He suggests that 'a conservation ethic can develop not as a code from absolute premises but in the manner of common law, with the aid of case histories' (Wilson, 1984: 124). Another intriguing observation is the one he offers about science. Wilson proposes a new division of labour between the First and Third Worlds stemming not out of cultural differences but from economics:

The exploration of natural resources is the kind of research most readily justified in the underdeveloped countries, especially those in the tropics . . . while these nations occasionally need accelerators, satellites, mass spectrometers . . . the economically less developed countries can do better with skilled and semi-skilled workers who make expeditions into the wild, collect and prepare specimens, culture promising varieties and spend the long hours of close observation needed to understand growth and behaviour. This kind of science is labour intensive, best performed by people who love land and organisms for their own sake. Can there be an Ecuadorian biology, a Kenyan biology? Yes, if the focus is on the uniqueness of indigenous life. Will such efforts be important to international science? Yes, because evolutionary biology is a discipline of special cases woven into global patterns, nothing makes sense except in light of the histories of local faunas and floras. (Wilson, 1984: 137–8)

One could easily be disturbed by Wilson's sociobiology and his theory of comparative advantage in science. But can we subvert the idea without losing a sense of the centre–periphery model within which it is articulated? I believe so. First, we must note that Wilson rarely mentions indigenous systems of knowledge. He does not realize that other cultures have different ways of looking at the forest and nature. What if the forest is not wilderness in the American sense but a dwelling for communities who have lived and understood the forest? Maybe they can be trustees, better stewards than our scientists. What if the ecumenism of science is actually broken into a plurality of sciences? What if gene diversity needs a diversity of knowledge-forms? What if Western science were to use the assumptions of these alternative life-forms for its research programmes? These questions will arise repeatedly during the following discussions.

There is one final point about *Biophilia*. Basically, Wilson's science, like his Judeo-Christian framework, finds it difficult to abandon a humanism which sees man as the goal and centre of creation and evolution. Yet, Wilson is embarrassed by man and his destructive capacities but proud of the power that science has created. He remarks sadly that 'the wilderness of the world has shrivelled into timber leases and threatened nature reserves' (Wilson, 1984: 11). Yet he claims, 'nature is to be mastered but (we hope) never completely. A quiet passion burns not for total control, but for the sensation of constant advance' (Wilson, 1984: 10).

Wilson's is a humanism that does not fully encode the need for caring in the will to power. As a result, the notion of stewardship he proclaims dangles helplessly and this is partly why his *Biophilia* remains a plea for a science of ecology but not an ecological science. A humanism based on interest alone cannot go too far. Eventually he sees the forest as a paradise for the food and pharmaceutical industry. When natural products are the sleeping giants of the pharmaceutical industry (Wilson, 1984) nature immediately becomes a resource; in fact the metaphor is that of a mine to be dug up and spoiled. It is this transformation of nature into resources that humanism has not been able to contain. What Wilson notes delicately as a concerned and passionate scientist, a multinational like Anaconda would state brutally with even greater aphoristic power,

> Nature creates ore deposits.
> Anaconda creates mines.
> (Alderman, 1978: 34–50)

It is this mining of the forest that Wilson's biophilia is powerless to stop. In the next section we shall examine Edgar Anderson's attempt to reflect on agricultural diversity.

DIVERSITY IN TRADITIONAL AGRICULTURE: ANDERSON'S *PLANTS, MAN AND LIFE*

Despite its deceptive simplicity, Edgar Anderson's *Plants, Man and Life* is one of the finest scientific reflections on agriculture. To appreciate Anderson's book, we have to understand that there have been three major revolutions in agriculture: the first began about 10,000 years ago; the second took place roughly over the last hundred years, and the third, is occurring at this present moment. Yet, what has been described diachronically must be read synchronically, for the inheritors of the three revolutions exist now in the same time and place. Anderson writes as a participant in the second revolution reflecting on the first. The experience is similar to a post-Newtonian scientist discovering the world of the Ptolemies and Aristotles and realizing that they were also right. To do this, Anderson confesses that one must move beyond the ethnocentrism of specialized science and the world-view of European and American Europeans 'too accustomed to thinking of agriculture in terms of one kind of plant, of one variety of wheat . . . of one hundred acres of maize all of one variety and weed free' (Anderson, 1967: 84).

Anderson observes that the end-products of agriculture are artefacts and that these artefacts, called cultigens, are as dependent on man for their continued existence as 'a temple or a vase or an automobile'. These crops, man, and his beasts, constitute a mutually dependent but unnatural complex of beings (Anderson, 1967: 9). The standard example is maize. Its female inflorescence, a pathological characteristic, has no equivalent among grasses, and if man were to stop planting it, it would disappear within six years. All known living maize, the world's third most important crop, is dependent on man for survival.

Anderson emphasized that while all agriculture is a disturbance of nature, each agricultural revolution disturbed nature in a uniquely different way. The first agricultural revolution helped catalyse nature's diversity and then operated by mimicking nature as far as possible. The later revolutions found nature unacceptable: the second sought to transform parts of it through mechanization and fertilizers, while the third attempted to rewrite nature by reconstructing genetic architecture in a laboratory.

The radicalism of the first agricultural revolution is captured succinctly by Erna Bennett:

Just as the chemical activity of a substance is enormously enhanced by the reduction to colloidal dimension, so the greatly fragmented patches of cultivation created by man enhanced the genetic activity of the plants he cultivated and the plants that mingled with them. The patchwork of cultivation sown by man unleashed an explosion of hybridization and a flood of evolution that found expression in literally inestimable numbers of new races of cultivated plants and their relatives. Nowadays in an age when weedy fields and fragmented cultivation have yielded to wide expanses of uniform cultivars, we cannot hope to repeat this experiment. Its products, the evolutionary consequences of a unique genetic explosion are the principal component of our genetic resources today. (Bennett, 1978: 113–22)

Anderson's book is a celebration of the innovative genius of the first agricultural revolution, and a recognition that the later revolutions are still scavenging off the first. He emphasizes the continuity of innovation in traditional agriculture. It is not the eponymic work of individual scientists but the work of generations of farmers working in communities. He savours major moments in it like the American celebration of sweetcorn, the Italian discovery of the tomato, which was as historically 'important as Garibaldi or Victor Emmanuel' (Anderson, 1967: 110). He cites his old teacher Ames Oakes as observing that 'Primitive man located all five natural sources of caffeine: tea, coffee, the cola plant, Yerba maté and its relatives . . . and that biochemical research has not added a single new source' (Anderson, 1967: 127).

I listed three examples not to perform a *Ripley's Believe it or not* but to emphasize the innovativeness of agriculture and also to suggest that it operates in terms of a different framework of understanding. The word diversity comes closest in contemporary science to grasping it but as a philosophical idea it must mean more than the mere existence of variety of a genetic or ecological kind. Diversity, like entropy, is an antiseptic but world-shattering concept. If entropy demolished the world of mechanistic physics and provided a virtual theology of limits to modern industrial civilization, diversity, if unravelled, might lead to a virtual recovery of the agricultural world-view within modern science. Apart from occasional and long-surviving monocultures like those of Java, the notion of diversity virtually encodes traditional agriculture at several levels.

Probably the easiest introduction to this alternate life-world is Anderson's classic description of a Guatemalan garden, which he first thought was 'a dump heap the size of an American city lot covered with such riotous growth, that it appeared planless and deserted to those accustomed to the puritanical primness of North European gardens' (Anderson, 1967: 137). Yet, when he went through it carefully he could find no plants which were not useful, in one way or another. There were no noxious weeds, and the return per man-hour of effort was high. I shall quote Anderson in detail:

Though at first there seemed little order, as soon as we started mapping the garden, we realized it was planted in fairly definite cross-wise rows. There were fruit trees, native and American in great variety: annonas, cherimoyas, avocados, peaches, quinces, plums, a fig and a few coffee bushes. There were giant cacti grown for their fruit. There was a large plant of rosemary, a plant of rue, some poinsettias, and a fine semi-climbing tea rose. There was a whole row of the native domesticated hawthorn, whose fruits like yellow doll size apples make a delicious conserve. There were two varieties of corn, one well past bearing and now serving as a trellis for climbing string beans which were just coming into season, the other a much taller sort which was tasselling out. There were specimens of a little banana with smooth wide leaves, which are the local substitute for wrapping paper, and are also used instead of cornhusks in cooking the native variant of hot tamales. Over it all clambered the luxuriant vines of the various cucurbits. Chayote when finally mature, has a large nutritious root weighing several pounds. At one point there was a depression, the size of a small bath tub where a chayote root had recently been excavated; this served as a dump heap and compost for waste from the house. At one end of the garden was a small beehive made from boxes and tin cans. In the terms of our American and European equivalents, the garden was a vegetable garden, an orchard, a dump heap, a compost heap and a bee yard. (Anderson, 1967: 140)

Anderson's note on the Guatemalan garden can probably serve as a text of which the rest of the book becomes a series of fascinating footnotes. They reveal that diversity is not the mere presence of variety; it virtually encodes the grammar of traditional agriculture.

Diversity first of all demands an understanding of the multi-dimensionality of natural processes. C. H. Waddington has observed that both the inputs and the outputs of natural process were extraordinarily complex (Waddington, 1978: 248). Traditional agriculture mimicked this multidimensionality, the classic examples being the maize–bean–squash complex of Central America, the elaborate systems of mixed cropping in India, or even the Guatemalan garden where a multiple canopy of plants was created to exploit every available niche. Waddington bemoans the fact that multidimensionality is mere noise to the world of modern science and the intellect. It is essential to note that this agriculture is multi-layered both in terms of space and time. First, as in the Guatemalan garden, along with the fruit tree, several other kinds of crop are grown adding to several canopies of crop on the same piece of land. Not only is there multidimensionality of several plant and several varieties of the same plant in one space (multiple-cropping), but multidimensionality in time through crop rotation. So successful in imitating nature are these gardens that often such native orchards have been mistaken for part of natural woodlands by European and American plant collectors (Anderson, 1976)!

There is a second kind of multidimensionality in agriculture where a crop is never conceived purely in the economic dimension. It is always part of a wider agricultural complex cutting across several frames. A plant cuts across the world of magic, science and religion, work, play, music, and medicine. It is precisely this multidimensionality of the plant that provides the sources of resistance to monoculture. The kind of selective harvesting mixed cropping requires, is also impossible with the machine. It is interesting to note that modern scientists are tapping these very sources of resistance—the sacred complex of the American maize, the sunflower dance of the American Indian, the sacred groves of India—for sources of gene plasm.

Thirdly, a plant is never conceived purely as a plant. Just as a car cannot be conceived without simultaneously thinking of an energy system, a system of roads, possibly even a system of advertising, in a similar way it is incorrect to think of a plant as an isolated unit. It has to be thought of as being in harmony with nature. As Aldo Leopold asked, 'Is it sound economics to think of any plant as a separate entity, to proscribe or encourage it on grounds of individual performance. One has to think of what its effect will be on animal life, on the soil, on the health of land as an organism' (Leopold, 1973: 195).

Diversity also involves multiplicity of uses. This involves not only a multiplicity of uses for the same plant but the use of the plant or part of it through every stage from seed to final maturation. Probably the two best examples one can think of are the coconut and the maize. Sigmar Groeneveld (1984) makes a devastating analysis of how modern economic botany and tropical agriculture have thought of the coconut. Treatises in economic botany define the coconut purely as an oil-yielding plant. Yet Groeneveld shows that the coconut is an integrated plant of rural culture with over a hundred uses for which there are few national and international statistics. He adds that the coconut is not just the tree of life, it is a way of life and to call it a mere coconut blinds one to the emotional and moral economy of the plant, to uses which are built into the very life-cycle rituals of the society (1984: 47). In fact, he makes a second fascinating link between use and language usage. The uses of the coconut cannot be appreciated through the language of economic botany. One must go beyond secular language and the shopping lists of modern science to the polysemy of native terms where there is a real celebration of diversity. In fact it is this (ethno-botanical) usage that captures the complexity of diversity which is lost in the aridity of economic botany.

Carl Sauer makes the same point for maize, which in America is conceived mainly as feed for livestock. It was only native Indians who conceived it as food and adapted it to the native diet and local soils. As a result, while only a small part of genetic wealth is preserved in commercial varieties, it is the local grower who has sustained the enormous diversity of maize. It is not accidental that a single native village may contain more kinds of maize than the corn-belt has ever heard of, each having a special place in the household and field economy. It is to these Indian varieties that geneticists turned when they sought to understand maize as a species complex.

Diversity in traditional agriculture also involves a framework of attitudes to weeds, disease, and risk. Anderson remarks that the attitude to weeds is one of the Rorschachs of modern science. For most taxonomists a weed represents something ubiquitous, mundane, yet irritatingly unknown. Anderson cites the case of a famous taxonomist with an almost encyclopaedic knowledge of the flora of Asia and the South Pacific, and the reputation of being able to name more species by sight than any American taxonomist. 'Yet, when confronted with plants associated closely with man, he would mutter "pantropic weed" and throw it into the waste basket' (Anderson, 1976: 35). In fact, it is interesting that a weed in science is defined as 'a plant out of place' (Anderson, 1976: 73) and there is even legislation banning certain forms of weeds in farms. This attitude of the taxonomist reflects the attitude of clear farming agriculture which celebrates the weedless field. Yet the history of weeds is virtually the history of modern agriculture and it is only today that scientists are realizing the creative role of weeds. Anderson cites the fact that modern sugar-cane came into being through a series of crosses between weedy grasses. 'Modern sugar cane breeders are now using one of India's greatest pests (*sic*), the Khas grass, in turning out improved varieties of cane' (1976: 73).

Traditional agriculture has been a celebration of the weed. It realized that nature knows no plants as weeds and left the boundary between weed and cultivated crop more open. This comes out clearly in Ugent's study of the Andean potato (Ugent, 1970). Ugent emphasizes that while the traditional farmer devoted considerable care to the preparation and planting of the field, he was relaxed, almost indifferent, to the presence of wild and semi-wild (weedy) potato species that grew in between the rows of potatoes and even in the thickets around them. As a result these wild-weedy species not only flourished but hybridized with the crops.

The quiet wisdom of this move has two consequences both of which are important for the perpetuation of the Andean potato. The hybridization of wild and weedy species with cultivated plants not only created greater cultivar diversity but also provided for resistance against disease and adaptability to climatic changes. Secondly, these fields constitute natural gene-pools, a legacy on which modern agriculture, committed to clean farming and monoculture, can draw upon. Homogeneous or uniform potato fields are more prone to disease. Ugent speculates that the Irish potato famine of 1845 might have been avoided if the fields had been planted with many different cultivars with varying degrees of resistance or susceptibility to disease.

It is as a method of insurance against crop failures that the system of mixed cropping finds its greatest justification. Diversity, both interspecific and intraspecific, provides insurance against the inclemencies of weather, pest, and diseases. In sustainable agriculture, there is in general a dynamic balance between host and pathogen. A. K. Yegna Narayan Aiyer in his classic monograph on mixed cropping notes 'The insurance afforded by mixtures in respect of wilts and rusts especially is worthy of notice' (Aiyer, 1949: 439–543). Perhaps the best illustration is the caster semi-looper pest that defoliates the crop so thoroughly leaving only the bare stem. 'A mixed crop of horsegram and groundnuts when grown as a mixture between castor rows serves as an effective insurance as they yield a crop and money return although the castor may be a complete failure' (Aiyer, 1949: 473). Varietal cropping thus guarantees the farmer some food at all times. Even if some plants fail to germinate or others become susceptible to disease, the overall harvest is enough to sustain the life-style.

Varietal cropping also guaranteed a balanced diet in traditional agriculture. In almost all mixed cropping systems in India both food grains and pulses are included in the diet of the population. There is always wheat and gram, castor and horsegram, or bajra and groundnut . . . but whatever the combination the main cereals grown in the tract are always supplemented by the main protein supplement, 'with other grain and pulse crops which are grown to a smaller extent providing the appropriate variety' (Aiyer, 1949: 473) in diet.

Anderson's reflections on the wisdom of agriculture reads like a slow rewind. The story of the latter two agricultural revolutions appears in fast forward. He has little to offer on these two except two statements which capture deep tensions. He remarks that while agriculture as an art began in the tropics, the scientific understanding of agriculture developed in the temperate zones and the tragedy lay in the imposition of one life-world on the other. He confesses that when an agricultural scientist goes to the tropics, he has more to unlearn than to teach. Yet his last chapter is a disturbing one. Anderson like many scientists has a naïvety, 'an immaculate innocence', while pursuing knowledge. He talks enthusiastically about the need to study common weeds, ornamentals, and crops and dreams of building a herbarium of specimens to catalogue and understand this diversity. He bemoans the lack of money available for such an enterprise and adds that as a Quaker he always felt 'a way will be opened'. Eventually he manages to set up such an enterprise in Latin America, with the help of Escuela Agricola 'a remarkable institution' established to bring about 'the rational development of natural resources in Latin America' (Anderson, 1976: 224). It was established by the United Fruit Company!

DIVERSITY AND THE GREEN REVOLUTION

David Selbourne somewhere makes a distinction between the world of life and the world of the book. This essay on gene diversity is a fragment of the second. The major critique of the Green Revolution will come from the world of life, from peasants, tribals, ecologists, and other Third World activists. The questions I have asked are more modest and stem from a reading of the books on the Green Revolution. Rather than replicate its elaborate histories or critiques from the field of political economy, I ask a simpler question. I regard the archives of the Green Revolution as particular kinds of narrative and ask what are the conditions, the basic elements that constitute any official narrative of the Green Revolution. What are the stock situations that go into the making of the modern fairytale, the Green Revolution?

The Green Revolution possesses at least five stock elements without which no narrative is possible. The first consists of a false history of the other, especially conceived as the tropics. The second is what one might call the recalcitrance of nature and the need to rationalize it through industry. Thirdly, the act of diffusion is seen as philanthropy, where the Taylorization of agriculture is justified as good science. Incidentally, the scientist is never seen as an epic hero, a liberator from old epitomes, but merely as a facilitator providing one more avenue for productive agriculture. Fourth, this demands in turn an attempt to dissolve the embeddedness of agriculture as a system by celebrating or privileging some form of economic calculus. Fifth and finally, there is what I call the myth of constant advance. The other as nature or agriculture is never totally controlled. New problems arise which once again need science.

Diversity in terms of the above constitutes a mode or site for resistance that needs to be made redundant or eliminated. Any attempt at recovering the category of diversity must begin by deconstructing the above assumptions.

The World of the Tropics

One must begin with the false history embedded in the construct called tropical agriculture and also reflected in manuals of economic botany. Sigmar Groeneveld once again provides a superb example. He remarks that the 'tree of life' called the coconut, has been a part of traditional agriculture for millennia, its repertoire of uses cutting right across the cosmology of traditional life. Yet the semantics of modern economic botany and tropical agriculture projects an entirely different picture. He considers a scientific study, Franke's *Useful Plants in the Tropics and Sub-tropics* to explore the tacit knowledges of tropical agriculture (Groeneveld, 1984).

Franke contends that 'although the coconut palm has been cultivated on an economic basis, little has been done up to now to cultivate this valuable oil plant systematically. Organized cultivation, care, fertilizing of new varieties were not given somewhat greater consideration until the past decades' (quoted in Groeneveld, 1984). Groeneveld observes that such a text was not a mere colonial tract but a scientific manual, and then explores the various forms of distortion and reductionism that this involves.

Consider first the word cultivation. It has a Eurocentric bias. It assumes that the term 'cultivation' cannot apply to the way in which the coconut palm has been grown in the tropics for centuries. Consider next the phrase 'economic plant'. An entire cosmology, a celebration is reduced to a single grid—an economic plant—and to a single use—oil. Thirdly, ordinary language names for the coconut are not cited. Any folk poem on the tree of life would have a more accurate celebration of its uses. Fourthly, the coconut is still nature, it enters history and science through 'organized care, fertilizing and breeding' of tropical agriculture. The process of abstraction becomes obvious here for not only does the term rob the plant of its full significance, it transforms an icon into an economic index. Groeneveld notes that there is hardly any reference to the ecological significance of traditional cultivation methods, to the fact that the coconut creates around it a micro-climate. Niched under and around it are the farmers' maize, peas, beans, and cassava. Once the coconut is seen as a disembodied category, isolated from its myriad traditional uses, and the innumerable plants that grow around it, the coconut is further opened to the clinical gaze of modern agriculture. It is as if the plant is moved from the field to the laboratory table. The predictable diagnosis is then the need for the dwarf palm, a fast-growing, short-trunked variety of the plant.

Groeneveld remarks that the request for this new variety did not come from traditional growers. It was possibly a plea from plantation growers who, impatient with labour, wanted such a product. Secondly, such an industrial product created a preference for monoculture as it allowed for more systematic harvesting. But the dwarf palm destroyed the traditional micro-climate around the plant. It lacked the height of the traditional plant, under which cashews, bananas, manioc, and other crops grew so well.

Groeneveld suggests a final point, that nowhere in Franke's manual are his basic assumptions clearly articulated. One wonders whether Franke's manual, like other tracts of agriculture, are as much a part of an imaginary science as Lysenkoism. Is tropical agriculture becoming such a science?

The Need to Rationalize Recalcitrant Nature

The fundamental threat to agricultural diversity comes from a world-view that privileges industry over agriculture. Cedric Stanton Hicks has observed that underlying the Green Revolution is a carry-over of unexamined assumptions from the eighteenth and nineteenth centuries that industry is the essential means to prosperity, that people engaged in agriculture must move to factories, that small farms must be merged into large farms and that agriculture must be converted into industry (Hicks, 1975: chs. 5–6). The controlled fury of the narratives of the Green Revolution comes from impatience with nature and its refractoriness to industrial time.

The first assaults against agriculture failed to convert it into an industry. What they did was to appropriate sectors of agricultural life. Through mechanization various parts of the labour process, particularly tools and instruments, were replaced. Thus broadcast sowing gave way to the seed-drill, the horse to the tractor. The second major revolution came through the production of synthetic fertilizers. But neither the mechanical or chemical revolutions affected the basic biological processes of agriculture or its repertoire of diverse performances (Goodman, 1987: chs. 1–2). Hicks observes that science's confrontation with agricultural diversity was full of ironies and missed chances. It was in 1887 that the German chemists Wellfarth and Hellreiger worked out the role of leguminous roots in nitrogen fixation. This memorable discovery, one of the most illuminating glimpses into the complexity of agriculture, should have had a revolutionary impact. Yet 'it lost out to the burgeoning science of chemistry more in tune with the materialist philosophy of the time' (Hicks, 1975: 88) and the attention focused on soluble nitrate as a fertilizer.

But the greater irony came from biology itself. Instead of celebrating the wisdom of diversity and providing the controls physics and chemistry so desperately needed, it was biology that provided the conditions for the industrialization of agriculture. The development of new hybridization techniques enabled the integration of genetic, chemical, and mechanical packages into one whole (Goodman, 1987). The hybridization of corn made the industrialization of agriculture a distinct possibility. Through genetics, crop characteristics could be adapted to the machine. Whether it was maize, tomato, or cotton, the crop could be designated as a standardized hardware to be picked and harvested by the machine. To the compact between the genetic and the mechanical was added another contract with the chemical, as fertilizer and herbicide.

Traditional agriculture was never responsive to fertilizers. A large intake of fertilizers caused excessive growth of the stalk and plant collapse. What one needed was a plant that was higher yielding but responsive to fertilizers. This was the achievement of the Japanese imperial experiments in Taiwan. The Japanese agricultural experiments created a seed that was a virtual sponge for fertilizers. Calestous Juma points out that 'while the average Japanese rice yield increased almost 50%, artificial fertilizer use increased by 254%' (Juma, 1989: 78). This integration of the genetic, chemical, and mechanical packages produced the star for the Green Revolution programme, the HYV, seed that allegedly could produce a short-stemmed, stiff-strawed plant, strong enough to carry a heavier grain cluster, which could be harvested mechanically and yet be responsive to fertilizers and herbicides. The other major invention required was a method of altering the photosensitivity of the plant so that it could mature in a definitive period unaffected by local variations in climate or day length. Once the biological time of agricultural transformations was reduced, labour time and biological processes could be synchronized, bringing agriculture closer to industry. Stanton Hicks notes that the possibility of diversity in agriculture is doomed as long as modern economics and science fail to accept the difference between industry and agriculture. Diversity can only emerge when an agricultural view of life is recovered and he sees this recovery as the major quest for modern science.

Agricultural Taylorism as Philanthropy

There is another point one immediately notices about the narratives of the Green Revolution: it is always portrayed as logical and inevitable. And when critics accuse the executives of the Green Revolution of failure or corruption, the responses of the latter always come out as technical answers to technical questions. I think these definitions must be taken seriously. The Green Revolution represents the extension of accountancy and instrumental reason to agriculture. The scientists no longer feel responsible because they are strictly 'appliers of formulas and recipes' (Gorz, 1989: 122–4). The Green Revolution scientist is not an *episteme* breaker like Galileo, he merely extends the domain of cognitive instrumental reason. New problems do create ethical problems, but these merely necessitate technical fixes. The rationality of Green Revolution is a kind that does not allow for self-reflection. Both resistance and critique and heroism lie in languages and worlds beyond it.

A part of the inevitability of the Green Revolution is its Taylorization. What inaugurates the Taylorization of agriculture is the hybrid seed. It not only facilitated monoculture but also created a monoculture of knowledge. Hybridization reduced the viability of seeds over generations. This ensured that every season the farmer had to return to the breeder for seed. Calestous Juma notes

the adaptive knowledge that had hitherto been accumulated at the local level for dealing with a wide range of problems such as pest, drought and disease was scrapped and improved varieties came with new techniques of how to handle problems. It made the farmers less adaptive as they had no control over the knowledge related to these inputs. Whenever the new varieties failed, the farmer was left with few options but to wait for solutions from the research centres. (Juma, 1989: 79)

But the greatest ignominy is the manner in which generations of knowledge are wiped out with a classificatory stroke. The classification of gene-plasm is an indication of this. Genetic resources are classified as wild species, improved land races including primitive cultivars, advanced

cultivars and breeding lines, etc. The point to note is that the label 'primitive cultivar' is a highly biased term and it is advantageous for the genetic
industry to label it so. The term 'primitive' hides the sophistication, the
millennia of work farmers have put into it (Mooney, 1983: 56). Mooney
adds that many of these 'primitive' varieties become modern merely by
crossing the border. A stroke of the pen and cosmetic variation leads to the
plant being listed as a new patent by a gene multinational.

The history of the Green Revolution becomes a Kafkaesque story. It is
one where Johnny Appleseed is now a multinational. The Green Revolution
is read as a modern success story. If Max Weber were to write about
capitalism and science today, he would make a study of the Green Revolution. His analytical focus would be different. Instead of the Protestant as
individual he would write about the bureaucrat scientist as functional
agent. Instead of citing Benjamin Franklin's *Poor Richard's Almanac* he
would be citing the annual reports of the IRRI and CIMMYT and would
refer to technocrats like Borlaug and Swaminathan. However he would not
talk of them as charismatic heroes, *Reader's Digest* style, but as functional
operators applying the recipes of technical reason.

Dissolving the Embeddedness of Agriculture

Success for the Green Revolution was gauged by increases in productivity
and profits. Accountancy was interested only in more or less, not in the
meaning of work, the diversity of nature, or the quality of life. This
privileging of the quantitative had definite consequences for diversity and
sustainability. Andre Gorz in his *Critique of Economic Reason* observes:
'Quantitative measure inherently admits no principle of self-limitation. The
category of the "sufficient" and the category of the "too much" are equally
alien. No quantity is the greatest possible, no success is so great that a
greater success cannot be imagined' (Gorz, 1989: 113). Gorz and Weber
realized that economic calculation was a rebellion against the constricting
orders of feudal society. It not only made efficiency measurable but turned
it into a scientific virtue. Yet Weber was a man attuned to ironies. He might
have realized that economic rationality, while a liberating category historically, might be read as destructive when confronted with the embeddedness
of traditional agriculture.

The Indian feminist and philosopher of science Vandana Shiva shows
how the abstracted categories of economic calculation virtually perform a
conceptual rape of agriculture (Shiva, 1989: 37–8). Agriculture as a conceptual system involves an interaction between plants, soil, farm animals,
and humans. Green Revolution reductionism substitutes for this symbiotic
interaction a formal integration at the level of seeds and chemicals. The
long-range impact of the seed-chemical package is never considered in
this reductionist assessment of yields. Secondly, the Green Revolution

concentrates on visible short-term economics and fails to assess invisible economics. It is illiterate when it comes to measuring the ecological contribution of nitrogen fixation or the prevention of diseases by mixed cropping.

Shiva insists that instead of isolated parts it is the two systems of agriculture that must be compared. She might have added that what is then compared is an impoverished innovation chain with a living chain of being which includes soil, plants, animals, and man as a living covenant. What one needs to measure is the sustainability of one system against the market life of the other. Mere radical critiques of political economy will not suffice. Merely to raise the questions about the percentage of people below the poverty-line after the Green Revolution mimics the language of economic calculation.

The Myth of Constant Advance

The history of gene diversity reveals how the dualism of power and caring is skilfully woven by science to create new spaces for policing. What appear as items for concern and crises for the paradigm are reduced to everyday problems for the next decade. The structure of science operates to create three permissible strategies in reaction to a problem. First, and what is of greatest interest to us, are the dissenting imaginations within science, the works of Ehrenfeld, Stanton Hicks, Anderson, Richard Levins, and others committed to transforming Promethean science into a caring Hermes. Their danger lies in their continuous marginalization while simultaneously providing normal science with a liberal air. The second model involves the juxtaposition of hard technology with environmental concern and these are reflected in the writings of advocates of gene reserves like Franke, Hawkes, etc. The third tactic is an attempt by scientists to claim that the crises created by science can only be solved by more science. Problems like pollution, disease, and falling productivity, rather than being mere concerns, also become pretexts for opening out new spaces for science in its perpetual quest for constant advance. What appears as a philosophy of concern and caring is the opening gambit of science clearing a new space for itself, using the impending threat of scarcity or disaster to wipe away questions of ethical concern. This is precisely how gene technology has approached the critique of the Green Revolution. It treats the Borlaug revolution as primitive and offers the epigones of Watson and Crick as the real revolutionaries. The new techniques of recombinant DNA or even tissue culture can create within the genetic architecture itself, seeds which are disease-resistant or less affected by herbicides.

A comparison can be made with equivalent occurrences in the development of child welfare. Jacques Donzelot in his *Policing of Families* (1979) shows that when eugenics was being condemned as a nightmare, a series of so-called Keynesian strategies incorporating social work, child psychology, and pedagogy provided a frame within which these disciplines sustained control over the family.

In a similar manner Cary Fowler and colleagues (1988) suggest that it is the genetics industry which is now talking the 'genespeak' of organic agriculture and environmental sensitivity. They observe that, 'although a billion pounds of toxic active ingredients were poured into American crops, only 1% hits the target'. 'Previously the American industry used to deny or play down such observations. Today it used this fact as a part of its new strategy to breed pesticide resistant varieties'. Structured in all such narratives is this act of erasure, a science forgetful of its past depredations, where herbicide damage alone cost American farmers 4 billion dollars annually. A comment by Horkheimer and Adorno sums up this attitude. They claim that 'loss of memory is the transcendental condition of science. All objectification is forgetting' (Jung, 1989: 39). To counter this Fowler offers a quote from Kundera, 'the struggle of the people against power is the struggle of memory against forgetting' (Fowler et al., 1988).

GENETIC LOSS AND SCIENCE AS A SYSTEM OF KNOWLEDGE

The crisis of diversity has created a strange kind of self-reflexivity, fumbling, tentative, and with none of the imperiousness of radical critiques or normal science. It is a search marked by despair, which is sometimes self-inflicted. Richard Levins in 'Genetics and Hunger' (1974) elaborates the two interlocking dimensions of the problem. He claims that agriculture poses a problem of two kinds of politics. There is first the common externalist assumption that modern science is a captive of business interests. But scientific knowledge itself is a map of life-chances which can pre-empt certain kinds of futures. So critiques of knowledge have to operate self-consciously across both internalist and externalist dimensions. Levins asks rhetorically, 'if the locus of hunger lies in political economy rather than entomology why look at genetics?' (1974: 67), and answers that the fact that agriculture is a social and political science does not make it less a biological science. What he insists on is 'the inseparability of biology and politics within a single science' (1974: 68).

To Levins, an agriculture that serves people's needs requires a base broader than plant biology to provide a more complex view of the world. To Levins, the most surprising thing about agriculture is that it still feeds people. Agricultural research, he claims, is oriented to the production of marketable commodities like insecticides, fertilizers, machines, and hybrid seeds. The feeding of people is incidental to all this or a mere by-product. 'The Linear syllogism that food relieves hunger, crops yield food, improving yields reduces hunger is inadequate' (Levins, 1974: 67). Such Green

Revolution syllogisms are based on too narrow a notion of agriculture, too simplistic a notion of politics. To recover an agricultural view embedded in sustainability and diversity necessitates an alternative imagination poised between realism and utopia.

Such a search for possibilities is limited by a certain sense of professional pragmatism and empiricism. Pragmatism is a belief that only the real is rational and relevant, and that incremental changes can be generated within the system. Such a pursuit of science ultimately reinforces existing conditions. Supplementing the self-reinforcing effects of pragmatism is empiricism as a professional style. This seeks a professional identity in the specialized and small. Such research also reinforces current hegemonies.

What Levins looks for is a halfway house that opens doors to an alternative imagination. He suggests three simple projects:

1. Agricultural systems based on integrated pest control.
2. The application of variability of micro-climates.
3. Breeding plants for mixed cropping.

Each of these modest research programmes challenges the real-is-rational approach of agribusiness and refuses to accept that the boundary concepts of research are those of the prevailing models of agricultural production and land use.

What Levins suggests is a series of research programmes which simultaneously emphasize the cognitive and ethical. One needs to dream beyond the hegemony of the system and incorporate the sensibility of the other into the research programme. He makes an eloquent case for this approach. The feedback loops of science traverse deep into politics, and a scientist can no longer claim innocence about the various implications of his work. He considers the importance of multi-cropping in this context.

Disease, today, is not only a logical consequence of monoculture but also a weapon of conquest. The necessity of multicropping becomes a cognitive and ethical imperative because war on crops is an accepted part of state policy. The Portuguese used it as a part of their policy to control an empire. Levins adds that 'at least one American scientist has won a medal for improving rice blast and at least one pilot run of insect pests have been used against rice crops in the Quan Ngai province in Vietnam'. Given this, it is irresponsible for any scientist to recommend the planting of single varieties.

In Levins's essay one can find what might be called the search for a plural framework for science, where the local and concrete can be celebrated as such. The three suggestions he makes in this context require further elaboration.

There is first the question of how scientific specialization can become more sensitive to diversity. This involves in turn a search for a site which allows science to be more open to diversity. Thirdly, he emphasizes the need for liberating tropical agriculture from the ethnocentrism of current practices. This takes us back to the question of the classification of knowledge itself. Beyond the vertical classification of scientific knowledge into archaeology, anthropology, physics, chemistry, biology, etc. are the specializations within biology itself. Here the notions of levels or organization reign supreme. The levels range from the molecules, cells, organelles, and organs, to organ-systems, populations, and communities and to the ecosystem itself. The vocabularies and techniques of practitioners at each level lead to mutual incomprehension. While each biologist attempts to give centrality to his level, a pecking-order has emerged where it is the reductive that is legitimated as powerful, because it claims wider applicability. As a result notions of diversity and variety are restricted to the higher levels of biology.

Implicit in the reductionist zeal of which monoculture is but one consequence is a belief in generality, in a science which conceives of order merely as central tendencies, where variance is viewed with despair. George Bartholomew suggests that the time for such adolescent scientism is over. Biology is mature enough to accept diversity as a basic fact of evolution, even if it is not amenable to the generalizing impetus of science (Bartholomew, 1968).

Edward Wilson pushes Bartholomew's ideas further but approaches the necessity of understanding the concrete in a different way (Wilson, 1989: 242–5). He argues that the difficulty lies in the formulation of the problem itself, basically in internalizing the themata of the levels of organization in biology. What he suggests are disciplines cutting across levels, where one studies an organism or organelle right across the levels from molecules to ecosystems. The division of labour changes from a stress on levels of biological organization to an emphasis on taxonomic groups or organisms. This valorizes the old-style field biologist, the herpetologist, the hematologist, who would regain ground lost to the ecologist and the geneticist. The word fundamental in this context could then be applied not just to work which leads to broad generalization but to studies of individual taxa, even if the information is not readily applicable to other taxa (Wilson, 1989: 243). 'This 45% reorientation', as Wilson calls it, reflects a move away from the search for generality in modern biology.

Wilson is frank enough to contend that this reorientation stems from two reasons, one pragmatic and the other cognitive. Biology of late has produced few general principles which can be applied widely, fruitfully or interestingly. Secondly, there is the recognition that 'the laws of biology are written in the laws of diversity' (1989: 244). This suggests that a plurality of biological approaches is required for understanding the variety of species and organisms. 'When you have seen one species of chrysomelid beetle, you *have not* emphatically seen them all' (1989: 245). There is more than the first glimmer of the celebration and understanding of the object for itself.

Yet in celebrating diversity, Wilson still operates within the permissible spaces of dissent in science. He still accepts the divide between science and the humanities that might emphasize magic, religion, or myth. Consider the snake or coconut. *Biophilia* contains a succinct essay on myths of the snake across cultures (Wilson, 1984). But while celebrating the mythology, he also reduces myths about the fear of snakes to an expression of a primordial biological instinct. For Wilson such myths could add to the aesthetics of the snake, even to poetry—but it would not be relevant to science. In his search for the concrete and the variable, Wilson would study a snake or hopefully a coconut across the levels of biological organization but he would not integrate the political, religious, or mythological understanding of them within scientific knowledge. It is the old dilemma of parts and wholes. It needs the recognition of three kinds of wisdom: first, the ecological wisdom of the whole being greater than the sum of the parts. Secondly, the biological wisdom that parts have to be celebrated as parts and not reduced to impoverished wholes. There is also a synecdochal understanding where every part represents the whole. Here the coconut is simultaneously myth, food, music, economic product, and art but as resonators of a more mystical notion of the whole, not the holisms of systems and cybernetic views but of a cosmology that simultaneously speaks secular, religious, and magical languages.

The second approach for a constructive understanding of diversity is in the work of Eugene Odum (Odum, 1984). The importance of diversity in agriculture needs a site apart from the laboratory where the wisdom of nature can be understood without succumbing to reductionist genetics. One needs a notion somewhere between natural systems and molecules and open to both. This is necessary, for the history of science has swung undialectically between holism and reductionism. Such a dialogical and dialectical site is the 'mecocosm'. Though mecocosm sounds occult, Odum, who sticks to systems terminology, would not call it a dialogue site. For him it is a world of feedback loops, halfway between laboratory microcosms and large complex real world macrocosms. The answer he suggests, and it is one also argued by Stanton Hicks and Levins, is the field, provided 'fields themselves are treated as part of the biological cycle' (Hicks, 1975: 120).

At one level, banal, even prosaic, a field is a profound entity. Cultivated fields are ideal mecocosms. They raise issues of genetics which are ignored when the field is generally reduced to a starch factory. The field is a system where all the parts are evolving, where pests are adapting to control techniques like insecticides. The field, unlike the laboratory with its one-step model of causation, is far more complex in its interactions. Instead of a reductionism that pits crops against herbicide, the field as a mecocosm consists of 'predators-parasites, nitrogen fixing bacteria, mites and collembola carrying out preliminary decomposition of residues, the earthworm and nematodes, all as active participants of a system. Their indirect effects on crops may be as great as the less remote one step causation models of the laboratory' (Levins, 1974: 74). The field as an open system is sensitive to issues like multiple cropping. As Levins observes, one understands the wisdom of how 'even a modest increase in the distance between the fields of a given crop might exclude a pest species completely' (1974: 75). Or how 'the migratory rate of a pest may be reduced by interplanting other plants whose odors can confound the sensory apparatus of a pest. Levins adds that cultivated fields are ideally suited for understanding biogeographic principles and even the issue of seasonality in a way that current models of genetic change and population fluctuation cannot handle.

The third major approach to diversity within science concentrates on a recovery of the tropics for science. Both Levins and Daniel Janzen (1973) have insisted that the transfer of temperate sciences to the tropics is unethical. They note that US models of high-energy, high-fertilizer monoculture are not only destroying the tropics ecologically but disrupting them as sites for alternative imaginations. The notion of the tropics raises once again the need for a pluralized approach both to diversity in nature and to the diversity of agricultural practices.

The tropics, by definition, allows as many different solutions to resource use, each of which may be as profitable as the other. Given this diversity of tropical systems, the conventional scientific approach of creating a generalized ecosystem model upon which to base resource-use planning is highly impractical. Its structure would necessarily be based on statements of central tendency, as would its predictions. But the needs of the tropical man frequently deviate from generalized ecosystem models. What one needs again is a movement away from generality towards sustainable yield solutions for each region. Such a regional approach, understanding the complexities of local interactions, and seeking optimum models for each region or even locality, would be a trend away from the reductionism of present-day tropical agriculture which focuses predominantly on one variable, yield improvement. Janzen admits that when each tropical system is treated as unique, charges of parochialism can be made. Responding to this requires both a cognitive and an ethical imagination. Janzen suggests that the scientist must openly decide whether a tropical station is to help a self-contained agro-ecosystem, or whether it should produce work like the International Research Institutes, which integrate the agrosystem into the world economy. He laments that there is no moral code preventing the injection of temperate-zone science and technology into the tropics. These methods include the Peace Corps, military bases, tractors, miracle seeds, grain surpluses, and hydroelectric dams. Each aid or transfer prevents the possibility of real alternatives developing in the tropics (Janzen, 1973: 1217).

342 DECOLONIZING THE TRANSFER OF TECHNOLOGY

In this last part of the essay we move from a reflection of knowledge to a consideration of nature in science, which has become captive to economics. This problem becomes obvious as scientists try to create a theoretical rationale for sustaining diversity in nature. This involves two separate kinds of argument. The first demands that one face up to the fact that nature does perform an economic function through activities like soil-binding, absorbing radiation, etc. The ecologist is aware of it in a generalized form and Walter Westman's 'How much are nature's services worth' (1977: 960–4) is a good demonstration that nature's services are too complex to fit the monetary matrix of cost–benefit analysis (CBA).

The problem becomes more specific when it comes to evaluating the loss of a particular object. Implicit in this is a set of axioms which is itself questionable. This reflects what might be called the great chain of being argument, where man, generally modern Western man, is seen as the crown of creation. Secondly, all nature is seen as being created for his use. This turns nature as forest, sea, or soil into a mine to be exploited and abandoned. Also implicit in this is the notion of obsolescence, of valueless objects that can be abandoned or forgotten. One is not confronted merely with the ethnocentrism of Western Judeo-Christian cosmology but also of cultural codes within it. How does one guarantee the objectivity of particular preferences, what does one save? Ecologists have shown that protecting one 'specimen' virtually writes the death-warrant of the other by default. Robert Leo Smith remarks that arguments for preserving a living organism can be based on the fact that it is a luxury, a necessity, or an asset. 'By such criteria', he adds, 'society can be rallied to save the bald eagle, for example, or come to the rescue of whales or seals. But it is extremely difficult to rally public support to save the blunt nosed leopard lizard. The eagle has merit in the public mind, the lizard has none' (Smith, 1986). It is not just true of particular animals or plants; it can extend to the selection of habitats. 'Habitats rich in birds and mammals are more likely to be saved than those that are rich in insects and plants. The legitimate concern on avoiding extinction of species leads automatically to less concern over the ecologically spectacular but species poor habitats like dry forest, swamps, high elevations, poor soils' (Janzen, 1986: 305–24). The logic of conservation based on utility can produce strange ironies, especially when men assume that they can evaluate the full value of a species, including its future utility. Ecology shows nature to be complex enough to make such evaluations sadly facile.

One of the saddest stories in this context relates to the *Raphus Cacullatus*, the dodo. This much maligned bird, a native of Mauritius, became extinct in 1681, less than two centuries after it was 'discovered'. The posthumous apology to the dodo begins almost three centuries later, with the discovery that there were only thirteen trees of the *Calvaria Major* left. Each of these trees was over three hundred years old. The trees did produce well-formed seeds yet the total absence of young plants puzzled botanists. Even when planted under nursery conditions, the seeds remained dormant. Stanley Temple, a University of Wisconsin biologist, felt that there was a correlation between the disappearance of the dodo and the slow extinction of the tree. He discovered that while the seed of the *Calvaria* had a thin exocarp, and a fleshy mesocarp, it had a hard thick-walled endocarp. The dodo ate these seeds, which it probably retained in its digestive tract, and it was here that the process of seed germination was accelerated through the abrasion of the seed-coat. Temple force-fed the seeds to turkeys and successfully germinated the first Calvaria in three centuries. (Too late, however, to save the dodo.)

The choice of what to save still operates in terms of some notion of the chain of being. In its modified versions it still holds that the creatures are made for man's use but man is regarded as a trustee, responsible for the stewardship of the earth. What is missing, however, is not the criteria of selection but some wide cosmological notion of kinship which sees the earth itself as alive. Unfortunately the establishment of science led to the abandonment of the *anima mundi* idea which saw the whole earth as alive. The mechanical world-view has turned nature into a tool-shed. Within the tool-shed view, the general argument for saving species takes on either an aesthetic or utilitarian dimension. The two can overlap as when nature is seen as having a recreational value, which will attract tourists, and tourism is then assigned an economic function, which is quantifiable.

The problem of looking at economic value is three-fold. First, the fact of talking in terms of economics is itself a metaphysical trap that scientists get embroiled in. The language of economics may fail to provide the life-giving assumptions required for ecology. Even if we accept the economist's attitude to nature, other problems arise (Ehrenfeld, 1986: 38–43). The first can be dubbed the non-resource problem and the second the substitutability assumption. Aldo Leopold in his 'Land Ethic' provides the classic formulation. 'One basic weakness of the conservation system wholly based on economic motives is that most members of the land community have no economic value. When one of these economic categories is threatened and if we happen to love it we invent subterfuges to give it economic importance' (Leopold, 1973: 246).

Also as Ehrenfeld and others have noted economism forces science to speak not the ordinary language of conservation ethic but the formal equations of cost–benefit analysis. It assumes that money can evaluate all aspects of nature, past and future, and that its benefits for every section can be graded. Such a CBA framework has also entrapped science into the substitutability problem. For example, when an economist like Simon advocates the destruction of Amazonian forests by claiming that the forests are not really being degraded because they are being replaced by valuable plantations of pine or eucalyptus, the ecologist gets involved in scholastic

334   DECOLONIZING THE TRANSFER OF TECHNOLOGY

exercises about the economic functions of nature, attributing anthropo-
morphic values to soil-binding, hydrological functions and so on
(Ehrenfeld, 1986). But by doing this he slips back into the mining model of
nature. Such economistic functions of substitutability, first applied to min-
erals, are now being applied to tropical forests. What Ehrenfeld is suggesting is that the language of economism is not really the language of nature.
In fact a philosophy of a money economy only resonates with the philosophy of a Western science which has been hostile to nature. Both combine
to dissolve the very ecologies they are trying to defend.

If nature cannot be saved at the level of production, conservationists seek
to protect it at the level of consumption by giving it a pedagogic, recreational, or aesthetic value. The notion of aesthetics tries to treat a part of
nature as a cultural artefact. Rarity is not viewed biologically as something
restricted but as something equivalent to a painting or a stamp. Endangered
species are viewed as analogous to a work of art. The economic substrate
produces ironies, because once a species is declared rare it becomes even
more vulnerable, subject to the attack of collectors and poachers. Secondly,
just as art is not seen as part of living tradition but as an alienated object in
a museum, the species is not seen as part of a living process or live
agricultural tradition. It is cut off, and embalmed in time in a reserve or a
museum. Aesthetics, like science, still smells of formaldehyde.

The irony of attributing economic values is that the very act of attributing
value on the basis of scientific research leads to eventual extinction. When
a Norman Meyers or an Edward Ayensu lists out a huge cornucopia of what
a tropical forest can provide, they are eventually inviting the exploitation of
the forest not its preservation.

A tropical rain forest being tapped for its exotic fuels, chemical precursors, rubber,
unusual hardwoods and drugs and filled to the brim with researchers, agronomists,
organic chemists, ethnobotanists, ethnologists and photographers is not likely to
keep its diversity much longer than one that is napalmed or burnt to produce
transient pasture for fast food hamburgers-on-the-hoof. (Ehrenfeld, 1986: 42)

One had merely to think of the destruction of the *Rauvolfia serpentina*. Once
common in the forests of India, it was hailed as the source of reserpine, a
drug effective against hypertension. The plant has been hunted so systematically that it has the dubious honour of being on the endangered list.

Ehrenfeld shows that the rationale for diversity cannot be built on a
science arguing for the economic, pedagogic, or aesthetic criteria for
nature. The problem also lies in the language and perspective from which
this is articulated (Ehrenfeld, 1986: 43).

Ehrenfeld argues that today 'generality is the theme and power of the
technological era, the key to our ability to manipulate the environment'
(1986: 43). Generality reeks of the reductionist and the universalizable.
Ehrenfeld adds that 'in biology diversity held its own until the rise of

reductionist molecular biology. From then on diversity makes its descent into the second rate and the second class' (Ehrenfeld, 1978: 178).

The taxonomist whose task it was to link the general and the concrete is today a neglected scientist and an object of fun. In fact *Taxon* recently published a story of the disappearance of the last taxonomist. Following Philip Wylie's best-seller, it was entitled *The Disappearance*. What characterized taxonomy was the search for order in the celebration of diversity. Characteristic of this genesis was Linneaus himself, whose work was marked by a celebration of detail and the language of detail. Yet today this preoccupation with the local and the detailed is frowned upon, even condemned. Scientists repeatedly refer to James Watson's attack on the taxonomic old guard of Harvard and their vested interest in mosses.

Ehrenfeld eventually contends that the theoretical rationale for diversity cannot be derived from science. His comment is very similar to that of the great soil scientist Hans Jeny, who remarked that the language of soil chemistry talking of colloids cannot provide the basis of a soil ecology. Jeny was one of the first advocates of the rights of different kinds of soil to exist and he carried slides of soil samples to demonstrate that they could be as beautiful as the work of the Impressionists.

Like Jeny, Ehrenfeld feels that the language of molecular biology is semantically inadequate and that the search for such a framework has to be sought outside science in the realms of religion, poetry, or local knowledges which can provide thirty different words for soil (Stuart, 1984). There is a despair in Ehrenfeld's writing. He exclaims that the humanist world 'accepts the conservation of nature only piecemeal and at a price'. He admits science has no way of saying, as Goethe did of nature, that 'each of her creations has its own being, each represents a special concept, yet together they are one' (Ehrenfeld, 1978). Ehrenfeld believes that one has to wait for a new phase of science. In the meanwhile it is only groups outside science, activists involved in politics, religion, and in local bodies who can recapture the love of diversity for its own sake.

The tensions of evaluating nature economically are caught in the literatures on parks and reserves. I do not propose to examine the conventional critiques made of reserves. What I wish to do is to examine parks and reserves as collective representations. The park as embodied in the ideological landscaping epitomizes the industrial ideal of arcadia (Williams, 1973). Its morphology has to be understood in relation to the urban industrial system. The park and factory town represent complementary parts of the same process. They seem overtly opposed to each other because, while the factory is organized for production, the park is being organized for consumption. In the primary grid of production the relation to nature is openly exploitative, in the secondary grid the facts of production are forgotten and nature becomes an aesthetic delight to be consumed at leisure. It is the economics of aesthetics that captures the two basic roles of the park today.

There is first the relation of production to consumption and second of production to preservation. Here nature is preserved not only to be consumed by tourists but kept in reserve for later industrial use. Preservation thus combines both the function of maintenance for later production and consumption through leisure and recreation.

The movement of a park to what is now called a 'biosphere reserve' captures this both at the classificatory and morphological level. Laura Tangley claims that a biosphere reserve is a more ambitious concept than a park (Tangley, 1988: 148–55). While parks focus on aesthetics and recreation, reserves claim additional functions. Basing herself on Michael Batise's work, Tangley shows that a biosphere reserve can be visualized as three circles performing three different functions. The first is an attempt to preserve a minimally disturbed ecosystem large enough to ensure genetic and species diversity. The reserve also plays a logistical role, providing for a whole range of education, training, and research activities. These include environmentally non-manipulative activities like measurement of acid-rain precipitation. But the reserve moves beyond the park in also having a development role. Beyond the core and buffer zones is a transitional zone where the reserve reacts with the neighbourhood areas attempting to work out new models of sustainable development. Thus unlike parks, which exclude humans except as tourists or officials, reserves try to involve local people as contributors of reserve activities. Outstanding examples of such reserves include the 52,800 ha. Sean Ka'an reserve in Mexico and the great reserves of Costa Rica. Here, under the guidance of Daniel Janzen, the entire reserve is being turned into a classroom which can create in Costa Rica a generation of environmentally sensitive scientists.

Yet the reserve is not only a piece of consumption, it is being preserved for production, and it is here that a certain uneasiness enters. There is something about it that reminds one of a future mine, something waiting to be plugged into the industrial system, so much gene-plasm awaiting the giants of the pharmaceutical industry. There is a strange dualism, a tension present. While a tropical ecologist talks of the density of the tropical forest and its diversity, the geneticist might want to rip off a plant for his latest lego set. The scientist himself suggests that the celebration of technological progress and the sense of loss is part of the same mind-set. Daniel Janzen has also hinted that the 'replacement of fresh oranges by pasteurized orange juice in paper containers and the adoption of the national park concept' (Janzen, 1986: 320–1) might be part of the same development frame.

There seem to be two notions of reserve which can be best understood in terms of an example Heidegger once gave. He compared an old bridge across the Rhine and a modern power-plant. One kind of reserve like the bridge lets nature be. The other is like the hydroelectric plant. Heidegger observes that the plant builds the Rhine river into the plant itself 'so that the river becomes merely a part of the machinery needed to generate electricity. The riverly character is denied as it becomes a mere resource used to turn generators' (Alderman, 1978: 48). Similarly many a reserve, or even more the much touted gene-banks, become the equivalent of the hydroelectric plant, technologically identified with industry.

CONCLUSION

There are several issues that this chapter has not touched upon, not because they are not important but because the professional scientist fails to develop them. There are three aspects which are more the work of people's science movements. There is first the need to develop a sense of juridical domain within which science works. What happens when life-forms themselves get patented? Professionalized science has no equivalents to the work of Jeremy Rifkin or Cary Fowler and Pat Mooney (Rifkin, 1984). The latter two have explored in detail how the concept of patenting seeds and other life-forms has altered science juridically. Mooney and Fowler still operate within the domain of the contract but hint that what one needs is the language of the commons, where past and present constitute parts of one community. The idea of commons defines access in terms radically different from those of contract. Rifkin adds to it an ethical imperative that the scientist cannot understand, a plea to renounce the pursuit of genetic engineering.

There is a third dimension that people's groups emphasize. They contend that ecology is the privileging of civil society against the state and challenges the contract between nation-state and modern science. People's movements need local knowledges, and religious fervour which professionalized science cannot provide. Ecology is a dialogic and for such dialogues Western science has to converse with traditional knowledges. A recovery of the agricultural world-view in science presupposes an encounter with the diversity of traditions, techniques, and knowledges that constitute agriculture. Dissenting science needs to enter these spaces. If not, there might come a time when peasant society confronted with modern science might have a new vision of the four horsemen of apocalypse as four scientists: Karl Marx, Charles Darwin, Albert Einstein, and the meek figure of the Czech monk, Gregor Mendel—carrying in their wake, plague, death, desolation, and destruction.

REFERENCES

AIYER, A. K. Y. N. (1949), 'Mixed Cropping in India', *IARI Bulletin*, 19/1: 439–543.

ALDERMAN, H. (1978), 'Heidegger's Critique of Science and Technology', in M. Murray (ed.), *Heidegger and Modern Philosophy: Critical Essays*, New Haven, Conn.: Yale University Press.

ANDERSON, E. (1967), *Plants, Man and Life*, Berkeley, Calif.: University of California Press.

BARTHOLOMEW, G. (1968), 'The Role of Nature History in Contemporary Biology', *Bioscience*, 36/5: 324–9.

BENNETT, E. (1978), 'Threats to Crop Plant Genetic Resources', in J. G. Hawkes (ed.), *Conservation and Agriculture*, London: Duckworth: 113–22.

BERNSTEIN, R. (1983), *Beyond Objectivism and Relativism*, Oxford: Basil Blackwell.

DONZELOT, J. (1979), *The Policing of Families*, London: Hutchinson.

EHRENFELD, D. (1978), *The Arrogance of Humanism*, New York: Oxford University Press.

——(1986), 'Thirty Million Cheers for Diversity', *New Scientist*, no. 1512: 38–43.

FOWLER, C., LACHKOVICS, E., MOONEY, P., and SHAND, H. (1988), 'The Laws of Life: Another Development and the New Biotechnologies', *Development Dialogue*, 1–2.

GOODMAN, D., SORJ, B., and WILKINSON, J. (1987), *From Farming to Biotechnology: A Theory of Agro-Industrial Development*, Oxford: Basil Blackwell.

GORZ, A. (1989), *Critique of Economic Reason*, London: Verso Books.

GROENEVELD, S. (1984), 'Lessons from the Tree of Life in the Context of Ecofarming and Development', in B. Glaeser, (ed.), *Ecodevelopment: Concepts, Projects, Strategies*, Oxford: Pergamon Press.

HICKS, C. S. (1975), *Man and Natural Resources*, London: Croom Helm.

ISAAC, E. (1970), *Geography of Domestication*, Englewood Cliffs, NJ: Prentice-Hall.

JANZEN, D. (1973), 'Tropical Agro-Systems', *Science*, 182: 1212–19.

——(1986), 'The Future of Tropical Ecology', *Annual Review of Ecology and Systematics*, 17: 304–24, 315–16.

JUMA, C. (1989), *The Gene Hunter: Biotechnology and the Scramble for Seeds*, London: Zed Books; Princeton, NJ: Princeton University Press.

JUNG, H. Y. (1989), *The Question of Rationality and the Basic Grammar of Intercultural Texts*, Tokyo: IUJ Monographs.

LECOURT, D. (1977), *Proletarian Science? The Case of Lysenko*, Norwich: New Left Books.

LEOPOLD, A. (1973), *A Sand Country Almanac*, New York: Ballantine Books.

LEPPIK, E. E. (1969), 'The Life and Work of N. I. Vavilov', *Economic Botany*, 23: 128–32.

LEVINS, R. (1974), 'Genetics and Hunger', *Genetics*, 78: 67–76.

MOONEY, P. P. (1983), 'The Law of the Seed: Another Development and Plant Genetic Resources', *Development Dialogue*, 1–2: 13.

ODUM, E. (1984), 'The Mesocosm', *Bioscience*, 34/9: 558–63.

RAVEN, P. (1988), 'Tropical Floristics Tomorrow', *Taxon*, 37/3: 549–60, 554.

RIFKIN, J. (1984), *Algeny*, Harmondsworth: Penguin.

SHIVA, V. (1989), *The Violence of the Green Revolution*, Dehradun: Vandana Shiva.

SINGER, P. (1975), *Animal Liberation*, London: Jonathan Cape.

SMITH, R. L. (1976), 'Ecological Genesis of Endangered Species: The Philosophy of Preservation', *Annual Review of Ecology and Systematics*, 7: 33–5.

——(1986), 'Ecological Genesis of Endangered Species: The Philosophy of Preservation', *Annual Review of Ecology and Systematics*, 7: 33–55.

SOLZHENITSYN, A. (1973), *The Gulag Archipelago*, New York: Harper and Row.

STONE, C. D. (1975), *Should Trees have a Standing? Towards Legal Rights for Natural Objects*, Los Altos, Calif.: William Kaufman.

STUART, K. (1984), 'My Friend, the Soil: A Conversation with Hans Jeny', *Journal of Soil and Water Conservation*, 39/3: 158–61.

SULLIVAN, W. (1967), 'The Death and Rebirth of a Science', in H. Salisbury (ed.), *The Soviet Union: The Fifty Years*, New York: The New York Times Company.

TANGLEY, L. (1988), 'A New Era in Biosphere Reserves', *Bioscience*, 38/3: 148–55.

UGEN, D. (1970), 'The Potato', *Science*, 170/3963: 1161–15.

WADDINGTON, C. H . (1978), 'Summary of Discussion Part VI', in I. G. Wakes (ed.), *Conservation and Agriculture*, London: Duckworth: 248.

WESTMAN, W. (1977), 'How Much are Nature's Services Worth?' *Science*, 197: 960–4.

WILLIAMS, R.(1973), *The Country and the City*, London: Chatto and Windus.

WILSON, E. (1984), *Biophilia*, Cambridge, Mass: Harvard University Press.

——(1989), 'The Conceptualization of Biology and the Stewardship of Systematics', *Bioscience*, 39/4: 224–45.

10

The Savage Freud: The First Non-Western Psychoanalyst and the Politics of Secret Selves in Colonial India

ASHIS NANDY

Among the nineteenth-century European schools of thought which claim to shape our self-definition in this century, the two most influential in-house critiques of modern Western civilization are Marxism and psychoanalysis. Both nurture a deep ambivalence towards their culture of origin. They seek to bare the normative and institutional anomalies of the Enlightenment and to demystify the bourgeois culture that has inherited the anomalies, but they do so in terms of the values of the Enlightenment itself. This is what makes the schools internal, rather than external critiques of the modern West.

One aspect of this ambivalence in Marxism and psychoanalysis has begun to attract some notice. Many in the southern world have become aware that the schools own up to their cultural roots by building into their theoretical frames aggressive Eurocentric critiques of the non-Western cultures. For both, the primitive world, especially the Orient, is an anachronistic presence and represents an earlier stage of cultural order that social

This essay was originally written for the conference on Development and the Transfer of Technology, organized at Karachi in January 1989 by the World Institute for Development Economics Research (WIDER) and the UN University. Subsequently, the paper was also presented at the Department of South Asian Studies, University of Virginia, Charlottesville, and at the Department of Politics, University of Hull. I am grateful to the participants in the Karachi conference, especially Durre Ahmed, and to the audiences at the Universities of Virginia and Hull for their criticisms and suggestions. The work on this began when I was a Fellow in 1988 at the Woodrow Wilson International Centre for Scholars, Washington, and a part of it was done at the Department of Politics, University of Hull, when I was Charles Wallace Fellow there in the summer of 1990, I am grateful to these institutions for the facilities they provided. Neither of the institutions are in any way responsible for the contents of the chapter.

The chapter has also gained much from my long interviews with Debiprasad Chattopadhyay, Vijayketu Bose, Bhupen Desai, Charuchandra Bhattacharya, and others, and from the help given by Tarit Chatterji, Hiranmay Ghosal, Heather Harlan, Amit Das, Sajal Basu and Sujit Deb. A section of the paper was presented at the Delhi Group for Psychoanalysis in November 1990, where it benefited from the comments of S. K. Mitra, Indrani and Ashok Guha, Ashok Nagpal, and Veena Das. As with a number of my recent works, Surabhi Sheth has helped with the various possible meanings of the Sanskrit *slokas* used in the chapter. I would not perhaps have used the idea of secret self as an organizing principle in this chapter but for a long discussion on the subject with Noel O'Sullivan.

evolution has rendered obsolete. Through this second criticism, that of the non-West, the schools pay homage to their first target of criticism, the West, and atone for being the dissenting children of Enlightenment.

Both schools, it is true, have their self-doubts, expressed in the lurking nostalgia towards the cultures they try to relegate to the dustbins of history or—it comes to the same thing—the waste-paper baskets of the clinic. Apart from the personal fascination their founders had for the Orient— viewed as a victim of imperial Europe or as an anthropological field populated by the 'natural', the antiquated, and the exotic—both schools have produced ideas such as primitive communism and regression at the service of ego as latent reparative gestures, to correct for or work through the arrogant social evolutionism that structures their theories of progress. It is the obverse of Albert Schweitzer's famous reparative gesture towards the West, to disabuse all those who thought that his medical mission to Africa was a homage to human dignity or an atonement for colonial violence. The African was his brother, the intrepid missionary said, but only a younger brother.

When Marxism and psychoanalysis were imported into the savage world at the high noon of imperialism, this racial arrogance was not obvious to their native converts. For the main attraction of these schools of thought in the tropics was their bidirectional criticism—of the contemporary European society and the savage world. Afro-Asian scholars and activists attracted to the new schools found them excellent instruments of self-criticism. In fact, when it came to the native ways of life, such scholars and activists rejected or undervalued ideas that softened the critical thrust of the two schools. Thus, psychoanalysts such as Carl Jung, who were especially open to the Indian world-view, found few adherents in India; Marxist scholars such as Ernst Bloch, who sought to establish a continuity between the Marxist vision and the older religious world-views, never enjoyed a vogue in non-European societies organized around religion. Such 'returns to tradition' were considered legitimate attempts to enrich social criticism in the modern West, not in societies bogged down in traditions.

Of the two schools, Marxism was to have a much more serious impact on the intellectual and political life of the South than psychoanalysis. The latter, after an early flurry of activity in a few societies—after, as it were, an Indian summer lasting about two decades—gradually became peripheral to the culture of public life in the South. Was this because Marxism became a political movement in Asian and African societies, at a time when politics was about to become the most important sector of these societies? Or were there other reasons that had to do with the culture of psychoanalysis, the conflicted personalities of those who tended it in its new habitat, and the persisting indigenous theories of mind that, like a chronic illness, resisted the Western remedies prescribed for the problems of living in the backwaters of Asia and Africa?

This essay pursues the second set of questions. It does so by focusing on the cultural meanings psychoanalysis acquired in its early years in India, after it first established a bridgehead in the country in the 1920s. The essay examines these meanings through the prism of the personal experiences, intellectual concerns, and metapsychology of the first non-Western psychoanalyst, Girindrasekhar Bose (1886–1953), who pioneered the discipline in India.

Bose began trying out psychoanalytic concepts and methods in his clinical practice towards the end of the first decade of this century when, following the partition of Bengal in 1905, the Swadesi movement had become a significant political presence. He founded the Indian Psychoanalytical Society in 1921, when the non-cooperation movement had started and Mohandas Karamchand Gandhi had assumed the leadership of India's freedom struggle. Both these political events had their cultural co-ordinates, such as the renewed efforts among Indians to revalue indigenous systems of knowledge and the growing awareness among them that the West's intellectual domination depended not so much on the new educational institutions in South Asia as on the philosophy of science and analytic categories popularized by the European culture of knowledge. Psychoanalysis in its early years reflected these changes in India's intellectual climate. Despite the efforts of many, the young discipline came to represent something more than a therapeutic technique that could be adapted to the mental health problems of India's burgeoning, partly decultured, urban bourgeoisie, although that is the way Bose often talked about the discipline, especially when writing for his international audience. Psychoanalysis also had to serve as a new instrument of social criticism, as a means of demystifying aspects of Indian culture that looked anachronistic or pathological to the articulate middle classes, and as a dissenting Western school of thought that could be turned against the West itself.

The following story tells how Bose's unique response to Freud's theories was shaped by the psychological contradictions that had arisen in the Indian culture due to the impact of colonialism and by the cultural contradictions within psychoanalysis itself. As a result, the usual encounter between an ancient culture with its distinctive culture of science and an exogenous science with its own distinctive culture fractured the self-definitions not only of Bose but also of many others involved in similar enterprises. At the same time, the encounter initiated a play of secret selves which widened as well as narrowing the interpretations of both Indian culture and the culture of psychoanalysis. The story suggests that the disreputable 'secret self' of psychoanalysis—the more speculative, political, cultural-critical aspects of the young science—gave greater play to non-Western psychoanalysis in the early years and might even have given it a stronger creative push under another kind of political-intellectual dispensation.

PART ONE: THE PSYCHOLOGY OF MORALITY

Sarvilaka's Gita

In ancient Magadha in eastern India, there lived a powerful, learned, highly respected, rich Brahmin, Sarvilaka. Disciples came to him from distant lands and his house resonated with recitals and discussions on sacred texts. Sarvilaka had a gifted son called Pundarika. Though young, Pundarika had already mastered the religious texts. When he reached the age of sixteen, Sarvilaka told him, 'Son, today is an auspicious day. You fast for the entire day and maintain your purity by following right practices. At 2 o'clock tonight, when the moonless night begins, I shall initiate you into our *kaulika pratha* or family custom. From evening onwards you stay secluded and meditate.'

At 2 am Pundarika was still reciting the name of God when, suddenly, the doors of his room opened. In the faint light of a lamp, he saw a huge man entering the room. The intruder wore a loincloth, rubbed oil shone from his body, and he held two axes on his shoulders. With a shock Pundarika recognized that the visitor was his father. Sarvilaka said, 'Son, do not be afraid. The time for your initiation has come. Dress like me, hold one of these axes, and follow me.' Pundarika followed as if mesmerized. Through a maze of streets, Sarvilaka led his son to the highway connecting Magadha to Varanasi and stood under a banyan tree. He then said, 'Pundarika, stand quietly in the dark, so that nobody can see you.' Pundarika stood trembling with fear, shock, and the strain of the long walk.

A rich merchant was travelling from the palace of Magadha to Varanasi on a horse-drawn carriage. He was carrying with him 10,000 gold coins. The route being dangerous, he had before and after his vehicle eight armed guards. As soon as the vehicle reached the banyan tree, Sarvilaka attacked it with a mighty roar. In the faint light of the vehicle, he looked even more fearsome. The driver and the guards immediately ran off. Sarvilaka decapitated the merchant with his axe, picked up the heavy bag containing the gold coins on his shoulders, and came back to the banyan tree. Pundarika by then was shaking; his axe had fallen from his hand. Sarvilaka picked up the axe and led Pundarika by hand towards home. He then pushed his son into his room and latched the door from outside.

After a long while, Pundarika regained some of his composure. By now, his mind was churning with contempt, anger, and hurt. He decided not to stay at his father's home even for a moment. In this state of high tension, he fell asleep. When he woke up in the morning, he found the sun's rays coming into his room. His father was standing near the bed, his usual serene self, wearing his usual dress. For a moment Pundarika felt that his memories of the previous night were part of a nightmare. But his own oily body and loincloth told him all. Sarvilaka broke the silence to say, 'Son, do not be unnecessarily perturbed. Nothing has happened which should cause you heart-burn.' Pundarika said, 'I don't want to stay in your house even for a moment.' His father said, 'You are not in a right state of mind because of fasting, absence of sleep, and tension. Take your bath, eat, and rest. Then I shall tell you about our family custom. If after hearing me you want to leave my house, I shall not stop you.'

Sarvilaka returned in the afternoon and had a long conversation with the son. In that conversation, Sarvilaka first narrated how the family had followed the same *kaulika pratha* from the time of the Mahābhārata and how he himself was initiated into the custom by his father. He said he knew he looked a hypocrite, robber, and a murderer to his son. But he also had faith in his son's intellect and knowledge of sacred texts. Sarvilaka then went on to justify every act of his by the tenets of Gita, for he felt that Pundarika's moral anxieties were similar to those of Arjuna before the battle of Kuruksetra; they were born of *moha*, attachment. Arjuna, too, had felt like living on alms rather than killing his own relatives for material gain.

Sarvilaka's arguments were sophisticated and they could be summed up in three broad propositions. First, Sarvilaka agreed, he did not openly talk of his *kulacara* (family practices) because he feared public censure and torment. He followed *lokacara* (customary practices) by day and *kulacara* at night. As a result, he now looked a hypocrite to his own son. Yet, no one could survive in the world by being totally truthful. All human beings were weak to a degree; to defend themselves they had to lie. Even Lord Krsna had to hide his intentions when he killed the demon Jarasandha. In addition, untruth was of divine origin. The creator of the universe had equipped some of his creations with the capacity to lie and cheat. The lions and the tigers hid their motives when stalking their prey. Human beings were too insignificant a species to invent by themselves the idea of falsehood.

Second, everyone was a robber to an extent. When one ate fruit, one deprived the trees of their fruits or even animals of their lives. Living meant living off other lives. Moreover, God had not sent anyone to earth with property or riches. One won worldly success by depriving others. *Vasundhara virabhogya*—the earth was for the enjoyment of the brave.

Third, one had to overcome the fear of being called a murderer. Arjuna feared the epithet when the battle of Kuruksetra was imminent and the response to that fear, Sarvilaka felt, was best given in Krsna's sermon to Arjuna in the Gita. The oppressor and the victim, the Gita said, were both unreal because *atman* (soul) was the sole reality and it was indestructible— *na hanta na hanyan*. None should rue the loss of a destructible, transient body. The opulent merchant killed on the road to Varanasi was aged yet attached to worldliness. The destruction of his body had only done him good. If Sarvilaka had forsaken his *kuladharma* or family's code of conduct to spare the traveller, that would have been more sinful. Human beings were mere agents of divinity—*nimittamatra*. Pundarika had been listening to the moral discourse with rapt attention. Already the doubts and contradictions in his mind were dissolving. At the end of the discourse, he touched his father's feet to pledge undying loyalty to their family custom.

With this story of homicide, secret selves, a seductive 'immoral' father, his vulnerable 'moral' son, and their final Oedipal compact, the world's first non-Western psychoanalyst, Girindrasekhar Bose, begins in 1931 his interpretation of the Gita in the pages of *Pravasi*, the influential Bengali journal of the pre-Independence years (Bose, 1931: 9–16). Bose was already a famous psychiatrist and founder of the Indian Psychoanalytic Society. By the time he began his work on the Gita, he had been exposed to psychoanalysis for nearly two decades. Yet, the work shows odd anomalies. Though one commentator has called it 'perhaps his most significant work' and an attempt 'to correlate Hindu philosophy to Western psychology' (Bhatia, 1987), the interpretation is more socio-philosophical than psychoanalytic. Though Bose claims to be motivated by psychological curiosity rather than religious faith (Bose, 1931: 15) in many places psychology enters the interpretation inadvertently and, one might say, diffidently. Was Sarvilaka's interpretation of the Gita correct? Did Gita permit him the interpretation he offered? And if he was wrong, on what grounds was his interpretation flawed? What were the real meanings of the *slokas* Sarvilaka cited? Bose interprets the Gita to respond to these questions.[1] In a society where texts survive as living texts mainly through interpretations and re-interpretations, Bose could create a space for his new science of interpretation only by enunciating and demonstrating its principles. Yet, he ventures his interpretation of Gita without a single open reference to any psychoanalytic concept.

To find out how Bose relates his interpretation to his own theories of consciousness, especially psychoanalysis, we shall therefore have to go to some of his other writings. Before we do that, however, we should know the broad outlines of the personal and social background he brought into psychoanalysis. For we must remember that while the story of Sarvilaka affirms the emergence of a new exegetic voice, that of an Indian psychoanalyst, it also enforces on Bose strange silences. It remains unexplained why Bose has nothing to say about the passive resolution of the Oedipal encounter that takes place in the story, or about the inverted relationship between a weak son personifying his father's manifest moral self and a powerful father personifying moral seduction and the amoral rationality latent in the son. Was Bose's psychoanalysis a defiance of the son's weak defiance of a strong, amoral authority? Did that defiance of defiance make Bose's cognitive venture an ethical statement? Why Bose refuses to consider the possibility that Sarvilaka's secret self, the one that his son finally owns up to, represents the unmediated primitive impulses of the kind that psychoanalysis subsumes under the category of the id? Is it because there is in Sarvilaka a complex structure of rationalization, including an element of controlled, dispassionate violence, that defies the conventional definition of the id and the primary processes?

Nor does Bose explain why his partiality for Pundarika's early Oedipal dissent is justified not in the language of the ego but that of the super-ego, whereas Pundarika's moral seduction by Sarvilaka is cast not in the language of the super-ego but that of the ego. It was as if the triumph of the therapeutic in South Asia heralded not so much a new bridgehead of the ego in the realm of the id, but an empowerment of the super-ego through an abridgement of the sphere of the unencumbered, psychopathic ego. The rest of this essay can be read as an attempt to work out the full implications of these abstract and somewhat opaque formulations.

The Rediscovery

Girindrasekhar Bose was probably born on 30 January 1886, the youngest of four brothers and five sisters. Two details about his first years he often told his students and trainees with great relish. First, he was a breech baby. As he loved to put it, he was born feet first, holding his head high. He paid dearly for the privilege: the associated birth injury ensured that he had to live, throughout life, with one foot slightly shorter than the other. Second, he was breast-fed until he was five. Defying psychoanalytical wisdom, Bose claimed that the prolonged breast-feeding had not heightened his oral dependency needs, but contributed to his psychological well-being and optimism.

The Boses originally belonged to Nadia, West Bengal. Girindrasekhar's father Chandrasekhar had worked for an English landlord in his early life, but was a Diwan to the Maharaja of Darbhanga when his youngest son was born. As a result, the son ended up spending much of his formative years outside Bengal, in northern Bihar. Bihar survived in his memory and was to occasionally re-emerge as a symbol of folksy, pastoral wisdom, laced with wit, and as a part-comic counterpoint to the urbanity of the babus in his works of fantasy.

Chandrasekhar conformed to the Bengali urban élite's ideal of a rounded gentleman. He was known for his managerial efficiency, financial probity, and Vedantic scholarship. This public image did not go unrewarded. By the time he was in his middle years, the Boses were a rather successful Kayastha family—respected, prosperous, and committed to learning. Chandrasekhar himself, however, despite his obvious social status, was the target of some ambivalence among the local Brahmins for his attempts to break into traditional scholarship. Perhaps that explains why the family, though orthodox in its beliefs, kept the social company of the reformist Brahmos once they moved to Calcutta. Many actually mistook the Boses for Brahmos. That did not improve matters much: the Brahmos now began to make fun of the orthodox ways of the Boses, especially their faith in gurus, *Purohitas*, *kuladevatas*, *istadevis*, etc.

Chandrasekhar's first two wives had died young and childless. He had a daughter by his third wife but she, too, had died early. In his middle years he married for the fourth time—a young girl, twenty-two years younger than him, Laksmimani. She bore him all his nine children. If Chandrasekhar had scholarship, Laksmimani had imagination. Superbly well read, especially in the *puranas*, she was a poetess and retained a life-long interest in matters of mind. Between the two, they ensured for their children a potent intellectual atmosphere, enlivened by the stories and the idioms of India's two greatest epics, the Ramayana and the Mahabharata. Two of Girindrasekhar's brothers were to become writers, too, Sasidekhar and Rajsekhar. The latter turned out to be the most successful of the siblings. He became famous as a satirist, classical scholar, translator, grammarian, and, paradoxically but reflecting Chandrasekhar's range of interests, a practising applied chemist and industrial manager. He also became an early patron of the Indian Psychoanalytic Society: the first psychoanalytic clinic in South Asia, probably the first in the non-Western world, was established on a piece of land donated by him.

Rajsekhar also remained, with the many personality traits that he shared with his youngest brother, the closest to Girindrasekhar among the siblings. In Rajsekhar's literary works, there are clues to the style of self-articulation Girindrasekhar assumed in his scientific discourse. There is in them a similar mix of rigour, parsimony, and directness, on the one hand, and a dependence on the idiom of the epics and the philosophical visions of the classical Sanskritic heritage, on the other. Both brothers worked at the nearly unattainable—an austere, rationalistic discourse that would reflect the moral urgency and the poetry of the classics. Both, one suspects, were searching for culturally rooted moral codes appropriate for their times, outside the puritanical moralism of the reformist Brahmos and the defensiveness of the orthodox Hindus.

Few details are available on Girindrasekhar Bose's childhood. Though a psychoanalyst, he showed a South Asian reticence about his own personal life, born partly out of a sense of defensive privacy and partly out of a casual disregard for history. Even his own psychoanalytic comments on himself, of the kind I have mentioned at the beginning of this section, were off-the-cuff, capsuled, witty remarks. They were gulped as such by his students, trainees, and admirers. So much so that today, no enterprising clinician can easily produce a psychoanalytic case-history of the southern world's first psychoanalyst. The reader may have noticed that one cannot be absolutely certain even about the exact date of Bose's birth. By way of a life history, one is mainly left with the memories of a few surviving contemporaries and the biographical notes of some of his students and trainees, notably that of psychoanalyst Tarun Chandra Sinha, his closest associate (Sinha, 1954:

62–74). In addition, there are the outlines of Bose's educational career, which followed a course partly similar to that of his chosen guru, Sigmund Freud.

According to Sinha, Chandrasekhar was a 'true' father who exercised 'full authority and control' (1954: 62). He was a strict disciplinarian and a conservative who conformed to family traditions 'fairly rigidly' (1954: 62). Though Sinha hastens to add that Chandrasekhar was no autocrat, as if apprehensive that he was hinting at a classical Oedipal situation, something of the father's style rubbed off on the son. Girindrasekhar, it seems, was a domineering child who enjoyed exercising authority. This was probably tolerated by the family because the future psychoanalyst was not only slightly handicapped physically, but also had fragile health after he suffered from blood dysentery in the first year of his life. The little despot, we are told, went to school in a palanquin.

Girindrasekhar's early schooling was entirely in Darbhanga. As a result, for a long time he retained a good command over Hindi. He also acquired a good knowledge of Sanskrit from his school and his father, though Girindrasekhar would later claim inadequate knowledge of the language in a couple of his Bengali essays and take the help of traditional Sanskrit scholars in his scholarly work. (Perhaps he was in awe of Rajsekhar who, as an author, was to make superb use of his Hindi and Sanskrit.) We also know that Girindrasekhar was a handsome, self-confident child despite his physical handicap and, perhaps because of the handicap, protected by and close to his mother. The self-confidence might have helped him, basically a village boy brought up in a culture rather marginal to the world of the Bengali babus, when he later entered Calcutta's intellectual life.

In 1904, when still 17, Girindrasekhar was married off to Indumati, a girl of 10. They were to have two daughters, one born in 1908, the other four years later. From the beginning, it seems, Bose maintained a separation between his family life and his academic life. The former was private, the latter public. But for a few rare exceptions, Bose's students and trainees never had a glimpse into his family. Many of them never saw his wife or daughters even once. This may or may not have anything to do with his attitude to women. His brother and ego-ideal, Rajsekhar, was a bachelor; yet he maintained a similar, if not stricter, separation between the private and the public.

After completing his schooling, Girindrasekhar went to Calcutta and joined Presidency College, the city's premier educational institute and its main intellectual hub. Bose chose to study chemistry, a discipline that became Rajsekhar's vocation. From there Girindrasekhar graduated in 1905, and joined the Medical College, Calcutta. At about this time his father retired and the family moved to Calcutta, more or less winding up their affairs in Bihar. They purchased a house in north Calcutta at 14 Parsibagan Street, and settled down there. The house was to become famous afterwards as the citadel of psychoanalysis in India. In 1910 Girindrasekhar got his medical degree and started private practice.

Bose's earliest passion was yoga and a focus of his scholarly curiosity in his teens was Patanjal's Yogasutra. Bose's nephew Bijayketu Bose, a psychoanalyst himself, believes that his uncle's fundamental search at this point of time was for supernatural or magical powers, *aloukika ksamata*.[2] Later on, when about 14, Bose developed a keen interest in magic and hypnotism. For all practical purposes, he could be called an amateur practising magician and hypnotist. This was not particularly uncommon in Calcutta at the time. Many middle-class Bengalis had begun to take an interest in these pursuits, perhaps attracted by their liminal stature. In Bose's case, following his nephew's account, there was also a direct continuity between the choice of magic as a vehicle of self-expression and the earlier search for magical powers.

Bose did make a success of his venture. When a medical student, he gave occasional public performances of magic, and even won a prize for writing an original article in a journal of magic. He went further with hypnosis. Encouraged by some of his teachers, he used hypnotic therapy with partial success in cases of insomnia, nausea in pregnancy, and, more dramatically, in an instance of cardiac asthma. This was while he was in his late teens (1902–7). When in 1909 Bose first learnt about psychoanalysis, he did not entirely give up on hypnotism in deference to the psychoanalytic belief in the absolute superiority of free association.[3] He retained, as a part of his analytic repertoire, hypnotic suggestion as an occasional therapeutic tool. He even made good use of the differences between two types of hypnosis: the father-type and the mother-type. One was more didactic; the other more persuasion-based.[4]

After taking his medical degree, Bose quickly established himself as a general practitioner. Within a decade, he was one of Calcutta's leading doctors, with a large private practice. When in 1926–7 he decided to restrict his general practice to concentrate on cases of mental illness, he was barely forty.[5]

Bose's fascination with Freud's new science began on the basis of casual acquaintance. Though he had heard of psychoanalysis as early as 1905–6, he first became interested in it in 1909, when only Brill's translation of a selection of Freud's papers was available in English. (Bose did not know any German then; be began to learn German in his middle years.) The preface to *Concept of Repression* suggests that, when he started psychoanalytical work, Bose had not even read Brill (Bose, 1921: pp. v–viii). The preface, in fact, reveals that some of the concepts Bose thought he had developed he found had already been developed by Freud. He was not defensive about the discovery; he accepted the superiority of the psychoanalytic concepts and began to use them in his work. He was actually better off in this respect than his more famous Tamil contemporary, the untutored mathematical genius Srinivasa Ramanujan (1887–1920). A huge majority of Ramanujan's discoveries were later found out to be rediscoveries. He had to be reconciled to being an immortal in the history of mathematics on the basis of the remainder.

Over the next five years, three more translations of Freud's books came out: *The Three Lectures on Sexuality* (1910), the lectures at Clark University in the United States, published as *Five Lectures on Psychoanalysis* (1910), and the *Interpretation of Dreams* (1913). By that time Bose was committed to the new science. One suspects from the sequence of events that the reasons for his decision to switch from conventional psychiatry were not purely intellectual, and that he gave his allegiance to Freud even before reading him systematically. Something in the framework and concerns of psychoanalysis had deeply touched the young Indian doctor. The strange, new-fangled ideas of the controversial Viennese physician had something to say about Bose's own world.

Bose's conversion did not mean much to his community. At the end of the first decade of the century few in India had heard of Freud. Rabindranath Tagore (1861–1940) recounts in a letter that the Bengali admirer of Freud, while speaking to Tagore about psychoanalysis, consistently pronounced Freud as if it rhymed with 'fruit'. Bose, however, found in Freud a kindred soul and saw immense possibilities in psychoanalysis. He quickly read up everything available on the subject and, on his own, began to apply the method in his psychiatric work. It seems he was satisfied with the results. At any rate, given his background and the intellectual position he had been moving towards before discovering psychoanalysis, he did not have to make too many modifications in his therapeutic style.

Bose's new passion heightened his curiosity about the discipline of psychology in general. From his early years, he had been an orderly person and, in many respects, a perfectionist. Once his interest in psychology was aroused, he began to feel handicapped by his sparse knowledge of abnormal psychology. What he knew was derived from the undergraduate courses in medicine he had attended. That knowledge was obviously geared to produce rounded general practitioners. It could not serve the purposes of one especially interested in the theory and practice of psychiatry.

So in 1915, when Calcutta University opened a new department of psychology, Bose enrolled as a student. He got his Master's degree in two years, once again doing well in the examinations. The same year he was appointed a lecturer in the department. One of the first things he did on his appointment was to make courses in psychoanalysis compulsory for all students of psychology, one of the first academic establishments to do so in the world (Hartnack, 1988: 85). He was now 31.

After four years, Bose completed a doctoral thesis which was published as *Concept of Repression* (Bose, 1921). Though fascinating in many ways, it is a clumsy work, made to look clumsier by Bose's cluttered English. One is sometimes surprised by the good reception it had. The thesis was reportedly dictated out to a stenographer in a week, in response to a bet taken with a fellow member of the Utkendra Samiti or Eccentric Club that Bose and some of his intellectual friends had founded at his Parsibagan residence. The friends had ragged him by claiming that his disregard for degrees and formal qualifications was a pose, meant to hide his incapacity to get a doctorate (Sinha, 1954: 64). Bose's dissertation was to remain the only doctoral dissertation in psychology completed at an Indian university during the 1920s, and this further underwrote the pre-eminence of psychoanalysis in Indian academic psychology. Perhaps in no other country was psychoanalysis to register such easy dominance as in India.

When his thesis was published, Girindrasekhar sent a copy of the book to Freud. It bore the inscription: 'from a warm admirer of your theory and science'. Freud was pleasantly surprised and wrote back almost immediately. The old dissenter was not used to easy acceptance; he was genuinely intrigued that in far off India psychoanalysis should have met with so much interest and recognition so early in its career. Thus began an intermittent correspondence between the two, lasting nearly two decades.[6] Bose was to never meet Freud. Going to the West for education and proper recognition of one's worth was popular among the Westernized élites of colonial India and this put Bose's back up. Despite a personal invitation from his guru, he refused to go abroad because that would be 'more of a fashion than need'.[7] There were also, according to Ernest Jones who invited Bose to Europe several times, Bose's numerous duties in India and 'perhaps a certain shyness' (Jones, 1954: 1).

In 1922, barely three years after the British Psychoanalytic Society was formed, Bose founded the Indian Psychoanalytic Society in Calcutta at his own residence. Of the fifteen founding members of the group, nine were college teachers of psychology and philosophy, five doctors, and one a business executive who also happened to be a generous patron of the Society. Thirteen of the fifteen members were Indians, twelve of them upper-caste Bengalis, and two were whites. The social origins of the thirteenth Indian member is not obvious from his name. Of the five doctors, two were British. One of the two was a relatively nondescript doctor in the colonial health service; the other was Owen A. R. Berkeley-Hill (1879–1944), also a member of the health service but already famous as the psychiatrist who had made the Ranchi Mental Hospital one of the best known in the East. Berkeley-Hill's name is inextricably linked with the history of modern psychiatry and psychoanalysis in India, and in many ways he epitomized some of the central problems in the culture of the two disciplines in South Asia. He was the first Westerner to attempt a psychoanalytic study of Hindu modal personality and the first Westerner to use psychoanalysis as a form of cultural critique in India. Probably a word on him will not be out of place as a counterpoint to Bose's philosophy of knowledge.

Berkeley-Hill was no ordinary migratory bird in India. The son of a wealthy and famous English physician, he was educated at Rugby, Gottingen, Nancy, and Oxford, from where he received his medical degree. Berkeley-Hill entered the Indian Medical Service in 1907 and, except for a four-year stretch during the First World War, spent the rest of his life in India. He lived in India, complaining all the while about the living conditions in the colony, and he married a Hindu, despite his preoccupation with the distorted personality and culture of the Hindus. The marriage and its Eurasian offspring were an almost sure indicator, during the period we are talking about, of both social defiance and uncertain social status among the whites in the colony. Neither the defiance nor the uncertainty were missing in Berkeley-Hill. Christine Hartnack points out that in Berkeley-Hill's autobiography, which includes open discussion of his pre-marital sex life and ends with 'a detailed description of the character and look of his horses, there is less mention of his wife than of [his] extra-marital affairs' (Hartnack, 1988: 28–9).[8]

Perhaps as a result of his liminal stature, Berkeley-Hill showed in many of his papers an aggressive psychoanalysism. And given his fractured self, simultaneously repelled and seduced by Victorian England and Brahminic India, this analysisism had to take a particular form. As befitted an Edwardian gentleman educated in an English public school and at Oxford, he showed a deep concern with the vicissitudes of anal eroticism and found in its patterning among the Hindus the clue to their cultural pathology and moral depravity. He had to pass a final judgement on their character, on behalf of all other cultures, in the following words.

It is not unlikely that the strange antipathy that is felt for the Hindus by most, if indeed not all, the races of the world is nothing more than an expression of an unconscious feeling of antagonism brought about by some of the peculiarities of the manifestations of anal eroticism as met with among the Hindus. It is certainly a fact that wherever the Hindu may go, no matter whether it be in Asia, Africa or Europe, he is to the inhabitants of that country a veritable Dr. Fell. We must therefore assume that this obscure but nevertheless very real dislike which is shared by all races of mankind for the Hindu, must, from its very nature, have its roots in some deeply buried source of feeling. Books on India teem with references to this singular 'otherness', if I may use the term, of the Hindu as compared, for instance, with the Muslim or Christian Indian (Berkeley-Hill, 1933: 75–112).

On the basis of the theoretical work of his mentor, Jones, Berkeley-Hill then goes on to identify, rather charmingly and with the full confidence of one advancing a dispassionate scientific thesis, the two ways anal eroticism may go (1933: 107). The valuable qualities thrown up by anal eroticism are 'individualism, determination, persistence, love of order and power of organisation, competency, reliability and thoroughness, generosity, the bent towards art and good taste, the capacity for unusual tenderness, and the general ability to deal with concrete objects of the material world' (1933: 108–9).

The despicable ones are the obverse of the above: 'incapacity for happiness, irritability and bad temper, hypochondria, miserliness, meanness and pettiness, slow-mindedness and proneness to bore, the bent for tyrannising and dictating and obstinacy.' Predictably, the Hindus suffered from a 'metapsychosis' featuring the second set of traits. On the other hand, 'the character traits of the English people as a whole belong for the greater part to the first of the two groups distinguished by Ernest Jones' (Berkeley-Hill, 1933: 111).

Berkeley-Hill, however, was not as one-sided as these extracts from his papers suggest or as Hartnack would have us believe. On occasion, his defiance overcame his social insecurities and he could be remarkably incisive in his cultural analysis. Nearly twenty-five years before novelist James Baldwin made such ideas a part of American folklore, Berkeley-Hill suggested that colour prejudice among the whites sprang from a deep fear of the perceived greater potency of the blacks and from the fear that the whites would lose their womenfolk to the blacks (Berkeley-Hill, 1923: 139–48).

The aggressive psychoanalysism was, however, the dominant tone. Like Kipling's imperialism, it reads today like an overdone gesture of allegiance by a man marginal to the culture of a ruling community, though at one time it must have read like a pungent exercise in social criticism and demystification. As if Berkeley-Hill, like Kipling, was fascinated and repelled by India at the same time, and the fascination was more painful to bear. It cut him off from his own kind and tainted him as culturally impure. His writings make it obvious that to him India was a living negation of the Victorian ideal of a moral self, and Indian culture a seductive presence that had to be fiercely repudiated.

This is understandable. For Berkeley-Hill to pursue the cultural-critical aspect of psychoanalysis to its logical conclusion would have meant taking a political position against a part of himself and against the social evolutionism that underpinned Victorian morality and sanctioned colonialism. He could not afford to own up to that responsibility. He had to defend himself by turning his new-found critical apparatus against the Indian culture itself, both with a vengeance and an immense effort of will, the way Kipling had earlier turned against that part of himself which constituted his Indianness.[9]

Berkeley-Hill had begun his personal analysis at London with the well-known Welsh psychoanalyst, Ernest Jones, and he probably completed his training with Bose at Calcutta. Along with his lesser-known compatriot Claud Dangar Daly, another erstwhile protégé of Jones and subsequently an analysand of Freud and Ferenczi, Berkeley-Hill defined for his generation of psychoanalysts the domain of psychoanalytic studies of modal personality or national character in India.[10] We have already told a part of that story. The political psychology of that pioneering effort—especially the links between psychoanalysis, colonialism, and the culture of science in the inter-war years—is neatly summed up in Christine Hartnack's verdict on the two British psychoanalysts. After analysing their works and interpretive styles, she concludes:

there is an unquestionable tendency in both writers to find in psychoanalysis a new scientific tool for getting a grip on problems of public order that were getting out of control . . . This explicitly political appropriation of psychoanalytic theory . . . co-incided in the 'twenties and 'thirties with the first successes of the newly formed Indian independence movement. In line with European thought at the time, Berkeley-Hill and Daly conceptualized a moral hierarchy with white men at the top and dependent women, infants, so-called primitives, and neurotics at or near the bottom. (Hartnack, 1988: 5)

Thus,

Berkeley-Hill's and Daly's writings on Indians had in common that they . . . both failed to note any achievement or positive aspect of the Indian culture . . . Both men identified themselves fully with British colonialism. For them, Indians were a source of threat and had thus to be combatted, and resistance had to be smashed not only on a military but also on a cultural level. Unlike Orwell, who left colonial India in order not to cope with the dual identity of a colonial bureaucrat by day and a questioning and critical human being by night, Daly and Berkeley-Hill worked to . . . contribute to a properly functioning colonial world.

Contemporary psychoanalytical thought offered them models to legitimize their . . . separation from Indians. If one was not a British (i.e. Christian) adult healthy male, one was in trouble . . . Victorian women, Anglo-Indians, Irish, Moslems, Children, sick and old people could to some extent still be accepted, as there were some common denominators between them and the British ideal. But women who did not obey the Victorian mores, mentally disturbed British subjects, Hindus and people of colour . . . were not only perceived as entirely different and thus inferior, but were also considered to be dangerous. They were not only in the majority, but there was the potential hysteria, violence, revolution, sexual seduction and other supposedly irrational acts, which would be difficult to control. Therefore, it was the 'white man's burden' to keep them under surveillance. (Hartnack, 1988: 73)

One should not be too harsh on the two well-meaning, simple-hearted practitioners of the young science of psychoanalytic psychiatry when the dominant culture of the now fully grown science has not done much better and when all around them the two could find even Indians lovingly embracing the same overall perspective. It is fairly obvious that both the British psychoanalysts were strictly allegiant to a transfer-of-technology model that had already become popular in the Indian scene and would remain paramount in Indian intellectual life even four decades after formal decolonization. Berkeley-Hill and Daly, like many before them and after, saw psychoanalysis as a state-of-the-art therapeutic device and hoped to introduce it with minor modifications into India as a partial cure for the worst affliction the Indians suffered from—Indianness. The exclusive universality imputed to most systems of modern scientific knowledge was a function, then as now, of the political privileges such a transfer created for specific individuals and groups.

With hindsight, is it fair to ask if the early Indian analysts were adequately aware that they were caught in a colonial grid of knowledge? Did they sense that analytic responsibility in the hot and dusty tropics had to own up to a new political responsibility? They did not and they did.

Manifestly, they did not react at all to the colonial psychology of Berkeley-Hill and Daly. To the first generation of Indian psychoanalysts, such politically loaded cultural interpretations were not uncommon and they blended with the dominant tone of the humanities and social sciences in the Indian universities. Berkeley-Hill and Daly must not have looked particularly vicious or scathing compared with many others. Also, the Indians attracted to analysis were themselves searching for new modes of social criticism that would make sense to their community; they were themselves given to provocative and arrogant psychoanalytic summary trials of Indian culture and personality. To them their British colleagues might have looked like two slightly over-enthusiastic white associates of Bose having their fling at psychoanalysis *vis-à-vis* Indian culture. After all, their formal status was high but not formidable in Bose's circle.

But psychoanalysts, too, have their unconscious. During the early years of the Indian Psychoanalytic Society, one member of the society did an imaginary portrait of Freud, for the artist had neither seen the master nor any photograph of his. This portrait, a near-perfect test of projection, was, appropriately enough, gifted to Freud. Freud was pleased, but complained in a letter that he looked a perfect Englishman in the portrait.[11] No one pointed out to the ageing patriarch the analytic implications of his casual remark and the political tragedy that lay inarticulate in it.

Some questions, however, still remain unanswered. Were Berkeley-Hill and Daly merely tropical extensions of the arrogantly international, universal culture of knowledge of which psychoanalysis was trying to be a part? Or were they adapting to the stress induced by the colonial situation with help of the existing psychoanalytic categories and by seeking sanction from the acceptance of psychoanalysis by some 'learned Hindus', as Freud described them (in his letter to Andreas Salome)? Were the attempts by Bose to locate psychoanalysis in the Vedantic tradition and give it a distinct non-progressivist language an unintended response to the colonial psychoanalysis of the two white colleagues and the social evolutionism implicit in the dominant culture of psychoanalysis?[12] Is it coincidental that some methodological comments in his *Purana Pravesa* read like a direct response to Berkeley-

Hill's interpretive style? Was it significant that both the British psychoanalysts in India had a record of mental illness and therapy under Jones? Were they both infected with the hard-boiled social evolutionism and positivism of Jones and the 'imperious', 'opinionated', and 'spiteful' aspects of his self? (Roazen, 1976: 345–6) Did they pick up from Jones his fear of ideas, metaphysics, and, above all, the fear of a reading of psychoanalysis that would allow one to turn the discipline upon itself? Or was the problem deeper, stemming from Freud himself? I shall attempt an indirect answer to a few of these questions later in this essay.

Berkeley-Hill and Daly did not entirely define the culture of psychoanalysis in India. Other psychoanalysts were also to leave their mark on the history of psychiatry and psychology in India, though in different ways. Tarun Chandra Sinha was one of the pioneers of psychoanalytic anthropology in India; Harpada Maiti and Pars Ram were to be associated with the founding of major institutions of psychoanalysis and psychology at Patna, Ahmedabad, and Lahore; Bhupen Desai contributed handsomely to the growth of psychoanalysis in Bombay; Suhrit C. Mitra and S. K. Bose became central to the growth of professional psychology in the country. Two of the most important pioneering figures in the Indian social sciences and humanities were also in the psychoanalytic movement: Nirmal Kumar Bose, in later life the doyen of social anthropology in the country, and Debiprasad Chattopadhyay, who was to make signal contributions to the philosophy and history of science in India. Others like Rangin Halder and Sarasilal Sarkar made vital contributions to the cultural life of the Bengalis. Many of them were not merely Bose's students but carried the imprint of his intellectual and clinical concerns in their work, including some of the limitations of Bose's distinctive style of psychoanalysis. Of his students and trainees, the allegiance of Sinha was to prove particularly dynamic organizationally. Sinha himself had had psychological problems and had been Bose's analysand. He used his therapeutic experience creatively to become a talented psychoanalyst and a gifted institution-builder. He gave psychoanalysis a continuing presence in Bengali social life after Bose's death.

Through Freud and Ernest Jones, then the president of the International Psychoanalytic Association, the Indian Society soon became affiliated to the international brotherhood of psychoanalysis. And Bose joined two others, Freud himself and August Aichhorn, as one of only three psychoanalysts ever to be recognized as psychoanalysts, on the basis of his self-analyses. Bose remained the president of the Indian Psychoanalytic Society until his death in 1953.

It is not easy to pass judgement on Bose as the founding father of the Indian Psychoanalytic Society. One obtains diverse estimates of him as an ideologue, an organization man, and as a person. Some say he was indiscriminate in his admissions policy and too eager to spread psychoanalysis to all corners of India. Others point out that in reality he never had that many trainees and many dropped out in any case. Of two things one can be more certain.

First, the formal requirements of psychoanalysis were often diluted for organizational and logistic reasons in India, resulting in the technical aspects of psychoanalysis remaining under-developed. This may not have been entirely a tragedy. The underemphasis on technique allowed psycho-analysis to retain the potentiality, never realized, of becoming some-thing more than an Indian subsidiary of a multinational professional corporation.

Second, as a pioneer in matters of mind and as an organizational inno-vator, Bose showed remarkable ideological tolerance. He was an easy person and, according to one of his students, a self-contained man of knowledge. It is doubtful if he saw psychoanalysis as an ideological move-ment, with a core of inviolable dogma. He used to say, an associate remembers, that psychoanalysis was a medical system like ayurveda or homeopathy; it worked with some people, while other systems worked better with others. Others mention that Bose never pushed psychoanalysis with his students of psychology, nor did he push his own psychological theories with his analytic trainees or colleagues.

This non-ideological stance was mirrored in Bose's politics, or anti-politics. Psychoanalysis became established in India at politically tumultu-ous times, when Gandhi was emerging as the new leader of the anti-imperialist movement, displacing both the moderate and extremist leaders. Among those being threatened by such displacement and facing political demise were the entire old leadership of Bengal, with their base mainly among the Hindu middle classes and the cities. Before their very eyes politics was becoming mass politics, bypassing them to reach into India's sleepy villages. Even in the metropolitan cities, the political atmos-phere was no longer what it had been only five years earlier. Though there is controversy among those who knew Bose about his response to Gandhi, he probably did believe that Gandhi represented the 'well-sublimated', rational, healthy personality.[13] Otherwise, but for a vague patriotism, Bose remained quite apolitical throughout life. Even that patriotism was, accord-ing to some, methodologically open. He was never particularly enamoured of political movements or the nitty-gritty of politics.

This apolitical attitude might have under-written the low salience of the cultural-critical aspects of the new science in India, but it allowed Bose to hold the loyalty of a wide variety of young enthusiasts holding diverse ideological positions. These ranged from India Sen, one of the first transpersonal psychologists of our times and later on a prominent mystic at the Pondicherry Ashram, to Debiprasad Chattopadhyay, then a budding radical philosopher of science, as well as a practising psychoanalyst. The latter, however, did have to bear Bose's aggressive interpretation of the

Oedipal roots of Marxism.[14] Bose's belief that psychoanalysis was primarily a method probably helped him to be ideologically open. He expected a method to have limitations and be controversial. (Apparently, the Indian Psychoanalytic Society failed to retain its intellectual catholicity after Bose's death. Chattopadhyay was excommunicated soon after his mentor died. His Bengali book *Freud Prasange*, an early Marxist interpretation influenced by the likes of John Somerville and Joseph Needham, was considered to be too critical of Freud, though it was certainly less so than many works produced by the pillars of the psychoanalytic establishment. *Freud Prasange* paid handsome tributes to Freud's method and accepted it fully but faulted the master on his philosophical assumptions. That did not help Chattopadhyay: he was expelled all the same. Apparently, there was a stylistic similarity between the psychoanalytic movements in India and the West. Both shared the same internal contradiction when it came to dissent—limited theoretical tolerance but unlimited organizational intolerance.)

It also says something about Bose's organizational skills that, unlike its Western counterparts, the Indian Psychoanalytic Society quickly acquired a sound financial base. In fact, once when the parent body was in financial trouble, the Indian branch sent it some money as a contribution. It is not known how his friend Berkeley-Hill reacted to such evidence of Bose's organizational ability, whether he attributed the trait to Bose's deviation from Hindu culture through self-analysis or to the persistence in him of the Hindu anal-erotic style.

Bose himself, however, changed in the process of becoming a psychoanalyst and institutionalizing the new discipline, at least according to his wife. From an 'energetic' and 'jolly' person he became a 'thoughtful' one (Sinha, 1954: 68). He also, it appears, began to keep separate his styles of management of the Indian Psychoanalytic Society and the Department of Applied Psychology at Calcutta University, which he headed after its establishment in 1937. While in the Society he was easy and egalitarian; in the university he was more paternalistic, socially withdrawn, and unwilling to share power. When Sinha says in his biographical note that some considered Bose to be money-minded, devoid of human touch, and mechanical, he was probably speaking of Bose in the University setting. Some who knew him in the University compare him in this respect with his friends J. C. Bose, whom we have already mentioned, and P. C. Mahalanobis (1893–1972), a pioneer of modern statistics and development planning.

However, it was not so much the Society or the Department which ensured the early success of psychoanalysis in the metropolitan culture of India. It was the personal intellectual presence of Bose and, later, that of some of his talented students and admirers such as Tarun Chandra Sinha, Harpada Maiti, Pars Ram, Rangin Halder, Indra Sen, and others. Bose's own intellectual range was formidable. He was a man of many parts—

chemist, Sanskritist, historian of ideas, experimental psychologist, doctor, teacher, artist, translator, and litterateur. In addition, he wrote scholarly commentaries on sacred texts and was the author of a highly popular children's tale, *Lal Kalo*, which included some lively, witty poems and a drawing that would have done justice to a Gothic horror story (Bose, 1956). His very personality attracted some of the better young minds of metropolitan India. (Bose had a ready Freudian explanation of the careerism which did not allow the brightest of Bengali youth, with a few exceptions, to come to psychoanalysis.)

This intellectual presence was underscored when the Indian Psychoanalytic Society belatedly brought out its journal, *Samiksha*, in 1947. The journal was an immediate success and its early days were to be the final golden years of Indian psychoanalysis. Apart from the Indians, the contributors included Geiza Roheim, David Rapaport, Clara Thompson, George Devereaux, Edmund Bergler, K. R. Eissler, Jules Masserman, and Fritz Wittels. Moving evidence of how seriously the journal was taken is a contribution by one James Clark Moloney, who wrote from aboard a warship approaching Okinawa before one of the climactic battles of World War II (Moloney, 1949: 104–24).

Bose was a gifted therapist, too. Some of the cures he affected were nothing less than spectacular. His writings give the impression that he was overly didactic, in the sense in which the same expression is used by some of the erstwhile colleagues of Erich Fromm to describe Fromm's therapeutic style. Such directness is said to have been not entirely alien to Freud's own therapeutic style, either (Jahoda, 1977: 10). It has also been said that Bose reinvoked the *guru–sisya* relationship in his analytic encounters (Kakar, 1990: 427–45).[15] Perhaps he did. But the result of the mix was Bose's dramatic therapeutic successes. As a result, by the time he was in his late 40s, he had already entered the imagination of the urban Indians as a legendary doctor of the mind.

This directness, however, also introduced into Indian psychoanalysis a theoretical twist. Therapy was viewed primarily as a cognitive venture, involving the acquisition of knowledge or information, and secondarily as a matter of rearrangement or reinterpretation of emotions. His success as a therapist suggests that he may have deviated from this view in practice, but the view did have an influence and, according to some, lowered the standard of analytic training in India.

As a person, Bose was, like many successful clinicians, a bundle of contradictions. As many of those who knew him well belong to the fraternity of psychoanalysts, he also comes across as a repositary of neurotic symptoms. A few remember his pronounced orality—his love for food, culinary art, and the spoken word; his language skills; and his emphasis on the core fantasy of the split mother, what Sudhir Kakar calls the 'hegemonic myth' of the Indian culture. A few others remember Bose's long struggle with the hypertension that finally killed him. (The concern with the fantasy of the split mother has proved particularly resilient. From Berkeley-Hill, Claud Dargar Daly, Philip Spratt, and G. Morris Carstairs, to John Hitchcock, Leigh Mintern, Monisha Roy, Susan Wadley, Sudhir Kakar, and Alan Roland—a wide range of social scientists influenced by psycho-analysis, including this writer, have returned to the myth with the feeling of making a new and important discovery (Berkeley-Hill, 1923; Daly, 1947: 191–6; Spratt, 1966; Carstairs, 1957; Hitchcock and Mintern, 1963: 203–361; Roy, 1975; Wadley, 1975; Kakar, 1979; Roland, 1988; Nandy, 1980a and 1980b). They have been strengthened in their belief by a galaxy of Indian writers and artists, myth-makers in general, who have regularly reinvoked the fantasy of a partitioned mother in their creative works and autobiographies.)

Most remember Bose's obsessive-compulsive ways—the meticulous records, the orderly minutes, the spotlessly white, immaculately starched, Bengali dress that was virtually his uniform, the frugality and—as with many nineteenth-century Indians being exposed to the Western concept of time for the first time and seeking to over-correct for the perceived Indian emphasis on 'timelessness'—the fanatic devotion to timeliness. His order-liness extended even to his taste in North Indian classical music. He liked *dhrupada* with its austere, orderly, rigid frame and not the flamboyant *kheyal* with its greater emphasis on fluidity and the imagination (Sinha, 1954: 68–9). As he once bluntly told his trainee Desai, 'I am obsessive-compulsive.'

Whether the orderliness interfered with his own creativity or not, he retained a sharp sensitivity throughout life to the obsessive-compulsive traits of his students and analysands. Remarkable stories are told about how he would keep his desk scattered with coins and draw diagnostic con-clusions from the way some of his visitors handled them. Indian psycho-analysis inherited this sensitivity; some of the most fascinating works on individual cases and cultural patterns in India centre around the analysis of the same psychopathology.

Others have livelier memories. Debiprasad Chattopadhyay remembers Bose even washing with an antiseptic lotion the goat which was eaten on the occasion of his daughter's marriage. Charuchandra Bhattacharya remem-bers how he went, armed with a stop-watch, from Bose's home to the Howrah railway station on two subsequent days, once without and once with luggage, as a rehearsal for Bose's planned train journey the following day. Desai remembers Bose once saying that, for his holidays at Deoghar in Bihar, he pre-calculated all possible expenses, including that on the wear and tear of his car tyres. Many speak of the twelve goats that Bose pur-chased for Vijayketu's marriage and had gram-fed for the improvement of the quality of their meat. Though he planned the marriage and the marriage reception with meticulous care, he could not attend the actual ceremony.

He had to go to bed at his usual hour, exactly at 8 pm. All this contributed to Bose's mythical stature.

There might have been a weightier reason, too, for the emergence of Bose as an important cultural figure in Bengal. Bose turned to psychoanalysis at a time when the traditional relationships that took care of most of the everyday problems of living—the neuroses and the less acute forms of psychosis—were breaking down in urban India. The place of these relationships and the world-view that informed them was being occupied by a new network of social relationships sanctioning a new set of 'superstitions'— constructions of mental illness derived from remnants of the traditional ideas of lunacy and available scraps of modern psychiatric knowledge. The first victims of this change were the psychologically afflicted: they were no longer seen as aberrant individuals deserving in their own right a place within the family and the community, but as diseased and potentially dangerous waste products of the society. As Bijayketu Bose puts it, the shock-absorbing capacities of the society had declined considerably at the time. And as a Michel Foucault or a Ronald Laing might have said, the dialogue between sanity and insanity had broken down; the society was now dominated by a monologue of sanity.

Girindrasekhar Bose took it upon himself to attack these perceptions and to offer the mentally ill a more humane treatment and voice. In 1933 he established India's first psychiatric out-patient clinic in Calcutta's Carmichael Medical College and hospital and research centre at Calcutta's Lumbini Park. In 1949 Bose founded a school for small children organized along psychoanalytic lines.

A word on the early impact of psychoanalysis on urban India, in contrast to that on Europe and North America, may be appropriate at this point. Freud's explosive emergence in the European intellectual scene had shaken up the Victorian world image. That image, as Carl Jung often pointed out, was not merely a feature of the Anglo-Saxon societies but of much of Protestant Europe, though in the continent 'it never received such an appropriate epithet'. Along with that image went a concept of bourgeois respectability, built on the attempts to keep artificially alive through repression a set of anaemic ideals. These ideals were, Jung felt, the remnants of the collective ideals of the Middle Ages, badly damaged by the French Enlightenment (Jung, 1973: 49–50).

When Freud challenged this respectability, he seemed to flout the basic tenets of social decency and challenge that moral universe of nineteenth-century Europe that framed and stabilized the everyday culture after the disruptions and uprooting brought about by the Industrial Revolution. In this stabilization, along with the concepts of nation-state and progress, a central role had been played by the concept of scientific rationality, viewed as a tool of knowledge and power but serving as a moral fulcrum. The concept might have been thrown up by the Enlightenment but ensured now, independently, a certain moral continuity and social sanction. By invoking this concept of rationality, Freud sought to legitimize a new concept of self that would accommodate a rediscovered, previously disowned underside of the self—a 'more real self' operating according to principles the 'apparent self' knew nothing about or rejected as immoral.[16] The Victorians could neither ignore him nor gulp him.

Freud's ideas were much less controversial in India. He might have seen himself as one of those who had disturbed the sleep of the world, but he did not disturb many Indians even in their waking hours. Only small sections of the Indian middle classes had deeply internalized the Victorian moral codes. Even fewer were exposed to the Victorian social norms relating to sexuality. Among them, objections to psychoanalysis were often strong and impassioned. Many of them saw Bose's love for psychoanalysis as moral betrayal and the content of psychoanalysis as dirty. (For instance, one well-known Bengali writer, Saradindu Bandopadhyaya, in one of his plays compared the Freudian with a pig enjoying itself in a sewer. And a Marxist outfit named after Ivan Pavlov kept up the barrage until the late 1950s by rejecting psychoanalysis as bourgeois and pornographic.) Otherwise, the Indian academics did not find Freud's ideas particularly wicked. Psychoanalysis might not have made much headway in India as a discipline, but the opposition to it could hardly be called frenzied. Most Indians, perhaps even most Indian psychoanalysts, would have been perplexed by Freud's famous statement to Jung as their ship approached the New York Harbour *en route* for Clark University in 1909, 'They don't realize we're bringing them the plague' (Kirsner, 1990: 197). Why this nonchalance?

The easy answer is that there were both a casual unconcern with the content of the discipline and a widely felt need for an updated, reasonably holistic theory of mental illness in urban India. The need was strong enough for many to ignore the actual content of psychoanalysis. While this might have been on the whole true, there can be a less pleasant answer, too. The bourgeois respectability that Freud attacked and which paradoxically defined him—the way industrial capitalism defines trade-unionism—came to India as part of the colonial cultural baggage, intertwined with other forms of respectability. But these other forms—colonialism itself, secularization, scientism, and impersonalization of social relationships are four examples that immediately spring to mind—were rarely the targets of the social criticism psychoanalysis offered in the southern world. As a result, psychoanalysis was bound to come to look like another tame professional enterprise, another of those many new sciences being imported by Westernized Indians, rather than critical, subversive presence. For a discipline that was a double-edged weapon—a means of exploring the human mind and a means of avoiding such exploration—this could not but lead to loss of selfhood. Let me spell out the first, and easier, answer here because it relates directly to Bose's life. I shall return to the second answer in the last section of the essay.

It was from Bengal that the British Empire had started expanding after the Battle of Plassey in 1757. It was the region where colonial intrusion was the deepest and the most disruptive in South Asia. Calcutta was not only the capital of British India, it was the second largest city in the Empire and probably the liveliest market-place of ideas from the East and the West in the world. Already some of the modern institutions—such as Western education and law—had entered the interstices of Bengali society and created a burgeoning, Westernized, middle class that sustained a variety of cultural forms, neither exclusively Western nor Indian. From theatre to food, from family dynamics to sports, and from dress to style of scholarship, every area of middle-class life in Bengal carried the imprint of the West and showed its mixed cultural parentage.

Living in two worlds is never easy, and the new middle class in Bengal had lived, for decades, with deculturation, break-down of older social ties, and disruption of traditional morality. In response to these, the class had even produced a series of highly creative social thinkers and reformers who sought to design new world-views and new moral visions for their fellow Indians.

As it happened, none of these reformers had directly attacked the psychological problems that were being thrown up as by-products of the break-down of social ties and uprooting. Modern Bengal was waiting for someone to explain or give a meaning to the psychological forces by which it was being buffeted. Not through literature, social analysis, or theology, in all of which some of the great Bengalis had tried their hands, but through an open-ended yet systematic theory of personality and selfhood. Bengal, and for that matter urban India, already had at least the rudiments of new social and political theories and theologies to cope with the new problems of an old civilization, but it did not have a new theory of consciousness, a new psychology—a culturally rooted, yet contemporary and self-assured theory of individuality and subjectivity—to go with them.

This was the need Bose was trying to meet with the help of psychoanalysis. There might also have been a vague awareness in him that the sectoral, one-dimensional approaches of the various schools of conventional academic psychology could not really grapple with the psychological problems of Indian society or establish durable links with Indian traditions. Psychoanalysis with its complex, holistic approach to human personality—with its invocation of the person as a thinking, feeling, driven individual—at least allowed one to reinterpret its interpretations and to adapt them to the complexities of Indian society. To turn the discipline on itself, psychoanalysis could allow itself to be used as a projective medium for parts of Indian society, while being simultaneously used as a critique of that society.

It was this potential of the young discipline that Bose exploited, and that gave the discipline its early start in India. Even Freud, no stranger to theoretical speculations, was impressed by the vivacity and intellectual power of the first Indian psychoanalyst and recognized the Indian's philosophical acumen. On receiving *Concept of Repression*, he wrote,

It was a great and pleasant surprise that the first book on a psychoanalytic subject which came to us from that part of the world should display so good a knowledge of psychoanalysis, so deep an insight into its difficulties and so much deep going original thought . . . [the author] is aiming at a philosophical evolution . . . of our crude, practical concepts, and I can only wish psychoanalysis should soon reach upto the level to which he [Bose] strives to raise it. (Freud, 1956: 108)

Of course, there was a touch of politics in the enthusiasm of Freud and, later, Ernest Jones, who reviewed Bose's book in the *International Journal of Psychoanalysis* (Jones, 1921: 453). Both were happy to see psychoanalysis spread to India while it was still beleagured in Europe and North America. Hence also Freud's emphasis, in a letter to Lous Andreas-Salome, on the fact that most members of the newly founded Indian Psychoanalytic Society were 'learned Hindus', not white expatriates or semi-literate native dilettantes (Freud, 1972: 1). Its cultivated Indian converts gave psychoanalysis, apart from ethnic colour, a look of cross-cultural validity.

However, there might also have been in such estimates of Freud and Jones a mix of awe and ambivalence that Bose spanned so effortlessly the worlds of psychoanalysis, philosophy, and cultural traditions. Certainly Jones, nurtured in an atmosphere of heady, Anglo-Saxon positivism, might have found Bose's speculative bent of mind a bit of a trial. He needed, by his own admission, 'the sense of security which the pursuit of truth gives'— in this instance, the certitudes produced by science—and he lived in an intellectual atmosphere in which Bertrand Russell was to soon call J. B. Watson the greatest scientist after Aristotle and compare the ultra-behaviourist with Charles Darwin.[17] For Jones, as for James Strachey, even Freud's cultural origins were an 'eccentricity' rather than a 'living factor in his life' and all religions were superstitions (Roazen, 1976: 347). But then, Jones also had a more mundane reason to tolerate Bose's flirtation with philosophy. In another few years, he would want to make the British Society the psychoanalytic regulating body for the British Empire, with the societies in the colonies as subordinate groups. The support of someone like Bose in this venture might have been seen as vital (Roazen, 1976: 346).

Freud, on the other hand, was brought up in an intellectual culture in which the pedagogic split between philosophy and science had not ossified. It was typical of the 'temperamental differences' between Jones and Freud, Roazen says, 'that whereas the former feared religion's anti-naturalism, the latter was more afraid of the dangers of medicine's scientific materialism'.[18] Freud could not but be intrigued by Bose's daring. Though he claimed to avoid philosophy, Freud was always impressed by it; it was with some difficulty that he kept his interest in metapsychology in check.[19]

Neither this support from Freud nor its precocious growth and cultural distinctiveness saved Indian psychoanalysis from exhaustion within a few decades. So much so that Alan Roland has recently asked in surprise: 'Why psychoanalysis developed so early in India, and why it has not grown there as it has, for instance, in America or even France since the late 1960s?' (Roland, 1988: 57).

Roland gives the answer on two levels. He notes the ease with which a theory of the unconscious can be integrated within a culture demanding 'extraordinary interpersonal sensitivity' from those living in extended families and other traditional groupings as well as the 'highly particularistic emphasis on a person's development through the combination of their qualities (*gunas*), powers (*sakti*), effects of familial and individual actions (*karma*), and attachments (*samskaras*) carried over from past lives' (1988: 57). Roland's answer to the second part of the question is sociocultural and it supplements what has already been said about the noncontroversial impact of psychoanalysis in Indian society. Comparing India with the Western developed societies, Roland speaks of the 'deconversion' that has taken place from the belief systems and symbols of the traditional communities in the West and of the basic shift to a culturally less integrated society that shares only the symbols of science and where each individual must create his world-view of symbols and meaning (Roland, 1988: 58). The person has been thrown back, as it were, upon him or herself in the West, not in India.

In other words, the factors which gave vibrancy to psychoanalysis in its early years in India may also have handicapped it as a profession. The individuation that has taken place in the West remains in India the characteristic of a small segment of the society. In such circumstances psychoanalysis as a therapeutic technique has to remain a matter of cognitive choice; it cannot resonate with the private search for self-definition or a theory of life for a majority of Indians. In a paper on the early years of psychoanalysis, Kakar says,

Cut off from the thrust and parry of debate, controversy and ferment of the psychoanalytic centres in Europe, dependent upon not easily available books and journals for outside intellectual sustenance, Indian psychoanalysis was nurtured through its infancy primarily by the enthusiasm and intellectual passion of its progenitor. (Kakar, 1990)

It probably was. Probably, for the same reason, psychoanalysis in India never grew spectacularly as a clinical discipline. In a culture in which complex, often ornate, theories of consciousness of both right- and left-handed kinds were an important component, neither did psychoanalysis have enough philosophical punch as a theory of the person threatening to supersede all other theories of the person, nor did it carry a strong enough impress of the evil and the smutty, in a society that treated the *Kamasutra* as a sacred text, to become the subject of a highly charged ethical debate on the nature of the human mind. Psychoanalysis rather quietly became the best-known school of Western psychology in India, controversial but not particularly live politically.

Christiane Hartnack says that 'the reception of psychoanalysis in British India varied from outright rejections of Freud's concepts as inappropriate for Indian conditions to unquestioned transfers.' (Hartnack, 1988: 151). Actually, the 'outright rejections' here means in most cases nothing more dramatic than a certain unconcern. Only a few pages after she has talked of such rejections, Hartnack herself shows surprise at the public response to Rangin Halder's paper on the Oedipus complex in Rabindranath Tagore's poetry: 'Halder's attempt to demystify the writings of this celebrity, the first Indian Nobel prize winner, who was seen as a kind of national hero in his country, do not seem to have caused any negative reaction from the Bengali side' (Hartnack, 1988: 161–2). So much so that Halder presented the same paper a few years afterwards to a wider audience at the Indian Science Congress—this time in English.

A partial explanation for such a state of affairs also lies in the public ignorance about Bose's world-view. It is doubtful whether Bose was known to the urban middle classes of India as a psychoanalyst, though that is usually what he called himself. Some knew him as such, but most Indians knew him as a doctor of the mind. They were relatively unconcerned, *udasina* is the expression Bijayketu uses, about psychoanalysis. Girindrasekhar himself, as we shall see below, may have been obsessive about many things, but not about the purity of psychoanalytic concepts, their philosophical roots in Western thought, or about the therapeutic tradition being built in Europe by the Freudian movement. Nor did he heavily stress the uniqueness of psychoanalysis as a particular school of psychology.

Was psychoanalysis, then, merely an artefact in urban India's attempts to explore its own soul? Was it severely refracted through and, hence, incidental to Bose's personal quest for selfhood as a healer? That, too, is doubtful. It says something about the young science that Bose, already exposed to a wide range of Eastern and Western options—from Patanjal's Yogasutra to academic psychiatry to behaviourism and experimental psychology—preserved his fondest feelings for psychoanalysis and called himself a psychoanalyst. Somewhere, at some level, the young discipline's concerns and implicit social-critical thrust had crossed the boundaries of culture, though not in the sense in which its Viennese founder's Eurocentric world-view would have it.

On the other hand, one must hasten to add that Freud's Eurocentrism also had its in-built checks. The most conspicuous of them was his concern with the worldly welfare of his own brain-child, psychoanalysis. He did want the young discipline to cross cultural barriers and become a true international citizen. When faced with a choice, therefore, the old war-horse did try to create a space for Bose's concerns within the mainstream of psychoanalysis. But that in turn had its own limits.

After corresponding with Bose and confronting his publications . . . Freud could no longer easily defend his claims for the universality of his concepts. Confronted with Bose's deviant theory, Freud considered working aspects of Bose's concepts into his system. He evidently intended to functionalize Bose's contributions like some kind of intellectual raw material, and to incorporate them into his own theory, not realizing that these were based on an entirely different conceptual system. (Hartnack, 1988: 192)

PART TWO: THE MORALITY OF PSYCHOLOGY

The Relegitimation

The compliment from Freud notwithstanding, Bose's English papers on the range and concerns of psychology, especially psychoanalysis, lack something of the philosophical imagination and elegance of his Bengali papers on the same subject. The reasons for this are not clear. Bose did not deliberately keep double ledgers and use roughly the same set of concepts in both languages. Perhaps he was less at ease with English than with his native Bengali. Perhaps he felt more self-conscious and burdened by the presence of an international audience when he wrote in English. Thus, 'The Aim and Scope of Psychology' (1932) and 'A New Theory of Mental Life' (1933) are both competent and fresh, but one misses in them the touch of the theoretical daring born of cultural self-confidence that one finds in some of his Bengali papers (Bose, 1932: 11–29; 1933: 37–157).

Both papers introduce the reader to the broad disciplinary framework within which the first non-Western psychoanalyst worked and the cognitive map that marked out the boundaries of his in-depth psychology. 'The Aim and the Scope of Psychology' specifically seeks to create a legitimate place for psychology in the world of knowledge by anticipating and resisting attacks on the infant discipline on three fronts. First, the paper rejects as invalid the behaviourist approach in psychology, for behaviourists deny the existence of mind on the ground that mind cannot be perceived without the intervention of matter. Bose considers the denial analogous to a physicist's rejection of the existence of matter on the ground that matter cannot be 'seen' without the intervention of mind (Bose, 1932: 13). Second, the paper tries to reclaim from physiology the terrain which rightfully belongs to psychology. Bose rejects the attempts to reduce psychology to the functions of the brain and the nervous system; he shows that, using the same arguments, one could claim endocrinology to be a branch of psychology. If changes in psychological states follow changes in the brain, glandular changes also follow from psychological changes. The paper does not obviously suffer from the positivist modesty which sometimes afflicted Freud. It does not even hint that in some distant future psychology will in effect become a biology of mind (Bose, 1932: 14). Finally, the paper takes on 'the oldest claimant to the psychological terrain', philosophy. Here Bose is more tolerant, given his own bent of mind, and he makes his point with qualifications. 'I am quite willing to admit', he says, 'that philosophical studies afford an excellent discipline to the science students but I cannot understand why it should be tacked on to psychology alone and not to any other science such as physics' (1932: 16).

The second paper recapitulates Girindrasekhar's once-popular theory of pan-psychic psychophysical parallelism, first propounded in *Concept of Repression*. Now entirely forgotten, the theory at one time was taken seriously in many circles. It also subtly influenced the course of his friend Jagadis Chandra Bose's (1858–1937) vitalistic biophysics, which took the world of knowledge by storm in the inter-war years (see Nandy, 1980b: pt. 2). The theory has parallels with Freud's belief in his student days, that 'the physiological processes of the brain and the psychological processes of the mind were not parallel and causally linked but, rather, were identical. They were one and the same thing apprehended by the scientist in two different ways: through external observation in the natural sciences and through inner perception in psychological investigation.' (McGrath, 1986: 18). But even a sympathetic psychologist reading 'A New Theory' in the 1990s is unlikely to be terribly impressed. It is likely to interest only the historians of science. For though it is the handiwork of a psychologist well versed in and committed to the non-dualist Vedantic tradition, it can be read as making a systematic case for a dualist psychology rooted in the Vedanta. The dualism, however, is a qualified one; it is set within the frame of a non-dualist vision and idiom.

In sum, neither of the two papers reveals Bose's hand fully. But within that limit, both show that, unlike Freud and some of the early analysts, Bose made no attempt to underplay the philosophical and social meaning of the new science. Nor did he share Freud's belief that psychoanalytic theory 'would be overtaken within half a century by biochemical therapies' (Freud and Pfister, 1963; quoted in Jahoda, 1977: 10). Whatever else Bose was, he was not apologetic about the larger ambitions of his discipline. 'We can look forward to the day', he says grandly at the end of 'The Aim and Scope', 'when Psychology [note the capital] will establish itself as our guide, friend and philosopher in all human affairs, and will be looked upon as the greatest of sciences' (Bose, 1932: 29).

In Bengali, Girindrasekhar Bose wrote voluminously and with enormous intellectual energy. Most of these writings are now out of print and not easily available; some of his essays and important letters are lost. The most remarkable feature of his Bengali writings is that, though a psychoanalyst, Bose often wrote on the Indian sacred texts and epics surprisingly unencumbered by his disciplinary faith. Thus, his *Purana Pravesa*, a 300-page tome on Indian epics, is mainly a meticulous—some might say Teutonic—study of genealogy, a chronological dynastic history of the *puranas*, not a study of fantasies or defences (Bose, 1934). There are, however, in the book fascinating comments on the politics of scholarship and the responsibility it imposes on Indian commentators on the *puranas*. We shall have occasion to touch upon them later in this section. Similarly, there is the low-key presence of psychoanalysis in his commentary on the Gita, as we have already noted at the beginning of this paper. All this restraint obtains at a time when the analysis of myths and religious texts had already become, thanks to Freud himself and to younger psychoanalysts like Ernest Jones and Geiza Roheim, an important and fashionable part of psychoanalysis. And even in distant India some analysts had experimented with such interpretations.

However, Bose did write a few perceptive essays in Bengali which help link his reading of Indian culture with the Freudian theory of mental life. Unlike Berkeley-Hill and others who followed him, in these essays Bose does not use psychoanalysis solely to demystify Indian culture and everyday life or to bare the pathologies of Western middle-class culture in the colonies. He also uses Indian cultural categories to domesticate psychoanalysis for the Indians. From this point of view, his two most important papers are: 'Sattva, Rajah, Tamah' and 'Manuser Mana', both written in Bengali and published in 1930 (Bose, 1930a: 1–5; 1930b: 339–53). Some of the ideas in the essays were later included in his English works but never with the same degree of directness. The first essay offers an understanding and justification of psychological knowledge in native terms, leading up to the Freudian tenet that the ego should ultimately supplant or supersede the id. The second extends the argument further and defines psychology as a science of persons, a personology, as Henry A. Murray might have described the venture.

Both papers depend on Indian classical texts and on a particular reading of India's past. The second dependence has to be, however, gleaned from Bose's other Bengali writings. Thus, from *Purana Pravesa*, also written in 1933 though published the following year, we come to know of Bose's conviction that foreign—read Western—histories of India are bound to be partial. They just cannot be fair to Indian texts because they think of themselves as a superior race. To expect an impartial history of India from the *videsis* or foreigners is, Bose says, the same as expecting the British to protect the self-interest of the Indians in politics (1934: 212). Bose tries to correct for such racist interpretations by proposing that the *puranas* are supported both by reason and empirical data (1934: 1, 3), and that there is no need to study the history of these epics, for they themselves are the Indian equivalent of history (1934: 179).

Then, responding as it were to Berkeley-Hill, Bose mentions the two kinds of exaggerations in the *puranas* (*atiranjana*) and the exaggeration of the past achievements of their culture. As for the former, Bose believes that the stylized exaggerations of the *puranas* can be handled through *atiyukti vicara*, analysis of over-statement. It is a matter of appropriate and empathetic reading of texts. Bose's response to the second issue is more political. He traces the hostility of Western scholars to things Indian to two main reasons. First, the Indians, unlike the ancient Babylonians or Egyptians, have survived to flaunt their glorious past against their inglorious present status as colonial subjects (1934: 212–13). This cannot but irritate many Westerners. Second, the Western scholars project onto the Indian situation the enmity between the Church and the State in Europe. This makes them hostile to Hinduism and virulently anti-Brahminic. Under such circumstances, given that the organizing principle of Indian culture has always been religion, any serious consideration of India's past cultural achievements is bound to look like an exaggeration.

'Sattva, Rajah, Tamah' (1930*a*) discusses *gunas* (traits, attributes, or qualities) in *prakrti* or nature. The concept of *guna* is notoriously complicated and, some may say, slippery. The essay mentions in a footnote that even Max Muller found it difficult to understand the concept, but found the Indian philosophers so clear about it that they did not need any explanation (quoted in Bose, 1930*a*: 3). The essay proposes that these qualities are of two kinds. The first kind consists of qualities that control *ajnana* or the absence of knowledge (in a person) and *aprakasa* or the non-manifest (in nature). These controlling *gunas* are classified as *tamah*.

The second kind of *gunas* control *jnana* or knowledge (in human personality) and the manifest (in nature). These *gunas* can, in turn, be of two types: *bahirmukha*, literally outer-directed or extroverted, and *antarmukha*, inner-directed or introverted. The essay identifies the former as *rajah*; and the latter as *sattva* (Bose, 1930*a*: 3); this is illustrated in Table 1.

TABLE 1   The *Gunas* or attributes of nature

which controls knowledge (*jnana*) and the manifested (*prakasa*)		which controls ignorance (*ajnana*) and the non-manifested (*aprakasa*)
introvert (*sattva*)	extrovert (*raja*)	(*tama*)

It is not clear whether Bose borrows the second-order dichotomy—that between extroversion and introversion—from Carl Jung. Bose's paper was written in 1930, and Jung had published his work on personality types in 1923. The work should have reached Calcutta by the time Bose wrote his essay. On the other hand, the impact of Jung on the first generation of Indian psychoanalysts was limited, despite the overlap between his theories and aspects of traditional Indian thought. This becomes surprising when one remembers that Bose and some of his associates were well versed in traditional philosophy and should have found Jung especially attractive. As inexplicable seems the fact that, although Jung visited India in 1938 and it was a triumphant visit, Bose probably did not meet him (Hartnack, 1988: 93).[20]

Were these measures of the loyalty of the Indian group to psychoanalytic orthodoxy, as Hartnack assumes? (Hartnack, 1988: 93). Or did Freud meet some deeper needs of Indians, searching at the time not so much for in-house criticisms as for a critical theory adequately discontinuous with a psychologically minded culture and able to serve as a radical critique of it? Probably the latter; Jung was probably too close to India to serve as a baseline for social criticism or to avoid cultural incorporation of the kind Bose nearly brought off in the case of Freud. We shall come back to this point.

What emerges clearly is the hierarchy Bose imposes on the entire set of *gunas*. Like Freud, he believes that the unconscious and the non-manifest (together constituting the *tamah*) represent an inferior level of personality functioning. Unlike Freud or Jung but like a true Hindu, Bose extends this hierarchy to extroversion and introversion. In his model, the extroverted or *rajasic* becomes inferior to the introversion, seen as definitionally more *sattvic* (Bose, 1930*a*: 3). However, the hierarchy has no social-evolutionist thrust, of the kind that permeates the work of psychologists such as Abraham Maslow. Nowhere does Bose imply that only after the basic needs of a person have been met can he or she graduate to introversion as part of a developmental profile. As in Jung, the hierarchy remains in essence a classificatory scheme.

Bose goes on to say that the *atma* or self is *bhuma* or all-pervasive; it pervades all nature (Bose, 1930*a*: 3). Compared with *atma*, nature is narrower and more limited. And it is not so much the knowledge of self but the mutual relationship between self and nature that is the stuff of genuine knowledge. The *sastrakaras* or writers of sacred texts in India were primarily concerned with this relationship, according to Bose. For the knowledge of this relationship can be truly emancipatory.

Note that the few concepts verging on technical psychoanalytic terms in the above paragraphs are mine, not Bose's. The entire essay, though it provides an excellent indirect comparison between some aspects of the traditional Indian theory of the person and psychoanalysis, seems strangely oblivious of its own scope. There is no direct mention of any psychoanalytic concept in the essay.

Bose offsets his typology of *gunas* against the proposition that the awareness of—or encounter with—the self is the same as the awareness of the ultimate reality of being and God. In his scheme, the *atmasakstkari*, the one who encounters one's own self, is automatically a *brahmasaksatkari*, the one who encounters or confronts the absolute, and *atmajnana* (self-knowledge) is *brahmajnana* (knowledge of the absolute). One must, therefore, know *atma*; *atmanam viddhi*, know thyself.

Further, *antarmukha jnana* or inner-directed knowledge is the knowledge of pure experience or awareness. Whereas *bahirmukha jnana* is material knowledge. 'From pure experience gradually grows pure knowledge . . . In pure knowledge there is no plurality (*nanatva*). *Na Iho nanasti kincana*' (Bose, 1930*a*: 3–4). This pure knowledge is self-knowledge and, therefore, knowledge is absolute. It defines the nature of the soul. So the non-duality that is sacrificed for the sake of the mind–body duality in Bose's concept of psychology is restored at another level. (Elsewhere, Bose equates pure consciousness with the state of *samadhi* as described in Patanjal's Yogasutra; quoted in Hartnack, 1988: 98.)

Obviously, here Bose is trying to locate contemporary psychology in Indian experience and legitimize the discipline as a natural outgrowth of traditional knowledge. As it happens, the space thus created for psychology also accommodates a heavily textual version of the *advaita* as the core of Indian consciousness. The psychologist is the ultimate scientist because he or she tries to look within. Psychology is *sattvika*; so is the psychologist's work. The work of the psychiatrist and the psychotherapist, like that of the physicist and the chemist, is applied or instrumental and hence, *rajasika* (Bose, 1930a: 5). When counterpoised against Bose's formal emphasis on the therapeutics of psychoanalysis, this proposition makes strange reading indeed. As if, after justifying psychoanalysis in terms of its *sattvika* content, Bose is pleading for a less exalted *rajasika* role for it.

The second proposition of the essay is to define the individual as the ultimate unit of the intellectual and, presumably, social analysis. Bose quoted from the *Kausitaki Upanisada*.

Do not try to understand speech; try to understand the speaker. Do not try to know smell; try to know the smeller. Do not try to know beauty; try to know the beautician. Do not try to understand words; try to understand the listener . . . do not try to know the deed (*karma*); try to know the doer (*karta*). Do not try to understand the mind; try to understand the thinker.

As opposed to the first proposition, which is clearly identifiable with aspects of Vedantic thought, the second goes directly against some of the most influential readings of the Vedanta. For Bose does not emphasize essence or platonic quality; he emphasizes the carrier of the essence. One suspects that he needed this sanction for using the individual as the basic unit of analysis both as a psychologist and as an urban Indian being constantly exposed to a wide variety of new institutions ideologically wedded to individualism.

A few other propositions emerge from 'Manuser Mana' (1930*b*), as by-products of Bose's unselfconscious attempt to break out of the regime of the positive sciences. Science has become a fashionable word, Bose says, and it is invoked as an 'explanation' of even magical episodes in Indian epics and rituals by defensive Indians seeking to give the episodes and rituals some respectability in contemporary times. This is natural, Bose feels, for whenever a science becomes popular, it produces its counterpart, an *apavijnan* (false or bad science) (Bose 1930*b*: 339, 349). To avoid the pitfalls of such cheap scientism, he justifies psychoanalysis, and psychology in general, in broader philosophical terms.

To Bose it is natural that psychology is a new science, the last science to crystallize out as a separate discipline. Human beings are by nature more interested in the outside world than in the inner world (Bose, 1930*b*: 339). According to the Kathopanisada, God has created human beings as *bahirmukha*. Our sense organs are oriented towards externalities. Rarely, a few serene persons (*dhiravyakti*) cross the barrier of attachment to the outside world, to face and examine the self. From the wishes of this minority, the need for *atmadarsana* arises. According to the sacred texts, *atmajnana* or self-knowledge is impossible unless mind becomes inner-directed.

> *Parancikhani vyatrnat svayambhu*
> *Tasmat parat pasyati nantaratmana*
> *Kascidivan pratyagatmanamaiksa*
> *davrtta caksur mrtatvamichchan*

Hence the number of psychologists in the world is small. Bose implies that most people, being extroverted, are driven by emotions like anger and fear; when angry and fearful, we do not examine the internal changes in us.

In other words, from the point of view of the Hindu *sastras*, psychology is the highest of the sciences (Bose, 1930*b*: 340). The growth of psychology is not merely an expression of the intrinsic power of the Indian civilization but also a marker of the intellectual and cultural maturity of the Indians. The growth has a disciplinary meaning, too. Bose believes that as a science progresses, its boundaries become better defined. By better defining the boundaries of psychology, he is helping the science to grow.

'Manuser Mana', a slighter essay, makes three other points. First, it relates psychological awareness to the study of sensibility and draws the reader's attention to the scientific works of Jagadis Chandra Bose, which show that there can be sensibility even in inert objects. After Jagadis Chandra, to assert the presence of such sensibility is no longer a form of mysticism, the essay claims (Bose, 1930b: 346–7). Second, there is an unbreakable (*acchedya*) chain of causality which ties together the entire material world (1930b: 347). This makes causality—presumably a scientific category—a special case of and intrinsic to the monistic vision of life. Third, at a more practical level, the essay affirms that the idea of unconscious unburdens the individual of the need to believe in superstitions such as ghosts. Acceptance of the unconscious does not secularize one's world, for the unconscious is not particularly incompatible with spirituality, but it cures one of pseudo-spirituality.

Human beings usually try to attain happiness by extending their control over the external world. All the material sciences help men in this endeavour. The Hindu *sastras* advise that there is no permanent happiness in external objects; genuine happiness comes from restraint over mind (*manahsanjam*). The serene person (*dhiraprajna*) is happy under all circumstances. To keep the mind under control, many pieces of advice are given for rituals, institutions, and asceticisms. Reduction and ignorance [unconscious?] is a way of attaining happiness and peace. The scientists of the unconscious (*nirjnanavit*) assures us that when the damned instincts subside, the conflicts of mind dissolve and all sorrows are eliminated. Until now, the source of peace for the disturbed mind, tortured by mourning, anxiety, and tiredness, lay in the moral lessons given by the religions. In this respect, the material scientist had to admit defeat at the hands of the religious preachers. Today, psychology, by offering human beings words of assurance and peace, has moved ahead to establish the dignity of science. (Bose, 1930b: 353)

Thus, the fate of the science of the unconscious, human happiness, and the dignity of science converge in the step-wise unravelling and transcendence of the *gunas*. According to the *sastras*, Bose acknowledges, all three *gunas* are hindrances to self-realization but, of the three, inner-directedness poses the least problem (1930b: 5). Ultimately though, he says, one must rise above one's attachment to the way—even when it is inner-directedness and even when it goes with the analytic attitude—to reach one's destination. But, in the meanwhile, the unravelling of the *tamasic gunas* by focusing on inner experiences must become an important part of the agenda of any worthwhile theory of consciousness. Psychology, when it establishes the dignity of science, is presumably no longer a positivist science, but science is a philosophy of consciousness. It emancipates science from its own strait-jacket, as Jagadis Chandra Bose's plant physiology had done.

Apparently, the latent critical-moral stance of early psychoanalysis in India came from this tacit equation between the *tamasic gunas* and the instinctual impulses. Analytic interpretation became not merely a cognitive venture or an instrument of therapy, but also a moral statement and a form of social criticism. Freud did not like to view his infant science as a philosophy of life and he would have shuddered to think of it as a moral statement—Philip Rieff or no Philip Rieff (Rieff, 1959). Some of Freud's early patients were even made to feel that 'he was not at all interested in politics, ethics or philosophy of life' (Roazen, 1976: 512). And the admiring Fritz Wittels, despite his belief that the master was 'too profound a person not to grasp the need for a *weltanschauungen*' (Wittels, 1956: 52), could not avoid confronting Freud's own statement made in 1926: 'I must confess I am not at all partial to the fabrication of *weltanschauungen*. Such activities may be left to philosophers.'[21]

Bose had no such inhibitions when writing in the vernacular. The limits of the critical-moral stance he had imposed on psychoanalysis and the therapeutic role of the discipline that he stressed were not evidently the whole story. Nor, for that matter, was Freud's avoidance of philosophy and world-views. I like to believe that the works of Berkeley-Hill and Daly had shown Bose that the declared value-neutrality of psychoanalysis was no guarantee against latent moral judgements tilted in favour of the powerful. But one can never be sure that the Indian read his British colleagues that way. What we know for certain is that, at least one part of Bose, a part that was a not-too-secret self either, would have ceased to be what it was, if it had given up its philosophical and ethical moorings. Like some of the early analysts such as Wilhelm Reich and Karen Horney, who sought an element of social criticism in their therapeutics and even at the cost of therapeutic 'finesse' and methodological 'sanity', Bose would have found psychoanalytic ego psychology, in particular, and the highly professionalized psychoanalysis of the Anglo-Saxon world, in general, anti-analytic. This despite the subsequent career of the discipline in his own country, a career that he himself helped to shape.

The Fate of Psychology

Girindrasekhar Bose was not the only person to create a space for Western psychology in Indian public life and its culture of healing. Nor were his works, especially his English works, free of inelegance, crudity, and simplification. But he was certainly the most colourful and robust figure to emerge in the world of Indian psychology in the first half of this century. No one since his time has oscillated so daringly and freely between the implicit psychology of traditional Indian thought, academic psychology, and psychoanalysis. He obtained this freedom by operating at two levels: by emphasizing the organizational needs and the therapeutic role of psychoanalysis for his Western and Westernizing pan-Indian audience and by disembedding the young discipline from its cultural moorings in the West to relocate it in Indian high culture and in the bicultural life-style of the urban middle classes in colonial India.

The former was by design, and it made him another high priest of the transfer-of-technology model that was regnant in the academic circles of India at the time. The latter was by default, and the unintended dissent gave him his intellectual robustness. But the dissent, by the logic of his life experiences and personality, had to remain partial. Bose did believe the Sanskritic tradition to be the core of Indianness, and his exposure to and assessment of the little traditions of India being the way they were, he could not help looking at the world of knowledge through the eyes of the babus. On the other hand, even this partial dissent paid him rich dividends. Though he often was 'too logical' and 'mechanical'—the judgement was Freud's—when writing in English, he wrote in Bengali as if he had anticipated the adage of Christopher Lasch that, in an age that had forgotten theory, 'theory had to begin in remembrance' (Lasch, 1975: pp. vii–xv; esp. p. vii).

As this narrative has shown, the memories Bose chose to excavate were not random. They were selective and shaped by his personality, in turn mirroring the experiences of a civilization and the anguish of an age and a class. Naturally, the memories had their own half-life. While they let modern psychology go native and acquire a moral standing in local terms, they also narrowed the discipline's social base. This base sustained the young discipline as a sectarian profession and therapeutic technique, not as a cultural critique. Like many other imported systems of knowledge and some of the new theologies, reform movements, and refurbished cults in South Asia that began spectacularly and then withered away, psychology, too, gradually lost its sense of adventure and wider social appeal to become a proper vocation.

During his lifetime, however, Bose did manage to keep the discipline a significant presence in Indian intellectual life. That would have been a harder task had he not been living at Calcutta in near-total isolation from the day-to-day culture of psychoanalysis in Europe and North America. For the isolation allowed Bose to take advantage of a contradiction in the European culture of science which got telescoped into Freud's self-definition and which the late-nineteenth-century Viennese medicine man could never reconcile in his life or work. It was the contradiction that made Freud's vision a Shakespearian one for some like Lionel Trilling.

The contradiction was defined by a number of polarities, not all of them orthogonal: the metaphysical versus the applied or the narrowly empirical; the clinical versus the experimental; the intuitive and the aesthetic versus the tough-minded and the objective; and, above all, between Freud the holistic healer and social critic inspired by the romantic tradition of science versus Freud the heroic, masculine scientist-engineer and pioneer of a new theoretical school, self-consciously speaking the language of hard-eyed positivism.[22] Some of these polarities were to survive in a few of his followers and in the disciplinary culture they built, though they had to drive underground the culturally less acceptable ends of the polarities, afraid of the social and professional costs of their dissenting philosophy and politics (see e.g. Jacoby, 1983).

But first a word on Freud's self-definition as a scientist. Freud was a product of a culture of science within which German romanticism was not quite dead. For though he lived well into the twentieth century, he really belonged to the previous one. By his own admission, he decided to study medicine after reading Goethe's evocative essay on nature, and he was exposed through his friend Wilhelm Fliess to romantic medicine, many of the assumptions of which came from the *Naturphilosophie* of Schelling (Holt, 1963: 364–87). The exposure was deep enough for Robert Holt to trace to it one entire genre of Freud's work. Holt calls the genre 'phylogenetic theory' and includes in it books such as *Totem and Taboo, Beyond the Pleasure Principle, Group Psychology and the Analysis of the Ego, The Future of an Illusion, Civilization and its Discontents*, and *Moses and Monotheism*.

Holt's paper was published in 1963 and there is in the author, as in Freud, a clear touch of ambivalence towards such speculative stuff. Within ten years, Iago Gladston is already less apologetic on behalf of Freud and considers the romantic tradition so central to Freud as to call him 'an ethologist and ecological and holistic scientist' (Gladston, 1973).

The culture of science that sustained Freud as holistic scientist was, however, one into which the experimental method and the idiom of positivism had made heavy inroads. George Rosen succinctly invokes the changing culture of science when Freud was a student and a young researcher, especially the way four young experimentalists—Ernst Brucke, Emil du Bois-Reymond, Hermann Helmholtz, and Carl Ludwig—came to set the tone of late nineteenth-century German science (Rosen, 1972: 21–39; see esp. 27–9). Within twenty-five years these four men had realized their youthful dream: they had not merely become the leaders of scientific physiology in the German language area, they and their students were a major influence in the entire community of medical researchers in the Western world. As it happened, it was in the laboratory of Brucke that the young Freud honed his self-concept as a scientist. Holt, in fact, considers it ironic that the 'attraction to a poetic, metaphysical, grandiosely encompassing approach to nature led Freud into medicine and thus into the University of Vienna Medical School, a hotbed of physicalistic physiology.' (Holt, 1963: 370).

The heart of the project of the four researchers was their tough-minded experimentalism. They had prised out the disciplines of physiology and pathology from the clinic and relocated them in the laboratory. These were now independent basic sciences which employed the precise methods of the natural sciences. Clinical observations were now at a discount. Rosen writes,

Brucke and his friends were in the forefront of a generational movement. They were members of a generation of young physicians who insisted that medical problems receive scientific treatment based more on laboratory experimentation and less on clinical observation.

Underpinning this mode of thought was a philosophical position . . . Life was equated with matter and energy, so that their genesis and development had to be studied and explained in material terms, that is, in terms of the chemical and physical forces that determine these processes, and thus ultimately on the basis of the impersonal, objective laws of nature. Intention and purpose had no place in such an approach to biological phenomena. This doctrine, comprising positivism, mechanism and materialism, was the philosophy to which Freud was exposed during his formative years as a medical student and young physician. Transmitted to him by those with whom he had chosen to identify, it was a major factor in the formation of his mode of thought and his self-image as a scientist (Rosen, 1972: 28–9).

The basic contradiction in Freud, in other words, was between the inner logic of clinical work which demanded a set of categories that came from myths, fantasies, and self-analysis, and a philosophy of science which demanded a different language of self-expression. The contradiction was sharpened by the discrepancy between his emotions and reason. The former pushed him in one direction, the latter in another. Billa Zanuso goes so far as to suggest that 'there is not a single trait of his character, nor a decision he made nor an incident in his life, that cannot be interpreted in two different ways' due to this discrepancy (Zanuso, 1986: 64–86; esp. 73–5).

For an outsider to the Western world, these fissures within Freud opened up immense possibilities, some of them invisible to those close to Freud culturally. The most important of them was the scope to construct a Freud who could be used as a radical critic of the savage world and, at the same time, a subverter of the imperial structures of thought that had turned the South into a dumping-ground of dead and moribund categories of the Victorian era. Whether the possibility was fully explored by the likes of Bose or not is, of course, another issue.

Before we deal with that issue, let me spell out the nature of the conflict within Freud himself in some more detail.

As a school of thought, psychoanalysis acquired its political thrust from being a part of the Western critical tradition. It was a tradition to which a galaxy of thinkers from Giovanni Vico to Frederich Niezsche to Karl Marx had contributed handsomely. As a part of the tradition, Freud expanded the Enlightenment vision of a desirable society and sharpened its major methodological weapon, demystification.

However, this participation of the Enlightenment project was overlaid by certain insecurities and ambivalences in Freud towards the relationship between science and philosophy. Even a person as blinkered as Jones, who spent all his life reading and defending Freud as a hard-boiled positivist, admitted that as a young man, Freud had an early but 'thoroughly checked tendency to philosophize'. (Jones quoted in Roazen, 1976: 24) Only after a decade-long detour by way of the medical-biological sciences had Freud been able, at an advanced age, to return to the problems of philosophy and religious psychology (see his letter to Eckstein quoted in McGrath, 1986: 94). Holt is truer to the grain of psychoanalysis when he turns to the problem. He points to the

> ... many indications that Freud's earlier inclination towards speculative psychology was something against which he felt a very strong need to defend himself... [The] involvement of conflict and defence is perhaps more convincing when one reflects that Freud took no less than five courses in philosophy ... during his eight years in the university, when he was supposedly studying medicine. (Holt, 1963: 371)

Others have contextualized this defensiveness by identifying cultural influences on Freud that were of older, less respectable pedigree, against which he also had to defend himself. David Bakan, for instance, has made an impressive case that Jewish mystical traditions found identifiable, if convoluted, expression in the master's work (Bakan, 1958). Still others have discovered in Freud the negation of at least some aspects of the Enlightenment culture of science. Some of them have used the discovery to denigrate psychoanalysis as anti-positivist and counter-modernist (e.g. Eysenck, 1965; 1985). However, as the nineteenth-century concept of science itself has suffered a decline, scholars in recent decades have been more tolerant of these disreputable aspects of psychoanalysis. Thus, unlike his forebears, Gladston is neither deriding nor defensive when he says,

> Freud has been compared to Darwin, to Newton, and to Copernicus. I concur in these comparisons. Yet, to my mind there is one man he truly resembles—not in any other respect—but in the signature of his personality—that man is Paracelsus (Gladston, 1973: 121).

Nor is Frederich Heer hesitant to admit that Freud's tragic vision implied a rejection of 'the simplest Anglo-American belief in the virtues of progress' (Heer, 1972: 22–39; esp. 24).

Freud himself, however, having driven underground his other self, worked hard to retain and use the idiom of tough-minded psychology. He was always fearful that psychoanalysis might otherwise be accepted not as a positive science but as a cultural artefact of philosophical speculation. One suspects that he avoided developing a world-view because he feared the outlines of the world-view he sensed within himself. 'Is Freud ... a metaphysician?', Egon Friedell asks and goes on to answer, 'Yes, but he does not know it' (quoted in Rosen, 1972). Perhaps Freud knew but feared the knowledge.

The world-view Freud disowned was 'rooted in the culture of the late German Enlightenment with its interest in the exploration of dreams, emotions, and other mysterious phenomena in man's inner world.' (McGrath, 1986: 93). To the first psychoanalyst, seeking academic credibility, that world-view must have looked overly open to the culture of science associated with the German romantic tradition. He could warmly endorse Bose's work, blatantly philosophical though it was, because that was what the Hindus were known for and could get away with. He himself had to be more circumspect.

This other Freud, who emerged from the shadows only when he was in his late 50s, was unknown in the popular cultures of the West and the East during the days psychoanalysis was spreading to the distant corners of the globe. To most Western-educated Indians, as to much of the Anglo-American world, what mattered were the comparisons being made between Freud, on the one hand, and Copernicus, Newton, and Darwin, on the other. These comparisons invoked connections that made psychoanalysis a positive science, an exportable technology, and an index of progress. They tied mainstream psychoanalysis not merely to the European Enlightenment, but also to the triumphalism of nineteenth-century European science. The other psychoanalysis survived, as did the other Freud, in the cracks of the modern consciousness, as reminders to an underside of the discipline that regrettably existed, but could not be owned up to.

As it happened, the Enlightenment vision, of which the dominant culture of psychoanalysis and the positivist sciences were now valued parts, came to India neither through apolitical cognitive choices nor through natural cultural diffusion. They came to India through colonialism, riding piggy-back on Baconian science, the Utilitarian theory of progress, evangelical Christianity, and their practical extension, the British colonial theory of a civilizing mission. Together they sought to systematically subvert a way of life and devalue all surviving native systems of knowledge. When the vision won over sections of the Indian middle classes, it also won over people who, however creative in other ways, were to constitute an emerging class of intellectual compradors. As if the new psychological man in India had to be, by definition, a colonial subject. As if psychology had to be, by definition again, the latest in a series of techniques of retooling the Indians into an edited version of the nineteenth-century European.

The vernacular self of Bose tried to find a way out of the predicament by rediscovering an older version of the psychological man in a traditionally psychologically minded society. He probably hoped that this rediscovery would anchor the new discipline outside the colonial progressivist discourse. It did not. In his own professional life itself, there were signs that the culture of Indian psychology was being integrated within the dominant global culture of psychology, its fangs safely removed. By the time Bose died, after being felled by a stroke in 1949 and becoming bedridden for some four years, he was already being seen, both in India and abroad, as a pioneer whose days were past. It is not insignificant that when he died, most of the major international journals of psychoanalysis did not care to carry obituaries. Such slights did not burden the Indian psychoanalysts overmuch. Even in Calcutta, where it all began, any 'critical engagement with received theory' was soon to almost disappear (Kakar, 1990: 433).

For the moment, let us not ask whether or not such a colonial connection was inevitable for the Enlightenment values, given their links with three processes that were to ensure the creation and substantiation of the concept of the Third World as a territorial and cultural category in the post-colonial dispensation: the search for the absolute secularization and objectification of the world and for total control of nature, including human nature, through science; the primacy given to history as a form of consciousness and as a way of constructing the past; and the hierarchy of culture and the social evolutionism written into the bond the Enlightenment forged between power and knowledge. The fact remains that the Enlightenment vision—especially its progeny, the Baconian philosophy of science—did systematically underwrite in Asia and Africa the colonial theories of progress and hierarchy of cultures and races (Bajaj, 1988: 24–67). Even granting the emancipatory role the vision might have played in Europe, it was impossible to miss its racist content and oppressive associations in the southern world.

Any serious critique of cultures in British India had to take into account this anomaly. Even when accepting psychoanalysis as liberative in principle, such a critique had to turn it into a means of concurrently criticizing the native culture and the progressivist discourse available in a packaged form as a legitimating ideology for colonial domination. That is, the analytic attitude, which Philip Rieff believes lies at the heart of the Freudian project (Rieff, 1968), had to bear a dual responsibility in India. It had to be self-critical at two levels: it had to demystify aspects of Indian culture and it had to demystify the proxy-West, constituted by the interlocking cultures of the colonial state and the Westernized, middle-class Indians.

Many psychoanalysts—and social critics—chose the easy way out. Their self-criticism was directed against non-modern India, as if they were an organic part of it, and they exempted every category dear to the Westernized, middle-class India from criticism. As against them, Girindrasekhar Bose unwittingly—probably against himself—owned up to this dual responsibility of the Indian psychoanalyst. This may be the other reason for his desperate attempt to reread psychoanalysis as a revised version or logical conclusion of some of the older theories of consciousness in India. Bose's rereading was backed up by two methodological deviations from mainstream psychoanalysis, both prompted by the need to situate the new science in an old cultural milieu.

Freud was fond of saying that he did not discover the unconscious; it was discovered by some of the great minds of antiquity. All he had done was to invent a method for studying the unconscious. When he said this, he had in mind the technique of free association. The technique was a response to two felt needs. One, the need to avoid the limits of the method of hypnosis with which he had started his career. Two, the need to go beyond the method of introspection developed by experimental psychologists such as

Wilhelm Wundt and E. B. Titchener towards the end of the nineteenth century. This method, the European academic circles now felt, had run its course. Freud himself said, 'It is . . . an illusion to expect anything from intuition and introspection; they can give us nothing but particulars about our own mental life, which are hard to interpret, never any information about the questions which religious doctrine finds it so easy to answer' (Freud, 1929; quoted in Roazen, 1976: 513).

Bose did not feel burdened by either of the two needs. He never felt called upon to transcend either hypnosis or introspection. He was not fully exposed to the culture of academic psychology in the West, and such tides and ebbs in methodological fashion might have looked to him, undersocialized to the modern academe, sectarian. He had been a hypnotist himself and, to him, free associations did not supersede hypnosis, but built on it. Most psychoanalysts believed, following Freud, that hypnosis disguised, psychoanalysis revealed (Freud, 1963: 448–53). Wittels acts as their spokesman when he says,

Hypnosis is one of the states in which the secondary function is put out of action. The secondary function is delivered over to the hypnotist. He assumes the testing of reality, decides between fantasy and actuality, logical and ethical problems, and precisely in the degree in which the medium renounces his own use of the secondary function (Wittels, 1956: 302).

Bose was a practising psychoanalyst. He was also exposed to psycho-analytic literature, being one of the editors of the *International Journal of Psychoanalysis* until his death. It is unbelievable that he was not aware of Wittels's argument. More likely, Bose sensed the presence of, and was impressed by, Freud's other, less socialized self, more open to methodological adventures. As early as 1905, emphasizing the ancient origins of psychotherapy, Freud had said, 'There are many ways and means of practising psychotherapy. All that lead to recovery are good' (Freud, 1905; quoted in Jahoda, 1977: 10). Fourteen years afterwards, he was to restate that faith in a context that must have sounded strikingly familiar to Bose:

it is possible to foresee that at some time or other the conscience of society will awake and remind it that the poor man should have just as much right to assistance for his mind . . .

We shall then be forced by the task of adapting our technique to the new conditions . . . It is very probable, too, that the large-scale application of our therapy will compel us to alloy the pure gold of analysis freely with the copper of direct suggestion; and hypnotic influence, too, might find a place in it again . . .[22]

As for introspection, Bose never disowned it. To him, viewing introspection as only a method of psychology was a trivialization. Introspection had behind it the authority of at least two thousand years of India's past, besides the association with some of the European philosophers found relevant by the Indians (such as David Hume, George Berkeley, and John Stuart Mill).

It was a method that had shown its possibilities over and over again. Fifty years of academic psychology in one cultural region of the world could not wipe out those possibilities.

Hartnack notes Bose's commitment to introspection, but fails to gauge its full meaning. When Bose said in 1938, surveying the work in psychology in India during the previous twenty-five years, 'psychological truth can *only* be discovered through introspection', (Bose, in Prasad, 1938: 336–52, esp. p. 345), he was in effect conveying four messages. That he was unaware that the free-associative method had grown partly in reaction to introspection in Western psychology and he saw free association mainly as an extension of introspection. That, to him, the discipline of psychology was inextricably associated with introspection, which in turn represented insight in its grandest philosophical sense. That, as a trained academic psychologist, he was aware of but uninterested in the transient Western academic debates on method. That, though he casually used the language of progressivism he had acquired from his Western education, he judged all techniques in terms of the philosophical quest that had continued unbroken in his society over the centuries, unimpeded by the rise and the fall of dynasties and regimes. To Bose, 'India's ancient learned men had a genius for introspective meditation and the Indian psychologist has that heritage. In this respect, he enjoys an advantage over his colleagues in the West' (Bose, in Prasad, 1938: 336–52).

In the case of a person as bicultural as Bose, it would be too easy to explain this away as nationalism. It would have to be read partly as a statement of intent, a construction of the past oriented to a preferred future to serve as a critique of an imperfect present.

Was the tradition of introspection that dominant in Indian civilization? Was traditional India that psychologically minded and was colonized India its true heir? When Bose opted for psychoanalysis, was it psychoanalysis he opted for? When he anticipated the other Freud whom historians of ideas identified some three decades afterwards, what empirical and conceptual clues did Bose use? Or was he reading Freud, too, as a classical text open to diverse interpretations, because he had more freedom as a *bhasayakara*, a traditional commentator on texts partly cut off from the modern West, than as a formal psychoanalyst?

These questions remain unanswered in this chapter. The issues they raise, I am also aware, are debatable ones. Without rejudging the issues or foreclosing the debates, however, it is still possible to propose that, at one level of the intellectual culture Bose created, such questions were less than important. Bose, at this level, true to his vocation, was not concerned with unearthing the objective past, but with working through the remembered past. He seemed to know that, as with the individual, in some societies at some points in time, the past flows out of the present as easily as in other societies, at other points of time, the present flows out of the past.

NOTES TO CHAPTER 10

1. Bose, 1931: 13. For those interested, Bose's commentary is based on the following principles he enunciates in the opening paragraphs of his work on Gita. Wherever more than one meaning of a *sloka* is possible, the simpler and more easily comprehensible meaning is taken. Gita, it is presumed, is meant for the ordinary people and the author of Gita did not lack the skill to write lucidly, If an interpretation of a *sloka* contradicts other *slokas*, it is rejected. So are all internally inconsistent interpretations. Also rejected are all supernatural meanings. As a general principle, the commentary also tries to be impartial and non-sectarian (Bose, 1931: 15).

2. Psychoanalyst Bhupen Desai believes that an analogous search for magical powers explains the choice of psychoanalysis as a career by many Indians. Desai says that he himself was motivated by the search for omniscience and gives the examples of others whose unconscious goals were similar.

3. See a brief discussion of Bose's long-term interest in hypnosis later in this chapter.

4. The classification was borrowed from Sandor Ferenczi: See Bose, 1921: 140–1.

5. This account by Bijayketu Bose is not consistent with Sinha's claim that Bose had to undergo economic hardship in his early years as a doctor. Probably, when Bose concentrated on psychiatry, his average income declined dramatically to about Rs. 100 a month: Sinha, 1954: 64.

6. Sigmund Freud to Girindrasekhar Bose, 29 May 1921, in Freud, 1956.

7. Bhatia, 1987; also Freud to Bose, 1 Mar. 1922, in Freud, 1956: 108.

8. Most of the biographical material on Berkeley-Hill used in this paper is from Hartnack's comprehensive work on the shadow of colonialism on the early years of psychoanalysis in India.

9. For a brief sketch of Kipling from this point of view, see Nandy, 1983.

10. See, for example, Berkeley-Hill, 1913: 97–9; 1921. One wonders after reading the last paper if its diagnosis was not partly influenced by Berkeley-Hill's long personal acquaintance with Bose. See also Daly, 1927: 145–98.

11. Sigmund Freud to Lous Andreas-Salome, 13 Mar. 1922, quoted in Harnack, 1988: 1. One wonders if this is the same portrait that the well-known illustrator Jatindra Kumar Sen did of Freud.

12. Bose claimed to be Vedantist, even though he reportedly helped his wife in her *puja* or worship: Sinha, 1954: 69.

13. Debiprasad Chattopadhyay believes that Bose was a *nisthavana* or loyal Gandhian; others like Bijayketu Bose and Charuchandra Bhattacharya strongly disagree. An indirect but important clue to Girindrasekhar's attitude to Gandhi is in Rajsekhar Bose's futuristic, comic fantasy, 'Gamanus Jatir Katha' (1950: 1–19). The fantasy lends indirect support to Chattopadhyay, rather than to Bose and Bhattacharya. On the other hand, Bhupen Desai, himself a Gandhian and coming from a family of Gandhian freedom fighters that has made major sacrifices for the Gandhian cause, remembers the touch of sarcasm with which Bose once talked about Gandhian asceticism. Desai believes that Bose, though he admired Gandhi, rejected the Gandhian attitudes to sexuality and the *varna* system.

14. Chattopadhyay recounts his debate with Bose on the subject. It seems he once asked Bose why, if Bose was so keen on an Oedipal explanation of communism and the indigenous 'terrorist' movement, he exempted Gandhi from it, even though Gandhi had also risen against authority. Bose's reply was that Gandhi had been effective because of his rationality and his cool, dispassionate, efficacious politics. This conversation seemingly confutes Vijayketu Bose's belief in the methodological openness of his uncle's politics.

15. On the *guru–sisya* relationship as a possible model for therapeutic work, the best-known paper is Neki, 1973.

16. Cf. Roland, 1988: esp. chs. 1 and 2, for insights into the comparative impact of psychoanalysis in India, Japan, and the West.

17. Jones on his own admission, 1959: needed 'the sense of security that the pursuit of truth gives': Jones, 63; quoted in Roazen, 1976: 346; Cohen, 1979.

18. Roazen, 1976: 354–5. Roazen bases himself on a letter of Ernest Jones to Sigmund Freud, 10 Jan. 1933 (Jones Archives).

19. On Freud's attempts to distance himself from philosophy, see below.

20. Bose's student Charuchandra Bhattacharya says that Bose probably met Jung but did not have any extended exchange with him.

21. Freud, 1925: 75–175, see p. 96. Freud had already declared a year earlier, 'even where I refrained from observation, I carefully avoided approach to actual philosophy. Constitutional incapacity rendered such self-restraint easy for me' (Freud, 1925; quoted in Wittels, 1956: 50).

22. A roughly comparable dichotomy is between critical and professionalized psychoanalysis used by Kirsner (1990). Kirsner's dichotomy hinges on his understanding of where Freud's real interest lay. He quotes Freud's statement that the analytic relationship is based on 'a love of truth' and the prime interest of psychoanalysis is to find out what resistances this love of truth met and the 'mental, theoretical and institutional formations based on our need to *avoid* the truth' (Kirsner, 1990: 181). Professionalized psychoanalysis on the other hand, is heavily dependent on what Freud calls 'therapeutic ambition', which he sees as 'only halfway useful for science'. For such ambition is 'too tendentious' (Kirsner, 1990: 182).

23. Freud 1919: 157–68; 167–8. Jahoda (1977: 26) adds that, after Freud's death, 'some psychoanalysts reverted to hypnosis and could overcome its disadvantages, even its boredom'.

REFERENCES

Most of Freud's work are cited from *The Standard Edition of the Complete Psychological Works of Sigmund Freud*, ed J. Stachey, London: Hogarth.

BAJAJ, J. K. (1988), 'Francis Bacon, The First Philosopher of Modern Science: A Non-Western View', in A. Nandy (ed.), *Science, Hegemony and Violence: A Requiem for Modernity*, New Delhi: Oxford University Press.

BAKAN, D. (1958), *Sigmund Freud and the Jewish Mystical Tradition*, Princeton, NJ: Van Nostrand.

BERKELEY-HILL, O. A. R. (1913), 'The Psychology of the Anus', *The Indian Medical Gazette*, 48: 301–3.

—— (1913), 'A Report of Two Cases Successfully Treated by Psychoanalysis', *The Indian Medical Gazette*, 48: 97–9.

—— (1921), 'The Anal-Erotic Factor in the Religion, Philosophy and Character of the Hindus', *International Journal of Psychoanalysis*, repr. O. A. R. Berkeley-Hill, *Collected Papers* (1933), Calcutta: Book Co.

—— (1923), 'The "Colour Question" From a Psychoanalytic Standpoint', *Collected Papers*, Calcutta: Book Co.

BHATIA, J. (1987), 'Pioneer Who Explored the Psyche of India', *Far Eastern Economic Review*, 13 Aug.

BOSE, G. (1921), *Concept of Repression*, Calcutta: Sri Gauranga Press and London: Kegan Paul, Trench, Troubner and Co.

—— (1930a), 'Sattva, Rajah, Tamah', *Pravasi*, 30, Pt. 2(1): 1–5.

—— (1930b), 'Manuser Mana', *Pravasi*, Asad 1337, 30, Pt. 1(3): 339–53.

—— (1931), 'Gita', *Pravasi*, 31, Pt. 2(1): 9–16.

—— (1932), 'The Aim and Scope of Psychology', *Indian Journal of Psychology*, 9 (July-Aug.): 11–29.

—— (1933), 'A New Theory of Mental Life', *Indian Journal of Psychology*, 10: 37–157.

—— (1934), *Purana Pravesa*, Calcutta: M. C. Sarkar.

—— (1938), 'Progress in Psychology in India During the Past Twenty-Five Years', in B. Prasad (ed.), *The Progress of Science in India During the Past Twenty-Five Years*, Calcutta: Indian Science Congress Association; quoted in Hartnack, 1988: 97–8.

—— (1956), *Lal Kalo*, Calcutta: Indian Associated Publishing Co.

CARSTAIRS, G. M. (1957), *The Twice Born: Study of a Community of High-Caste Hindus*, London: Hogarth.

CIOFFI, F. (1973) (ed.), *Freud: Modern Judgements*, London: Macmillan.

COHEN, D. (1979), *J. B. Watson—The Founder of Behaviourism: A Biography*, London: Routledge.

DALY, C. D. (1927), 'Hindu-Mythologie und Kastrationkomplex', trans. P. Mandelsohn, *Imago*, 13: 145–98.

—— (1947), 'Hindu Treatise on Kali', *Samiksha* 1/2: 191–6.

EYSENCK, H. J. (1965), *Fact and Fiction in Psychology*, Baltimore: Penguin.

—— (1985), *The Decline and Fall of the Freudian Empire*, London: Viking.

FREUD, S. (1905), 'On Psychotherapy', *Standard Edition*, vii; quoted in Jahoda, 1977.

—— (1925), 'Inhibitions, Symptoms and Anxiety', *Standard Edition*, xx.

—— (1956), to Girindrasekhar Bose in 'Correspondence Regarding Psychoanalysis', *Samiksha*, 10/2: 104–10; 10/3: 155–66.

—— (1963), 'Lecture XXVIII: Analytic Therapy', *Standard Edition*, xvi.

—— (1972), to Lous Andreas-Salome, 13 Mar. 1922, in Ernst Pfeiffer (ed.), *Sigmund Freud and Lous Andreas-Salome Letters*, trans. W. Robson-Scott and E. Robson-Scott, New York: Harcourt, Brace and Jovanovich; quoted in Hartnack, 1988.

—— and PFISTER, O. (1963), *Psychoanalysis and Faith: The Letters of Sigmund Freud and Oscar Pfister*, London: Hogarth; quoted in Jahoda, 1977: 10.

GLADSTON, I. (1973), 'Freud and Romantic Medicine', in Cioffi (1973).

HARTNACK, C. (1988), 'Psychoanalysis and Colonialism in British India', Ph.D diss. (Berlin: Freie Universität).

HEER, F. (1972), 'Freud the Viennese Jew', trans. W. A. Littlewood, in Miller (1972).

HITCHCOCK, J. and MINTERN, L. (1963), 'The Rajputs of Khalapur', in B. Whiting (ed.), *Six Cultures*, New York: John Wiley.

HOLT, R. R. (1963), 'Two Influences on Freud's Scientific Thought: A Fragment of Intellectual Biography', in R. W. White (ed.), *The Study of Lives: Essays in Honour of Henry A. Murray*, New York: Atherton.

JACOBY, R. (1983), *The Repression of Psychoanalysis: Otto Fenichel and the Political Freudians*, New York: Basic.

JAHODA, M. (1977), *Freud and the Dilemmas of Psychology*, London: Hogarth.

JONES, E. (1921), 'Review of Concept of Repression', *International Journal of Psychoanalysis*, 2: 453.

—— (1954), 'Foreword', *Samiksha*, Bose Sp. No.

—— (1959), *Free Associations: Memories of a Psycho-Analyst*, London: Hogarth; quoted in Roazen, 1976.

JUNG, C. G. (1923), *Psychological Types*, New York: Harcourt Brace.

—— (1973), 'Sigmund Freud in his Historical Setting', in Cioffi (1973), 49–56.

KAKAR, S. (1979), *The Inner World: A Psychoanalytic Study of Childhood and Society in India*, Delhi: Oxford University Press.

—— (1990), 'Stories from Indian Psychoanalysis: Context and Text', in J. W. Stigler, R. A. Shweder, and G. Herdt (eds.), *Cultural Psychology*, New York: Cambridge University Press.

Kausitaki Upanisada, trans. Sitanath Tattvabhusana; quoted in Bose, 1930a.

KIRSNER, D. (1990), 'Is there a Future for American Psychoanalysis?', *Psychoanalytic Review*, 77/2: 176–200.

LASCH, C. (1975), 'Introduction' in R. Jacoby, *Social Amnesia: A Critique of Conformist Psychology from Adler to Laing*, Hemel Hempstead: Harvester.

MCGRATH, W. J. (1986), *Freud's Discovery of Psychoanalysis: The Politics of Hysteria*, Ithaca, NY/London: Cornell University Press.

MILLER, J. (1972) (ed.), *Freud: The Man, his World, his Influence*, London: Weidenfeld and Nicolson.

MOLONEY, J. C. (1949), 'The Biospheric Aspects of Japanese Death by Suicide', *Samiksha*, 3/2: 104–24.

NANDY, A. (1980a), *At the Edge of Psychology: Essays in Politics and Culture*, New Delhi: Oxford University Press.

—— (1980b), *Alternative Sciences: Creativity and Authenticity in Two Indian Scientists*, New Delhi: Allied.

—— (1983), *The Intimate Enemy: Loss and Recovery of Self Under Colonialism*, New Delhi: Oxford University Press.

NEKI, J. S. (1973), 'Guru-Chela Relationship: The Possibility of a Therapeutic Paradigm', *American Journal of Orthopsychiatry*, 43: 755–66.

PRASAD, B. (1938) (ed.), *The Progress of Science in India during the Past Twenty-Five Years*, Calcutta: Indian Science Congress Association.

RIEFF, P. (1959), *Freud: The Mind of the Moralist*, New York: Doubleday.

RIEFF, P. (1968), *The Triumph of the Therapeutic: Uses of Faith after Freud*, New York: Harper.

ROAZEN, P. (1976), *Freud and his Followers*, London: Allen Lane.

ROLAND, A. (1988), *In Search of Self in India and Japan: Toward a Cross-Cultural Psychology*, Princeton, NJ: Princeton University Press.

ROSEN, G. (1972), 'Freud and Medicine' in Miller (1972).

ROY, M. (1975), *Bengali Woman*, Chicago: University of Chicago Press.

SINHA, T. C. (1954), 'A Short Life Sketch of Girindrasekhar Bose', in N. Dey (ed.), *Samiksha*, Bose Special No.: 62–74.

SPRATT, P. (1966), *Hindu Culture and Personality*, Bombay: Manaktalas.

WADLEY, S. (1975), *Shakti: Power in the Conceptual Structure of Karmpur Religion*, Chicago: University of Chicago Press.

WITTELS, F. (1956), *Freud and his Time: The Influence of the Master Psychologist on the Emotional Problems of Our Lives*, London: Peter Owen.

ZANUSO, B. (1986), *The Young Freud: The Origins of Psychoanalysis in Late Nineteenth-Century Viennese Culture*, Oxford: Basil Blackwell.

INDEX